ASIA

by

Will Fieldhouse

Thracians, Scythians, Cimmerians, Seres, Parthians, Goths and Amazons

Copyright © Will Fieldhouse 2024. All rights reserved. No part of this book may be reproduced, copied, broadcast, stored, or shared in any form whatsoever without written permission from the author, except in the case of brief quotations in articles and reviews, and in the case of illustrations licensed by separate copyright-holders, as noted.

Cover Copyright © Ivan Zanchetta 2023

ISBN 978-0-646-89541-3

The purpose of this book is to fill in long-neglected details about the period of time from roughly a thousand years before Christ until the time of Christ. In particular to tell the history of a large group of nations that conventional history would label 'European', but who at that time did not yet live in Europe but still lived, under different names, in Asia. We know quite a lot about them in fact, but curiously their story during this epoch is rarely told, until now.

"From the north and all down over the eastern part, even to the south, is called Asia. In that region of the world is all fairness and pride, and the fruits of the earth's increase, gold and jewels. There also is the centre of the earth; and even as the land there is lovelier and better in every way than in other places, so also were the sons of men there most favoured with all goodly gifts: wisdom, and strength of the body, beauty, and all manner of knowledge."

Prose Edda, Chapter 2

"there is nothing covered that shall not be revealed; and hid, that shall not be known; because whatever in the darkness ye said, in the light shall be heard; and what to the ear ye spake in the inner-chambers, shall be proclaimed upon the house-tops."

– Jesus Christ

Contents

Introduction 1
   The Trojan War... 1
Part 1: "Settlement 1" 3
   The World Immediately Before the Trojan War... 3
   The Forgotten Black Sea World...................... 14
   a) Mysia.. 15
   b) Paphlagonia... 15
   c) Moschoi, Tiberenoi, Chalybes 17
   d) Armenia.. 19
   e) Kaskia.. 26
   f) Kartli-Iberia... 29
   g) Colchis... 32
   h) Khazars... 33
   i) Amazons... 34
   j) A Word About the Goths and their History.... 38
   k) Scythians.. 43
   l) Sarmatians... 45
   Maeotian Lake... 45
   Ancient Weather... 47
   m) Thrace... 50
   n) Troas/The Troad.................................... 56
   What is Asia? 56
   Pressure on Troy.. 58
   o) The Greeks... 62
   The Events of the Trojan War...................... 70

Part 2: Panic and Revenge, 1200-640 BC 73
The 'Bronze Age Collapse'. 73
The Sea Peoples. 75
Sea Peoples raids on Hatti. 77
Sea Peoples raids on Greece. 80
Sea Peoples raids on Ugarit, Alashiya, Cilicia and
    Carchemish 84
Sea Peoples raids on Mitanni and Amor. 89
Sea Peoples raids on Assyria. 95
Sea Peoples raids on Phoenicia. 96
Sea Peoples raids on Egypt. 98
Greeks among the Sea Peoples. 106
Israelites among the Sea Peoples. 108
Settlement of the Sea Peoples 109
Sherden. 110
Shekelesh. 114
Peleset. 114
Denyen. 117
Irish, British and Scottish origin stories. 120
Roman origin story. 128
Iron Age Anatolia. 135
The March of the Cimmerians. 136
The Identity of the Cimmerians 143
The Saka. 151
Altai/ Afanasievo. 154
The Tarim Mummies. 160
Tocharia. 162
Yuezhi and Issedones. 166
Analysis of the Claims of 'British Israelism'. 175

PART 3: Decline and Migration, 640-350 BC...... 181
   Orientalisation and 'Homersexuality'.................181
   Greek colonization of the Aegean Coast of Asia...186
   As Rich as Croesus..188
   The Two-Horned Ram..................................189
   The Scythian Empire...................................196
   The Second Horn.. 200
   The History of Iran....................................205
   BMAC... 219
   The Kayanian Kings................................... 224
   Cyrus's encroachment beyond Sogdiana
   and Khorasan... 237
   Darius' encroachment into Thraco-Cimmeria..... 240
   The Classical Era...................................... 249
   The Hellenization of the Black Sea Coast......... 252
   The Odrysian Kingdom.............................254
   The Bosporan Kingdom............................ 259
   Pontus... 264
   Macedon.. 265

PART 4: Exit Strategy, 350 BC-100 AD............ 269
   The He-Goat from the West........................ 269
   The Greco-Bactrian Kingdom..................... 275
   Greece turns into Rome and Persia turns into Parthia... 277
   The Parthians: Indo-Iranians take back Iran...... 279
   Identification of the Turans and Afrasiab.......... 282
   Shennong and the Foundations of China.......... 283
   The Battle that defined China....................... 287
   Sino-Babylonianism.................................... 289
   The Yellow Emperor and Early China............. 303
   The European Civilization that lived in China.... 307
   The Xiong Nu..332
   The Great Yuezhi move house...................... 339
   Finding Odin... 341
   The Historical Kayanians............................. 350
   The Canter of the Sarmatians.......................363
   Roman Encroachment................................373
   Northward to Liberty.................................375
   The Cimmerians announce their arrival in Europe..384
   The Founding of Sweden........................... 390
   The End of Thrace and Dacia....................... 396
   More About the Goths................................ 399
   The Yuezhi Part Ways................................. 409
   The Kushan Empire................................... 410
   Scandinavian Family Portrait.......................417
   What Happened to the Scythians? 441
   The Japhetic Spread.................................. 443
   The Telescoping of Generations and the 'gods' of Ancient Pantheons.................................447
   Conclusion... 449

APPENDIX 1:
Plato on the 'gods' of Super-Ancient History.................. 451

APPENDIX 2:
The Trojan War Through the Eyes of the Hittites.......... 455

APPENDIX 3:
Logic Chain on the Cause of the Bronze Age Collapse..... 467

APPENDIX 4:
Investigation into the Trojan Roman origin story............ 471

APPENDIX 5:
Historical Correction in Classical Chinese chronology..... 479

APPENDIX 6:
Zoroaster Revisited... 503

APPENDIX 7:
Who was who in Dark Ages Europe?........................ 527

Bibliography... 569

Introduction

The Trojan War

Judging by the number of European nations who would later claim descent from the Trojan refugees of this war, including Italians, Franks, Goths, Turks, Macedonians, Britons and Scandinavians, it must have been a fairly big deal. Indeed, it was an event that ushered in an entirely new era in the west. In a short period of time it transformed the geo-political and cultural world catastrophically from the way it had been for roughly a thousand years before then, stretching back into what we might call deep antiquity, into the newer Classical era of antiquity, which slowly and carefully developed itself into the conventional narrative of history that we know about today; a different narrative arguably from the one that had existed before.

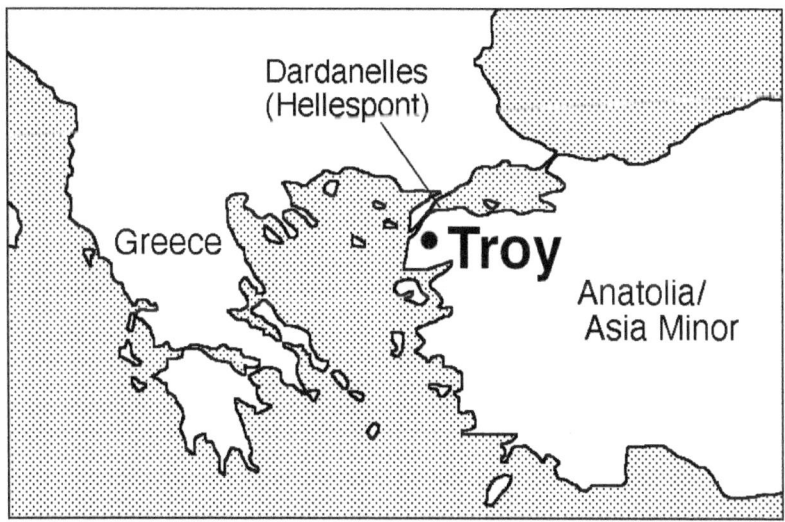

Fig. 1: The Dardanelles Strait

Very basically, the Trojan War swung the centre of power and commerce for what we shall tenuously call 'proto-Europeans' Westward, to the Mediterranean Sea, away from their traditional and long-established centres of power in Anatolia and Asia. The fulcrum of this shift was the Dardanelles straight, the waterway between the European and Asian landmasses that had long controlled trade between the two. When the Greeks, a peripheral, frontier nation far to the West of this 'main stream' took control of the famous trade route, the result was a devastating death-blow to an entire way of life for most 'proto-Europeans'. It instantly disenfranchised their economic and cultural lifestyle and turned their world upside down. They now found themselves geopolitically on the outside looking in. It also spectacularly announced the entrance onto the world stage of a cultural force we shall call Greco-Roman Homosexual Fascism (GRHF), and produced shockwaves and ramifications that we still feel today, not least in the fact that most of our history even now is fed to us through the prism of this 'GRHF' worldview. That is why we are told so little of the following and indeed prior history of that multitude of other nations whom after the Trojan war were shut out of the conversation between the major players of the global economy.

Where are the annals of Troy? A city and civilisation that was as central to its era as Rome was to a later one. Yet we know so little of its history, and almost all we do know is communicated to us by the very powers that conquered it and sought its cultural annihilation. In many ways they succeeded, at least temporarily. This book is not a complete history of all of those 'investor' nations in the city of Troy, for whom it provided the main if not the only window and marketplace onto the wider world, but rather a focus on the regional ecosystem around the Black Sea, that was in immediate proximity to this 'sea-change' in world history, and arguably most affected by its events.

PART 1: 'Settlement 1'

Fig. 2: Map of nations and cities surrounding Troy at the time of the Trojan War

The World Immediately Before The Trojan War

Before the Trojan War and the climactic events that followed it, the Western world was a very different place from how it appears to us later during the much better known Classical era. To a significant extent, Western history as most people learn it today 'starts' only after this event, with the rise of the Hellenic (Greek) civilization. Most of what happened before then is 'invisible' to the general consumer of mainstream history, and is usually dismissed with the keywords, 'mythological', 'tribal' or 'prehistoric'. There is an aggressive and sustained effort to enforce acceptance of the tacit platitude that history 'starts' with the Greeks, or even with their successors the Romans. Unfortunately for those who would airbrush away our common human heritage, we live in an age of accelerating informational availability, and a flood of facts are now

3

coming to light very quickly that allow us to see back into this 'prehistory', or rather 'forbidden history', and reveal it to have been anything but unimportant, but rather to have had dramatic and decisive bearing on the world that came later, the world of today.

Before the Trojan war therefore we are looking at a global human social and political 'settlement' that we are often unfamiliar with. This settlement was in fact already on its way out at the time of the Trojan war, since the dramatic volcanic explosion on the island of Thera (today's Santorini) in the Eastern Mediterranean, around 1600 BC. That volcanic eruption destroyed the Minoan Civilization of Crete and set the Greeks on a trajectory of rebuilding that would culminate in Empire. It was roughly contemporary with the Exodus of the Israelites from Egypt, and it signalled the beginning of the end of what we shall call 'Settlement 1'.[1]

A settlement of nations that had lasted from roughly 2000 BC to 1000 BC, Settlement 1 would be decisively broken by the 'Indo-European' (i.e. Japhetic) 'invasions' that came after 1300 BC. It had been the 'first' (to use very general terms) settlement of the nations after the Tower of Babel incident C.2100 BC. After that event, most of humanity spread out in separate directions from earth's first post-diluvian capital city 'Babel' (meaning 'Confusion' - probably today's Eridu in Iraq) and settled in various parts of the Eurasian landmass and Africa, the fastest of them continuing on much further afield.

---

[1] The period before 'Settlement 1', known to conventional history as the 'Sumerian' era of world history, is largely outside the scope of this book. During it the majority of the human population migrated South-Eastwards along the course of the Euphrates and Tigris rivers towards their river mouths on the Persian Gulf and settled in the area between them, called 'Mesopotamia' (a later Greek word meaning 'between the rivers'). The community they established there was called 'Sumer'.

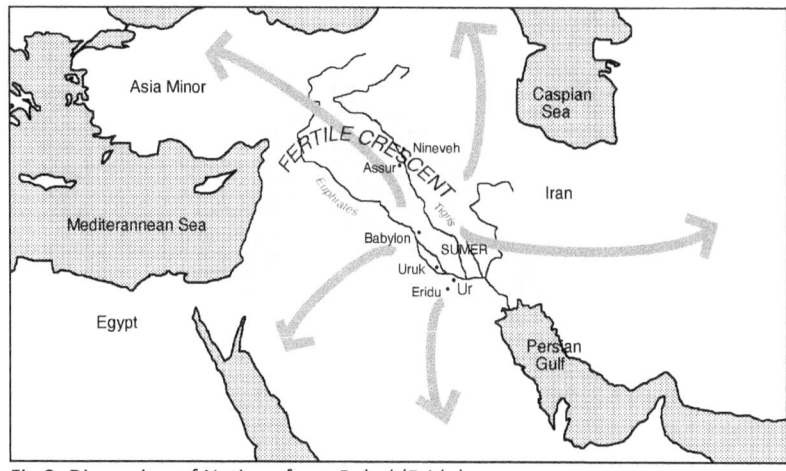

Fig.3: Dispersion of Nations from Babel (Eridu)

With few exceptions, we tend to think of nations as having existed only where they are today, and having 'arisen' there somehow. This is a grave error. In fact there have been multiple 'settlements', wherein today's nations or their direct antecedents lived in other parts of the world and were every bit as established in those places (if not more so) as they are today in the geographical locations we find them in now. We just don't *know* about those earlier epochs of history like we know about the 'settlement' we live in today. These 'big moves' or 'ages of migration' provide a natural barrier to history because much of the nation's story in its previous location tends to be lost or devalued in the course of the move. Nevertheless, it is important to understand that ethnicity is not geographical. When we speak of 'nations' we are speaking of families, people who are ethnically descended from the same patriarch or father. The modern era's fallacy that a 'nation' is essentially a region on a map, needs to be replaced with the truth that a nation's history can be traced by ethnic descent quite clearly and with a high degree of cultural and linguistic continuity, despite that nation having moved around dramatically from place to place. The fact that today's culture struggles to trace that story beyond a current or recent dwelling place has been a significant bar to a true understanding of the history of nations.

This book will focus on the history of 'Asia'. That is to say that region that the ancients would have understood by the term. Namely today's Turkey or Western Anatolia and its surroundings, the area immediately around the Black Sea. We will look at the changing national populations within the area during this roughly thousand-year epoch. The 'Asia' in question was populated previously and for thousands of years by people whose descendants would later become known as 'European'. Indeed it can be said to have been the 'first Europe'.

By the terms 'European', 'proto-European' or 'Indo-European' we intend to mean descendants of the patriarch Japheth, and of his sons Gomer, Magog, Madai, Javan, Tubal, Meshech and Tiras. As we shall see, some of their descendants were the real 'Asians', and the originally intended meaning of the term.

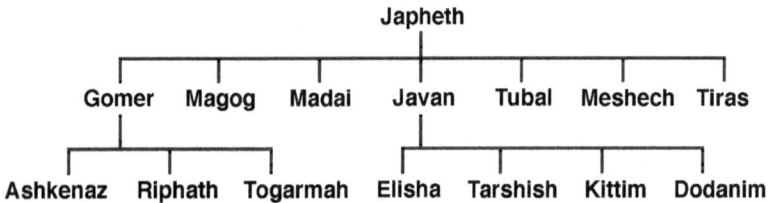

Fig.4: The Table of European Nations descended from Japheth[2]

The bizarre idea perpetuated by Victorian evolutionists and promoted in recent centuries that insidiously suggests that 'Europeans' somehow 'evolved' in the period *since* 'other' human beings 'evolved' (and are therefore 'more evolved') is a pseudoscientific fiction. For an example of this kind of thinking, witness how conventional history would have us believe that humanity 'started' in Africa and developed from there. Examine the inferences that such a theory entails. In reality, 'Europeans' were there all along, much as we would recognise them today.

---

[2] Tanakh, p.6. Note: the 'im' at the end of 'Kittim' and 'Dodanim' is the Hebrew signifier for plural. So these two patriarchs were probably named 'Kitt' and 'Dodan' or 'Dardan'.

They were merely living in another part of the world, and their story in those places has regrettably become as distant to us in understanding and awareness as it is in time and geography. As we shall see, this little-understood reality is borne out by the plain testimony of history when studied rationally and free from long-used and assumed prejudices.

Along with all other nations, the 'European' nations emigrated from the Babel debacle in Southern Iraq on the Persian Gulf around 2100 BC or shortly before. They tended to settle in remote, rural regions, and generally towards the North of the liveable area of the Eurasian landmass, with isolated settlements on the European peninsula. These were the descendants of Japheth, and they were fully 'evolved' from the very beginning. However, it is true (and somewhat embarrassing to Europeans!) to say that they didn't write much down. They seem to have overwhelmingly preferred a pastoral, rural life and strongly eschewed the urbanisation of what is customarily called 'civilization', along with the writing systems, usually a product of urban commerce and/or self-aggrandisement, that went with them. Therefore, 'Europeans' of today may view their ancient ancestors only from a distance, almost exclusively through the eyes of their neighbours, and more often than not through the eyes of their enemies.

During Settlement 2, the Earth's urban civilizations were in fact almost exclusively Hamitic, led or dominated by descendants of Japheth's brother Ham. This fact is one of the distinctive characteristics of this era of human history. Up until around 1500 BC, the 'imperial' heritage had come down from the Babel incident generally through Hamite-led civilizations, and it was they who 'ruled the world'. These were: in North Africa, the Egyptians; in Anatolia, the Hittites; in Crete, the Minoans; in Mesopotamia, the 'Babylonian continuum' of Akkad, Assyria and Babylon; in northern India, the Harappans, and in China, the Shang' An Chinese. These Hamite cultures were at that time the sole (that we know of) custodians of what are today called development and urbanisation. In other words they built cities:

large, permanent and perpetuating, urban, institutional settlements. This is being somewhat challenged by the discoveries of BMAC (the 'Bactria-Margiana Archaeological Complex' of the early Iranian civilization) but generally speaking during this thousand years cities, empires, most writing and most technological innovation (a Hamite speciality) were the preserve of the Hamite nations, while Shemites (descendants of the probably eldest brother Shem[3]) wandered in the Middle Eastern desert at the centre of the world (and right in the centre of the area between the domains of these Empires) and Japhethites spread out to the farthest reaches of the habitable earth in pursuit of liberty, as far away as they could get from the urban, imperial centres.

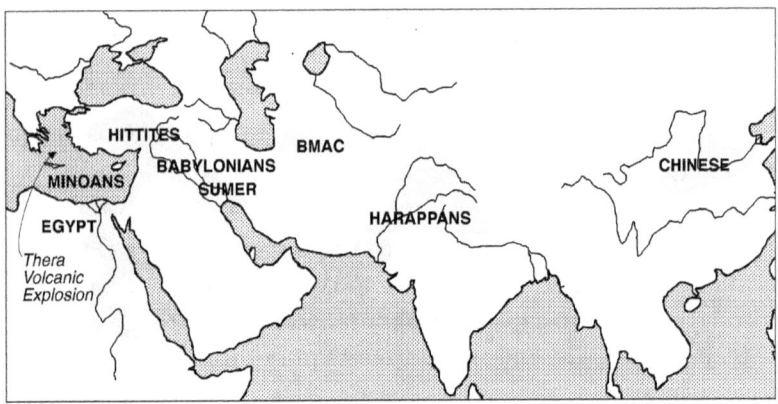

Fig.5: Map showing the main urbanized civilizations of the world C.2000-1500 BC

The reason for this Hamite dominance was that these multiple Hamitic Empires had descended quite directly from the original empire, the post-Babel one, centred probably at Akkad in today's Iraq, with its tyrannical King Nimrod, probably secular Mesopotamian history's 'Naram-Sin' (or possibly his grandfather,

---

[3] Opinion is divided over whether Japheth or Shem was the eldest son. In the Genesis Apocryphon, a narrator who claims to be Noah states that Shem was 'my first son' (Dead Sea Scrolls, p.451), and this is confirmed in the Book of Jubilees that states that the order of birth was: Shem, Ham, Japheth (Jubilees, p.42). This would be consistent with the witness of Moses of Khorene that Shem (Zrvan) initially reigned over the other two brothers, becoming a tyrant. (p.78)

Sargon the Great[4]). The figure of Naram-Sin was the first to wear the characteristic two-horned bull-like headgear that was the spiky prototype of what would later be called a 'crown'. This had been the first Empire of the post-diluvian era, known to secular history as the Akkadian Empire, and had produced its first post-Babel city and its first King. The entire imperial system was (and is – see for example the hexadecimal, 360 'degree' system used in angles of direction and units of time even today, the same degrees by which the Tower of Babel was attempted) descended directly from Nimrod's evil Empire[5]. This then was the basis of the 'Babylonian' or imperial system

'Empire' as a concept comes directly from the devil, with its unspoken assumption that pursuit of dominion over and enslavement of others for the purposes of obtaining 'glory' for oneself and thereby for the spiritual power behind one – Satan - was the purpose of life. As Napoleon Bonaparte memorably

---

[4] There remains a question as to whether Sargon the Great himself or his (probable) grandson Naram-Sin was the Biblical Nimrod. Despite Sargon being claimed in some sources to have been the first ruler of an empire, more elements of Naram Sin's story bear closer resemblance to Nimrod, such as the 'N-R M' features of his name, his claiming for himself the title of 'god', and his horned headgear. Nimrod was the son of 'Cush', probably secular history's 'Gushur', the first post-diluvian King of Sumer mentioned in the 'Sumerian King List', that memorably states: "after the flood had swept over, and the kingship had descended from heaven, the kingship was in Kish" (Sumerian King List, p.9). The City of Kish also was likely named after this same Cush, son of Ham.

[5] Although the Bible states that Nimrod was Ham's Grandson (Tanakh, p.6), the language of the empire was 'Akkadian', a Semitic language that took over from the Sumerian language (a language isolate), a pattern that was to continue for millennia in the Mesopotamian region, where by the time of the Persian empire 1500 years later another Semitic language, Aramaic, had replaced it. The empire's writing system, one of the earliest attested, was 'cuneiform', allegedly invented by Enmerkar, an earlier King and founder of the Mesopotamian city of Uruk. David Rohl has argued that Enmerkar was himself the Biblical Nimrod, based on Enmerkar's reputation as a hunter and his association with the city of Uruk (Rohl, 1999, p.215-217). However, while the Bible states that Nimrod conquered Uruk, it does not claim he founded it, whereas it does claim he founded the city of Nineveh (Tanakh, p.6), a feat also claimed for Ctesias' later, legendary version of Nimrod, 'Ninus' (Ctesias, p.115). This suggests that Enmerkar was an earlier, Sumerian figure than the post-Sumerian Nimrod. It is not impossible, though unlikely, that they were the same person.

distilled it: 'more and more wealth, more and more power, everything else is meaningless'. Most of the systems of Babylon had simply been copied and continued by Nimrod's spiritual descendants as their domains spread west to Africa, north to Anatolia and east to India and China.

These cultural systems that had perpetuated themselves from Babel dominated Babylonian culture at that time and were its de facto way of life. They included the imperial cultural hegemony of pursuing power by the oppression of others through slavery and the suppression of the individual.

This included the continuation of the Babylonian pagan spiritual system, that is argued to have been established by Nimrod's wife after his death, a pagan fertility cult system based on a worship of 'progress' (AKA technology, AKA knowledge) by degree under the guise of a primary sun god (Nimrod), secondary moon god (Semiramis[6]) and 'more highly evolved' 'child' 'product'

---

[6] This female fertility deity, the 'Queen of Heaven' aka Ishtar, Astarte, Aphrodite, etc. was later symbolised by Semiramis/Shammuramat, the Queen of Babylon, C. 824-811 BC, possibly one of the main builders of that particular city, that would be the capital of the later 'Neo-Babylonian Empire'. Semiramis's image forms the basis of both New York City's Statue of Liberty and the logo of the 'Starbucks' Corporation. This Shammuramat apparently married, then later killed and usurped, Assyrian King Shamshi-Adad V, who partially provided the model for the figure of 'Ninus' familiar from the ancient record of Ctesias (Ctesias, p.113). Ninus however has become all but irrevocably confused and synthesised with his direct ancestor Nimrod/Bel/Baal, with whom he shared a similar career trajectory. Hence Semiramis is often called the wife of Nimrod. This identification is such that when Ctesias was speaking of Ninus, he was almost certainly describing Nimrod. In particular he credits Ninus as founding the city of Nineveh (Ibid), a feat the Bible ascribes to Nimrod. It should be noted that some ancient authors continued to maintain that Semiramis indeed lived in far ancient antiquity (roughly contemporary with Abraham) and was married to Nimrod, for example Eusebius (325, p.519-520). Although the Babylonian 'Sun/Moon/Child' trinity system became ubiquitous from Nimrod's reign, its particular constituent characters varied over time, and may have preceded it. At the time of the rise of Nimrod and the Akkadian Empire, a main idol worshipped in Babel appears to have been 'Enki' (whom Langdon believed represented the antediluvian fallen angel Oannes (Sumerian King List book, p.4) but was perhaps more likely a version of Cain's son Enoch), who was credited with the founding of Eridu and central to the Babylonian worship of knowledge. The name of 'Tammuz', Nimrod's child in the pagan pantheon (often

(apotheosis of 'progress') god (Tammuz). This was carried on using sex worship (sex being seen as the mechanism for forward evolutionary 'progress'), with 'temple' institutions of pagan 'learning' and 'knowledge by degree' that were something akin to today's universities, but with a more overt pagan sex-cult and pagan deity (i.e. avatar of the devil) worship element, that often involved human sacrifice and always involved perverted sexual practices with temple prostitutes, male and female. This is the ubiquitous ancient system eulogised by enthusiasts of neo-paganism in the 20th Century such as Manly P. Hall. The Hamite Empires of Settlement 1 may have changed the names of the three primary deities of this pantheon to those of their own culture to reflect their newly separated languages (for instance the Canaanite Baal/ Ishtar/ Horon or the Egyptian Osiris/ Isis/ Horus) but they were still very recognisably using the same system.

This hegemony began to change around 1500 BC. Spiritually the Egyptian grip on power that they had enjoyed since Babel, largely by the exploitation of their possession of the pyramids and of the Nile River, was spectacularly broken by the exit of the 'Hyksos' Israelites and Egyptian impotence to stop them[7]. Meanwhile two new Japhethite 'Empires' were now emerging in the remote corners of the world, with their own writing and their own fledgling 'urban' imperial centres, that were taking on more of the imperial, Babylonian, pagan system. They had a different kind of perspective from the older Hamite Empires, in their record-keeping, in their spiritual beliefs, and in their views of the great mass of their 'uncivilized' cousins living 'without civilisation' in the rural North, but they were Empires nevertheless, and would eventually come to conquer the Hamite ones....but not yet. These

---

depicted as a single eye), also derives from an antediluvian figure, the King 'Damuzid', whose reign was most associated with subsequent fallen angel visitations (Sumerian King List book, p.4). The 'evil prostitute queen' archetype later known as Semiramis was embodied possibly even before Nimrod, in the person of Enki's daughter and Damuzid's consort 'Inanna' (Sumerian Documents, 1.3.1;1.3.5; 1.1.3)

[7] If the Israelites were not the 'Hyksos' rulers (Josephus states they were: Manetho, p.77-91; cf. 97) then they were intimately involved with their emergence (Rohl, 1995, p.271; 2007, p.66)

two new Empires, one in the West and one in the East, were characterised or came to be characterised and distinguished from their rural cousins by one of the salient cultural signifiers of all empires: homosexuality. This was a currency of urbanisation that provided the way for rural peoples to submit themselves to urban 'civilization'. It was part of the sexual deviancy at the heart of the imperial concept of domination, with its pagan spiritual component. Essentially they were corrupted by 'empire'. For this and other reasons, these new Japhethite empires and those who submitted themselves to them were considered with the utmost contempt as 'turncoats' and 'traitors' by the northern 'Europeans' who remained yet free.

The two new Japhetic cultures of imperialism were, firstly, in the West, 'Greco-Roman Homosexual Fascism' (GRHF) and in the East, the 'Bactria-Margiana Archaeological Complex' (BMAC). A third developing Japhetic empire yet further east, the 'Sanskrit Hindu Vedic Aryan' (SHVA) empire of India, that to some extent was a subculture of BMAC, is outside the scope of this book. The Hellenic or Western Japhetic 'Empire' only developed into an Empire proper under Alexander in the 300s BC, after a process of what is termed 'orientalisation' (for which read: pagan homosexualisation) in Greece during the first few hundred years of the 1st millennium BC, a prerequisite process for the development of 'empire'. It and the Eastern Empire would meet one another many times on the battlefield from around 550 BC to around 700 AD, alternately possessing the South Central Asian landmass around Babylonia, the original seat of empire....but not yet.

The aforementioned Empires, both initial Hamitic and later Japhetic, although they represented a relatively small slice of the human population and indeed of human culture and learning in general, are nevertheless overwhelmingly the cultures of the era that we know the most about. If you open a mainstream history book, you will almost exclusively find yourself reading about these Empires. That is firstly because of the pressure on history-writers to construct a narrative of 'progress, development and civilization by degree', i.e. technological improvements leading towards urbanisation and standardization - this flatters both the reader and the current era by presenting them as the apex and highest point of human 'progress' - and secondly because that narrative is easier to construct because we have so much larger a record of these 'Imperial' cultures from any given time period by virtue of their urban lifestyle and better preserved, more voluminous writing. Whether or not this is a case of 'the winners write the history', this overwhelmingly more extensive archaeological and historical footprint tends to dwarf any other voices from the period both intentionally and unintentionally. In other words, we know about them because they left records of themselves, whereas the rural 'Europeans' of the time generally did not - or if they did, we don't have them.

What we know about the 'Asian' or 'Trojan' nations, as we shall call them, we therefore know basically through the eyes of these foreign Empires: the fast-disappearing residue of the old Hamitic Empires from Settlement 1, and the boldly self-glorifying, new, increasingly homosexual Japhetic Empires who would make up the bulk of the recorded history we have of Settlement 2. Both types of Empire left copious written testimony about their dealings with the 'Asians', and that makes it even more interesting to consider why the 'Asian' history of the period is generally not taught. Perhaps it is because the picture that emerges is necessarily an imperfect patchwork, and we tend not to have the story in the subjects' own words. We must therefore content ourselves with piecing it together from multiple independent witnesses. And this book will attempt to do just that.

The Trojan War then may be seen as the major threshold event dividing 'Settlement 1' from 'Settlement 2' in human history. After the previous whistle-stop summary of the history of Settlement 1 up until the time when the Trojan war began, let us take a closer look at Troy; what conceptually it was, and why it was so important to so many people and so many cultures. That means taking a closer look at its main 'investor' nations, in other words the people who lived on the shores of the Black Sea.

The Forgotten Black Sea World

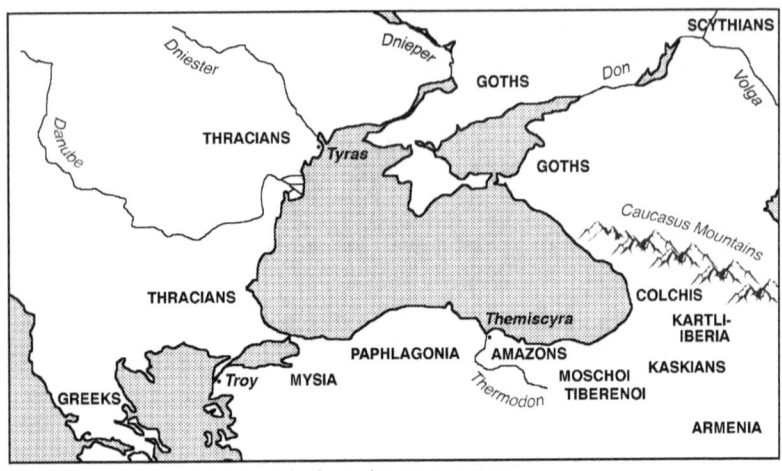

Fig.6: The Black Sea Nations before the Trojan War

Two things need to be said about the cultures that lived on the shores of the Black Sea during the era leading up to the Trojan War. Firstly they were all without exception what we would call Europeans or what are generally termed from the field of linguistics 'Indo-Europeans' i.e. descended from Japheth. And secondly the Black Sea was absolutely the Western centre of this Japhetic or European culture. From this, one can see that the Mediterranean world by contrast was a foreign one to these cultures. The Mediterranean was dominated by Egyptian, Hittite and Phoenician (Hamite and Shemite) traders, only in the North of which some of their European cousins, the island-dwellers we know as the Mycenaean or 'proto' Greeks (descended from Japheth's son Javan) had built small outpost settlements of Indo-Europeanism, arguably at a moral hazard to themselves in terms of their exposure to the pagan imperialist culture of the Mediterranean. The suspicion of such danger to Black Sea World eyes was thoroughly borne out by the events of the following millennium. The Mediterranean therefore was kept at arm's length by the majority of Japhethites and only entered into for the purposes of trading the wares of the Black Sea World to these distant and alien foreigners.

To get better acquainted with these Black Sea dwellers, let us take a counter-clockwise tour of the Black Sea Coast, starting at the Hellespont, at the outset of the Trojan War.

a) Mysia

This area, the far North-West of Anatolia (today's Turkey), was more a geographical location than a culture, however the 'Mysians' were a people group who periodically joined together politically. They were part of the wider Trojan 'nation', sphere of influence or culture[8], i.e. they spoke the ancient Indo-European Anatolian language, later best known by its variant 'Luwian' form from South-Coastal Anatolia, Luwian being one of the very few versions of this language that survived the Trojan War era.

b) Paphlagonia

Another of the 'ancient' Kingdoms of Anatolia: those who had settled on the peninsula at the beginning of Settlement 1, after the very first migration after Babel, directly from Babylonia. And indeed, there is even the possibility that some of these nations had settled in Anatolia *before* Babel. This group of nations spoke variations of the Anatolian subfamily of Indo-European languages like Trojan, a language group that has a claim to being one of the original European languages and attests to the fact that Anatolia was overwhelmingly inhabited by Japhethites in far ancient antiquity. Indeed, it can in many ways be viewed as the original Indo-European or Japhethite homeland, the 'first Europe', along with the area to its immediate North-East, Caucasia, of which more later.

---

[8] Strabo, vol.1, p.453. The Prose Edda describes the Trojan system: "There were twelve kingdoms and one High King, and many sovereignties belonged to each kingdom" (p.6)

The Hittites, who had come to dominate the central-southern portion of Anatolia by the beginning of the war, were new in relation to this primary Japhetic settlement, the Hamite super-Empire ruled by the ancestors of today's Cathays of Western China and descended from Heth, the son of Ham's son Canaan, having only begun its meteoric growth around 1600 BC. Interestingly the Hittites had discarded their own Hamitic language, 'Hattic', for everyday use and had adopted a variation of the prevailing ancient Anatolian language of the surrounding area.

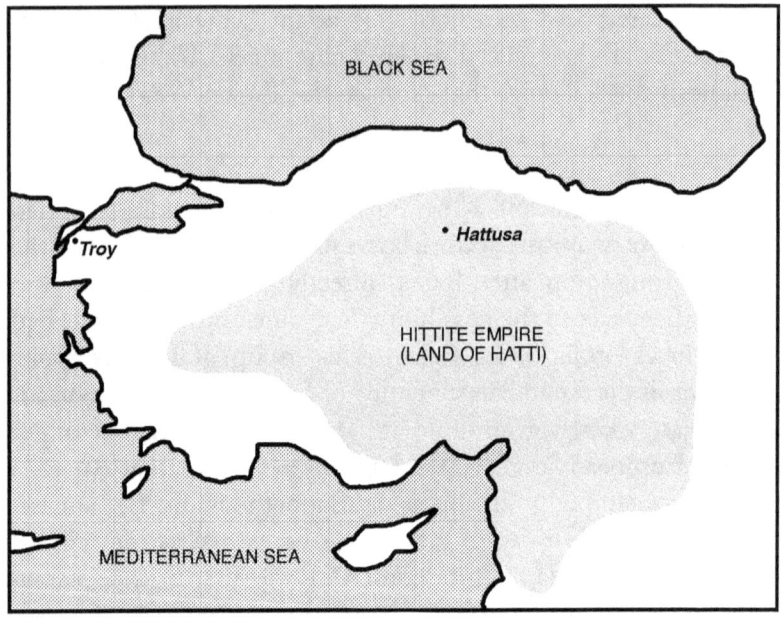

Fig.7: Extent of the Hittite Empire C.1350 BC at the outbreak of the Trojan War

A mention should be made here of Galatia, a nation that would eventually dwell to the immediate South of Paphlagonia in central Anatolia. The consensus view is that the Galatians or Gauls invaded sometime after 350 BC as part of the military conquests of Bren, who also conquered Rome at that time. This is probably accurate, however it is not completely impossible that this was the original homeland of the Galatians, from where they migrated West to the Southern and Eastern slopes of the Alps (probably the

'Mountains of Qelt' mentioned in the Book of Jubilees[9]) to found the Celtic Civilization. The Celts or Gauls are generally thought to have descended from Ashkenaz, son of Japheth's son Gomer, or at least from Gomer[10], who (via a Roman General) gave his name to one of the capitals of Galatia, Germanicopolis. It would make sense for these Galatians to settle next to the descendants of Ashkenaz's brother Togarmah, whose descendants the Phrygians had occupied this area by that time[11].

c) Moschoi, Tiberenoi and Chalybes

The region of the North-Central coast of Anatolia, a region that would later become the Northern extent of 'Cappodocia' and later still the Greek colony of 'Pontus' was at this point in history apparently blissfully unaware of such foreign imperial political structures. So much so that it does not seem really to have had a 'state' as such. The region to its immediate South was thoroughly conquered by the Hittites by this time, but the coastal area was not, and apparently never had been. There is good reason to believe the populations there, in loose tribal groupings, were the original settlers from the Babel dispersion.

The three main population groups were the Amazons[12] who had settled around the Thermodon River (of whom more later). To the East of this river (that we will take as being roughly in the same location as today's Yeşilırmak River) were settlements of Moschoi (AKA Mosynoeci), descended from Japheth's son Meshech, who later went on to found the city of Moscow, and Tiberenoi, descended from Japheth's son Tubal. These two sons' descendants seem to have stuck together, and their histories are fused almost indistinguishably in this part of the world. One might even say there were 'forged' together, as this culture is generally credited with being the first to smelt steel from iron ore in significant

---

[9] Book of Jubilees, p.74
[10] Josephus, vol.4, p.59
[11] Moving back closer to the area that Togarmah himself initially settled and where he probably founded the city named after him, 'Tegarama' (today's Gürün in East-central Turkey, an ancient city of Armenia)
[12] Apollonius Rhodius, p.65

quantities, and this occurred just at this time, around 1300 BC. The fourth term used for people of this area, 'Chalybes' was an umbrella term for 'steel-smelters', 'Chalybs' being the Latin for 'steel' from the Greek Χάλυψ.

Following the Trojan War, all three groups would increasingly seek refuge in the Caucasus Mountains from the encroaching Mediterranean empires that followed in the wake of the fall of Troy, and they would become major elements of the future state of Georgia.

Fig.8: The South and East Coasts of the Black Sea featuring the territories of the Moschoi, Tibarenoi and Amazons on a 1624 AD map by Abraham Ortelius, of the C.1350 BC voyage of Greek hero Jason and the Argonauts from Greece to Colchis[13]

---

[13] Public domain image from Wikimedia Commons (https://en.wikipedia.org/wiki/File:MapoftheVoyageoftheArgonauts_Caucasus.jpg)

d) Armenia

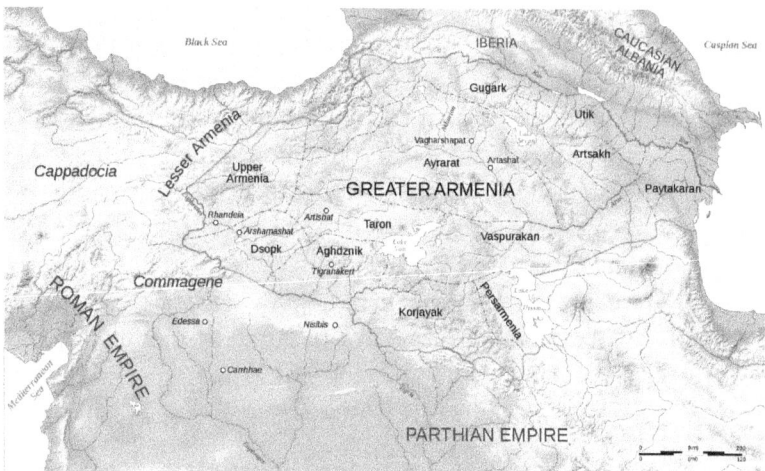

Fig.9: Showing the later location of Armenia[14]

Although the area of the Armenians, the Armenian highlands and the area of Lake Van, is South-East of the Black Sea and does not reach it, it is important to understand this nation as it is ancient and was often involved in the very convoluted politics of the region, being as it is close to the Middle-Eastern 'crossroads of the world'. While Armenia has a well-established historical tradition, as well as its own language, writing system and even chronology, it is nevertheless not straightforward to trace this history through to its claimed deep antiquity. What can be said is that a nation with roughly the same name existed around Lake Van from the earliest times, around 1800 BC at least, that would place it amongst the most ancient cultures of the area established at the beginning of Settlement 1 or before it. However the continuity of this culture, and even perhaps its origins, are not entirely clear, although it is generally accepted that the continuity did and does exist. What this probably means is that, understandably for such a fought-over part of the world, the Armenian regional tradition survived with multiple ethnic components and multiple restorations of the proto-nation, with various emphases and leadership groups over the years.

---

[14] Public domain image from Maptsof.net (https://www.mapsof.net/copyright)

The later state of Phrygia's claim was that Armenia was seeded as a colony from Phrygia (of Japheth's son Togarmah), itself a late (roughly 14th Century BC) arrival into Anatolia. As with many of these 're-invasions' of ancient territory however, further investigation often reveals that the nation in question was already there before the time of such events, and indeed many of these 're-invasion' explanations are ultimately exposed as attempts to explain the presence in Anatolia or its environs of many very early roots of nations otherwise than having to admit that all humanity has a common recent heritage in Anatolia, as it arrived in the Mountains of Ararat aboard the Ark of Noah, sometime around 2350 BC[15].

Armenian history itself has a different story to tell from the Phrygian origin one, a history that is emphatic and detailed. It says (Moses of Khorene) that Armenia is the nation of the descendants of Hayk, son of Togarmah, son of Tiras (sic – as this is the only deviation from the Table of Nations, where Tiras is a separate son of Japheth, we can perhaps theorise that it is a mistake, and remove Tiras from this genealogy), son of Gomer, son of Japheth, son of Noah[16]. According to this history and the related Georgian history 'Life of Kartli', Hayk lived with his brothers in Babylonia. Hayk "was prince of the seven brothers and stood in service to the giant Nimrod ('Nebrovt') who first ruled the entire world as king. Now after a few years had passed, Hayk assembled his brothers and said to them: "Hear me, my brothers. Behold, God has given us might and many people. Now, for the mercy upon us, let us not serve a foreigner but rather the true God."[17] As Moses writes:

---

[15] This is taking the Masoretic Text chronology rather than the Septuagint. The Septuagint would add 600 years to the antiquity of this event. For consistency the Masoretic chronology will be followed primarily in this book, as it appears (marginally) to be the most consistent with all available corroborating historical evidence, such as that of ancient Egypt and Babylon, and allows for the 'Newton principle' that historians throughout history have tended to elongate rather than shorten the antiquity of their nation's history (Newton)
[16] Moses of Khorene, p.74
[17] Life of Kartli, p.3

"This was at the time when humanity began to scatter over the face of the earth among the multitudes of the giants who were immensely dumb, yet powerful. For every one of these giants had flown into a rage, thrusting his sword into the other's flank in striving to rule over one another. Thus the whole land came to be dominated by Bel, to whom Hayk did not consent to submit. After the birth of his son Aramaneak in Babylon, [Hayk] went north to the land of Ararat together with his sons, daughters, their children, and powerful men, about three-hundred strong, together with additional servants, newcomers, and all their equipage. He encamped in a valley at the foot of the mountain where a few of the scatterers had previously encamped. Hayk subjected them and built an estate that he bequeathed to Aramaneak's son, Kadmos...Then he advanced...northwest with his children, encamped on a high plain and called it Hark ["Fathers"], for that is where the fathers of the line of the house of Togarmah dwelt. He also founded a village and named it Haykashen ["built by Hayk"] after himself."[18]

Here we once again encounter the 'Sargon/Naram-Sin' issue with the Babylonian tyrant in question: was it Nimrod or Bel, or were they the same person? There is a persistent effort among commentators to represent Bel, the antagonist of Hayk and the Armenians in Moses' account and in 'Life of Kartli', as the grandson of Nimrod, but not Nimrod himself. However those two primary sources themselves are unanimous in their agreement that Bel is Nimrod. The Iberian (Georgian) history 'Life of Kartli' states outright that Hayk battled Nimrod[19], and Moses gives it as his opinion that Bel and Nimrod were one and the same[20], the dictator giant 'who first ruled the entire world as king'. This makes it highly likely that Nimrod is conventional history's Akkadian emperor 'Naram-Sin', as Naram-Sin's career trajectory mirrors closely that of 'Bel' in the Togarmanian histories. It is also an

---

[18] Moses of Khorene, p.85-86
[19] Called however in the text, 'Nebrovt' or 'Nebroth'. Life of Kartli, p.15, 20
[20] Moses of Khorene, p.75. Also: "There have been various accounts by different authors about Bel, with whom our ancestor Hayk was a contemporary. To me, the names Cronus and Bel both refer to Nimrod." p.81

excellent fit as Naram-Sin's characteristics are very like those of the Biblical 'Nimrod', including his bearing the Canaanite name for Nimrod, 'Bel' (aka 'Baal'[21]), and being the first Akkadian ruler to claim for himself the title of 'god'[22].

Fig.10: 'Naram-Sin'/'Bel' – probably the Biblical Nimrod. From the victory stele of Naram-Sin. Note the horned helmet, prototype of the 'crown' and symbol of being a (self-proclaimed) 'god-king'. Note also the great size portrayed. Whilst ancient documents often portrayed kings as physically larger, the depiction is nevertheless highly consistent with Moses' account of Bel as a 'giant'[23].

---

[21] In fact 'Baal' simply means 'lord', but its use was understood in antiquity also to refer more specifically to Nimrod.
[22] Steinkeller, 2017, p.107-157
[23] From the 'Naram-Sin Victory Steele' in the Louvre, Paris. Public domain image from Wikimedia Commons (https://commons.wikimedia.org/wiki/File:Stele _Naram_Sim_Louvre_Sb4.jpg)

Either way, the story continues with Hayk leading his people, about 300, to Ararat. Moses records the message sent to Hayk from Nimrod:

"You went to dwell in the icy cold" he said. "Live wherever you'd like in my land, but melt your icy pride. Submit to me and live in peace. Hayk sent Bel's messengers away with a harsh reply and the delegation returned to Babylon."[24]

The incensed Babylonian dictator follows to force him back into service, but Hayk's grandson Kadmos warns of his approach. Hayk meets Bel in battle at a mountain pass southeast of Lake Van and prevails by means of a miraculous arrow shot that kills Bel[25]. This is known as the 'Battle of the Giants' and is stated to have taken place near Julamerk in Armenia[26] and is dated by the Armenian chronology to August 11, 2492 BC.

This corresponds in conventional history to the defeat of Naram-Sin and the fall of the Akkadian Empire (that is dated to approximately 2218 BC), following which the entire of Mesopotamia was overrun by the 'Gutians', virtually the very Mountain-dwelling people whom Bel is depicted trampling upon in the above picture. The Gutians destroyed the initial Akkadian/Babel empire and took control of its territory for several generations[27].

---

[24] Moses of Khorene, p.86
[25] The 16th Century work 'Book of Jasher' claims that Esau was the one who eventually killed Nimrod. However the chronology of that account is somewhat problematic: for Esau to have ended Nimrod's rule it would have had to have occurred as late as 1800 BC. Yet the Bible mentions nothing of Nimrod (the supposed King of all the earth) during the narratives of the lives of Isaac and Jacob, leading to a presumption that this is because his story on earth was over by then. There may be multiple claims to Nimrod's scalp because of its noteworthiness. Also it should be noted that this 'Book of Jasher' (that was claimed to be the 'Sefer HaYasher' referred to in the Bible) is not generally credited with having a genuine ancient source, and this account of Nimrod's death is consistent with that book's preoccupation with the doings of Esau, and thus possibly a fabrication.
[26] Today's Hakkari.
[27] Sumerian King List, p.17-19

The Akkadians recorded their annoyance at the Gutians' non-compliance with Babylonian pagan (Marduk-worshipping) imperial behaviour:

"Naram-Sin destroyed the people of Babylon, so twice Marduk summoned the forces of Gutium against him. Marduk gave his kingship to the Gutian force. The Gutians were unhappy people unaware how to revere the gods, ignorant of the right cultic practices."[28]

In other words they were not willing to bow to the pagan idols of empire. The Akkadians also recorded the Gutians as having a language that sounded to them like a confused babble[29]. This is incredible early evidence of what must have been the shocking new experience of not being able to understand the speech of other nations. It confirms the basic state of affairs in the post-Babel world: an oppressive attempt by the Nimrodians to maintain the tyranny of a one-world government (ruled by them) despite the disintegration of the Tower of Babel project; with this attempt similarly collapsing in the new multilingual conditions,[30] but not

---

[28] Weidner Chronicle, p.469. The reference to Marduk is an anachronism as Marduk only came to be worshipped as a major deity in Babylonia later, after the rise of the city of Babylon (whose patron idol he became) in the 19th Century BC, at least a hundred years after the demise of Nimrod.

[29] Glassner, p.97-98. This phenomenon is the source of the exonym 'barbarian'.

[30] Although the Bible record does not state that Nimrod was involved with the building of the tower of Babel, the two events are listed very near one another as though closely contemporary and related (Tanakh, p.6). The Book of Jasher (at least the book we have that claims to be the ancient work of the same name) states that Nimrod was already King before the tower and that it was his project, along with his brothers. However this Jasher volume has a number of discrepancies with other sources and this is one of them. Instead a popular interpretation is that the separation of languages was followed very quickly by the tyranny of Nimrod. Pseudo-Philo adds considerable detail regarding the tower of Babel project, stating that it was a community undertaking (motivated by a general lust for status and fame) that began after Noah had passed away, following a similar community project to count the human population to present the results to Noah in time for his passing (with the final tally being 914,000). And that the tower project was supervised by the same three patriarchs who had supervised the counting project: Joktan representing the Shemites, Phenech (son of Dodan) representing the Japhethites and Nimrod representing the Hamites. It also describes how Abraham was persecuted for not supplying the bricks or stones with his name written on

before contributing in no small measure to the spread of the nations out from Babel as they fled away from it.

'Life of Kartli' states that following the Battle 'Hayk ruled his brothers and all the neighbouring peoples as king.'[31] It is possible then that Hayk and the Armenians were the 'Gutians'. Although arguably the Gutians most resemble the Zagros Mountain-dwelling Medes[32]. In any case, the many witnesses testify to a general overthrow of the Nimrodian regime, and a primary loss of control for the Babylonian imperial system in the wake of the downfall of Nimrod (quite possibly caused by Hayk in the manner described by Moses of Khorene and 'Life of Kartli') resulting in a restoration of liberty to the nations of earth, at that time still mostly dwelling in or near the Mesopotamian region.

Moses of Khorene goes on to describe the descent of Hayk's sons as the founders of Armenia and its first Kings: "Hayk begot Aramaneak. Aramaneak begot Aramais. Aramais begot Amasya. Amasya begot Gegham. Gegham begot Harma. Harma begot Aram. Aram begot Ara the Handsome."[33] In terms of the establishment of Armenia, the following are some of the remaining problems with this narrative aside from those already stated. Whilst the names of Hayk's sons clearly contain the etymological requirements for 'Armenian', it is somewhat suspicious how comprehensively they cover it. Which one of them, for example, was the nation named after? Also, Book of Jubilees gives an entirely different ethnic origin for a nation that is indistinguishable from Armenia, stating that the name comes from Aram, son of Shem, after whom 'Aramaic' is named:

"And for Aram there came forth the fourth portion, all the land of Mesopotamia between the Tigris and the Euphrates to the north of the Chaldees to the border of the mountains of Asshur and the

---

them with which everybody was instructed to memorialize themselves in the monument. (Pseudo-Philo p.86-90)
[31] Life of Kartli, p.4
[32] From the name, the Gutians may also have been early Goths.
[33] Moses of Khorene, p.74-75

land of 'Arara.'"³⁴

Josephus also describes a portion of land South of this as the main estate of Aram, Shem's son (today's Syria) but says that Aram's other son 'Ul' founded Armenia.³⁵

So these discrepancies are fairly stark and it seems that for the moment the controversies will rage. Of course it is understandable to have many claimants to an area that contained the resting place of Noah's Ark. For now, we will accept the 'Hayk' story, as it fits with the general 'Togarmah' regional identity, although it is entirely possible that this is a later innovation of Japhetic settlers and that the origination of Armenia was Semitic. This kind of confusion is compounded by the fact that the Lake Van/Ararat area Kingdom went by many different names over the centuries and millennia, including the 'Kingdom of Van', 'Azzi-Hayaza' and 'Urartu', as well as half a dozen different variations of 'Armenia' such as 'Armani' and 'Arme', that may or may not have had exact continuity with the original Armenia. A word should also be said about Moses' dating. As comprehensively covered by Isaac Newton³⁶, nations tend to extend their history rather than shortening it, as antiquity is seen to enhance grandeur. To match other sources and to maintain the continuity of the Masoretic Text timeline we will pencil in for these events an approximate date of 2100 BC, which accepts that they followed immediately upon the separation of human languages at Babel.

A picture emerges from this story: from the earliest times, the Black Sea region was populated by people who did not like empires!

e) Kaskia

East of the Moschoi/Tiberenoi region and North of Armenia there was something of a no-man's land, as is often the case on the borders of large Empires and Kingdoms. The South-Eastern tip

---

[34] Book of Jubilees, p.76
[35] Josephus, vol.4, p.71
[36] Newton. See also Kramer, p.32

of the Black Sea area seems to have been disputed, and certainly it was a zone that proved too difficult for the Hittite Empire to penetrate and therefore formed its Eastern border, just as the area would later form the Northern border of the Assyrian Empire. However the 'border tribes' that kept the Hittites at bay in the foothills of the Caucasus can be described with some degree of confidence. Chief among them were the Kaskians. This group are mysterious. While they formed the main antagonist force to the Eastern Hittite Empire, invading and even sacking its capital Hattusa numerous times in the 15th and 14th Centuries BC, they were not a 'state' in that they did not have a King (until much later, as reported by the Assyrians), but rather were a loose confederation of tribes.

The second entity mentioned frequently in the Hittites' annals as being troublesome on this border was Azzi-Hayaza, normally discussed as an area rather than a people group. However this is now understood to have been one of the incarnations of Armenia ('Hayaza' referring to Hayk, and for a discussion of 'Azzi' see later). It is likely that Kaskians were of a different ethnicity to both the Armenians (Hayk) and the Moschoi/ Tibernoi (Meshech and Tubal) as they are listed as a third nation allied with the other two during a later invasion of Assyria in the 12th Century BC. After that invasion, that was defeated by the Assyrian Emperor Tiglath-Pileser I, the Kaskians formally disappear from history. The Iberian 'Life of Kartli' may provide the answer. It lists one of the sons of Togarmah, and Hayk's younger brother, as 'Kavkas' or 'Caucas'[37]. This surely is the most likely explanation of the Kaskians' ancestry, that fits perfectly with their neighouring 'brother' nation the Armenians.

There are two other later entities in the area that are likely related to the Kaskians. Firstly the Circassians, Circassia being a state along the Eastern Black Sea Coast North of today's Georgia that came into being later. Despite the somewhat strange appearance of the 'Kaskians' North of the Caucasus after they previously lived

---

[37] Life of Kartli, p.1

South of it, it is hard to ignore the similarities in name and general regional geography, nor indeed the similarity in name with the iconic mountains themselves. Clearly, the Kaskians/Circassians were closely associated with the Caucasus mountain range, and it is likely that the etymology is one and the same. Secondly the Cossacks. This group, who emerged from an area on the North side of the Black Sea during the renaissance era after the entire Caucasus region had been conquered by the Mongols and had become a part of the Tatar Khaganate in the 13th Century AD, seems also to share features with the ancient Kaskians. In particular they were fiercely independent and came from the Northern Caucasian isthmus. Notwithstanding the centuries under Mongol rule and probably intermarriage with them, it is highly plausible that the Cossacks are the cultural and ethnic successors to the Kaskians. And that this nation later formed the main identity of today's Kazakhstan. During the historical era under discussion however, they were a loose confederacy of mountain guerilla warriors who kept the Hittites at bay at the South-East corner of the Black Sea.

And so we come to the Caucasus mountains themselves. It is impossible to overstate the significance of this mountain range to the ancient world. There is a reason 'European' people of today are said to be ethnically 'Caucasian', it is because the Caucasus mountains were the defining geographical feature that divided the world of Ham and Shem from the world of Japheth. North of this mountain range was mysterious and alien territory to the empires of the Middle-East, whose records alone we are able to access from that time. It was the exclusive domain of people whose ways, histories and even existence were so foreign and threatening to the very core identity of the Southern, urban empires who peered at them over their city walls that even today they have to label them 'mythological' or 'tribal' in an attempt to downplay their significance and erase the testimony of their descent (and the admonition of the witness of their efforts against imperial tyranny) from history. But they were a vast multitude, a huge swathe of the world's population, and as we shall see, they were the ancestors of such nations of today as the English, the Americans, the Russians, the Australians and the Scandinavians. And it is into this heretofore historically neglected region, the primary subject of this book, that we now step.

f) Kartli-Iberia

Fig.11: Early Georgian states[38]

The Caucasus mountains constituted a unique defensive barrier that allowed nations to exist in them unmolested by the Mesopotamian empires to their South to an entirely greater extent than any of their Southern neighbours. The Hittites and Akkadians could not breach them, the later Assyrians only partially and the Persians and Greeks not without significant and sustained effort. The nations inhabiting them also thereby controlled the gateway between the Southern, settled and agrarian

---

[38] Image by Deu via Wikimedia Commons (https://commons.wikimedia.org/wiki/File:Georgian_States_Colchis_and_Iberia_(600-150BC)-en.svg) under CC BY SA 3.0 (https://creativecommons.org/licenses/by-sa/3.0/deed.en)

Hamitic/Shemitic world and the Northern, nomadic, Japhetic world, by the great 'gate' Caucasus mountain passes such as the central 'Scythian' or 'Caucasian' Gate and the eastern seaboard 'Darband' or 'Caspian' Gate, rendering them considerable influence as well as defensive security. It is for these reasons that a truly incredible level of cultural continuity has been maintained in the area in the region of today's Georgia, from very ancient times even until today.

Iberia AKA the land of Kartli was the main precursor state of Georgia. It arguably was and is the pre-eminent nation to guard both the Caucasus mountain range and the political and cultural heritage of Togarmah (whose other descendant nations include Armenia, Kaskia and Azerbaijan). Although it should be noted that the name 'Iberia' probably comes from the Patriarch 'Tubal' whose descendants on the north shores of Anatolia may have been the first to spread eastwards and occupy this territory[39].

Whilst as we have seen the Armenians were descended paternally from the (probably) elder brother Hayk and the Kaskians from a younger brother Caucas; the second brother was Iberia's famous patriarch Kartli, whose story is related in the colourful 'Life of Kartli' by the medieval writer Juansher.

Furthermore, whereas the Armenian language is undoubtedly ancient, it has admittedly been more influenced over the millennia by the sweeping geopolitical changes that Armenia has seen, with influences as diverse as Greek, Phrygian and Parthian adding to it, than Kartvelian, the language of the Mountain-defended ultimate Togarmanian stronghold of Iberia. This gives Kartvelian a claim to being a remnant of the original language of Togarmah, entrusted to Him as one of the seventy national Patriarchs listed in the Table of Nations at the time of the dividing of the languages at Babel. And indeed Kartvelian is a singular language with its own very unique script that unlike Armenian cannot easily be related to

---

[39] The Georgian capital of 'Tibilisi' is also named after Tubal.

any other existing language[40].

'Life of Kartli' confirms the Togarmanian story from Armenian history, describing Togarmah thus:

"He was a brave, gigantic man. At the time of the destruction of the Tower [of Babel] and the division of tongues and the dispersion of mankind throughout the world, [T'orgom] came and settled between the Masis and Aragats mountains. He had many women; sons and daughters of his sons and daughters were born, and he lived for six hundred years. But the country did not suffice for the multitude of his folk. Therefore, they spread out and enlarged their boundaries: from the Pontic sea to the sea of 'Heret and Kasp and by the mountains of the Caucasus.

"They selected eight of the bravest and most renowned of his sons. First was Hayk, second K'art'los, third Bardos, fourth Movkan, fifth Lekan, sixth Heros, seventh Kovkas, and eighth Egres. But Hayk was the strongest and bravest. There was no one like him on earth, not before the deluge nor after it, to the present. T'orgom divided his land among them: half he gave to Hayk and half to the seven sons, according to their merit."[41]

Hayk, therefore, is still described as the strongest, a giant who took down Nimrod. But the story continues with Kartli. He establishes his 'home and fortress' on the mountain Amraz/Armaz, the 'head of Kartli', where he dies and is buried by his sons, the 'senior' of which is Mts'xet'os. Mts'xet'os, his brothers and their mother proceed to build multiple other mountain fortresses. These fortresses would become famous symbols of defense for thousands of years, still putting up stiff resistance to Alexander's army in the 4th Century BC more than a thousand years later. Juansher relates: 'The T'orgomeans built fortresses out of fear of the Nimrodians, who harassed them to exact blood vengeance for their ancestor

---

[40] Although 'Life of Kartli' does state that to some extent the language became an amalgam of later incoming nations seeking sanctuary from the South (p.10).
[41] Life of Kartli, p.1

Nimrod. But until Mts'xet'os' death they were unable to conquer them because of their unity.'[42]

After the passing of Mts'xet'os' however it all went pear-shaped for the Iberians. 'They forgot God their creator, worshipped the sun, moon and the seven other stars, and they swore by the grave of their father K'art'los'. The surviving brothers argued and civil war ensued, followed by conquest from the Khazars to their North, then the Nimrodians to their South under one Arbitron, and finally the 'Iranians', which we can reasonably assume to refer to the embryonic Medo-Persians to their South-East, coming from BMAC. This state of affairs more or less continued until the time of the Trojan War. Around this time an 'Iranian' prince K'ue Xosrov reconquered Iberia building an (assumedly Zoroastrian) 'house of prayer' in Atrpatakan.

g) Colchis

As can be seen from the above map, Colchis was in many ways simply coastal Iberia. However as such it was the cosmopolitan, ethnically and linguistically diverse and exotic component. It was here that the descendants of Meshech and Tubal slowly migrated to following the Trojan War (though there were many of them still on the North-East coast of Anatolia in the days of Greek writers Xenophon and Herodotus even up to the Roman era)[43]. And many other Anatolian nations also ended up in Colchis, that became a sanctuary for those who had previously lived in Anatolia before the War.

The Colchian state was an industrial and mining powerhouse, a place famous in its time. It was here that Achaean (Greek) hero Jason went to obtain the Golden Fleece in the famous legend of the Argonauts[44]. Gold was sifted from rivers using fleeces in

---

[42] Life of Kartli, p.5
[43] Xenophon, p.371, Herodotus, p.458
[44] Herodotus, in the opening of his famous 'Histories', alleges that Jason's trip to Colchis and his marriage (seen by the Asians as an abduction) of Colchian princess Medea played a crucial role in causing the Trojan War, as it was part of a tit-for-tat,

Colchis, a possible connection to the story. The language of this strong and efficient Colchian State was Kartvelian, the language of Iberia its close neighbour, and its ethnic basis was probably the Laz-Mingrelian people, descended from Meshech.

Both Meshech and Tubal have strongly-held traditions of widerspread travels and achievements. Meshech as the Patriarch of the far-North Indo-Europeans, as the founder of the city of Moscow and the nation of the Muscovites; Tubal in the West as the Patriarch and founder of the Spanish (and probably the eponym of 'Iberia' that was taken with his descendants to Spain). Both of these traditions have multiple controversies and complicating factors but are probably too widespread not to have some basis in truth. However it is proposed that these Anatolian Meshech/Tubal settlements are the earliest, where the pair put down roots before spreading their wings further afield.

Tubal's connection to metallurgy and industry are interesting in that an antediluvian namesake 'Tubal-Cain' was famous for exactly this activity. It is possible that the later Tubal was named after the earlier one for this reason. It is notable that wheel technology is first evidenced in the Northern Caucasus (Maykop Culture) and the earliest claimed (spoked-wheel) chariots have been found at Sintashta in Russia, on the way to Moscow

h) Khazars

An amazingly central and influential group, the Khazars are a favourite of anti-Semitic propaganda as they converted to the religion of Judaism around 900 AD, apparently in a commercial and strategic decision to allow them to remain a neutral trading party between the 'Christian' Byzantine Empire to their South and West and the Seljuk Sultanate and other Muslim entities to their East. The argument is that they were a huge avenue of entry into Europe for people of Turkish ethnicity in the guise of Jews throughout the medieval era. However the account from 'Life of

---

escalating series of woman abductions/elopements that eventually led to war. (Herodotus, p.1-2)

Kartli' causes huge problems for this Turkish Khazar theory, as the Khazars were apparently living on the Northern slopes of the Caucasus Mountains very early on, immediately after the passing of Mts'xet'os', so perhaps 1300-1400 BC. A descent from Togarmah's son Caucus is suggested by their name, though unlikely in the light of their very early warring with and conquest of what would be their near relatives the Iberians. Others have proposed a descent from Meshech finding similarities in the names. For the moment we will merely note that according to Life of Kartli they dwelt somewhere North of the Caucasus at this early point in history.

i) Amazons

The Amazons are a perfect example of the kind of historical group that conventional history has attempted to 'mythologise' out of existence. Of course the Amazons are the subject of many a Hollywood paeon, and the nature of their society is so dramatic that it seems hard to believe, but that doesn't mean they didn't really exist and didn't really live like that. Indeed, if the overwhelming weight of perfectly authoritative historical records is not to be abandoned, they certainly did exist and were a fact of life in the Black Sea world for over a thousand years.

The Amazons were a feminist warrior society that eschewed their need for men and fiercely asserted their equal standing with them particularly in the art of warfare[45]. Their whole culture was dedicated to warfare and they subdued every other aspect of life to this one end[46].

In keeping with the history of an all-female society, there is a capriciousness to the story of the Amazons that makes it flighty, varied and hard to pin down. As with many of the nations catalogued here there is some evidence that the Amazons originally had a homeland in Southwestern Anatolia[47], later

---

[45] Iliad, p.135 & 201
[46] Apollonius Rhodius, p.86
[47] Strabo, vol.2, p.298

migrating perhaps more than once Northward and Eastward as the 'GRHF' imperial creep slowly overran their previous territory.

For instance Homer seems to believe their dwelling place was in Lycia/Lukka on the South Coast of Anatolia, at the time of the Trojan War. And this is also where the Greek hero Bellerophon fought them before the war[48]. This would be in keeping with strong tradition that Amazons worshipped at the Temple of Artemis (an avatar of Semiramis) in Ephesus, up the coast from Lycia. Artemis was a female deity idol based around a meteorite that had the shape of a woman's breast, so it certainly fits that Amazons would have sought it out[49]. And indeed there are claims that it was founded in the first place by Otrera, one of the earliest claimed Amazon Queens, whose daughters provide the Amazon Queen foils for many a Greek legend involving the Amazons.[50] The Amazons also fought on the Trojan side in the war, that also makes sense if they were defending their homeland. Queen Penthesilea (a daughter of Otrera) led an Amazon force against the Greeks in the war, dying in single combat against Achilles[51].

Perhaps following the war this location became untenable for the Amazons, as after this they are referred to as living much further away. Even before it they seem to have had colonies in multiple locations. In the Argonautica[52], probably based on events in the few hundred years before the war, Achaean hero Jason in the ship Argo visits what the book claims is the capital of the Amazon state, Themiscyra at the mouth of the Thermodon River on the central north coast of Anatolia, that would later be part of the Hellenic

---

[48] Strabo, vol.2, p.328
[49] It is probable that we have a record of that meteorite hitting, in the Annals of Hittite King Mursili II, who describes a 'a lightning bolt, and my army saw the lightning bolt, as did the land of Arzawa. The lightning bolt traveled and struck the land of Arzawa, (in particular) Apasa [Ephesus – Ed], the city of Uhha-ziti'. This would place the meteorite strike, cause célèbre of the Temple of Artemis/Diana, around 1322 BC. (Hittite Correspondence, p.15)
[50] Indeed, Strabo claims that the Anatolian cities of Ephesus, Smyrna, Cyme and Myrina were all named after Amazons (Strabo, vol.2, p.237)
[51] Aethiopis, p.111
[52] Apollonius Rhodius, p.64-65; p.85-86

colony of Pontus, north of Cappadocia. This was already understood to be an Amazon homeland earlier, in Greek stories featuring earlier heroes Heracles and Theseus. (The all-woman city seems to have been a regular target for Greek heroes endeavouring to prove their courage!) This location is also confirmed by other Greek sources Bacchylides (6th C BC)[53] and Herodotus (5th C BC)[54]. Strabo (1st C BC) visited the location but by that time he states the Amazons had long since retreated into the mountains[55].

And those mountains were the Caucasus Mountains. One can see from this path of the Amazons the consequences of the Trojan War for many Asian nations: an invasion of their previous life of liberty resulting in an enforced exile further North. It is quite possible that the Amazons had always had some settlement in the Caucasus as this is arguably the location most often associated with them[56]. Strabo relates a tale from other authors that the Amazons chose to resettle beyond the borders of the Gargareans, an all-male tribe who dwelt in the foothills of the Mountains. Famously this was how the Amazons perpetuated themselves: by meeting in secret once a year to mate with the Gargareans, female children being raised by the Amazons and males by the Gargareans (or in more grisly versions, males being killed by the Amazons)[57].

According to Jordanes, Goths also provided the male component of the Amazons[58], whether this was during a different era or otherwise. This he says occurred in the Gothic homeland of Lake

---

[53] Bacchylides, p.24
[54] Herodotus, p.588
[55] Strabo, vol.2, p.237.
[56] Indeed there is more than a suggestion that their presence in Southwestern Anatolia was solely as a result of a military campaign they had undertaken from a base in the Caucasus (possibly the aforementioned Mount Amraz/Armaz, explaining their name) following which they held the area in subjection for 'almost a hundred years' before retiring back to the Caucasus (Jordanes, p.64). This is likely to be the same incident referred to by Strabo who records that the Amazons 'ventured to invade' Caria/Lycia, causing Priam and Bellerophon to undertake an 'expedition against these women'. (Strabo, vol.2, p.328) (See also Iliad, p.127)
[57] Strabo, vol.2, p.236; Russian Primary Chronicle, p.58
[58] Jordanes, p.62

Maeotis (see the Herodotus story below). And according to the epic cycle Queen Penthesilea was of Thracian extraction[59]. So it is likely that the Amazons found male companions from multiple sources over the millennia.

It has even been suggested, based on extraordinary archaeological finds of female warriors in Russia such as at Voronezh that this arrangement was a more widespread one among the wider Scythian horse cultures of the Eurasian Steppe, with men and women living separately except for the purposes of copulation.

Herodotus relates a story of how the Amazons came to be in 'Scythia' (that we can assume is shorthand for 'north of the Caucasus Mountains') in the first place. A group of them having been captured at Thermodon by the Greeks, they overcame the Greek sailors of the ships they were being transported back to Greece upon, turned the ships around and having no navigational skills ended up on the Scythian shore. Having caught enough horses, they eventually assimilated with the Scythians.[60]

Either way, the Amazons were famous and well-known constituents of pre-war Asia.

And so, passing through the Caucasus Mountains and their great mountain pass 'gates', guarded largely by the sons of Togarmah and Meshech, we come to the first of the four 'Northern sons' of Japheth, whose descendant nations took the lead in pioneering the settlement of the northernmost reaches of the habitable world at that time: Magog, Ashkenaz, Meshech and Tiras. As these early pioneer nations pushed through the Caucasus for the first time, very generally speaking the descendants of Ashkenaz went West (possibly also via the Bosporus), settling in the Alps and establishing the Celtic Civilization of central Europe that is largely outside the scope of this book, and the descendants of Tiras went

---

[59] Aethiopis, p.111
[60] With the offspring of this union being the nation of the 'Sauromatae'. (Herodotus, p.284)

37

East, albeit borne separately by water. But it is to the famous sons of Magog, many of whom stayed put in this area to the North of the Caucasus and made it their homeland, others spreading Eastwards and Northwards, that we now turn.

j) A Word about the Goths and their history

The Gothic nations are a fairly spectacular and dramatic part of this section of history. Certainly they play perhaps the defining role of the later 'Dark Ages' (roughly from the time of Christ to 800 AD), that can very loosely be summarised as being the period of ascendancy in Europe of the Gothic nations and their Arian form of Christianity. During that time the Goths achieved the following notable political feats:

- The decisive, historic defeat of the Roman Empire on the battlefield of Adrianople in South Eastern Europe in 378 AD, by Ostrogoths under Fritigern
- The conquest of the Roman Empire, including the permanent occupation of its capital Rome and the dissolution of its thousand-year old civic institutions by Odoacer in 478 AD, including its sacking by Visigoths under Alaric I in 410, by Vandals under Genseric in 455 and by Ostrogoths under Totila in 546
- The conquest of a large part of North Africa by Vandals under Gaiseric by 435 AD
- The final defeat of the reviled oriental invader Attila the Hun at the Battle of the Catalaunian Fields in 451 AD in Northern France where the cavalry charge of Theodoric's Visigoths was decisive. From this soon followed the wholesale expulsion of the Huns from Europe
- The conquest of Spain and Southern France by 500 AD, by the Visigoths
- The famous destruction of the dragon 'Grendel' that had been terrorizing the Danish court, by the Northern Goth Beowulf around 500 AD.

These startling military victories attest to the Goths' swashbuckling and warlike culture and way of life. In keeping with this 'easy come easy go' attitude however they were largely unable to hold on to their great gains, losing practically all of them by around 600 AD (losses that interestingly coincided with them abandoning their Aryan beliefs.)

The Gothic nations (an umbrella term for the Visigoths, Ostrogoths, Vandals, Gepids, possibly the Massagetae, Alans, Avars and Roxalani and possibly also the mysterious Sarmatians/Sauromatae) were descendants of Magog (Jordanes[61]) and as such were 'horse people'. That seems to be the overwhelmingly defining characteristic of the Magogians. These Gothic nations represent roughly one half of the famous horse riding Magogian culture, whose riders at one point or another seem to have reached and conquered virtually the entire Eurasian landmass.

The 'urheimat', 'original homeland' or cradle of the Magog nation appears to have been the shores of the Maeotic Lake at the North-East corner of the Black Sea (today's Sea of Azov), that they dominated during early antiquity, whilst retaining significant connections with the lands stretching back down to the Caucasus Mountains, whose 'Caspian Gate' pass was partially controlled by their sometime concubines the Amazons[62]. It is likely that they were either there before Babel – more or less straight off the boat, or they came there immediately after it. Their institutionalization in this part of the world suggests it was before. Indeed it is possible that Magog himself settled at the Lake. The Bible's prophetic reference to an 'end-time' army of 'Gog and Magog' sweeping Southwards towards Jerusalem from the North (presumably through the Caucasus Mountains) most probably refers to 'Goth' and 'Magoth', a description of the descendants of Magog many of whom became known as 'Goths'. While we do not have the exact information, it is possible that 'Goth' represents an early male

---

[61] Jordanes, p.58

[62] Jordanes states that the Amazons only later moved to the Caucasus Mountains, from Scythia, after they had been married to the Goths there, although this is hard to reconcile with their timeline from other sources. (Ibid, p.64)

descendant of Magog, or that it is simply a derivation of 'Magog'.

From here some descendants of the Gothic nations continued further North perhaps as part of archaeology's wider Japhetic Yamnaya horizon that emerged as the earliest post-diluvian Northward migration from the Caucasus, very early on, perhaps 2000 BC or before. Some continued North-East establishing or at least being very associated with the metallurgical manufacturing centre of Sintashta (near today's small Russian town of Bredy, about 40 miles from the Kazakhstan border) where chariots were first developed around 1750 BC, and some continued further East, to a second cradle of the Magogian civilization, in that patch of land, all but completely foreign and unknown to modern Western history, that lies to the East of the Caspian Sea and to the South of the Aral sea. The Aral sea is now all but dried up but during the period under review it was a huge inland lake, and the land between it and the Caspian was a lush and fertile paradise.

These Eastern descendants of Magog[63] were split into distinctive Northern and Southern Magogian heritages, divided roughly by the Oxus River. It appears to have been along the lines of the familiar urban/rural one, with the more free-spirited, nomadic branch remaining further to the North of an urbanized centre that developed in the South. That urban centre, roughly on today's Turkmenistan/Iran border, is one of the most singular archaeological discoveries of the Twentieth Century (mainly the work of Russian archaeologist Viktor Sarianidi), the 'Bactria-Margiana Archaeological Complex'. This is an hitherto completely unknown network of large, sophisticated, incredibly ancient and apparently long-used cities, built on elegant grid patterns, that emerged and are still emerging from the desert sands of the region. The substantiality and astonishing antiquity of the archaeological finds are consistent with the theory that this was a

---

[63] Magog is probably one and the same with the Greek character or 'god' 'Dionysius', AKA 'Bacchus', who famously travelled to the East and to India and conquered it very early on in post-flood history (Diodorus Siculus, vol.1, p.23-27). 'Dionysius' is very likely to have been the progenitor of the 'eastern' Magogians, AKA the Indo-Iranians.

major centre of the Magogite culture (although note Josephus' claim that Bactria was actually founded by a Shemite 'Gather').

The BMAC civilization was the cradle of what linguists call the 'Indo-Iranians'. These Eastern descendants of the Magog family consisted of two of the most famous horse riding nations in history. Firstly a group that dispersed and increased generally southward and westward, the Avestan-speaking Zoroastrian civilization that became the Persian Empire and its successor states the Parthian Empire and the Sasanian Empire, that would war with the Mediterranean GRHF Empires to its West for a thousand years for control of the known world. Secondly a more far-flung group who had as their homeland what they called 'Airyanem Vaejah' on the eastern side of BMAC in today's Tajikistan. Both groups were heavily involved with the Silk Road merchant culture and its nascent Buddhist philosophy, but this second branch probably more so, as they would incorporate elements of it into their own hybrid spiritual system. The Aryans migrated from the Tajik foothills of the Himalayan Plateau to the Indus Valley basin around 1300 BC, dramatically conquering ancient Harappa, bringing to an end its meticulously organised urban civilization and imposing over the top of it their own Sanskrit-speaking, Aryan, quasi-Buddhist culture. From this amalgam later emerged the nation of Hindu India. We know about these events from the Aryans themselves, through their own (probably quite one-sided) records, the Sanskrit Vedas, that subsequently became the foundation texts of Hinduism.

For the purposes of this work, our focus however is on the Northern, rural settlers, who congregated in the area that came to be called Sogdiana close to the oasis of Khorasan, just to the North of Bactria, over the Oxus River in today's Uzbekistan. This Northern branch of the Eastern Magogians appear to have contributed a significant element to that swathe of Northern horse confederacies known to history as the 'Scythians', the vast scope of which label we shall discuss in greater detail later. Josephus states that the Scythians were also descended from Magog[64], however Jordanes insists the Scythians were *not* Goths[65]. Meanwhile Herodotus describes a distinct and less nomadic group within the Scythians who ruled over the others whom he calls the 'Royal Scythians'. It is conjectured here that the Royal Scythians were Magogian (and associated at this time with the Sogdiana region), while the greater and more nomadic body of Scythians were not.

Most of the Gothic nations we therefore find well established North of Caucasia at the time of the Trojan War, in particular settled around the Maeotic Lake, the Goths' ancient homeland, as Jordanes insists. He states that they were attacked there in ancient times by Egyptian Pharaoh Senusret III (whose reign is dated to C.1800 BC). He also mentions an early Gothic leader when they lived in this region, one 'Telefus'[66] whose son 'Eurypylus' took part in the Trojan War. Suffice it to say that the tough Goths dominated the Caucasian isthmus from the Mountains up to Lake Maeotis, and their sister nations to the East essentially 'owned' the Eastern Caspian Sea coast region as well, through the trading centres of BMAC and Sogdiana, as well as producing metal and the world's first chariots at Sintashta, settling Tajikistan and roaming Eurasia's 'Sea of Grass' as a significant component of the countless Scythian hordes.

---

[64] Josephus, vol.4, p.59-61
[65] In fact he takes issue with Josephus' characterisation of them as such (Jordanes, p.58)
[66] According to Jordanes, Telefus (whom he calls a 'Goth') was a son of Heracles by Auge. If true this raises questions of Heracles' ancestry as possibly a descendant of Magog. In Jordanes' account Telefus married a sister of Priam of Troy and founded Moesia, an area in the Balkans that the Goths would later migrate to (Jordanes, p.67). However, Strabo also discusses a Telefus from a similar era, but says he was a son of one 'Teuthras', whom he succeeded as King of Mysia in Anatolia (vol.2, p.327)

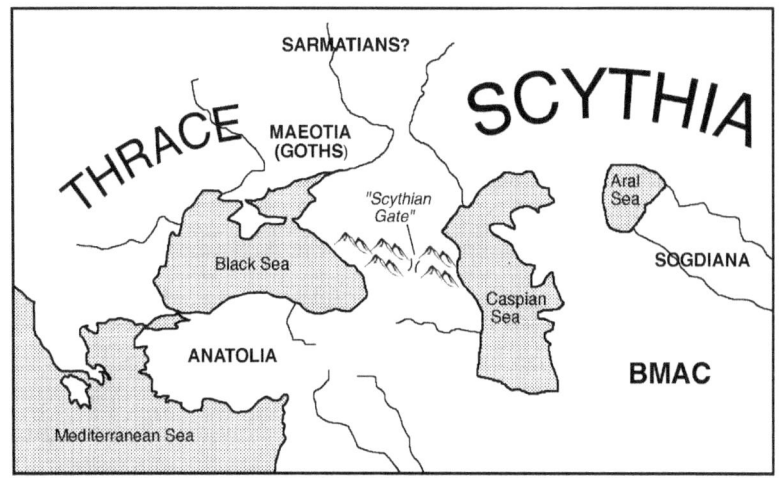

Fig.12: Map showing the approximate locations of Sogdiana, Bactria/BMAC and the Scythians at the time of the Trojan War

k) Scythians

Despite the intriguing possibility of the 'Royal Scythians' being Magogian, the major part of the famous Scythians was almost certainly of another derivation. The Scythians were geographically and probably by population the largest and also the least homogenous group we will discuss in our tour of the pre-Trojan War Black Sea coast. They roamed the 'Sea of Grass' North of the Black and Caspian Seas from China to Thrace for millennia on horseback. It is also hard to call them a nation exactly as they were an agglomeration or continuum, almost certainly containing aspects of many different nations[67]. The name derives from 'rider-shooter', the English words 'shoot' and 'scoot' having the same origin[68], and this describes their characteristic nomadic lifestyle, rather than a particular ethnic origin.

---

[67] Strabo says: 'The ancient Greek writers called all the nations towards the north by the common name of Scythians' (Strabo, vol.2, p.240)

[68] Oswald Szemerényi's exhaustive study of the roots of the term 'Scythian' found that 'Scythian'-type names (including the root of 'Sogdiana', original homeland of the Scythians) all stem from from *skeud-, an ancient Indo-European root meaning "propel, shoot" (cf. English shoot) (Szemerényi, p.45-47). Herodotus describes their self-identifying term as 'Scoloti, after one of their kings' (Herodotus, p.247)

However, while there seems to have been elements of Magog and also Uralic-speaking peoples of the far North (descended from Meshech) amongst the Scythians, and while many commentators have associated them closely with proto-Russian peoples like the Slavs[69], there is one ancient Patriarch they are more closely identified with than any other: Riphath, the second son of Gomer. Gomer, being the oldest of the sons of Japheth, had perhaps the widest-spread and most prodigious legacy. His eldest son Ashkenaz (whose descendants also undoubtedly formed some element of the Scythian hordes) famously went West and founded the Celtic civilization of central Europe, the ethnonym 'German' deriving from 'Gomeran'. Riphath, whose nomadic descendants surely made up the greater part of the 'Yamnaya' archaeological horizon that first spread Northward from the Caucasian Isthmus into the vast Eurasian Steppe, instead seems to have decided to make the 'Sea of Grass' his playground.

There are multiple corroborating historical witnesses to this identification. Greek sources speak of the 'Riphean Mountains' that are most associated with the Ural Mountains of Russia[70], although a second identification with the Carpathian Mountains of South-Eastern Europe exists. Either attests to Riphath being the main Patriarch of the Scythians, as they later swept into Europe to join their cousins the descendants of Ashkenaz in places like Austria and Germany, where after being Romanised they became known as 'Ripuarian Franks'. But the clearest attestation comes from the Middle Irish work Lebor Gabála Érenn that gives 'Riphath Scot' as the name of Gomer's son, a Scythian ancestor of the Goidels (Gaels)[71].

Riphath's offspring were essentially cowboys. Beef-eating, wagon-

---

[69] MacKenzie, p.14-15
[70] Book of Jubilees, p.69. Jordanes also equates them with the Urals (p.59)
[71] Lebor Gabála Érenn, vol.1, p.37. This could make Riphath identical with, or closely related to, the legendary Scythian progenitor 'Targitaus', whom Scythians reported to Herodotus as having lived exactly one thousand years before the invasion of Darius (515 BC), thus dating Targitaus to C.1500 BC (Herodotus, p.247)

trailing, cattle-droving nomads. The Sea of Grass was ideal territory for their way of life. And from them derived the nation of the Scots - their name having this same derivation of 'Scythers'/'Shooters'/'Scooters'), as the Irish records attest, who migrated via the Mediterranean to Ireland C.600-300 BC, and from whom indeed the most famous cowboys of all are descended, these same Scots being the main ethnic component of the population of the United States of America.

The proto-Scottish cowboy Scythians then were busy roaming the Eurasian Steppe at this point in history, on the eve of the Trojan War. It should be noted that they also had a significant connection to Sogdiana, that some have claimed to be the 'original Scotland'.

1) Sarmatians

The mysterious Sarmatians at the time in question were located possibly where they appear in the above map, and possibly to the east of the map, near Sogdiana. Later they would migrate Westward. Their ancestry is problematic, as they are equally claimed to be descended from Magog and Riphath (much like the Scythians). They were also a horse people, and are credited with inventing the heavy cavalry style of warfare that would come to dominate medieval Europe. Herodotus claimed that the Sauromatae/Sarmatians arose from a union between Scythians and Amazons. This doesn't particularly help with identifying their ancestry however, as both Scythians and Amazons had various ethnic components. We will look into the Sarmatians more later.

Maeotian Lake

The Maeotian Lake, AKA the Maeotian Swamp, AKA today's Sea of Azov, looms huge in ancient maps of the region. This was for two reasons. Firstly, it *was* bigger in those days, possibly a lot bigger, encompassing much more of the delta of the Don River (the traditional dividing line between Europe and Asia)[72] than it does today. When we consider far ancient history, it is instructive to remember that the world's natural features and coastlines

---

[72] Josephus, vol.4, p.59; Book of Jubilees, p.69-71

undergo considerable change in what might seem not a huge amount of time. 3000 years ago, who knows exactly what the Northern coastline of the Black Sea looked like. The second reason was its significance. In many ways the Maeotian Lake was the cultural centre of the Black Sea's northern nations, and had a unique status as a locality of particularly exotic mystery and dread to the Mediterranean imperial civilizations. It epitomised the far, far north to them, the dwelling place of fearsome warrior cultures like the Scythians. No-one really knew how big the lake was, with some even believing it continued into the arctic ocean. The whole area was foreboding to them because of its peculiar geography. Mud volcanoes, strange currents, shifting sands and an irregular, swampy depth made it a hazardous and uncertain destination for foreigners, but prime real estate for liberty-seeking freebooters and privateers.

At this time it was the headquarters of the Goths, AKA the Getae, the warlike Western offspring of Magog.

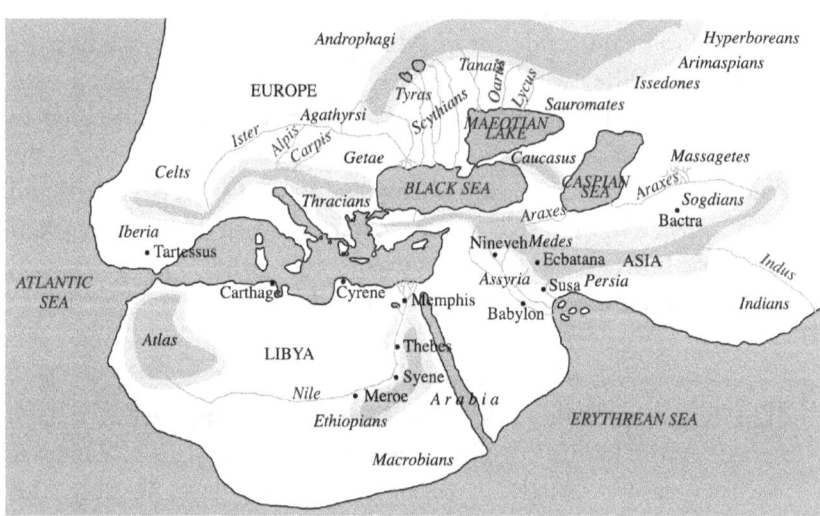

Fig.13: The world according to 6th Century BC Greek historian Hecataeus. The Maeotian Lake is huge![73]

---

[73] Public domain image by Bibi Saint-Pol (https://www.worldhistory.org/image/159/world-map-of-herodotus/) after Cram, p. 568

Ancient Weather

At this point we should take a moment to consider further the question of the environmental conditions during the very ancient period in history that we are discussing. It was not only the geography of the coastlines of the day that were dramatically different to how we see them today, but also the weather.

Such recent attempted revisions of history as Bernard Jones' 'Discovery of Troy and its Lost History' argue that the Trojan War cannot have taken place in the Mediterranean region, amongst other reasons because of its descriptions of cold weather, icy seas, harsh winds, et cetera, when the Mediterranean has a balmy and sunny climate. Yes, it has now. But it wasn't always so. 'Climate change' is a subject that causes much hand-wringing today. And it is a fact that areas of the Earth are warming up and Arctic and Antarctic ice caps are slowly melting and reducing. What often isn't fully understood is that this slow and steady rate of change and ice melting, that can be measured and modelled, is not a new phenomenon of the last couple of centuries, but has continued at virtually the same rate uninterruptedly for millennia. The only reason for today's panic is that western science has only been able to measure it reliably for the past couple of centuries, so people have assumed that it has been caused by modern industrial pollution.

They have assumed this because of the relatively dramatic rate of temperature change and ice sheet melting. That rate can only be extrapolated back a few millennia before causing vast changes to the topography and livability of the globe, and that would be starkly incompatible with the Victorian 'evolution' theory's now conventional narrative of the human historical timescale, that reigns tyrannically amongst today's academic priesthood. That timescale demands that humans evolved hundreds of thousands of years ago in Ethiopia (more or less), and have been walking the Earth since then. However, this is utter nonsense, and completely impossible scientifically when tested against actual evidence. When one takes a more pragmatic and realistic view, drawn from the dates we acquire from scientific facts rather than from dogmatic ideology, we can see that everything points to human existence on this Earth for less than ten thousand years. Startling to those who have been indoctrinated with the academic dogma throughout their school years, but true nonetheless[74].

When we take a sensible approach and apply the model we get from extrapolating back today's rate of climate change, we arrive at the 'Ice Age' somewhere around 2500-2300 years BC. And that is roughly when it happened. The catastrophic global flood involved enormous tectonic and seismic shifts of the Earth's surface. It also involved an unprecedented amount of rain and ice falling from the sky. During this maelstrom, the magnetic pull of the North and South Poles drew a gigantic amount of water to themselves, and this is the source of the polar ice caps we see there today.

After the flood, when the waters receded, what we call the Ice Age followed immediately afterwards. A period when, as we know, the northern glaciers were around the line of 55° latitude, somewhere around today's Poland, and everything above that was ice sheet and all but unlivable for human beings.

This model perfectly explains the record of history. Places like the Maeotian Lake were considered the far North of human habitation at this time, because they were. It explains many anomalies in the history of civilizations, like why the flag of Lebanon has a cedar tree on it when cedar trees can no longer be grown there because it is too warm, or why the Mesopotamian delta of the Tigris and Euphrates in the Persian Gulf became the cradle of human urban development and farming settlement, when today Iraq is largely an arid desert. It wasn't at the time.

---

[74] One can, for example, look at the rate of coastline erosion, that is measurably vastly too rapid to be consistent with hundreds of thousands or geologically millions of years of Earth history, but like the climate change evidence, is perfectly consistent with less than 10,000 years of Earth history.

So when we are discussing the Northern Black Sea coast around 1000 BC, we are indeed talking about an area of rain, snow and icy conditions that was barely habitable and had the climate and wildness of today's Scandinavia. And 'Asia' itself, today's Turkey, was not only culturally the equivalent of the modern era's Europe, it shared its temperate, frosty and verdant climate as well. 'The past is a different country, they do things differently there' is highly relevant to ancient weather.

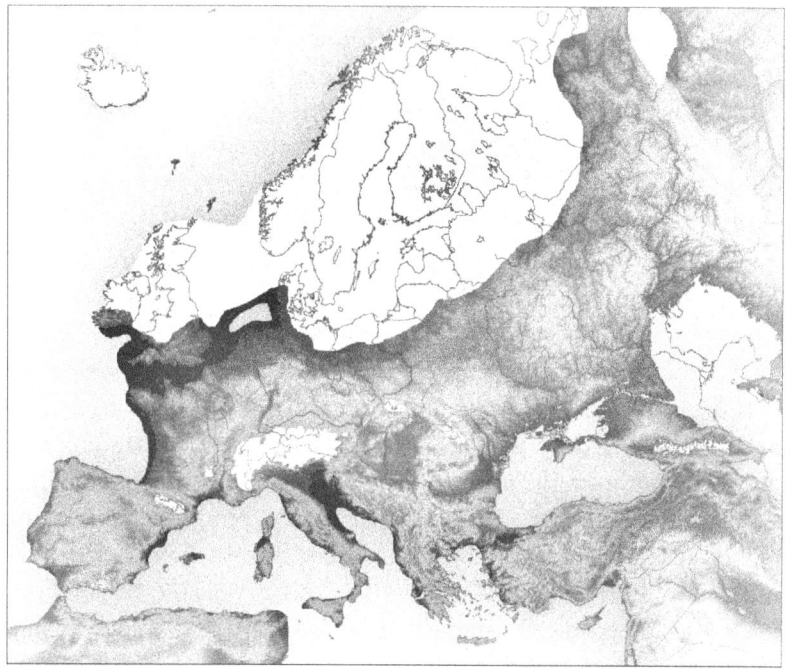

Fig.14: Europe during the last Ice Age. Conventional history demands that this state of affairs existed as far back as 110,000 years or more, only beginning to melt around 20,000 years ago. But the evidence including from human history shows that it began after the flood only 4,000 to 5,000 years ago, and was melting from approximately 2,300 BC[75].

---

[75] Image by San Jose (https://commons.wikimedia.org/wiki/File:Weichsel-W%C3%BCrm-Glaciation.png) used under CC BY SA 3.0 (https://creativecommons.org/licenses/by-sa/3.0/deed.en)

m) Thrace

Later the western borders of the Goths would amalgamate into a new polity known as Dacia, but before then, at the time of the Trojan War, westward of the Maeotian Lake (land of the Goths and Scythians) began Thrace. Its story is a remarkable one. From here on round to Troy, the territory of the time was dominated by the nation we can call 'greater Thrace'. That is, those people who were descended from its famous founder. This founder of the Thracian nation can be identified by the countless number of place and people names spread not only around this region, but around the whole of Asia. This includes the City of Troy itself, that etymology surely renders all but impossible not to have been founded by this same culture, that was descended from the same founder.

Here are a few of those names: 'Tiras' (the Greek name for the River Dniester, in Thrace), 'Thrace', 'Troy', 'Troas'/ 'the Troad' (the area surrounding Troy), 'Thuringians' (perhaps the remnants of Thracians in later centuries) and 'Teucrians'. The distinctive 'TR-S' sound among place names is amazingly ubiquitous in this part of the world. It is argued here that this is a consequence of descent from a single ancient patriarch who bore such a name, as this is overwhelmingly the main reason behind the naming of places and settlements, as we have already seen. This individual must have lived very early in post-flood history, as the city of Troy itself was already well established by 1600 BC. All the evidence points to the fact that this was Tiras, the youngest son of Japheth, known to the Greeks as Thrax or Ares[76], to other groups as Teuter or Teucer, and to his Scandinavian descendants as 'Thor'[77].

Scandinavian records are quite clear that Thor was a real person, who lived in 'Turkland' and was a famous warrior and leader[78]. Japhetic culture has always been very prone to ancestor worship,

---

[76] See also Gill, commentary on Genesis 10, verse 2 (Gill, Vol.1)

[77] Pronounced 'Tour'. His name is possibly also the origin of the 'tour', a mode of life much associated with him.

[78] Prose Edda, p.6

and many of the deities of its pagan pantheons, as we shall see, were in fact real ancestors, whose expoits were passed down the generations until they attained the status of 'gods' within the culture of their descendants.

Snorri Sturluson's history however has Thor as the maternal grandson of King Priam of Troy, the King of the City during the time of the Trojan War, and the son of one Mennon[79]. Similarly Greek history has a Teucer of that generation as well (let's call him 'Teucer 2'), a son of King Telemon of Salamis and his wife, the daughter of King Laemedon, Priam's Father[80] (who despite this fought on the Greek side in the war). However there is a big problem with this theory, that Thor/Teucer lived in the era of the Trojan War. What about all the names? Even granting that there was a Thor/Teucer alive and active during the war (and this Teucer while fighting in the war is not particularly prominent amongst his contemporaries), all reason requires that the name of the City of Troy itself, Thrace, Thracians, the Troas, etc, must have come from some earlier source, as they predate him by as much as a thousand years and by at least 600. This creates a presumption that there must have been an earlier Thor/Teucer, who gave his name to and originated all these ethnonyms.

And indeed, Greek history has multiple other characters bearing virtually the same name from earlier eras, that could point to this originator of the ubiquitous 'T/R/S' place and people names. Firstly there is Tros, three generations back from Priam, whom the Greeks credited with founding the Kingdom of Troy (whose capital they called 'Ilus' after Tros's son 'Ilios'[81].) Even further back however is another Teucer, Tros's great grandfather. This Teucer (son of Scamander[82] and Idea), let's call him 'Teucer 1' was of the generation before Dardan (son of Javan), six generations back from Priam according to classical Greek records, and he inhabited the

---

[79] Prose Edda, p.6
[80] Iliad, p.240
[81] Ibid, p.511
[82] AKA Xanthus (not the historian)

Troad before the arrival of Dardan (after whom the Dardanelles Strait is named), having come there from Crete[83]. Upon Dardan's arrival in Anatolia Teucer gave him land there and also his daughter in marriage, and Dardan became King after him[84]. This Teucer, claim the Greeks, gave his name to what would later be called the Troad, AKA Teucria and to its inhabitants his descendants, who became known as Teucrians[85]. Really, any one of these three options could be the Scandinavian 'Thor'. However, it is argued here that only the earlier two would adequately explain the very early existence of the T/R/S place names in the area. And really only the earliest Teucer would explain the great reputation of 'Thor' as being the *originator* of the 'T/R/S' 'nation'. – It is difficult to believe, though not impossible, that later descendants named after him would eclipse his fame. The early Teucer would also match the dating of the Biblical character Tiras, whom Josephus states plainly was the ancestor of the Thracians[86]. And then there is 'Thrax', the 'god version' we would suggest of this same early personage (possibly one and the same with the more famous 'Ares' of Greek mythology[87]). This all adds up to a reasonable presumption, despite the Prose Edda, that the founder of the Trojan 'nation' was Teucer son of Scamander of Greek history, AKA Tiras, youngest son of Japheth, AKA 'Thor', legendary ancestor of the Scandinavians. If not, it is still more likely that Snorri's Trojan War-era 'Thor' was named after some much earlier 'Thor' ancestor.

---

[83] Strabo, vol.2, p.373.
[84] Diodorus Siculus, vol.1, p.285
[85] Ibid
[86] Josephus, vol.4, p.61
[87] The description of the ethnicity of Penthesilea the Amazon Queen from the Aethiopis runs thus: 'The Amazon Penthesilea arrives to fight with the Trojans, a daughter of the War god, of Thracian stock.' Here then is a descendant of 'the war god' (Ares) described in the same sentence as being 'of Thracian stock'. Which is it? Or indeed are Ares and Tiras the same person? (Aethiopis, p.111) Gill also thought so (Gill, vol.1, note under Genesis 10:2)

While the nations of Magog were 'horse people', the nations of Ashkenaez were 'earth people' and the nations of Riphath were 'cow people', the nations of Tiras were very definitely 'sea or ship people'. The maritime tradition among the descendants of Thor is crystal clear and distinct from the very beginning. The Black Sea was their initial stomping ground, and they dominated its logistics and trade. In particular the city of Troy through its control of the Dardanelles strait enjoyed as decisive and pre-eminent a trading crossroads role between Mediterranean and Black Seas, and between European and Asian continents, as Constantinople (that was built probably at a location better suited to the changed coastline) enjoyed two thousand years later.

Seaborne ship transportation and trade was the speciality of the descendants of Thor, and they roamed the seaways of the time very broadly. Those seaways were not necessarily the Mediterranean. In fact all the evidence is that Troy was about the furthest South that Tirassian sailors ventured. Again we must remember that the topography of the era was very different to how it appears to us today. The entire of Asia Eastward from the Black Sea was one long sequence of seas and inland lakes all joined by a vast, seemingly endless network of rivers and tributaries. Whoever could master the navigation of those waterways, had at their disposal a transportation network as extensive and almost as fast as a modern motorway system. The Tirassians were those people. Their ship trade was done mostly by river, honing the skills of rowing that would become a stock in trade of the Scandinavian people. While the 'old Thrace' of Western Anatolia and South-Western Europe was booming with its capital Troy, this Eastward exploration was perhaps less important. But there is no doubt that very early on this vast waterborne expansion made its way across to the silk road, founding eastern Tirassian outposts of great wealth and prestige, a civilization almost completely unknown to modern scholarship, in the area around the Tarim basin in today's North-Western China, whose cultures and descendants bear the familiar etymological link to the ancient Patriarch: they are called the 'Tocharians', the 'Turans' and perhaps even the Turks.

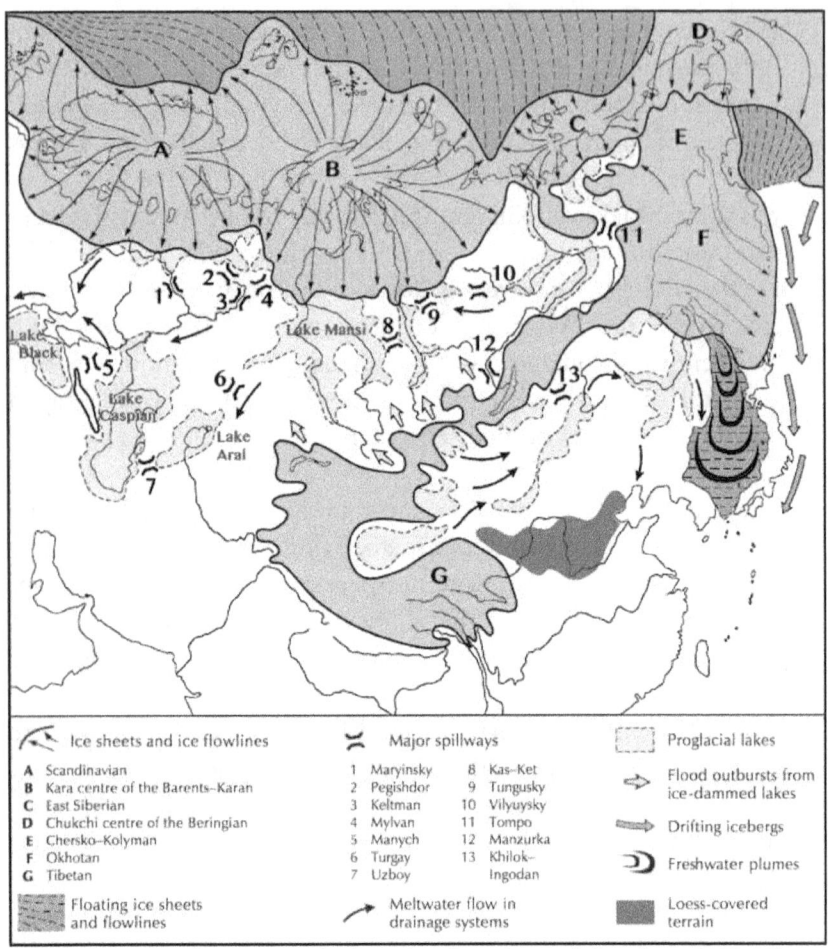

Fig.15: this map of Eurasia at the last glacial maximum (of perhaps 2200 BC) gives some idea of the greatly increased extent of its waterways in ancient history, including the remarkably arctic conditions that must have still have prevailed in North-West China and today's Kyrgyzstan and Uzbekistan at the time of the Trojan War (C. 1200 BC)[88]

---

[88] Image by Grosswald, p.210. Adapted by Huggett, p.232. © Wiley Publishing Corp. Used under licences

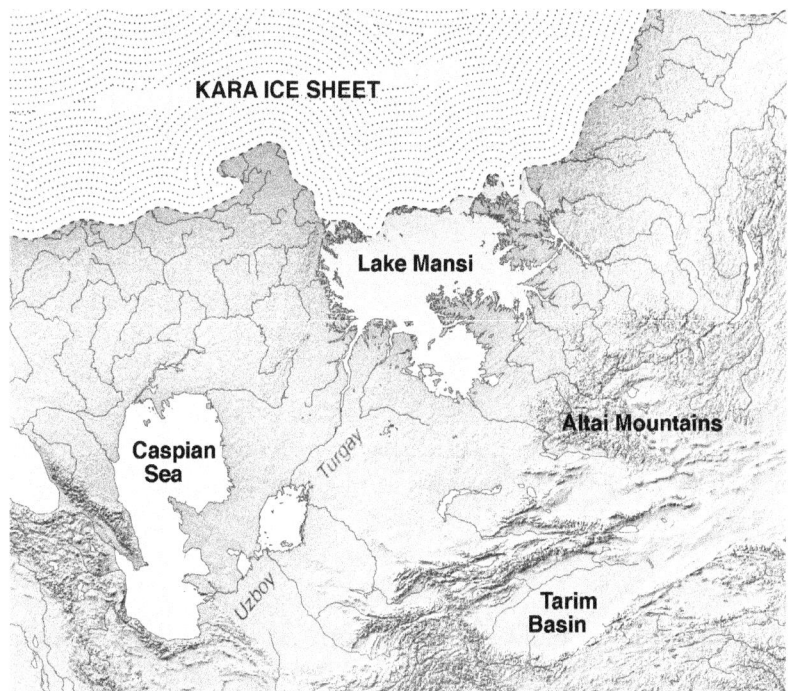

Fig.16: This map shows some of the major river systems utilized by the Tirassians in their vast trade Eastwards. Note the enlarged Caspian and Aral Seas, and the river system joining them, the 'Uzboy Pass'. Note also the Turgay River and the huge Lake Mansi (now disappeared), that would have facilitated maritime transit from the Black Sea to the Altai Region[89]

In the West of European Thrace, in what was later called Moesia, Thracians lived alongside Celts/ Germans, descendants of Ashkenaz. And from there along the waterway systems of Asia there were Tirassian settlements and trading posts all the way to China.

Now we are starting to understand the significance of the City of Troy to the ancient world. It was possibly *the* trading City of the entire globe, and must have been a glittering prize to its Western Japhetic neighbours the Mycenaean Greeks, for whom it would

---

[89] Image by Hellerick, with all labels added by the author. From Wikimedia Commons (https://commons.wikimedia.org/wiki/File:Ice_Age_glacial_lakes_of_Siberia_and_Central_Asia_-_ru.svg) used under CC BY SA 3.0 (https://creativecommons.org/licenses/by-sa/3.0/deed.en)

have appeared as a tantalizing gateway to unknown wonders of the East.

n) Troas/ The Troad

So passing over the Dardanelles Strait we come to Troas, that is the ancient name for today's Biga peninsula of Northwestern Turkey, the region or province of the City of Troy, and very likely the original homeland of Thor and the Thracians, who spread out from there Northwest across the Dardanelles strait into South-Eastern Europe, but retained this foothold in Anatolia, the ancient and original homeland of the Europeans. A foothold that was, however, increasingly under pressure from its neighbours. The region of Troas was also known at this time as 'Assuwa' and later part of 'Arzawa'.

What is Asia?

At this point we should discuss the term 'Asia'. As we have seen it did not mean then what it means to us generally today, and its true meaning has more or less been lost over the millennia. Now it refers to a vast geographical region that stretches from the Dardanelles Strait to Japan. But back then it referred to a people group. The people group most associated with this region, because its people transversed it like no other. Throughout this period of history, we encounter the prefix or suffix 'Az' that is a reference to them.

As we have seen, Western Anatolia was named for this people, both by the Greeks to their West (Ἀσία) and by the Hittites to their East (Assuwa). This was the area of the 'Az'[90]. But not only this area. Let's look at some of the other 'Az' names:

We have of course, Asia, in both its Greek and Hittite forms, then there is the Sea of Asov, so-called today, a confluence of 'Az' people in later eras, after they had fled their ancient homeland in

---

[90] Herodotus while admitting ignorance of the subject relates that in his day the Lydians claimed the name came from the 'Asias' tribe at Sardis, that 'Asies' was the son of Cotys, grandson of Manes (Herodotus, p.261)

'Asia'. There's also 'Azerbaijan', the region to the South-East of the Caucasus Mountains, East of Iberia. We saw that the Hittites also called Armenia to their East 'Azzi-Hayaza', so there were 'Az' there also. But we can go much further afield. The name of the Roxolani, one of the later possibly Gothic nations of upper Caucasia, has been translated as meaning 'Rukh-Az-Alani', meaning 'the fair-haired-Az Alans'[91]. And it is proposed that this 'Rukh-Az' construction may be the origin of the name 'Russia'[92]. One element of the Sarmatians that later entered South-West Europe were the 'Iazyges'. And the name that the Scandinavians of ancient times knew themselves as according to their records is quite clear: they were the 'Æsir'.

So what did it mean? Well, it is the contention of this book that the 'Az' of 'Asia' was well known during the era of ancient history we are looking at to refer to either Europeans (descendants of Japheth) in general, or to the descendants of Thor in particular, AKA Tour-Az or 'Tiras', from whom comes the ethnonyms 'Tirassian', 'Thracian' and 'Trojan', that can clearly be seen to be variations of the same term, as well as the place name 'Tro-Az'. In other words the Scandinavians. And that this generality of awareness of their common cultural connections across what is now 'Asia', as well as the vast significance of their historical tradition and heritage in this area, has been all but lost to history, until now. Why is this story such 'forbidden history'? Who knows. Quite possibly it suited everybody including the 'Azians' themselves for them to disappear not only from the Asian continent but also from the pages of history altogether, as we shall see.

---

[91] MacKenzie, p.16
[92] Although an alternative derivation from a later Finnish name for Swedes: 'Ruotsalaiset' also exists (Russian Primary Chronicle book, p.48)

Pressure on Troy

The Hittite Empire to Troy's East was the big boy on the block during this era. It called the region of Troas 'Taruiša' and its capital Troy 'Wilusa' (interestingly following the Greek name for Troy, 'Ilios').

Around 1400 BC Hittite expansion Westward was such that Troy formed the 'Assuwa Confederation' of the 22 states of the Troad and its surrounding area for mutual defence against the Empire, including such Southern neighbours as Lukka/Lycia (speakers of the ancient Anatolian language Luwian, a relative of Trojan), the Leleges/Caria, Mira and also Mysia. It didn't work. The Confederation was defeated by the Hittite Emperor Tudhaliya I and broken up[93].

The Assuwa League was replaced/ re-organized by the Hittites as 'Arzawa', a wider political grouping based further South that was probably something of a puppet regime and had as its 'capital' 'Apasa', AKA Ephesus, in Mira. This later state subsequently also rebelled against the Hittites, requiring significant military effort by Hittite Emperors Suppiluliuma I and Mursili II around 1300 BC to subdue it.

---

[93] Hittite Correspondence, p.6, 135-8

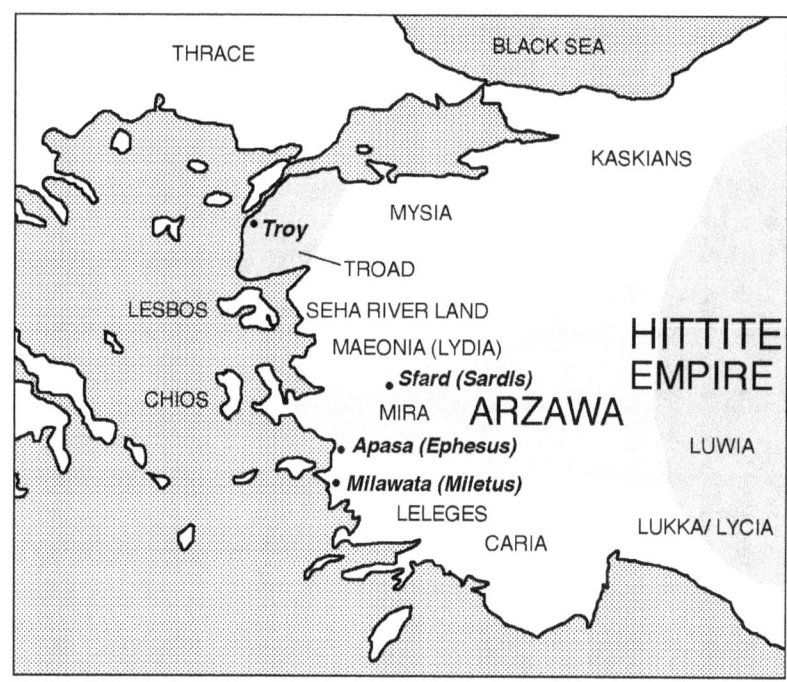

Fig.17: A reminder of the situation in Western Anatolia in the lead up to the war

Troy itself meanwhile had been forced to make terms with the Hittites, typified by the Aleksandu Treaty of around the same time between the Trojan King Aleksandu and the Hittite Emperor Muwatalli II[94]. This required the Trojans to provide intelligence and some soldiers for Hittite battles, and indeed soldiers from the area numbered amongst the Hittite forces when they fought the Egyptian army of Ramses II at the titanic Battle of Kadesh in C.1274 BC[95].

---

[94] Hittite Treaties, p.87

[95] Ramses' 'Poem on the Battle of Kadesh' lists amongst the Hittite army Dardanians, Mysians, Lycians, Pisidians (near Lukka) and Arzawans (Egyptian Inscriptions, vol.3, p.138, 141). While many have read into this that Trojans fought in the battle, in fact the name of Wilusa does not appear. Dardanians are distinct from Trojans in the Iliad (p.125-126), and the absence of Wilusa/Trojan forces in the list rather suggests that Troy/Alaksandu was independent of Hatti at this time. That would fit with the somewhat pleading tone of the Alaksandu Treaty for Alaksandu to be an ally of the Hittites and support their Arzawa political structure in the area.

But this seems to have been a shifting arrangement that may only have lasted for that generation. Arguably bigger problems were developing for the Trojans from their neighbours to the West.

And this is where the politics gets muddy. Because it appears there may have been major support for military activities against the Hittites from Mycenaean Greece, known to the Hittites as 'Ahhiyawa', their rendering of 'Achaea', the Achaeans being at that time the most dominant of the four main Greek ethnicities.

Both Greek and Hittite history records significant Greek activity in Anatolia before the war, but it is far from easy reconciling the two versions. Way back in 1500 BC the Hittite history reveals a major invasion of Western Anatolia by the Achaeans under a leader 'Attarsiya'[96], often thought to correspond to Greek history's 'Atreus', the father or Grandfather of Agamemnon, King of the Greeks in Homer's epochal account of the Trojan War, the 'Iliad'[97]. It is even suggested by some that this invasion was the war itself, with 'Attarsiya' meaning 'those of Atreus', but this is unlikely, in that this earlier invasion took place much further South than Troy. Atreus, if it was he, conquered Miletus (AKA 'Milawata') in South-Western Anatolia, establishing the first Greek colony there that displaced the Anatolian-speaking Leleges (who had themselves settled there as part of a Minoan colony centuries earlier)[98].

---

[96] Hittite Correspondence, p.69
[97] Iliad, p.78, 80-81
[98] According to Strabo (vol.2, p.328), the Carians AKA Leleges "settled on the continent [i.e. Asia/ Anatolia – Ed.] with the assistance of the Cretans," and Miletus was built by the Cretan Sarpedon, the brother of King Minos. Thus continues an ongoing theme of early settlement of Anatolia from Crete, including by Thor himself, if he is to be identified with the Greek Teucer '1', who lived first at Crete, only later to move to 'Teucria' AKA Asia after a famine (Strabo, vol.2, p.373). This is highly consistent with the seafaring culture of Thor's descendants, as the Minoans of Crete had a maritime monopoly during super-antiquity, at least in the Mediterranean and Atlantic (in particular running the transatlantic copper trade), and Thor may have learned his seamanship from them. Hamites had gained sea experience through their initial colonisation of Africa by ship from Sumer (Rohl, 1999, p.252), 'Poseidon', the Greek 'god' of the sea, representing Ham (see for example Odyssey, p.80). Strabo also says the leaders of the Leleges were 'a Trojan

Moreover, there was considerable Achaean (Greek) involvement in the wars against the Hittites, firstly by the Assuwa League and then by Arzawa. Indeed, the war against the Hittites by Arzawa C.1300 BC can more or less be stated to have been an Achaean campaign against the Hittite Empire, launched from their new Anatolian stronghold of Miletus and led by an Achaean King.

Other Greek adventures in Anatolia are recorded in Greek history, such as Heracles' attack on Troy and Bellerophon's quest to Lycia where he battled the Amazons[99]. While Hittite records speak of one 'Piyamaradu', a warlord of Western Anatolia in the mid to late 1200s BC who also caused problems for the empire, and was a sometime ally of the Achaeans[100]. It would appear that Piyamaradu was considered 'part' of the Hittite world but nevertheless conquered multiple cities including Troy and claimed a level of independence from the empire over a period of 35 years. It is argued with some substance that this figure is one and the same as King Priam of Troy, recorded in the Iliad as being King at the time of the Trojan War[101]. His complex political manoeuvrings between the Greeks and Hittites would be very consistent with the pre-war power struggles of an increasingly desperate local ruler[102].

Because it would seem that the ancient trading state of Troy was increasingly finding itself caught in the middle of a growing regional power struggle between the two local heavyweight states: the Hittites and the Greeks. The established Hatti to their East and the burgeoning Mycenaean Greeks to their West, who were apparently spoiling for a fight.

---

dynasty' (Strabo, vol.2, p.344)
[99] Ibid, p.328
[100] Hittite Correspondence, p.140
[101] Iliad, p.100
[102] For a fuller discussion in detail of the activities of Piyamaradu and the chronology and dating of the lead up to the Trojan War and the war itself from original sources, see Appendix 2: The Trojan War through the Eyes of the Hittites.

o) The Greeks

And so finally we come to the Greeks, who dwelt in the mountainous Thessalian peninsula and the Aegean islands to the immediate West of the Trojan World we have reviewed. Descended from Japheth's fourth son Javan, one might have thought they would have kept their place leaving leadership of the Japhetic nations to descendants of the older sons Gomer, Magog and Madai. But the Greeks had a reason why they felt they should vie for and deserved pre-eminence among the sons of Japheth: they had a secret weapon - they had Japheth!

Whilst the idea that 'gods' of ancient pantheons often represent memories of real people, usually 'kept alive' by their descendants, is dismissed by some as 'euhemerism', taking the evidence logically there is really no other explanation that fits the facts. Japheth was well known, under various names, to all the descendant nations of his offspring. And the linguistic evidence is overwhelming that they refer to the same person. The Vedic Aryan 'Pra Japati[103]' is the same person as Roman 'Jupiter' and Scandinavian 'Tyr'[104]. The Greek histories, though an immense quagmire of soap-opera-like poetic additions and confusing artistic licence-taking are crystal clear about one thing. The undisputed ruler of their realm was called Zeus (from Indo-European 'Deus Pater' meaning to them

---

[103] Rigveda, vol.4, p.273, 356, 404. According to Griffith's sources, Prajapati has seven sons (Rigveda book, vol.4, p.155), and according to Griffith, one of his sons is named 'Prajavan' (Ibid, p.413)

[104] Poetic Edda, p.140-142. This section of the Edda (Hymiskvitha), though confusing, appears to suggest a family relationship between Hymir (probably one and the same with 'Ymir' (Noah), described as a 'giant', who dwells 'to the east'), Hymir's son Tyr, and Tyr's son or at least confidante Thor. Thor goes to Tyr for advice on how to acquire a large 'kettle' in which to brew ale, Tyr advises him to seek out 'my father' Hymir. The two go together on a trip to visit Hymir to get the kettle. 'Tyr' is the origin of the English day name 'Tuesday'.

'Sky Father'[105]) and he lived with them upon Mount Olympus[106].

A made-up fantasy dwelling place of the imaginary 'gods' perhaps? Well no, Mount Olympus is a real place, it is the highest Mountain in Greece, and you can visit it today.

The facts have to be faced. Japheth was a real person. He really was the father of the European nations, and he appears to have chosen as his permanent home the mountain towards the East of the Thessalian peninsula that became the starting point of Greek Civilization. It was here that he held court and where his sons and daughters visited and interacted with him. No wonder the Greeks believed they had a head start in Western Civilization!

One aspect of the residency of Zeus on Mount Olympus should be noted. One might wonder why Zeus would be seen as such a 'god' among Greeks and many Japhethites, even perhaps during his own lifetime. Well, a person who has survived a global cataclysmic flood, and has lived in an era before it so different as to be virtually a separate state of existence in what must have seemed like a different universe, would be a figure of some standing in the community. Add to this the tremendous additional information, 'wisdom', quite possibly technology (his abilities concerning the manipulation of weather are almost always mentioned) that such an upbringing would furnish Japheth, that would give him unassailable advantages over younger men, none of whom could ever claim anything approaching such insight, and all of whom were if not his own direct offspring then at least his dependants and subordinates, such that his abilities and know-how could quite easily appear to them supernatural or superhuman.

---

[105] Zeus is credited with unusual expertise with weather, particularly lightning (Hesiod, p.9, 43), and is usually pictured holding a lightning bolt. This is highly appropriate for someone who spent a formative part of his life on the ocean! The title 'Sky-Father' denotes both Zeus's particular domain of the sky (rather than the ocean or the underworld, given to his brothers (Apollodorus, p.11)) and also his association for the Greeks with God Almighty, who is usually termed (e.g. in Hesiod, p.21, 53) some variation of 'their father, Sky'.
[106] Hesiod, p.5-7

Then there are the copious evidences that human beings of this super-ancient era were physically larger than those of today. The environmental conditions before the flood, as evidenced by the hugely larger bones and remains of every type of animal discovered from that time, were overwhelmingly more conducive to growth. The grave of Noah's wife at Sagliksuyu in the mountains of Ararat is over fifteen feet long. A similar height is ascribed to the bed of Og King of Bashan (13 ½' long and 6' wide[107]), an opponent of Joshua's Israelite force occupying Canaan sometime around 1600 BC. And then there's Goliath, the Philistine champion defeated by King David around 1000 BC, whose height was recorded as 9 and a half feet[108].

Finally, what if you encountered such an unusual man 500 years later? Living on a mountain, surrounded by hundreds of years of his own descendants. According to the Bible, sometime after the flood humanity was limited to an approximately 120 years' lifespan. But not before that. If these characters were real, and the record of written history attests overwhelmingly, repeatedly and with multiple cross-referenced sources that they were, there are not many rational reasons to disbelieve what it says about their lifespans. And it says that Japheth's (probably elder) brother Shem lived for 502 years after the flood[109]. There are also multiple corroborating witnesses that record similar lifespans for the early generations after the flood, for example Togarmah in 'Life of Kartli' (600 years)[110], the many Kings of the Sumerian King list, and others[111].

Japheth or 'Zeus' seems to have settled into his mountain retirement home soon after the flood. It is unlikely that he would have been much involved in the tumultuous events of younger generations at Babel, so he may have been there before the Babel

---

[107] Tanakh, p.121
[108] Tanakh, p.194
[109] Tanakh, p.7
[110] Life of Kartli, p.13
[111] see also Josephus, citing multiple other historians (Josephus, vol.4, p.51-52). For more on this see Appendix 1: Plato on the 'gods' of super ancient history

dispersion. Mount Olympus seems to have been a meeting place not just for Japheth and his offspring but for all 'gods' as the early generations after the flood were known by the Greeks[112]. In particular Japheth and his two brothers Poseidon (probably Ham, or possibly Canaan) and Hades[113] (probably Shem) and their immediate family. 'Titans' was the term used by the Greeks to refer to the pre-flood generations[114], of whom only Cronus, the brothers' father (AKA Noah) survived[115]. The rest having been imprisoned in 'Tartarus' (basically hell), under the earth's surface[116].

It would appear that Japheth departed from his father's faith in God, increasingly taking advice from an 'oracle' witchcraft system located at Dodona in Epirus[117], that was later transplanted further South to Delphi and continued on throughout Classical Greek history[118].

---

[112] Hesiod, p.12-13, 35 and Lactantius, vol.1, p.30-31
[113] Ibid, p. 39
[114] Ibid, p.21. Meaning 'strainers', i.e. for their own glory, with whom 'their father, great Sky' was angry. Presumably the equivalent of 'Anunnaki', the Sumerian term for the antediluvian 'gods' (Epic of Gilgamesh, p.711)
[115] Hesiod, p.55. Greek mythology records some element of 'overthrow' of Cronus by Zeus (Hesiod, p.9, 35, 41, 43) (following on from the bizarre story of Cronus' emasculation of his father by which Zeus is conceived – see also the same story with the Hittite version of Japheth, 'Tarhunta'/'Teshub', whom the Hittites adopted as their own 'storm god' from their Japhethite neighbours the Hurrians). However this may have been a one-sided view from Japheth's and/or his descendants' perspective only. No other testimony of Noah's life describes any particular disempowerment of him by any of his sons. The fact that Japheth dwelt in the far north-west of the habitable world while Noah continued to live near the centre of human civilization suggests rather that it was Japheth who was the perhaps self-imposed exile.
[116] Hesiod, p.61-63
[117] Iliad, p.420. 'Dione' or the first 'Sibyl', was the diviner or witch that Japheth consulted. Later, according to Greek legend, slain by 'Python', son of 'Gaia'. The later Delphic 'oracle' was recorded as having been established or run by 'Apollo' (possibly Javan, although other sources cite him as a son of Magog).
[118] Euhemerus relates that Jupiter, AKA Japheth, ended his life in Crete, and that his sepulchre was at Knossos (Lactantius, vol.2, p. 101)

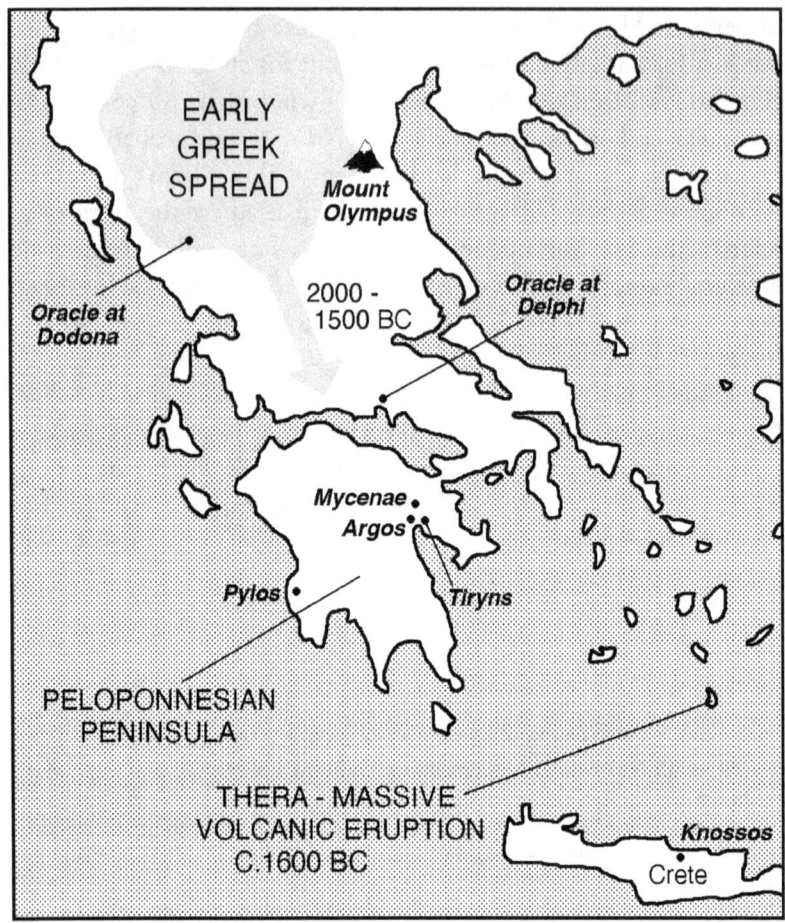

Fig.18: The development from the proto-Greece of C.2150 BC to Mycenaean Greece by around 1500 BC.

Greek civilization spread out Westward from Mount Olympus, as seen in the above map. It would appear that Javan was either a favourite son or just a sycophantic one. Either way he stuck to his father's side and settled right there with him, while his sons settled the Aegean islands, Elisha and Kitt settling Cyprus and Dardan giving his name to the Dardanelles strait[119].

---

[119] The Greek 'god' 'Adonis' may be Dardan's grandson by Erichtonious, 'Ganymede' (Iliad, p.511), kidnapped and brought to Mount Olympus because of his beauty.

It should be noted that this was quite far from the Hellenic Greece of the later Classical period. This culture was not particularly homosexual; there was yet an almost complete absence of pagan shrines in Mycenaean Greek archaeology, and one look at the brutal boar-tusk helmeted war-gear of a Mycenaean panoply, unrecognizable from the familiar Greek Hoplite armour, lets us know that this proto-Greek society was a world away from the effete narcissism of later Classical Greece.

Hellen, the eponymous founder of the Hellenes, whom we know as the Greeks, whose sons and grandsons supposedly founded the four main ethnicities of the Hellenes: the Dorians, the Achaeans, the Ionians and the Aeolians, was a descendant of Japheth, perhaps born later of Javan. Unfortunately Greek history and genealogy is a convoluted mess. Millennia of dramatic re-interpretations all with their own separate artistic nuance have left us with an incredibly confused record of whose children were whose, and often with multiplications of the same person into separate poetic, spiritual and historic versions. For example Japheth is known as the 'god' Zeus, the more prosaic, historical ancient father figure 'Iapetus' and also possibly 'Pronous'. Meanwhile in the traditional version Iapetus is the father of Prometheus whose story most resembles that of Ham[120], who in turn is the father of Deucalion, who is unmistakably the Greek (historical) version of Noah![121] Deucalion is usually given as the father of Hellen, or in some versions the father of Pronous[122], father of Hellen. In this case Hellen himself is most likely to be the Biblical Javan. However the name of Hellen's Grandson 'Ion', patriarch of the Ionians, also bears close resemblance to 'Javan'. In short despite the copious number of ancient primary sources on the subject we are regrettably left with an embarrassingly

---

[120] Other 'versions' of Ham include Poseidon, Pluto (Apollodorus, p.11) and Hephaestus (at least Moses of Khorene thought so (p.81), see also Apollodorus, p.25)
[121] Apollodorus, p.55
[122] Hecataeus (Greek Historical Fragments, vol. 1, p.2)

incomplete and unreliable record of early Greek genealogy[123].

The first known capital of Greece was established at Argos, considerably to the South of Mount Olympus, on the Peloponnesian peninsula (that would have been a much warmer and easier climate to settle) sometime between 2000 and 1500 BC by its first King, Inachus[124], who may have been a descendant of Iapetus or may have arrived from Africa[125].

The Javanic or Greek culture grew slowly over the next 500 years. It was overshadowed by and was a client state of the Minoan Empire of Crete, one of the early civilizations. The Minoan capital of Knossos was the leading local power centre (the basis of the legend of Theseus and the Minotaur) and possibly one of the first post-diluvian islands settled.

But something dramatic happened to Crete and the Minoan Civilization around 1600 BC. One of its nearby outlying islands, 'Thera', exploded in a spectacular volcanic eruption. The Cretan Empire was totally destroyed[126]. This left a power vacuum in the

---

[123] The identification of Ion with Javan is etymologically very likely. But if the family tree structure is retained around it, Japheth would be Hellen and the other three proto-Greek nations essentially 'other' nationalities who either co-existed from early times with, or 'invaded', Javanian culture (see later re: Dorians). Josephus states plainly that the Aeolians are descended from Javan's eldest son Elisha (vol.4, p.63), while the (somewhat dubious) medieval source 'Book of the Bee' states persuasively that Elisha is himself Hellas AKA Hellen (p.38). In light of this perhaps also Aeolus, making Elisha/Hellen the 'true' progenitor of the Greeks, Ionians a generic term for Javanians, and Achaeans and Dorians as yet unaccounted for.
[124] Augustine of Hippo, vol.2, p.221
[125] Apollodorus, p. 297. Inachus may then have been a 'Pelasgian'. The Pelasgians inhabited the Peloponnese before the Greeks arrived.
[126] Thera and its eruption are often thought to be the model for Plato's island of 'Atlantis' that 'disappeared into the depths of the sea' after exerting an imperial influence on Mediterranean states including primaeval Athens (Plato, vol.3. p.446; p. 527-543). While Atlantis is undoubtedly partially inspired by the Minoan Empire and shares details with it (notably the bull sport popular in Minos) it is also described as an island of vast size that is specifically located 'beyond the pillars of Hercules' (Gibraltar) i.e. in the Atlantic Ocean. Plato's 'tall story' therefore is likely a hybrid memory of both the antediluvian civilization in toto and prehistoric America, whose Midwest 'Ohio Mound Builder' and/or Bolivian Lake Titikaka cultures were almost certainly clients of the Minoans in the super-ancient

region. The Greeks, now firmly based in the Peloponnese with a new capital at Mycenae seven miles from Argos (founded by the city's first King Perseus around this same time), were there to fill that vacuum. In many ways they piggy-backed off the Minoan way of doing things, arguably learning from them the idea of Empire. They quickly occupied Knossos and all of the previous Minoan colonies and started building grand or 'palatial' architecture, including for the first time installing a throne room at Knossos.

Fig.19: the extent of Mycenaean Greek influence at the outbreak of the Trojan War[127].

---

transatlantic copper trade that fed the Bronze Age, the apparent severing of the communication with whom (resulting from the natural disaster) contributed significantly to the devastating 'before and after' impact of the Thera eruption on the Mediterranean world.

[127] Image by Alexikoua/Panthera tigris tigris/Reedside from Wikimedia Commons (https://commons.wikimedia.org/wiki/File:Mycenaean_World_en.png) used under CC BY SA 3.0 (https://creativecommons.org/licenses/by-sa/3.0/deed.en)

Culturally the Mycenaeans were an heroic or warrior elite culture with a strong emphasis on regular interaction with the 'gods' who dwelt on Mount Olympus, and with a string of famous heroes that come down to us as all but superhuman, many of whom are claimed by Greek mythology to be the direct sons of Zeus; the likes of Perseus, Hercules/Heracles, Theseus, Bellerophon and Jason.

The rise of Mycenaean Greece was fairly meteoric. By 1450 BC they had begun making trade overtures into Asia Minor, with Mycenaean pottery being found at Troy, Miletus, Cyprus, Lebanon and Egypt. Island by island they were approaching the Western Asian coast, with Miletus in particular being their notable pre-war colony. By 1300 BC they were well known to the Hittite Emperors in Hattusa, who were also aware of some disturbance happening between the King (Mycenaean 'Wanaka') of Ahhiyawa (Achaea) and the Hittite Emperor's Western vassals in Wilusa (Troy). They probably didn't suspect that the turmoil that was to follow would bring down the entire Hittite Empire and many others besides.

The Events of the Trojan War

This history will not rehearse in great detail the events of the war. Suffice it to say that it is recorded as the first great event of European history, in the oldest work of literature of the Greek civilization, Homer's 'Iliad', and the other seven poems of the 'Epic Cycle'.

The significance of the war has already been discussed. But here we will simply note that one of the shocking and monumental elements of this conflict that seems to have stunned the Japhetic world, is that it was an invasion and conquest of one Japhetic nation, indeed of one of Japheth's sons, over another. Had this happened before? Perhaps not on a level of this magnitude. Everywhere in the history we have reviewed ethnic relations of the sons of Japheth had lived in apparent harmony, such as the sons of Togarmah living with the sons of Magog in Caucasia, Magog with

Riphath in Scythia, Magog bordering Tiras on the Northern Black Sea coast, and Ashkenaz living next to Tiras in Moesia. Of course there would have been conflicts before. But this was an inter-Japhetic war, invasion and takeover on an inter-continental scale. Not only against a sizeable demographic or people group of another brother nation, but even including the conquest of their ancient homeland and capital city. Had this happened before? Or was this an unprecedented crime akin to Cain's murdering of Abel that sent shockwaves around the Japhetic world and led to widespread revulsion and a shared consensus that something had to be done about it.

PART 2: Panic and Revenge, 1200-640 BC

The 'Bronze Age Collapse'

The Bronze Age Collapse of C.1177 BC[1] was caused by the fallout of the Trojan War. The ludicrous pretence that some other explanation is to be sought, still kept up by many arbiters of the modern academic priesthood, is just that and nothing more. It must be dismissed as surely as their predecessors' insistence that the City of Troy never actually existed. Until Calvert and Schliemann unearthed its remains on the shores of Western Anatolia exactly as described by Homer[2]. The attempt to find another fundamental cause for the Bronze Age Collapse stems from an unwillingness to face the true history of the world, and more importantly to let others face it, matched with a terror that common people might find out that ancient written witnesses can really be believed, and come to know their own history.

All evidence points overwhelmingly to the fact that the epochal events recorded by Homer in the 'Iliad' and also in the other seven works of the 'Epic Cycle'[3] were the very cause of the destruction of Mycenaean Greece, and of the Bronze Age Collapse and subsequent 'Greek Dark Ages' that followed it.

---

[1] (Cline) It should be noted that the 'New Chronology' of Egyptologist David Rohl (Rohl, 2007, p.20-22) may well redate the Trojan War and the subsequent 'Bronze Age Collapse' forward to the 9th Century BC. Remarkably such a revision would dispense with the requirement for much of the 'Greek Dark Ages' that followed the Bronze Age Collapse altogether, by largely explaining away the 'cultural gap' in Western Civilization currently understood to have existed between the 12th and 9th Centuries BC, as nothing more than a dating error. The 'New Chronology' debate however is beyond the scope of this book, therefore conventional dating will be used here for convenience.

[2] Whether Homer himself ever went there is uncertain. He may actually have used the citadel at Karatepe, where he worked as an Assyrian scribe, as the model for the Troy of his epic poem

[3] The Epic Cycle consists of the books: Cypria, Iliad, Aethiopis, Little Iliad, Sack of Ilion, Returns, Odyssey and Telegony (Aethiopis book, p.12-19)

Well, what happened? According to the Epic Cycle, the Achaeans led by their King Agamemnon invaded and conquered Troy under its King Priam, in a ten year war. They took captive much of the Trojan ruling class and accelerated the process of colonizing the Western Coast of Anatolia. This is usually understood as corresponding to the destruction of layer 'VIIb' of the archaeological site of Troy, the zenith of its extent, estimated as having been destroyed around 1200 BC[4]. However the Trojans and their allies were not finished yet. The Mycenaean Greeks would get more than they bargained for.

---

[4] For a fuller discussion in detail of the chronology and dating of the war from original sources, see Appendix 2: The Trojan War through the Eyes of the Hittites.

The Sea Peoples

The mysterious 'Sea Peoples' whose large-scale 12th Century BC invasions of all the major empires of the Mediterranean world that caused the end of the Bronze Age and many of its civilizations including the Mycenaean Greek, Hittite and very nearly the Egyptian and Middle Assyrian empires ushering in an age of migration that would last for hundreds of years, have been called the Bronze Age equivalent of the Vikings, and that is precisely what they were.

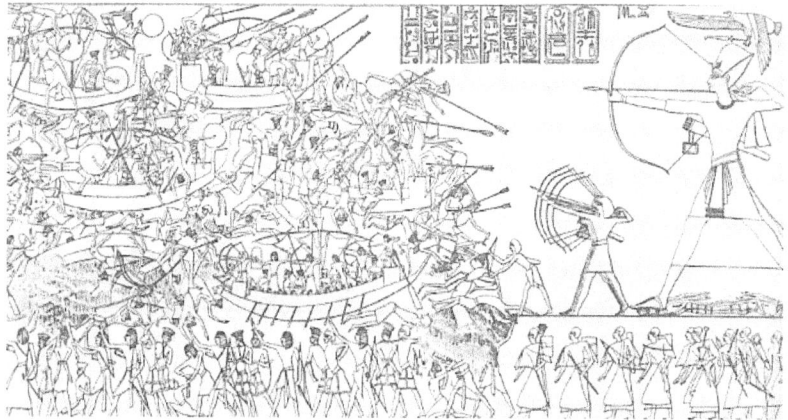

Fig.20: Vikings invade ancient Egypt.[5]

The inability to accept this rather straightforward explanation comes from a reluctance to comprehend that the Scandinavians of two thousand years later were already fully in existence and active at this very early date. Their whereabouts were simply unknown in the urban centres of the Middle East and Mediterranean at that time, because they didn't live in the Mediterranean nor in Europe. Hence the 'mysterious' Sea Peoples. Where can they possibly have come from?

---

[5] From the great relief depicting the Battle of the Delta on the outside of the North wall of Ramses III's mortuary temple at Medinet Habu, near Luxor, Egypt. This is a public domain {{PD-1996}} image from Wikimedia Commons (https://commons.wikimedia.org/wiki/File:Seev%C3%B6lker.jpg)

One only needs to look at the names used for one of the leading groups of this naval confederacy that swept into the Mediterranean Sea in the wake of the Trojan War apparently bent on wanton destruction, to understand immediately who they were and where they came from: 'Tershi', 'Tirsa', 'Thyrsenes', 'Tyrrhenians', 'Tursha'[6], 'Tyrsenoi'[7] and 'Teresh of the Sea'[8]. The Sea Peoples came into the Mediterranean from the Black Sea, and they were led by the descendants of Thor, who were very angry that their capital city Troy had been destroyed. The Egyptian history of the enormous invasion that occurred during the Reign of their Pharaoh Ramses II describes the raiding 'Teresh' thus: 'they were always drunk and lived on boats'. Can a more perfect description of Viking culture be attempted?[9]

As the Tirassians were the major logistical trade transport network for the Black Sea and Asia, it is highly likely that refugees from the Trojan War had gone far and wide, recruiting for this gigantic revenge mission many other peoples, their clients and allies, from the Black Sea world and beyond to join them. This accounts for the many other nations that history records were also among the 'Sea Peoples', who were then transported to the Mediterranean battlefront aboard Tirassian ships and led by them in raids or undertook their own.

The imperial powers' reactions to the Sea Peoples' attacks were very similar to the reactions of the established states to the Viking raids of a later era. They were astonished and taken completely by surprise, having been perfectly unsuspecting that any human cultures could possibly have existed in such numbers outside the scope of their own knowledge and writ.

---

[6] The rendering of Gaston Maspero (Maspero, vol.2, p.471)
[7] Egyptian Inscriptions book, vol.3, p.239
[8] Great Inscription in the Second Court, Medinet Habu (Egyptian Inscriptions, vol.4, p.76)
[9] The extreme similarity between the two cultures has been noted among others by nautical archaeologist Shelley Wachsmann (Wachsmann)

It should be noted that while the subsequent few hundred years are often mournfully described as a 'Dark Ages', in fact this is really the voice of GRHF historiography talking. In that it was primarily a 'Dark Ages' for the Greeks only, who let's face it had brought it upon themselves. Their new 'palace economy' was thoroughly demolished. However it did also signal a decline for many of the other large, regional powers. But many non-Imperial cultures thrived during this time, in particular the Phoenicians and the Israelites.

Let us look in detail at the many witnesses to these events, taking them in order of the respective regions affected. The Sea Peoples' invasion was often the very first sighting by the inhabitants of the Mediterranean world of 'Asian' culture, and their records of what happened were their first descriptions of it.

Sea Peoples raids on Hatti

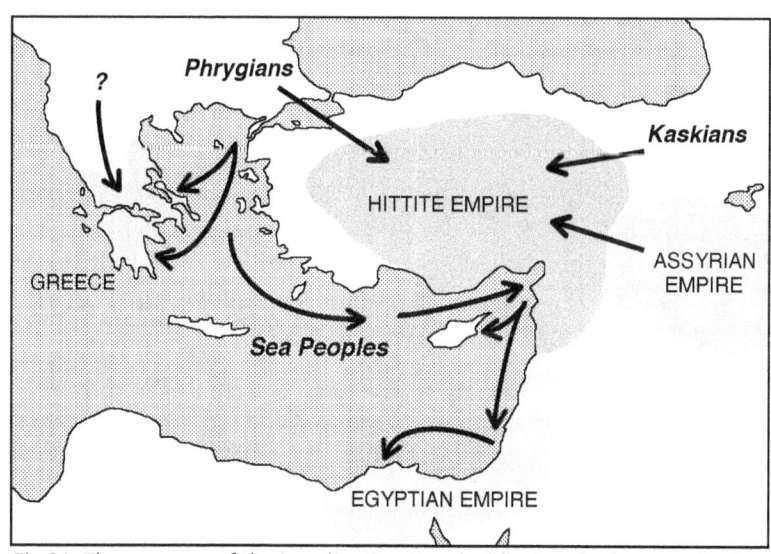

Fig.21: The progress of the invading Sea Peoples' fleet and other attacks that precipitated the 'Bronze Age Collapse' traditionally dated to 1177 BC

The Hittite Empire was one of the first casualties of the Sea Peoples' attacks, being closest to Troy, the epicentre of the naval invasion-quake, and to the Hellespont, perhaps the entry point into the Mediterranean for part of the Sea Peoples' fleet. The Hittites were mainly the victims of a massive invasion force from Thrace by a nation who would become known as the Phrygians (the 'Thyni' (who became the Bithynians[10]) and the 'Bryges' (who became the Phrygians[11]). While most scholars would say this Phrygian migration happened before the war, it is increasingly likely that the main thrust of it was afterwards, in response to the war, and part of the wider Thracian/Trojan counter-strike that we know as the invasions of the Sea Peoples[12].

There had been some Phrygian activity in Anatolia beforehand. The Phrygian leader Gordias had established a city, Gordium, on the Sakarya River[13]. A famous Phrygian King in the years before the war was Mygdon, who warred with the Amazons and the Mysians and was killed, allegedly by Heracles, during this Mysian war in a battle in North-West Anatolia[14]. The Phrygians fought alongside the Trojans in the war[15], with Mygdon's son Coroebus fighting and dying and King Priam of Troy marrying Hecuba, daughter of the Phrygian King Demas.

But the Phrygians were newcomers to Anatolia. Their language, possibly 'paleo-Baltic' was not mutually intelligible to the ancient and well-established Trojan/Luwian language of Assuwa/Arzawa. The Phrygians were descended from Togarmah, and this Anatolian Togarmah colony was known to the Hittites as Tegarama. The Phrygian colony would soon grow into an empire of its own occupying most of Western Anatolia.

But first the Phrygians quickly got busy invading the Hittite Empire from the West. The Hittites had already been somewhat weakened by the growth of the Middle Assyrian Empire to their

---

[10] Possiby descended from Tubal or Meshech
[11] Herodotus, p.457
[12] See for example Strabo, vol. 2, p.316 and vol.3, p.66, quoting Xanthus
[13] Gordias' son was the famously wealthy King Midas, of the 'Midas touch' (Herodotus, p.6)
[14] Apollodorus, p.205
[15] Iliad, p.127

east and were in no state to sustain substantial and unexpected invasions from the West as well.

The Sea Peoples' fleet had invaded around the Eastern Coast of the Aegean and along the Levant coastline conquering Cyprus and Cilicia. This was the coastline of the Hittites' precious trading ports and they were now cut off. In its heartland, Hatti was caught in a pincer movement. As Assyrian Emperor Ashur-resh-ishi I took over large swathes of Hittite territory from the East, the Phrygians and Bithynians from the West joined with Kaskians from the North-East and burnt Hattusa to the ground C.1180 BC. The once mighty Hittite Empire was no more. In subsequent centuries its leading families are said to have migrated Eastward along the Silk Road to join their Hamite cousins the Shang'An Chinese (also descended from Canaan) in the Far East, becoming known there as the 'Cathays'[16].

Meanwhile a new, 'neo-Indo-European' era began in Anatolia, an era unmistakably changed from the Settlement 1 situation. It would be dominated by 'immigrant' nations that had left and come back, instead of the indigenous populations that had dwelt there since the flood. It would be one where the influence of the city of Troy, rebuilt but never regaining its pre-war status, was relegated mostly to the past. Many of its traumatised populations and dependents were gone; either taken captive, marauding the Mediterranean in revenge or otherwise caught up in the maelstrom of turmoil and war, or having fled the region as refugees seeking new lands elsewhere. Where the hieroglyph and cuneiform writing systems of the old era were replaced with a new, Indo-European-modified Phoenician communication system called 'the Alphabet' that would become a symbol of this new millennium of Japhetic, rather than Hamitic, empires. The Phrygians proceeded to conquer large parts of central and Northern Anatolia[17], while Tabal, a state derived from the descendants of Japheth's son Tubal,

---

[16] Strabo, vol.3, p.92
[17] Strabo, vol.2, p.191

spread out over the Southern half, possibly associated with the Bithynians.

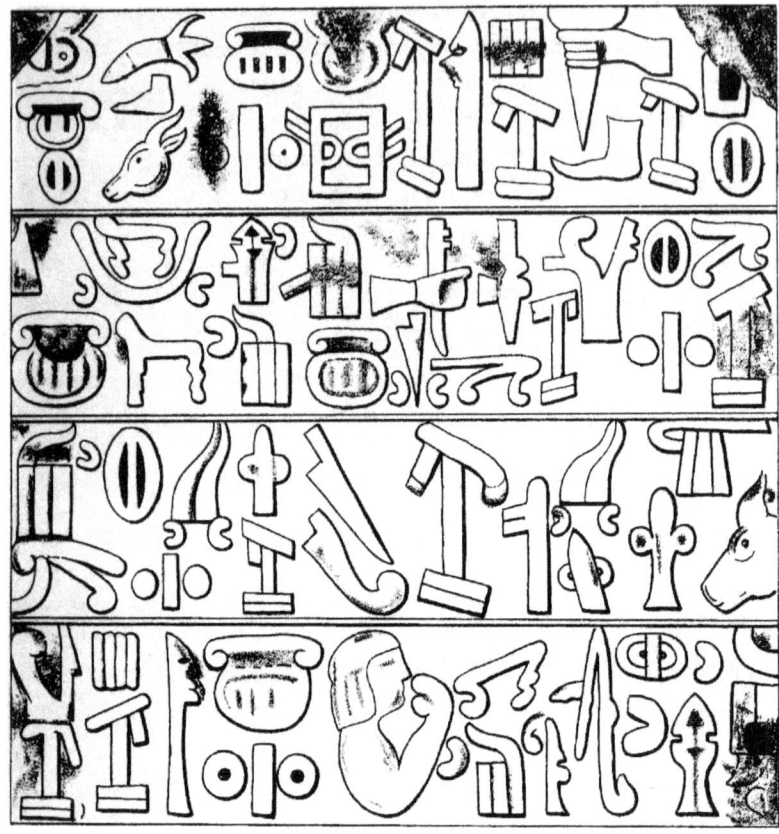

Fig.22: Luwian hieroglyphs. Likely the writing system of ancient Troy and the whole Anatolian language family related to it that occupied Anatolia during Settlement 1 from prior to the rise of the Hittite Empire up to the time of the Trojan War[18]

Sea Peoples raids on Greece

In many ways Homer's 'Iliad', published around 750 BC, was the first opportunity for the Greeks to celebrate their short-lived 'victory' in the Trojan War, after having lived for 400 years in

---

[18] This is a public domain image from Wikimedia Commons (https://commons .wikimedia .org/wiki/File:Hamath_inscription.jpg)

ignominious defeat and poverty because of it[19]. Certainly the consequences of the war were cataclysmic for the nascent Mycenaean Empire. Its growing, Achaean-led 'palace economy' copied arguably from the Minoan arrangement at Knossos on Crete was brought to an abrupt end. Linear B, the Mycenaean administrative writing system, also derived from Minoan Linear A (as yet undeciphered) disappeared without trace. No evidence of the use of writing survives from the subsequent 'Greek Dark Ages'. When the Greeks re-emerged from them with Homer, they would be communicating in a very different, European, proto-Greek script bearing a language based on the Ionian and Aeolian dialects of Greek not the old Achaean.

As with everything in Greek history, its record of what followed after the Trojan War is confused and highly over-dramatised. The utter destruction of the Greek Empire that followed the war is known in Greek history as the 'Return of the Heracleidae' or the 'Dorian Invasion'.

Very basically, what the Greeks understood to have happened was a major 'revolution' in Greek Civilization wherein the Achaean ascendancy of the Mycenaean era was violently overthrown by Northern 'Dorian' Greeks. Before we delve into this story it should be pointed out that the self-obsessed ancient Greeks were notorious for always preferring to discover native Greek origin stories for famous foreign figures and events, reluctant to admit that anything strong, successful or notable could have come from the world outside of Greece[20].

So the event that catastrophically ended the Mycenaean Greek Civilization and plunged Greek history into a Dark Ages is taught by Greek legend to have been caused by the return of the rightful rulers of Greece, heirs to the throne of Perseus, the sons of

---

[19] Although the New Chronology's possible revision of this dating might make the gap known as the 'Greek Dark Ages' considerably shorter (Rohl, 2007, p.20-22)
[20] Josephus comments on this phenomenon (vol.4, p.59). As for example in the suspiciously thorough 'embedding' of the Trojan royal house of King Priam into Greek Genealogy.

Heracles (the 'Heracleidae'), who had been persecuted and driven from Mycenae by Eurystheus, who then became King of Mycenae. Eurystheus was later left without an heir, leaving the exiled Heracleidae as the only rightful Perseid heirs remaining. But the throne had been taken by a different family, the Pelopids. Heracles' son Hyllas then lost a duel against the Pelopids, the terms being that if he lost, his brothers would have to leave Greece for three generations. These sons of Heracles then went into exile in the Northern lands of the Dorians, whose King Aegimius, having been helped by Heracles, had previously adopted Hyllas as his son and given the Heracleidae one third of his Kingdom. So the Heracleidae were not Dorians, but they lived with them[21].

When the three generations were over, the Heracleidae, now considerably strengthened and accompanied by their Dorian allies, re-invaded the Peloponnese and conquered it, led by one Temenus who took over the Greek throne[22].

It's a very interesting story, one that cleverly and poetically renders the destroyers of Mycenaean Greek Civilization the previously exiled 'true, rightful' rulers of Greece. What it doesn't explain is why such a triumphant, happy occasion resulted in utter economic devastation in the country and the total collapse of its power. Perhaps, indeed, what we are told was a 'Dark Age' was in fact only Dark in the same way that the later 'Dark Ages' was dark: dark as in opaque, i.e. we don't have much information about it, and in fact this was a golden age; a return to Perseid and Heracleid heroic, rural values that eschewed and ended the slowly corrupting influence of Minoan Imperial ambitions that had resulted in the fratricidal invasion of Troy.

But this just does not fit with the evidence of the massive devastation of the Mycenaean Empire. The city of Mycenae itself, like so many other cities, was comprehensively destroyed by unknown forces, never to rise again as a great city, C.1200 BC,

---

[21] Strabo, vol.2, p.128; Apollodorus, vol.1, p.263; Diodorus Siculus, vol.1, p.251
[22] Strabo, vol.2, p.53-54

exactly the time of the Sea Peoples' rampage. The other major Mycenaean cities suffered a similar fate, such as the main port city of Pylos whose complete destruction by sudden invasion occurred around 1180 BC. Tiryns, home city of the famous Heracles, was utterly destroyed as well. Why, if its destroyers were the returning Heracleidae? Miletus, the Achaean colony in Asia, was burnt to the ground. The same problem arises with the theory that the Sea Peoples mainly or substantially consisted of Mycenaean Greeks themselves[23]. If this was true, why would their own civilization be so utterly destroyed by the Sea Peoples' attacks, when it had previously been burgeoning and on the increase?[24]

The fact is we don't really have much in the way of reliable sources about this 'collapse' in Greece, and Greek Classical history is extremely reluctant to give away too many specifics about such a miserable period in its history. What we can say is that there was a large-scale invasion from the North and/or from the sea, resulting in the Achaean hegemony with its capitals of Argos/Mycenae, being overthrown permanently with significant ethnic change and economic desolation following.

Who were the Dorians? We (think we) know that they dwelt to the North of Mycenaean Greece, closer to the original Greek lands in Thessaly. It is surely not too much of a stretch to propose that this 'Dorian Invasion' while being an invasion from the North was perhaps from outside the Greek world entirely, possibly including disaffected rural relatives from its Northern periphery like the Heracleidae/Dorians, but consisting largely of the Thracians who lived to the North-East of Greece, 'descending' down into the Peloponnese and invading, conquering and destroying it. Indeed, it is entirely possible that these were one and the same; that

---

[23] As for example in the argument of Michael Wood (Wood)
[24] It is notable that in the 'Chronicle' of Greek historian Eusebius, one of the most important works of Western history ever written, if not the most important, the chronology of events across four columns is interrupted around the year 1180 BC by the huge words 'TROIA CAPTA' (Troy captured), treatment that not even the birth of Jesus Christ is afforded by this Christian writer. This shows the significance of the event in the Greek mind. (Eusebius, Chronicle, p.96/97))

'Dorians' should be read *'Tourrians'*, so that they were not Greeks at all, but rather 'Sea People' (i.e. Thracians) who reasoned that they could also attack over land[25]. If indeed the attack was an invasion from the north at all, and not solely from the sea.

There is some evidence suggesting that the 'Dorians' could have been Sea People based at Dor on the Mediterranean Phoenician coast near Israel[26]. All of this strongly calls into question the domestic nature of the Greek explanation and argues instead for a devastating foreign invasion or conquest of some kind. And that the 'return of the Heracleidae' story was a nice way of putting a positive spin on things, particularly for the proud classical Greek culture that wanted to renew its imperial ambitions and draw a veil over previous failures.

Considering the devastation to the Mycenaean Greek state and culture, this seems like the only rational explanation considering the context of the times. Every other Empire of the day was under massive attack by the Sea Peoples. It would be some kind of incredible coincidence if the classical world's attempt to dismiss this disaster in Greek history as a purely internal affair was really true, and it just happened to coincide with the wider regional turmoil of the era that had identical characteristics.

Sea Peoples raids on Ugarit, Alashiya, Cilicia and Carchemish

After trashing the Greek and Hittite Empires, the Sea Peoples' main fleet continued further South into the Mediterranean proper, turned East along the Southern Anatolian coast and smashed into the Eastern Mediterranean coastal trading HQ at Ugarit, in the

---

[25] This is supported by the Sea People origins theory of Woudhuizen (p.116) that also adds weight to the argument that the 'Dorians' were not truly ethnic Greeks but rather foreigners

[26] In the Egyptian 'Report of Wenemon', dated C.1100 BC (around a hundred years after the destruction of Mycenaean Greece), Wenemon describes how he travelled north to Dor, that was at that time a 'city of Tjecker', the Tjeker being one of the Sea People nations (Egyptian Inscriptions, vol.4, p.278). However it would seem that this settlement was subsequent to the Sea Peoples' invasion.

north-west of what is now Syria.

Ugarit, probably the major business hub between the Hittite and Egyptian Empires, that also traded extensively with Alashiya (Cyprus) and Mycenae, was totally destroyed by the Sea Peoples, never to recover, at an approximate date of 1190 BC.

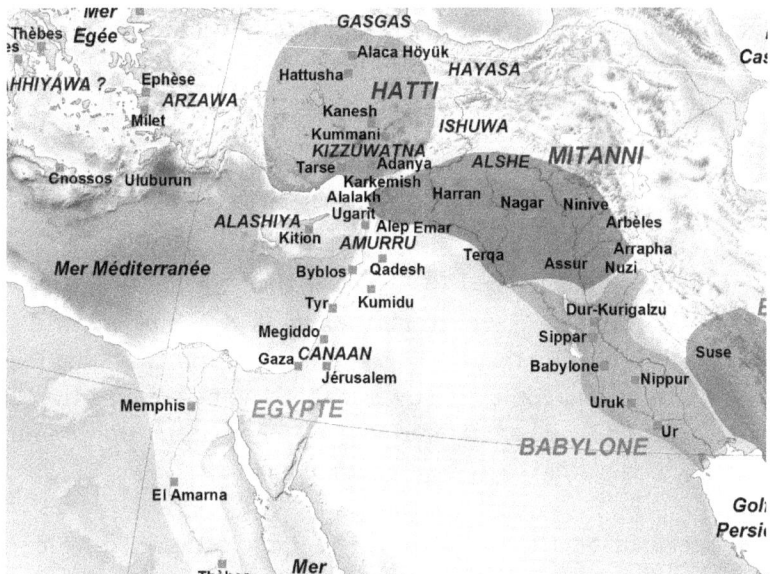

Fig.23: One can see from this representation of the state of affairs a little before the time of the Sea Peoples attack, the central position of Ugarit and the surrounding area to the great Empires of the day. It was the economic hub of the Mediterranean[27]

Besides being one of the major events of the Sea Peoples' campaign, the invasion of this corner of the world, the 'cluny' or Bay later called the Marandynian Bay (today's 'Iskenderun Gulf') repays closer inspection because there are some strange details in the story of the Sea Peoples' interactions here, arguably one of the most ethnically and culturally diverse and complex regions of the entire world, at that time and even today.

---

[27] Image by Zunkir from Wikimedia Commons used under CC BY SA 2.5 Generic (https://creativecommons.org/licenses/by-sa/2.5/deed.en)

Look at this communication from the Governor of Alashiya (Cyprus) to Ammurapi, the last King of Ugarit, in response to the latter's distress call about the devastations wrought by seven ships of the Sea Peoples:

> "As for the matter concerning those enemies: (it was) the people from your country (and) your own ships (who) did this! And (it was) the people from your country (who) committed these transgression(s)...I am writing to inform you and protect you. Be aware!"[28]

What could this mean?

Well, Ammurapi had said in his letter that "all my troops and chariots(?) are in the Land of Hatti, and all my ships are in the Land of Lukka?[29]" so that could explain the ships part, in that the invasion ships had come directly from Lukka and were partly his own ships. But what is meant by 'the people from your country...committed these transgression(s)'?

Well let us first set the scene of the multiple compacted nations that were squeezed into this small corner of the world. One can see from the above map that it was a confluence of three major empires (the Mitanni Empire had by this time largely been displaced by the Middle Assyrian Empire, see below), but there were many more cultures in this zone than just these heavyweights.

---

[28] Cline, p.151.
[29] In a letter to King Ammurapi of Ugarit from the Hittite court from this period, the Hittites demand that Ammurapi send copper (perhaps to make bronze weapons) to Achaeans who were then in Lukka, using the ships of Ugarit under a leader Satalli (Hittite Correspondence, p.257). Is this why the ships were in Lukka? And could this letter be part of defence arrangements against the encroaching Sea Peoples' fleet? This strong possibility implicates the Hittite Empire, the Achaeans and Ugarit as being in collusion against the Sea Peoples/Troy on the very eve of their destruction by the Sea Peoples. It therefore constitutes evidence, though tenuous, that they also combined together in the earlier defeat of Troy.

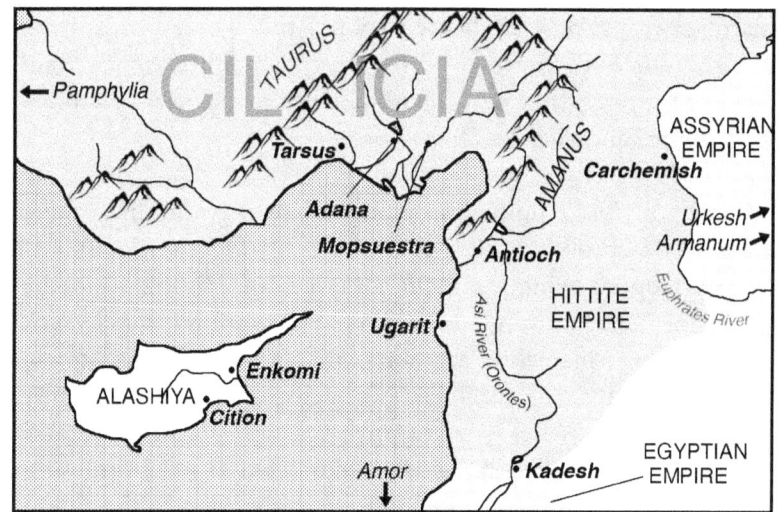

Fig.24: the complicated situation around Cilicia and the Marandynian Bay, with the Taurus and Amanus Mountain ranges at the top and the island of 'Alashiya' (Cyprus) at bottom left.

Most straight-forwardly, the island of Alashiya (today's Cyprus), with its capital city of Enkomi, was primarily populated by descendants of Elishah, the eldest son of Javan, son of Japheth, hence the name, and was therefore likely a close ally of the Greeks. The other major city of the island was 'Cition', named after Elisha's brother Kitt[30], from whom quite possibly our English word 'city' derives[31]. The next brother Tarshish had settled immediately across the water on the Southern coast of Anatolia, founding the city of Tarsus. Josephus says that Japheth's sons originally settled Asia 'beginning by inhabiting the mountains of Taurus and Amanus'[32]. So this may have been the very first area settled by the sons of Japheth, possibly even before Japheth's move to Mount Olympus.

So these were Indo-Europeans, but they were in an odd position. During deep antiquity it would not have been so odd, in that

---

[30] Josephus, vol.4, p.63
[31] Kitt is closely associated with cities. Not only Cition but also the later city of Rome is usually linked with his descendants.
[32] Josephus, vol.4, p.59

Anatolia was almost exclusively populated by descendants of Japheth. But with the rise of the Egyptian, Hittite and Neo-Assyrian Empires, they now found themselves the meat in a three-way Empire sandwich[33].

But this was not a problem, because they had a trading niche. Alashiya was probably the Mediterranean's biggest exporter of Copper. Copper being the main component of Bronze, and this being the Bronze Age, Alashiya was doing very nicely economically. Meanwhile around the Taurus Mountains to the north of the city of Tarsus was the region the Egyptians called 'Kode' and the Hittites 'Kizzuwatna', but is better known in the West as 'Cilicia'. Cilicia became a major exporter of Silver, as the Taurus Mountains were the centre of Silver mining in the region. So this whole area was the fulcrum not only of the Mediterranean economy, but arguably of the whole Bronze Age!

Indeed, the fallout from the Trojan War and subsequent Sea Peoples' campaigns in the Mediterranean is generally seen as the threshold event that marks the end of the Bronze Age (usually termed the 'Bronze Age Collapse') and the beginning of the Iron Age. It is entirely possible that the economic devastation of this area in particular contributed to the change from the Bronze technology of the earlier era to the use of the Black Sea's steel technology in the Iron Age. It is thought that this change occurred in part because of the increased difficulty of acquiring the materials necessary for producing Bronze, namely tin and copper, leading to a greater impetus to find an alternative technology, that turned out to be better, resulting in the permanent abandonment of bronze. The sacking and destruction of Alashiya and its key trading partner Ugarit would have played a major part in the disruption of the Bronze trade that catalyzed the onset of the new Iron Age. Archaeological level IIIA of the Enkomi site on Cyprus corresponds to the Sea Peoples' raid C.1190 BC. Subsequently it was rebuilt but the rebuild only lasted until 1125 BC. Later it was

---

[33] The border between the Hittite and Egyptian Empires had been established at the nearby city of Kadesh, the site of a major battle between the two C.1274 BC

occupied by the Greeks who brought a somewhat different culture to the Alashiyan one, but an earthquake in 1050 BC finally put paid to Alashiya's position as a trading hub.

We do not have much information on the Sea Peoples' attack on Kode/Cilicia, but Egyptian Pharaoh Ramses III's Medinet Habu inscription lists it as being destroyed by the Sea Peoples as well[34].

Carchemish was another hugely significant trading centre in the area, its speciality being timber. The Hittites conquered it in the 1300s BC and made Carchemish the main imperial Hittite establishment in this 'world trade crossroads' region. Carchemish sent reinforcements to Ugarit but it was too late to stop the city's destruction by the Sea Peoples. Carchemish was also then sacked, but survived the destruction to continue trading on into the Iron Age.

As we move on to the Sea Peoples' attack on Mitanni, we can start to understand the massive regional impact of the sudden shock destruction of this global trade region. Enough to shake the world and bring to an end an entire 'age' in the history of civilizations.

Sea Peoples raids on Mitanni and Amor

But what did the Alashyan Governor mean that the raids were by the Ugaritans 'own people'? Who were the Ugaritans? Well, the Ugarit people were primarily Amorites, that is, like the Hittites, descended from Ham's son Canaan, but from his fourth son Amor[35]. The Sea Peoples made the area of 'Amor' or 'Amurru', home of the Amorites, their local base of operations in the region[36]. As we shall see, Amorites even joined them in their subsequent invasions. Why was Ugarit targeted while other Amorites became allies?[37] We don't know. Possibly because Ugarit was within the Hittite sphere of influence, whereas its southern

---

[34] Egyptian Inscriptions, vol.4, p.37
[35] rather than from Canaan's second son Heth, the ancestor of the Hittites
[36] Egyptian Inscriptions, vol.4, p.37
[37] Although the capital city of Amor, 'Sumur', was also destroyed

neighbour Amor was closer to the Semitic-speaking world of coastal Canaan, AKA 'Phoenicia', with whom the Sea Peoples seem to have had an affinity.

The Sea Peoples stationing themselves at Amurru would likely have come after their sacking of Ugarit, so that still doesn't fully explain the Alashyan Governor's letter. Perhaps he had become aware that the Sea People/Amorite alliance was already in the works.

Another large local power was also in the region that until recently had had a major stake in this economic nexus: the 'Mitanni' Kingdom run by the Indo-European-speaking Hurrians, a smaller Empire that had existed between the larger Egyptian, Hittite, Assyrian and Babylonion Empires surrounding them. This ancient people is worth discussing in greater detail. While some have claimed that the Hurrians, for whom chariot warfare was a speciality, were Indo-Aryans (the culture that invaded India around this time) they may also have had ties to Medo-Bactria and been a remnant of the very earliest Japhetic cultures who had fled North from Nimrod's Babyonian tyranny[38].

This is because their language, Hurro-Urartian, appears to have been very old, part of the 'Kura-Araxes' archaeological culture that, with its sister culture 'Shulaveri-Shomu', centred on the Ararat plain and in Azerbaijan, Armenia and Northern Iran, may represent the language of Japheth and his family in the earliest years after the flood, or if not perhaps after the Babel dispersion[39]. The 'Kura-Araxes' culture and Hurro-Urartian language[40] has been linked to Kartvelian, the mountain-protected language of Kartli, brother of Hayk, son of Togarmah, son of Gomer, son of Japheth, who is recorded in Armenian and Georgian history as

---

[38] Or they may have been an offshoot of the super-ancient Indo-European 'Gutians', of whom more later

[39] If one can conjecture credibly that the Japhethites returned directly to Ararat, the location of the Ark, after previously migrating to Shinar.

[40] Although largely uncategorized, it has been tentatively labeled 'Alarodian' or 'Northeastern Caucasian'

having slain Nimrod.

Hurrian culture therefore provides evidence of a super-ancient Indo-European heritage in this part of the middle-east. For example, the 'gods' that the Hurrians worshipped are strangely familiar. A primary God, 'Alalu' had a son 'Kumarbi', and he had a son 'Teshub' (Hittite 'Taru', Luwian 'Tarhunt'), who became the Hurrian 'storm god' who carried around a thunderbolt[41] and was understood to have supernatural powers over the weather. These three bear more than a passing resemblance to Lamech, Noah and Japheth, the 'Sky-Father' of the Indo-Europeans. The origin story of Teshub is also very similar to Zeus's in Greek mythology.[42] The attribution can be extended to other local places of interest named after this 'god' like the Taurus Mountains themselves and the nearby region or city of 'Tarhuntassa'.

This all shows that before the relatively new Hittite empire, Western Anatolia had been thoroughly Indo-European and Japhetic in culture and heritage. Indeed the Hittites had themselves borrowed the 'Teshub' version of Japheth-worship from the Hurrians, so that by the time of the Trojan War 'Taru' had become the Hittites' main idol. This along with their adoption of the Anatolian language is why they are often misidentified as Japhethites, when in reality they had simply 'gone native' during their occupation of Antatolia.

The distinctiveness of the 'Teshub' version of Japheth, with its origins specifically in this area and not apparently deriving from the Greek 'Zeus' tradition, as well as multiple witnesses of super-ancient Japhetic settlement, suggest strongly that Japheth lived here before he moved to Mount Olympus in Greece, and that

---

[41] Also an axe or mace – shades of Thor here as well
[42] According to the 'Song of Kumarbi', Teshub was conceived when the god Kumarbi bit off and swallowed the chief God Anu's genitals (Hittite Myths, p.42-43)—in the same way that Cronus (Noah) did to Sky (God) in Greek mythology (Hesiod, p.17-19; p.39-41); apparently a metaphor for the antediluvians' loss of earthly sovereignty to Noah. Like Noah, three sons ('gods') are named as being the offspring of Kumarbi (Hittite Myths, p.43; Pritchard, p.120-121)

therefore the Hurrian 'Teshub' is a memory of an even earlier era in the life of Noah's probably youngest son.[43]

Teshub, the Hurrian Japheth, holding lightning bolt and axe/ hammer[44]

---

[43] Some of the rowdy family relationship narratives concerning Kumarbi, the 'Storm God' and the Storm God's offspring in Hittite records probably relate to this period (Pritchard, p.125-128). The Amanus Mountains, called 'Cedar Mountain' and 'Mount Lebanon' are also described as 'the dwelling of the gods, the throne-dais of the goddesses' in the C.1800 BC 'Epic of Gilgamesh' (p.603)

[44] Public domain image by Maur from Wikimedia Commons (https://commons.wikimedia.org/wiki/File:Weather_God.jpg)

This also fits with the evidence that Elisha, Tarsus, Kitt and whoever was the ancestor of the Hurrians, all resided in this area in deep antiquity. Additionally, an important local river, the 'Orontes', was known in ancient times (and even today in Arabic and Turkish) as the 'Asi' river, that could be the very origin of the 'Asia' name. If as seems likely 'Asian' usually refers to descendants of Thor, it is possible (as per Josephus) that Thor also settled here before moving on to Crete.

While at this point in history the Asi river marked the point where 'Amurru' began, and also formed the boundary between the Hittite and Egyptian Empires (at Kadesh), traditionally it had been the boundary between Indo-European (Japhetic) settlers to its North and Hamitic and Semitic settlers to its South[45]. Perhaps this explains why the Sea Peoples devastated the area North of the river but allied with the nations to its South: because North of the 'Asi' was considered to be traditionally Japhetic territory and therefore currently under foreign imperial occupation, from which it needed to be liberated. This agenda of liberation from slavery and Empire could also explain the Sea Peoples' alliance with the Shemites – the 'Shasu' often harboured escaped slaves from Ugarit and other imperial centres[46].

Indo-European Hurrian/ Mitanni dominance in the area stretched back to the era of Nimrod[47], but had recently come to an end. Around 1360 BC the expansionist Hittite Emperor Suppiluliuma had defeated the Hurrians and conquered the region, so that by the time of the Sea Peoples' invasion the Mitanni Kingdom was a shell more or less controlled by the Assyrian Empire to its east. Like the Trojans in the North-West, the Hurrians were being pushed out of original Indo-European lands.

---

[45] Over a thousand years later this ethnic border would still be significant. The city of Antioch was also located on the Asi river. Antioch became the second base of the early followers of Jesus Christ after the destruction of Jerusalem in 70 AD, and the jumping off point for the subsequent evangelization of the non-Jewish, 'gentile' world to its North.

[46] Ganor

[47] with Naram-Sin eventually marrying his daughter to the Hurrian King after warring against an early Hurrian capital 'Armanum'

Is it possible that some Hurrians joined the Sea Peoples' invading forces? It may be a coincidence but the name of the Mitanni Kingdom's ancient capital city 'Urkesh'[48] calls to mind the name of one of the Sea Peoples nations: 'Ekwesh'.

A word should be added here about a local warlord 'Mopsus' (AKA 'Moxos' or 'Muksa'). Probably of Thracian, Luwian or Lydian extraction, Mopsus was a big noise in the region around this time. He battled Amazons during their sojourn in Southern Anatolia (perhaps as part of the mission to vanquish them), may have been one of the Argonauts, established Pamphylia to the West of Cilicia, founded the city of 'Mopsuestra' in the middle of it, and all in all was a significant figure in the pre-war Anatolian-speaking world. He may have been a contemporary of Atreus, but also may have lived later. Eusebius records for the year 1185 BC, immediately before the Sea Peoples' invasions, that 'Mopsus reigned in Cilicia'[49]. The 8th Century BC Karatepe inscription shows that 'Muksa's House' (i.e. the nation or people of Muksa) were still dominant in the area some three hundred years later[50]. In other words Mopsus continued to thrive after the Sea Peoples had swept through. Being part of the wider Trojan culture, he may well have joined the fleet as it invaded Eastward along the Southern Anatolian coast, from the direction of Pamphylia. In light of this Mopsus is perhaps one of the only ancient figures with a credible claim to have been one of the leaders, or at least an important ally, of the Sea Peoples.

The extremely complicated political context of this 'Ugarit corner' region all adds up to the fact that it would have been a veritable hotbed of support for the Sea Peoples' huge invasion. Was this what the Governor of Alashiya was referring to, that many of the invaders of Ugarit had been recruited from its own local populations!

---

[48] This city, located about halfway between the Marandynian Bay and the Ark's resting place in the mountains of Ararat, was particularly associated with Teshub's father Kumarbi (i.e. Noah).
[49] Eusebius, Chronicle, p.96/97
[50] Karatepe Inscription, p.125. Although, cf. the New Chronology

Sea Peoples raids on Assyria

The Assyrian Empire based in the northern Mesopotamian city of Asshur, founded by Shem's second son of the same name who was born almost immediately after the flood (making the Assyrian Empire an anomaly as being a Shemite-originated Empire), the predecessor state of today's 'Syria', was also apparently substantially affected by the 'bronze age collapse' brought on by the turmoil in the Aegean and Mediterranean Seas.

For most of the city of Asshur's existence it had been subject to the empire of Akkad/Babylon to its South, and the nearby Babylonian city of Ninevah was a major imperial centre. But around 1600 BC the surrounding empires fought and this gave Asshur an opening to copy Babylon and become an Empire of its own, based of course on the Babylonian satanic spiritual system. The Hittites to the West invaded and defeated the previously dominant Babylonians, who were replaced in the area by the smaller Mitanni Empire, but this in turn was also invaded and destroyed by a Hittite attack around 1360 BC. Assyria established its independence from Mitanni and began its own imperial domination.

A serious dent was put into this trajectory by the Sea Peoples' invasion of the Mediterranean. Essentially the empire collapsed and retracted back to the area immediately around Assyria, during a period exactly corresponding with the invasion and its aftermath (1207 BC-1050 BC). Although there were no direct Sea Peoples' attacks on Assyria, it is highly likely that the immense economic disruption of the coastal region particularly in the Mediterranean Sea's North-East corner, such a crucial concentration of trading centres and import/export hubs, landed a heavy blow to the burgeoning Assyrian economy. It would seem that the entire Western ancient world was stunned and halted in its tracks for some time by this upheaval, even a massively centralized state far to the East like the Assyrian Empire.

Sea Peoples raids on Phoenicia

As has been discussed, while the major empires of the region were destroyed or severely weakened, the settlements on the cosmopolitan strip of land on the East coast of the Mediterranean known as 'Canaan', peopled by Shemites or Semitic-speaking Canaanites, by contrast came out of this age of conflict very well. In fact long-term the Phoenicians were the big winners of the whole invasion era.

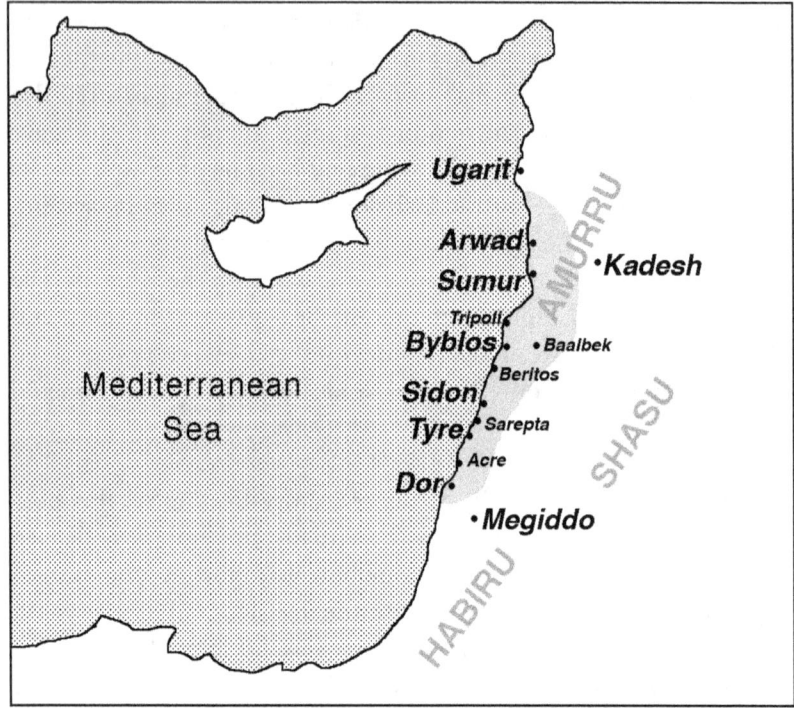

Fig.26: Phoenicia, with the surrounding Shemite-speaking populations. Note the Amorite capital of Sumur, destroyed in the invasion

Following the Sea Peoples' devastating attacks, the coastal cities of Byblos, Tyre and Sidon, collectively known as Phoenicia, became the dominant economic force in the Mediterranean world for the next thousand years. Glassware from Sidon and purple dye from Tyre, combined with a highly effective, advanced and organized maritime distribution system, formed the basis of a vast and expanding trade network that made a speciality of being the intermediary between other civilizations, connecting them together through trade. On top of this it was the Phoenician script, the first real alphabet, that came out of this 'sea-change' era as the revolutionary new and dominant writing system, replacing the old hieroglyphic systems in the Western world and forming the basis of all modern Western writing.

How the Sea Peoples interacted with the Phoenicians is highly complex, as this whole coastline was a major 'crossroads of the world', particularly with respect to trade. It was the area that joined the Egyptian, African world to the South, the Hittite Empire and 'Asian' seafarers to the North, and the Babylonian and Assyrian Empires to the East, that intersected with the Mediterranean via trade along the 'fertile crescent' up the Tigris River that came most of the way up from Babylon, arriving at the top of this coastal strip of land at Ugarit and Amurru. This transport funnel into the Semitic-speaking coast of Phoenicia also brought Indo-European chariot warriors from the North-East, the likes of the Hurrian, Mitanni and Kassite cultures. Such was the centrality of the region that the two titanic battles of the Bronze Age, the 16th Century BC Battle of Megiddo (between Egypt and a Canaanite confederacy) and the C.1274 BC Battle of Kadesh (between Egypt and Hatti) both took place in this area. It was a melting pot. And into this melting pot arrived the Sea Peoples.

Ugarit was totally destroyed but from there on South the invaders seem to have found common cause with much of this Semitic world, whose trade rival, Ugarit, they had just knocked out. There was of course a shared interest in seafaring and mercantile trade between the two, that one can propose may have been a significant bond between Troy and Phoenicia before the war. The Sea Peoples based themselves at the North of the 'Semitic strip' at Amurru for the duration of the hostilities. But, as in the 'report of Wenemon', they also made themselves at home further South in places like Dor[51]. And the cities of Phoenicia down the coast,

---

[51] Egyptian Inscriptions, vol.4, p.278

Byblos, Sidon and Tyre, do not appear to have suffered the wrath of the invasion fleet much, if at all. Indeed Phoenician growth and trade supremacy can be dated exactly from the time of the Sea Peoples' raids.

In particular, the Sea Peoples' massive attack on Egypt led to that civilization's 'Third Intermediate Period' or era of malaise and decline, that allowed Phoenicia/Canaan, that had been an Egyptian vassal, freedom and independence to branch out on its own. That included arguably providing breathing space for its Israelite settlers (called 'Habiru' or 'Shasu' to the surrounding cultures[52]) who had been in the area for some hundreds of years, to form a Kingdom of their own in Canaan[53].

Sea Peoples raid on Egypt

While there are scant original sources about what exactly happened to the Mycenaeans for example, the activities of the Sea Peoples in Egypt by comparison are a luxurious vista of detail. The Egyptian Civilization was, with Sumer/Shinar (Mesopotamia) one of the very oldest and earliest established after the flood, and by the time of the Trojan War around 1200 BC it was flush in its 'New Kingdom' phase, a period of energetic prosperity and vigour typified by the famous Ramses II (often wrongly associated with Moses' Exodus from Egypt, that took place some 450 years earlier) and very well set up with writing and efficient administrative records to give us a bird's eye 360 degree view of the tumultuous events of the 12th Century, complete with pictures. Most importantly, they weren't defeated and destroyed by the Sea

---

[52] Anson Rainey has argued against 'Habiru/Apiru' being identified with the Biblical Israelites (Rainey). However the data for either view are extremely minimal and other scholars have pointed out the close linguistic and referential similarities between the 'Apiru' referred to in the Ras Shamra (Ugarit) writings for example, who often sheltered runaway slaves from Ugarit and other empires, and the Israelite settlers. And also the extraordinary similarities between the Ugaritic proto-Phoenician language and ancient Hebrew (Ganor, p.229-230)

[53] The 'Israel Stele' of Pharaoh Merneptah (C.1200 BC) is the earliest independent witness of the nation (i.e. ethnic grouping) of Israel (Egyptian Inscriptions, vol.4, p.263-264; Karatepe Inscription book, p.40)

Peoples[54], unlike the unfortunate Greeks, Hittites and others, so they were able to leave records of them.

The Egyptian records are therefore overwhelmingly our primary sources for what we know about the Sea Peoples, and they make fascinating reading.[55] This was a culture clash of epic proportions.

Over a period of about 110 years, the Egyptians of successive dynasties detail their interactions with a group of peoples described very definitely as 'of the sea', or 'of the countries of the sea'[56], in contrast to other nationalities like Hatti, Israel or Armenia who are described as 'of the land'. They are also routinely described as 'Northerners'[57] and the Egyptian scribes often scold them as being 'unruly' or hard to handle. As in this example:

'the unruly Sherden whom no one had ever known how to combat, they came boldly sailing in their warships from the midst of the sea, none being able to withstand them.'[58]

Their relationship to imperial Egypt is not exactly straightforward. While they are definitely always described as 'foreign' and clearly very alien to the Egyptians and hostile to them, nevertheless they are known to them, with their 'ways' and national characteristics as above, even before the attacks of this era. As this century-long period of interaction went on, the tone of Egyptian commentary treats them more like a constantly harassing nuisance, and there is significant Egyptian investment put into actually rehousing and relocating them, once defeated, in the periphery of the Egyptian sphere of influence, around the Southern Mediterranean. But something definitely seems to have happened up North to cause

---

[54] However the huge attack on Egypt has been described as 'dealing Egypt a blow from which it never recovered' (Woudhuizen, p.9)
[55] These records are the Tanis Stele, Kadesh Inscriptions, Great Karnak Inscription, Athribis Stele, Medinet Habu incriptions, Papyrus Harris I, Rhetorical Stela and the Onomasticon of Amenope
[56] for example Egyptian Inscriptions, vol.4, p.76 & vol.3, p.249 & 255
[57] Ibid, vol.4, p.24, 37
[58] Tanis Stele (Egyptian Inscriptions, vol.3, p.210); Kitchen, p.40–41

this major and sustained population movement. A lot of people apparently became stateless at this time and roamed the Mediterranean searching for plunder and also for places to settle. It could quite easily be the case that once in the alien territory of the Southern Mediterranean, many of these raiders couldn't find their way back!

As time went on, detonated by the fallout from the Trojan War, the refugee/raider-quake expanded. Increasingly different people groups are found among the Sea Peoples. As states fell to them, more newly stateless nationals were added to the seaborne horde.

Here is a list of the Sea People nations, as set out in the Egyptian records:

Teresh, 'of the sea'[59]. As already discussed, this nation is perhaps the easiest to identify. These were Thracians/Trojans, probably from north of the Dardanelles Strait. Almost certainly identical with the later Thracian ethnonym: 'Treres'.
Tjeker. Likely a variation of the Teresh. 'Tjeker' is most similar to 'Teucer' or 'Teucrians' i.e. residents of Assuwa; or Thracians from Thrace.
Sherden, 'of the sea'[60]. While their post-invasion identity is known with some confidence, the origins of the Sherden are more obscure.
Shekelesh. Same as the Sherden.
Lukka. Lycians, from Arzawa.
Peleset. Later identity well known, origin less so.
Weshesh, 'of the sea'[61]. Assuwa or Wilusia. Maspero identified them as Carians from Wassos, though these raiders are less understood and competing theories exist[62].
Denyen, 'in their isles'[63]. Previously thought to be 'Danaans', one of the names for Greeks in the Iliad.
Ekwesh, 'of the countries of the sea'[64]. Thought possibly to refer to Achaeans, although this is somewhat problematic in that the traditional Egyptian name for Achaeans was 'Tanayu' ('Danaoi' – reflecting Danaus's African origins), not 'Achaeans'[65]. They could also be people from the Hurrian capital of Urkesh.[66]

---

[59] Great Inscription on the first pylon of Ramses III's mortuary temple at Medinet Habu, near Luxor, Egypt (Egyptian Inscriptions, vol.4, p.76)
[60] Ibid, p.76, and Papyrus Harris (Ibid, p.201)
[61] Ibid, p.201
[62] Woudhuizen perhaps less plausibly believed they were Oscans from Italy
[63] Egyptian Inscriptions, vol.4, p.201
[64] Great Karnak Inscription (Egyptian Inscriptions, vol.3, p.249)
[65] Woudhuizen, p.77
[66] Another group occasionally mentioned as part of the various confederacies attacking Egypt, sometime dwellers in Libya, are the 'Meshwesh' or 'Mashuasha' (e.g. Egyptian Inscriptions, vol.4, p.61), usually identified with the 'Maxyans' stated by Herodotus to be dwelling at his time in Libya and to 'say that they are descended from the men of Troy' (Herodotus, p.314)

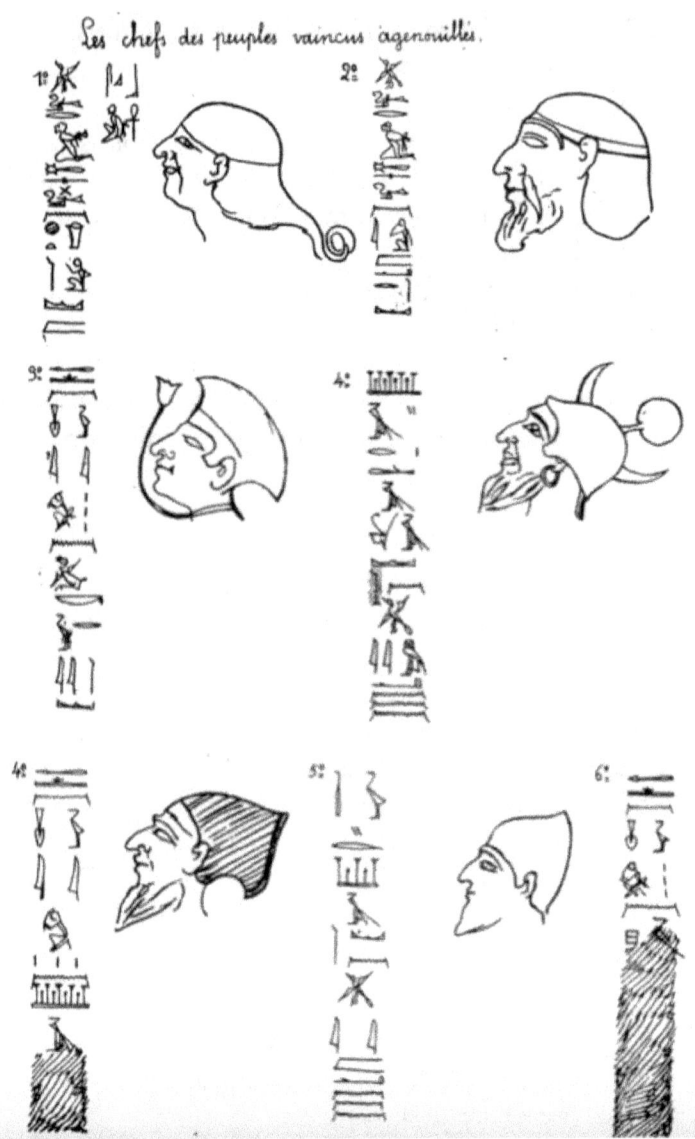

Fig.27: Captured Sea People leaders[67]. 1 = Hittite; 2 = Amorite; 3 = Tjeker (the characteristic 'plumed head-dress'); 4 = Sherden – (this horned headgear of the Sherden is probably the origin of the Viking horned helmet idea that later Vikings rarely actually wore); 4/5 = Shekelesh (or Shasu); 5/6 = Teresh[68]

---

[67] Jean-Francois Champollion's images taken from reliefs at Medinet Habu (Champollion, p.721-722). Public domain image from Wikimedia Commons.
[68] Translations of the labels from Maspero, vol.2, p.471

Fig.28: The plumed 'flat-top' head-dress of captured Tjeker and/or Peleset in detail. Or is it actually spiky hair?[69]

The first Egyptian contact we have recorded dates to around 1277 BC. This was a raid by the Sherden on the Nile Delta. It was defeated by Ramses II, who then pressed some of the captured Sherden into service for him, including at the Battle of Kadesh that occurred just three years later, which ended up as a draw between the Hittite and Egyptian Empires. The Poem of Pentaur describing the battle even suggests that the captured Sherden helped design the Egyptian Battle order[70].

The next mention of Sea Peoples occurs during the reign of Merneptah, who suffered a synchronized attack by a confederacy led by the King of Libya called the 'Nine Bows' that included Gaza, Ashkelon, Yenoam and Israel. Some Sea Peoples are mentioned amongst the vanquished after Merneptah successfully resisted the attack at the Battle of Perire in 1207 BC: Ekwesh, Teresh, Lukka, Sherden and Shekelesh, 'Northerners coming from all lands'.[71] It also adds that 'He has brought his wife and his children'.[72]

---

[69] From the first courtyard at Medinet Habu. After Foucher-Gudin's drawing of Insinger's photograph (Maspero, vol.2, p.699)
[70] Egyptian Inscriptions, vol. 3, p.136-7
[71] Great Karnak Inscription (Ibid, p.241)
[72] Ibid, p.243. This refers to all of the Sea Peoples' nations mentioned collectively

However all of this was merely preamble. It was during the reign of the next Pharaoh, Ramses III, that the floodgates opened and all hell broke loose upon the Mediterranean.

Specifically the year 1178 BC, the fifth year of Ramses' reign. Perhaps a date around 1218 BC is a reasonable estimate for the date of the beginning of the Trojan War, taking it as having lasted for 10 years[73]. The disturbance in Egypt involving Sea Peoples in 1208-7 (that included amongst the Shekelesh 'men and women') would then correspond to the immediate fallout from the conquest of the Trojan State. If the classic narrative is to be believed, the victory was won by treachery, the Greeks deceiving the Trojans with the Trojan Horse gift and thereby taking the city. The existence of an actual 'Trojan Horse' is hotly disputed (the story does not come from the Iliad, which doesn't mention the Trojan Horse at all, but rather comes down to us through remnants of other lost works, copied or referenced by later writers like Virgil). Today's commentators believe the Trojan Horse was some version of a siege engine, or if it was a gift was in fact a ship, a type of gift-ship known as a 'horse'. But if the Trojan Horse story preserves an element of truth in that the victory was the result of trickery, the defeat and capture of Troy would have been a sudden, shocking and unexpected blow to the Trojans, unrepresentative of the relative military strengths of the two armies and leading to a fast exodus away from the insurgent Greek occupiers.

Having then taken stock and mustered forces from the Black Sea and beyond for a major expedition, that may have taken another ten years, the Trojans and their allies might have commenced their invasion of the Mediterranean around 1198 BC. The much, much bigger invasions of Egypt starting in 1178 then would correspond to the fallout from the collapse of the Hittite Empire under the first wave of attack from the Sea Peoples that had begun in perhaps 1195. This enormous Empire falling so suddenly would explain

---

[73] Although the Hittite chronology of events would suggest an earlier date, around 1240 BC, for the war; see Appendix 2: The Trojan War through the eyes of the Hittites

the huge knock-on effect of the subsequent major invasion of the Southern Mediterranean, as the conquering Sea Peoples' main force swept down into the Sea, pushing refugees now from multiple conquered territories before it.

Whilst the Egyptians were aware of some of the Sea Peoples' nations beforehand, particularly from their brush with the Sherden a century earlier, the arrival on their doorstep of a full-scale invasion force in such numbers was clearly unprecedented, and such an extremely distant foreign adventure for so many invaders suggests a major disruption in their home nations.

> "The northern countries are unquiet in their limbs, even the Peleset, the Tjeker, who devastate their land. Their soul came, in the last extremity. They were warriors upon land, also in the sea[74]...The countries..., the [Northerners] in their isles were disturbed, taken away in the [fray] - at one time. Not one stood before their hands, from Hatti, Kode, Carchemish, Arwad, Alashiya, they were wasted. [The]y [set up] a camp in one place in Amurru. They desolated his people and his land like that which is not. They came with fire prepared before them, forward to Egypt. Their main support was Peleset, Tjeker, Shekelesh, Denyen, and Weshesh. These lands were united, and they laid their hands upon the land as far as the circle of the East. Their Hearts were confident, full of their plans."[75]

It appears that this massive maritime invasion force then carried all before it along the Eastern Seaboard of the Mediterranean, conquering everything that lay in its path. The Medinet Habu Inscription also relates:

> "Now the northern countries, which were in their isles, were quivering in their bodies. They penetrated the channels of the

---

[74] Great Inscription in the second court (year 5), Medinet Habu (Egyptian Inscriptions, vol. 4, p.24)
[75] Ibid, p.37

Nile's mouths. Their nostrils have ceased (to function, so that) their desire is [to] breathe the breath."[76]

This is interesting language. 'Quivering in their bodies' suggests anger and discontent. 'Their nostrils have ceased (to function, so that) their desire is [to] breathe the breath' indicates a desperation or suffocating.[77]

Successive waves of attacks on the Nile Delta began, in 1178 BC (Peleset and Tjeker), in 1175 BC (the main invasion, comprising the 'Nine Bows' again as a 'conspiracy in their isles': Peleset, Tjeker, Shekelesh, Denyen, Weshesh and some Hittites are narrowly defeated at the 'Battle of the Delta') and in 1171 BC (Tjeker, Sherden, Teresh, Peleset). The first two major naval attacks were defeated by the Egyptians in the 'Nile's mouths', while separate land attacks, including forces from 'Hatti (Hittites), Amor (Semitic Amorites) and Shasu (Israelites or other Shemites) were also defeated. As discussed, the fleet had based itself at 'Amor', the coastal city of the Amorites, seemingly forming an alliance with the Semitic peoples of the area. Sometime after these major battles Ramses records "I slew the Denyen (D'-yn-yw-n) in their isles"[78], suggesting a return raid possibly using the captured fleet, and that the Denyen were from a place navigable to by Egyptian sailors.

Greeks among the Sea Peoples

There is no doubt that this epochal seaborne movement of peoples during the 12th Century BC involved Greek people as well as Trojans to some extent. It is very likely that Michael Wood's theory is true: that Homer's 'Odyssey' that follows Trojan War hero Odysseus' roundabout journey by sea back to Greece, taking in adventures all over the Mediterranean including Egypt, is a

---

[76] Egyptian Inscriptions, vol.4, p.44. Pritchard, p.263
[77] Although it could also be the hyperbole of the hagiography, intended to convey how scared Ramses' enemies were of him.
[78] Papyrus Harris (Egyptian Inscriptions, vol. 4, p.201)

'memory' of involvement in Sea Peoples' naval expeditions[79]. There is also significant connection between events on Crete and the Sea Peoples[80]. However attempts to make the Sea Peoples Mycenaean Greeks or even one and the same with the Greek fleet of the Trojan War do not bear scrutiny.

Firstly the convulsions of the Mediterranean under the Sea Peoples' campaigns occurred very definitely after the war; the war does not follow from them. An attempt to find common headdress and war gear among images of the Sea Peoples made by the Egyptians to later Greek Hoplite soldiers forgets that the culture of the Mycenaean Greeks was not that of classical Greek Hoplite culture. The Mycenaeans wore boar's tusk helmets that are not in evidence at all in images of the Sea Peoples. The distinctive Sea Peoples 'plumes' are more likely to have been Thracian or Trojan, whose style was later copied by Classical Greeks during the rebuilding and reinventing of their culture based on Homer's 'Iliad' in the 8th Century BC, much of their subsequent sense of themselves and national identity deriving from the epic poem.

---

[79] Wood

[80] It has been argued that the Sea Peoples were none other than the Atlantic fleet of the (previously) Crete-based Minoans, attacking directly from America; a largely Scandinavian mercenary force now disenfranchised, unemployed and economically cut off following the Thera eruption's destruction of the Minoan empire, and with it that empire's extensive transatlantic copper trade that had both powered the Bronze Age and employed the sailors. This, it is claimed, is the explanation for Plato's description of the invasion of the Mediterranean by the 'Atlantans', that, he says, was defeated by the Greeks (Plato, vol.3, p.444). While it is probable that the Sea Peoples had been involved in this trade, and reasonable to assume that the destruction of the Minoans caused a shift in the balance of power in the Mediterranean to the detriment of the now leaderless Sea Peoples, that must have contributed significantly to Troy's decline and Greece's rise (the Greeks took over Crete and with it made a tacit claim to the mantle of the Minoans' Mediterranean supremacy), possibly precipitating the Argives' newfound belligerance towards Troy, yet the theory has a problem: the Thera event happened at least 200 years before the Sea Peoples' campaigns and the subsequent Bronze Age Collapse. Therefore they must have had a more immediate cause. Perhaps the Trojan War was an attempt to shore up the old Bronze Age political status quo. When the Trojans were defeated, the old era was well and truly over. The Sea Peoples' entry point into the Mediterranean can also arguably be seen (by mapping their trajectory) to have been the Dardanelles strait (although possibly not the initial Sherden attack C.1277 BC). See also Appendix 3: Logic Chain of the Bronze Age Collapse

Secondly, while mercenary veterans of the war from both sides were surely enlisted for the Sea Peoples' adventures – it would be amazing if they weren't as the Sea Peoples' fleets passed right through the Aegean Sea where all these veterans, the likes of Odysseus, would have been stationed - any explanation for truly large-scale Greek-led naval activity must surely include the fact that their own country, the Peloponnesian Peninsula, was at that time or had just been itself destroyed and conquered by foreign peoples from the North and/or from the sea. That still requires this definitely non-Mycenaean primary invasion, the initial thrust of the Sea Peoples' invasions, to be accounted for other than as an action of Greek forces.

Israelites among the Sea Peoples

As the historicity of ancient Israel has become better evidenced[81], the theory that some of the Sea Peoples may have been Israelites has been put forward. For example the Denyen as the Israelite tribe of Dan, and the Weshesh as the Israelite tribe of Asher; 'Sherden' seems almost to be a conflation of the two: 'Asher-Dan'. While this seems unlikely, it is not impossible. The record of the Battle of Perire in 1207 BC includes the information that the Ekwesh were circumcised[82], perhaps calling into question their identification as Achaeans. The inscription appears to state that the Sherden, Shekelesh and Teresh were also circumcised, though this is less clear. That would suggest an even closer association between the Sea Peoples and Northern Shemites, even arguably placing them within the boundaries of the Afro-Semitic world of Egypt, Israel and Arabia where this practice was ubiquitous. Or perhaps they got circumcised on their way South though Canaan! Or, Trojan culture may have included circumcision.[83]

---

[81] Israel is mentioned in the 'Israel Stele' of the reign of Egyptian Pharoah Merneptah (1213-1203 BC) as being one member of a combined resistance to Egyptian power that also included Hittites and Syrians (Egyptian Inscriptions, vol.4, p.263-264).
[82] Great Karnak inscription of the Pharaoh Merneptah (Egyptian Inscriptions, vol.3, p.249)
[83] Notably, it was the Semitic Phoenicians, with whom the Sea Peoples were in alliance, who ultimately inherited the Minoans' transatlantic shipping trade

The presence of Israelites among the 'Nine Bows' is also intriguing. Their being part of the 'land force' is more in keeping with the wider historical context as no other sources suggest that Israelites were ever particularly maritime nations. Except that is for the tribe of Dan[84]. Ramses III's claim of a return raid to the 'isles' of the Denyen is fairly clear, although this could conceivably be an Egyptian term for anywhere arrived at by sea, that therefore could include the Israelites' homeland in Canaan.

What is clear is that the Sea Peoples, of Northern and many of them of Scandinavian origin, made some level of common cause with the Semitic and Canaanite nations of the Eastern Mediterranean during this expedition. Amorites, Israelites and other Shemites ('Shasu' or 'Sheshu'[85]) appear to have made up much of the land assault force on Egypt. As they traced their respective paths across Asia over subsequent millennia, Scandinavians and Israelites would have many opportunities to interact, some of them highly controversial, as we shall see.

Settlement of the Sea Peoples

Large numbers of Sea Peoples stayed in the region after the failed attacks on Egypt, possibly against their will, and the Egyptians appear to have taken it upon themselves to re-house them in the Mediterranean[86]. In fact we have quite a clear understanding of where they went.

---

[84] Woudhuizen, p.78
[85] Anson Rainey has argued that 'Shasu' and 'Habiru/Apiru' were different groups, and that 'Shasu' is more likely to refer to the Israelites (Rainey)
[86] The Peleset in Askelon, the Tjeker in Dor (Maspero, vol.2, p.697) Possibly also some Sherden at Akko (Woudhuizen, p.112)

Sherden

After the Battle of the Delta many Sherden famously settled on the island of Sardinia[87], giving it its name and coinciding with the record of 'giants' moving there at that time, who are associated with the 'Nuragic' archaeological finds on the island. The Sherden are arguably the 'most alien' of all the Sea Peoples to the Egyptians and the most recognizably Scandinavian or northern European, with their horned helmets, round shields and long swords. This suggests a pre-Sea Peoples' homeland further to the North.

The best lead as to Sherden origin is the city of Sardis in Western Anatolia, that became the capital of the future state of Lydia. Around the city are various toponyms like Mount Sardena and the Sardanian Plain. 'Sherden' would therefore be a perfectly reasonable Egyptian ethnonym for people from this area. And this Luwian/Trojan-speaking Arzawa homeland would be in keeping with what we have discovered about the other Sea Peoples, most of whom appear to have been from this same region, the area of the wider Trojan 'nation'.

There is an additional aspect to this identification relating to pre-war Greek hero Heracles, who is recorded in the Iliad as being very active in this area in the generation before the war, himself sacking Troy and slaying all of Priam's brothers leaving only Priam (AKA Podarces)[88] alive.

---

[87] Egyptian Inscriptions book, vol. 3, p.239
[88] Apollodorus, vol.1, p.245-247; Iliad, p.378. This could potentially explain the destruction of Troy VI in the archaeological record at Hisarlik C.1300 BC

Moreover, Herodotus records that the city of Sardis was founded by guess who: the Heracleidae, the sons of Heracles, beginning with 'Akron' in 1220 BC. And there's more. Diodorus Siculus records that once Heracles finished his famous twelve 'labours', an oracle tells him that before he can ascend to Mount Olympus, he must create a colony at Sardinia and make his sons (with the daughters of Thespis, of whom there were fifty) its leaders. Together with Heracles' nephew Iolaus, forty of the sons settle the island[89].

This is an unmistakable connection between the Heracleidae and the Sea People. Could the Sherden have been amongst the 'Heracleidae' who 'returned' unexpectedly to Mycenaean Greece in the proposed 'Dorian Invasion' that destroyed the civilization at exactly this time? And could Heracles sending his sons to Sardinia be associated with the Sherden settling there after the war? Or indeed before the war, at or before the time of the first Egyptian interaction with the Sherden C.1277 BC[90].

---

[89] Diodorus Siculus, vol.1, p.243-244

[90] Such an association would help to explain persistent connections between Heracles/ the Heracleidae and northern, Tirassian and/or proto-Scandinavian peoples. As for example in his pre-war involvement in Trojan politics. However as to Heracles' origins, Siculus adds that 'they say that Hercules was born amongst them [the Indians – Ed.]' (Ibid, p.133). This is not the only reference to suggest that Heracles may have been descended from Magog (Greek Dionysius). Diodorus Siculus states about Dionysius that Heracles was "his near kinsman" (vol.1, p.24). Greek mythology is adamant that he was directly a son of Zeus (Japheth), but the (admittedly approximate) gap in time between the estimated death of Japheth (C.1900 BC) and the estimated era of Heracles' majority (C.1500-1300 BC (Herodotus, p.159)) make this appear implausible. A more prosaic ancestry of Heracles is suggested by his birth to Alcmene, supposedly 'secretly' by Zeus, disguised as her husband Amphitryon, but perhaps actually by Amphytryon. Indeed Herodotus describes him plainly as 'son of Amphitryon' (Ibid) and this would fit with the Heracleidae's claims to the throne of Mycenae as 'Perseids' i.e. descendants of its founder Perseus (C.1500 BC) father of Alcaeus (King of Tiryns), father of Amphitryon. Perseus' own heritage however remains obscure. Claimed by the Greeks, inevitably, as a direct son of Zeus, this is slightly more believable, but not much. However, the narrow possibility exists that Perseus was another name for Magog/Dionysius, or one of his sons. This would for example explain the Greek claim that the Magogian Persians were descended from Perseus.

Indeed, this Heracles story not only connects the Heracleidae with the Sherden, it also connects the Sherden of Sardis with the Sherden of Sardinia, as both groups were sons of Heracles. This must surely also explain the similarity in name. The dates would suggest that Sardis was settled from Sardinia, not the other way around. i.e. the Sardinia colony being started C.1280 BC and Sardis founded C.1220 B.C., exactly prior to the Sea Peoples' invasion and close (most likely just after) to the date of the Trojan War. It is entirely possible that these two Sherden branches were still in communication with one another and coordinated together for the giant strike against Egypt.

An even further conjecture would be to propose that the Heracleidae of Greek history, having like their brethren in Sardis gone to be hosted by allies in the Trojan/Thracian world (AKA possibly the 'Tourrians' or 'Dorians') were also acting as part of this same combined Thracian-led campaign when they invaded Greece from the North in the famous 'Return of the Heracleidae'.

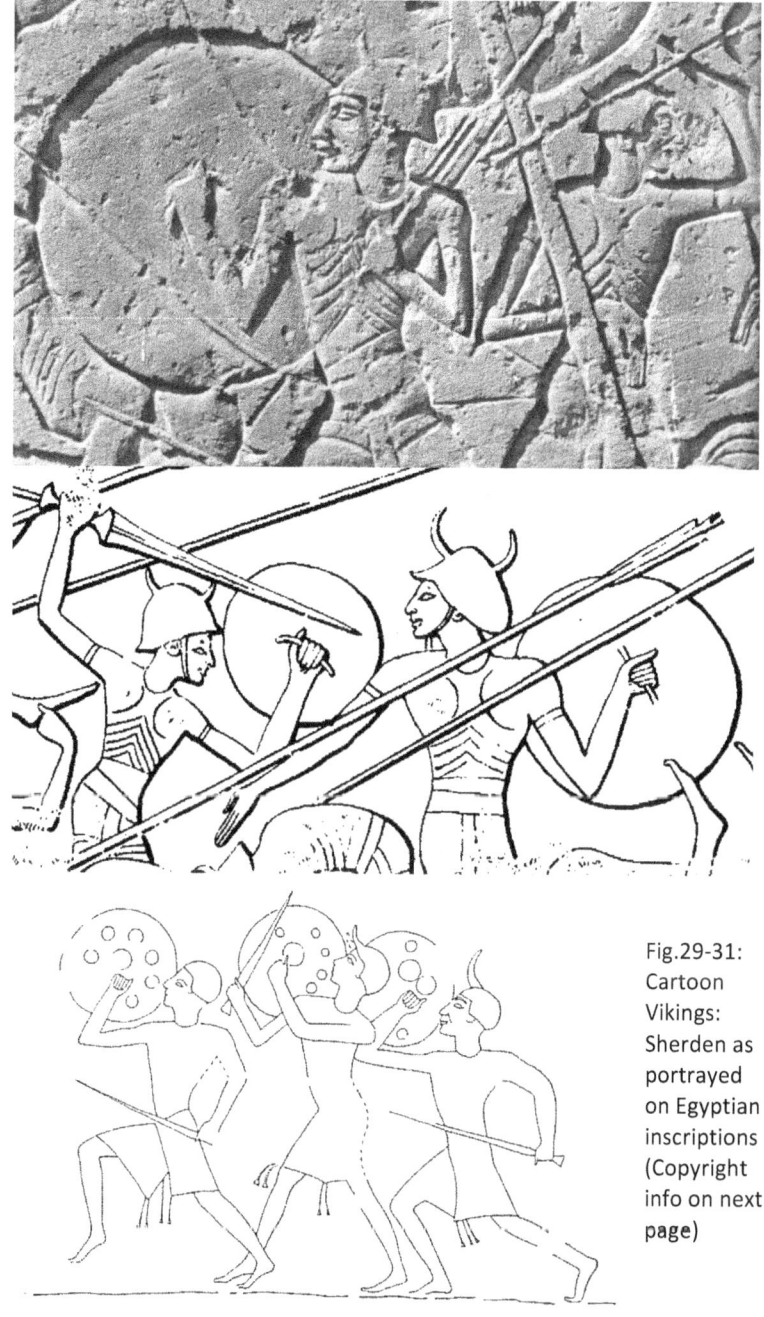

Fig.29-31: Cartoon Vikings: Sherden as portrayed on Egyptian inscriptions (Copyright info on next page)

Shekelesh

The best lead we have for the Shekelesh is that probably the name refers to the same group as 'Tjeker'[91], i.e. Teucrians/Trojans. Maspero believed they were from Sagalassos in south-central Anatolia, but Woudhuizen has credibly argued that this doesn't make sense as they were strangers to the Hittite Emperor Suppiluliuma II[92]. However this is explained perfectly if they were one and the same with the 'Tjeker' or Trojans/Teucrians, and were Scandinavians of the Black Sea culture of Troy, that was as we have seen largely outside the scope of awareness of the Mediterranean Empires. This fits exactly with the Ugaritic characterisation of the Shekelesh as people who 'live on ships'[93]. After the war, we know with some confidence where the Shekelesh went: the island of Sicily, giving it its name.

Peleset

Initially the Peleset were linked with the Pelasgians, i.e. proto-Greeks, but there is no real evidence of this other than the dubious similarity in name. What we do know very clearly is where they went after the war. After participating in the Battle of the Delta, the Peleset were forcibly relocated to Southern Canaan[94], and

---

Fig.29-30: Details from the Battle of the Delta relief at Medinet Habu (Egyptian Wall Reliefs, plate 50(c) and detail from pl. 39) reproduced courtesy of the Institute for the Study of Ancient Cultures of the University of Chicago. Fig.31: after Wreszinski, pl.78.

[91] For example Maspero renders Tjeker as 'Zakkala' (e.g. vol.2, p.698), while Breasted's version is 'Thekel' (e.g. Egyptian Inscriptions vol. 4, p.47). Therefore the ethnonym 'Tjeker' is practically indistinguishable from 'Shekelesh'

[92] Woudhuizen, p.114. However it is perfectly credible that some of them settled there after the invasion. Furthermore, Woudhuizen's statement that the pre-invasion Suppiluliuma was 'in full control of western Asia Minor' (p.114), justified by the fact of his recent conquest of Miletus and partial expulsion of the Greeks from Anatolia, is not accurate. The Greeks were not the Trojans, and they certainly weren't the Trojans' allies in the Black Sea. Rather Western Anatolia, in particular North-West Anatolia, was very much on the periphery of Hittite control, part of a foreign culture substantially not understood by the Hittites, hence their still being the target of its piratical raids, and hence their unpreparedness for the massive and fatal Sea Peoples/Phrygian invasion from that direction.

[93] Wachsmann, p.297

[94] Maspero, vol.2, p.697

became the 'Philistines' of Bible history, famously defeated by King David approximately two hundred years later. They subsequently gave their name to the Greco-Roman imperial designation for Canaan, 'Palestine'. This migration is confirmed by genetic archaeology that has identified a European (Japhetic) influx into the area at this time in history[95].

However, this recognition of them as the Biblical Philistines opens up a further can of worms, because the Bible identifies the Philistines as being descended from the 'Casluhim', that is from the sons of Ham's son Mizraim, AKA Egypt.[96]

This in turn embroils the discussion in an even muddier historical quagmire, involving the location and identification of 'Caslu' and his younger brother Caphtor. For these two brothers seem to be closely associated, in that a famous Egyptian City on an Eastern bank of the Nile, 'Pelusium', that must surely be the original dwelling place of the Peleset, and a similar location argued by some to be the home of the descendants of Caphtor, AKA Egyptian 'Keftiu', are right next door to one another.

But, this location has increasingly been challenged by many arguments that the nation of Caphtor really lived in Cilicia on the Mediterranean shore of Anatolia, or on Crete. Confusion is added by the whole issue of deciphering and interpreting ancient Egyptian texts, for example whether the phrase 'the great green'[97] refers to the Mediterranean Sea or to the vegetation of the Nile Delta!

---

[95] Feldman, et al; Wilson
[96] Tanakh, p.6
[97] Dickinson, p.243-4

The general consensus is that Caphtor/Pelusium was probably somewhere in this North-East Corner of the Med, basically Cilicia. This would make great sense in that:

a) Cilicia would have been within the sphere of influence of Troy/Arzawa
b) the Peleset are depicted as sporting the same 'plume' or spiky hair and headband look as the Tjeker AKA Teucrians. This is perfectly consistent with them being from the same area of Southern Anatolia.
c) The sweep of the Sea Peoples' main fleet around the South Coast of Anatolia made particular landfall in this region, near Ugarit and Kode, and made its base of operations in nearby Amurru, home of the Amorites. So the Peleset coming from nearby fits. This would be another local recruitment to add to the Alashyan Governor's statement that the invading force was from the Ugaritans' 'own people'.

Another name connection could add more weight to this theory. After the Sea Peoples' invasions, there was major population change in the area of Cilicia. Many of its people went North into central Anatolia, the region that the Hittites had previously controlled, and this area later became known as 'Cappadocia'. Clearly there is a similarity with the name 'Caphtor'.[98]

There is one final element to the Peleset/Caphtorim story. There has always been a persistent association of Caphtor with the island of Crete – a location that the Old Testament gives to the descendants of Caphtor. But no corroborating smoking gun evidence has been found. If the Caphtorim and Philistines settled in Anatolia from Crete, after the great disasters that Cretan Civilization had suffered, particularly the Thera volcanic explosion of 1600 BC, but also the subsequent takeover by the Mycenaean Greeks, this would fit with the long-held theory that the original Minoan Civilization of Crete was African in origin. Linear B, the

---

[98] Pseudo-Philo (C.100 AD) agrees with this: "Mestram begat Ludin and Megimin and Labin and Latuin and Petrosonoin and Ceslun: thence came forth the Philistines and the Cappadocians." (Pseudo-Philo, p.88)

writing system of the Mycenaeans has been deciphered, because the language it encodes is proto-Greek. But Linear A, the writing system of the Minoans, encodes a totally unrelated language (usually termed 'Eteo-Cretan') that has not yet been deciphered. Could this have been the Hamitic language that came from Caphtor and Caslu, the first Patriarchs of the Minoans?

This theory fits with the founding legend of the city of Miletus: that it was built by immigrants from Crete[99] - far from Cilicia but towards that direction. The Carians also (Caria being west of Cilicia on the south coast of Anatolia) were stated by Herodotus to have been of Minoan descent[100]. It would even then perhaps work with 'Pelasgians' as this broad term for indigenous Greeks was often used for people of the far ancient cultures of Greece, including the Minoans.

Denyen

By far the most difficult Sea Peoples nation to identify. 'Danaans' is one of the main terms Homer uses to describe Greeks in the Iliad (the others being Achaeans or Argives, i.e. those from Argos). The term comes from Danaus, the very ancient founder of Argos, who, like the proposed founders of Minos above, was not himself a son of Japheth but rather the son of King Belus of Egypt (possibly Biblical Mizraim), son of Poseidon (Ham), who had fled Egypt and settled in the Peloponnese. This makes 'Argives' exactly cognate with 'Danaans'. The Egyptian connection is one reason why the Egyptians may have called people from Greece 'Tanayu' ('Danaans') rather than 'Argives' or 'Achaeans'.

One intriguing detail in support of this identification is that the city of Argos, only seven miles from Mycenae, was not apparently completely destroyed by the Sea Peoples, unlike Mycenae, Pylos, Tiryns and Miletus. It also had a later trend of siding against the

---

[99] And indeed even Thor himself ('Teucer') is said by Greek mythology to have lived first at Crete, only later to move to 'Teucria' AKA Asia after a famine (Strabo, vol.2, p.373).
[100] Herodotus, p.76

Greeks with their enemies, famously in the Greek-Persian wars of the 6th Century BC. Also in 468 BC Argos completely destroyed both Mycenae and Tiryns, wishing to dominate the 'foundation city of Greece' market. This is very thin but it could possibly be an echo of the Danaans/Argives joining the Sea Peoples. On the other hand it would still be a highly unlikely shift of sides.

Other theories can only offer similar speculation. As above the Denyen could be the Israelite tribe of Dan, after the war going back to a similar location as the Philistines. Or the term could potentially refer to 'Dardanoi', i.e. descendants of Dardan, son of Javan, who settled in the Troad in far ancient times, welcomed by Thor, after leaving Greece because of rising sea levels/ floods according to Greek mythology. His descendants (including according to the classical narrative the Trojan royal family) would certainly be among the Sea Peoples.

Meanwhile the stomping ground of the warlord Mopsus, the Cilicia region, also has a mention of a people who could be the Denyen: the Karetepe Inscription in its Phoenician version calls the people of the 'House of Mopsus' (located basically in Mopsuestra/Adana in Cilicia) 'Danunians'[101]. Perhaps a compromise theory would identify the Denyen (and possibly the Ekwesh) as Achaeans/Danaoi not directly from Greece, but of the contingent who had just been defeated in Southern Anatolia[102] by the Sea Peoples' invasion, turned soliders of fortune, who were now blow-ins arriving in Cilicia from the West, possibly with Mopsus.

However it should be noted that the Danunians/Danuna of Adana are also mentioned in the earlier Amarna letters (C.1350 BC)[103], suggesting they may have already been in Cilicia prior to the Sea

---

[101] Karatepe Inscription, p.149; in its Luwian version 'Adanaweans' (Ibid, p.125), that has also been translated as 'Hiyawans' as in 'Achaeans' (Woudhuizen, p.74) as also in the Çineköy inscription (Hittite Correspondence, p.263)

[102] Maybe the very force in Lukka whom Ammurapi had sent his ships to earlier to prepare the defence (Hittite Correspondence, p.257)

[103] Egyptian Correspondence, p.238

Peoples' campaign. For example Woudhuizen notes that 'the form Danuna corresponds to the root of Dnnym "people of Adana" as recorded for the Phoenician version of the bilingual Karatepe text (late 8th century BC), and has nothing to do with the Danaoi of mainland Greece'[104]. In light of this, and considering that Adana, the land of Mopsus, was directly in the path of the Sea Peoples' fleet, it seems much more likely that the Denyen were from Adana than from Greece, which was itself also under attack at exactly this time.

All of this adds to the conclusion that the Sea Peoples, although perhaps ethnically disparate, nevertheless were all rooted in a common Trojan/Thracian cultural outlook, homeland and possibly language, that was the underlying impetus for this vast invasion. This is reflected in their leadership group that was a combination of Scandinavian Thracians/Trojans (Teresh, Tjeker, Shekelesh, Dardanoi) and Heracleidae (Sherden, Dorians)[105], carrying along with them as culturally assimilated Anatolian confederates disaffected Pelasgians (Peleset) and Cilicians or Cilician Greeks (Denyen, Ekwesh)

---

[104] Woudhuizen, p.77

[105] An alliance apparently forged between Heracles and Aegimius around 1300 BC in the war against the Lapiths (Apollodorus, vol.1, p.263; Diodorus Siculus, vol.1, p.251)

Irish, British and Scottish origin stories

This book will not go into too much detail on the ancient history of the British Isles, but it is worth noting the tremendous range of the migrations from the Mediterranean that resulted from the Trojan War and its aftermath.

The ancestors of many later European nations left the Asian area at this time, presumably to escape the associated turmoil and to find new lands where they could dwell in peace. As the ice caps slowly melted, Northern regions that had been uninhabitable gradually thawed and presented themselves as new options for settlement.

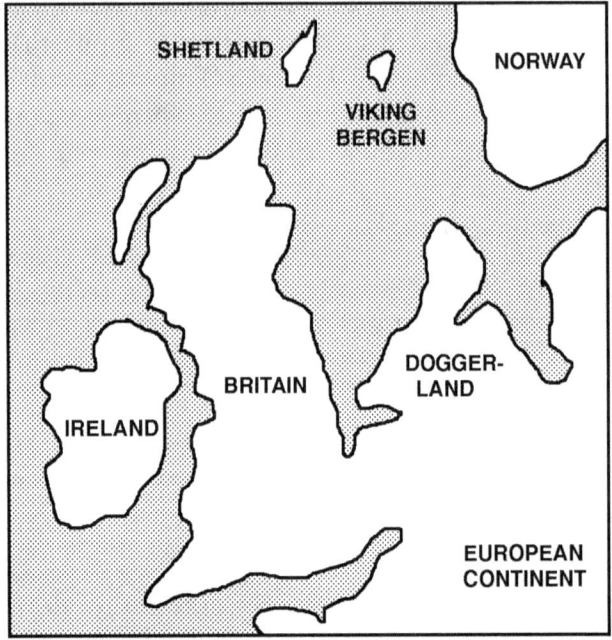

Fig.32: Estimated map of the British Isles showing the lower sea level that would have remained during the thousand years or so after the last glacial maximum AKA 'Ice Age' that followed the flood, including the hypothesized land bridge to the mainland known as 'Doggerland'.

The British Isles had already been settled to some extent by the descendants of Gomer, the red-headed 'Cruithne' whom the Romans called 'Picts', who may have walked over the land bridge that had previously joined the islands to the mainland[106]. As the ice melted and the sea level rose and they became islands, new immigrants would have to arrive by boat.

The island of Ireland therefore became the first stop for people sailing north from the Mediterranean. This situation resulted in multiple waves of immigration/invasion of Ireland by sea, colourfully chronicled in the 11th Century Irish history Lebor Gabála Érenn ('The Takings of Ireland').

The writer is essentially documenting a history of the Scots AKA the Irish AKA the Gaels (not to be confused with the 'Gauls' AKA the Celts of central Europe) who would arrive from northern Spain in roughly 600-350 BC. But, displaying a very Irish/Scottish preoccupation with family and clan, the author also tries to make all previous immigrant waves into Ireland, about whom he has significantly less detail, relatives of the Gaels as well. But it is extremely unlikely that all of these invaders, openly hostile and alien to one another, were so closely related. Especially as the first four groups in the story all died out or were expelled from the island, so it is difficult to see how this Gaelic historian could know about them one way or the other!

The first settler, Partholon, from 'Mygdonia', arriving 'when Abraham was in his 60th year'[107], dies in a plague. Five hundred

---

[106] Although see notes below on Partholon
[107] (LGE, vol.2, p.269) i.e. around 2000 BC. Partholon is claimed here to be 'son of Sera, son of Sru, son of Esru, son of Brament, son of Eochu, son of Magog' (vol.3. p.5). His arrival is stated to be 300 years after the flood. However in one of many chronological contradictions in the LGE it is then immediately stated (vol.3, p.3) to have been 1002 years after the flood, there being 942 years from the flood to Abraham (a discrepancy that reflects the Masoretic/Septuagint controversy). At Partholon's death 30 years after coming to Ireland the LGE states that 'Ninyas s. Ninus s. Belus was in the High Kingship of the Orient' (vol.3. p.19) The Pictish Chronicle and Scottish additions to Nennius (Pictish Chronicle p.4 and 24) give a different genealogy for Partholon: they say the eponymous leader of the Picts,

and fifty years later, so do all his offspring[108]. Thirty years after that Partholon's claimed relation[109] Nemed arrives. He also succumbs to the plague and his people have to defend themselves from the Fomorians, a hostile native people who may be the Picts/Cruithne, but other sources call them Hamites.[110] The survivors leave the island.

But it is the next wave of immigrants whose journey may have been part of the Sea Peoples' diaspora in the wake of the Trojan War. This group, called by the Irish records the 'Fir Bolg', are quite possibly part of the same fleet described in detail in the Welsh Chronicle[111] as being led by King Bryt (Hellenized 'Brutus'), son of Silvius, son of Ascanius, son of Creusa the daughter of King Priam of Troy and Aeneas, and part of the captured Trojan royal family[112]. The Welsh Chronicle records that Priam's family were

---

'Cruithne' ('father of the Picts living in this island' (i.e. Britain – Ed.)) was the son of Cinge, son of Luctai, son of Partalan, son of Agnoin, son of Buain, son of Mais, son of Fathecht, son of Jafeth, son of Noe. Therefore possibly a Pictish leadership group may have been descendants of Partholon, so that his progeny did not all die out. However while the identity of 'Fathecht' is a mystery, the first half of his name appears to memorialize Riphath. If true that would mean Partholon was more of a Scot than a Pict. It is suggested that, like the Magog attribution above, this may not be accurate. The Pictish Chronicle states that the Cruithne came to the British Isles from the region of Thrace and 'are the children of Gleoin, son of Ercol. Agathirsi was their name' (Ibid, p.30). Agathyrsus/Leipoxais, one of three brothers, was the grandson of Papaios (Celto-Scythian Japheth) and son of 'Targitaos' in Scythian mythology (Herodotus, p.247-249). While 'Targitaos' could be any one of Togarmah, Gomer, Thor or even Heracles (see Herodotus, Ibid), the name Agathyrsus is most suggestive of Ashkenaz, son of Gomer, son of Japheth. This would fit with the stated generations, the three brothers (the youngest is named 'Scythes' (Ibid, p.249), that fits exactly with Riphath), and the geography.

[108] LGE vol.3, p.29. This is stated to be when 'Hercules captured Troy' so there would appear to be some conflation of time here (as this would have been C.1300 BC, some 700 years after Abraham). The detail is added that it was 50 or 60 years after this that 'Troy was captured for the last time'.

[109] However he is also called 'son of Agnomain of the Greeks of Scythia' (LGE, vol.3, p.121)

[110] Keating, vol.1, p.179. This early Hamite presence in the British Isles echoes claims that the 'giants' encountered by Bryt on the mainland (Welsh Chronicle, p.9) may also have been Hamites. Perhaps this remembers colonists from the many and powerful Settlement 1 Hamite empires that made it this far north.

[111] Welsh Chronicle, p.2-10

[112] The LGE's account of this is confused but partially agrees. Firstly there are the

taken back to Greece and kept captive for generations, until his relation Bryt hatched a plot to obtain Greek ships and escape. This was done, and the flotilla made its exit through the Straits of Gibraltar northwards, around 1100 BC. The memory of the captivity in an unenviable area of the Greek islands is preserved by the Irish history, that relates that the Fir Bolg were forced to haul endless sacks of earth to their assigned territory in order to build up enough topsoil to grow food, hence 'Fir Bolg' meaning 'those of the sacks'.[113]

Bryt and his fleet continued on to the island that would from then on bear his name: Britain, establishing the city of London as 'New Troy' AKA 'Trinovantum'.

The generations from Priam to Bryt in the Welsh Chronicle are widely thought to be romantic additions[114], almost certainly lifted wholesale from Virgil's dubious 1st Century BC poem the 'Aeneid' (of which more later), so the Irish history's alternative descent of Bryt from Nemed's son Fergus Redside[115] may therefore be more factual[116]. However as to the concept that Bryt and the early Britons were descendants of Trojan refugees, this is confirmed by

---

customary dating contradictions regarding the arrival of the Fir Bolg: they are stated to have arrived both 'in the end of the rule of the Chaldeans' when 'Baltassar' (Belshazzar) was Emperor, just before the rule of the Persians (so C.550 BC) (vol.3. p.35), but also '230 years after Nemed' (Ibid, p.125), who arrived C.1270 BC, so C.1040 BC. The earlier date will be preferred here. The story of the Fir Bolg and their captivity in Greece is very similar to that of the Britons, the LGE reporting that they 'stole the pinnaces of the King of Greece for coming therein' (vol 3, p.125). However it also claims that the Fir Bolg were descendants of Nemed, led by his grandson 'Semeon'/'Semul', who fled Ireland at the time of the war with the Fomorians. Meanwhile it plainly states that 'Britain Mael' 'of whom are all the Britons in the world' was the son of one Fergus Redside, a son of Nemed (and uncle of Semeon). Therefore the LGE makes the Britons Nemedians, but intertwines the histories of the Nemedians and the Fir Bolg. In light of this the coincidence between Nemed's arrival in Ireland and the Heraclean disturbance in Troy is hard to ignore. Was Nemed a first generation Trojan refugee?

[113] LGE vol.3, p.147
[114] Petrie
[115] LGE vol.3, p.127
[116] The writer of the LGE tries to resolve the two traditions by arguing somewhat implausibly that there existed two Bryts at exactly the same time (Ibid, p.149)

none other than Julius Caesar, who in his 'Gallic Wars'[117] states that the leading 'tribe' of Britons he faced in the area of London when conquering the island a thousand years later in 50 BC were the 'Trinovantes', meaning 'New Trojans'.

As the Welsh Chronicle describes in detail, Bryt founded a dynasty that, although conquered by Roman invasion, would continue in power until pushed into Wales by the arrival of the English some 1500 years later.

Some time after this, (perhaps as much as 250 years[118]) Ireland is again the target of invasion, this one the oddest and most dramatic of all. These invaders are called the Tuatha De Danann. The name evidence causes one to question whether they were related to the 'Danaan' of Greece, and/or the 'Denyen' of the Sea Peoples. As discussed 'Danaans' is one of the main terms Homer uses to describe Greeks in the Iliad (the others being Achaeans or Argives, i.e. those from Argos).

The 'Danann' who arrived in Ireland are described in the most dramatic terms as people with an advanced knowledge of sorcery and dark arts, so highly skilled and so far in advance technologically of the existing Irish populations that they are suspected of being demons. They are simultaneously described as having learnt these dark arts 'in the far North' but also having come 'from the Greeks'. They proceed to vanquish the Fir Bolg to the islands of the Irish Sea and dominate Ireland until the arrival of the Gaels.

Other theories of their origin include a possible association with the Israelite tribe of Dan. Although this sounds like a stretch, there are intriguing correlating details. Firstly, unlike all the other

---

[117] Caesar, p.259. All the more credible as he is both a hostile and an oblivious witness.
[118] The LGE has mixed witnesses for the date of the coming of the Tuatha De Danann (though not as glaring as the contradictions in the dating of the Fir Bolg's arrival), but in general it states they came in the 'eighth year' of the reign of 'Cambyses son of Darius' (the Persian Emperor), so roughly 520 BC

Israelite tribes, the Tribe of Dan's primary trade was seafaring[119]. Secondly, after partaking in the unified Israelite state of King David around 1000 BC, Dan becomes part of the northern breakaway state of Israel/Samaria. The Bible's records of the ten northern tribes famously ends when they are conquered in 721 BC by the Assyrian Empire[120]. Based on the coast and with a handy fleet, could the Danites have made an escape by boat from the coming invasion?

The timing of their arrival in Ireland would be just about perfect to coincide with the Irish records[121], that also mention that they appear to have burnt their boats as soon as they landed in Ireland to prevent them returning[122]. What were they running away from? Finally, what about the 'devilish' dark arts of the Danann? Well, the Book of Revelation lists the Twelve Tribes of Israel who will receive the inheritance from God. But Dan (and Ephraim) are missing (replaced by Joseph and his son Manasseh[123]). Why no Dan? Many have concluded that this was because of the spiritual degeneration of the Tribe of Dan (whose symbol is a serpent), away from God and towards paganism.

To finish the story of ancient Irish settlement: finally arrive the Gaels, AKA Scots, AKA 'Milesians' (no relation to the city of Miletus, but rather named after 'Mil', the leader of their expedition). This testimony is fascinating and detailed as it is one of the few records to give us an inside witness into Scythian culture. The main hero of the 'Lebor Gabála Érenn' and the ancient Patriarch of the Gaels is one Feinius Farsaid, an early 'prince' of the Scythians. What the writer is less sure of however is whether Feinius Farsaid was a descendant of Magog or of Riphath; the perennial Scythian ethnic confusion persists. The writer offers alternative genealogies of each:

---

[119] See for example Woudhuizen, p.78
[120] Tanakh, p.261-262
[121] Considering the looseness or at least multi-faceted nature of the Irish Chronology
[122] LGE vol.4, p. 109
[123] Brit Chadashah, p.170

"As for Feinius Farsaid, he was son of Baath s. Magog s. Iafeth. Others say however that Feinius Farsaid was s. of Baath s. Ibath s. Gomer s. Iafeth."[124]

'Ibath' is identified elsewhere in the text as Riphath[125]. What is crystal clear however is that the language spoken by the Scythians and by the Kingdom or principality of Feinius Farsaid was 'Scottish' (i.e. Gaelic), the language of Riphath, who had brought it personally from the tower of Babel into Scythia as one of the 70 human languages of the dispersion[126]. The name 'Riphath' is said to be related to the word 'spoken' or 'language' in Hebrew.

A compromise may be arrived at then that while the Scythians spoke Gaelic and most of them may have been descended from Riphath, their leadership group including the later Patriarchs of Ireland were Magogian. This would fit perfectly with other accounts of the 'Royal Scythians' being sons of Magog[127] while the great majority of the population and its culture was Riphathian. Feinius Farsaid is also recorded as being an expert in languages. The 'Riphathian nation' then was apparently led by Magogites.

The trip for the Scythians that finally ends up in Ireland is a long-winded one that takes in multiple voyages on the Caspian, Mediterranean and Black Seas, with at least one visit to Sri Lanka

---

[124] LGE, vol. 1, p.155-157. It is proposed here that the second reading is the correct one, for these reasons: FF is always named as being a son of Baath; Baath must surely be the son of Ibath because of the name similarity, and Ibath is identified as Riphath. Additionally Riphath is stated plainly in vol.1, p.37 to be 'the grandfather of Feinius Farsaid'. Whether the patriarchs Esru, Sru and Sera were from Magog or Riphath is an interesting question. As per the genealogy of Partholon, it is suggested they may be from Magog.
[125] Ibid, p.153. Quite possibly Greek mythology's 'Iobates' (Apollodorus, p.151-153)
[126] LGE vol.1, p. 37
[127] The famous Irish/Scottish prefix 'Mac' could be a claim of patrilineal descent from 'Magog'. Especially as, if the identification of the Royal Scythians as Magogian as compared to the Riphathian main population is correct, denoting oneself as a 'Mac' would signify that one belonged to this high-status group, possibly explaining the longevity of the term's usage. Similarly, Sanskrit has a word for a patrilineal descendant of Magog: 'Gotra'.

(AKA the 'Island of Tabropane') and to Egypt where Mil famously marries the Pharoah's daughter, named 'Scota' (the text actually relates this Egyptian marriage story twice, the first time the groom being Feinius's eldest son Nel – some 1500 years earlier[128]), and a westward invasion into Germania the land of the Gomerans (Celts) with some Thracians tagging along, through 'Pict-land' before finally ending up in Galicia in northern Spain around 600 BC (although it could be as late as 350 BC[129]). It is from here that one of the Scots spies Ireland from a tower. They set off by boat and, after much battling with the Danann, finally settle and take over the island.

The many previous settlements detailed in Lebor Gabála Érenn may be remembered from travellers from whom the Scythians learned about the island's existence, and indeed the story is full of 'seers', particularly their Druid 'Caicher', telling them that 'Ye shall not rest till ye reach Ireland.'

It is quite possible that the Scythians were involved to some extent in the Sea Peoples' raids, or if not they were aware that navigators could transport them great distances. With the fall of Troy that had been the gateway to the Black Sea, the Northern Black Sea Coast, stomping ground of the Scythians, was now open to invasion by Mediterranean Empire builders. The Scots apparently didn't want any part of that and, over successive generations, many of them migrated to the British Isles.

---

[128] The first 'Scota' that Nel marries is stated to have been a daughter of Pharaoah Cineris. Whether this is a 'double-memory' of the same event (there are multiple parallels between the two narratives, such as the stopover in Sri Lanka) or whether there genuinely were two separate sojourns in Egypt and two separate dynastic marriages, is uncertain

[129] This is due to the mention of Mil leaving the service of Egyptian Pharoah 'Nechtenebus' (after staying in Egypt only 8 years) because the Pharoah was losing his power to Alexander the Great (LGE Vol.2, p.39-41). In fact this Pharaoh (Nectanebo II) was not conquered by Alexander but rather the previous generation's Persian Emperor Artaxerxes III. However this would still date the life of Mil much later than the LGE states, as Nectanebo II ruled Egypt 358-340 BC.

Roman origin story

The origins of the city of Rome and therefore of the Roman Empire are as shrouded in mystery as just about anything in ancient history, being as they are intensely sensitive for the continued promoters of and lobbyists for the 'Greco-Roman Homosexual Fascist' idea.

Because of this, the circumstances surrounding the true history of early Rome are highly opaque and cannot conclusively be described here. What can be said is that an isolated, aggressive, urban centre dedicated to the 'city' concept and to military domination grew up and became a political entity to be contended with in the midst of today's Lazio region of Western Italy, during the 8th Century BC. There are rival theories mostly involving an origin among the multi-ethnic surrounding rural populations, but none really stand out, especially considering the subsequent particularly aggressive and anti-social Roman expansionist bent, that does not find a very satisfactory explanation in the pastoral, rural settlements that surrounded it.

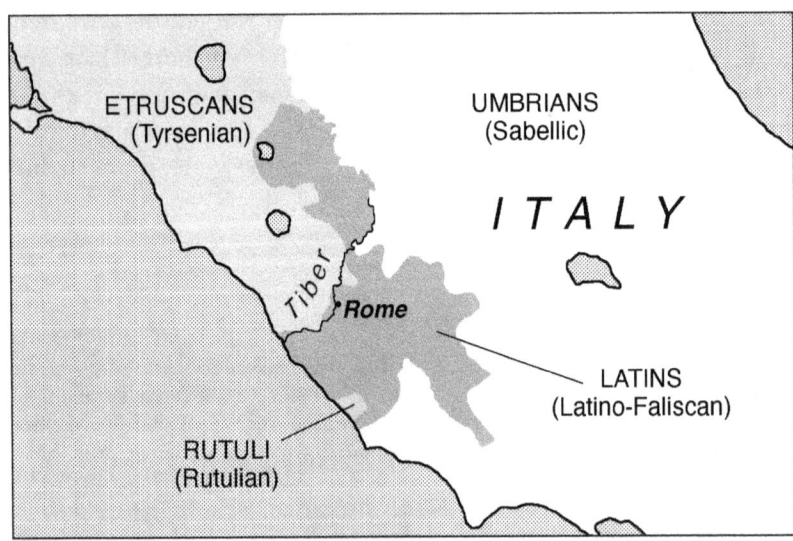

Fig.33: Linguistic landscape of central Italy at the beginning of Roman Expansion
(C. 700 BC) (copyright info on next page)

The origin and nature of Rome is emphasized by its foundation story, probably the best-attested of all early events in Roman history: 'The Rape of the Sabine Women'.

This new and unusual city, apparently a foreign culture, was founded sometime in the mid-8th Century BC[130]. The city grew through energetic trade and military activity, but had very few women. It was more or less an all-male society, lending credence to the theory that this was a homosexual colony, with the suggestion that it was significantly composed of 'male bandits' i.e. criminals[131]. None of the surrounding rural populations such as the Sabines, the Etruscans and the Rutuli, would have anything to do with it, least of all let their women intermarry with the questionable denizens of the new city. This inability to breed was recognised by the Romans as a long-term danger to the survival of their colony, so a plan was hatched.

The originator of the plan may have been Romulus, who would become celebrated as the first leader and 'founder' of Rome, as he seems to have come to power and notoriety largely through the incident. It was a founding event that would come to define both Rome and Romulus, as it simultaneously 'saved' the new colony and provided the despicable model for the imperialistic and fascist character and values of the future Roman state. Basically, all the surrounding nations were invited to a festival devised for the occasion. At a given signal by Romulus, the Sabine women were violently abducted and dragged away, subsequently raped to populate Rome.[132]

This is an independent adaptation of a Wikimedia Commons map by Susana Freixeiro (https://en.wikipedia.org/wiki/File:Linguistic_Landscape_of_Central_Italy.png) used and published under CC BY SA 4.0 (https://creativecommons.org/licenses/by-sa/4.0/deed.en)
[130] Cornewall-Lewis, vol.1, p.267
[131] Mathisen, p.60.
[132] Livy, vol.1, p.35-37. The Sabine women story occupied a central position in the cultural tradition of Rome's foundation, often memorialised throughout its history in pornographic theatrical productions performed at festivals (Holden)

There are four main competing origin stories as to who the Romans were and in particular what was the ethnic ancestry of Romulus. Firstly the later Roman imperial story, most famous from Virgil's epic poem the 'Aeneid', written around 20 BC. According to Virgil, Romulus was a descendant of Aeneas, a minor character in Homer's 'Iliad', that the 'Aeneid' was a proposed sequel to; an attempt to create a similarly epic poem in the Homeric style that would glorify Rome and give it an heroic and legendary status equal to that of the Greeks. In the Aeneid, Aeneas, a Trojan soldier, flees the burning city of Troy with his family and after some adventures lands in Italy and founds the city of Rome[133].

Although this is often related as the 'primary' Roman origin story, it can really only be seen as having the same tentative authority as the other three, for the following reasons. Firstly it was written 700 years after the fact, in a period where it played an extremely political propaganda role in shoring up the tenuous state control of first Roman 'Emperor' Augustus[134], by providing a 'fitting' and 'honourable' backstory to the Roman state that emphasized the legitimacy of Augustus's Julio-Claudian dynasty and reassured everybody that Rome's future was steady because its past was settled and that they should prioritise stability and not overthrow Augustus. In particular, dynastic continuity and its claimed benefits were the number one priority that Augustus wanted to impress upon the people in support of his reign, so finding a 'legitimate' dynastic succession (such as from Trojan hero Aeneas) for both his own family and the foundation of Rome was essential.

Secondly the idea that Rome was seeded from Trojan refugees does not seem compatible with the highly distinct, imperial Roman culture that had very little in common with the mercantile, sea-faring Trojan one (that was indeed more like that of Rome's

---

[133] Or at least its predecessor city, Lavinium
[134] AKA Octavian, the son of the military dictator Julius Caesar, who had 'broken' the Republican constitution by crossing the Rubicon River in 49 BC and establishing for himself autocratic rule by fiat, thereby beginning the decline in fortunes of the Roman state.

adversary, Carthage, a colony of Troy's allies the Phoenicians). Nor is there much in the way of other evidence of a common heritage with Troy, until this 'noble' history was 'found' by Roman historian Fabius Pictor around 200 BC, before which it is notably absent from contemporary sources[135]. Moreover, the Aeneid was composed very much in the wake of the Roman conquest of Britain, where Roman forces had encountered the 'Trinovantes' ('New Trojans') who themselves claimed ancestry from Trojan refugees. Could such a glamorous backstory have been a further inspiration for Virgil?

Thirdly there is a much better evidenced Trojan colony in the area: the Etruscans, whose name is derived from 'Trojans' or 'Troas', who settled there at the time of the destruction of Troy and who had a long and well-evidenced history in the region stretching back to at least that time.[136] But that was not Rome. As per the Sabine Women story, the Etruscans, who lived to the north of Rome, were entirely hostile to the new city, and indeed it was not until the Roman-Etruscan wars of the late 4th Century BC that Rome

---

[135] For a fuller discussion of the evidence, see Appendix 4: Investigation into the Trojan Roman Origin Story. Virgil's main historical support was Dionysius of Halicarnassus. But Dionysius, writing at the same time as Virgil, was engaged in the same Augustinian propaganda effort as he was, i.e. hagiography and flattery of the then-reigning Julian family in an attempt to legitimise Augustus's regime. Indeed Dionysius and Virgil (and historian Livy) were personal associates of Augustus.

[136] Herodotus relates an origin story of the 'Tyrrhenians' (aka 'Tyrsenoi'), the Mediterranean pirates believed to be the ancestors of the Etruscans (the name is a Greek exonym, therefore including the meaning of 'not Greek'); that they came from Lydia (western Anatolia, around Sardis) and emigrated to 'Umbria' (Western Italy) for economic purposes (Herodotus, p.44). Josephus claims Lydia was founded by Lud, son of Mitzrayim, son of Ham (vol.4, p.143-146). But Herodotus disagrees, making them instead descendants of Lydus, son of Atys, son of 'Manes' (Herodotus, p.457) The departure of the proto-Etruscan, Tyrrhenian migrants, he says, took place 'in the days of Atys'. Regardless of Lydian origins, at this time the area was still very much part of the Trojan sphere of influence, hence the 'Trojan' name of the leader of the migrants 'Tyrrhenus' (the son of the Lydian King, says Herodotus). Woudhuizen argues against this 'early' migration from Asia to Italy, and instead accepts a later, post-war migration (Woudhuizen). However both are possible. It would be entirely natural for refugees from the war and/or piratical Sea Peoples to find their way to colonies previously established by their countrymen. Interestingly, Scandinavian runes are most commonly associated with the alphabet of the Etruscans, who are likely to have had a Trojan heritage.

finally subdued the Etruscans, forcibly, into its empire. This may however have provided another inspiration for Pictor and Virgil's explanation, in that the Etruscans, being a famous nearby settlement with a noble pedigree back to precisely the mythic events of the Iliad that Virgil wished to emulate, were a handy source for an origin story for the parentless and delinquent early Roman state.

There are more problems with the conventional narrative. In that Rome is considered to have been an outgrowth of an earlier culture known as the 'Latins', who had already been in the area for hundreds of years when the new city was formed. But we can see from the Sabine Women story that when that event occurred Rome does not appear to have had existing relations or family ties with the surrounding cultures, hence the story. How can this be explained if the Latins had been respectable, even leading, members of the community for four hundred years?

For example, Virgil and other Roman sources such as Livy state that Romulus had come from the royal dynasty of Alba Longa, a city twelve miles from Rome that was much more ancient and a leading member of the 'Latin League' of local cities. But if this was true why couldn't the Romans intermarry with women from that city? Instead all the evidence points to Rome being an entirely new, alien and unwelcome innovation in the region.

This anomaly might be explained by the other sources for the origins of the Romans. Lebor Gabála Érenn states that the 'Epirotae' were descended from Tubal[137] 'from whom sprang Ianus, king of the Epirotae. He is the first king who took over the Romans. From him is named the month of January, and from him are the Quirites.' [138] ('Epirotae' and 'Quirites' are both terms for Romans.)

---

[137] Son of Japheth
[138] LGE, vol.1, p.155

Meanwhile the medieval work 'Yosippon' relates how descendants of Tubal built 'Sabino' while the 'Kittim' (descendants of Kitt) built 'Posomanga' with the Tiber river between them. The writer identifies the Romans with the 'Kittim'[139], who subsequently committed the rape of the Sabine women. Later after an occupation by Agnias King of Carthage, the Kittim end up appointing Zepho, grandson of Esau, as their king, with the title 'Janus Saturnus', with Romulus a distant descendant of this line, or at least its political successor. The timing makes it impossible for a grandson of Esau to have been alive at the time of the Sabine Women attack if it was in the 8th Century BC, however Yosippon would seem to be arguing for a many hundreds of years earlier dating for the rape of the Sabine women, contemporary with Zepho. If Romulus was descended from Esau, the ancient enemy of the Israelites, it would explain the pervasive anti-semitism of Romanism, but it could also be a medieval invention for the same reason.

These sources point to an association of Romulus with Quirinus, a deified version of him later worshipped by the Romans, and also with Janus, another deity of the early Romans that probably represents Romulus as well. Or, if the Yosippon version is to be believed, perhaps Zepho or the 'Zepho line' of Romulus' descent. Janus is the 'god of two faces', this could certainly be a memory of the evil trickery of Romulus and/or a proposed primaeval Kittim predecessor[140].

---

[139] Yosippon, p.94-95 The Kittim's association with our words 'city' (Italian: 'Citta') and 'citizen' adds weight to the argument for the Romans as Kittim. And this is also how they are referred to in some of the Dead Sea Scrolls (another Jewish source), such as the 'Nahum Commentary' and the 'War Scroll' (Dead Sea Scrolls, p.473 and p.163-165)

[140] Janus also regularly invites the 'god' Saturn to Rome. Saturn appears to be the Roman version of Greek Cronus, AKA Noah, with this claim associated with a somewhat improbable 'Saturn' version of Noah's story involving his overthrow by his sons and then his sojourning as an outcast and fugitive in Europe.

Finally Strabo relates a fourth origin story, that Rome was a Greek colony planted by the Arcadian Evander at the time of Heracles' visit to Italy to recover the cattle of Geryon.[141]

In light of the difficulties with the official account of the Sabine women incident related above, it is possible that the Yosippon version of the story may be essentially correct but rather than the foundations of the city of Rome itself, it recalls the original arrival into Italy of the Latins, AKA the Kittim, as an all-male colony possibly directly from Cition in Alashiya (Cyprus), that would have been much earlier. This is consistent with the 'beachhead' appearance of the Latins' territory in the above map, as they attempted to establish a settlement in a hostile region already long occupied by Umbrians, Etruscans and Rutuli. It would also explain the 'alien' nature of the newcomers in the Sabine women story[142].

While it is not completely impossible that the new city of Rome established in the 8th Century BC (essentially by a gang of thieves and criminals[143]), could have been considered enough of an anti-social entity by the Romans' own relatives in the surrounding Latin cities to cause them to refuse to give their daughters in marriage to the Romans, it is highly unlikely[144]. However there clearly remained a remarkable level of hostility between Rome and its 'parent' cities in the Latin League surrounding it. The Latin League would later contract with Rome as though it was contracting with a foreign entity, and Alba Longa itself was

---

[141] Strabo, vol.1, p.343. This would have been C.1350-1300 BC

[142] Romulus may or may not have existed. Some early sources refer to the founder of Rome as 'Romus', a name more suggestive of a token figure used because the true founder was not known (for example Antigonus (Greek Historical Fragments, vol.4, p.305, Fr.1)). Or he may have lived earlier and was an indistinctly remembered version of Zepho. Or, earlier still, the leader of the original Latin colony in Italy, such is his association with the Sabine women incident. Remus, traditionally the twin brother of Romulus, is almost certainly a poetic addition (see later re: Tiridates and Horsa)

[143] See for example Livy, vol.1, p.21

[144] Although the 'homosexual runaway' subtext of Rome's foundation could perhaps add to the plausibility of this idea

destroyed by Rome in the mid 7th Century BC with its inhabitants forced to settle in Rome.

The murky details of exactly what occurred to spawn the city of Rome and why it was so hated by its neighbours will have to be left for future chroniclers. For the moment we may simply note the rise of this militaristic, homosexual-fascist colony from the mysteriously isolated urban settlement of Rome.

Iron Age Anatolia

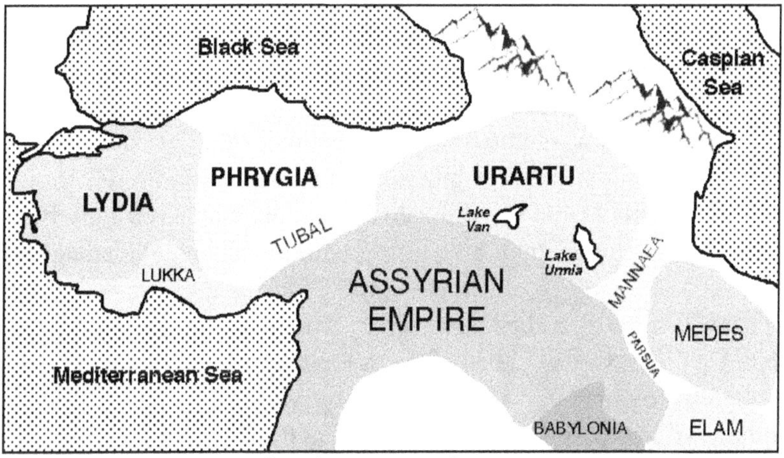

Fig.34: the approximate political status quo of Asia in 722 BC

After the Sea Peoples' invasions and the subsequent 'Bronze Age Collapse' there was what is referred to as a 'Dark Age' for a few hundred years in Asia[145]. This 'lull' in major events was probably a blessed relief for its inhabitants!

Having apparently expelled both the Hittites and the Greeks for the time being, from roughly 1150-750 BC a period of some kind of stability ensued for the inhabitants of Anatolia. In the centre of the peninsula, the Phrygians held sway, based in their capital Gordion. To the West the Kingdom of the descendants of

---

[145] Although as previously discussed if the 'New Chronology' dating revision of David Rohl is applied, this Dark Age may actually only have lasted 100-150 years.

Heracles, now called 'Lydia' (the derivation of this name is disputed[146]) had also expanded and prospered, with its capital at Sardis (AKA 'Sfard', almost certainly the origin of the 'Sherden'). To the South-East Lukka/Lycia/Tabal became a buffer state to the customary imperial aggressions of Mesopotamia. The big player there at this point in history was the neo-Assyrian Empire, the superpower of the age. After the setback to its ambitions caused by the Sea Peoples' raids, it was once again pushing westward. The north and south-west coasts of Anatolia were still probably inhabited by indigenous Carian, Amazon, Tubalic and Meshechian nations. At the east of Anatolia and to the North of the Assyrian Empire, another large empire called 'Urartu' had grown around Mount Ararat covering roughly the territory of historical Armenia. Although it is possible that Armenia proper was then known as the smaller Kingdom of 'Mannaea', while Urartu was a puppet of the burgeoning Assyrian Empire. This set-up was largely stable for about four hundred years, during which time Lydia, Phrygia and Urartu had something of a golden age.

This was to be disturbed however, by the tumultuous events of the late 8th Century BC. The newly Indo-European-dominated Iron Age was particularly characterised by wild invasions from the unknown north, and the next major event in the region would fit this type exactly. It was the arrival into history of an intensely controversial nation who would cut a swathe through Asia: the Cimmerians.

The March of the Cimmerians

The Asian 8th and 7th Centuries BC were dominated by the Cimmerians, whose transit straight through the middle of Anatolia was as shocking to the people of the era as the Sea Peoples' raids were to their ancestors 400 years earlier[147].

---

[146] As discussed Josephus claims Lydia was founded by Lud, son of Mitzrayim, son of Ham (vol.4, p.143-146), but Herodotus disagrees, making Lydians instead descendants of Lydus, son of Atys, son of 'Manes' (Herodotus, p.457)
[147] Or, in the new chronology, only 100-150 years earlier

The Cimmerians had a lot in common with the Sea Peoples. Like many of those nations, we can trace the Cimmerians' later settlement and movements with a reasonable degree of accuracy, but we don't really know where they came from. Indeed, the origins of the Cimmerians constitute arguably the most controversial aspect of this book.

Essentially, horse-riding archers with characteristic pointy headgear, coming from the North-East, conquered the entire Anatolian peninsula (today's Turkey) for a hundred years. Then they were expelled with extreme difficulty, before migrating back up North again, once more disappearing out of the sight of mainstream history.

Fig.35: the archetypical image of the Cimmerians, from an Assyrian relief[148]

Because of their later identification with subsequent nations, their origins have come in for the most intense scrutiny.

---

[148] This a public domain image of a relief in Nimrud, Iraq, from Wikimedia Commons (https://en.wikipedia.org/wiki/File:Kimerian.jpg)

The issue is that, while for all intents and purposes they were some kind of 'Scythians', clearly exhibiting the same nomadic, horse-archer lifestyle, that general explanation is somewhat insufficient and unsatisfactory in this case. This is because the Cimmerians had characteristics that show them to have been a specific nation, and those distinctions lead to questions about the vast, expansive variety and multi-faceted nature of the 'Scythian' hordes. In other words: what kind of Scythians were they?

Opinion about this is divided, with little agreement. What can be said is that the emergence of the Cimmerians from the Eurasian Steppe began an entire era when Indo-European horse cultures from the north came to dominate the central Eurasian plains of Anatolia and Babylonia. Following the Cimmerians would come their friends the Medes, then the Persians, then the Parthians, all of whom had significant links to the greater Scythian or 'Indo-Iranian' equestrian states centred around Sogdiana and BMAC and led by descendants of Magog.

The first record of the Cimmerians as a military threat to the Iron Age status quo comes in the 720s BC in the form of reports from Prince Sennacherib of Assyria to the Assyrian Emperor Sargon II citing severe resistance to attacks by Assyria's client state Urartu's forces against Colchis and its surrounding areas. It seems that the empire of the day was attempting to expand and annex/enslave more of the indigenous inhabitants of Asia. But the Colchians had unexpected allies in this campaign from an unknown Scythian-type force dwelling there in today's Gori in Georgia, known then by the Assyrians as 'Gamir', on the Kura River[149].

---

[149] The name of this region, 'Gamir', possibly the origin of the label 'Cimmerian', has led many to assume an ethnic derivation of the Cimmerians from Gomer. Although the main body of the Scythian nation was indeed 'Gomeran' (from Gomer's second son Riphath), the specifics of the Cimmerians point to them belonging to a different culture, but one previously under the feudal or federal headship of Scythia. This association may explain the term 'Gamir' or it may refer to previous Gomeran residence in the area earlier in history.

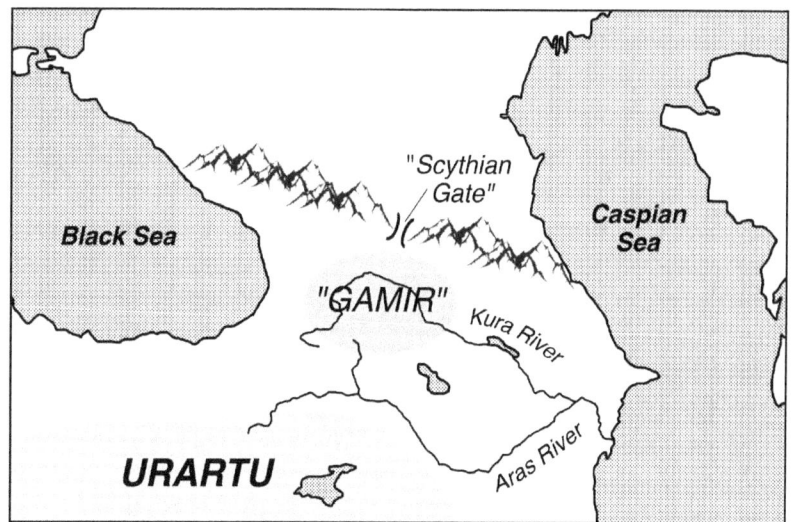

Fig.36: the location of 'Gamir' south of the Caucasus Mountains

Apparently spurred on by their ease in resisting the Urartian King Rusa I's depredations, these newcomers quickly became too much for King Rusa to handle. They counter-attacked Urartu between 720 and 714 BC, so King Rusa in turn counter-attacked Gamir, but with disastrous results for his forces. The entire Urartian army was wiped out, including Rusa's Commander in Chief and thirteen Urartian regional governors[150]. The total destruction of its army allowed for Urartu's immediate conquest by and assimilation into the Assyrian Empire, shortly after which King Rusa died. Urartu for all intents and purposes was finished.

The Cimmerians then drop from the record for a few generations. They appear to have split into two streams. An eastern stream settled among their allies in Mannaea, around Lake Urmia (arguably the 'real' Armenians). From this strategically critical spot they fed strongly into the Median kingdoms to the south-east, descendants of Japheth's son Madai, likely becoming a significant catalyst to the Medes' growth from a northern province of the Assyrian Empire into a major state in their own right, beginning under Median King Kashtariti (Phraortes). Once again, the

---

[150] Assyrian Correspondence, p.30-32

Cimmerians were a part if not the instigators of this resistance effort towards the Assyrian Empire. In 676 BC they helped the Mannaeans fight off an Assyrian attack. A year later, the Assyrian records are concerned with whether they will be able to extract their tribute from Media itself, because of the Cimmerian presence[151].

Similarly the Assyrian vassal city of Cybistra/Hilakku in Cilicia was also being menaced by a different group of Cimmerians and their Scythian allies. In 679 BC Assyrian Emperor Esarhaddon managed to defeat the Cimmerians there in battle, killing their King Teuspa, but he was still not able to reoccupy Cybistra nor completely subdue the Cimmerians in the area. Instead Esarhaddon cannily married his daughter to the Scythian King Prutava[152], that proved to be a turning point in the Cimmerians' Anatolian fortunes, as the marriage gained for the Assyrians the Scythians as allies, splitting them from the Cimmerians. This demonstrates the critical distinction between Cimmerians and Scythians - these were two separate groups, albeit previously affiliated.

The Cimmerians do not join the truce, remaining loyal to the Ellipi and the Medes, and carrying on with them a major, successful campaign lasting until 671 BC that rolls back the Assyrian Empire on its north-west border.

Meanwhile the Western stream of Cimmerians are on the march. They now ally with Urartian King Rusa II and/or become mercenaries for him[153], invading and conquering the Kingdom of Phrygia in central Anatolia in 675 BC, completely destroying it.

This mercenary force once again however quickly gets out of hand and seemingly out of the control of the Urartians, as it subsequently attacks and conquers Bithynia, Paphlagonia, the

---

[151] Ivantchik, p.127-154
[152] AKA 'Bartatua', 'Protothyes' or 'Partatua'. Assyrian Divination Records, p.24-5
[153] Sulimirski & Taylor, p.559

Troad and the recently-founded Greek colony of Sinope, that is also completely destroyed. It then prepared to take on the largest Kingdom of Anatolia: Lydia.

It should be noted that while Lydia was the Kingdom of the Heracleidae (whom we are identifying as 'Sherden'), there had been dynastic regime-change in Lydia since then. The period of the Cimmerian invasion of Anatolia is in fact exactly contemporary with the Heracleidae being overthrown from the Lydian throne, suggesting an alliance of interests between the Cimmerians and the Heracleid Kings of Lydia, whose aggressive usurper Gyges/Kukas was the main target of the Cimmerian attacks.[154].

Gyges quickly mobilises to resist the Cimmerian assault, calling for help from the Assyrian Empire in 667 BC. But in 665 without its help he defeats the Cimmerians and stops the invasion by himself.

In the East however, the Assyrians have to some extent been forced to recognise a Cimmerian King as 'Kissati' ('King of the Universe' in the Mesopotamian conception), requiring the Assyrians to win the title back from him. So they are in no state to help the Lydians. A new leader of the Cimmerians, Tugdammi, attacks the Lydians again in 644 BC and finally overcomes them, killing Gyges and sacking Sardis. He also destroys the famous Temple of Artemis in Ephesus, then promptly invades and kicks out the Ionian and Aeolean Greek city-state colonies on the West coast of Anatolia, whose colonists once again flee back to the Aegean islands.

The Cimmerians have now conquered the entire of Anatolia. But their anti-imperial activities do not let up. Tugdammi moves to the region of Cilicia around 640 BC and allies with the Kingdom of Tabal in continued fighting against the Assyrian Empire,

---

[154] Gyges was previously the servant of the last Heracleid King Candaules, killing him and taking his throne in 687 BC (Herodotus, p.4-6)

although he eventually swears an oath to the Assyrians, dying soon afterwards.

In 637 BC Tugdammi's son Sandaksatru participated in another successful invasion of Lydia, this time led by King Kobos of the Thracian Treres (almost certainly the 'Teresh' of the Sea Peoples) whose forces had hopped over the Bosporus from Thrace apparently to help out their allies the Cimmerians. This very close relationship with the Treres is extremely telling when identifying the roots of the Cimmerians. Another Sea Peoples nation, Lukka/Lycia also participated in this attack. Sardis was again sacked and Ardys, Gyges' son, killed.

Enough was enough for the Assyrians. They finally took advantage of their marriage deal with the one group they knew could handle the Cimmerians: the Scythians, whose King Madava/Madyes entered Anatolia in C.620 BC with his forces, duly expelling the Treres back to Thrace and defeating the Cimmerians in battle. This Scythian ascendancy in Asia would last for a generation - traditionally 28 years - before the Cimmerians' allies the Medes in turn invaded and conquered the territory themselves, pushing the Scythians out by around 590 BC. The Cimmerians remained in Anatolia, Cappadocia and the Troad for a while yet, but were finally forced to emigrate in ships from the North Anatolian coast, from where they landed on the peninsula next to the Maeotian Lake and settled there, giving it its name, 'Crimea'[155].

---

[155] Asimov, p.50.

The identity of the Cimmerians

So the famous march of the Cimmerians was over. But where had they come from? This question requires a deep dive into the vast and constantly shifting sandstorm that is Scythian history.

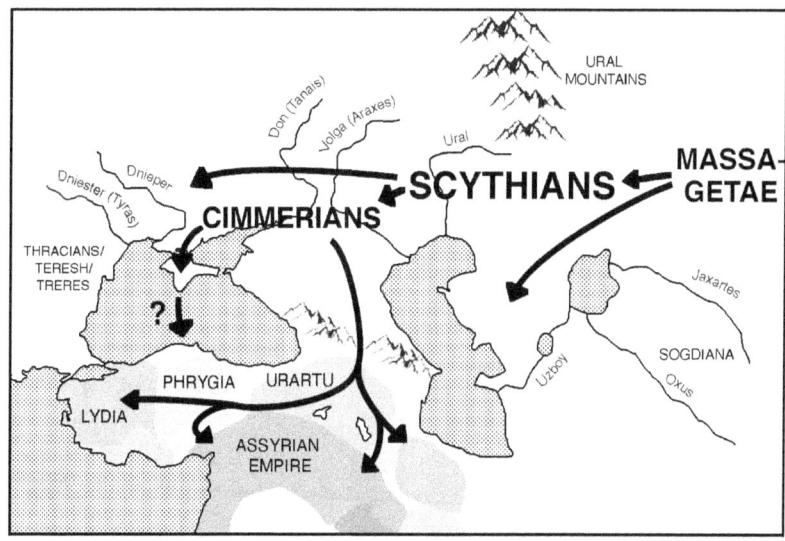

Fig.37: The traditional understanding of the Cimmerians' origin and route

The conventional answer is that the Cimmerians, previous to their Anatolian adventure, lived in an area of the 'Sea of Grass' with the Maeotian Lake to its west and the Volga River to its east. The history of the Volga (known to the Greeks as 'Araxes'), the main River of Russia, is closely linked to the history of the Scythians[156], as many commentators consider the area around it to have been the original Scythian settlement[157]. According to Herodotus, during the 8th Century the Scythians 'proper' who lived to the east of the Volga, pushed westward across the Volga, under pressure from the 'Massagetae' to their east (of whom more later), who were pushing westward into Scythia[158]. The Scythians consequently

---

[156] Sulimirski & Taylor, p.553
[157] For example Diodorus Siculus, vol.1, p.136. Although Sogdiana (at the right of the above picture), little understood by the Greco-Romans, is more probably the primaeval 'homeland' of the Scythians
[158] Herodotus, p.249-250

invaded the territory of the Cimmerians, causing them to migrate Southwards into Anatolia.

It should be noted that all three of these groups were regularly termed 'Scythians' by outsiders[159]. But there was clearly some distinction between them, hence the hostility. Also as we have seen it was 'Scythians' who eventually expelled the Cimmerians from Anatolia, therefore they must have been a different group. We can perhaps conclude then that the 'Scythians proper' who dwelt east of the Volga in this model were the Riphathian Scots, led by the descendants or heirs of Fenius Farsaid, according to the Irish history. Whereas further investigation of the Cimmerians shows that they probably had a different ethnic origin.

Lebor Gabála Érenn, one major window into the convoluted Scythian politics of the day, provides evidence of major dynastic upheaval amongst the Scythian nations in this 'north of the Caspian' Scythian homeland at roughly this time. Although the chronology is highly problematic, it describes how after a long absence mainly in Egypt[160], descendants of Fenius Farsaid's eldest son Nel returned back to Scythia just as the King of Scythia, a descendant of Fenius's younger son Nenuel, dies. This leads to a dynastic dispute that the authors assert lasts for nine hundred years[161]. This seems to be rather an exaggeration as the generations listed can't really cover that period, but there was clearly a long feud between the two branches of Fenius's family for control of the Scythians at roughly this time in history. The eventual 'founder' of Ireland, Mil (a descendant of Nel), is exiled from Scythia for his dubious killing of one Refloir (a descendant of Nenuel) at the tail end of the feud, leading to Mil's flotilla of Scythians leaving the Sea of Grass 'nine hundred and fourteen years after the drowning

---

[159] This makes sense when we remember that, as per Oswald Szemerényi, the term 'Scythian' is ultimately derived from 'Skuda' that is simply a term for an archer (i.e. 'shooter') (Szemerényi, p.45-47), and would therefore probably be applied casually to any group who utilised this Indo-Iranian style of warfare.
[160] The Egypt story, despite seeming unlikely, is affirmed by Diodorus Siculus (vol.1 p.136)
[161] LGE vol.2, p.37-39; 65-67; 73;

of Pharao Cineris in the Red Sea'[162]. That would be approximately 750 BC. There follows in the account a somewhat confused travelogue describing how the Milesians eventually returned to the region via the Caspian Sea, battled with Sirens and Amazons on its West coast (who may have been one and the same), before 'the sons of Mil left the crews of twenty ships of their people there, and forty-four companies from that back to Scythia.'[163]

Mil then crosses Caucasia and settles in Asia 'for one month' before crossing the Bosporus northwards and going through 'Germania' westwards ending up in Northern Spain.

How this dynastic struggle impacted on the Scythians pushing the Cimmerians westward is not clear, but the Irish history corroborates that there was indeed turmoil and migration in the greater Scythian world at this time, with apparent ease of transport for Scythians and their associates throughout the Asia Minor region. It shows that there was significant movement around the Caucasus and Anatolia of various leadership groups with various different affiliations, that fits broadly with Greek accounts of the tumult that preceded the appearance of the Cimmerians in Anatolia. One can speculate how the adventures of the Milesians on their way to Ireland may have intersected with the 28-year ('one month'?) Scythian reign in Anatolia and the people movements in the eastern Caucasus where they left the 'crews of twenty ships', but we simply do not at this time have the details of what happened.

When we look at Classical Greek sources on the Cimmerians, Herodotus' description of the Cimmerians' political structure is familiar from that of other Scythians. He relates that the ruling class or 'Kings' of the Cimmerians were ethnically different from the 'commoners'. Just like with the Scots it appears that an Indo-Iranian (Magogian) leadership group may have had an early kingship role among the Cimmerians, following the general

---

[162] LGE vol.2, p.67. See also p.73-75
[163] Ibid, p.71

Gothic or Indo-Iranian ascendancy in the Sea of Grass at that time. The Magogians appear to have pioneered the 'Scythian' horse-warfare style, and welcomed all comers into their confederacies, as long as they submitted to Indo-Iranian rule. Judging by the Scottish example, it is possible that the Cimmerians retained much of their own culture, including possibly language, and that this was a distinguishing factor between them and the Gaelic/Scottish speaking 'Scythians proper'. Greek sources go on to say that when the Massagetae pushed westward into Scythia, and the Scythians in turn pushed across the Volga/Araxes River, conquering Cimmerian territory, the hitherto Cimmerian leadership group made up of Magogians refused to leave their lands in surrender and killed each other instead, being buried in a kurgan near the Tyras River[164] (today's Dniester River in Moldovia/Ukraine).

There is much about this story that lends itself to the other facts. Firstly the burial at the Tyras River is a long way from the Volga. And it suggests that the Cimmerians' Westward border was not in fact at the Maeotian Lake (HQ of the Goths) but rather continued on much further west. To Thrace, and indeed the River Tyras, named after Thor/Tyras himself. This is perfectly in keeping with two other significant pieces of evidence: a) the remarkable alliance of the Cimmerians with the Treres/Teresh from exactly this Thracian region only a hundred years later (who crossed the sea and migrated to hostile, foreign territory apparently completely assured of finding friendship with the Cimmerians there). And b) the very strong identification of the Cimmerians with the Chernogorovka-Novocherkassk archaeological findings, that were also directly found in this spot, around the Prut River, a few miles South-West of the Dniester. This archaeological horizon is in fact often termed 'Thraco-Cimmerian'.

A second aspect of Herodotus' 'Scythian leadership group of the Cimmerians falling on their swords' story that has the ring of truth to it is how this sudden loss of leadership would have left a

---

[164] Herodotus, p.249-50

somewhat delinquent, battle-happy group of 'commoners', exiled from their lands in the north, as orphan soldiers of fortune in the South. This is exactly the character of the Cimmerians we find in Anatolia, and would also to some extent explain their sudden, inexplicable appearance[165].

This understanding is highly consistent with Assyrian Emperor Assurabi's reaching out to the Scythians, if they were the Cimmerians' erstwhile leadership group, to come and fetch them from Anatolia where they were causing trouble.

Homer's Odyssey, one of the oldest Greek sources, mentions the Cimmerians as well. It relates that they lived at the Ocean river[166], in a land permanently deprived of sunlight at the edge of the world and close to the entrance of Hāidēs[167]. This is a typical Greek description of Scandinavian or Hyperborean cultures, that fits with the Northern derivation of the Cimmerians, and of course would have perfectly described the climate of the area to the north of the Black Sea at this time. He goes on to describe "their realm and city shrouded in mist and cloud". Probably the best guess as to the 'city' of the Cimmerians would be 'Kimmerikon' (today's Psoa) on the South shore of the Kerch peninsula, on the north coast of the Black Sea, in Crimea. Claimed by the Greeks to have been founded by them in the 6th Century BC, it was nevertheless likely a Cimmerian stronghold before this. That means that when the Cimmerians eventually embarked from Anatolia to make their escape across the Black Sea, their arrival in Crimea was not an accident, rather they were going home.

---

[165] It is not beyond the bounds of possibility that the Scythian leadership group of the Cimmerians was somehow connected to Mil and his party, who also left the Sea of Grass roughly around this time, although in fact probably centuries later
[166] The River 'Oceanus' was thought by the Greeks to flow around the outside of the whole world.
[167] Odyssey, p.250, See also Strabo, vol.2, p.221

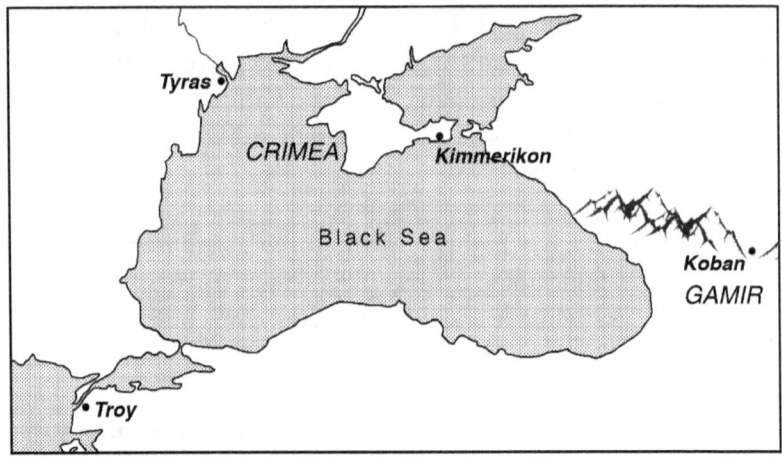

Fig.38: The location of Kimmerikon on the Crimean Peninsula

There seems to be no clear evidence then for the insistence that the Cimmerians *only* came from further East. Rather we can with some confidence theorise that the Cimmerian nation were descended from Tyras/Thor and were Scandinavians, originating from Thrace and Troy in the West and venturing eastward, quite probably as part of a general exodus after their defeat in the Trojan War, and basing themselves at the maritime ports of Crimea, particularly Kimmerikon, whence some of them went on to became a part of the Sea of Grass-based, Magogian (Indo-Iranian)-led larger Scythian hordes, but dwelling to the west of the 'true' Scythians from whom, though they shared similar Gothic leaders to some extent, they were nevertheless distinct. The Scythians were descended from Riphath and spoke Gaelic, whereas the Cimmerians were Thracian/Tirassian and most likely spoke a Scandinavian language.

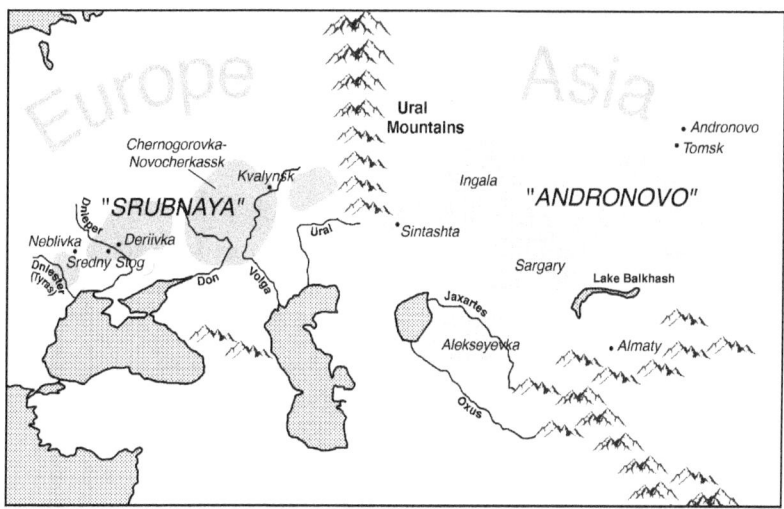

Fig.39: The proposed approximate border between descendants of Tyras (Srubnaya – Thraco-Cimmerian) and descendants of Riphath/Magog (Andronovo - Scythian) prior to the 8th Century BC westward migration of the Scythians. They were apparently divided by the Ural Mountains, much as the Urals traditionally divided Europe and Asia. Significant archeological sites are shown[168].

---

[168] The archaeology of these groups is highly complex and the above illustration is in general terms only. It is likely that the original, Dniester ('Tyras')-based settlements of Thor are known today as the 'Cucuteni-Trypillia' archaeological culture (dated conventionally to 5500-2500 BC). This location would make sense as having been settled by ship across the Black Sea. This was a separate group from the 'Yamnaya' culture, the land-based Indo-Europeans who first migrated northward through the Caucasus (it is suggested here under the leadership of Magog or Gomer). There was interaction between the groups, in particular around 3500 BC (conventional dating) when the Yamnaya apparently invaded and conquered westward, firstly defeating the 'Sredny Stog' culture, the partial eastern offshoot of Cucateni-Trypillia, then later the 'Trypillians' themselves, moving the western side of the above map into the 'Srubnaya' era. Converted into more realistic dates, this invasion could have occurred around 1500 BC and may have been the initial conquest of the Thraco-Cimmerians by Indo-Iranians that led to the 'Scythian' (i.e. Indo-Iranian) leadership group we see attested in Thraco-Cimmeria at the beginning of the 8th Century BC.

Archaeo-genetic studies (though some have questioned the reliability of DNA extracted from deceased persons) have yielded Y-DNA haplogroups for the 'Trypillians' of G and I (Gelabert, Mathieson), suggesting the possibility that one or both of these could be the genetic marker for descendants of Thor. Meanwhile the descendants of 'Yamnayans' are overwhelmingly Y-haplogroup R (Allentoft); potentially Magog, Riphath or Gomer.

This also fits perfectly with the Cimmerian behaviour in Anatolia: the apparent support for native Anatolian and 'Trojan' remnant allies such as the Sherden dynasty of Lydia and the Lycians and Tabalans, against usurpers like Gyges and the Neo-Assyrians[169].

The Cimmerians then, it seems, were elements of a central Scandinavian group that had come east from the Dniester and the Crimea. Suddenly bereft of the moderating influence of Magogian, Scythian leaders, they were now marooned in Caucasia, and with nothing to lose felt liberated to go on a rampage around Anatolia, with unexpectedly successful results.

---

[169] The Cimmerians as successors and descendants of earlier 'Sea Peoples' also makes sense linguistically, as the Anatolian language family is strongly connected with the 'Cernavodă' archaeological culture of the Danube river mouth and associated Black Sea coastal region (Kroonan). Where the Phrygians feature in this is less clear however, as they also supposedly emigrated from Thrace. Gill (Commentary on Genesis 10:2-3, Gill Vol.1) believed the Phrygians were Gomerans/Gauls. This agrees with the conventional view (Josephus) that they were descended from Togarmah, Gomer's son. Gill also believed the Cimmerians themselves to have come from Gomer and that this was the origination of the name 'Cimmerian'. It may well be the origin of the name (that may be an ethnonym applied by others, possibly because of their residence in 'Gamir'). However, as we have seen, the activities of the Cimmerians are strong evidence that they were in fact Thracians, much more aligned politically and culturally with the descendants of Tiras, who in fact warred extensively with both the Gomeran (Togarmanean) Phrygians, whom they destroyed in Asia, and the Gomeran (Riphathian) Scythians.

The Saka

But the story does not end there. Because this whole chain of events was apparently caused by the westward expansion of the 'Massagetae'. Who were they, and why were they moving West?

Well, conventional opinion is that the Massagetae were a separate group again, one who lived further east than the Scythians, and who were at that time pushing westward, in what would be the first of many major westward migrations/invasions across the Sea of Grass, around the area north of the Aral Sea in today's Kazakhstan. The Massagetae are thought to be identical with the 'Saka', the most exotic and eastern of the Indo-European horse nomad cultures, with the two words seen as cognate (i.e. Ma-Saka-Tae). Of course this is primary Scythian territory and many would see 'Saka' as simply the exact Persian cognate of Greek 'Scythian', a generic term for the Indo-Iranian led Scythians. However there is usually some idea of a distinction between the two[170], with Saka as a more eastern group.

In the conventional theory of a westwards expansion at this time across the Steppe (Massagetae/Saka >Scythian > Cimmerian), the Saka would be fully Indo-Iranian, i.e. descended from Magog, not only in their leadership (as we are seeing, horse cultures with Magogian leadership groups controlling large swathes of nations of different ethnicity is a recurring pattern), but in their main population as well. And this would make sense with the name 'Massagetae', i.e. their being 'Getae' AKA Geats or Goths of some kind[171]. These then would be the eastern branch of the Magogians who went east from Caucasia after the flood, settling around Khorosan and perhaps Sogdiana. But this may be an oversimplification.

---

[170] Oswald Szemerényi's exhaustive study of the roots of the term 'Scythian' found that 'Scythian'-type names (including the root of 'Sogdiana', original homeland of the Scythians) all stem from *skeud-, an ancient Indo-European root meaning "propel, shoot" (cf. English 'shoot'). But 'Saka' is not part of this group and has an entirely different derivation: *sak-, to go, flow, wander, roam. (Szemerényi, p.45-47)

[171] Jordanes claims the Massagetae (but also the Scythians) as Goths (p.67-68)

This is because the Saka exist slap bang in the middle of the 'Asian Continuum' of that Eastern wing of 'Asians' that were virtually unknown to European historians until very recently. Looking at the famous 'golden warrior' armour unearthed at Almaty in Kazakhstan, the quintessential image of the Saka, most Western commentators up until recently would have ascribed this to an oriental culture related to the Han Chinese or Mongolians. But as more evidence comes to light, it becomes increasingly clear that the Chinese and Mongolians simply did not dwell in this region to the East, North and South of the Aral Sea at this point in history at all. Instead, the startling picture emerges that this entire area of Asia was during most of the thousand years before Christ and before, inhabited by what we would call Europeans. Could the straight-laced denizens of today's Europe once have been so outlandish as to wear this far-out, exotic gear? It seems increasingly inescapable that this was indeed the case.

Fig.40: the 'golden warrior' 'Saka' armour found in the Issyk Kurgan at Almaty in Kazakhstan[172]

---

[172] Although this is obviously a ceremonial and/or special set of armour, its use of gold is compatible with Herodotus' extraordinary descriptions of the Massagetae's war gear: "Their arms are all either of gold or brass. For their spear-points, and arrow-heads, and for their battle-axes, they make use of brass; for head-gear, belts, and girdles, of gold. So too with the caparison of their horses, they give them breastplates of brass, but employ gold about the reins, the bit, and the cheek-plates. They use neither iron nor silver, having none in their country; but they have brass and gold in abundance." (Herodotus, p.95) Picture from Wikimedia Commons by Derzsi Elekes Andor (desaturated). Used under CC BY SA 3.0 Unported (https://creativecommons.org/licenses/by-sa/3.0/deed.en)

153

One curious factor in studying these eastern Indo-Europeans, is the extraordinary theme when tracing their path that one is always being led further and further North-East in search of their origins. So let's go there.

Altai/ Afanasievo

The very earliest settlements of the eastern Indo-Europeans, in extremely ancient antiquity, were in the area around the Altai Mountains, the crossroads between today's Russia, Mongolia, China and Kazakhstan. It is no coincidence that this area even today is such a significant international border. Because arguably it was a major cradle of all those nations.

This point is the far North-Eastern tip of all Indo-European archaeological remains, an archaeological horizon labelled 'Afanasievo'. And it is arguably the 'ground zero' of all of the Scythian, nomadic, steppe cultures.

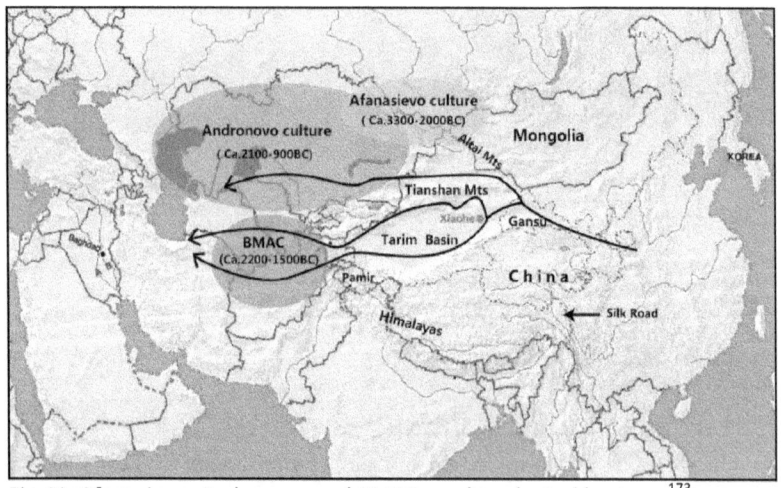

Fig.41: Afanasievo, Andronovo and BMAC arachaeological horizons[173]

---

[173] Image by Chunxiang Li, Chao Ning, Erika Hagelberg, Hongjie Li, Yongbin Zhao, Wenying Li, Idelisi Abuduresule, Hong Zhu and Hui Zhou, from Wikimedia Commons (desaturated). Used under CC BY 4.0 Unported (https://creativecommons.org/licenses/by/4.0/deed.en)

This is not to say that it preceded the 'Yamnaya' horizon made up of descendants of Japheth first exploring North from Caucasia. However, a very early offshoot group from those explorations apparently went very very early, very very far east.

They established a major focal point of Indo-European culture around the Altai Mountains, that was nevertheless continually in communication with the Western roots of these Indo-Europeans in the Magog horse cultures around the Maeotian Lake, and their neighbours the Tirassian ship cultures around the Black Sea. A topographical map of the region might be instructive in understanding how they got there:

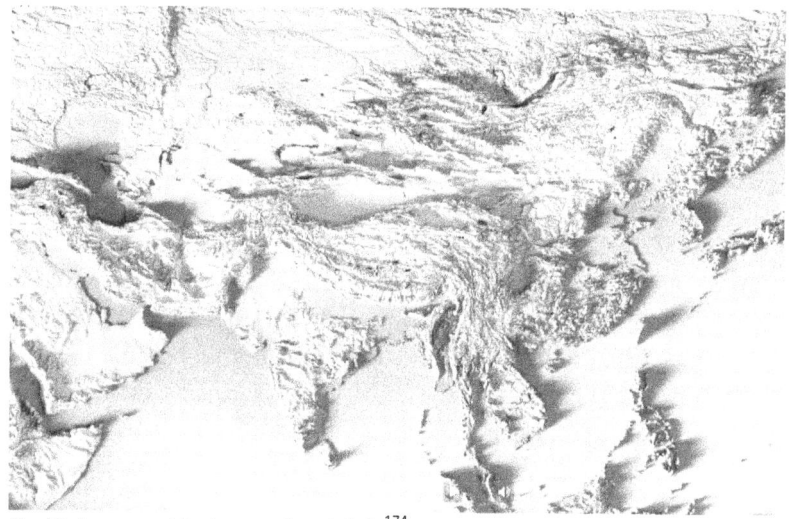

Fig.42: topographical map of east Asia[174].

The above map gives a wonderful view of the 'Sea of Grass' steppelands (top left, that indeed stretched much further west than this, all the way to Europe), where the descendants of Magog and Riphath roamed. One can see how this Sea of Grass region was significantly cut off from Southern, imperial settlements by huge mountain ranges to its South and East. In particular from the Mesopotamian Empires (at the bottom left of the picture) by the

---

[174] © Getty images. Used under license

Iranian Plateau and Zagros Mountains, from the Mediterranean Empires (out of frame left) by the Caucasus Mountains and Black Sea, and from the nascent Chinese Empire, located in the fertile lands at the far right of this picture, by the gigantic Himalayan plateau and the Pamir, Tian Shan and Altai Mountains further north. This explains much of the reason why the cultures dwelling to the north of these natural barriers, that as we now know were 'Europeans' or 'Asians', the ancestors of many of today's Europeans, Scandinavians, Americans and Australasians, remained entirely hidden from the mainstream civilizations of the Mediterranean world that formed the foundations of our modern Western history. Until now.

It is as yet hard to say what nations were the prime movers of the Altai 'Afanasievo' settlements. The exact ethnic make-up of this complex of Japhetic North-East settlements is still lost in the mists of time. Was it the proto-Scythian 'horse' Magogians, who may have domesticated the horse at Deriivka near 'Yamnaya' before riding east south of the Urals; or the proto-Scandinavian 'ship' Tirassians? And there was also in the area the Uralic-speaking 'Finno-Ugrian' descendants of Meshech who pioneered much of Siberia, probably represented by the 'Okunev' archaeological remains[175]. Finally there was another ethnic heritage in the region, a substantial and extensive one: the eastern-venturing descendants of Joktan, the great, great grandson of Shem.

In the Table of Nations, the largest number of sons (and therefore nations) of any one person are the sons of Joktan (13 sons, beating out Sidon with 11). This translates to a huge number of people,

---

[175] The Okunev culture of Southern Siberia has links with other northern Uralic-languages like Finno-Ugric (Peyrot). Some of the Okunevans are thought to have interbred with the Afanasievans to produce the Andronovo (Scythian) culture, while others are believed to have continued on eastward eventually crossing the Bering Strait and colonising America as Paleo-Indians. They are associated archaeo-genetically with Y-haplogroup N that could represent Meshech. Notably, though, Okunevs and other Siberian cultures famously did *not* take the domesticated horse with them to America. Unless their horses did not make it over, this suggests the American Okunevs split with the Afanasievan Okunevs before contact with Steppe horse-nomad (i.e. probably Magog/Riphath) 'proto-Scythian' cultures

assuming each son went on to become a nation in his own right. Josephus states that some or many of these sons - probably in particular 'Ophir'[176] - went east towards India and further, somewhere Josephus calls 'Seria'[177]. How many others went with him? Today's DNA evidence offers some suggestion that indeed Joktanian DNA could have been in the mix as part of the super-ancient 'Afanasievo' culture.

The primary genetic Y-chromosome to have been extracted from human Afanasievo remains is R1A. While expressing disbelief in the reliability of DNA sampling from long deceased persons, geneticist Nathanael Jeanson at the University of Minnesota has identified Y-Haplogroup R as signifying a descent from Joktan. As we have seen though there is also strong circumstantial evidence that 'R' was Magog, as R is overwhelmingly prevalent in the Yamnaya culture as well as its offsoot Andronovo/ Indo-Iranian cultures. However, the R-derived haplogroups (chiefly R1a and R1b) are in fact so vastly ubiquitous – eventually blanketing the entire Eurasian landmass from Spain to China – that it becomes all but impossible from historical sources to speculate accurately what ancient Patriarch was their original source. At the current state of historical evidence, realistically 'R' could be Magog, Joktan, Gomer or even Japheth himself.

It is notable though that the 'oldest' version of 'R' ever extracted from human remains, nicknamed 'Mal'ta Boy' (MA-1), who lived before R even split off into R1 and R2, was found around Lake Balkhai in Siberia[178], even further northeast than the Altai Mountains, suggesting that the 'R' community went all the way out there first, before massively multiplying and sweeping back westward later.

---

[176] Thackeray, the translator of Josephus, basing his comments on the Septuagint and other sources, states that Joktan's son 'Ophir' in particular can be identified as one who went east (Josephus book, vol.4, p.72)
[177] Josephus, vol.4, p.73
[178] Raghavan

Regardless of whether 'R' represents Magog, Joktan, or any other ancient patriarch, it was R's primaeval horse culture that would be taken on by other ethnic groups moving into the region; 'N', 'Q'[179] and elements of the Hamitic Shang'An Chinese settlers to the South-East (possibly Y-haplogroup 'C'), producing the famous 'horse Asian' steppe nation confederacies that would in the future emerge from the area: the 'Xiong Nu', known to history as the *Huns*, the Turks and the Mongols. These groups would have a vast impact on the history of Asia, as we shall see. The picture however remains complex of exactly who were the original, post-diluvian settlers of Altai/Afanasievo, the primary eastern terminus of the horse cultures, whence eons of vast waves of invasion would eventually pour westward over the millennia, inexorably pushing all other Steppe nations before them. It is probable that Magogians, Joktanians, Tirassians and Meshechians were all involved one way or another in this amazing nexus point of super-ancient history.

Afanasievo would be displaced by a second wave of immigration from the South-West, the main line Indo-Iranian-led Scythian i.e. 'Andronovo' culture[180], who may have had more of a Riphathian element than the original explorers. Tirassians also made the trip to the area at some point, but by a different route. From their settlements around the Crimea and Black Sea, they could explore into both inland Russia and the Caspian Sea via The Don and Volga rivers, that intersect at today's Volgograd[181] and constituted the main transit 'superhighway' east for the ancient Scandinavians. From there the vast rivers of Russia – significantly more numerous and connected in ancient antiquity as the Ice Age receded – would have allowed for perfect transport to and from the Altai region, as previously discussed.

---

[179] If R is not Joktan, 'Q' may be (see for example Jeanson, plates 80 and 187)
[180] Allentoft
[181] The river connection between Black and Caspian Seas in super-ancient times is known as the 'Manych Pass'

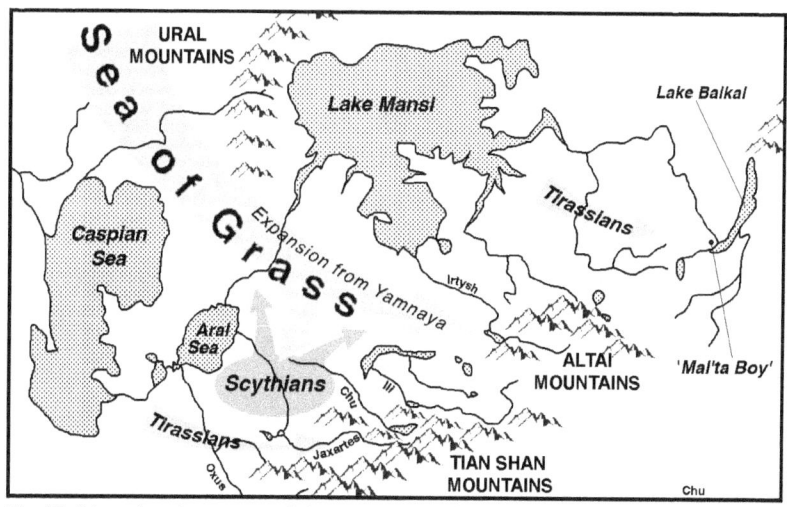

Fig.43: Map showing some of the waterways the Tirassians would have utilised on their journey east[182]

The Magogian proto-Scythians having theoretically displaced the more primaeval Afanasievo 'exploration' culture, that included some Tirassians and/or Joktanians, the Tirassians must have moved somewhere else to avoid the Scythian hegemony in the Sea of Grass. Unlike the Magogians, the Tirassian MO was not really nomadic. Rather they favoured established settlements, 'homelands', usually tucked somewhere out of the way, from where they could venture out far and wide by boat, trading and exploring, to then periodically return with their profits.

If one looks again at the topographical map above (Fig.42), one glaring geographical feature presents itself, that is yet to be explained. Something that we can see, but the 'civilized' world of the day could not. A giant eye-shaped hole right in the middle of the monolithic Himalayan mountain wall, a hiding place simultaneously shielded from and invisible to both East and West; both the Steppe and the Southern Empires, but highly accessible to both equally. This is the *Tarim Basin*, today's Taklamakan Desert, and that was where the Tocharians lived.

---

[182] Map uses material from the map by Hellerick (see p.55), used and published under CC BY SA 3.0 (https://creativecommons.org/licenses/by-sa/3.0/deed.en)

The Tarim Mummies

The findings of the earliest 'Afanasievo' archaeological horizon are directly North of the Tarim Basin. It is proposed here that the primaeval Afanasievo culture interacted significantly with the maritime descendants of Tyras/Thor, and that from Lake Balkhash those descendants and possibly some Afanasievans subsequently sailed South via the Ili River system to settle the Tarim Basin, making it and the region around it their base of operations for the foreseeable future.

That the Tarim basin could have been the location of a secret but extensive Indo-European settlement that had dealings with the eastern terminus of the Steppe-nation continuum from far ancient antiquity but was virtually unknown to the major civilizations of the day, would have been laughed off as preposterous until as recently as 1900. While Western historians knew something about the Trojan War and the Cimmerians and the Goths in the West, the entire eastern wing of 'barbarians', as they would have called them, that now appears to have been quite possibly the *larger* of the two, remained all but invisible to them. That is until the discovery of the Tarim mummies.

From around 1900, explorers in Asia such as Sven Hedin and Aurel Stein described discovering desiccated bodies in the Tarim basin region. Because of the particular environmental conditions of the basin, it is one of the very driest places on earth. That means that organic remains, deprived of moisture, are preserved to an incredible age without decomposing. This phenomenon has left one of the most astonishing records of history to us, one that spectacularly belies the obfuscations and erroneous assumptions of conventional Greco-Roman history: the Tarim Mummies.

Very basically, a large number of extraordinarily well-preserved human remains, that can only represent a sizeable and long-lasting human settlement, have been discovered around the eastern end of the Tarim Basin[183]. They have been dated to between 2100 BC and 1500 BC, and, crucially, they are unmistakeably *European*.

That is, they are not of the ethnicity of today's Chinese (that at this time were mainly descended from Ham) but rather they are tall, with generally red, blonde or brown hair and high cheekbones, and clothed with European-style textiles such as woven, patterned twill, otherwise known only from European archaeology.

Since their discovery, much of conventional historiography has fallen over itself in an attempt somehow to undiscover this evidence and to show that they can't possibly have been Europeans (because they are too far east and were all but unknown to the Greeks). But the attempt is futile: they clearly were. As Mair has said:

"The new finds are also forcing a reexamination of old Chinese books that describe historical or legendary figures of great height, with deep-set blue or green eyes, long noses, full beards, and red or blond hair. Scholars have traditionally scoffed at these accounts, but it now seems that they may be accurate."[184]

Not only, then, is it shown that Europeans once lived extensively in this region of China; but, staggeringly, it is shown that they lived there *first*. That is, a) this area of Afanasievo/Tarim can only have been settled very soon indeed after the dispersion from Babel C.2100 BC by certain descendants of Japtheth, and b) that it was settled by them *before* anyone else settled there – they were the first settlers of the Tarim Basin[185]. Therefore, it can genuinely claim to have been an original homeland for these people. What happened to them? We will soon find out.

---

[183] Mair. They are centered around Xiaohe, near the ancient cities of Loulan and Karashar, and the impressive fortress city of Jiaohe. At this time, C.2000 BC, this area was not desert, but rather a verdant freshwater environment, fed by the abundant nearby post-glacial lakes of the melting 'Ice Age'.
[184] Mair, p.30
[185] Mallory & Mair, p.281

Tocharia

The discovery of the Tarim Mummies unmistakably unearthed the existence of a concentration of colonies, indeed entire cities and a civilization, of 'Westerners' living way over in the Tarim Basin of what is now China as early as 2000 BC. They were far, far out of the bounds of traditional history. What were they doing there?

Well, in a word, trading. Jade mined in and near the Tarim Basin was exported to the slowly growing faraway Chinese civilization centre at Shang'An[186]. In China, Jade had a status similar to gold in the West: it was the basic means of monetary exchange - the basic money. In exchange the Chinese traded back a unique textile secretly made from the larvae of worms - 'silk'. The trade secret of silk's method of manufacture was guarded assiduously by the Chinese, and silk trading would slowly become the basis of their entire contact with the outside world, a trade that was carried out exclusively with the Japhetic/Joktanite inhabitants of the Tarim Basin. Thus this many millennia-long trade relationship was crucial to the development and prosperity of the two civilizations and slowly became the basis of vast wealth for both parties.

This trade, along the Xiang-Chu corridor that crossed the arid desert between Shang'An and the eastern end of the Tarim Basin became the first leg in a pan-Asian transport route that would later become known as the 'Silk Road'[187]. As time went on this trade only expanded more and more.

Jumping forward in time a millennia or so, Chinese history was of course well aware of the extensive civilization of the Tarim, but it was as yet virtually unknown to Westerners. When a people from

---

[186] The original settlement of the Chinese civilization, AKA 'Chang'An' or 'Xi'an', meaning 'Perpetual Peace'.
[187] In fact there were two or three Silk roads, some going to the north and some taking a more southerly route, but the one section for which there was no alternative route, in other words that was an absolute monopoly, was the section from Shang'An (China) to the Tarim Basin, i.e. the one controlled by the 'Tocharians'.

the Tarim Basin conquered Bactria in the 2nd Century BC, a region known to the Greeks, they were called *Tókharoi*, an ethnonym indistinguishable from the origins of 'Turk' that will be discussed later. Documents subsequently found in the Tarim Basin from the 1st Millennia AD showed that these people spoke an Indo-European (Japhetic) language, that was consequently labeled 'Tocharian'[188]. Internal evidence from the documents also confirms that this term was known in antiquity, with references to the Tarim Basin civilization as "the land of the Four Toghar"[189]. We will therefore refer to it as 'Tocharia' and to its people as 'Tocharians'.

Fig.44: the famous picture of the Tocharians who lived in the Tarim Basin. From a 5th Century AD tapestry[190]

---

[188] First by linguist Friedrich W. K. Müller. The actual term found by Müller in an Uyghur (Turkic) note about the language a Buddhist text was in, before it was translated into Turkic C.800 AD, was "toxrï" (Mallory & Mair, p.281). This is by far the furthest eastern culture yet discovered that spoke an Indo-European language.
[189] Beckwith (2009), p.380-381
[190] This is a public domain image from Wikimedia Commons (https://en.wikipedia.org/wiki/File:QizilDonors.jpg)

The Tocharian civilization was known to the Mediterranean world only peripherally, as 'Serica' – this was the mysterious "Seria" spoken of by Josephus - and its people as 'Seres', and was only indistinctly understood by them to be separate from the Chinese 'Sinae'. The Mediterranean world's conflation of the two demonstrates how completely the Tocharians controlled all silk trade to the West (the 'Seria' name is derived from the word for 'silk'), and so all communication between east and west and therefore knowledge by one of the other, for at least a thousand years. By the time of Ptolemy's 'Geography' around 100 AD, he is able to write more extensively about 'Serica', listing fifteen 'important towns' of the area and its surrounding or associated nations, notably the 'great race' of the 'Issedones', who according to Ptolemy had one of the towns of 'Serica' named after them, "Issedon Serica"[191]. However 'Serica' was still clearly at that time the furthest extent of Ptolemy's geographical knowledge; he is not able to describe anything beyond it, adding only that it was bordered at its north by 'unknown lands', before turning his attention back towads more Southern regions.

The civilization of 'Tocharia' then, known to the Greeks as 'Serica' and to the Chinese when they arrived there to annex the region from 100 BC onwards as the 'Kingdom of Shule', was in fact a massive trading nexus, the main bottleneck of the Silk Road's passage West, that brought together all the major Indo-European nations of the area into a greater Tarim Basin conurbation that constituted a giant Eastern hub of 'Asian' settlement for the entire first half of post-diluvian human history, but hitherto virtually unknown. Including to most of the descendants of the inhabitants of that civilization. And if you're reading this, that probably includes you.

---

[191] Ptolemy, p.145-146

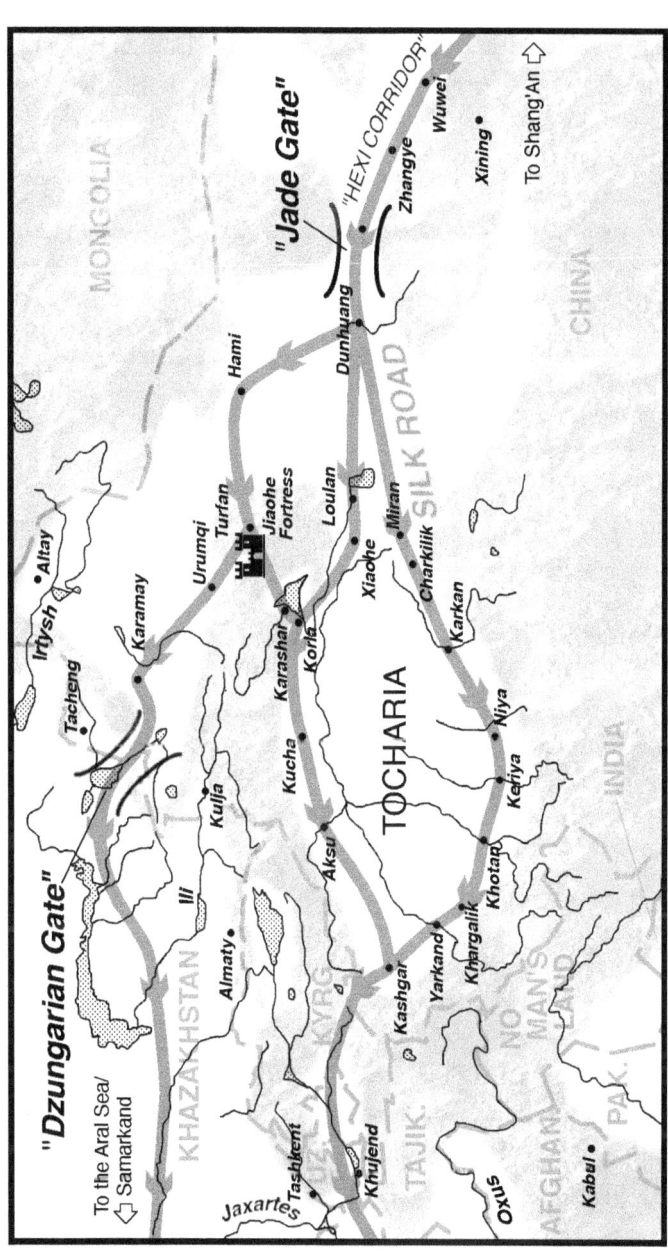

Fig.45: The major cities of 'Tocharia', the civilization of the Tarim Basin; eastern economic hub of the Indo-Europeans in ancient antiquity. No fewer than 10 modern day countries are featured on this map. The major 'Tarim Mummies' discoveries were unearthed in the cemetary of Xiaohe (centre right), while the richest images of 'Tocharians' (though from millennia later) including the one above were found at 'Kizil' near ancient Kucha (centre top). (For Copyright info see footnote on page 167)

Yuezhi and Issedones

While the westernmost cities of 'Tocharia', such as Kashgar, were undoubtedly significantly influenced by the Indo-Iranian (Magog) horse cultures to their West, the Zoroastrian Bactrians, the Vedic Aryans of Tajikistan and Northern India and the hordes of Scottish Scythians on the Steppe and around Sogdiana, it is probable that Indo-Iranian Magogites were not the group that dominated the trading centre of Tocharia. One can understand this by observing that culturally the Magogites were horse warriors, not specialists in trading and logistics.

One group that did specialise in this very thing, were the ship-based Tirassians, descendants of Tyras/Thor. As we saw earlier, their initial expansion northward from Ararat was by boat, using the superhighways of the day: rivers. In particular they went north-east up the Don River at the top right-hand corner of the Black Sea. The post-glacial rivers and lakes allowed the descendants of Thor to navigate far and wide virtually anywhere on the Eurasian continent. And this they did, charting courses far to the North and East of the understanding of the more settled Southern trading routes that were bound by roads and mountains. They made their way to Lake Balkhash and possibly even Lake Baikal, the largest lake in the world (although of course the maritime map of the region has been hugely transformed since that time- there was a lot more water back then!) By this method the Tirassians made contact with the Shang'An Chinese, then entirely unknown to the Western Civilizations of the Mediterranean, and were consequently able to become the primary trading middle-men between East and West.

The later Tarim Basin Silk Road civilization we are calling 'Tocharia' that arguably developed from Afanasievo, shows identification with proto-Scandinavian cultures in the West. The Tarim mummies have been found paternally to be 92% Y-DNA haplogroup R1a1-M17[192]. While this indicates a descent from Joktan or Magog, it is the Y haplogroup that also characterises the Don-Volga region, home of the Thraco-Cimmerians. The mummies are dated provisionally to 1800 BC[193], and 'Tocharia' was inhabited continually from 2000 to 150 BC[194], a timeline that fits exactly with the history of a group that the Chinese called the *Yuezhi*. The Tocharians spoke or developed into speaking (in this isolated civilization somewhat separated from other Indo-Europeans) the famous 'Tocharian' languages. These were Tocharian A (AKA *Ārśi-kāntwa*; "tongue of Ārśi"), Tocharian B (AKA *Kuśiññe*; "of Kucha, Kuchean/Kushan"), and Tocharian C (which is associated with the city-state of Krorän, also known as Loulan)[195]. The 'Arsi' is almost certainly one and the same with the Chinese 'Yuezhi', and it is proposed here also the same as the 'Asia' or 'Asians' known from earlier Anatolian history.

Here for example is a description of the 'Seres' from a Sri Lankan (Tabropane) embassy to the Emperor Claudius around the time of Christ, as reported by Pliny:

"beyond the Emodian Mountains [Himalayas] they look towards the Serae, whose acquaintance they had also made in the pursuits of commerce; that the father of Rachias [the ambassador – Ed.] had frequently visited their country, and that the Serae always came to meet them on their arrival. These people, they said, exceeded the ordinary human height, had flaxen hair, and blue eyes, and made an uncouth sort of noise by way of talking"[196]

'Mountain Stone Rock' by the3rdSequence (https://www.the3rdsequence.com/texturedb/) is licenced under CC BY 4.0 (http://creativecommons.org/licenses/by/4.0)
[192] Li, et al., 2015
[193] Mair, p.31
[194] Li, et al., 2010
[195] The three languages are evidenced mainly in the cities of Karashar/Turfan, Kucha and Loulan respectively (see above map) (Mallory and Mair, p.121-3, 274, 277-279)
[196] Pliny, vol.2, p.54-55

Such testimonies contradict the absurdity that Alexander the Great was the first 'Westerner' to make contact with the Far East. The Greco-Romans were simply ignorant of the primaevally established trade and cultural connections along the Silk Road, including the major 'Asian' civilisation of the Seres/Tocharians of the Tarim Basin, masters of the ancient Silk Road trade, that neither Alexander's nor later Greco-Roman expansions ever reached nor learnt about during their ascendancy.

Whether the 'Tocharians' are exactly to be identified with the Seres is an interesting question. 'Tocharia', the Tarim Basin civilization, in fact included a variety of different but probably related nations, dwelling nearby one another in a close-knit trading confederacy. The largest and most powerful of these was reported by the Chinese as dwelling initially in Dunhuang around the 'Jade Gate' at the east of the basin (controlling trade with the Chinese)[197], then later or at the same time at the Ili and Chiu rivers around the 'Dzungarian Gate' near the Tian Shan mountain range of today's Kyrgestan, north of the basin (controlling the trade with the Scythians). They are therefore likely connected to the extensive archaeological remains known to be as yet submerged under the Issyk Kul Lake, right next to Almaty, where the 'golden warrior' 'Saka' armour was found. Located at these strategically critical points of access into and out of the Tarim basin, this nation likely provided 'security' for the haven, allowing its trading cities to go about their business unmolested. It is proposed here that this powerful and extensive nation, that would later become known to the Chinese as the 'Great Yuezhi' is most associated with the proto-Scandinavian settlements of the region, and was the leading military state of Tocharia, under whose protection the other states existed.

In other words the vast Scythian hordes of the Steppe had Scandinavian centres of maritime culture to both their West and East, one around the Black Sea and Don River and one, hidden

---

[197] For this purpose it is possible that they built the Jiaohe fortress in Turfan (see for example Book of Han (C.100 AD), Vol.10, p.21)

by the Tian Shan and Pamir Mountains, around the Tarim Basin. As we shall see these Western and Eastern wings of Tirassians were in communication with each other by the waterways of the South through the Aral Sea, and possibly also by the waterways of the North through passes in the Ural Mountains. The Scythians then were in some ways the meat in a Tirassian sandwich.

So what does this have to do with the Saka? Well the Saka were stereotypical of exactly the equestrian steppe culture of Magog, but there were a couple of differences. As we have seen they were distinguished from the 'Scythians proper' that were to their West, whom they pushed westward across the Araxes/Volga River C.750 BC. They could have been an entire nation of Goths/Magogites, but this is not particularly in keeping with the Indo-Iranians' MO that we have seen so far: the Magogite Indo-Iranians specialized in forming horse-aristocracies that controlled other nations and populations. This happened in India (where they became the rulers of the Harappans), in Scythia (where they became the rulers of the Scots) and in 'Cimmeria', where they had previously been the rulers of the Cimmerians. It would also be odd for an 'eastern Magogian influx' to attack Scythia (their own people) from the North-East when the Indo-Iranian centres were to the South (in Sogdiana). What was to the North-East of Scythia and the Volga region? Well, precisely this Scandinavian/Joktanite complex of Tocharia and its surrounding, dependent nations.

Nagging issues with a purely Indo-Iranian identification for the Saka persist. In particular the Behistun Inscription of Persian Emperor Darius the Great (C.520 BC) lists 'Saka' and 'Gamira' (i.e. Cimmerians) as two different terms for the same people, with 'Gamira' being the Assyrian name and 'Saka' being the Persian name[198]. There's also a similar appearance. Here is the Behistun Inscription's image of captured Saka King 'Skunka':

---

[198] Behistun Inscription, p.4 (lines 16-17) and p.161-2 (line 6)

Fig.46: King 'Skunka' from the Behistun Inscription[199]

Look familiar? In other words, when it comes to the identification of the Cimmerians, there is significant evidence that they *were* the Saka. Or at least some element of the Saka were known as the Cimmerians. This might explain the strong alliance between the Cimmerians and the Medes when the Cimmerians came in from the West, i.e. they already knew the Medes from their dwelling in the East. What divided these two areas after all, the area of the Cimmerians and the area of the Saka, was nothing but the Caspian Sea, easily navigable by the ships of the Tirassians.

---

[199] Image from Wikimedia Commons courtesy of Livius.org (https://en.wikipedia.org/wiki/File:Behistun.Inscript.Skunkha.jpg)

This would also explain some of the Saka's 'far-eastern' distinctives, with their close association with Kashgar and the Western cities of Tocharia (Almaty where the 'golden warrior' was found is right next to the Issyk Kul lake of the Yuezhi[200]). Namely if there was a Scandinavian element to the Saka as there was with the Cimmerians, they would have had a closer relationship with the Scandinavian Yuezhi[201]. We previously learned from Ptolemy about the 'Issedones', one of the nations that lived under the protection of the Tocharia-ruling Yuezhi, but also roamed westward from Tocharia.

We also discussed Herodotus' famous description of the knock-on effect of the invasion from the North-East by the mysterious Massagetae, who pushed the Scythians westward across the Volga who in turn pushed the Cimmerians out of their ancestral lands north of the Black Sea. A couple of pages later however Herodotus relates an alternate version of the story deriving from Greek explorer Aristeas[202] who 'went as far as the Issedones'. Aristeas states that 'above' the Issedones dwelt the 'Arimaspi' (of whom more later), and continues:

"Hence it came to pass that the Arimaspi drove the Issedonians from their country, while the Issedonians dispossessed the Scyths; and the Scyths, pressing upon the Cimmerians, who dwelt on the shores of the Southern Sea, forced them to leave their land."[203]

In this version, it is clear that Aristeas is simply replacing the term 'Massagetae' with 'Issedones'. Thus Herodotus' text is evidence that the Massagetae, and therefore the Saka, were one and the

---

[200] Issyk Kul may only have been a temporary home of the Yuezhi, it is usually more associated with the 'Wusun' (Book of Later Han (C.440 AD), Section 1), another name for the Saka (Book of Han, Vol.11, p.83-84).
[201] Although as we shall see the later migration of the Yuezhi would push the Saka before it. Ptolemy in his 'Geographia' (p.144) also mentions a tribe called the 'Sasones' in the east Asian Saka lands, that is almost certainly the Saka, near other tribes like the 'Aorsi' (Yuezhi) and 'Machetegi' (Massagetae).
[202] Aristeas of Prokonnēsos (6th C BC)
[203] Herodotus, p.250

same with the Issedones. Meanwhile as we have seen the Behistun inscription and other evidence strongly links the Saka with the Cimmerians. It therefore seems likely that Cimmerians, Saka, Massagetae and Issedones were different names for the same group or nation, or at least very closely connected groups. The Saka and Cimmerians therefore appear to have been eastern and western branches of essentially the same widespread but water-connected polity, one strongly associated with and perhaps derived from, and perhaps also the *communication link between* both the Scandinavian Treres/Thracians in the west and the Scandinavian Yuezhi in the east.

Then there's this from Roman historian Strabo in the 2nd Century BC:

"The Saki raided like the Cimmerians and Trers; some raids were long-distance, others - at close range. So they captured Bactriana and took possession of the best land in Armenia, to which they left the name in their own name - Sakasena."[204]

This is another strong connection between these named groups (Cimmerians, Treres and Saka) indicating some kind of common identification. It is also further evidence for a Scandinavian connection to the Saka, as this witness identifies the 'Saki' with those who 'captured Bactriana', and as we have seen the origins of the term 'Tocharian' was as a label for precisely this nation: the one that subsequently captured Bactria from Tocharia, the area controlled by the Scandinavian Yuezhi. With the Saka also now identified as Issedones and therefore at least semi-Scandinavian, this fits perfectly with Ptolemy's description of the Issedones having a city named after them in Tocharia, a civilization dominated by the Scandinavian Yuezhi.

In addition, the Strabo text identifies a region on the Kura River in modern-day Azerbaijan as 'Sakasena', a place so associated with the Saka that it is named after them, and whose inhabitants Pliny

---

[204] Strabo, vol.2, p.246

called 'Sacassani'[205]. Remarkably, this is virtually the exact same location, between the Kura and Araks rivers near Lake Sevan, that was the early base of operations of the Cimmerians, an area called in other sources 'Gamir'[206]. This is strong evidence that for Strabo at least the Saka and Cimmerians were one and the same group.

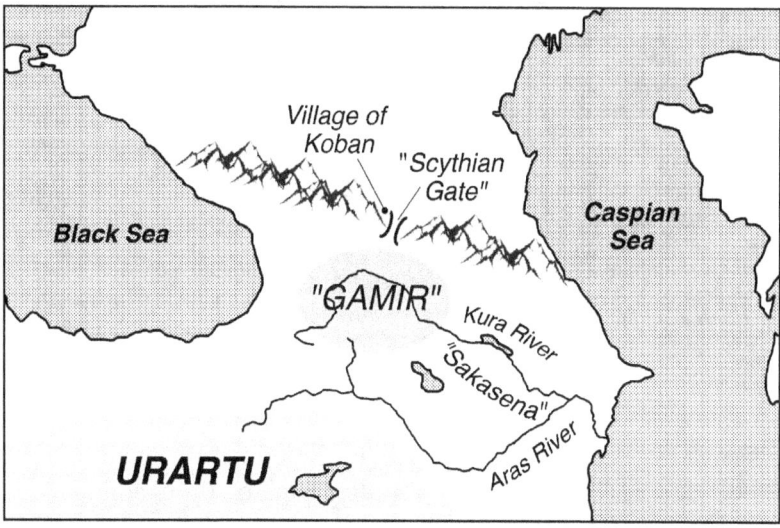

Fig.47: Location of 'Sakasena' between 'Gamir' and Mannaea

The usual understanding is that the Cimmerians came through the Scythian Gate southward through the Caucasus, settling in 'Gamir'. Interestingly, this area of today's Georgia is close to the village of Koban in North Ossetia (near today's city of Vladikavkaz) where the 'Koban' archaeological finds were discovered. These axe-heads and other artifacts are part of the Srubnaya, Chernogorovka and Novocherkassk archaeological horizons, that are generally associated with the Thraco-Cimmerians[207].

---

[205] Pliny, vol.2, p.21. Note the similarity with Ptolemy's 'Sasones'
[206] While many have seen a 'Gomeran' origin for the Cimmerians based on 'Gamir', on closer inspection most 'Gomerans' had emigrated north by this time with the 'Yamnaya' horizon. The Cimmerians, by contrast, were new arrivals there.
[207] Olbrycht, p.102

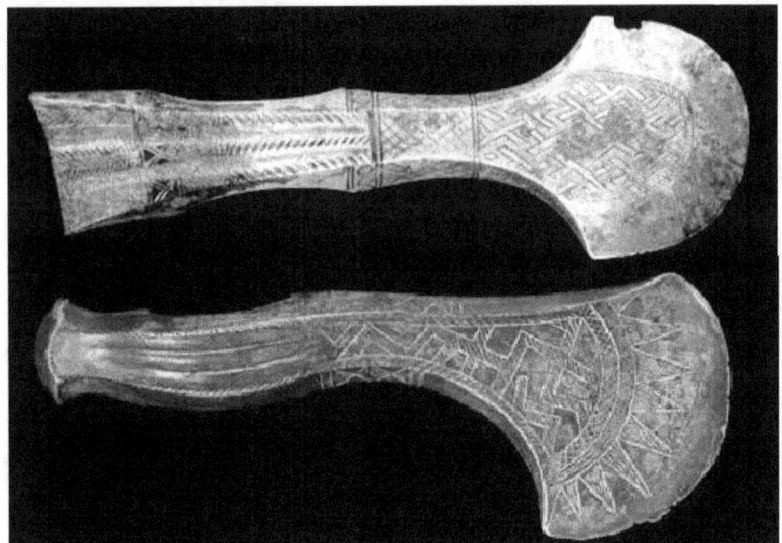

Fig.48: Axe-head finds from Koban bearing what are believed to be 'proto-Scandinavian' patterning.[208]

They were believed by Norwegian experimental archaeologist Thor Heyerdahl to be 'proto-Scandinavian' in origin, and the area was a focus of his book 'The Hunt for Odin' ('Jakten På Odin'). As we shall see, Heyerdahl was looking in the wrong place. Nevertheless, this is more evidence that the Cimmerians, and therefore the Saka, Massagetae and Issedones, had Scandinavian roots.

Why is the identification of the Cimmerians so important? Well, one reason is that the term 'Sacassani' would eventually become 'Saxon', the term for the southern English, of whom, as we shall see, the Cimmerians/Saka were the direct ancestors and forbears.

The origins of the Cimmerians are debated even more hotly because of a highly controversial theory put forward by some commentators.

---

[208] Images © Finch and Co London. Herodotus confirms that the Massagetae "use bows and lances, but their favourite weapon is the battle-axe" (Herodotus, p.95). The axe being a Scandinavian distinctive, this is another piece of evidence that the Massagetae were Scandinavians.

Analysis of the Claims of 'British Israelism'

This quasi-religious theory proposes that all the Scythians, but particularly the Cimmerians and/AKA the Saka, 'are' England, America and possibly Scandinavia ('Nordic Israelism'). But most importantly, that these nations are the direct descendants of the Biblical 10 'Lost Tribes of Israel'[209]. It is proposed here that these claims are not particularly persuasive.

However, there is a lot to the argument, and some of the evidence for it is startling, requiring perhaps the acceptance that rationally, there was very likely some cross-pollination and an exchange of ideas and perhaps leadership groups between these two peoples. Therefore it is worth unpacking.

The Bible records how as a consequence of Israel's idolatry, the Kingdom of Israel was split into two Kingdoms, a Northern Kingdom, 'Israel' (later known as Samaria) consisting of ten of the twelve Israelite tribes, and a Southern Kingdom, 'Judah' (whose inhabitants would become known as 'Jews') consisting of the tribes of Judah, Benjamin and part of Levi. This occurred in roughly 930 BC when the usurper Jeroboam established a separate Northern Kingdom from that of David's son Solomon's son Rehoboam[210].

Both Kingdoms went downhill morally and consequently in fortune, with Israel's slide into idolatry faster than Judah's. In 721 BC, the Assyrian Empire ultimately conquered Israel, taking its people off into captivity in the Northern part of its Empire, near

---

[209] This is purported by proponents of British Israelism to be the explanation for the Coat of Arms of England, the Lion of Judah and the Unicorn of Ephraim. Ephraim is claimed to be today's England, whilst Manasseh is more dubiously promoted as representing the United States. One problem with this is that Judah was not one of the Ten Lost Tribes.
[210] Tanakh, p.237-238

Urartu, as a bulwark against Northern invasion, never to be seen again. The theory is that these Northern tribes 'were' the Cimmerians, who, it has to be admitted, do appear in Assyrian records at precisely this point in history.[211]

The fulcrum of the argument is the name 'Cimmerian' and its derivation. This rests essentially on one ancient source: the Black Obelisk of Assyrian Emperor Shalmaneser (C.825 BC). This text calls the Israelites of the Northern State 'Beth-Omri'[212] (or, it is claimed, 'Khumri' or at least 'Humri', is the correct pronounciation), i.e. 'the people of Homri'. This then is held to be the origin of the ethnonyms 'Cimmerian' and 'Cimbri' (whom we shall encounter later), and cognate with the 'Gimiri' of the Behistun Inscription two centuries later, that makes 'Gimiri' equivalent to 'Saka'. There are multiple other claimed evidences of 'British Israelism', for example that the terms 'Saka' and 'Saxon' (and sometimes also 'Scythian') originally come from 'Isaac's son' or 'Isaachar's son'[213]. But the evidence from Shalmaneser's Obelisk is really the key issue.

---

[211] And the Bible specifically mentions the Northern ten tribes being moved to the 'cities of the Medes': right on time to catalyse the Medes' subsequent rebellion/attack on the Assyrian Empire (Tanakh, p.261)

[212] Black Obelisk of Shalmaneser, p.211

[213] The argument that 'Saxon' comes from 'Issachar's sons' or 'Isaac's sons' is in fact one of the strongest arguments in favour of the BI theory. At least in combination with the geotemporal proximity of the Cimmerians (aka 'Sacassani') with the 10 Lost Tribes of Israel around 721 BC. 'Isaachar's Sons' is eminently plausible as an origin of 'Saxon' and 'Saka'. The strength of this argument is that there remains no particularly convincing alternative explanation for the extremely strong demonym 'Saxon', that has lasted multiple migrations since we first hear of its usage in Caucasia in the early centuries BC. As has been clearly demonstrated, 'Saxons' connotes the fundamental meaning that these were 'Sons of the Saka'. But precisely where does 'Saka' come from? The explanation put forward conventionally is that it derives from the 'Seax' (pronounced 'Sax'), a short sword used by the Saxons, but this is rather unsatisfactory in that the suffix 'sson' is well known to mean 'son of' in Scandinavian culture, where also the vast majority of national names come from the names of Patriarchs. Therefore it is unlikely to have come from an everyday item. As previously discussed, we also have the argument that 'Saka' was merely a shortened form of 'Ma-Saka-tae', but then we are presented with the same question as to the origination of the term 'Massagetae'. Arguably until we find a fully sufficient source meaning for 'Saka' and/or 'Massagetae', BI theories will persist.

There are many arguments against the British Israel theory and the discussion is too extensive to be entered into in depth here. But the main ones can be summarised as follows:

i) The etymological connection is too tenuous. Even if 'Omri' is to be read 'Khumri' this is still only one witness to the idea that the Northern Israelites were known to the Assyrians as 'Khumri', and that by this they meant the same group that the Persians later referred to as 'Gimera'.

ii) King Omri (reigning over Israel 884-873 BC), a successful military campaigner, was quite possibly not an Israelite himself but a usurper, being listed in the Bible unusually without a tribal designation. He was 'commander of half the King's chariots' when the rightful King Elah (descended from King David) was deposed and murdered by one Zimri, the soldiers electing Omri instead, who still had to fight for another four years before his Kingship of Israel was established[214]. All the evidence does suggest, however, that if he was an Israelite he was probably of the tribe of Issachar.

iii) the identification of the Cimmerians as Scandinavians ('Tirassians') is fairly strong, in particular their close alliance with the Treres of Thrace, the Scandinavian Koban artifacts found in Azerbaijan and their emigration to the Crimea. Even more so the highly Scandinavian nature of later Danish and English language and culture.

iv) the identification of the Lost Tribes with all Scythians is arguably not compatible with history, in that the existence of the Scythians preceded the 721 BC exile of the Ten Tribes to the North of Assyria. Lebor Gabála Érenn, for example, gives a detailed history of a Scythian leadership group going back to the time of the Tower of Babel and descending from Riphath and Magog.

v) One version of the BI theory ('Nordic Israelism') attempts to argue that Scandinavians in general are descended from the ten lost tribes. This is even less likely (than just the Cimmerians) in that as has been covered in this book, there is extensive evidence of Scandinavian culture preceding by thousands of years the exile

---

[214] Tanakh, p.241

of the ten tribes to the northern Mesopotamian region.

vi) another problematic piece of evidence for the British Israelite theory is the mention of the Cimmerians in Homer's 'Odyssey'[215]. While dating authorship in such ancient times is far from an exact science, it does appear that the Odyssey was written around the same time if not before the Assyrian conquest of Israel. (The Odyssey is usually dated to around 725 BC). This suggests that the Cimmerians were in residence in Crimea/Asov from very ancient times, *before* being displaced by the Scythians and entering Anatolia, and that therefore their subsequent evacuation there after being kicked out of Anatolia was a return *back* to their homeland.

vii) in terms of tracing the main populations of the Ten Lost Tribes of Israel, Simcha Jacobovici in his documentary 'Quest for the Lost Tribes'[216] presents highly persuasive evidence for the current geographical locations of sizeable remnants of the descendants of the peoples that made up the Ten Lost Tribes, as follows:

Dan = Falachas of Ethiopia
Mannaseh = Manmasseh people of the India-Burma border region of Manipour
Issachar = Bukhara, Uzbekistan
Naphtali = Hephthalite Kingdom of Bukhara (Shubinski)
Zebulon = Zavula of India/Pakistan, Ben Israel of today's Bombay
Reuben, Levi, Shimon, Gad, Ephraim = Pathan/Pashtun people of the Khyber pass region of Afghanistan/ Pakistan[217].

---

[215] Odyssey, p.250
[216] Jacobovici
[217] A note about 'Arzareth', the traditional name for the region where the Ten Tribes were sent by the Assyrians, mentioned most prominently in the Apocrypha (p.65) and thought to correspond also to the Tanakh, p.141. Clearly this relates in some way to 'Asia' or 'Asians'. With 'erets' meaning 'land' in Hebrew, it really translates as 'Az' or 'Arz'- land. This could refer to the lands of the 'Az' people AKA the Scandinavians, but could also refer to Assyria. It has also been interpreted as simply 'another land'. Columbus famously though unaccountably (aside from his Templar beliefs) identified it with America. Generally it is seen as a term for the mythical place where the Ten Tribes went, its only real contribution aside from the name being the description of it as being 'beyond the Euphrates', in the Apocrypha (p.65), so much as a year and a half's journey beyond it. Josephus states the Ten

Of course these identifications do not preclude the possibility of other branches of these tribes having broken off with the Cimmerians or other groups over the millennia, but it is extremely noticeable how much closer are the ethno-cultural similarities between for example the Pathan/Pashtun people of the Khyber Pass region and ancient Israelites, than any proposed connections between Anglo-Americans and ancient Israelites.

However, it is certainly interesting that these two groups of migrants dwelt in the same locations at the same time. And from this it is plausible that there was at least some memetic if not genetic cross-pollination between them. The 'leaderless' Cimmerians may indeed have taken upon themselves ideas and even leaders from among the exiled Israelites.

As time went on and the Israelites went east (though many of them also stayed within the bounds of Mesopotamia, with some being reunited with their Jewish neighbours when the latter were exiled to Babylon in 589 BC), there is every reason to believe that these Semites crossed paths with many Scandinavians and Scythians over the centuries in key Asian Silk road trading cities[218] such as Samarkand, Tashkent, Ferghana and later Afrasiah.[219]

Tribes were still living there 'in countless numbers' in his day (Vol.6, p.377-379). This is highly consistent with the identification of the descendants of the lost tribes made by Simcha Jacobovici, indeed a perfect description of the lands around Afghanistan, Bactria, Sogdiana etc.

[218] The locations of Jacobovici's Ten Tribes mirror in particular the territories of the later Kushan Empire

[219] Other Semite groups were also already very active in the far east right from the era of super-ancient history (<1750 BC), for example Shem's son Elam, founder of the South Iranian Elamite Civilization, Shem's son Aram's son Gether/Gather, whom Josephus states founded Bactria (vol.4, p.71) and as previously discussed descendants of Shem's Great Great Grandson Joktan, whom Josephus states settled around the Cophen River in India and in 'Seria': North-West China in and around the Tarim Basin. (Ibid, p.73).

This interaction could have contributed to or sprung from a collection of shared values and codes between Israelites and Scandinavian cultures throughout history, such as Patriarchy, Heterosexuality (and the associated wearing of trousers rather than skirts), the use of twelve judges or peers in the deciding of legal cases and a revered tradition of the rule of law and equality before the law in general.

However, exactly to what extent the 'House of Omri' contributed to the Cimmerians and Saxons will remain a mystery until more evidence comes to light.

PART 3: Decline and Migration, 640-350 BC

Orientalization and 'Homersexuality'

Well what of the Greeks? The 'Bronze Age Collapse' had caused an enormous, 400-year hiatus in the march of their imperial ambitions[1]. Finally they were starting to rebuild. But it would be a decidedly different culture from the Achaean, Mycenaean one of heroic Greek legend that would eventually emerge from the 'Greek Dark Ages'. The Greek culture that rose to prominence from the 6th Century BC onwards would come to be known as the 'Classical' or 'Hellenic' civilization.

Hellenic culture was built on Homer. His work was the defining statement of its grandiose imperial ambition. After all, his was an unapologetic celebration of the conquest and occupation of their neighbour and brother nation. The shamelessness of classical Greek and GRHF culture all followed from this tale. And indeed, even if the Trojan War was an ethno-cultural disaster of epic proportions that resulted in the utter destruction of the perpetrators' civilization, the publication in the 8th Century BC of Homer's poem would be the catalyst and propagandic encouragement for a new and different culture to arise, a self-aggrandising culture of imperial domination and homosexuality based on Homer's poetic re-imagining of the disastrous events of 400 years earlier. Classical, imperial Greece was born out of 'The Iliad'.

---

[1] Unless the Rohl 'New Chronology' is correct, in which case it was only about a hundred to a hundred and fifty years.

A word should be added here about the ongoing 'homosexual' theme of Greco-Roman culture (present in the Iliad for example in the relationship between Achilles and Patroclus[2]) and the direct discussion of it here. There may be some who object to the term 'Greco-Roman Homosexual Fascism', querying whether sexual orientation (or rather, institutional sexual orientation culture) is relevant to political history.

To answer that criticism one needs only to point out that fourteen of the first fifteen Roman Emperors were practicing homosexuals[3], as was Alexander the Great. That homosexual sex played a central role in the urban, bathhouse, toga-wearing culture of the Greco-Romans, which developed to facilitate it, and that later variations of the same fascist ideology such as Mussolini's Fascist movement in Italy and the Nazi movement in Germany also had deep and unmistakable roots in homosexuality[4]. Adolf Hitler, one of the epitomes of fascism, had himself emerged from the homosexual, criminal underworld of post-World War I Germany when he became the poster boy of the Nazis through his position as the homosexual lover and protégé of Ernst Roehm, founder of the

---

[2] The elaborate descriptions of the close relationship between Achilles and Patroclus (for example Iliad, p.415, 468, 470) are perhaps not in themselves strong evidence of homoeroticism, but they certainly gave adequate reason for later Greeks of the Classical era overwhelmingly to interpret them as such (Iliad book. p.53)

[3] Lively & Abrams, p.100

[4] Lively & Abrams, p.129. Homosexuality played a central role in the tragic change in German fortunes that occurred in 1890, when the brilliant Chancellor Otto von Bismarck whose sober realpolitik had seen German prestige steadily increase during the Victorian era, was abruptly fired by homosexual Kaiser Wilhelm II, who subsequently ruled by autocratic fiat. This change of direction plunged Germany into the fascist militarism that precipitated World Wars I and 2. The homosexual cabal who had procured the change was exposed in the famous 'Eulenburg Affair' in 1906 by Jewish journalist Max Harden, whose articles, amongst others, so enraged the young Adolf Hitler (then a Vienna-based rent boy) that they significantly contributed to his later anti-semitism (Igra, p.30-33, 59-60, 67; Domeier). These comments are not intended to demonise homosexuals, but rather to highlight the specific danger of homosexual *political* leadership. Unfortunately, the correlation between homosexual rule and fascist tyranny is an undeniable historical fact, and it cannot be ignored in any serious study of human dignity, liberty and freedom from oppression. This is not a criticism of the persecuted, but of the persecutors.

Nazi Party[5]. There is indeed an absolute connection between fascism and homosexuality, and Greco-Roman culture was a major archetype of this.

During the period from the 10th Century BC to the 6th Century BC, an era known as 'archaic', major cultural changes occurred in Greece.

This process is often termed 'orientalization', by which is meant a change in Greek art from specializing in geometric shapes and patterns on vases, etc, to borrowing different forms from surrounding imperial influences. From the Minoan Civilization Greek art had already taken the Griffin, a lion's body with an eagle's head and wings. Now influenced by the Assyrian Empire, lions, sphinxes and humans began to be depicted. The move from abstract patterns to increasingly elaborate and lifelike representations of real-world animals and people would culminate in the ubiquitous statues worshipped throughout the Classical world and the frescos and paintings of the renaissance mirrored a moral degeneration from the making of innocent patterns to 'idolatry': a full-scale manufacturing of life-like statues and forms as the fanciful, imagined embodiment of the superstitiously feared pagan idols, through which (via 'priests') the devil would demand and receive human sacrifice in satanic rituals.

---

[5] Strasser; Lively & Abrams, p.87; Igra, p.63.

This change in art was also highly evident in Greek culture. This period saw a huge increase in the urban culture of vanity, sexual perversion, homosexuality and slavery that would characterise the Classical era. Public nudity[6], statue-making, self-aggrandisement and pleasure-seeking became central to its lifestyle, rationalised by the concept of 'Greek idealism' whereby one's actual behaviour and use of the body could be separated and disconnected from 'ideal' conceptions of art by high-minded, 'cultured' thoughts. This culture developed into two main streams, distinct and later antagonistic to one another but equally addicted to homosexuality and slavery. The Attican city-state of Athens in the east of Greece gravitated towards art, philosophy and pleasure, whilst the Laconian city-state of Sparta[7] in the south became obsessed with a communistic form of homoerotic militarism.

---

[6] This habit, though often presented as 'natural' or even 'primitive' by Classicists, was in fact a perverse innovation, a degeneration from earlier, more circumspect Greek habits. Public nudity only became fashionable and acceptable in the Greek world (before which it was seen as shameful) after its introduction into the Olympic Games by competitors Orsippus of Megara and Acanthus, traditionally in 720 BC (Dionysius, vol.7; Scanlon, p.73-74). Notably both athletes were from Sparta, a State where homosexuality and pederasty were a national obsession. Athletic 'Gymnasia', where athletes were also nude, became centres of Greek homosexual activity. Scanlon writes: "a critical mass of evidence indicates that athletic nudity and artistic male nudity were adopted at the same general time as the emergence of pederasty, namely in the first or possibly the second half of the seventh century."
[7] AKA 'Lacedaemon'

In Sparta children were taken from their parents and raised by the state. Both genders were then subjected to semi-formalised state-approved child sexual abuse. Chosen boys were entered at age seven into the 'apoge' system of 'military' training to become 'hoplites' (Greek soldiers), where they were usually raped by an older male 'mentor' in an organised system of paedophile pederasty that was promoted and condoned throughout the Classical world[8]. As adolescents the youths participated in the 'Crypteia', a secret (to mask its homosexual nature) rite-of-passage initiation process that is imitated to some extent by the fraternal society 'Greek system' of today's American colleges, where the 'Cryptai' were sent out into the countryside armed with daggers and encouraged to steal from and murder 'helots' (the slaves of Sparta) with impunity[9]. Such evil practices, substantially hidden from modern audiences that would reject Greco-Roman Classical culture and its many offshoots in today's society with revulsion if it knew about them, were in fact entirely central to that culture and indivisible from it[10]. Indeed, they 'are' Classical culture.

---

[8] Scanlon, p. 64–70; Bloch
[9] Life of Lycurgus (Plutarch, Vol.1, p.86-87). Plutarch's narrative of the life of Lycurgus (C.800 BC), the architect of Spartan society, is a good description in miniature of the process of orientalization that overtook the whole of Greece during this time. Lycurgus's innovations tended towards corruption, beastial self-interest, criminality and paganism, but were presented in the posture of an amoral communistic rationale that a state-controlled society could impose on individuals better 'virtue' by taking away their liberty. In reality it appears to have been little more than a cover for abuse, perversion and exploitation, a legitimisation that the 'Classicist' Plutarch is only too happy to go along with. Plutarch points out that many of Lycurgus's innovations were inspired by his visits to Egypt, his adulation of the works of Homer and his visits to consult the oracle witchcraft divination system at Delphi (Ibid, p.63-64).
[10] Pollini

Greek colonization of the Aegean Coast of Asia

Between the destruction of the Mycenaean Greek Civilization C.1200 BC and the rise of the Classical Greek Civilization C.700 BC, a complex history of local politics was played out in the Western half of Anatolia with many ups and downs, but throughout this period and despite many reverses, the slow, dogged settlement of the Anatolian coast by the Greeks, from the ashes of their primary settlement of Miletus on the Meander River, continued apace.

The Achaean primacy of the Mycenaean age was no more. Achaeans were relegated now to a footnote in mainstream Greek history. This new era would be led by the Ionians, Dorians and Aeolians, speaking an entirely different Ionian version of Greek and using the earliest Greek Alphabet (developed from the Phoenician) to write, instead of the earlier hieroglyphics. From the 8th Century BC the Ionians accelerated their colonisation of the Aegean coast.

As well as the rebuilt Miletus, new cities like Smyrna were set up and ancient Anatolian centres like Ephesus were increasingly 'Hellenized' and incorporated into the Greek 'League' system of groups of city-states.

While original Anatolian nations such as Caria, Luwia, Mysia and the Troad had persisted in some much weakened form of independence as trading centres since the Bronze Age despite the destruction of Troy, during the 8th and 7th Centuries BC they now increasingly came under the direct, systemic control of the Greeks.

The Greek City-States organised themselves in 'Leagues' of cities, the most powerful being the 'Ionian League' associated with the prosperous leading city of the Greek colonies, Miletus. This league took over the central section of the Anatolian Coast, with Dorian colonists invading Luwia/Lukka in the South and Aeolians the Northern section up to the Troad.

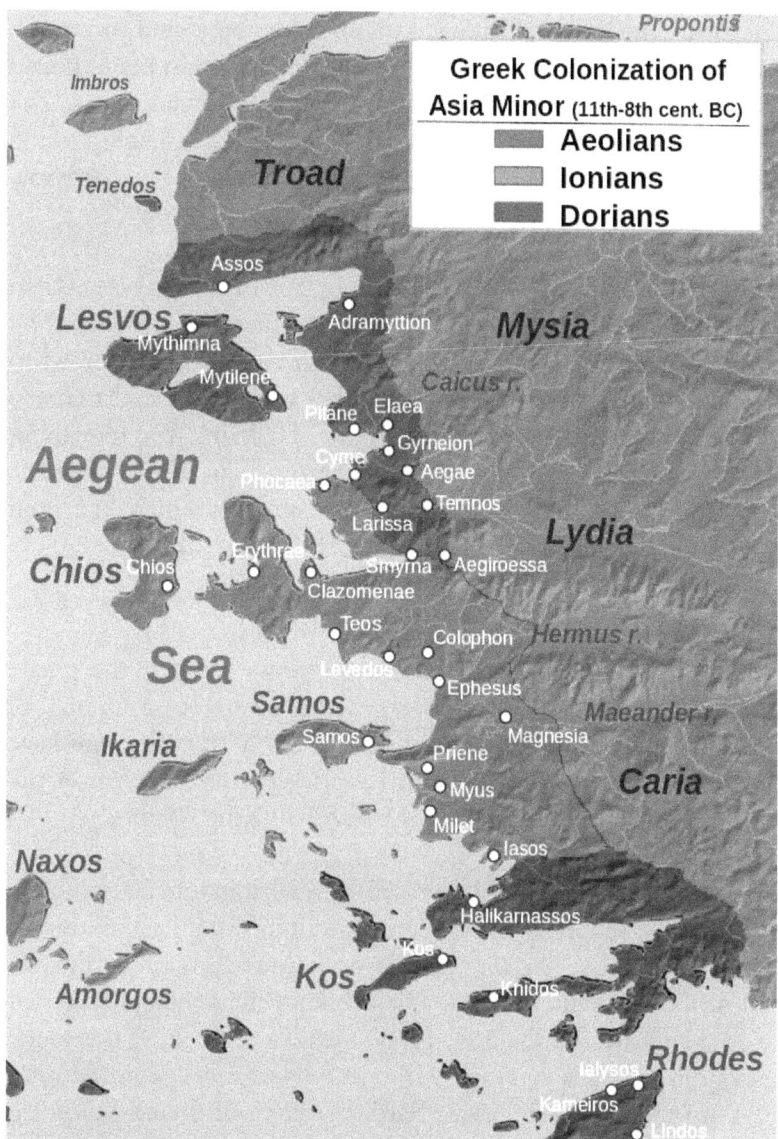

Fig.49: Greek Colonization of Asia Minor[11]

---

[11] Image by Alexikoua from Wikimedia Commons (https://commons.wikimedia.org/wiki/File:Western_Asia_Minor_Greek_Colonization.svg) (desaturated), used under CC BY SA 3.0 Unported (https://creativecommons.org/licenses/by-sa/3.0/deed.en)

Classical Greek Civilization can arguably be dated from the Meliac War of the mid 7th Century BC, when the last major power of Caria, the city-state Melite was defeated by Ionian forces. The war would result in the Ionian League of twelve Ionian-speaking city-states including Miletus, Ephesus, Chios, Samos and Smyrna.

However, though ascendant, the Greek colonies were overthrown, destroyed, had to flee or were incorporated into larger Anatolian States for many hundreds of years. Firstly they were dependant on Phrygia, then they were conquered with their citizens forced to evacuate back to the islands by the Cimmerians. After the Cimmerians had been defeated by the Scythians, the remaining dominant power of the region was Lydia, that rebuilt after the Cimmerian invasions and grew to become extremely rich and influential during the first half of the 6th Century BC.

As rich as Croesus

The King of Lydia that achieved this was Alyattes, the great-grandson of Gyges. The three generations before him had all probably died fighting the Cimmerians, and Alyattes may have taken part in the final, Assyrian Empire-sponsored defeat of the Cimmerians in 635 BC led by the Scythian King Madyes.

From there Alyattes rebuilt the Lydian Kingdom into an economic and trading superpower whose innovations would revolutionize world commerce. The Pactolus River that ran through Sardis was full of the mineral electrum, a valuable precious metal composed of gold and silver. Somebody hit on the idea of smelting this metal into uniform balls stamped with symbols of the Lydian King to back up their authenticity as Sardian electrum, thereby allowing these units of precious metal to be traded as stand-ins for the value in goods that they were worth. This was the invention of coinage.

The invention of money or currency as we know it today saw Lydia become fantastically wealthy. The only problem was that gold and silver had different values, so the stamped balls of electrum that would become known as 'coins' still varied substantially in their value. This problem was solved during the reign of Alyattes' son Croesus who reigned from C.585-546 BC. Heating the electrum with common salt removed the silver, allowing Croesus for the first time in recorded history to mint gold coins with a standardised purity, known as 'Croesids'.

This gold coinage and the trading advantage it brought saw Croesus become internationally famous for his great wealth, able to rebuild the Temple of Artemis at Ephesus (previously destroyed by the Cimmerians.) He was particularly highly thought of by the Greeks. Very quickly all surrounding Kingdoms adopted the minting of coins and the ability to do so quickly became understood to give a ruler overwhelming control of the economy and thereby of the lives of those who used the currency.

The Anatolian supremacy of Lydia was short-lived however, because the Scythian control of the region that had allowed for it had already before 600 BC been felled by a new and vast empire from the east, that was slowly rolling its way westwards.

The Two-Horned Ram

The period from 630 BC to 530 BC was an incredibly tumultuous one for the area that had been the original imperial centre or first urban settlement of human beings after the flood - Mesopotamia/Babylonia. It arguably signified the transition of this region into what we know as the Classical era, from the previous ancient era that had been typified by the hegemony of the Neo-Assyrian Empire with its many administrative systems and its Aramaic language.

Whilst the Assyrian dominance had been virtually unchallenged for five hundred years, during the hundred years from 630 BC onwards the territory that had seen the rise of empire under Nimrod 1500 years earlier would be possessed by no less than four empires in succession, culminating in the transition of power from the Hamite and Shemite older empires to the Japhetic empires that would characterise and define the Iron Age, a transition that had already occurred elsewhere. In other words the shift from settlement 1 to settlement 2, that had been postponed in this area by the intervening Shemite Neo-Assyrian empire, was finally coming home to roost in the region of the world's oldest post-diluvian civilization.

In keeping with this ethnic change, what made the difference in the complex politics of Mesopotamia was a new and unexpected incursion from the north at a crucial time when the Assyrian Empire was busy putting down a major independence movement from its Southern neighbour and ancient progenitor of empires, Babylon. Such conflicts had occurred before and Assyria might well have put this one down as well, had it not been for the intervention of this Northern, Indo-European culture, until then considered by the Assyrians to be disorganised, crude and 'tribal': the Medes.

The surprise sacking and capture of the ancient imperial capital of Assur in 614 BC by the Median King Cyaxares was crucial in undermining the Assyrian ability to defend itself against the Babylonian insurgency to its South, leading to the Neo-Assyrian empire's fast replacement by the Neo-Babylonian Empire[12] (whose period of rule would include the reign of the famous Emperor Nebuchadnezzar), that would itself soon be replaced within 80 years by the Medes themselves and their big brother nation the Persians, ushering in a period of Japhetic ascendancy in the region that would not be broken until the Arabic Mohammedan conquests of the 8th Century AD, 1400 years later.

So let us take a look at the Medes. Who were they? As their name suggests, they were descendants of the one son of Japheth not yet discussed, his third son, Madai. Unlike some of Japtheth's other

---

[12] An even more crucial intervention, without which the entire collapse of the Assyrian Empire probably wouldn't have happened, occurred in 622 BC when a thus far unidentified Assyrian general in the West unexpectedly marched on Nineveh and proclaimed himself King. This caused Emperor Sinsharishkun's until then successful mopping up of the Babylonian rebellion against Assyria to be halted for a decisive 100 days, reversing the course of history.

sons, the offspring of Madai did not disperse around the world to multiple distant lands. They contented themselves with dwelling in one location, the mountainous region to the South of the Caspian Sea, in what is now north-west Iran, around the area of today's Zarrin Rud. However, if they were hoping to be left alone up there they hoped in vain, because that region over the following millennia would become more and more a strategically crucial fulcrum in the shifting waves of Mesopotamian politics, and the Medes themselves, the ultimate imperial Kingmakers.

The Medes then were certainly 'mediators' and 'intermediaries'. A people who were frequently a nexus between the larger and more powerful empires around them. And this role seems to have been an early one. The Book of Jubilees relates that Madai married a daughter of Shem and essentially naturalized into the Shemite culture of his brother-in-laws Asshur (Patriarch of the Assyrians), Arphaxad and Elam (Patriarch of the Elamites) [13], requesting from them and being granted the aforementioned territory below the Caspian Sea, rather than dwelling with his Japhetic brothers further North[14]. And that Madai's daughter Melka married Cainam, Arphaxad's son, giving birth to Salah, father of Eber, Patriarch of the Hebrews[15].

---

[13] Jubilees, p.85
[14] The territory allotted to him by Japheth (following Noah's example) appears to have been somewhere in Europe (Jubilees, p.76)
[15] Jubilees, p.67

Fig.50: Map showing the location of Media and Persia, with particular reference to the surrounding mountain ranges that to some extent defined the Iranian world.[16]

The descendants of Madai thus were embedded into this North Iranian region of the Zagros Mountains for millennia, and were probably synonymous with or associated with the Guti and other small, independent, Japhetic nations of the area that crop up throughout history[17].

We have already seen how the chariot-riding 'Iranian' Mitanni Empire of the Hurrians facilitated the birth of the Assyrian Empire in the 14th Century BC by destabilising the preceding Babylonian Empire. It is entirely possible that the Hurrians and/or Mitanni Empire were connected with the Medes, or even *were* the Medes. Certainly Media must surely have provided the transit

---

[16] 'Mountain Stone Rock' by the3rdSequence (https://www.the3rdsequence.com/texturedb /) is licenced under CC BY 4.0 (http://creativecommons.org/licenses/by /4.0)

[17] The modern nation of the Kurds claim to be the descendants of the Medes, and this is probably accurate. Berossus (p.21) quoted in Josephus (vol.4, p.45) describes how after the flood 'Korduaians' of Armenia would raid the Ark site carrying off sections of bitumen which they made into superstitious talismans. This could well be an early reference to Kurds as they would have been in this area at the time. The 'Cadusians' are also mentioned as a closely related nation to the Medes who are confederates of Cyrus the Great in Ctesias (Ctesias, p.161).

corridor that joined Indo-Iranian BMAC with Indo-Iranian Mitanni, providing the only logical explanation for the presence of 'Indo-Iranian' (and even proposed Indo-Aryan) chariot culture so far West at this time in history. (A thousand years later the Medes would essentially reverse this process, facilitating the Neo-Babylonians' counter-displacement of the Assyrians.)

Then in the late 8th century BC the Medes were again at the crucible of history by hosting the nascent Cimmerians as they began their Westward march through Anatolia. The Median attacks on the Assyrian Empire from this period arguably constituted the beginnings of Media proper's involvement in the geo-politics of the region, raising the question of whether the Cimmerian presence among them played a part in catalysing their rise and consequently the entire Medo-Persian empire that resulted from it.

Indeed the presence of the Cimmerians coincides almost exactly with the emergence of Media as a definable and independent state. Before this time the Medes had existed as a loose collection of independent 'Shahs' or Kings united ethno-culturally but not politically.

The change occurred around 728 BC with the emergence of Media's first unified ruler, Deioces. Herodotus goes into some depth describing the rise of Deioces. The story is of note as it traces the beginnings of statehood from tribal villages, and the formation of a model that would be passed down and used by the Persians and Parthians for a thousand years from these humble beginnings. Because of this Deioces is often poetically identified with the semi-deified 'first legislator' figure of 'Hushang' in Indo-Iranian mythology described in the medieval Shahnameh[18]

Deioces (meaning roughly 'farmer') was the chief of his village, but had ambitions to 'sovereignty'. He also had strong beliefs about justice, seeing it as being in constant war against injustice. In

---

[18] Shahnameh, p.2-3

service to this belief he dispensed justice impartially and with studied intention as chief, exhibiting a Solomon-like neutrality. Slowly more and more of the surrounding Median peoples and chiefs came to him for arbitration and fair rulings in their disputes. Eventually he was administering justice over a wide area. At this point, he resigned, stating that to continue didn't 'square with his interests' as he was giving all his time to others' affairs and none to his own. Following his resignation as judge there was chaos and injustice in the land.

This appears to have been something of a canny strategy by Deioces to demonstrate his value to the Median community, because duly the idea arose (it is suggested by allies of Deioces) to appoint a King, with the name of the wise Deioces being advanced most prominently. Deioces said he would accept the Kingship upon certain terms: the Medes would have to a) give him a bodyguard of his choosing, and b) build a fortified capital city, eschewing their previous villages. All this was done. Deioces became the first Shah of the unified Medes, and the city that was built was Ecbatana (today's Hamadan – see above map), that would become the joint capital city of the vast Medo-Persian Empire.[19]

There followed the complex period of regional politics related earlier between the Medes, the arriving Cimmerians, Urartu, Mannaea and the Scythians for roughly a hundred years that would leave in its wake a Median state poised and perfectly placed to take advantage of internal division within the Assyrian Empire to its West.

Initially Deioces was allied with Rusa I, the Urartian King and first antagonist of the Cimmerians. When Rusa was defeated by them and Sargon II of Assyria assimilated his erstwhile vassal state Urartu, he also captured Deioces and exiled him to Hama (in today's Syria), apparently concerned by the growth of the new Median state at Ecbatana.

---

[19] Herodotus, p.45-47

But this was just the beginning of Assyria's problems. There followed a solid fifty years of major encroachment on the Assyrian Empire in the region, catalysed by the Cimmerians, who strengthened and inspired the Mannaeans and Medes to exert their own independence. Deioces' son Kashtariti (AKA Phraortes) took over from him C.675 BC. His career was one of warfare and conquest. In particular and primarily he subjugated the Persians, the Medes' neighbours to their South. 'Being now at the head of two nations'[20] Kashtariti proceeded to attack the Assyrians, still formerly the overlords of Media.

These two nations, from then on united in a common state, would go on to conquer the whole region, as prophesied by the Biblical prophet Daniel around 550 BC who described a 'two-horned ram':

"and the two horns were high; but one was higher than the other, and the higher came up last.

I saw the ram pushing westward, and northward, and southward; so that no beasts might stand before him, neither was there any that could deliver out of his hand; but he did according to his will, and became great."[21]

This Median 'rebellion' against Assyrian rule was temporarily put down by Assyrian Emperor Esarhaddan's strategic marriage alliance with the powerful Scythians, who by his agency entered Anatolia in a 'bouncer' capacity to evict the Cimmerians[22]. Kashtariti was killed probably fighting them around 650 BC and there followed the 28-year rule of the Scythians in Anatolia and north-western Iran. This little-known Scythian ascendancy bears closer scrutiny.

---

[20] Herodotus, p.47
[21] Tanakh, p.551
[22] Herodotus, p.47-48

The Scythian Empire

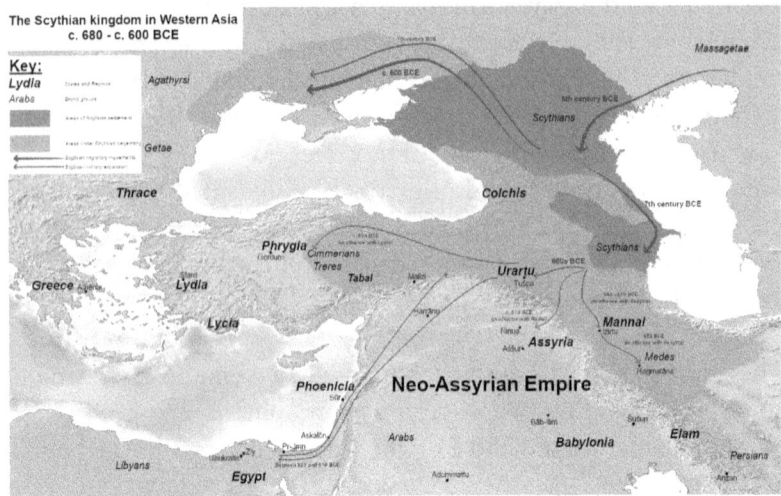

Fig.51: The little-known and short-lived but influential Scythian Empire of the 7th Century BC[23]

Not much is written about the Scythian Empire, but should be. Perhaps it doesn't fit with many chroniclers' understanding of the way the world worked. The Scythians were savages, right? But although it was short-lived – traditionally lasting for only 28 years (the exact dating is obscure, but some time between 650-590 BC), it was highly influential on events that came later. The Scythians essentially swarmed South in the wake of their erstwhile allies the Cimmerians. The unprecedented Cimmerian intervention in Mesopotamian and Anatolian politics had opened the door for their neighbours the Scythians, who by their great numbers and martial superiority, in particular the use of the horse, quickly conquered the hugely contested zone in pale shading at the centre of the above map.

---

[23] Image by Antiquistik from Wikimedia Commons (https://commons.wikimedia.org/wiki/File:Scythian_Kingdom_in_West_Asia.jpg) (desaturated) used under CC BY 4.0 International (https://creativecommons.org/licenses/by-sa/4.0/)

The Scythian ascendancy in this area was the next and incredibly key phase in a transition to Indo-European rule in Mesopotamia and the Levant. If the Cimmerians' brief adventure was proof of concept, the Scythians' invasion showed it could be more established and long-lasting. Many historians take great pains to downplay the twenty-eight years of Scythian rule in this 'centre of the world' region as merely a 'phase' or 'temporary arrangement' with unruly northern 'savages'. But this characterisation really only holds up when applied to the Cimmerian phase. The Cimmerians may only have crashed through but arguably the Scythians who followed in their wake betrayed the spirit of liberty of the Northern free peoples and fully embraced the satanic formula of 'empire' by establishing the first Indo-European empire in world history. Without question it paved the way for the subsequent Indo-European, equestrian empires that would control the region for most of the next 1300 years.

Certainly the Scythians 'took the Queen's shilling' in the sense that in order to carve out this 'empire' they had to swap sides in the conflict, accepting the deal offered by the clever Esarhaddon to marry his daughter and turn on their previous allies and closer ethnic relations the Medes and Cimmerians. As can be seen from the above map, the Scythian expansion not only pushed Southward into Media and Anatolia but also pushed westward, north of the Black Sea, overrunning much of what was previously 'Thraco-Cimmeria'[24], the traditional western wing of the territory of the descendants of Tyras, who would have had particular reason to feel betrayed by these neighbours (who had also kicked them out of Anatolia at the behest of the Assyrians). As we shall see from Herodotus' account of later communications between these northern Black Sea coast-dwelling nations, this betrayal would not be forgotten.

---

[24] This effectively was a continuation of the long-term (for at least a thousand years) westward push of the border between the 'Srubnaya' (Tyras) and 'Andronovo' (Magog) archaeological horizons referred to earlier, seemingly motivated by a constant expansion of nomadic 'Scythian-type' peoples from the Altai area.

It also appears that the Scythian expansion at this time pushed the 'Getae' i.e. the Goths west from their traditional homeland around the Maeotian Lake into South-Eastern Europe next to the Thracians.

Finally we cannot move on from the 'Scythian Empire' without mentioning the Lebor Gabála Érenn narrative. As discussed, according to its history at roughly this time there was dynastic turmoil among the Scythians between the descendants of Nel and the descendants of Nenuel. While the records are yet too scant to establish any specific connection, we can speculate that it may have played a part in the Scythians' expansion. Perhaps the moderating influence of the Nelites, now banished, would have prevented the deal with the Assyrians, that would turn out to be not such a wise one for the Scythians in the long term. As previously mentioned, however, it seems beyond dispute at this stage that the departure of the Nelite Mil, at least, was three hundred years later, approximately 350 BC.[25]

Assyrian Emperor Esarhaddon had made a very shrewd deal to turn the Scythians against their allies. Yet history records that it would only buy the Assyrian Empire a generation. The steadying of the Assyrian ship of state under its capable Emperors Esarhaddon and his son Ashurbanipal would end with Ashurbanipal's demise in 630 BC. In 625 BC the Median King Kashtariti's son Cyaxares invited the Scythian leaders to a banquet, got them drunk and murdered them all, including probably their leader Madyes.[26]

---

[25] Because of LGE Vol.2, p.39-41 that associates Mil's visit to Egypt with Persian Emperor Artaxerxes III, who reigned C.350 BC.
[26] Sulimirski & Taylor, p.547–590

Cyaxares and the Medes were now free from Scythian rule. Cyaxares[27] immediately began a huge expansion effort including a comprehensive reorganization of the Median military forces. This was the true beginning of the Medo-Persian Empire, the first large-scale Indo-European-led empire, that would become the largest the world had ever seen. The Medes conquered the surrounding Kingdoms of the Mannaeans and Parthians (also warring against the Parthians' eastern neigbours the Saka, AKA the 'eastern Cimmerians')[28]

After this they marched on Assyria proper, resulting in their surprise conquest and sacking of Assur in 614 BC. There Cyaxares joined forces with the Neo-Babylonian Emperor Nabopolassar, marrying his daughter (or granddaughter) and giving his daughter Amytis in marriage to Nabopolassar's son Nebuchadnezzar. The combined Medo-Babylonian forces conquered the Assyrian capital of Nineveh in 612 BC.

Aided by the Babylonians, the Medes then conquered Urartu and together they finished off the remains of the Assyrian state with its Egyptian allies at the battle of Carchemish in 605 BC.

Cyaxares then warred with Lydia, eventually fixing a border between Media and Lydia somewhere in central Anatolia in 585 BC after the Battle of the Eclipse, sealed with a marriage between Cyaxares's son Astyages and King Croesus' sister Aryenis.

---

[27] Almost certainly the same figure called in Ctesias' version of the story 'Arbaces' (Ctesias, p.133 onwards)
[28] Diodorus, vol.1, p.129

The Second horn

There was now a three-way power split in Asia between the Empires of Lydia, Media and Neo-Babylon, ruled by three brothers-in-law: Astyages of Media, Croesus of Lydia and Nebuchadnezzar of Babylon.

Of the three the relentless roll of the Medo-Persian imperial expansion would be the one that continued apace, enveloping the other two. But its leading edge would henceforth not be the Medes but their southern partners, the Persians.

Astyages' daughter Mandane was married off to King Cambyses of Anshan, AKA Persia (the original 'Parsua' was probably in the Zagros Mountains near Media, but the Persians had migrated South-East to Elam, inhabiting the Elamites' ancient city of Anshan). According to Herodotus, following a dream that Mandane's offspring would destroy his empire, Astyages ordered his general Harpagus to kill her son Cyrus. Echoing Biblical stories of Moses and Jesus, Harpagus instead gave the infant Cyrus to a shepherd to raise. Whether this legendary story is true, upon his adulthood Cyrus indeed confronted Astyages in battle[29]. Following a mutiny by Astyages' troops apparently instigated by Harpagus, Astyages was defeated by Cyrus at the Battle of Pasargadae in 550 BC, and the Persian Empire was born. Cyrus would go on to defeat King Croesus and conquer Lydia in 546 BC and to capture the city of Babylon itself in 539 BC, an epochal event in world history.

Cyrus was allegedly descended from a great-grandfather 'Achaemenes' about whom very little is known (and who may have

---

[29] Ctesias in his 'Persica' has a different version of Cyrus's origin story, naming his father as one Atradates, a thief 'through poverty'. In this version it is Cyrus's mother Argoste who has the dream presaging Cyrus's future Kingship (Ctesias, p.159-161). While Ctesias is often seen as an unreliable source, he resided at the Persian court (of the later King Artaxerxes II) and supposedly had access to the Persian royal records. His proximity to the narrative in 'Persica' (in contrast to his other famous work 'Indica' which famously contains many tall stories based more on remote hearsay) is arguably reason to believe his version may be the truer one in this case.

been an invention of the later Persian Emperor Darius in an attempt to justify his rule). The paternal descent of Cyrus and therefore of the Persian 'Achaemenid' Emperors is thus lost to history for the moment, although the Indo-Iranian language and culture of the Persians suggest they descended from Magog[30]. The Greeks, based on the name 'Persia', believed the dynasty was descended from Perseus, understood by them to have been a later son of Japheth himself[31].

The Medo-Persian Empire as it was called, because it retained the essential state operations of the Median Empire but now transferred to the Persian 'Achaemenid' dynasty of Cyrus, had a number of distinguishing features. Being the first large-scale Indo-European empire its spiritual beliefs were markedly different from the Babylonian satanic system (albeit within the confines of 'Empire'– no empire can truly be separate from Babylonianism). The Persian system was called Zoroastrianism and had developed in BMAC. It was a monotheistic religion of sorts, that had recorded ancient truths about the creation of the world, the flood and the tyranny of Nimrod (very likely the Zoroastrian figure of 'Zahhak'[32]) by an ancient writer 'Zoroaster', writing in the 'Avestan' language – similar to Sanskrit – and that worshipped a single creator God whom they called 'Ahura Mazda'. Zoroastrianism did not sanction the worship of idols, instead its adherents lit perpetual fires or flames as the centrepieces of its places of spiritual worship.

However Zoroastrianism's quasi-monotheism was also characterised by Manichaean dualism: the idea that light and dark/ good and evil are simply two sides of the same coin, two equal and opposite forces (as in Taoism); a fundamental concept of

---

[30] Ctesias describes Cyrus as 'a Mard by birth' (p.159) and his mother Argoste as having been 'a goatherd among the Mards' (p.160)
[31] Greek assertions of this relationship are quite strident, and as we shall see, far from impossible. Cephalion (C.0 BC), as reported by George Sincellus (C.800 AD), calls him 'Perseus Dionysius the son of Semele' and also 'Perseus the Danae' (Greek Historical Fragments, vol.3, p.626)
[32] Although the Zahhak character in the Avesta and Shahnameh also incorporates elements of Satan.

witchcraft (AKA Satan worship), that is symbolised by the famous black and white checkered flooring utilized in its practice. The study of this dualistic teaching was a particular speciality of the Magi, one of the six original people groups conquered by Deioces the Mede[33]. Just as the denizens of the region of Chaldea had been the main practitioners of witchcraft in the previous Babylonian Empire, the name of the Magi would become synonymous with this satanic aspect of the Zoroastrian system in the Persian Empire: 'magic'.

Culturally then the Medo-Persians can arguably be seen as being a blend of the Indo-European heritage of Madai and Magog and the Shemite heritage, with its greater emphasis on God and law, of the surrounding Bactrian and Elamite cultures, with Elam in particular being geographically the predecessor state of Persia. It is notable that the Persian Empire is the only one spoken of highly by the Jewish writers of the Bible, whose people at this time were prisoners of the Neo-Babylonian Empire, but would soon be liberated by one of Cyrus's successors, Xerxes.

Another new aspect of the Medo-Persian Empire was that being an Indo-Iranian-led empire it 'automatically' incorporated a large swathe of the eastern Japhetic settlements around BMAC into its writ, people groups who had previously not been subject to the giant Mesopotamian Empires of the Akkadians, Assyrians and Babylonians (that had usually conquered Hamite and Shemite cultures). This pushed the imperial border as far as the Oxus River south of Sogdiana, incorporating much of the Silk Road up to the Hindu Kush and Pamir Mountains. The Medo-Persians' Indo-Iranian cousins in that area were to be fairly reluctant participants in the empire, and the Bactria region would continue to be a thorn in the side of the Persian empire and its successors, as it was essentially the border between the Indo-Iranian world and that of the ethnically diverse 'Scythian' hordes to its north, one of whose nations, the Parthians, would eventually replace the Persians as rulers of the Empire.

---

[33] Herodotus, p.47

The very vastness of the Medo-Persian Empire (that was also the first to specialize in making long roads or 'highways' to facilitate fast communication and travel between its disparate regions) makes it a threshold point in history that marks the beginning of the Classical era, as many of the widespread states it conquered had previously been free from foreign rule. Egypt, Thrace, to some extent Greece, India and Bactria would henceforth be forced to partake in some form of common culture, and that culture would turn out to be the homosexual 'Classical' culture of ancient Greece.

The Medo-Persian Empire then was something new in world politics: an Indo-European Empire that was organised and centralised. Contemporary Mesopotamia, Iran, Asia and Africa had no answer to its inexorable expansion. To cut a very long story short, over the next century from 550 BC to 450 BC during the reigns of four warrior Emperors: Cyrus, his son Cambyses, Darius (a usurper who claimed descent from a common ancestor Achaemenes), and his son Xerxes, the vast Medo-Persian organisation would go on to conquer Babylonia and the Neo-Babylonian empire, Parthia, Bactria, Sogdiana, Arya, the Indus Valley (today's Pakistan), Egypt, Carthage (today's Tunisia), Anatolia including Lydia, Colchis/Iberia, Cyprus, coastal Thrace, Illyria and briefly Greece. These conquests made it by far the largest empire in world history up til that point.

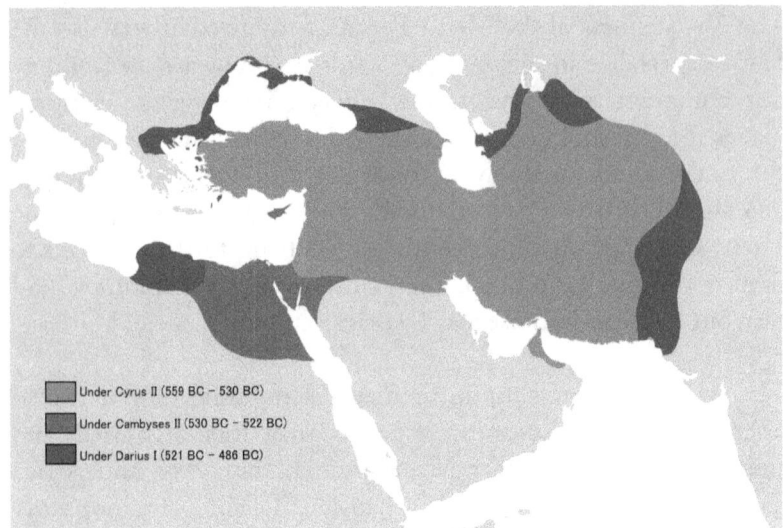

Fig.52: the Persian or 'Achaemenid' Empire at its furthest extent[34]

As one can see from the top left and top right sections of the above map, this was the beginning of the encroachment of Empire into 'Asian' territory, i.e. the dwelling places of the descendants of many of the Trojan nations during Settlement 2.

The Persian Empire as fully formed from Cyrus onwards was a vast institutional juggernaut. One of the many territories it enveloped was that to its north-east, the region including the ancient states of Bactria, Sogdiana and Khorasan. This was an odd situation because on the one hand it was almost an afterthought as these were in fact the ancient homelands of the Persian, AKA Indo-Iranian people and would assumedly be part of the empire automatically. But on the other hand there was an uncomfortable element to this occupation, as the child Persia, having moved to the west near Mesopotamia, was now exercising authority over its own parent.

---

[34] Wikimedia Image by Ali Zifan (https://en.wikipedia.org/wiki/File:Achaemenid _Empire_under_different_kings_(flat_map).svg) (desaturated) used under CC BY SA 4.0 International (https://creativecommons.org/licenses/by-sa/4.0/deed.en)

The History of Iran

To explain this unusual situation, we have to delve deeper into the colourful and rich history of Iran and the Iranian people, and their ancient development in this area. This is not an easy task. Much like the Greeks, the Iranians, being a Japhetic nation (but descended from Magog not Javan) had a poetic attitude to history, and their written history like the Greeks' is a convoluted muddle of melodramatic stories and characters interwoven together into a narrative where the truth isn't often allowed to get in the way of a good story. Extricating fact from the hagiography, national iconography, retrospective commentary and artistic licence is not for the faint-hearted. Especially as this poetic remembering of ancient history is also mixed up in this case (unlike in the Greek[35]) with the sacred writings of a complex monotheistic (or rather dualistic) belief system: Zoroastrianism.

The effort to understand the roots of Iranian civilization is particularly hampered by an extreme level of historical vandalism done to its written heritage, apparently in an attempt to stamp it out from history altogether, by two massive, successive waves of foreign occupation which both carried out wholesale cultural extermination policies towards Iranian, Zoroastrian history, the source culture of the Persian Empire. Firstly the Greek Empire, whose attempts between 330 BC and around 50 BC to 'Hellenize' eastern Iran were particularly virulent. The banal Greek takeover systematically attempted to destroy all copies of the 'Avesta'[36], the foundation text of both Iranian history and the Zoroastrian religion[37] that included the 'Gathas', Zoroastrianism's most sacred and ancient writings, claimed to have been penned by Zoroaster himself[38]. The 'Avesta' survived, but barely.

---

[35] The influence of the Greeks' pagan secularism on their history is arguably just as impenetrable, but not as complex, and less vandalised by later occupiers
[36] Bundahisn, p.173
[37] The Avesta is essentially a compendium of all the extant writings in the Avestan language.
[38] The Gathas basically consist of dialogues between Zoroaster and Ahura Mazda. Plato is thought to have been influenced by them in the writing of his 'Dialogues'.

Then, after a resurgence of Iranian national strength under the Parthian Arsacid and Sasanian rulers, a second vast invasion and occupation of Iranian culture by Arabic, Islamic conquerors from the 7th Century AD onwards destroyed many more countless artifacts of Iranian civilization. As a consequence of these two occupations, it is estimated that three quarters of all Avestan language material has been lost[39].

During the middle ages however something of a reconstruction effort was undertaken under the Samanid and Ghaznavid dynasties[40], and the oldest extant texts and compilations we have are from this period, around the 11-12th Century AD. All of this is the reason why a true appreciation of the vast scope of the BMAC-related civilization, and books such as this one incorporating its extensive history and heritage - in scale easily equivalent to an eastern version of the western Greco-Roman corpus - into a wider understanding of global history, are only now in the 21st Century being attempted for the first time.

What material we have is highly piecemeal, and later assumptions about it, in particular attempts to date the stories contained within it have often been little more than guesswork, as we shall see. What remains of the 'Avesta', for example, is an extremely fragmentary and esoteric text, with limited historical content[41].

---

[39] Boyce, 1984, p.3
[40] 819-999 AD and 977-1186 AD respectively. Notwithstanding that these dynasties were still under Muslim occupation, the culture from which the reconstruction effort was attempting to salvage its lost history.
[41] The extant Avesta only contains the tale of Ahura Mazda's creation of the sixteen lands plus the narrative of Yima (Noah) and the flood/ice age.

The most significant single source for Iranian history left to us is the 'Shahnameh' or 'Book of Kings', an epic poem from the 11th Century AD by the poet Ferdowsi that contains valuable information from previous now lost histories of Iran. There is also the Pahlavi-language 'Bundahisn' ('Creation'), written just before the Shahnameh, another Zoroastrian religious text that contains some sections of otherwise lost history, that was one of the sources for the 'Shahnameh'[42].

A good example of the patchiness of Iranian historical evidence is the dearth of data we have on the iconic figure of Zoroaster (AKA Zarathustra) himself, the founder of the Zoroastrian religion. He has a status within it equivalent to Siddhartha Gautama in Buddhism or Mohammed in Islam, but incredibly there is virtually no scholarly consensus on when he actually lived. It could have been any time between 2000 BC and 0 BC. As we shall see however, like much of the existing conventional digest of Iranian history, this is a somewhat disingenuous prevarication[43], that ignores the intrinsic clarity and internal consistency of the historical evidence that is available. Once the sand of millennia of obfuscation is brushed off, a realistic and satisfactory timeline can in fact be settled upon. By cross-referencing sources we can discern with some certainty when Zoroaster and other ancient characters lived.

Zoroaster then, allegedly receiving the text from a divine source, penned the 'Avesta' (or at least its oldest portion the 'Gathas'), in its unique Indo-Iranian source language 'Avestan', that is very close to Indian Sanskrit. A somewhat later-written section of it, the 'Vendidad', begins with a list of the 'sixteen perfect Iranian lands'[44], as seen in the following map:

---

[42] The Bundahisn is in fact probably a translation or summary of the now lost 'Dāmdād Nask', the 'Creation' section of the Avesta.
[43] Often by foreign historians, who for reasons either in concert with the destroyers of Iranian culture, or of romanticism, wish to keep Iranian history mystically opaque.
[44] Vendidad, p.4-10

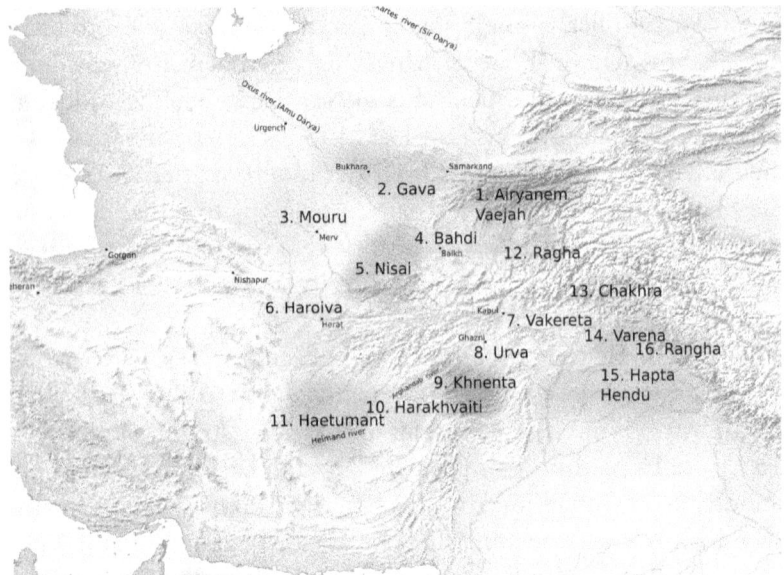

Fig.53: the '16 perfect Iranian lands' of the first verses of the Vendidad. Note in particular 1 (Arya), 2 (Sogdiana), 3 (Margiana) and 4 (Bactria).[45]

These were the homelands of the Indo-Iranians. First to be listed and given primacy among them was 'Airyanem Vaejah' (a root of our word 'area'), the cradle of Iranian civilization in the Pamir Mountains of today's Tajikistan. These then were the 'Indo-Aryans' who would spread westward to Persia and Southward into India[46]. To this extent Sanskrit can be seen as a derivative language and culture of Avestan. It is likely that Magogites first settled here as the furthest extent of their overland journey either North across the top of the Caspian Sea then southward, or through Mountain Passes along the South shores of the Caspian Sea through the primordial territories of the 'Gutians', Hurrians and Medes. Or, possibly via a Southern route through Mesopotamia.

---

[45] Wikimedia Image by Fhesse (https://en.wikipedia.org/wiki/File:Geography _avesta_grenet.png).svg) (cropped and desaturated) used under CC BY SA 4.0 International (https://creativecommons.org/licenses/by-sa/4.0/deed.en)

[46] The Oxus river of the BMAC/Iranian civilization and the Indus river of the SHVA/Indian civilization spread out from virtually a single (or very close) source in the mountains, suggesting that the Indo-Aryans inhabited that area in remote antiquity, with the two cultures diverging as they got further downstream.

It is instructive to remember when dealing with such super-ancient history (pre-1750 BC) that the first post-diluvian settlers in these regions would have been facing a very different topography from the present one - a topography with considerably more ice and water:

Fig.54: East Asia during the last glacial maximum (C.2300 BC). Note the gigantic post-glacial Lake Mansi in the North that stood between north-eastern 'Afanasievo' and Steppe 'Andronovo' archaeological horizons (labelled 'Possible IE Urheimat'). Also the presence of a proglacial lake in the Tarim Basin. Note also the greatly enlarged size of the Caspian Sea and the Persian Afghan glacier that would have made transit eastward directly South of the Caspian more difficult (though perhaps not impossible) at this time.[47]

---

[47] Image by Don Hitchcock (donsmaps.net), used with permission. Adapted from Huggett, p.232, adapted from Grosswald, p.210. © Wiley Publishing Corp. Used under licences

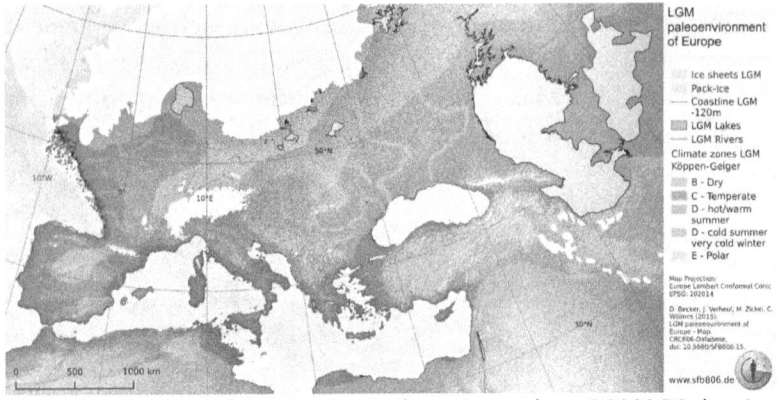

Fig.55: Another map of the situation in the region perhaps C.2300 BC showing the greatly enlarged Caspian and Aral Seas[48]

Fragmentarily in the Avesta, and more coherently but with more editorialising in Ferdowsi's 'Shahnameh', the story continues with Yima AKA Jamshid, the Iranian name for Noah (cognate with Sanskrit 'Yama' and Old Norse 'Ymir'[49]) being instructed by 'Ahura Mazda' to construct a survival sanctuary for a coming flood/ice age apocalypse[50]. Afterwards he rules the world for 300 years and towards the end of his life becomes involved with wine-making[51].

The Shahnameh has the reign of the evil tyrant 'Zahhak' AKA Nimrod basically follow on from the reign of Yima/Noah. Zahhak is defeated by one Fereydun, in a narrative that became confused with that of the later 'Shah' Cyrus the Great's overthrow of his uncle Astyages, complete with dream, etc. This is one of many historical conflations in Iranian history no doubt stemming from the paucity of accessible cultural material that has resulted for example in early modern Iranians believing that statues of Cyrus,

---

[48] Image by Becker, D; Verheul, J; Zickel, M; Willmes, C, of the CRC806 project (desaturated) (https://crc806db.uni-koeln.de/dataset/show/lgm-paleoenvironment-of-europe--map1449850675/). Used under CC BY
[49] Oettinger, p.169-183; Poetic Edda, p.4
[50] Vendidad, p.16-17
[51] Pellechia, p.11-12

Darius and other Achaemenid Kings in the Persian capital of Persepolis were representations of the primordial heroes Yima, Fereydun and the rest. Such has been the hidden nature of much of this history for millennia.

It is also typical of the highly 'repeating' nature of Iranian history, where ancient story arcs are synthesised with more recent history for symbolic emphasis. For example the founder of the Median Empire Deioces being identified with 'Hushang', an antediluvian figure some generations removed from Gayomart/Keyumars, the Zoroastrian 'Adam'. Or in the character of the wicked 'Afrasiab' who appears to be a composite of every powerful ruler of the Iranians' northern enemy over the centuries, cropping up again and again in generation after generation. As we shall see, this has led to great confusion and difficulty in correctly dating the various eras described in Iranian history, particularly the 'Kayanian' dynasty. For now, we will continue with the narrative as laid out in the 'Shahnameh'.

The defeat of Zahhak/Nimrod takes place in the mountains to the north of the Mesopotamian world as it does in the Armenian and Georgian accounts, but here it is in the Alborz Mountains[52] somewhat to the east of their Armenian location.

The character of Fereydun is not easily relatable to other super-ancient historical records. He is credited with defeating the evil Zahhak and re-establishing righteous rule on earth. But he is not named as Yima's son and really could be anyone from Hayk to Esau to Madai to Japheth to Magog, or a composite of more than one person[53]. In the story of his sons however he is reminiscent of Japheth, as the Shahnameh's description of how he divides up the land inheritance between them[54] is similar to how Japheth

---

[52] Zahhak is eventually bound at Mount Damavand (Shahnameh, p.27)
[53] In the Bundahisn there are 4 generations from Gayomart (Adam) to the significant figure of Hushang, then 3 more generations to Yima (Noah), then 10 more generations to Fereydun (Bundahisn, p.185)
[54] Shahmaneh, p.36

conducts the same process as described in the Book of Jubilees[55] (although this was probably done by all Japheth's sons following his example). To his favoured son Iraj[56] he gives Iran. 'Iraj' AKA 'Airyu' was later understood to be the eponym of 'Iran'[57]. Ferdowsi's epic alleges that Airyu is then killed by his brothers Tur and Salm out of their jealousy towards him because of his recieving the best land (Iran)[58].

Cross-referenced with other sources, this is strong evidence that at least at this point, the brothers represent the sons of Japheth[59]. Firstly, the Bundahisn states that 'the land of Salm' is the 'land of Rome'[60], suggesting that Salm is Javan (Greek and Roman were often conflated by the Persians). And, as we shall see, Tur is certainly Thor.

Secondly, the account in Diodorus Siculus of Dionysius's trip/invasion to the east and India in extreme antiquity, fits exactly with the evidence we have from the Indo-Iranian tradition. Diodorus relates how Dionysius (whom he equates with both Osiris and Bacchus), after growing up in Egypt, went on a great trip eastward, accompanied by his two sons. The trip went through Arabia[61] all the way to India, where he stayed for some time founding the City of Nysa[62] and introducing many ancient

---

[55] Jubilees, p.76-77

[56] AKA 'Airyu' or 'Erez'. One of the great causes of confusion in Iranian historiography is the different versions of names used in different texts. When those names are also carried over from the original Avestan, Pahlavi or Persian script into English, the confusion is only compounded.

[57] Note the similarity in the national names of 'Iran' and 'Éirenn' (Ireland). Although the Irish ethnonym supposedly comes from a female 'Danann' 'goddess' it is notable that the two nations' leaders, the Iranians and the 'Royal Scythians', were both likely descended from Magog's eastern 'Indo-Iranian' stream. As were the Indians, and the flags of India and Ireland have the exact same three colours - perhaps an echo of their shared Magogian heritage, that is also confirmed by similarities in language (Mallory, p.125)

[58] Shahnameh, p.36-44; Bundahisn, p.186

[59] Whether Fereydun is exactly cognate with Japheth is less clear, although the Bundahisn does state that Fereydun was one of three brothers (p.185)

[60] Ibid, p.79 In the Shahnameh Salm's portion is also 'the West' (p.36)

[61] Therefore apparently by the Southern route

[62] AKA 'Nyssa', 'Naishada', 'Nagara' and 'Dionysopolis' (Ptolemy, p.152)

customs there, in particular the cultivating and drinking of wine and the promotion of inebriated hedonistic behaviour[63], the planting of ivy and the growing of long hair for men. After this he went north-west through the rest of Asia[64], then 'transported his army' through the Hellespont to Thrace, where he killed a 'king of the barbarians' who 'opposed him in his designs'.[65]

When he returned to Egypt, Dionysius/Magog 'was murdered by his wicked brother Typhon'[66]. So not only was Dionysius a son of Zeus/Japheth, he also travelled early to the east, seeding a culture on the Indus and in Iran, before being murdered by his 'Ty/u'-named brother[67]. 'Iraj'/'Airyu' then, it is proposed, is Magog, AKA Dionysius, Patriarch of the Indo-Aryans, who formed both the Indian and Iranian nations, and also, through the 'Royal Scythians' of Sogdiana, the Irish and Scottish.[68]

As for Fereydun as Japheth, that is a little more problematic. Certainly the Shahnameh's description of Fereydun's 'court' is an exact fit with Japheth's retirement palace on Mount Olympus. Its descriptions of a priest's visit there have the same sense of the awe and gravitas in approaching the ancient Patriarch's throne that we

---

[63] Dionysius's 'Orgia' is probably the source of the word 'Orgy' (Diodorus Siculus, vol.1, p.206)
[64] Such a trans-Asian path would explain the otherwise odd presence of Indo-Aryans like the Hurrian Mitanni way over in the west around Armenia – precisely along the course of Dionysius's route back from India. As well as other Indo-Iranian cultures seeded along the way such as the Kassites, Gutians and Persians.
[65] Diodorus Siculus, vol.1, p.23-27
[66] presumably for the killing of the Thracian King
[67] In Greek mythology, the character of Typhon is highly consistent with being an unflattering and hostile depiction of the unruly Thor (Hesiod, p.29), who is associated with locations such as the Orontes River, Mysia, Thrace and Sicily (e.g. Strabo, vol.3, p.163, vol.2, p.406, vol.1, p.368). The 'youngest son' of Gaia (Earth), Hesiod reports that Typhon (the origin of our word 'typhoon') resists Zeus (Japheth)'s power grab where he wrested control of the world from Cronus (Noah), but is defeated (Hesiod, p.69-73).
[68] This would explain the Milesian Irish Scythians' frequent visits 'back' to Egypt, the homeland of their ancient father. Also the connection between the Irish and the 'Gypsies', i.e. 'Egyptians'. Indeed Magog's name may be connected to 'Magan', an ancient name for Egypt.

know from copious Greek tales of Zeus's descendants going on pilgrimages to seek his advice or intervention:

"He reached Fereydun's castle, which towered above him like a mountain, its battlements hidden among the clouds. Courtiers sat in the throne room, and beyond a curtain were the nobility; on one side lions and leopards were tethered, and on the other raging war elephants. The assembled warriors gave a roar like a lion's; it seemed to the messenger as though this were a celestial court, and that the warriors standing there were angelic beings."[69]

But Fereydun is listed in the Bundahisn as being ten generations after Yima/Noah, not his direct son. Also, according to the Georgian histories, Japheth did not kill Nimrod, although his great grandson Hayk did. Perhaps the garbled memory that a Japhethite liberated the world from Nimrod's tyranny was enough for Japheth to be awarded the credit by proxy, and the Bundahisn's extra generations can be attributed to the imperfections and disruptions in the Iranian historical record (that, as we shall see particularly with chronology, were substantial.)

More likely though, is that while Fereydun is meant to represent Japheth in the issue of his sons, the character is also a conflation of later Magogian figures. The Shahnameh's narrative constitutes a significant Indo-Iranian claim to involvement in the toppling of the Nimrod/Zahhak regime. Which sheds interesting light on the 'Gutians' who spread down from the mountains and destroyed the Akkadian throne of Nimrod after his defeat[70]. It adds to the likelihood that the Gutians were proto-Goths, descendants of the recently deceased Magog[71], who had left them there on his transit through the Zagros from India.

---

[69] Shahnameh, p.38. Compare for example the Odyssey, p.80, 126-7, 169; Hesiod, p.12-13, 35, 67-69; Lactantius, vol.1, p. 30-31; Moses of Khorene, p.78
[70] Sumerian King List, p.17-19
[71] Or Magog himself, on the return leg of his journey. The Shahnameh mentions that Fereydun celebrates his takeover of Mesopotamia with wine, and also does not stay there long, exhibiting a Dionysian penchant for wandering: "I am lord of the entire earth, and I should not stay always in one place, otherwise I would have lived here with you for many long years." (p.24 and 27, see also p.29)

The Shahnameh's account of Nimrod's overthrow is significantly different to the Armenian and Georgian versions – instead of being chased into the mountains, Fereydun 'invades' Mesopotamia and hunts a cowering Zahhak/Nimrod down, before taking him to Mount Damavand and imprisoning him there[72]. The differences suggest that the Shahnameh may be remembering an interaction with a different Akkadian ruler, perhaps the immediate successor of Nimrod[73], and that its narrative is in fact a description of the Gutian invasion and takeover of Mesopotamia in the wake of Nimrod's defeat.

The hypothesis would be that while the Togarmanians have a closer claim to toppling Nimrod himself, the 'Gutians' who swarmed down and kicked over the Babylonian Empire where it lived, were possibly a different group: the proto-Goths of Magog[74]. The Shahnameh relates for example how Fereydun crosses the Tigris and approaches the high-walled city of 'the world's king'[75]. He then proceeds, without much apparent effort nor resistance (as though the ruler had already been defeated and it was vacant), to occupy the throne and commence a reformatory deconstruction of Zahhak's evil system, essentially 'liberating' the country and immediately gaining the gratitude of the citizenry[76].

Here is the description of Fereydun by one of Zahhak's spies to Zahhak:

"He rode into the palace, accompanied by his brothers, and took his place on your throne; then he destroyed all your idols and spells

---

[72] Shahnameh, p.26-27; in an echo of the Biblical binding of Satan.
[73] Possibly 'Kondrow', Zahhak's inefectual minion in the Shahnameh (p.24)
[74] A near descendant of his (if not Magog himself) may have been the 'Erridupizir' of Mesopotamian history (presumably some version of 'conqueror of Eridu'), the first Gutian overlord of the region following Naram-Sin's fall.
[75] Named bizarrely in the Shahnameh as Jerusalem, but that would be quite far from the Tigris.
[76] Shahnameh, p.22-27.

and flung your courtiers, both men and demons, from the castle walls, mixing their brains and their blood in death."[77]

And the women of the harem to Fereydun:

"How wretchedly we've passed our days, mistreated by that fool of a magician; what sufferings we have endured at that monster's hands! We have never seen anyone strong enough or valiant enough to seek his throne."[78]

Here is Fereydun's proclamation to the city's inhabitants, interestingly referencing the 'confusion' (aka 'Babel') of Zahhak's international one-world government:

"You are wise and honored men; it is not right for you to be wielding weapons and riding out to war, in the same way that soldiers should not be artisans. Each group should follow its own calling, since if they follow one another's, the earth is filled with confusion. The evil tyrant has been captured, and the earth is cleansed of his power. Return in peace to your former occupations, and may you live long and happily!"[79]

As the Shahnameh continues, following Airyu's murder by his brothers, his rule over Iran is succeeded by his grandson Manuchehr, who avenges his father's murder.

But before continuing with this narrative, we must take a detour to consider the relationship of these events to primaeval India.

The understanding that Magog/Dionysius/Bacchus founded the Indo-Aryan colonies that became both India and Iran on his super-ancient trip east explains a lot about the historical and archaeological record in the area.

---

[77] Shahnameh, p.24-25. Nb. Dionysius was also accompanied by his brothers in the Diodorus version
[78] Ibid, p.23
[79] Ibid, p.26

For example the story of Fereydun and Zahhak is echoed in the Rigveda, the foundational writings of the Hindu belief system left to us by the Indo-Aryans who took over Northern India around 1300 BC establishing the 'Sanskrit Hindu Vedic Aryan' (SHVA) civilization that became India. The Rigveda's chief 'god' 'Indra'[80] (the eponym of 'India'), about whom a quarter of the Rigveda is written, is possibly a memory of Magog/Airyu as Indra is called 'Maghavan'[81], but also may be cognate with Japheth/Fereydun, as he is also called 'Thunder wielder'[82] and 'bolt-hurling thunderer'[83], who, 'with his lightning'[84] defeated the evil serpent demon 'Vritra', liberating humanity[85].

A similar name to 'Iraj', 'Viraj' describes the Rigveda's primordial man/ Adam figure or figure of benevolence and serenity/ breath of life. Meanwhile 'Gotra' is the Sanskrit word for patrilineal descendant, seemingly a memory of 'Goth' aka Magog their ancient father (with their cousins the Irish arguably having the other half of the name: 'Mac'). There is more evidence of 'proto-Gothic' influence in the Rigveda in that the writers of the poems describe themselves as 'Gotamas'[86].

Japheth is represented in the Rigveda in at least two forms, as the spiritual leader 'Prajapati'[87] and as the father figure or 'begetter' 'Dyaus', who is once called 'creator'[88], cognate with Greek 'Zeus Pater': 'Sky Father' and Roman 'Jupiter'. And as discussed the

---

[80] Rigveda, vol.1, p.3
[81] Rigveda, vol.1, p.183
[82] Ibid, p.56. If Indra is Japheth, Magog could possibly be represented by 'Agni', the Rigveda's spiritual leader priest or head soma-dealer (e.g. vol.1, p.1, 22-24)
[83] Rigveda, vol.2, p.224
[84] Ibid
[85] Rigveda, vol.1, p.27 and 56
[86] Ibid, vol.1, p.108
[87] e.g. vol.4, p.356
[88] Rigveda, vol.3, p.195. Although 'Dhatar' is possibly the Rigveda's closest thing to an 'ultimate' creator, see vol.4, p.416. But there are also some mentions of an 'Asura' (e.g. vol.1, p.65-66), cf. Zoroastrianism's 'Ahura Mazda'; and 'Varuna' also features as another, arguably more abstract, version of 'God'

lightning-wielding conqueror/hero figure of 'Indra' may also be Japheth[89].

The identification of Dionysius/Magog as the founder of India explains much of the evidence for the 'out of India' theory of Indo-European (by which is often meant 'Indo-Iranian') origin, as the Dionysian/Indo-Iranian culture did indeed apparently branch out from Northern India or Arya[90]. Possibly Magog transversed the Hindu Kush mountains via the meeting point of the Oxus and Indus rivers, but more likely through the Khyber Pass - the location of 'Nysa'[91] - visiting both Arya, the land that bears his name, and 'Mehrgahr' in today's Bolochistan in Pakistan, that both appear to be initial settlements from the Magogian expedition.

Archaeologists have discovered strong evidence that the farming methods and other cultural signifiers of Mehrgahr were brought from the Mediterranean and Mesopotamia, exactly in keeping with the Dionysius story[92].

For example, regarding a lactose tolerance genetic marker, one report states:

"the most common lactose tolerance mutation made a two-way migration out of the Middle East less than 10,000 years ago. While the mutation spread across Europe, another explorer must have brought the mutation eastward to India – likely traveling along the coast of the Persian Gulf where other pockets of the same mutation have been found."[93]

---

[89] Although at one point Dyaus is described as Indra's maker or begetter (Rigveda, vol.2, p.119), this may be in Dyaus's 'creator' capacity.

[90] Conversely, this makes the Yamnaya horizon (also technically Indo-European/Japhetic), that came north through the Caucasus, less likely to have been Magogian/Dionysian, and more likely to have been led by Gomerans, such as Ashkenaz and Riphath and/or their offspring.

[91] Nb. Jerahmeel records that Dionysius built the city of Nysa 'about the same time' that Troy was built in Dardania (Yosippon book, p.174)

[92] Gangal, et. al; Gallego Romero, et. al

[93] Mitchum

BMAC

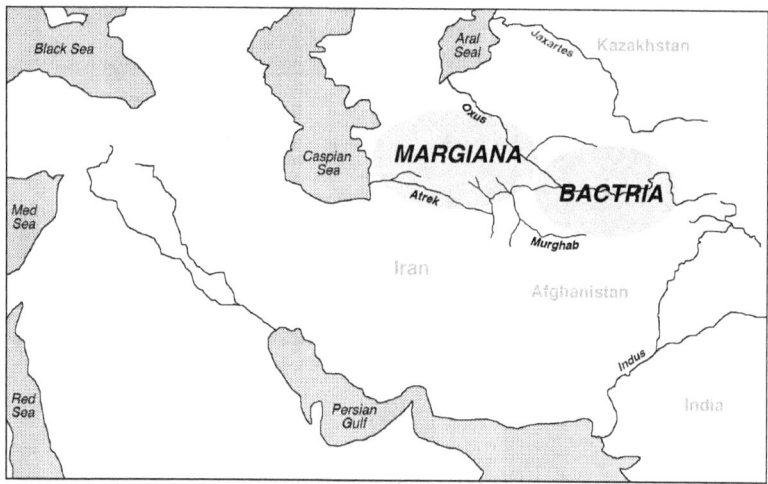

Fig.56: showing the approximate location of 'BMAC'

At this point we must look at the amazing BMAC, the Bactria-Margiana Archaeological Complex. This is the remains of what was once a super-ancient civilization in the Iranian area that would have been closely contemporary with 'Airyu' AKA Magog and his descendant Kings of about 2300-1700 BC[94]. Its existence was completely unknown to modern academia until the late 20th Century when Russian archaeologist Viktor Sarianidi began unearthing it from the desert sands. It is a perfect example of the surprisingly fast-shifting climate and its effects on historical awareness. Because the topography changed (in this case the course of the Murghab River moved to the west) the major sites of BMAC were completely abandoned for perhaps three thousand years, never suspected of being there because of the harshness of the arid environment.

---

[94] 'Marhaši', the name by which BMAC, or at least its south-western extent (i.e. 'Margiana'), was known to the Babylonians, is very present in Mesopotamian records as a powerful and exotic far-off land that both Sargon and Naram-Sin campaigned against, the source of precious gems, in particular Chalcedony and Lapis Lazuli. However it disappears from the records around 1700 BC, suggesting it ceased to be a political entity around that time (Steinkeller, 1982, p.263)

Fig.57: the remains of the fortress at Gonur Depe, a major citadel of BMAC.[95]

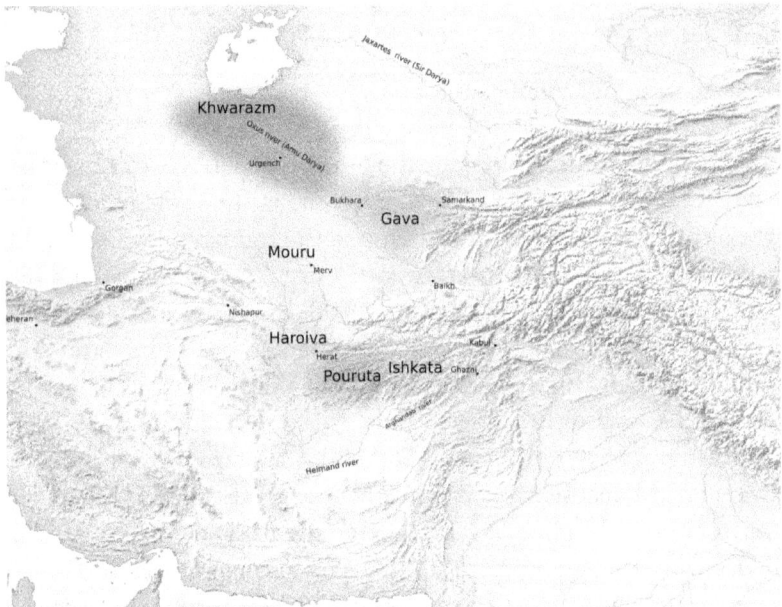

Fig.58: Margiana is labelled 'Mouru' on this map that shows the expansion of the Iranians northwards towards the oasis of Khorasan/Khwarazm. Iranians from Sogdiana (labelled here 'Gava') continued on into the Sea of Grass where they teamed up with eastward-moving Riphathites to form the Scythians[96]

---

[95] Sarianidi, 2008, p.242
[96] Wikimedia Image by Fhesse (https://en.wikipedia.org/wiki/File:Avestan_geography_mihr_yasht.png), (desaturated, cropped), used under CC BY SA 4.0 International (https://creativecommons.org/licenses/by-sa/4.0/deed.en)

The BMAC civilization was also contemporaneous and in communication with other super-ancient urban developments along the Indus River: Harappa and Mohenjo-Daro, the beginning of a long-standing association between the Aryans and northern India.

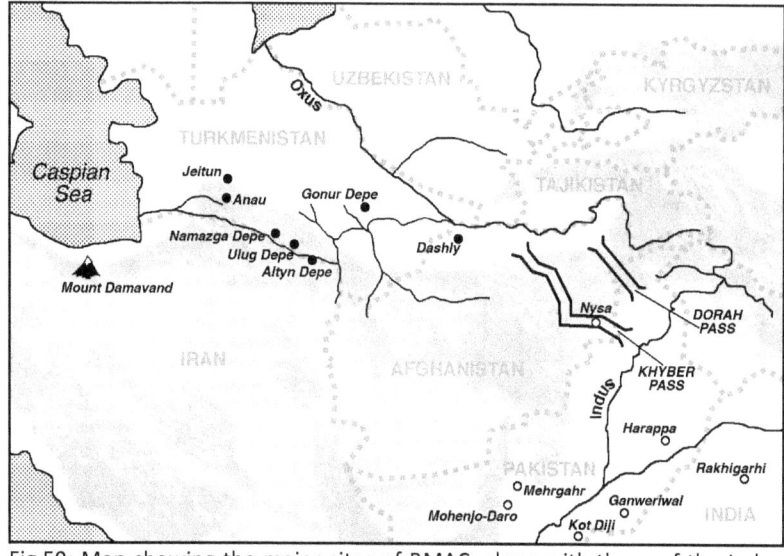

Fig.59: Map showing the major sites of BMAC, along with those of the Indus Valley or 'Harappan' Civilization, with whom they were in communication.[97]

Harappa and Mohenjo-Daro are generally understood to have been pre-Aryan Hamite settlements, although in fact their development, commonly called the 'Indus Valley Civilization', also probably grew initially from Magog's visit to Arya/ Mehrgahr, but over time became increasingly assimiliated into the culture of its key Hamite and Shemite trading partners. In particular its main clients Elam and Sumer/Mesopotamia to the far west (from the direction, indeed, that Magog had come from), to whom it became an agricultural production outsourcing centre. So much so that by the time of the arrival and takeover of the famous Vedic Aryans of Rigveda fame from the north in the mid 2nd Millennium BC, the

---

[97] 'Mountain Stone Rock' by the3rdSequence (https://www.the3rdsequence.com /texturedb/) is licenced under CC BY 4.0 (http://creativecommons.org /licenses/by/4.0)

Indus Valley cities had more or less been colonies of Elam/Mesopotamia for hundreds of years. And, despite the spectacular boasts of conquest in the Vedas, the Harappan civilization had already dwindled to almost nothing by the time the Aryans arrived, owing to the drying up of its ancient pasturelands[98].

It would be tempting to see BMAC in the same vein as largely preceding the arrival of the Indo-Aryans, were it not for the many evidences that the Aryans were indeed very definitely in residence there during its golden age. Particularly its being the apparent centre for the production of 'Soma', the famous soporific ritual drug drink frequently referred to in the Rigveda and (as 'Haoma') in the Avesta, whose name and proposed 'narcotic social control' function were borrowed by Aldous Huxley for his famous liberal utopian science fiction novel 'Brave New World'. Sarianidi found large boilers and tools for pressing the ingredients of 'Soma' at Gonur Depe and Ulug Tepe[99]. Its use is testified to as a major part of the spiritual life of both the Avestan culture and in particular the Vedic Aryan culture, where it was associated with their adopted chief deity Indra. For example:

"Mighty is Indra, yea supreme; greatness be his, the Thunderer: Wide as the heaven extends his power. Which aideth those to win them sons, who come as heroes to the fight, or singers loving holy thoughts. His belly, drinking deepest draughts of Soma, like an ocean swells, Like wide streams from the cope of heaven."[100]

and:

"We have drunk the soma; we have become immortal; we have gone to the light; we have found the gods. What can hostility do

---

[98] Madella & Fuller. This was because of reduced sea levels, due to the inexorable retreat of the Ice Age.
[99] Sarianidi, 2003, p.54-55
[100] Rigveda, vol.1, p.14. This is more than reminiscent of the heavily imbibing Magog/Dionysius and his western incarnation, Bacchus.

to us now, and what the malice of a mortal, o immortal one?"[101]

Lines such as this in the Rigveda have led to speculation that Soma had hallucinogenic properties. Sarianidi found dishes with traces of cannabis, poppy and ephedra and believed these to be the ingredients[102], while more conservative commentators note that Zoroastrians in Yazd in Iran were still using a drink called hum or homa in the late 19th Century, which only contained ephedra[103].

So the Iranians were certainly present at BMAC, if not its main residents. As Magogites are invariably a rural, equestrian people, it is possible that the cities of BMAC were founded by or in concert with Shemites, with Josephus testifying that Bactria was founded by Shem's son Gather[104]. But that their settlements provided an urban and trade network that allowed the Magogite, Iranian culture to flourish and grow around them[105]. Such is the antiquity and grandeur of BMAC, one can start to understand the claims of jealousy by the other brothers because of the verdant luxury of 'Airyu's' domain.

---

[101] Rigveda, vol.3, p.265
[102] Sarianidi, 2003, p.54-55; 2008, p.276-277
[103] The references to Haoma in the 'Yasna', the second tier of the Avesta after the Gathas, suggest that the drink, although perceived as bestowing many other benefits, may have been used primarily as an elixir: a health cure to heal the body, increase vitality and preserve long life. There is even a reference here to its use by Yima (Noah) as a method whereby the first generations after the flood lived to great ages: "What man, O H(a)oma! first prepared thee for the corporeal world?...Vivanghvant [the fifth from Gayomart, the Iranian Adam] was the first of men who prepared me for the incarnate world. This blessedness was offered him; this gain did he acquire, that to him was born a son who was Yima, called the brilliant, (he of the many flocks, the most glorious of those yet born, the sunlike-one of men), that he made from his authority both herds and people free from dying, both plants and waters free from drought, and men could eat imperishable food...In the reign of Yima swift of motion was there neither cold nor heat, there was neither age nor death, nor envy demon-made. Like fifteen-yearlings walked the two forth, son and father, in their stature and their form, so long as Yima, son of Vivanghvant ruled, he of the many herds!" (Yasna, p.231-239)
[104] Josephus, vol.4, p.71
[105] Possibly these Shemites were the early 'Jeitun' farmers who appear to have been the progenitors of BMAC.

The Kayanian Kings

As we read on in the Shahnameh we transition to a new phase in the King list. Although Ferdowsi's chronicle moves seamlessly from one era to the other, there is almost certainly a gigantic gap (unfortunately a consequence of the vast, lost portion of Iranian history) of at least a thousand years between the generations of Fereydun, Airyu and possibly Manuchehr (the 'Pishdadian' dynasty) and the next major dynasty in Iran's history, the Kayanians.

At this point in the narrative a new antagonist enters the scene, the 'Turans' to the north of Iran (descended from Airyu's brother and alleged murderer 'Tur', aka Thor/Tyras), with their hated King 'Afrasiab' (also called 'evil world ruler')[106]. Ferdowsi writes that Manuchehr is succeeded by his son Naotar/Nowzar, who is not a successful king. 'Afrasiab' invades from the north and defeats the Iranians. Here the 'Pishdadian' dynasty ends, as two unrelated rulers follow (Uzava and his son Keresespa, possibly transitional composites intended to mask the gap in the timeline), who are also failures. This leads to the election of a new dynasty, the Kayanians or Kayanids, beginning with Kay Kawad[107], who proves his mettle by overcoming Afrasiab's forces in battle[108].

The Kayanian Kings would come to symbolize a golden age in Iranian culture that was a kind of 'Camelot' for them when affairs were as they should be in their kingdom. The Shahnameh states that Kay Kawad moved 'to Pars' and all the Kayanids ruled from a city 'Estakhr' (5 miles from Persepolis) - perhaps symbolizing the beginnings of the western movement that would culminate in the Persian Empire. This was a high point then for Iranian civilization, seen as surpassing even the later heights of the Persian Empire in the nobility of its rule.

---

[106] Shahnameh, p.110-130; Yarshater, p.574
[107] AKA Kabod or Qobad. The 'Kay' comes from the dynasty's surname: 'Kaviani'
[108] Shahnameh, p.134-141. With help from the Afghan hero 'Rostam', the 'Iranian Hercules'.

Fig.60: The Indo-Iranians as they preferred to see themselves: Kayanian rulers exhibiting sumptuous, cultured and delicate finery. Indo-Iranian literature is full of descriptions of such civilized, courtly scenes as this.[109]

---

[109] Illustration by Mirza Ali Qoli Khoei from the 1850 illustrated lithograph edition of the Shahnameh by Kojuri (Kojuri). Also Shahnameh, p.362

Fig.61: The Kayanians at war, as always mounted on horseback and displaying the classic Indo-Iranian spiked head-dress[110].

The Oxus River (Iranian 'Amu Daria') formed the northern border of the somewhat urbanized Indo-Iranian civilization of the Kayanians[111]. Famously the border was established as such when Afrasiab was tricked into agreeing to set it wherever an Iranian archer's arrow would hit the ground after being fired from the Padašxwār mountains in Tabarestān (today's Mount Damavand).

---

[110] Illustration by Mirza Ali Qoli Khoei from the 1850 illustrated lithograph edition of the Shahnameh by Kojuri (Kojuri). Also Shahnameh, p.55
[111] Shahnameh, p.139

According to the legend the champion archer subsequently shot the arrow a huge distance north where it struck a tree on the Oxus[112].

Beyond the Oxus however was 'Turkestan', where dwelt the Turans and their leader Afrasiab, the mortal enemies of the Iranians. The Turans were not part of the Indo-Iranian world. They are very definitely described as 'Aniranian'. Unlike the Scythians to the north-west (who lived above the Caspian Sea around the Volga River moving further and further west towards Europe during this period) who were probably led by Magogites who had originated in Sogdiana, the Turans were apparently a completely alien race to the Iranians who shared none of their heritage and whose values as we shall see were antithetical to theirs.

Perhaps the most celebrated of the Kayanian Kings in the Shahnameh is Kay Kawad's grandson Kay Khosrow, who finally defeats and kills the wicked Afrasiab.

The Kayanian Kings that formed the 'Iranian golden age' were, in the order of succession listed in the Shahnameh:

Kay Kawād
Kay Kāvus
Kay Khosrow
Kay Lohrasp
Vishtaspa
Esfandiyar
Kay Bahman
Humay Chehrzad
Kay Darab
Dara II.

---

[112] Yarshater, p.572. This legendary archer is generally associated with 'Arash', the archer-hero archetype of the Iranian nation. The story surprisingly does not appear in the Shahnameh, but is a staple of other collections of Iranian folk tales, in which the location the arrow was shot from and where it struck sometimes varies. The best known version comes from the 10th Century AD Persian language 'Tarikhnamah' written by Bal'ami

There is some corroboration for the existence of these rulers in the Iberian national chronicle 'Life of Kartli', as some of the Kayanian names appear there as occasional conquerors of Iberia (Georgia). From this we can attempt to approximate a date for their reigns. In the Kartli narrative they feature some time after Iberia has broken free from the subjugation of the later 'Nimrodian' 'Arbitron', and after the news that 'Moses, the friend of God… had crossed through the Red Sea with the twelve tribes'. Of course the medieval chronicler Juansher, writing as part of 'Christendom', may have added that detail in for effect, but nevertheless he clearly had some reason to date the contemporary Iberian events roughly to that period. Juansher writes that at this time:

"Finding the time opportune, the Iberians, aided by the Ossetians, killed the chief of the Iranians while he was diverting himself in the country. They also killed others from his army, and remained unconcerned about the Iranians. However the country of Aghbania/Aghuania and Heret' remained with Iran. After this the king of Iran, named K'ekapos, once more grew powerful. He came to Movkan and Heret' and planned to enter Leket'. But the chief of the Lek was a relation of Xuzanix and a sorcerer. By enchantment he blinded K'ekapos and his soldiers. They turned back and thereupon their eyes were opened. Placing Iberia under taxation, they departed" [113]

The unnamed 'chief' of the Iranians may have been the last pre-Kayanid King of Iran, that would fit with Ferdowsi's chronology, as K'ekapos clearly refers to Kay Kawad/Qabod, whose relative strength in relation to previous Iranian rulers fits the Shahnameh account. Juansher goes on:

"In this period all the T'orgomean peoples, united with the Armenians, stood off from Iran, fortifying cities and keeps. The embittered K'ekapos sent his commander, P'araborot, against the T'orgomeans with many troops. The Armenians and Iberians went before them in Atrpatakan, and striking forth killed many of

---

[113] Life of Kartli, p.8

them. P'araborot fled with a few men. Angered, K'ekapos dispatched his grandson named K'ue Xosrov, son of Biuab the Fair (who was killed by the Turks). The Armenians and Iberians were unable to resist him and generally were trampled beneath his feet. [K'ue Xosrov] designated his officials and built in Atrpatakan a house of prayer, after their faith, then returned to his own country. He commenced fighting the Turks, who had slain his father. Some men of the Turks—twenty-eight houses fled from him and came to the *tanuter* of Mts'xet'a requesting of him a cave on the eastern side of the city. They walled this dwelling place of theirs and named it Sarakine, which means Iron Mine. Since K'ue Xosrov was too preoccupied to concern himself with the Armenians and Iberians, [the latter] gathered strength and killed the Iranian prince and built fortresses." [114]

This could not possibly fit the Shahnameh account more accurately, which leads many commentators to dismiss it as having derived from a proposed medieval Georgian translation of 'Shahnameh'.

After a brief description of Iberia's becoming a cosmopolitan sanctuary for oppressed peoples of the south, there is further mention of Iranian monarchs:

"Now after this, once more still another Iranian king named Spandiar, son of Vashdapish, came against Armenia and Iberia. But when he reached Atrpatakan, he heard the bad tidings that the nation of the Turks had killed his father's brother. He departed thence to T'urk'astan, while Armenia and Iberia relaxed. Following this, Spandiar's son Vahram (also called Artashesh), ruled Iran as king. He was stronger than all the [previous] kings of Iran. He took Babylon and placed under taxation Asorestan, Greece and Iberia."[115]

---

[114] Life of Kartli, p.9
[115] Life of Kartli, p.10

This then appears to refer to the Achaemenid dynasty of the Persian Empire, as only Cyrus conquered Babylon (as well as 'Asorestan' – probably Asia AKA Anatolia). That would date the Kayanians to the first half of the 1st millennium BC. Although approximate, this is key information in understanding the historicity of the Shahnameh. In particular as 'Vashdapish' AKA Vishtaspa (the grandfather of Kay Bahman in the narrative[116]) is well known as being the patron and contemporary of Zoroaster and chief sponsor of the early spread of Zoroastrianism[117]. Thus Zoroaster's life and work can provisionally be dated reasonably simply to around 650-600 BC. In addition, Vishtaspa would then be the real-life 'Achaemenes' of Darian hagiography. Although that does not in any way validate Darius's dynastic legitimacy, it is interesting that this figure, the first 'Zoroastrian' King[118], is the one who often features as the 'founder' of the Achaemenids, an attribution that would be attractive to later chroniclers not wishing to recognise a 'pre-Zoroastrian' Iranian Kingship[119]. Although, it is very odd that the earlier 'Kay' Kings are not generally mentioned in histories of Cyrus.

---

[116] It should be noted then that the Shahnameh's king list is far from exhaustive. There is no mention of Cambyses for example, and we can assume that many other generations are missing with only the most prominent characters featured. And of course only this 'telescoping' of history (a common feature of linear ancient King or ruler lists) could explain the great ages from the proposed Magog 'Iraj'/'Airyu' to Cyrus over a thousand years later.

[117] Vishtaspa is mentioned multiple times by name in the Avesta, including in the earliest 'Gathas', as being a 'friend' of Zoroastrianism. (Gathas, p.22, 142, 185)

[118] Although note the Iberian statement that Kue Kosrow built a house of prayer 'after their faith' - what faith this is is not stated.

[119] Although strangely other traditions like the Sistan (Afghan) history of the same period, codified in the Shahnameh, are by contrast highly critical and disparaging of Vishtaspa as an evil and scheming King (e.g. Shahnameh, p.417)

This rather prosaic evidence for an historical origin of Zoroastrianism nevertheless still often fails to satisfy, and there continue to be many attempts to establish a weightier antiquity to Zoroaster that perpetuate the mystery surrounding his historical origins.[120]

With this recognition then, 'Kay Darab' AKA 'Dara I' would quite sensibly equate to Darius the Great. This identification is confirmed by both figures being celebrated firstly for having established the Persian postal system, and secondly for having used Babylon as their chief residence. It also further illuminates the issue of Dara's parentage, as the Shahnameh states that his mother and predecessor monarch Humay Chehrzad had married her own father (and previous King) Kay Bahman (surely the 'Vahram' of the Iberian text and therefore Cyrus, although if generations have been missed this could be Cambyses) and Dara was the product of this incestuous union[121]. If true, it is no wonder that Darius took such pains to establish his ancestry, nor that a cloud of illegitimacy followed him despite those efforts![122]

---

[120] Moses of Khorene states that Zoroaster taught that Shem (whom he says was known as 'Zrvan' in the East) was the 'origin and father of the gods' and that a son of one of his younter sons 'Tarban' first settled Bactria (p.78-80). This would fit quite well with the dating and origins of the foundation of BMAC, traditionally ascribed to Shem's son Gather (Josephus, vol.4, p.71).

[121] Shahnameh, p.440-451. The question of the identity of Bahman is a difficult one. He has been identified here with Cyrus, based on the 'Life of Kartli' testimony. There is also one other partial corroboration: the incestuous character of 'Humay/Homay' in the Shahnameh bears a strong resemblance to one 'Atossa' in Herodotus and other Greek accounts. In both, she is strongly associated with incest (indeed Zoroastrianism in general has throughout its history been enmired in controversy regarding this practice, known as 'the custom of Pahlavi' (Shahnameh book, p.440)). In Herodotus, as in the Shahnameh, 'Atossa' is a kingmaker and wiley power behind the throne, who marries first her brother Cambyses (and the usurper 'Smerdis'), and then Darius (p.216). In the Shahnameh she bears Darius by her own father, Bahman. In both accounts this character is the daughter of a Persian King, named in Herodotus as Cyrus and in the Shahnameh as Bahman. If all of the incest allegations are true, not only was Humay/Atossa impregnated by her own father, she married that child (Darius) and gave birth to his heir, Xerxes! But regardless of the exact details, the incest assocation suggests strongly that 'Humay' and 'Atossa' are one and the same, and that therefore Cyrus is Bahman.

[122] See Herodotus' comment to this effect re: the Darius inscription (p.217)

Fig.62: Kay Bahman AKA Cyrus the Great, the Two-Horned Ram of Biblical prophecy[123].

The understanding that Kay Bahman (AKA 'Vohuman'[124]) is in fact Cyrus the Great was generally understood by the Sasanians of a later era[125]. Resistance to this rather clear-cut fact among modern and western academic commentators in part stems from their usual ideological reluctance to take historical texts at face value. But, here there is more to it. The sceptics in this case may have good cause to be hesitant about the identification of the characters in the 'Shahnameh', as there is evidence to doubt its chronology as

---

[123] From tiling in the Tekyeh Moaven al-molk in Kermanshah, Iran. This is a Wikimedia image by Farzaaaad2000 (https://en.wikipedia.org/wiki/File:Moaven_Almolk_Tekiye_(Kay_Bahman).jpg) (desaturated) used under CC SA 4.0 (https://creativecommons.org/licenses/by-sa/4.0/deed.en)

[124] The esteem with which this figure is regarded is suggested by his name: 'Vohu Manah' in the Avesta means 'The Good Mind', i.e. righteousness or the righteous path (Gathas, p.256)

[125] Khaleghi-Motlagh, p.489–490

presented. A number of things don't add up. Indeed when studying Iranian history in particular it is hard to escape the conclusion that the picture has been intentionally muddied, confused and misguided by successive chroniclers so as to make it as difficult as possible to see clearly. This is suggested by the relative clarity and utility of the picture that emerges when these impediments are removed.

As we shall see, while the later Kayanian Kings are almost certainly a memory of the Achaemenids, as discussed, there is a strong possibility that significant elements of the earlier narratives surrounding Kays Kawad, Kavus and Khosrow, particularly their interactions and famous feud with the nation of the Turans to their north and its leader Afrasiab, are actually a conflation of events from much later in Iranian history. And that indeed this out of sequence section of the narrative also found its way into the Iberian record during the medieval era, profoundly confusing the Iranian history up to this day. This explains for example why among the predecessors of Cyrus the Great in other sources there is no mention of such great figures as Kay Khosrow and Kay Kawad, nor any large-scale war with any northern neighbour, which has understandably led to the reluctance of conventional historians to recognise Kay Bahman as Cyrus. The generations before him as we have seen were actually dominated by the Cimmerian, Scythian and Median ascendancies, with his reign immediately succeeding that of the Median Astyarges whom he had to defeat in battle to take the throne, not a famous paternal lineage of earlier, 'golden age' Persian Kings. The 'missing Kayanians' are a major, if not the major, problem of ancient Iranian history.

This also explains some other jarring facts in the story. Firstly, the Kayanian Kings being based at Estakhr, basically the Achaemenid ceremonial capital city of Persepolis, from the time of Kay Kawad[126]. Conservatively (taking the Shahnameh narrative in sequence as read and with Bahman as Cyrus) this would put the move to Estakhr at around 700 BC. This is a fantastically early

---

[126] Shahnameh, p.140

point in history for the Iranians already to be based in 'Parsi' or Persia, i.e. Elam (Anshan), the territory the Persians migrated to from the original 'Parsua' in the Zagros Mountains. It is highly unlikely if not impossible.

Secondly the 'House of Prayer after their faith' mentioned as being built by Kay Khosrow in Iberia[127]. This sounds suspiciously like it must have been a Zoroastrian project, otherwise what belief system could this be referring to? But if Bahman is Cyrus and Dara is Darius, Vishtaspa didn't sponsor the beginnings of Zoroastrianism under Zoroaster until after Kay Khosrow's reign[128].

Thirdly the Oxus River as the northern border of the Indo-Iranians is way too far South for this early period in history. As we have seen by the time of the Achaemenid Emperors the original homelands of the Iranians had expanded northward establishing the Silk Road trading Kingdoms of Khorasan[129] and Sogdiana[130], that were flourishing at this time and had been, uninterruptedly, since far ancient times. These Kingdoms are more or less between the two famous rivers of 'Transoxiana': the southern River the Oxus/Amu Darya (these are the Greek/Iranian names) and the northern river the Jaxartes/Syr Darya.

---

[127] Life of Kartli, p.9
[128] The 'Denkard' Zoroastrian historical text first compiled during the 9th Century AD confirms the idea that Khosrow was a strong advocate and sponsor of Zoroastrianism (Denkard, p.5-7)
[129] AKA 'Kharazm', 'Kurasan' or 'Chorasmia'
[130] AKA 'Sogdia', 'Sogd' or 'Sugd'

Fig.63: the famous Oxus (Amu Darya, lower) and Jaxartes (Syr Darya, upper) twin rivers that flow from the Pamir and Tian Shan Mountains north-westwards to the Aral Sea, today encompass most of the territory of Uzbekistan. Anciently this region was known as 'Transoxiana' and contained the Kingdoms of Khorasan (the north-west half) and Sogdiana (the south-east half)

How were they not affected by the incursions as far south as the Oxus by the 'Turans' (indeed further – the arrow had to fly north to reach it)? The Turan war then must come from a different era entirely, as the Northern border of Iran at the time of Cyrus and Darius can be said rather to have been more or less at the Jaxartes, the northern of the two rivers, or at least in the centre of 'Transoxiana'. Between them still lay the ancient Indo-Iranian (not foreign) Kingdoms of Sogdiana and Khorasan that had never been substantially conquered nor overrun by northern enemies of the Iranians[131].

---

[131] Strabo, writing in the 1st Century BC but based on older sources confirms this: "the Oxus River, which forms the boundary between the Bactrians and the Sogdians, and the Iaxartes River. And the Iaxartes forms also the boundary between the Sogdians and the nomads." (vol.2, p.253. See also vol.3, p.248). Strabo also clearly states that Sogdiana was not 'foreign' to the Iranians, but a part of Iranian culture: "The name also of Ariana is extended so as to include some part of Persia, Media, and the north of Bactria and Sogdiana; for these nations speak nearly the same language." (vol.3. p.125)

235

This explains why the conquest of the previous Iranian homelands of Bactria, Margiana, Sogdiana and Khorasan by the Achaemenid Empire was a relatively straightforward one that Cyrus achieved during 546-539 BC[132]. The imperial Aramaic writing system and coin currency were introduced and the region duly became just another drop in the vast administrative ocean of empire (although Sogdiana would enjoy some independence again after 400 BC). There were no Turans on that border nor any record of them at that time to contend with. However, ten years later in his last campaign Cyrus would revisit the region and cross the Jaxartes, to his cost.

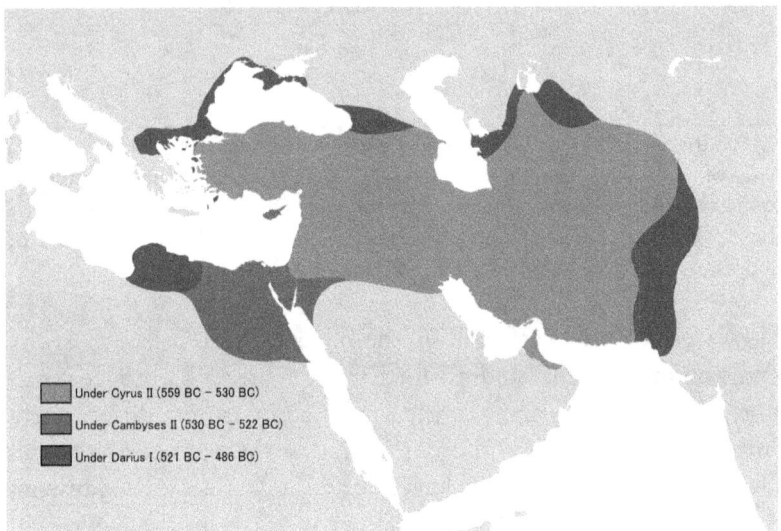

Fig.64: Once again, the Persian or 'Achaemenid' Empire at its furthest extent[133]

---

[132] Herodotus for example does not bother to describe Cyrus's conquering of Bactria (unlike his campaigns in Anatolia, Babylonia or against the Massagetae), merely listing it later as one of the 'Satrapys' or provinces of the Achaemenid Empire: "From the Bactrian tribes as far as the Aegli the tribute received was three hundred and sixty talents. This was the twelfth satrapy." (p.218) He later also discusses Parthians, Chorasmians and Sogdians as part of Darius's army (p.455)

[133] Wikimedia Image by Ali Zifan (https://en.wikipedia.org/wiki/File:Achaemenid _Empire_under_different_kings_(flat_map).svg) (desaturated) used under CC BY SA 4.0 International (https://creativecommons.org/licenses/by-sa/4.0/deed.en)

Cyrus's encroachment beyond Sogdiana and Khorasan

Another nation dwelt beyond the Jaxartes at this time. Not the Turans but the 'Massagetae'[134]; previously encountered pushing the Scythians westward during the 8th Century BC. Generally understood to have been some kind of bastardised and mysterious hybrid of Saka and Scythians, and with the epithet 'Getae' suggesting some relation to the Iranians' northern, wilder co-Magogians the Goths, we discovered earlier that in fact the Massagetae were more or less themselves the 'Saka'. In particular they were the 'Sakā tigraxaudā' or 'pointy-hat-wearing Saka'[135]:

Fig.65: 'Sakā tigraxaudā' on an Apadana relief in Persepolis, Iran, with characteristic pointy hats[136]

---

[134] Although the 'Massagetae' technically probably were 'Turans' (i.e. descended from Tur), they cannot have been the Turans of Kayanian history because they did not dwell on the Oxus River, but rather far to the north beyond Sogdiana.
[135] Olbrycht, p.109; Ivantchik and Licheli. p.19. This term may in fact have referred to all Saka.
[136] Wikimedia image by Mehr News Agency uploaded by Amin Berenjkar (desaturated) used under CC BY 4.0 https://creativecommons.org/licenses/by/4.0/deed.en

As such they were largely Scandinavians, and it is quite possible that they were identical with the Cimmerians, or at least were the Cimmerians' eastern cousins with whom they maintained communication. They are therefore to be distinguished from the Sogdians who were part of the Indo-Iranian (Magogian) civilization to their South[137]. This would make sense as Sogdiana with the other Iranian homelands had fairly easily been incorporated into the Indo-Iranian Persian Empire, but not so the Massagetae to the north of the Jaxartes, who were a completely different kettle of fish. Cyrus crossed the Jaxartes around 530 BC, with the intention of subduing the Massagetae[138].

---

[137] This throws interesting light on the emergence of the Cimmerians into Anatolia in the 8th Century BC. As we have seen that episode was caused by the Scythians pushing the Cimmerians westward from the east, because they were in turn being pushed westward by the Massagetae from their east. If the Cimmerians essentially were the same people group as the Massagetae, there may have been a pan-Steppe antagonism between the Saka/Cimmerians and the Sogdians/Scythians, that would be repeated in Anatolia in the 7th Century BC.

[138] The geography of this conflict, particularly with respect to the identity of the river that Cyrus crossed, is somewhat confused. Herodotus (and Jordanes, p.67) states that the river crossed in the campaign against the Massagetae was the 'Araxes', but that is in Caucasia, so this is generally thought to be a mistake (the Volga is also sometimes mistakenly called the 'Araxes' in Greek sources), especially as Herodotus previously describes the domain of the Massagetae as being 'eastward, toward the rising of the sun, beyond the river Araxes, and opposite the Issedonians'; and states: "On the east [the Caspian Sea] is followed by a vast plain, stretching out interminably before the eye, the greater portion of which is possessed by those Massagetae, against whom Cyrus was now so anxious to make an expedition." (p.89-90). Meanwhile Berossus locates the subsequent battle in the 'Plain of the Daas' (p.29) (probably the 'Dahae'), and Diodorus simply has Cyrus invading 'Scythia' (p.137). While it is not impossible that the river crossed was the Uzboy, between Caspian and Aral Seas, or the Volga, although there is no evidence of a Persian presence that far north, or that the Oxus was intended, with the plain referred to being today's Kyzyl Kum desert in central Transoxiana, it is argued here that it was the Jaxartes. Firstly because of Strabo's clear delineation, reviewed above in footnote 131, secondly because only the 'Sea of Grass' really constitutes a 'vast plain', thirdly because of Herodotus' reference to the proximity of the 'Issedones', and fourthly because of the mention of 'Cyropolis', the city founded by Cyrus (probably at today's 'Kurush', near Ferghana), as being on the Jaxartes in Arrian (vol.1, p.329, 343-355), whose account also has the river as the major border between the Iranians and the 'nomads' or 'Scythians'.

Both Herodotus and Michael the Syrian report that Cyrus the Great met his end campaigning against the Massagetae Queen 'Tomyris'[139]. As usual Herodotus has a colourful story to illustrate this: Cyrus makes a strategic offer of marriage to Tomyris as his army approaches the river. Tomyris rebuffs it and warns him not to encroach on her territory any further, instead challenging him to a pitched battle further south. The canny Cyrus leaves his camp with plenty of intoxicating liquor lying around (that the Massagetae were apparently unfamiliar with). The Massagetae general (and Tomyris's son) Spargapises overtakes the camp and he and his men proceed to drink themselves into a stupor at which point they are massacred by the Persians. Incensed at Cyrus's dishonourable tactics, Tomyris swears vengeance and leads a massive attack on the Persian forces in what Herodotus describes as the fiercest battle of Cyrus's career and of the ancient world, in which the Persians are routed with huge losses and Cyrus is killed, C.529 BC[140]. His body may or may not have been retrieved from the Massagetae but his tomb is in Pasargadae, the site of his victory over Astyarges.

---

[139] Chronicle of Michael the Syrian, p.37 and 1870 edition g92. Also Jordanes, p.67-68, who claims Tomyris as 'Queen of the Getae'

[140] Herodotus, p.91-95; see also Strabo, vol.2, p.246-247. As with the geography, it is also less than perfectly clear exactly who Cyrus fought against, although Herodotus' 'Massagetae' version is best supported. The presence of a female Queen in that version leads Diodorus to conclude that they were Amazons (vol.1, p.137, see also Olbrycht, p.110-111 re: the 'matriarchal' Sauromatae), Jordanes has 'Getae', whom he claims as Goths (p.67), while Ctesias has 'Derbices', aided by Indians with elephants (p.173). Berosssus' 'plain of the Daas' has suggested to some that Cyrus's opponents were the 'Dahae', who resided in Transoxiana and on the east coast of the Caspian Sea, from whom would later come the 'Parthians' (see also Strabo, vol.2, p.245, who puts the 'Dahae' on the west near the Caspian and the Massagetae/Sacae on the east near the Pamir Mountains), but this is unlikely, as the Dahae were also part of Indo-Iranian culture, not foreigners. However, the whole area was fairly fluid, with many bands of equestrian raiders who roamed widely.

Darius' encroachment into Thraco-Cimmeria

As one can see from the top left section of the above map (p.236), the Persian era also saw the encroachment of Empire into the 'Settlement 2' location of some of the Trojan nations in the West as well. Having been progressively pushed out of Anatolia, for five hundred years they had lived unmolested on the northern shores of the Black Sea, a region that was beyond the reach of both Greek and Assyrian imperialists. As we have seen this area of South-West Europe from Thrace next to the Dardanelles up to the Crimea was precisely where the Teresh/Treres and Cimmerians lived and had retreated back to after their last expulsion from Anatolia by the Scythian King Madyes in 620 BC[141]. This, their home base of 'Thraco-Cimmeria', the western territory of the descendants of Thor (including the river 'Tyras' aka the Dniester), had also suffered under the brief 'empire' of their neighbours the Scythians, as the Scythians had pushed westwards overlording much of northern Thraco-Cimmeria during their ascendancy. However, no large-scale Mesopotamian empires had made it so far north[142].

But with Darius's 'Scythian' campaign of 513 BC all that changed. Although as we shall see Darius was not able to find the enemy to face them in pitched battle, rather being subjected to 'Vietnam-style' guerrilla tactics, the fact of his incursion into the area was enough to signal the beginning of the end for the Thracians/Cimmerians/Scandinavians' ability to live in freedom there. The march into this once dreaded territory by imperial armies provided a beachhead that could be emulated and built upon by successive generations of imperialists such as the Greeks and the Romans, and it was.

---

[141] E.g. Strabo, vol.2, p.346: "Treres, who were also Thracians"
[142] Herodotus (e.g. p.136-137) near obsessively repeats the story of an ancient Pharaoh Sesotris who conquered Thrace and Scythia and affected the early population of the Colchians (whom Herodotus believes were descended from Egyptians). However no corroborating witness for this claim (taken from Egyptian priests) has yet come to light. The best guess as to the identity of this Sesotris is Senusret III (reigned 1878-1839 BC), but the evidence of his campaigns strongly suggests he only got as far as Syria.

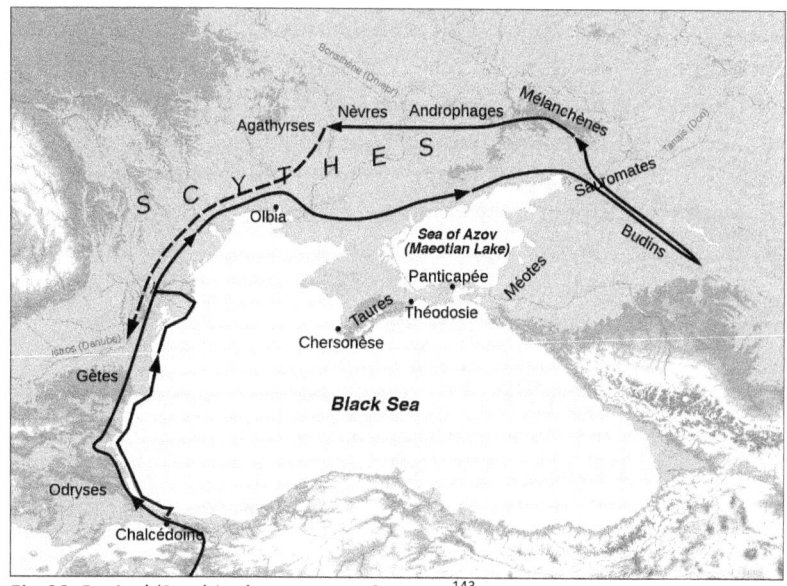

Fig.66: Darius' 'Scythian' campaign of 513 BC[143]

The above map shows how far Darius got, and it was pretty far. Although he stuck to the coast to allow for resupply or potential withdrawal, and being totally unfamiliar with the terrain was not able to find the enemy nor largely disturb their way of life (the previous map flatters Darius in claiming that this area was 'conquered', really only the section below the Danube was occupied or subjected in any real sense), nevertheless this was a shot across the bows to the entire 'Asian' world.

Because of this the campaign provides a fascinating window into that world, one rarely seen and recorded by the imperial civilizations to the South. Firstly it is instructive to note that Darius called this the 'Scythian campaign' and the resulting 'Satrapy' or province of Thrace he called 'Skudra', i.e. 'Scythia'. This of course reflects the Scythians' previous territorial gains over

---

[143] Wikimedia image by Anton Gutsunaev (translated by GrandEscogriffe) (https://commons.wikimedia.org/wiki/File:DariusScythes_fr.svg), desaturated, some labels changed and arrows emboldened. Used under CC BY SA 4.0 (https://creativecommons.org/licenses/by-sa/4.0/deed.en)

the Thraco-Cimmerians, although Darius calling all the nations encountered 'Scythians' was certainly an over-generalising misnomer. 'Scythian' was not necessarily for the Persians a catch-all label for all Northern nations[144], and many of the peoples met with in this 'Scythian campaign' were not 'Scythians' proper, i.e. Magogite-led Riphathians. They were also the descendant nations of (Gothic) Magog and Tiras at least, and possibly some Gomerans and Meschechians. The 'Scythian' label then referred only to the dominant group in the area.

According to Herodotus[145], who wrote extensively of the campaign, the first nation encountered by Darius north of Thrace (called in the above map 'Odryses') were the 'Getae' i.e. the Goths, with the Scythians in turn as their immediate northern neighbours. By this time then it appears the Goths had already moved westward from their previous Maeotic Lake HQ, presumably dislodged by the Scythians' recent expansion, and had settled north of Thrace, a settlement that would become known as 'Dacia'[146]. This migration was the first of many as Thrace/Dacia would become a perennial destination for westward-migrating steppe nations for the next 1500 years. The Goths, now sandwiched into this narrow strip of land below the Danube, were the only group who actually fought Darius, but they were quickly overcome by his massive imperial military apparatus[147]. We can surmise then that the maritime Tirassians (the original Thracians),

---

[144] Herodotus reports that the Persians by contrast did not call the Saka Scyths but rather 'Sacae', who 'had on their heads tall stiff caps rising to a point' and 'carried the battle-axe, or sagaris'. Herodotus disdains this, believing 'They were in truth Amyrgian Scythians, but the Persians called them Sacae, since that is the name which they give to all Scythians.' (Herodotus, p.455) However, he was clearly mistaken about this, as the western, Black Sea Scythians of Darius' campaign and Satrapy were called by the Persians 'Skudra' (Scythians), not 'Sacae'. Herodotus's comments are typical of Greek attempts to group all northern 'barbarians' under the umbrella term 'Scythians', even while his own details expose the folly of his over-simplification. For example his statement (see also p.95) that the 'favourite weapon' of the Massagetae was the battle-axe, a Scandinavian weapon all but unheard of amongst the Indo-Iranian-led Scythians proper.
[145] p.279
[146] Olbrycht, p.104
[147] Herodotus, p.279

had already also been substantially pushed out of the northern section (around the Tyras River) of their ancient homeland and were by that time largely confined in this region to Thrace in the south (the coastal part of which following Darius' invasion would fall under the puppet Odrysian Kingdom) and the Crimean Peninsula itself[148]. Herodotus puts the border between Thrace and Scythia at the Danube River[149].

He also describes the Kings of eight other nations involved in the deliberations on how to deal with Darius's invasion: the Tauri (to whom he gives a more maritime description consistent with their being the Treres or Teresh), the Agathyrsi[150], the Neuri, the Androphagi, the Melanchaeni, the Geloni (whom he states were Greek colonists), the Budini, and the Sauromatae (who were the descendants of the offspring of Scythian men and Amazon women). To all of these he ascribes sharply differing physical characteristics and cultures. And he lists them as 'neighbouring nations' to the Scythians and very separate from them[151].

---

[148] However there is some evidence that Tirassian holdings throughout 'Scythia' were often isolated port cities joined by water and maintained for trade, with the land being under the possession of other nations (see e.g. Herodotus, p.281-282)
[149] Herodotus, p.279, 281
[150] The patriarch of the Agathyrsi, 'Agathyrsus', may have been the biblical 'Ashkenaz'. The territory of the 'godlike Ascanius' (Strabo, vol.2, p.316), AKA 'Ascania', was certainly in this area, in 'Europe, the left side of the Pontus [Black Sea]' (Strabo, vol.3, p.66, quoting Xanthus), in other words almost certainly the civilization of the European Celts (and possibly this was also the origin of the Phrygians), although Olbrycht argues that the 'Agathirsi' were the Getae/ Goths/ Indo-Iranians, who had been pushed westward by the Scythians (Olbrycht, p.104).
[151] Herodotus, p.282-287

Messengers from the Scythians request help from the Kings of these nations. While the Sauromatae, Budini and Geloni are willing, the response from the other Kings, including the Tauri, is as follows (it should be noted that Herodotus' source for all this is not stated):

"If you had not been the first to wrong the Persians, and begin the war, we should have thought the request you make just; - we should then have complied with your wishes, and joined our arms with yours. Now, however, the case stands thus - you, independently of us, invaded the land of the Persians, and so long as God gave you the power, lorded it over them: raised up now by the same God, they are come to do to you the like. We, on our part, did no wrong to these men in the former war, and will not be the first to commit wrong now. If they invade our land, and begin aggressions upon us, we will not suffer them; but, till we see this come to pass, we will remain at home. For we believe that the Persians are not come to attack us, but to punish those who are guilty of first injuring them."[152]

This amazing statement shows how prominently the previous 'war' in Asia (635-590 BC) featured in the minds of these men. Particularly in that this was also the view of the King of the 'Tauri', who, if the Tauri are indeed to be identified as the 'Treres', that seems certain, would of course feel this way, as they had themselves been defeated and ousted from Anatolia and harassed in Thraco-Cimmeria by the very same invading Scythians who now asked for their aid! Who at the behest of the now extinct Assyrian Empire had defeated the Treres and Cimmerians and occupied the territory of their friends the Medes (and by association here the Persians) for 28 years, who in turn now some 75 years later were in a position to invade the Scythians' territory in retaliation.[153]

---

[152] Herodotus, p.287-288

[153] The Cimmerians themselves are absent from this list, but are apparently identical with the 'Tauri', as Herodotus' locates them precisely where 'Kimmerikon' is, at the east of the Crimean Peninsula near the 'Cimmerian Bosporus', and on the Peninsula in general, that he calls 'Taurica' (p.281-2).

Following this, the defenders resolve not to meet Darius in a pitched battle, but rather to harass his column with a scorched earth policy and guerrilla raids.

Suffering from the Scythians' scorched earth policy and unable to find them, apparently towards the easternmost point of the expedition, Darius in frustration sends a letter to the Scythian King Idanthyrsus. This is also highly illuminating as it shows that at the time the Persians at least were quite aware of who the 'Scythian' leaders were, information that for the most part by contrast comes down to us only very sporadically.

According to Herodotus, the communication between them was as follows. Darius sent the message:

"Thou strange man, why dost thou keep on flying before me, when there are two things thou mightest do so easily? If thou deemest thyself able to resist my arms, cease thy wanderings and come, let us engage in battle. Or if thou art conscious that my strength is greater than thine - even so thou shouldest cease to run away - thou hast but to bring thy lord earth and water, and to come at once to a conference."

To which Idanthyrsus replied:

"This is my way, Persian. I never fear men or fly from them. I have not done so in times past, nor do I now fly from thee. There is nothing new or strange in what I do; I only follow my common mode of life in peaceful years. Now I will tell thee why I do not at once join battle with thee. We Scythians have neither towns nor cultivated lands, which might induce us, through fear of their being taken or ravaged, to be in any hurry to fight with you. If, however, you must needs come to blows with us speedily, look you now, there are our fathers' tombs - seek them out, and attempt to meddle with them - then ye shall see whether or no we will fight with you. Till ye do this, be sure we shall not join battle, unless it pleases us. This is my answer to the challenge to fight. As for lords, I acknowledge only Jove my ancestor, and Vesta, the Scythian queen. Earth and water, the tribute thou askedst, I do not send, but thou shalt soon receive more suitable gifts. Last of all, in return for thy calling thyself my lord, I say to thee, 'Go weep.'"[154]

This shows how at this point in history the Scythians were still well aware that Jove AKA Japheth was their actual ancestor and a primary definer of their lifestyle and habits. 'Vesta' was a pagan goddess who is usually claimed as part of Greek culture but clearly is part of the Scythians' culture at this early date.

While the story of Darius' Scythian campaign is frequently referred to as being 'moderately successful' and 'forcing the Scythians to respect the Persian force'[155] in conventional summaries, in fact the account of Herodotus tells a very different story. He relates how the Scythians grew increasingly confident in their military superiority and very nearly captured and destroyed the Persian forces, who slowly came to realise that a military confrontation would not go their way, despite their great resources. And in fact that Darius had balked at a pitched battle with only half of the Scythian main force, after an incident where both sides had been arrayed for battle: some of the Scythians saw a hare and went chasing after it, which convinced Darius that his advisors were right and the Scythians were not scared of him at all.[156] Herodotus describes how the Persian army only very narrowly escaped Scythia with their lives, avoiding being totally massacred because of the actions of the recently-conquered Ionian Greeks, who did not withdraw from Darius's bridge over the Danube after sixty days as he had instructed them to do (and as the Scythians subsequently asked them to keep to, to which they agreed but later reneged).

---

[154] Herodotus, p.290-291
[155] Wikipedia.org: https://en.wikipedia.org/wiki/Scythian_campaign_of_Darius_I, retrieved 16/10/22
[156] Herodotus, p.293

The question of whether or not to leave the bridge and thus to leave Darius cut off and at the mercy of the Scythians was deliberated by the Greeks amongst themselves. The opinion of Histiaeus the Milesian carried the debate:

"It is through Darius," he said, "that we enjoy our thrones in our several states. If his power be overturned, I cannot continue lord of Miletus, nor ye of your cities. For there is not one of them which will not prefer democracy to kingly rule."[157]

Tragically, by this ignoble and ignominious rationale is tyranny always begot of empire.

Herodotus provides a backstory to King Idanthyrsus that further illustrates the perspective of the free and unconquered peoples of the north when faced with both BMAC and in particular GRHF imperial tentacles. In 589 BC one Anacharsis of this same part of Scythia north of the Black Sea, a world traveller, arrived in Athens. A lover of wisdom of sorts, he became a cause celebré of the philosophers there, famous for his droll 'Scythian' wit. However he also allowed himself to be initiated into the Athenian 'Eleusinian Mysteries' pagan cult of the 'mother of the gods' 'Cybele', a type of the Babylonian Queen Semiramis, and to receive Athenian citizenship. Upon his return to Scythia and as part of the deal he had made with the Athenians he attempted to set up worship of the goddess there. His (alleged) brother, King Saulius, upon discovering this, immediately shot and killed him with an arrow. King Saulius was the father of King Idanthyrsus[158]. Here we have a perfect picture of the very 'orientalization' process that the free nations wished to avoid[159]. Anacharsis had been 'assimilated' into a matriarchal pagan witchcraft system of the homosexual Greek culture that was viewed as undignified, dishonourable, treasonous and disgusting to the Scythians, and something that rendered him fundamentally untrustworthy.

---

[157] Herodotus, p.294
[158] Ibid, p.272
[159] See also later, the story of Scylas son of Ariapithes (Herodotus, p.272-275)

While their violence towards him is similarly disgusting and betrays their own equally evil, primitive, ancestor-worshipping paganism (that like all paganism involved human sacrifice), the incident demonstrates precisely the primary importance of the culture clash that was in effect here, that the Scythians clearly and profoundly believed to be absolutely critical to their retaining their liberty.

Darius had failed to secure the Black Sea for the Persian Empire, but he had conquered Thrace and made an imperial beachhead on the Black Sea Coast.

The Classical Era

And so we come to the Classical era, the era of the supremacy in the Mediterranean and Middle Eastern world of the Greco-Roman Homosexual Fascist weltschmertz.

Because of an interest in continuing its inherent vice and degeneracy amongst academics down the millennia, the era has often been euphemistically represented as the bucolic and rustic idyll that its own self-aggrandising propaganda in idols of marble and stone would like it to be seen as, whose pompous and grandiose vanity knew no bounds. In reality the Classical Age was a sewer of sleaze and corruption, during which humanity sunk to a new nadir of beastial violence, brutality and enslavement, characterised by the wanton abandonment of morality in service only to banal self-gratification, infantile vice, pride and human folly. The Greco-Romans were a bunch of unsupervised, foolish, irresponsible children, acting from their basest and vilest desires and lusts.

'Hellenism' was the system devised to allow them to do that. And it was also the process by which the GRHF empire was expanded, through the personal corruption of people in positions of power throughout the Mediterranean world, who would then in turn have to adopt, perpetuate and promote it themselves out of the worst kind of self-interest. Therefore colonies and conquered territories were immediately filled with bathhouses, gymnasiums, statues and the usual accoutrements of Greek homosexual perversion. It was of paramount and prime importance to them in the establishment of these outposts, even more so than trade. They were immediately made to be as much like Greece as possible, with the existing, ancient culture of the surrounding area kept out and walled off from the urban bathhouse 'Hellenic' activities conducted within as early as possible.

Their corruption, and the resulting evil and furtherance of the homosexual slave state was its primary aim. Once a political figure was corrupted into homosexuality and the indulgence of personal vice through mock-religious 'pagan' activities, this addiction was then used as a type of blackmail to turn them into new exploiters of their people and promoters of the Greek system themselves. To go against it or to make any kind of moral stand in the face of its evil was to have to abandon their own, personal self-indulgences and have their own moral failings exposed. This then was the cultural imperialism that had overwhelming primacy in the expansion of GRHF. The idea was to make 'new Greeks', by appealing to local potentates' basest desires. In this way Hellenism was 'franchised' out throughout the Asian world, wherever a local leader could be found who was willing to betray his people.

This was the meaning of the term 'Hellenistic' when applied to later non-Greek Kingdoms and fiefdoms. These outposts to export 'Hellenism' (read GRHF urbanism) were highly isolated to begin with. But after the all-conquering Persian Empire established imperial domination over the north coast of Anatolia, Egypt and the Middle East, and Alexander the Great reconquered virtually the same territory for Greece (with GRHF culture being essentially a creature of, and its promotion being very greatly assisted by, imperial subjugation) these Greek colonies grew fast into large, powerful and wealthy Kingdoms, subjects of whichever of the two imperial poles, GRHF or BMAC, waxed at the time, their loyalties for sale and blowing with the prevailing wind as long as the decadent and amoral, sycophantic creatures of domination who 'ruled' them as puppets were sustained in their tyrannies by the imperial military infrastructure necessary fascistically to oppress the people living under them, and kept amply supplied with wine, entertainments and boy lovers.

The minting of coins after the Lydian fashion became a mania in the Classical world, bringing with it a new level of power disparity between those who minted the coins (the 'Hellenized' rulers) and the general population who were forced to use them. Its popularity was also due to the unprecedented boost it gave to the narcissistic egotism of the grotesques who served the Greek system (very often by homosexual patronage) as the 'Kings' of these Hellenized fiefdoms. This was a new form of vanity whereby their personal face could now be in everybody's lives and hands every day, identified with what controlled their subjects' lives economically, what drove them and what they worked for. The Babylonian spiritual system was in full violence with many Hellenized rulers worshipping themselves as gods and demanding the same devotion from their subjects, on pain of death.

Minting coins was a status symbol and also a major source of evidence on the reigns of the various 'Kings'. However the method is highly flawed in that only those 'Kings' 'Hellenized' and vain enough to want to engage in the morally dubious pursuit of minting coins are thereby involved in the history, one of the gaping failures in conventional treatments of the period. Indeed that is what the vainglorious spirit of the age wanted. Unless a culture was involved in the bathhouse sodomising, idolatrous statue-building, coin-minting GRHF culture, it didn't exist. And that laughable affectation is still cultivated and has its adherents today.

Wealth, narcissistic self-promotion, exploitation of the 'non-Hellenized', the odious indulgence of personal vice and a lack of basic human decency were the order of the day in the 'Classical' world, and it plumbed new depths of human misery and the barbarity of each person against the other.

This catalogue of sordid filth and selfishness would only begin to be toppled around 600 years later by the influence of Jesus Christ of Nazareth[160] and other developments such as the Jewish revolts of 66 and 120 AD and the massive shock annihilation of the cream of the Roman legions by Herman of the Cherusci at the Battle of the Teutoburg Forest in Saxony in 9 AD[161].

---

[160] To a significant extent Gibbon attributed the decline and fall of the Roman Empire to Christianity (Gibbon, vol.3 (1 December 1789) p.632-633)

[161] The victory by the Cherusci was partially a result of the preceding 'Bato War' of 6-9 AD during which Illyrians attempted to win back their independence from the Roman Empire. That war was due to high taxes, food shortages and the cruel and oppressive behaviour of Roman tax collectors. Their leader Bato the Daesitiate is alleged to have stated "You Romans are to blame for this; for you send as guardians of your flocks, not dogs or shepherds, but wolves." This statement aptly describes the fate of all who acquiesce to the velvet chains of subjection to empire.

The Hellenization of the Black Sea Coast

As previously discussed, from very ancient times pre-Classical Greek heroes, notably Heracles and Jason, had ventured into the Black Sea and explored along the North coast of Anatolia. Jason and the Argonauts' voyage in particular made multiple stops on this coast, interacting with the Amazons on its way to Colchis. These isolated trade and exploration trips resulted in a Greek awareness to some extent of the Black Sea coast that was followed up in subsequent centuries by the slow founding of a very few Greek colonies, such as Sinope, founded in 731 BC[162] by Greeks from Miletus, and the aforementioned Gelonus near the Maeotian Lake of the Goths and Scythians, founded perhaps 600 BC. Of Gelonus Herodotus writes:

"The Budini are a large and powerful nation: they have all deep blue eyes, and bright red hair. There is a city in their territory, called Gelonus, which is surrounded with a lofty wall, thirty furlongs each way, built entirely of wood. All the houses in the place and all the temples are of the same material. Here are temples built in honour of the Grecian gods, and adorned after the Greek fashion with images, altars, and shrines, all in wood. There is even a festival, held every third year in honour of Bacchus, at which the natives fall into the Bacchic fury. For the fact is that the Geloni were anciently Greeks, who, being driven out of the factories along the coast, fled to the Budini and took up their abode with them. They still speak a language half Greek, half Scythian."[163]

In particular the areas around the two colonies above grew into Kingdoms that came to be known as the 'Kingdom of Pontus' (the Greek word for 'Sea') that grew around Sinope and its eastern offshoot Trebizond[164], and the 'Bosporan Kingdom' that grew around the north coast of the Black Sea next to the Crimea, home

---

[162] Hewsen, p.39. Although probably first by one of Jason's companions Autolycus (Strabo, vol.2, p.293).
[163] Herodotus, p.284
[164] Although it did not actually include the city of Sinope itself until 183 BC, but thereafter Sinope became its capital (Strabo, vol.2, p.292)

of the Cimmerians, situated to control the trade coming through today's 'Kerch Strait' (the 'Cimmerian Bosporus'[165]) between the Maeotian Lake and the Black Sea (no doubt significantly influenced by Darius' expedition into the region).

These two imperial prostitute states, whose leaders would plumb new depths of degeneracy, lasted throughout the era when the BMAC and GRHF empires alternated in their control of the north Anatolian region. The beginning of their residencies would mark the end of the independence of the ancient peoples of the north Anatolian coast, such as the Amazons, Tubali, Moschoi and Kaskians, who were forced to relocate into the Caucasus Mountains or north of them into 'Scythia' to maintain their liberty. Meanwhile the dwellers on the north coast, Scythians and others, would increasingly be curtailed and hemmed in by the syphilitic growth of the Bosporan Kingdom that attempted to turn them all into 'Greeks'.

There follows a brief summary of these hybrid Hellenic/Trojan states.

---

[165] 'Bosporus' was simply a Greek term denoting a crossing point (originally of cattle), mainly referring to the Dardanelles Strait, the crossing point between Asia and Europe in Anatolia/Thrace. This then was the 'Cimmerian version' of such a crossing point, hence 'Cimmerian Bosporus'.

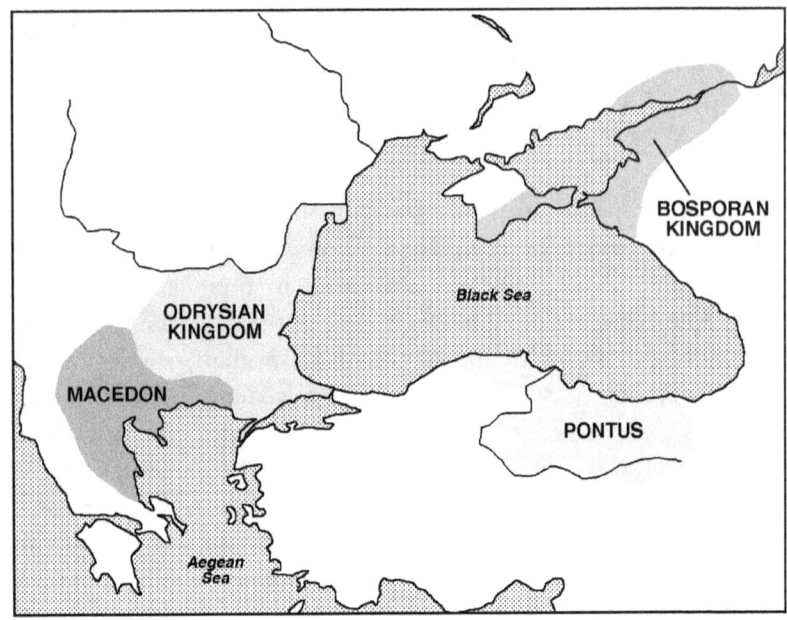

Fig.67: Map of the Black Sea region showing roughly the locations of the Black Sea Hellenistic Kingdoms during the period of approximately 500-100 BC following the Persian Empire's retreat from its zenith in the region.

The Odrysian Kingdom

In the wake of the failure of the Persians to conquer Greece[166], their foothold in Europe collapsed, leaving what is often euphemistically termed a 'power vacuum', which generally means that tyranny, once established, infects a people, so that even when the tyrant is gone, the apparatus of oppression remains, making it much more likely that it will be seized by another tyrant and the tyranny perpetuated, than that the population will be able to throw off tyranny and return back to liberty. This situation is of course in the interests of the larger empires, who would rather deal with petty local potentates as 'client' Kings in order to exploit and enslave that region (letting their 'franchisees' do it for them) than have to bother with the unpredictable qualities of a free people.

---

[166] Darius' son Xerxes had invaded Greece in 490 BC, famously failing to overcome them as his father had the Scythians

Thus, like a virus, Empire breeds Empire[167]. In this way, the zone west of the Dardanelles strait that Darius had been able however briefly to subjugate had been infected with the virus of empire, and the inhabitants of its two nations, previously free, in imitation of their erstwhile imperial occupiers, would now go on to form empires of their own, wittingly or unwittingly following the Greco-Roman and Persian mould, the abuse victim becoming the abuser. These two were Thrace and Macedon.

The first mini-empire to form, almost immediately following the Persian retreat, was the Odrysian Kingdom of Thrace. The apparatus of imperial control was hastily appropriated and used to consolidate a sizeable chunk of the famously disparate Thracians into a state by a warlord 'Odryses' about whom very little is known,[168] other than that he came from the west of the country at the Evros River near Sofia, the capital city of today's Bulgaria.

Ironically the resulting 'Odrysian Kingdom' of Thrace is often seen as the beginnings of Thracian history because of its entry into Mediterranean culture at this point in history (following the 'GRHF' concept of history as only including those cultures that partook in its own Bacchanalian urban bath-house culture), when in fact it was really the beginning of its end. The assumption, no matter how tentatively, of the Greek confines of statehood were not a good fit for the independent-minded descendants of Thor.

---

[167] This phenomenon can be seen throughout political history in the relationships between for example: Assyria/Media, Persia/Macedonia, Macedonia/Maurya, Macedonia/Greco-Bactrian Kingdom, Rome/France

[168] Although the name 'Odryses' is believed to refer to Thor (Gill, vol.1, note for Genesis 10:2)

The Odrysian Kingdom would be a desperate last hurrah for the Western Tirassians in this important section of Thor's ancient homeland, before within four hundred years it inevitably succumbed to the fate of all who fall for the 'you have to change it from the inside' argument for collusion with imperial dictates (i.e. the attempt to manifest one's own culture within a larger universalist power structure in the hopes that it will be respected): complete national annihilation.

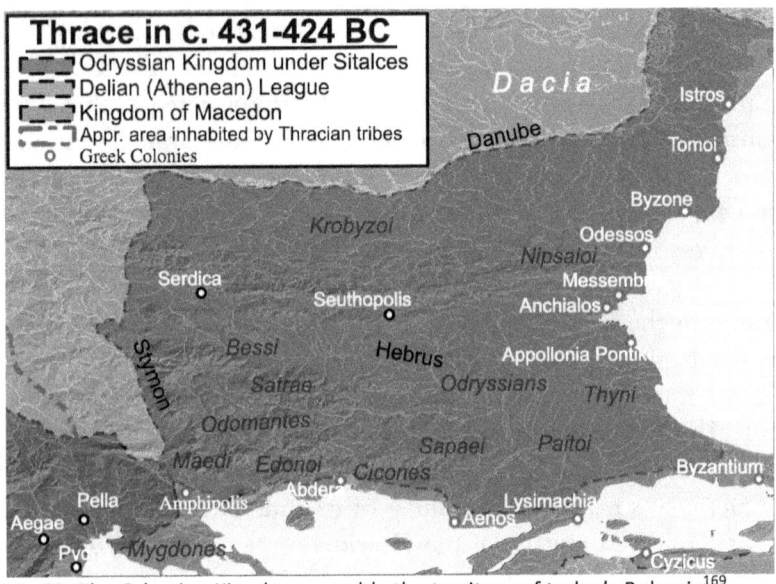

Fig.68: The Odrysian Kingdom, roughly the territory of today's Bulgaria[169]

Thrace of course was one of the super-ancient homelands of the Scandinavian people, and this was the first time it had been 'statised' in the Mediterranean fashion, its leaders before this time currently lost to history, the records probably destroyed as part of the cultural imperialism of later institutional occupiers. North of the Rhodopes mountains was free from the 'Aegean trade' until the invasion of Darius[170] as shown by the lack of any imported

---

[169] Wikimedia Commons image by Alexikoua (https://commons.wikimedia.org/wiki/File:Odrysian.svg) (desaturated) used under CC BY SA 3.0 (https://creativecommons.org/licenses/by-sa/3.0/deed.en)
[170] Archibald, p.93-94

artifacts in the archaeology before then. Therefore despite the fact that the Persians only built a couple of forts (Doriskos and Eion), Darius' brief conquest and subjection of the area to 'tax' extortion was the turning point in Thracian history and the end of Thracian liberty.

Following the Persians, the minting of coins by a Thracian junta began almost immediately. By the mid 5th Century BC the powerful warlord 'Teres I' (being original when it came to names was not one of the qualities associated with the ancient Thracians), a scion of Odryses, had established a mini-empire over the south-eastern section of Thrace and the Getae. We know about him primarily because of his involvement in two neighbouring civil wars of that time.

Firstly among the Scythians to his north. Teres made an alliance with his powerful northern equestrian neighbours by marrying his daughter to the Scythian King Ariapithes[171]. It was soon to be tested. When the Scythians overthrew their King Scylas, Ariapithes' heir, after the Scylian controversy (of which more later) Scylas fled to the Thracians. When he was pursued by his brother Octamasadas, Teres' son Sitalces swapped Scylas for a brother of his who lived among the Scythians. In 438 BC, the Thracian Spartakos (the same traditional Thracian name as the later Thracian freedom fighter and liberator of Roman slaves) seized power in the Hellenic Bosporan Kingdom to the east, further enhancing the power and influence of the Odrysian throne.

The second neighbouring civil war involving the Odrysian Kingdom, now ruled by Teres' son Sitalces, was to its south, a larger and more momentous contest of arms, the 'Greek Cold War' that broke out in 431 BC after centuries of tension between the 'Delian League' of the liberal/commercial city-state of Athens and the 'Peloponnesian League' of the communist/fascist city-state of Sparta.

---

[171] Archibald, p.102–103.

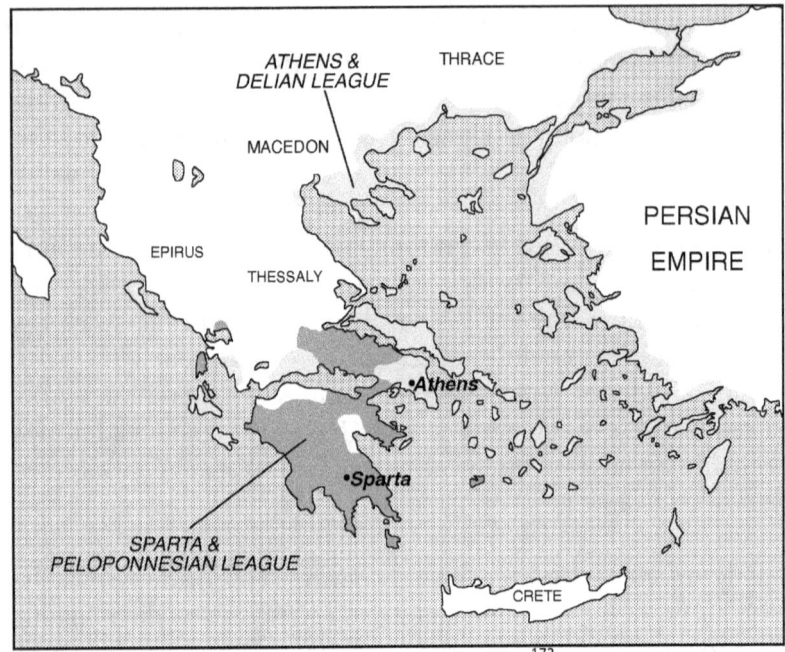

Fig.69: the opposing sides in the Peloponnesian War[172]

The Peloponnesian War is known to us in some detail as its history was recorded by the contemporary historian Thucydides[173]. From Thucydides we know of the great strength of Sitalces' Kingdom. Sitalces made another alliance with the Athenians at this time, marrying the Athenian ambassador's sister and proving a steady ally of the Athenians during the war, service that was not reciprocated when Sitalces went to war with his south-western neighbour Macedon in 428 BC. Athens lost the war to Sparta, and with it its primacy in Greek affairs.

The Odrysian Kingdom continued for some centuries, with notable Kings being Seuthes and Cotys, who defeated the Athenians and conquered the Hellespont in 363 BC. However

---

[172] Map traced from a Wikimedia Commons image by E. Lévy (https://commons.wikimedia.org/wiki/File:Map_Peloponnesian_War_431_BC-en.svg). Used under CC BY SA 3.0 Unported (https://creativecommons.org/licenses/by-sa/3.0/deed.en)
[173] Thucydides

after his death Thrace was conquered by the ambitious new Macedonian King Philip II in 340 BC. After the fracturing of the Greek Empire in 323 BC, a new Thracian King Seuthes III re-established Thracian 'independence'. Seuthes however was highly Hellenized and happy enough (after Thrace's conquest by Macedon) to be one of the 'client Kings' previously discussed, minting coins and building Greek-type towns, in particular his capital (named, in true Greek self-aggrandising style, after himself): 'Seuthopolis'. Duly Thracian fortunes waned and the Odrysian story became one of slow degeneration as the now vassalised Thrace became increasingly weak and dependent on its slave masters over the next 300 years, becoming a client state first of the Seleucids, then the Ptolemies, probably suffering during the Celtic invasion of 270 BC (the Celts subsequently built a Kingdom in the area, 'Tylis') then the Romans by 50 BC and finally was ignominiously made into a Roman province in 46 AD.

The Bosporan Kingdom

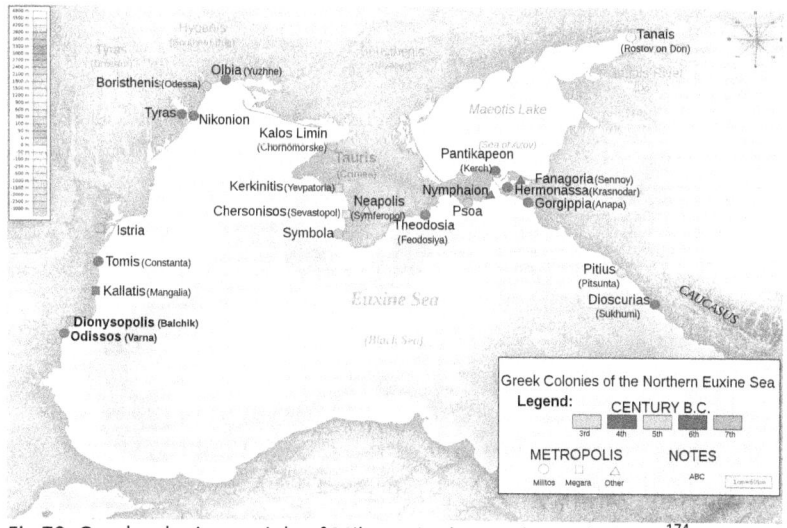

Fig.70: Greek colonies, mainly of Miletus, in the northern Black Sea[174]

---

[174] Wikimedia Commons image by George Tsiagalakis (https://commons.wikimedia.org/wiki/File:Greek_colonies_of_the_Northern_Euxine_Sea_(Black_Sea).svg) (desaturated) used under CC BY SA 4.0 Unported (https://creativecommons.org/licenses/by-sa/4.0/)

The Hellenized state that would most affect the zone of influence of the Scythians was the 'Bosporan Kingdom'.

Of the beginnings of GRHF imperial colonization of the north coast of the Black Sea, Herodotus tells the insightful story of the aforementioned Scylas, who lived C.450 BC. Although long, it is reproduced here in full due to its relevance:

"Ariapithes, the Scythian king, had several sons, among them this Scylas, who was the child, not of a native Scyth, but of a woman of Istria[175]. Bred up by her, Scylas gained an acquaintance with the Greek language and letters. Some time afterwards, Ariapithes was treacherously slain by Spargapithes, king of the Agathyrsi; whereupon Scylas succeeded to the throne, and married one of his father's wives, a woman named Opœa. This Opœa was a Scythian by birth, and had brought Ariapithes a son called Oricus. Now when Scylas found himself king of Scythia, as he disliked the Scythic mode of life, and was attached, by his bringing up, to the manners of the Greeks, he made it his usual practice, whenever he came with his army to the town of the Borysthenites [this is the Greek colony of 'Pontic Olbia' near the mouth of the Dnieper river in today's Ukraine – Ed.], who, according to their own account, are colonists of the Milesians - he made it his practice, I say, to leave the army before the city, and, having entered within the walls by himself, and carefully closed the gates, to exchange his Scythian dress for Grecian garments, and in this attire to walk about the forum, without guards or retinue. The Borysthenites kept watch at the gates, that no Scythian might see the king thus apparelled. Scylas, meanwhile, lived exactly as the Greeks, and even offered sacrifices to the gods according to the Grecian rites. In this way he would pass a month, or more, with the Borysthenites, after which he would clothe himself again in his Scythian dress, and so take his departure. This he did repeatedly, and even built himself a house in Borysthenes, and married a wife there who was a native of the place.

---

[175] Nb. his mother then was not the daughter of Teres, but a different wife

Fig.71: Coins from the Greek colony of 'Pontic Olbia' are a curious hybrid. While their conception is Greek, the Greeks have tried to make them attractive to local tastes as much as possible by featuring on the face of them the horned 'river god' (Hellenized) 'Borysthenes' and on the reverse an axe and a quiver, symbols of the traditional war gear of the Thracians and Scythians respectively[176]

But when the time came that was ordained to bring him woe, the occasion of his ruin was the following. He wanted to be initiated in the Bacchic mysteries, and was on the point of obtaining admission to the rites, when a most strange prodigy occurred to him. The house which he possessed, as I mentioned a short time back, in the city of the Borysthenites, a building of great extent and erected at a vast cost, round which there stood a number of

---

[176] Images used by kind permission of Classical Numismatic Group, LLC (https://cngcoins.com)

sphinxes and griffins carved in white marble, was struck by lightning from on high, and burnt to the ground. Scylas, nevertheless, went on and received the initiation. Now the Scythians are wont to reproach the Greeks with their Bacchanal rage, and to say that it is not reasonable to imagine there is a god who impels men to madness. No sooner, therefore, was Scylas initiated in the Bacchic mysteries than one of the Borysthenites went and carried the news to the Scythians "You Scyths laugh at us" he said, "because we rave when the god seizes us. But now our god has seized upon your king, who raves like us, and is maddened by the influence. If you think I do not tell you true, come with me, and I will show him to you." The chiefs of the Scythians went with the man accordingly, and the Borysthenite, conducting them into the city, placed them secretly on one of the towers. Presently Scylas passed by with the band of revellers, raving like the rest, and was seen by the watchers. Regarding the matter as a very great misfortune they instantly departed, and came and told the army what they had witnessed.

When, therefore, Scylas, after leaving Borysthenes, was about returning home, the Scythians broke out into revolt. They put at their head Octamasadas, grandson (on the mother's side) of Teres. Then Scylas, when he learned the danger with which he was threatened, and the reason of the disturbance, made his escape to Thrace.

Octamasadas, discovering whither he had fled, marched after him, and had reached the Ister [Danube], when he was met by the forces of the Thracians. The two armies were about to engage, but before they joined battle, Sitalces sent a message to Octamasadas to this effect – "Why should there be trial of arms betwixt thee and me? Thou art my own sister's son, and thou hast in thy keeping my brother. Surrender him into my hands, and I will give thy Scylas back to thee. So neither thou nor I will risk our armies." Sitalces sent this message to Octamasadas, by a herald, and Octamasadas, with whom a brother of Sitalces had formerly taken refuge, accepted the terms. He surrendered his own uncle to Sitalces, and obtained in exchange his brother Scylas. Sitalces took his brother with him and withdrew; but Octamasadas beheaded Scylas upon the spot. Thus rigidly do the Scythians maintain their own customs, and thus severely do they punish such as adopt foreign usages."[177]

From such inauspicious beginnings, but immediately after Darius' incursion into 'Scythian' territory on the north coast of the Black Sea, was soon founded the 'Bosporan Kingdom', based on economic ties mainly with Athens to whom the state exported fish, slaves and wheat, but as above heavily influenced by the Scythians, who had wiped out many early Greek colonies when they had conquered the area in the 7th Century BC. As Herodotus attests the Maeotian Lake was still entirely frozen during winter (except for the port of Theodosia), but due to Athenian demand for grain in the wake of the Peloponnesian war, despite Scythian depredations, the state grew - out of the lust for Athenian silver. Initially under a dynasty, the 'Archeanactids', but soon overthrown by Spartokus around 438 BC. The resulting 'Spartocid' dynasty would rule the Bosporan Kingdom slave state until 110 BC. Spartokus may have been Thracian or may have been a Scytho-Greek like many of the denizens of the Kingdom as indeed was its hybrid character in general.

Where exactly the Cimmerians/Tauri were during this time is unclear. They were apparently still in the area when Darius came according to Herodotus' story about their lack of enthusiasm for aiding the Scythians to resist him. Traditionally they resided on the Crimean peninsula itself (hence the common name for the Kerch Strait at that time: the 'Cimmerian Bosporus') and it is likely that the urbanist Greek client Kingdom of Bosporus did not actually extend far beyond the walls of its mercantile port cities. Indeed it had a very tough time even maintaining them against the more or less hostile Scythian culture surrounding them. In this atmosphere of relative liberty against GRHF aggression, the Cimmerians/ Crimeans were apparently able to live relatively undisturbed – for the moment.

---

[177] Herodotus, p.273-275. This quote taken from the 1862 John Murray Edition

Pontus

Fig.72: Map showing the Kingdom of Pontus in dark shading[178]

The Kingdom of Pontus that occupied the territory roughly from the Thermodon River that in ancient times had been the Amazon capital eastward to Colchis was a Persian project of the Achaemenid occupation and carried on Indo-Iranian culture internally. However its Kings were only too happy to play the part of Hellenists for the benefit of the Greco-Romans. In this way Pontus became a middle ground much like its neighbour Armenia that was both fought over and simultaneously played off both sides against each other, in the titanic contest between the GRHF and BMAC imperial continuums over the centuries.

Its dynasty, put in place by the Persians, continued through the ravages of multiple empires for five hundred years, many of the Kings being named 'Mithridates', highlighting the growth in

---

[178] Public Domain image from Wikimedia Commons, by Javier1212

popularity of the pagan sun (in the person of 'Mithras') worshipping cult around the middle east. It celebrated the 'birth of the sun'/Mithras on the winter equinox that was around that time on 25th December. In fact this sun worship had been part of the Babylonian satanic system from its beginning, with Nimrod having been worshipped as a type of the sun (the origin of today's festival of 'Christmas'), but the Mithridadic version of it became extremely popular during the Classical and Hellenistic eras.

After the splitting up of the short-lived Greek Empire, the double-sided Kingdom of Pontus became an influential node in the 're-Iranisation' process of the Zagros Mountains area, before being conquered by the Roman Empire in 66 BC.

Macedon

So the Persians had faltered in their attempts to conquer Greece. They would still enjoy close to that high water mark of territorial expansion for another hundred and fifty years, but slowly the momentum would swing against them as the GRHF culture in turn flexed its muscles following this demonstration of its own potency in stopping the Achaemenid Empire in its tracks. But there was one area to the north of the Greek world that had been conquered, and well-learnt the evil methods of empire: Macedon.

Diodorus states that Macedonia was founded by Dionysius' son Macedo, who went with Dionysius on the India trip and was left to rule this land above Greece when the return leg crossed into Southern Europe[179].

---

[179] This intriguing detail lends credence to the idea that Perseus, the founder of Mycenae, was also a son or descendant of Magog (Dionysius), sired or left in the area of Greece (or the Zagros mountains) during this same visit. This in turn raises the possibility of a connection between Dionysius and 'Danaus', legendary founder of Argos, both hailing from Egypt (although Manetho has a much later date for Danaus than Dionysius – by over 500 years), that in turn raises the further possibility of a connection between Greek Danaans or Denyen and Irish (Magogian) Tuatha de Danann. Eusebius: "[Cephalion] says...that [when Belimus ruled over Assyria,] Perseus, [son] of Danae arrived in his land with 100 ships. He was escaping from Semele's son, Dionysius. After describing the defeat of Perseus by Dionysius, [Cephalion] says that in later times, when Pannyas ruled over the

The Macedonians, previously a free people situated with Illyria to their west, Greece to their south and Thrace to their northeast, a buffer state between the Greek and non-Hellenized worlds, that had been peripheral to and ambivalent about the benefits of Greek bath-house culture, now after a period as a close ally of the Persian occupation embraced it wholeheartedly, and began a period of intense 'orientalizing' that would lead to its exporting of GRHF culture around the globe.

Macedonia warred with Athens during the 5th Century BC and sided with Sparta during the Peloponnesian war, before swapping sides to join Athens. From 399 to 393 BC a state of anarchy in the Kingdom ensued from King Archelaus I's assassination, resulting from the fallout of a homosexual affair with court page boys. And Macedonia was often in conflicts with the neighbouring states of Thrace, Illyria, Thessaly and the Chalcidian League.

Eventually in 359 BC the throne of Macedon fell fatefully to the twenty-four year old politician and diplomat Philip II. Philip was a gifted, energetic and highly ambitious, but also cynical and shrewd administrator, politician and diplomat as well as an excellent military planner. He transformed the Macedonian army into a ruthlessly efficient machine, influenced probably by the Theban General Epaminondas. To expand his holdings and placate erstwhile local enemies, he unashamedly married sisters and daughters of neighbouring Kings, seven in all. He also maintained ties with the Achaemenid Persian empire now having retreated back across the Hellespont to Asia, an awareness of Persian methodology that would come in handy for the Macedonians later.

Assyrians, the Argonauts sailed up the Phasis River to Mende' in Colchis." (Eusebius, Chronicle, Part 1, p.17) Wherever this 'defeat of Perseus by Dionysius' (whom we may now surely presume to have been his own paternal ancestor) occurred, the account appears to be describing the founding of Persia.

From 357 BC Philip began a programme of aggressive military action against surrounding states, with a particular penchant for founding or refounding cities named after himself. This included a successful war in 349 BC against the interests of Athens and the Chalcidian League. Philip formed the League of Corinth in 338 BC of most major Greek city-states together (except Sparta) for the purpose of nothing less than a wholesale invasion of the Achaemenid Empire to re-conquer the previously Greek Aegean colonies. The rationale for this was, aside from personal ambition and the wealth to be acquired from the project, the fear among Greeks of another Persian invasion, with the capable Persian Emperor Artaxerxes III tightening his grip on Anatolia.

Philip was the quintessential Hellenist. An obedient lackey of the GRHF system and an enthusiast of its repulsive methods for enslaving others. He retained the services of the Athenian philosopher Aristotle, who had been educated by a prior philosopher Plato, who had in turn been educated by a prior philosopher Socrates, to educate his son and heir Alexander.

PART 4: Exit Strategy, 350 BC-100 AD

The He-Goat from the West

Aristotle's cosmology would underpin GRHF theology for the next two thousand years, until his earth-centralism was superceded by the more scientific heliocentrism of Copernicus and Galileo during the renaissance, so it was appropriate that Alexander would become its biggest cultural exporter. Or at least its most geographically extensive, as the Greek hold on his conquests would be brief and somewhat shallow but nevertheless influential.

The Biblical prophet Daniel, writing around 550 BC, after describing the rise of the 'Two-Horned Ram', or Medo-Persia, continued:

"I saw the ram pushing westward, and northward, and southward; so that no beasts might stand before him, neither was there any that could deliver out of his hand; but he did according to his will, and became great.

And as I was considering, behold, an he goat came from the west on the face of the whole earth, and touched not the ground: and the goat had a notable horn between his eyes.

And he came to the ram that had two horns, which I had seen standing before the river, and ran unto him in the fury of his power. And I saw him come close unto the ram, and he was moved with choler against him, and smote the ram, and brake his two horns: and there was no power in the ram to stand before him, but he cast him down to the ground, and stamped upon him: and there was none that could deliver the ram out of his hand.

Therefore the he goat waxed very great: and when he was strong, the great horn was broken; and for it came up four notable ones toward the four winds of heaven."[1]

---

[1] Tanakh, p.551

From 336 BC when he inherited the Macedonian throne after Philip was abruptly murdered by his bodyguard (an assassination probably procured by Alexander and his mother Olympias), 'Alexander the Great' as he would come to be known immediately put into action his father's plans and aggressively began the invasion of Asia starting right next door to Macedonia. Full of youthful vigour and enthusiasm and in the first flush of enjoyment at having inherited the throne, he would try his luck to see how far he got. With the well-planned structure of Philip's military machine at his disposal, and serendipitously coinciding with ripe conditions for regime change in the moment, he got pretty far. Further than anyone imagined likely or even possible. The copious tinder of disaffection with the ailing and creaking Achaemenid system across the Middle-East went up like a powder-keg.

Alexander's genius was that he didn't stop to consolidate or slow down. The speed and momentum of his domino-toppling conquests did not give the next town or stronghold enough time to prepare a defence. He was at the gates almost before they had heard of his approach.

Alexander extraordinarily continued on until he had conquered virtually the entire territory previously conquered by the Persian Empire (except for northern Anatolia and Armenia), all the way to India and Bactria. Before long the whole Eurasian continent south of the Black and Caspian seas had been swept over by fast-moving, skirt-wearing Greeks (like most of the leaders of the Classical world, Alexander was a practising homosexual).

In reality the Achaemenid structure with its efficient roads, postage and administration systems provided extremely well for this fast transit through its territory, and the Macedonian familiarity with Persian methods did the rest. Once one Satrapy was conquered the set-up of most of the others was similarly understood and the pattern of conquest could be replicated ad infinitum with the momentum building upon itself.

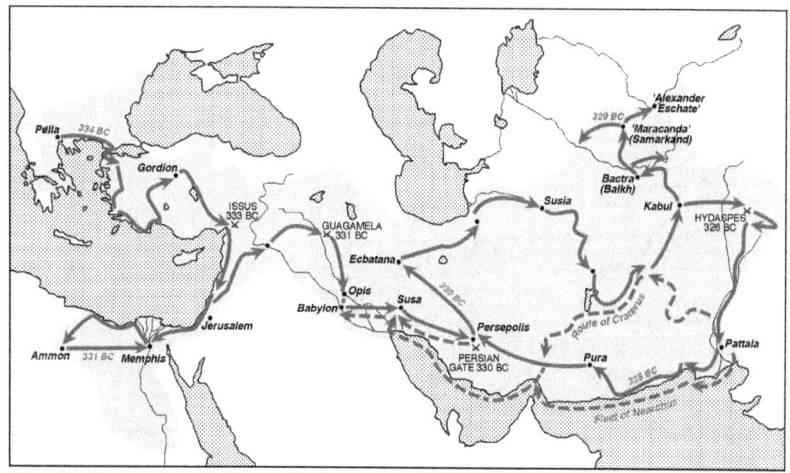

Fig.73: the path of Alexander's empire-busting and empire re-establishing route[2]

The impressive speed and extent of Alexander's military achievements (in fact owing much to the preparations of his murdered father) is too often allowed to gloss over the reality that Alexander was also a despicable tyrant, patricide, murderer and megalomaniac. In true Classical form he attempted to have himself worshipped as a god, ordering his men to bow down before him (which they refused to do). As is inherent in GRHF culture he would also frequently and arbitrarily murder underlings and members of his staff if they displeased him.

Like Philip, Alexander founded cities called 'Alexandria' after himself. He even got as far as Sogdiana (famously overcoming the 'Sogdian rock' fortress), founding a city in the lush Ferghana Valley called 'Alexandria Eschate'[3], meaning 'Alexandria the furthest'. Indeed it was, because the Greeks never penetrated the Pamir and Tian Shan Mountains at the end of the Ferghana Valley, remaining perfectly ignorant of the countless wonders and riches that lay just beyond.

---

[2] Map based on Wikimedia Commons image by Generic Mapping Tools (https://commons.wikimedia.org/wiki/File:MacedonEmpire.jpg), used under CC BY SA 3.0 Unported (https://creativecommons.org/licenses/by-sa/3.0/deed.en)
[3] Almost certainly on the site of Cyrus's previous 'Cyropolis' (today's 'Khujend')

Fig.74: the 'Alexandrias' in Indo-Iran. Most were established on the site of existing settlements that defaulted to their previous names within a few generations. Note also 'Bucephala', named after Alexander's horse.[4]

---

[4] 'Mountain Stone Rock' by the3rdSequence (https://www.the3rdsequence.com/texturedb /) is licenced under CC BY 4.0 (http://creativecommons.org/licenses/by/4.0)

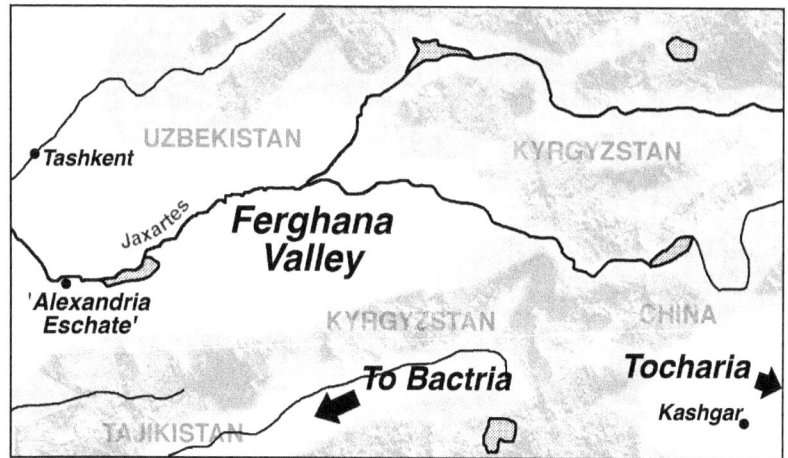

Fig.75: the lush Ferghana Valley. The great riches of Tocharia and China lay just beyond the mountain pass at its east, never dreamed of by the GRHF imperialists.[5]

As with all such fast conquests however, it didn't last long. Alexander's winnings would be for others to administer. He was struck down (appropriately enough in the palace of Nebuchadnezzar in Babylon) in 323 BC at the age of 32[6].

---

[5] 'Mountain Stone Rock' by the3rdSequence (https://www.the3rdsequence.com/texturedb/) is licenced under CC BY 4.0 (http://creativecommons.org/licenses/by/4.0)

[6] Probably of Malaria or Typhoid, although others have suspected poisoning, with Macedonian statesman Antipater most often accused of being the culprit.

True to the prophecy, the freshly conquered Greek Empire was then divided up amongst four of his generals: Cassander, Lysimachus, Ptolemy and Seleucus - AKA the four 'Diadochi' - who immediately fought against each other for twenty years, with their territories fast degenerating into the vile GRHF petty tyranny 'client Kingdoms' run by corrupt local potentates previously described, increasingly fracturing into smaller and smaller fiefdoms.

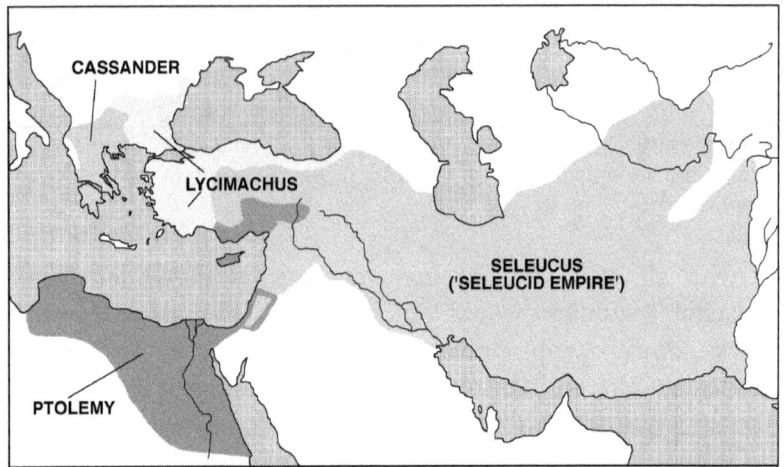

Fig.76: the Greek empire as split up after the death of Alexander the Great into the territories of the four 'Diadochi'[7]

---

[7] Map based on Wikimedia image by Captain_Blood, Luigi Chiesa and Homo Lupus (https:// commons.wikimedia.org/wiki/File:Diadochi_LA.svg), used and published under CC BY SA 3.0 Unported (https://creativecommons.org/licenses/by-sa/3.0/deed.en)

The Greco-Bactrian Kingdom

We have already looked at a few of these 'Hellenistic' Kingdoms, and there were many, many more over the following centuries. But for now our attention remains in this furthest north-east sector of the fragmented empire of Alexander, to study one in particular, the 'Greco-Bactrian' Kingdom:

Fig.77: The 'Greco-Bactrian' Kingdom at its geographical height around 170 BC[8]

This region, that included the ancient heartland of the Iranians in Bactria, Margiana, Arya and Khorasan, was tremendously wealthy. Bactria, the 'land of a thousand golden cities', was in particular a trading powerhouse because of its Silk Road location and its relatively protected shelter within a giant valley of the Pamir Mountains. This wealth was the reason why Diodotus, the Satrap of Greco-Bactria under the post-Alexandrian Seleucid Empire, felt able in 250 BC to secede from the Seleucids and form his own sub-empire. The splintering off of Greco-Bactria was part of a general disintegration of the Seleucid Empire during the 240s BC probably catalysed by the events of the Third Syrian War

---

[8] Wikimedia image by World Imaging (https://commons.wikimedia.org/wiki/File:Greco-BactrianKingdomMap.jpg) (desaturated), used under CC BY SA 3.0 (https://creative commons.org/licenses/by-sa/3.0/deed.en)

275

during which the Seleucids were decisively defeated by the post-Alexandrian Ptolemaic Empire of Egypt. Following this war in 247 BC the Greco-Bactrians' western neighbour Satrapy of Parthia also seceded under its Seleucid Satrap Andragorus, of which more later.

Diodotus, his son Diodotus II and Euthydemus, another Greek who in turn overthrew the Diodotian dynasty in 225 BC, withstood multiple invasions from the west by the Seleucids intended to bring them back into the Seleucid empire, particularly by Antiochus III in 210 BC. These failed and the Greco-Bactrian Kingdom was recognised by the Seleucids around 206 BC. Euthydemus claimed that his state should be applauded for being a buffer state seeing that great 'hordes of nomads' were close at hand[9].

The Kingdom then was a major exporter of 'GRHF' culture in the east. More so than many other Hellenistic Kingdoms further west, closer to Greece. One reason for this was the policy of the Achaemenid rulers of the old Persian Empire three centuries earlier to exile troublesome polities and resettle them at the other end of the empire, thus neutralising their potential to cause problems. This resulted in many Greeks over the centuries being sent to the Bactria region, so Alexander's conquest of it therefore met with greater recognition than in many other places, and subsequent attempts to 'Hellenize' it made more inroads.

The Greco-Bactrian Kingdom thrived following the peace treaty with the Seleucids. Using its wealth to expand, it pushed into India establishing the Indo-Greek Kingdom in 175 BC that was a major crucible of Buddhism. Various fallouts ensued: the Greco-Bactrian throne was once again overthrown by a general, who was then attacked by the Indo-Greek leader, who was defeated when the new Greco-Bactrian Emperor invaded India, where he was nonetheless eventually defeated as well and, in true Alexandrian style, murdered by his own son, who ran him over with a chariot.[10]

---

[9] Polybius, vol.4, p.301
[10] Justin, p.401

This infighting weakened the bastardised Greco-Bactrian state and by 141 BC it was subsequently conquered by its erstwhile western ally, the growing state of Parthia.

Greece turns into Rome and Persia turns into Parthia

The Parthian Empire is one of those historical subjects about which western awareness has been appallingly lacking for much of its history. Only now the true breadth of this extensive empire and the comprehensively Indo-Iranian nature of its culture are fully being understood.

This is because of historical propaganda wrought by its perennial enemy to the west, the Roman Empire. At this point in history, the mid 3rd Century BC, there was a transfer of power in both GRHF and BMAC imperial continuums at virtually exactly the same time. The Greek Empire was giving place to a new, even more virulently and cynically 'GRHF' power than itself, the aggressive Roman Republic based in west-central Italy. This change occurred over some centuries, with the epochal Roman victory over its nemesis the rival Carthaginian Empire and its leader Hannibal in the Punic Wars (264-146 BC) that resulted in Rome's unrivalled supremacy in the western Mediterranean region, being perhaps the turning point.

During the same period, Indo-Iranian dynasts in the east were throwing off the post-Alexandrian Seleucid occupation and re-asserting themselves as heirs of the once-all-conquering Persian Empire. The defeat of the Seleucids and thereby the re-establishment of Parthian and subsequently general Indo-Iranian independence by Arsaces I (aided by the Greco-Bactrian Kingdom) in 247 BC was considered by them the key date. This eastern transition has been obscured in conventional history, largely because of the exceptionally great pains taken by Roman leaders (particularly propaganda specialist Augustus) to mask the Parthian Empire's equivalence to Rome in size, power, prestige, longevity and cultural influence.

The reality is that the contest between these empires, that would last until the 3rd Century AD[11], was very close to being an even fight. In fact both empires attempted in their hagiographies to present the other as being their vassals or servants. Neither was ever really true. If anything Parthia may have had the slight edge because of its shocking total rout of the Roman forces in one of the major military confrontations between the two, the Battle of Carrhae in 53 BC. This defeat resulted in the death of one of the major figures of Roman history, who had been one of the three 'Triumvir' dictators to rule Rome (along with Caesar and Pompey) at the end of the Roman Republic: the big-city gangster Kingpin who had run the corruption rackets within the city of Rome itself, Marcus Licinius Crassus. Apparently his back-room wheeler dealing and slimy street-smarts had not equipped him for the open field of battle, where he was soundly and embarrassingly defeated, with the vast Roman Army he had taken command of totally destroyed.

Armenia in particular became a key battleground pawn in the struggle between these two empires, especially after Rome finally conquered the Kingdom of Pontus in 66 BC, that had alternately been possessed or controlled by one or the other.

On the whole though, the pair were evenly matched throughout their ascendancies and could not advance significantly upon one another. The Euphrates River became the default boundary between the two, rarely crossed for long by either empire.

---

[11] Longer if one includes the continuation of the rivalry during the era of the Sasanian Empire of the Persians and the Byzantine Empire of the Romans

The Parthians: Indo-Iranians take back Iran

It was from the area at the south-east of the Caspian Sea, near the ancient BMAC settlements of Gonur Depe and Altyn Depe, an area that had been a semi-nomadic, semi-Scythian outlying region of the Persian Empire full of rugged horsemanship and a healthy scepticism of empire, that would come the dynasty that would re-establish Indo-Iranian hegemony in Persia.

This was the territory of the 'Dahae', a confederation of three tribes including the Scytho-Iranian 'Parni'[12], who had possibly migrated from the north and perhaps were not even Zoroastrians or only recently so[13].

The catalyst for Iran's independence from the Greeks, that must have seemed like a serendipitous boon to them after 80 years of Greek occupation, was the secession of the Greek local ruler (Satrap) Andragoras from the Seleucid Empire, in the wake of a brief Seleucid succession crisis when Ptolemy III temporarily seized the Seleucid capital of Antioch in Syria around 246 BC.

Andragoras' opportunistic throne-grab would not prove to be such a great idea, as it also provided a moment of opportunity for the resentful Iranian populations now under his control. This opportunity was grasped by one Arsaces, leader of the Parni.

Around 238 BC Arsaces[14] invaded Parthia and took possession of its administrative capital Kabuchan, soon after hunting down and destroying the hapless Andragoras.

---

[12] Strabo, vol.2, p.245-246
[13] Historians such as Richard Foltz and Parvaneh Pourshariati have argued that the Arsacids were primarily Mithraists, i.e worshippers of Mithra (Foltz, p.22).
[14] Arsaces was previously thought to have had a brother, Tiridates, however more recent research has concluded that Tiridates is fictional. This is another instance of the curious phenomenon whereby chroniclers have added imaginary brothers (such as Remus and Horsa) to stories of famous founding figures, perhaps to add perceived lustre and credibility to the lineage.

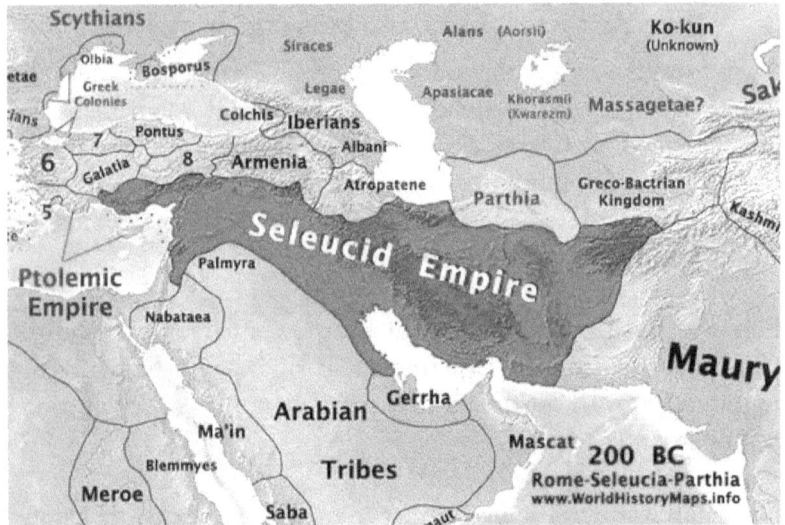

Fig.78: the location and position relative to the surrounding powers of Parthia c. 200 BC[15]

Iranians were once again in a position of independence and sovereignty in Iran. However the restoration of Iranian fortunes was by no means achieved. This was merely a foothold at the edge of a giant empire. The path to a status and national prosperity and security with any remote resemblance to the great Medo-Persian Empire of old was to be a long, uphill struggle that would take a hundred years or more.

Arsaces, from the position of a tribal chieftain now in tentative possession of a Greek state whose culture, coinage, administration and armed forces were thoroughly Greek, was however a dogged prosecutor of this very, albeit remote, objective.

But his reign would be characterised by continued guerrilla warfare against Seleucid attempts at reconquest and the new much more Hellenised Greco-Bactrian Kingdom to his east. In particular in 228 BC he was forced to retreat his mobile, equestrian forces

---

[15] Detail from Wikimedia image by Talessman (https://commons.wikimedia.org/wiki/File:Rome-Seleucia-Parthia_200bc.jpg) (desaturated), used under CC BY SA 3.0 Unported (https://creativecommons.org/licenses/by-sa/3.0/deed.en)

northwards into Khorasan/Scythian territory as Seleucus II briefly reconquered Parthia. But Seleucus soon had to withdraw allowing Arsaces to recover[16]. Nevertheless Arsaces managed to found multiple towns and over time strengthen the Parni government and its hold over Parthia.

While adopting the Greek state apparatus, in particular coinage, that bore inscriptions in Greek, Arsaces cannily and subtly (perhaps to avoid alienating the still-powerful Greek interests in the region) promoted ideas reminiscent of Iranian culture in his themes. He did not call himself 'King' (in the Greek sense) but rather 'Karny', a title for Achaemenid military commanders.

Fig.79: coin of Arsaces[17]

Arsaces was able to pass Parthia on to his son Arsaces II in 217 BC. His descendants, the Arsacid dynasty, would rule the Parthian Empire (Nb. this is an exonym, it should probably be called the 'Iranian' Empire) until 224 AD, and parts of Armenia, Albania and Iberia until as late as the 6th Century AD.

---

[16] The Seleucids would repeat this brief reconquest then withdrawal in 209 BC under Antiochus III
[17] Image used by kind permission of Classical Numismatic Group, LLC (https://cngcoins.com)

Parthia then, continued to grow and gain in strength, all the while increasingly making use of both the cultural and the military, diplomatic and administrative heritage of the old Persian Empire to expand its reach, slowly 'de-Greecing' the region and returning it to an Iranian zone.

This was largely the work of Mithridates I, Arsaces' supposed great grandnephew. While groundwork had been laid by his predecessor Phraates, it was Mithridates who fundamentally transformed the petty Kingdom of Parthia into something that began to look more like the ancient Persian Empire. He conquered the BMAC region, including the Greco-Bactrian Kingdom in 163-155 BC, then Media in 147 BC, and finally Babylonia the centre of empire itself in 141 BC. Mithridates finally pronounced himself 'King of Kings', the title used by Cyrus and the subsequent Persian Emperors.

Identification of the Turans and Afrasiab

Here we shall return to the story of Iranian history we left earlier, with its mysterious narrative of the Iranians' perennial struggle with their northern neighbours the Turans in Turkestan. One might think these were the Turks, but not so. The Turks had yet to emerge from the borders of China and Mongolia, though they would take their name from this culture. The Turks as we know them indeed were not 'Turkic', a name that came from the Turans, rather they were Xiong Nu, part of the para-Chinese bandit confederacies. Ehsan Yarshater writes:

"The identification of the Turanians, a rival Iranian tribe, with the Turks, and Afrāsīāb with their king, is a late development, possibly made in the early 7th century [AD], the Turks having first come into contact with the Iranians only in the 6th century. Mas'ūdī (*Morūj*, par. 540) shows awareness of the error of this identification, in contrast to Ferdowsī [writer of the Shahnameh – Ed.], who maintains it and wrote under the impact of Turkic invasions of Transoxiana in Islamic times and the prevailing negative sentiments among Persian nationalists toward the Turks.

But the Turks themselves cultivated the legends of Afrāsīāb as a Turkish hero after they had come into contact with the Iranians.[18]"

So who on earth were the original Turans? To answer this we must first tell the story of the great power slowly emerging to the east and the nations that lived near it.

Let us remember that the proto-Turks at this point were still confined to Mongolia and what is now Western China, continually harassing the northern Chinese plain with seasonal raids. But this would change, because the Chinese had an idea. They would build a wall. And this construction would start a chain reaction that would echo across the Eurasian continent to the farthest reaches of France and Ireland, transforming the world population in a vast age of migration.

Shennong and the foundations of China

China's history is blessed with a copious wealth of ancient written sources[19], primarily the epic 'Shiji' or 'Records of the Grand Historian' written around 100 BC, and the 'Classic of History' (AKA 'Book of Documents') and 'Classic of Mountains and Seas' that are considerably older[20]. However that has not necessarily produced a particularly coherent narrative when translated and editorialised into English, where the wood is often missed for the trees.

As always when studying super-ancient history:

---

[18] Yarshater, p.576

[19] Indeed, one of the unusual difficulties of Chinese history is that *too much* has been written down.

[20] There are five Chinese 'Classic' texts (purportedly edited by Confucius C.500 BC) of which the 'Book of Documents' is one. The others, that reflect to some extent on history, are the 'Classic of Poetry', the 'Classic of Changes' ('I Ching')– a work of witchcraft divination, supposedly partially deriving from 'Fuxi', i.e. Adam, and therefore thought to be of immense antiquity (Sima Zhen, p.271), the 'Book of Rites', and the 'Spring and Autumn Annals' with their equally reknowned commentary by Zuo; and there was also a now-lost 'Classic of Music'. The 'Ching' or 'Classic' designation was added later during the Confucian Han dynasty C.100 BC ('Documents' book, p.2). The 'Classic of Mountains and Seas', confusingly, is not one of the Five Classics.

"of all mythological themes of ancient China, the earliest and by far the most pervasive is that of flood."[21]

China's flood history is voluminous. From it emerges a number of figures that can be related to other cultures' written texts. The Chinese records tend to list a series of 'great leaders' or forbears, contributors to Chinese civilization through time, whose precise relations with one another are complex and have been fiercely controversial throughout China's history, but whose basic importance and relative significance to the history of China is beyond dispute. These are mainly grouped into two categories: firstly the 'Three August Ones' (aka 'Sovereigns', 'Rulers', etc) and secondly the later 'Five Emperors'. Chinese society, an insular, isolated culture from the earliest times, is understood essentially to be ethnically derived from these figures.

Firstly and most prominently is 'Fuxi', who represents Adam[22]. Fuxi was the primordial human in Chinese history from whom the world was populated[23].

Noah is represented by one of Fuxi's descendants, 'several generations' after him: 'Nuwa' AKA 'Nukua' or 'Nuhsi'[24], the 'wood king'. 7th Century AD chronicler Sima Zhen, in his introductory chapter to his commentary on the 'Shiji', continues,

---

[21] Bodde, p.398

[22] I Ching, p.382-3; Sima Zhen, p.269-272; Huainanzi, p.80,99, 208. Fuxi AKA 'P'ao-hsi' means 'Animal Domesticater' (Wu, p.50). There is an outside possibility that Fuxi is not Adam, but some other antediluvian figure more associated with righteousness, such as Enoch, based on the exuberant praise for his rule, for example in the Huainanzi (e.g. p.224, 230, 300)

[23] The serpent theme is present in the story of Fuxi and Nuwa, as they are described as having human heads but the bodies of serpents (as indeed all super-ancient Chinese forbears are from time to time) (Sima Zhen, p.271, 273; Huangfu Mi, section 1); possibly a memory of the fall of man, i.e. having been begun (at the 'head') as a human, but thereafter becoming increasingly serpent-like towards the tail end. The Huainanzi speaks lamentably of 'when the age declined, in the reign of Fuxi' (p.99)

[24] Some versions include 'Nuwa' as the 'sister-wife' of Fuxi and thus an 'Eve' figure. However this seems to be a later addition, and in fact quite appropriately 'Nuwa' is simply Noah. (For example Huainanzi, p.224-5, Huangfu Mi, s.1)

with what appears to be a description of the flood narrative, mixed with some elements of the Tower of Babel event:

"In his [Nukua's] last year one of the princes named Kung kung, whose duty it was to administer the criminal law, became violent and played the tyrant. He did not rule properly, for he sought by the element water to subdue that of wood. He also fought with Ch'uyung[25] and was not victorious, when, falling into a rage, he butted with his head against the Incomplete mountain, and brought it down. The 'pillar of heaven' was broken and a corner of the earth was wanting. Nukua then fused five-coloured stones to repair heaven, cut off the feet of a tortoise to establish the four extremities of earth, collected the ashes of burnt reeds to stop the inundation, and so rescued the land of Chichow.

After this the earth was at rest, the heaven made whole, and the old things were. Nukua died, and Shennung began his reign."[26]

The third of the 'Three August Ones' is Shennong[27], the founder of the Chinese nation. Shennong is most likely the eighth son of Canaan, son of Ham, listed in the Table of Nations as 'Sinites' (as being the nation that descended from him)[28]. As every anthroponym and eponym of 'China' including its people and first city are derived from 'Shennong' it is highly likely that Shennong himself was this patriarch, who first made his way eastwards along what would become the Silk Road, all the way to the site of the city he would found, 'Shang'An' (or X'ian) on the Yellow River[29], ground zero and ancient capital of the Chinese civilization.

---

[25] Chinese 'god' of fire, quite possibly Kung kung's own father (Classic of Mountains and Seas book, p.249)
[26] Sima Zhen, p.273-274, based on the Huainanzi, p.224-225. Kun-Kung is somewhat reminiscent of Nimrod, though the passage seems mainly a description of the flood. Nimrod may also be remembered in the figure of 'Archer Yi', whose dissolute hunting obsession is contrasted with Noah's humble reign (Zuo, p.919)
[27] 'Divine Farmer' (Huainanzi book, p.80) or 'Divine Husbandman' (Wu, p.50)
[28] Tanakh, p.6; Bamboo Annals book, p.189
[29] In fact on the Yellow River's tributary the Wei River, but the settlement began what would become the Yellow River Civilization, located in and around the large 'S' bend (incorporating the 'Ordus Loop') of the river, on the east side of China.

Shennong seems to have been a quiet, thoughtful type, qualities that transmitted themselves to his nation. Having found just about the most out of the way spot on earth, he dedicated himself to testing plants and cataloguing their medicinal benefits[30].

Fig.80: Shennong testing plants[31]

Other primordial figures following Shennong also have traditional significance such as Youchao, credited with inventing buildings, and Suiren, credited with coming up with the technique for drilling wood to produce fire for cooking.

---

[30] Huainanzi, p.766-767
[31] Public Domain image from Wikimedia Commons (https://commons.wikimedia.org/wiki/File:Shennong3.jpg)

But the next major figure and the fourth major character in Chinese history is the 'Yellow Emperor'[32] AKA 'Huang Di', who lived some hundreds of years after Shennong. He was first and chief of the 'Five Emperors' (the rest all being his offspring), and had many achievements including commissioning the recorder Cangjie to invent the Chinese writing system[33], first painted on tortoise shells hence its tile format, and then on bones.

The next contributor, according to the Shiji, was 'Yu the Great', a non-royal engineer who is credited with overseeing the construction of drainage and damn systems to redirect the flow of the Yellow and Wei rivers thus making the Chinese heartland fit for agricultural development and expansion[34]. However, this is in fact almost certainly a mistake by the Han era chroniclers (C. 200 BC-200 AD), and Yu is another, misplaced (in the historical chronology), version of Noah[35].

The Battle that defined China

This Battle, the Battle of Zhuolu, followed on from another major battle, the Battle of Banquan. These two battles together[36] form a pivotal, possibly even *the* pivotal, foundational moment of Chinese history, because they brought together the three ethnic strands of Chinese culture in the settlement that would define China.

At the Battle of Banquan, Shennong's original line of rulers, the Yan Emperors (Yan Di), under pressure from Indo-European raiders, led by the warlord 'Chiyou', were displaced and defeated

---

[32] It should be noted that 'Emperor' was not really a title that existed in China before C.200 BC, so the label is a later anachronism. 'Di' or 'Ti' is a more general term meaning 'Lord' or even 'great god', only later co-opted by an 'Emperor'. (Book of Documents book, p.xxiii-xxix; Classic of Mountains and Seas book, p.224-225)
[33] Wilkinson, p.666
[34] Shiji, 1, vol.1, p.22-36; Book of Documents, p.64-76
[35] See Appendix 5: Historical Correction in Classical Chinese Chronology. The Shiji relies heavily on the Book of Documents for this 'Yu' section of Chinese history. The descriptions of Yu's achievements in the Chinese sources seem particularly to have recorded Noah's indefatigable industry *after* the flood, to make the waterlogged land habitable for his descendants.
[36] In fact it may have been three or many more battles in what was a three-way war.

by the Yellow Emperor (Huang Di)'s line of rulers. Almost immediately following this the Yellow Emperor led the combined Huang and Yan force against Chiyou, decisively defeating him at the Battle of Zhuolo[37]. Thus providing for the future expansion, growth and survival of the Chinese civilization.

Fig.81: Chiyou, a warlord from super-ancient history who menaced China from the north[38].

The Huang and Yan nations then merged together under this Huang Di leadership to form the 'Huaxia' civilization that would go on to become Han China. The Han Chinese therefore call themselves 'Yanhuang', 'descendants of Yan (symbolically, red) and Huang (symbolically, yellow)'.

It is tentatively proposed that Shennong was the original of the Ham contingent of China, with the Yellow Emperor's nation representing a Shemite contingent, that took over after the Battle of Zhuolu possibly some hundreds of years later, merging with the Shennongites to form Huaxia and then Han[39].

---

[37] Shiji, 1, vol.1, p.2-3
[38] Wikimedia image by Kue Kid (https://en.m.wikipedia.org/wiki/File:Chiyou.gif) (desaturated) used under CC BY SA 4.0 Unported (https://creativecommons.org/licenses/by-sa/4.0/deed.en)
[39] Shennong's descendants might be represented by Y-DNA haplogroup C or D, while the Han Chinese could be O (see for example Jeanson, p.115-116; plates 139, 161, 164, 165).

Sino-Babylonianism

A spanner was thrown into the works of this nice Chinese history by Maverick French historian Terrien de La Couperie, who made waves in the late Victorian world with his idea that *all* of this history actually occurred in Mesopotamia, before the Chinese ever got to China. And, frustratingly, he was probably right[40].

Of course such an idea in general terms (that the Chinese came from Mesopotamia) is fairly obvious and well known (i.e. the dispersal from Babel), with no less an authority than James Legge[41] affirming it in 1865. But La Couperie put meat on those bones with detailed attempts to match Sumero-Babylonian King-lists with Chinese mythical King-lists.

Primarily he asserted that Shennong was in fact none other than Sargon the Great (i.e. either Nimrod, or his close predecessor and possibly father or grandfather[42]). La Couperie's proofs for this,

---

[40] La Couperie's disparate and unfocused ramblings tested the patience of his contemporary historians (and many since), but even his most ferocious and dismissive critics have had to admit that his theory contains undeniable elements of truth (Girardot, p.392-393: "creeping reappearance"). And indeed, 'Sino-Babylonianism', to give it its full ad hominem attack smear label, was already affirmed by Legge long before La Couperie came on the scene (Bamboo Annals book, p.189). It fell out of favour in China during the 1940s because of a new-found credulity towards evolutionist mumbo-jumbo following the discovery of 'Peking Man', pronounced to be 500,000 years old (Liebold, p.199-206). However that did not greatly impact its place in Chinese historical understanding, as it remains substantially unrefuted and is probably true. Schlegel's response to it (Schlegel) concerned the linguistic aspect only, leaving the rest untouched, and seems to have primarily been motivated by a personal irritation and the Sinologist's chauvinism that Chinese culture cannot have been predated by any other culture. Much of the commentary on the subject by modern writers seems at least in part to be an attempt to avoid having to admit that this annoying Frenchman (who appears to have been pathologically incapable of citing his original sources) was actually *right*. Unfortunately, that seems to have been the case.

[41] Translator into English of much of the ancient Chinese written canon (see above)

[42] As discussed, Nimrod was more likely 'Naram-Sin'. There is a suggestion that Sargon was a non-Cushite (Hallo, 2003, vol.1, p.461), i.e. not a son of Ham's son Kush (who was probably Gushur, first king of Kish), but that Naram-Sin *was* a Cushite. And that therefore Sargon's rule split the reigns of Gushur and Naram-Sin, who may have been father and son or grandfather and grandson. However, the Sumerian King List does clearly name Naram-Sin as the grandson of Sargon (p.17).

although never remotely adequately demonstrated by him, were of two kinds[43]. Firstly, similarity between the foundation legends of Sargon and those of Shennong. The 'Birth Legend of Sargon' runs thus (emphases added):

"Sargon, the mighty king, king of Agade [Akkad], am I. My mother was a high priestess, my father I knew not. The brother(s) of my father *loved* the hills. My city is Azupiranu, which is situated on the banks of the Euphrates. My mother, the high priestess, conceived me, in secret she bore me. She set me in a basket of rushes, with bitumen she sealed my lid.

She cast me into the river which rose not (over) me. The river bore me up and carried me to Akki, the drawer of water. Akki, the drawer of water lifted me out as he dipped his e[w]er. Akki, the drawer of water, [took me] as his son (and) reared me. Akki, the drawer of water, *appointed me as his gardener*. While I was a gardener, Ishtar granted me (her) love, And for four and [. . .] years I exercised kingship. *The black-headed [people] I ruled, I gov[erned]...*"[44]

Note the references to Sargon being a 'gardener' and his rulership of the 'black-headed [people]'. The Sumerian King List confirms this 'gardener' reputation:

"The rulership passed to Agade (Akkad). At Agade Sharrukin-ilubani [Sargon] a gardener, a cup-bearer of Ur-Ilbaba, the king of Agade, who built Agade, became king. He ruled 56 years."[45]

---

[43] In fact there is a wealth of circumstantial supporting evidence relating to cultural elements brought from Mesopotamia to China (La Couperie, p.9-25, 277, 291-302), but, though plentiful, it was all rightly thought too vague to persuade many of La Couperie's contemporaries.
[44] Birth Legend of Sargon, p.119. The character of Sargon here is somewhat different to more imperial, conquering versions of him known from later texts.
[45] Sumerian King List, p.17. Ur-Ilbaba is apparently Akki, founder of Akkad. Nb. the (post-diluvian) Sumerian King list is really multiple lists that ran in parallel at different Sumerian/Mesopotamian centres.

The Chinese description of Shennong in the I Ching runs thus (emphases added):

"On the death of Pao-hsi, there arose Shannang (in his place). He fashioned wood to form the share, and *bent wood to make the plough-handle. The advantages of ploughing and weeding were then taught to all under heaven*...He caused markets to be held at midday, thus *bringing together all the people, and assembling in one place all their wares.* They made their exchanges and retired, every one having got what he wanted."[46]

And in the Huainanzi (emphases added):

"In ancient times, the people fed on herbaceous plants and drank [only] water, picked fruit from shrubs and trees and ate the meat of oysters and clams. They frequently suffered tribulations from feverish maladies and injurious poisons. Consequently, the Divine Farmer [Shennong] first taught the people to plant and cultivate the five grains.

He evaluated the suitability of the land, [noting] whether it was dry or wet, fertile or barren, high or low. He tried the taste and flavor of the one hundred plants and the sweetness or bitterness of the streams and springs, issuing directives so the people would know what to avoid and what to accept. At the time [he was doing this], he suffered poisoning [as many as] seventy times a day..."[47]

And: "In ancient times, when the Divine Farmer *ruled the world*, his spirit did not lunge forth from his chest; his wisdom did not go beyond the four sides [of his body].

He cherished his humane and sincere heart. Sweet rains fell in their season; the five grains multiplied and prospered. In the

---

[46] I Ching, p.383. This reference to Shennong (possibly Sargon) taking over from Paohsi (Adam) may be a conflation of Adam with Noah. Possibly Sargon's rule closely followed the death of Noah. Or, as Huangfu Mi writes, all of the dynasties following Noah 'took the title of Pao Xi for fifteen generations' (section 1)
[47] Huainanzi, p.766-767

spring there was birth, in summer growth; in the fall, harvest; in the winter, storage. He inquired monthly and investigated seasonally; when the harvest ended, he reported the achievements...

He nurtured the people with public spiritedness; the people [in turn] were simple and steady, straight and sincere.

They did not engage in angry struggle, but goods were sufficient. They did not strain their bodies, but they completed their accomplishments. They availed themselves of the gifts of Heaven and Earth and lived in harmony and unity with them. Therefore, his awesome demeanor was stern but not exercised; his punishments existed but were not used; his laws were sparing and uncomplicated.

Thus [the Divine Farmer's] transformation [of the people] was spiritlike. His territory to the south went as far as Jiaozhi and in the north to the Youdu Mountains. To the east it stretched to Sunrise Valley, and to the west it reached to Three Dangers Mountain. There was none who failed to follow him. At that time the law was generous and punishments were lenient; prisons and jails were vacant and empty. *Throughout the world, customs were one*, and none harbored wickedness in their hearts...[48] In ancient times, the Divine Farmer used no regulations or commands, yet the people followed."[49]

Thus both Sargon and Shennong are strongly associated with gardening or agriculture. Note also the references to the 'whole world', and in particular that customs were 'one' throughout the world. This is highly suggestive of the pre-Babel Sumerian era.

And here are two of the many instances of the Chinese also being referred to as the 'black-headed people' in the 'Book of Documents':

---

[48] Huainanzi, p.297
[49] Ibid, p.496

"He [the Emperor Yao, one of the Five Emperors – Ed.] (also) regulated and polished the people (of his domain), who all became brightly intelligent. (Finally), he united and harmonized the myriad states; and so the black-haired people were transformed. The result was (universal) concord..."⁵⁰

"If the sovereign can realize the difficulty of his sovereignship, and the minister the difficulty of his ministry, the government will be well ordered, and the black-haired people will sedulously seek to be virtuous."⁵¹

All of this is suggestive of a strong sense of continuity between the Sumerian 'regime' of Government (and even the Babylonian, as the Lüshi reports that 'the house of Shennong possessed the world for seventeen generations'⁵²), and that of later China, that appears to have wanted to preserve the Sumerian mode of living.

More circumstantial evidence is found in the 3rd Century AD writings of physician Huangfu Mi. He lists fourteen dynasties following the demise of Noah (Nuwa)'s dynasty, with the 'Getians' i.e. Gutians as the twelfth dyasty after Noah's, then two more⁵³. Then the list stops and he starts discussing Shennong⁵⁴, whom, he adds, 'rules Xia'. Xia is the Chinese name for Sumer, and the dynasty or country founded by Noah (under his other name Yu the Great)⁵⁵.

---

⁵⁰ Book of Documents, p.32
⁵¹ Ibid, p.46
⁵² Lüshi Chunqiu, p.429. By contrast, the Sumerian King List, though not entirely clear, names 10 kings after Sargon, and apparently descended from him (though some are brothers) ruling before 'Agade was smitten with weapons [and] The rulership passed to Erech.' (p.17-18)
⁵³ Three in some versions of the text, that also have the Gutians at 11th (Section 1). This roughly agrees with the Sumerian King List that makes the Gutians the 10th distinct dynasty to rule in Sumer/Mesopotamia, with the Akkadians the 9th (Sumerian King List, p.22-26).
⁵⁴ Huangfu Mi, section 1. Whose family, he says, 'also has the surname Jiang'. Could this be a reference to one of the 'families' or dynasties previously named who ruled Sumer, perhaps the Zhuxiang who preceded the Getians? (Cf. Lüshi Chunqiu, p.720)
⁵⁵ See Appendix 5: Historical Correction in Classical Chinese Chronology. 'Xia' may be derived from 'Tianxia' meaning 'all under heaven'.

Meanwhile the traditional Chinese chronology of the 'Xia' (Sumer) dynasty also has 17 generations[56] from Yu (Noah) to Tang, who founded the succeeding 'Shang' dynasty. One of these Xia dynasts is himself named 'Xie', precisely the same name as that of the person named in the 'Book of Documents'[57] as being the ancestor of Tang of Shang, and who because of that association has tentatively been identified as Shennong himself[58]. 'Xie', like Sargon, was succeeded by two of his sons in turn[59], followed by the son of the second son to reign. So Both Xie and Sargon ruled Sumer a few generations after Noah, and both were succeeded in turn by their two sons. Xie was also rewarded by Noah (Yu) for helping to clean up the flood[60]. Additionally, the Shang dynasty, descended from Xie, were more associated than any other with Shennong[61] (not least in their name). This might have been because Xie and Shennong, and therefore also Sargon, were the same person[62].

---

[56] Shiji, 1, vol.1, p.36-38. Or nineteen, according to Huangfu Mi (section 3)

[57] p.42. Also Shiji, 1, vol.1, p.41. The Shiji here also relates how Xie, like Sargon, *did not know who his father was.* (Also in Bamboo Annals, p.128). A remark about Shennong from the Zhuangzi is perhaps relevant here, though general: "In the age of the Divine Farmer...people knew their mothers but not their fathers." (p.302)

[58] See Appendix 5: Historical Correction in Classical Chinese Chronology. There is an outside chance that Xie, and therefore also perhaps Shennong, could be Shem.

[59] Bamboo Annals, p.123; Wu, p.120. The eldest of these is known as (Bu) Jiang, a similar name as that described by Huangfu Mi as being the 'surname' of the family of Shennong (section 1). Sargon's sons are named in the Sumerian King List, p.17

[60] Shiji, 1, vol.1, p.41-42. This fits well with 'Xie' being Shennong/Sargon, the 'Divine Farmer' discipled by Noah to help with flood clean-up operations.

[61] As opposed to their successors the Chou and Han, who are seen as more associated with 'Huaxia' and the yellowite or Han ethnicity.

[62] The identification of Shennong as Sargon makes it hard to explain the overwhelming connection of Shennong with the founding of China specifically, with the city of Shang'An, the state of Shandong, the ethnonym 'Sinites' and also possibly the Shang dynasty all arguably named after him, that does not seem very compatible with a Shennong who spent his entire life in Mesopotamia and never set foot in China. Nonetheless, it appears that the Elamites felt such a strong connection to Shennong/Sargon (a special inheritance; that they, and perhaps they alone, were the 'Black-headed people' of his flock), that they took as their own his history and traditions with them when they emigrated to China, and indeed seem to have believed they were the sole and rightful possessors and custodians of his legacy and inheritance. Sargon was probably not part of the Cushite dynasty (famously not knowing his father), so it is possible that 'the Black-headed people' tied themselves ethnically to him specifically, rather than to Cush or Nimrod.

La Couperie's theory was that the Chinese people were descended from the Elamites[63] of Susa (that would later be an Achaemenid Persian centre). Elam was near Babylonia, just to its south-east, on the north shore of the Persian Gulf, along the Karkheh river.

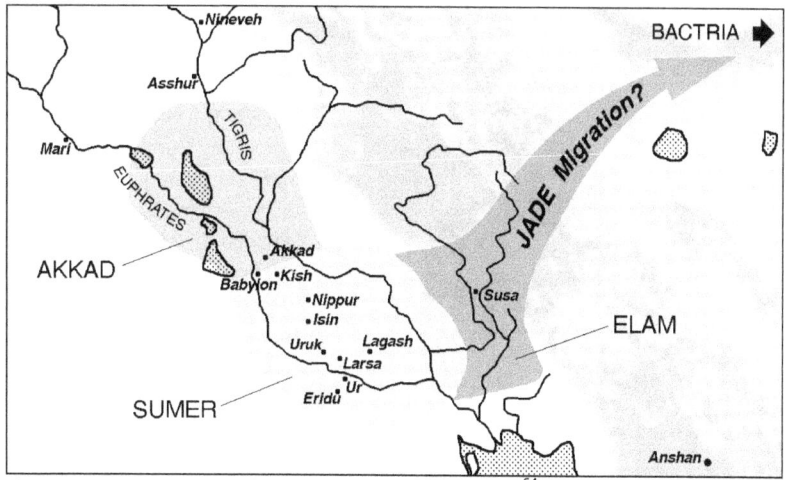

Fig.82: Mesopotamia at the end of the Sumerian era[64]

A settlement of the eponymous son of Shem, it was one of the lands involved in the primaeval This is reflected in Chinese history, in the Lüshi Chunqiu (C.239 BC):

"The people of Susha all took it upon themselves to attack their lord and shift their allegiance to the Divine Farmer [i.e. Shennong]."[66]

---

[63] And therefore were probably descendants of Elam, one of Shem's eldest sons (Tanakh, p.6), or as an outside possibility, of Joktan (Jeanson identifies Y-haplogroup 'O', one of the main signifiers of the Han Chinese, with Joktan.)
[64] 'Mountain Stone Rock' by the3rdSequence (www.the3rdsequence.com/textured/) is licenced under CC BY 4.0 (http://creativecommons.org/licenses/by/4.0)
[65] Or at least Shem, hence 'Sumer' (Kramer, p.298). The Sumerian record associates Noah particularly with the city of Shuruppuk (site of the earliest, 'Jemdet Nasr' and 'Ubaid', remains) (Epic of Gilgamesh, p.691-705; Sumerian Documents, 5.6.1)
[66] Lüshi Chunqiu, p.491, a phrase whose significance is heightened by its being repeated verbatim in both the Huainanzi (p.467) and the Wen-tzu (p.144)

Regarding this statement, Wu comments that "Of Shusha, however, we know nothing"⁶⁷ i.e. in conventional Chinese history⁶⁸. It is suggested that this is because the reference is to Susa in Mesopotamia.

Fig.83: The very Chinese-looking King Gudea of Lagash, one of the first Elamite Kings who were independent of Akkadian (Nimrodian) rule, following the Gutians' liberation of Mesopotamia. His reign is conventionally dated to C.2150 BC⁶⁹. Around 200 years later, according to La Couperie, 'Hu Nak Kunte', part of this same Elamite culture, left the area for the far east to become Chinese history's 'Yellow Emperor'.

Elam then was a spin-off state from the original Sumerian colony, and became a a semi-detached 'satellite' of Babylonia after Babel. Rulers of Lagash, the city at the border of Elam, are listed on the Sumerian King List from the time of Sargon⁷⁰. But Gudea,

---

⁶⁷ Wu, p.102

⁶⁸ In fact this is not entirely accurate. 'Shusha' is mentioned once in the very ancient 'Classic of Mountains and Seas', that states: "The country beyond the Flowing Sands (desert of Gobi) are those of Ta-hia, Shu-sha, Ku-yao, and Yueh-ti" (La Couperie, p.275, also Classic of Mountains and Seas, p.151). 'Ta-hia' is Sumer, i.e. ancient Mesopotamia, listed right before 'Shu-sha', in a list that appears to run from furthest to nearest in relation to the Shang'An Chinese, ending in 'Yueh-ti', i.e. the residents of Tocharia, who were directly on the other side of the Gobi Desert from them.

⁶⁹ Sumerian King List, p.25. Public domain Wikimedia image by Jastrow (https://commons.Wikimedia.org/ wiki/File:Gudea_of_Lagash_Girsu.jpg)

⁷⁰ As the 'Patesis' ('priest-king') of Lagash'. Sumerian King List, p.24-25

pictured above, was arguably the first to have any real independence; courtesy of the Gutians who had just liberated the whole of Mesopotamia including Elam from the tyrannical Akkadians, and under whose umbrella Gudea ruled[71]. Consequently his reign was a cultural golden age for the newly-free Elamites.

But that independence didn't last for long. A reconstituted Babylonian regime (known as 'Ur III', that became its last first-phase incarnation) soon reconquered Elam under a leader 'Utu-Hengal'[72] C.2115 BC.

La Couperie's secret weapon for establishing 'Sino-Babylonianism' was his second identification: the association of another figure on the Sumerian King List (from this 'Ur III' era) with a character from Chinese history. La Couperie proposed that 'Cangjie', the legendary inventor of Chinese writing[73] was one and the same with 'Shulgi' (AKA 'Dungi'), the second ruler of of the Ur III Mesopotamian Empire[74] (and therefore Elam) after the Gutians had been pushed back into the mountains.

Like the identification of Sargon as Shennong, there is perhaps no smoking gun evidence, but the two are certainly connected by their shared speciality of writing and teaching.

The linguist Xu Shen, around 100 AD, states: "The Yellow Thearch's recorder, Cang jie, seeing the tracks of birds and animals, knew how to distinguish them by their signs and first created writing (*shuqi*)...Cang Jie made characters by imitating the forms according to the unit [of each class]. Therefore, it was called *wen*. Later, when the picture and the phonetic were combined, it was called *zi*.[75]

---

[71] Sumerian King List, p.25
[72] Ibid
[73] Wilkinson, p.295, 666
[74] Sumerian King List, p.19, 25
[75] Wilkinson, p.666, translating from Xu Shen's 'Shuowen jiezi'. Note that the Chinese name for their original script was 'Shuqi', somewhat close to 'Shulgi'. Also

La Couperie believed that the 'forms' 'imitating' the 'tracks of birds and animals' were 'cuneiform', the famous wedge-shaped script of ancient Mesopotamia. Here is some late cuneiform script from the reign of Shulgi, of the type La Couperie argued was the beginnings of Chinese writing:

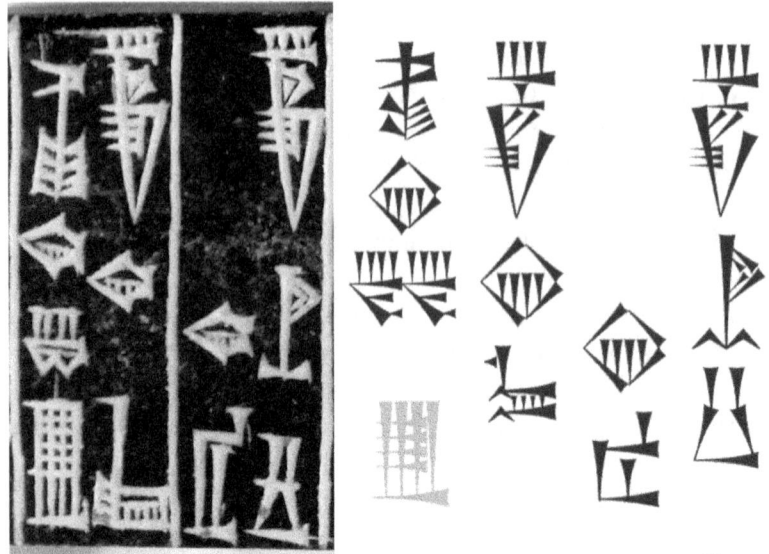

Fig.84: The name and title of a Mesopotamian King, on a seal of Shulgi[76]

---

that this witness seems to suggest that Shulgi/Cangjie was the Yellow Emperor's scribe or recorder. Great figures in Chinese history were often anachronistically given roles as bureaucratic functionaries by later Han-era writers (a habit of Chinese historians, ever eager to please the reigning monarch, see Appendix 5: Historical Correction in Classical Chinese Chronology). In the Lüshi Chunqiu (C.239 BC) an apparent version of Cangjie, 'Da Nao' is stated to have been taken by the Yellow Emperor as 'his teacher' (p.122, 420, 718). La Couperie wished to find a linguistic equivalence between 'Da Nao' and 'Dungi' AKA Shulgi.

[76] Wikimedia image by Marie-Lan Nguyen/Jastrow (https://en.wikipedia.org/wiki/File:Lugal_Urimkima_Lugal_Kiengi_Kiuri,_King_of_Ur,_King_of_Sumer_and_Akkad,_on_a_seal_of_Shulgi_(transcription).jpg) used under CC BY 2.5 (https://creativecommons.org/licenses/by/2.5/deed.en)

Shulgi was most famous for his achievements in education, having reformed the teaching curriculum of his state[77]. In general, he seems to have been a popular monarch, with a considerable number of cultural artefacts left from his reign[78].

He also has a couple of other points of contact with the primaeval history of China:
- He was particularly associated with Susa and Elam, making it his 'home from home'. He spent much time there, raising many monuments, and claimed he spoke Elamite as well as Sumerian[79].
- He probably married one of his daughters to an Elamite King[80]
- He took the Akkadian title 'King of the four corners of the universe', or 'king of the four quarters' that was remembered in the Chinese 'President of the four mountains' appellation[81]
- He called himself 'Pastor of the black-headed people'[82]

It appears that, some time after the reign of their beloved Shulgi, some of the Elamites (La Couperie specifically identified a sub-tribe of Elam, the 'Baks'[83]) wanted out of the increasingly dysfunctional Mesopotamian political scene, where 'good' Babylonian emperors, like Sargon and Shulgi, could easily soon be followed by 'bad' and tyrannical ones, like Nimrod, or indeed by foreign rulers, without them being able to do much about it. These intrepid souls apparently set out for China.

---

[77] Potts, 2016, p.124
[78] The Sumerian King List calls him 'the divine Dungi son of the divine Ur-Nammu' (p.19-20). Shulgi/Dungi's son Bur-Sin also gets this 'divine' title, but not from his son onwards. This however probably more likely reflects Shulgi's decision to proclaim himself a 'god'. (Potts, 2016, p.124)
[79] Ibid
[80] Steinkeller, 2018, p.195
[81] For example, Book of Documents, p.34-35
[82] Pritchard, p.585: "I, Shulgi...I am the king of the four quarters, I am a shepherd, the pastor of the "black-headed people""
[83] La Couperie, p.26

Unfortunately, while this emigration almost certainly happened between the reign of Shulgi C.2075 BC and the conquest of the region by the Babylonian Emperor Hammurabi in C.1750 BC, we do not know exactly how or when it occurred[84], nor who specifically the 'Yellow Emperor' was.

Candidates include Utu-Hegal (who defeated the Gutians under their final leader 'Terigan', possibly the Chinese 'Chiyou')[85], his successor Ur-Nammu[86], a beloved 'shepherd' of the 'black-headed people' who established a dynasty of five emperors, possibly the 'Five Emperors' of Chinese history (the 'Ur III' dynasty)[87]; Shulgi himself, or subsequent Elamite 'Shimashki' or 'Sukkalmah' dynasts, who dominated the region after Ur III[88], including the

---

[84] It is not clear whether the Yellow Emperor himself led the people movement, or whether one of his successors took his memory with them (as they did that of Sargon and Shulgi), or whether it was a leaderless, purely organic, slow drift of economic migrants and/or refugees over a long period of time. Such is the status of the relatively meagre written record that comes down to us from this extremely ancient era.

[85] This would suggest an identification of the 'Yan-ti' who could not handle 'Chiyou' and so lost the empire, with Naram-Sin.

[86] The Chinese sources suggest that Cangjie (probably Shulgi) was an appointee or subordinate of the Yellow Emperor, pointing tentatively to Yellow living immediately before him, hence perhaps Utu-Hegal or Shulgi's father Ur-Nammu.

[87] There is a very strong connection between the fledgling Chinese state and the Ur III dynasty of Mesopotamia – the final incarnation of the 'Sumerian' civilization. Above all because they seemed to consider themselves its heirs. The 'original', one-language Sumer ended with the Tower of Babel, but an attempted perpetuation of it continued on until the fall of Ur III, and arguably the establishment of China itself was yet a further attempted perpetuation. After the fall of Ur III rulers of Babylonia would all be Amorites for hundreds of years, a different ethnicity, as is generally understood, from the Sumerian kings. There is circumstantial evidence that China was founded in some way by refugees or exiles from the pre-Amorite dynasty, who were alienated from Mesopotamia by Amorites and taken to Elam as prisoners following the final destruction of the Ur III state. Such an emigration is suggested by the epic 'Lament for Sumer and Urim' (Sumerian Documents, 2.2.3).

[88] Some of the main names here are 'Yabrat'/'Ebarat' who may have been Shulgi's son-in-law (Potts, 2016, p.128-129) and guided in all things by him (Steinkeller 2007, p.225-227). The founder of the 'Shimashki' Elamite dynasty, Yabrat supported Shulgi's major operations to secure the north-east 'Great Khorasan Road' passage through the Zagros Mountains to Bactria, a route which an emigration from Elam to China would have taken. This 'trans-Iranian' connection between Ur III, Elam's Shimashkian dynasty and BMAC may be a key avenue of future investigation for discovering the Yellow Emperor in Mesopotamian history.

Sukkalmah warlord 'Kutir Nakhunte', who ruled Elam some 250 years after Shulgi[89]. La Couperie identified 'Nakhunte', the Elamite designation for ruler or 'god'[90], as the original of 'Huangti', meaning 'Yellow Emperor' or 'Yellow god'[91]. But he climbed down from an initial claim that Kutir was the Yellow Emperor[92] to focus on a more obscure leader of the 'Bak' Elamite sub-tribe that he called 'Hu Nak Kunte'[93].

Comments by both Potts (2008, p.194) and Steinkeller encourage such a proposition. Steinkeller writes: "the land of Marhaši [Margiana/BMAC, in the view of this author – Ed.] was a major political and economic power in the 3rd millennium Western Asia, which controlled the eastern section of the Iranian plateau and acted as an intermediary between Mesopotamia and Elam in the west and Meluhha [Harrappa] in the east." (Steinkeller, 1982, p.263). Yabrat's son Kindattu (a definite candidate for Yellow Emperor), who may have been Shulgi's Grandson, was the warlord of Elam who destroyed the Ur III regime (Van Dijk, p.197), and took its last dynast 'Ibbi-Sin' to Elam in captivity. A Shimashki-affiliated emigration would certainly fit with La Couperie's 'Bak' hypothesis, as the Elamite city or town of Shimashki (today's Masjed Soleyman) is even today the capital of the Bakhtiari people. Ancient Chinese culture has strong connections to Elam, such as its associations with jade, a speciality of the Elamites, and with Shulgi and Susa. Perhaps a remnant of the Ur III regime, after their captivity, embarked from there accompanied by Elamites.

[89] C.1800 BC. Not to be confused with the 700 years later Kassite-battling Kutir Nakhunte II of the same name (Potts, 2016, p.229-230). Although possibly La Couperie was confusing the two, in seeing the Sukkalmah Kutir as a warlord who had raided Babylonia, when this appears to have been an act of the later Kutir, unless these are somehow records of the same king, which may be the case.

[90] Nb. Shulgi, following the lead of Naram-Sin (probably Nimrod) had previously decided to call himself a 'god' (Potts, 2016, p.124). Many subsequent rulers would do the same.

[91] La Couperie, p.26

[92] Apparently still claiming this at p.6 and p.24 of his book (cf. p.320-1). The change was perhaps motivated by an incompatability of Kutir Nakhunte's career trajectory with an emigration to China. La Couperie's sources for 'Hu Nak Kunte' are obscure and difficult to replicate. This author has been unable to find any reference to a 'Hu Nak Kunte' (separate from the warlord Kutir Nakhunte) in any ancient source.

[93] La Couperie theorized that when the empire tried to re-assert authority over Elam under one 'Dan-tik' (presumably the Sumerian King List's 'Damik-ili-shu' (p.26)), 'Hu Nak Kunte' defeated Dan-tik (Chinese history's Battle of Banquan), and thereafter defeated Chiyou near the Tigris and Zab Rivers (Chinese history's Battle of Zhuolo). He suggested because of the return to Elam of 'Kutir Nakhunte' after his period of raiding Babylonia, 'Hu Nak Kunte' took a powder and left for China, dating this to 2285 BC, with the arrival of Hu Nak Kunte into China at 2282 BC (p.319-322). Regarding who might be the 'Chiyou' in this scenario, Potts points out that as late as C.1785 BC an Elamite Sukkalmah King Shiruk-tuh raised an army to

Whoever the emigrants were, they appear to have believed that the 'true' inheritance of the Sumerians resided with them, and that they had to take it far away from Mesopotamia for safekeeping. This is the real meaning of 'Huaxia', i.e. the 'Yellow' version or regime, of 'Xia', i.e. Sumer. They believed they were the genuine heirs of Sargon (Shennong)[94] and through him of Noah (Yu). But that his legacy would no longer be respected in Mesopotamia, so that it must be re-planted elsewhere[95].

The Yellow Emperor therefore seems to have established the fundamental basis of all Chinese culture, 'Huaxia' (i.e. 'Yellow Xia'), *in Mesopotamia,* not in China. It was probably a Shemite-led partnership between Yellowite (proto-Han) Shemites and Shennongite (proto-Shang) Hamites, a settlement that was an attempted continuity from the ancient Shennongite polity[96], and therefore already included many of the cultural elements that would define the future centralized Chinese state.

At some point following this creation of 'Huaxia' then, the emigrants made their way north-east, possibly led by a 'Nakhunte' of some description, who came to be remembered by them as the Yellow Emperor.

---

join with Assyria to expel and destroy the Guti, who were therefore apparently still a menace (Potts, 2016, p.156-157)

[94] As discussed, this could conceivably also be Shem

[95] A Chinese migration at an early date (for instance following the destruction of Ur III, around 2000 BC) would make great sense, as Chinese culture bears all the hallmarks of never having really experienced the post-Sumerian, international, multi-polar world. Hence its preoccupation with the pre-Babel 'sages' Noah, Sargon, etc. The Chinese never bought into the new international idea perhaps because they left Mesopotamia before it took hold, so for them, 'Isin-Larsa' (the regime that followed Sumer) hadn't happened, and they still perceived the world as a 'mono-state', a single ('middle') empire, of which they were the caretakers.

[96] AKA Sumer, known in Yu (Noah)'s day as the 'Middle Kingdom' (for example Liezi (C.300 AD), p.102), a term they attempted to transpose onto their transplant settlement in China (Ibid, p.67), perhaps one source of the confusion between 'Xia' (Sumer) and China.

The Yellow Emperor and Early China

The Sumerian/Elamite migration into China was probably a reaction to the political instability of the late Sumerian era in Mesopotamia, but it was also very likely a natural extension of the ('Bak') Elamites expansion north-eastward in search of their precious jade, in which they were already extensively trading, and possibly founded the city of 'Bactra' to expedite[97] (one strong argument that the emigrants were from Elam). The jade came from Tocharia, and that is where they went. That the Yellow Emperor came through Tocharia is attested by the Classic of Mountains and Seas, that (being generally obsessed with jade) records his interaction with the 'black and white' jade formations unique to the Yarkand area:

"Four hundred and twenty leagues further northwest is a mountain called Mount Secret...White jade is abundant on the central flank of this mountain. The River Cinnabar contains jade grease. It gushes up from its source and churns around. The great god Yellow ate this jade grease and enjoyed it as a ritual offering. Jade grease creates the dark jade."[98]

A little further on, the Yellow Emperor appears to have settled for a time in the Kunlun Mountains, at the south-eastern tip of Tocharia, as related in the narrative of a King Muh, C.950 BC:

"On Ting-tsze (221st day), the Son of Heaven [i.e. King Muh] started in a S.W. direction and ascended to the region where the ... [missing but probably read 'Hwang Ti']...had permanently settled. Here there are large trees and splendid plants....He then stopped at the outlying hills of Kwan-lun in front of the river [Red]...On a lucky day (specially selected)...the Son of Heaven

---

[97] See for example Potts, 2008, p.194, on the trade connections between Elam and BMAC. The Elamites probably also acquired tin from Afghanistan through Bactria, possibly controlling the tin trade westward to the Mediterranean, a powerful position to be in at the dawn of the Bronze Age. As well as Lapis Lazuli, ever present in Sumerian descriptions of luxury, from Badakhshan in Afghanistan (Potts, 2016, p.158-175).
[98] Classic of Mountains and Seas, p.21.

ascended the heights of Kwan-lun and viewed the palace of Hwang Ti...Whilst residing on Kwan-lun, the Son of Heaven occupied the palace of Hwang Ti."[99]

The Yellow Emperor may, as the above narrative suggests, have ended his life in this location[100]. But if not he, then certainly his heirs, continued on to the Ordos Plateau of the Yellow River, near Shang'An[101]. The arrival in the far east of a ready-made 'imperial' state explains something that has often puzzled Chinese historians: the pre-established, institutional nature of Chinese civilization from the very beginning, which never knew (in China) anything very primitive[102]. The emigrants' establishment of what would become China was self-consciously as an outpost of the original Sumerian authority of Noah ('Yu the Great' in Chinese history[103]), and the rulership of it would continue to be known as the 'Xia' or 'Sumer' dynasty (in its specific 'Huaxia'; 'Yellow-Red' or 'Yellow Sumer' configuration), complete with all the trappings, traditions and, as we have seen, history, of that earlier location; an

---

[99] Narrative of the Son of Heaven called Muh, p.229-230. The 4th Century AD 'Liezi' also suggests that the Yellow Emperor had a 'palace' that could be seen (only) from the summit of 'Mount Kunlun' (Altyn Tagh, or near it) (Liezi, p.64) These witnesses are hard to reconcile with Ur-Nammu or Utu-Hegal being the Yellow Emperor, unless somehow he visited this region at some point, pioneering an outpost, before returning to Mesopotamia. An extreme outside possibility is that the extensive description of Ur-Nammu's early death and journey to the 'Netherworld' (Sumerian Documents, 2.4.1.1) relate to a live capture and deportation to the far east. ('The abducted and the dead, how like they are!' (Gilgamesh, p.697)). The 'Netherworld', ruled by a powerful Queen, is described in other documents as being in 'the east'. (Sumerian Documents, 1.4.1)

[100] This stopover or settlement at the Kunlun Mountains is intriguing. The Chinese term for the mountain range is 'Offspringline'. This coud be simply because they are the source of the Yellow River, but could also refer to the fact that the Chinese nation 'sprung off' from these mountains. The settlement may also explain why Shaohao, the son of Yellow, did not inherit the imperial throne, but rather ruled a separate region that did not go on to become the central government. It could be that 'Shaohao' stayed in the west, while his other siblings continued east to establish Shang'An.

[101] Schlegel (p.246) claims an absolute proof by means of the recording of a solar eclipse by the Chinese, that they were in China by 7 May 2165 BC

[102] Laufer, p.29

[103] AKA 'Nuwa', see Appendix 5: Historical Correction in Classical Chinese Chronology

attempt at continuity with the past that would become a typical feature of the future Chinese civilization[104].

The Yellow Emperor's influence on this society was comprehensive, and he is given credit for many Chinese traditions, including, through his wife Leizu, the introduction of 'Sericulture', i.e. silk-making, into Chinese society, by having her teach the skill (that she invented) to the people[105]. It duly became the means of China's long-term prosperity

The Sumerian/Elamite colony slowly grew as a mercantile and textile manufacturing centre, ensconsed in a large fertile plain protected by the giant Himalayan Mountain Range to its West, and further mountain ranges to its North and North-West, making a "mountain-wall which stretches from Manchuria to Afghanistan, over a distance of three thousand miles" (Douglas Carruthers [106])

By the time of the mid-first millennium BC, although regularly harassed by bands of nomadic raiders from its North, it was generally prosperous and safe, busily exporting its speciality textile silk. It did not go outside the mountain wall to do this. For it must be remembered that the nascent Chinese Kingdom was not the only national occupant of this mountain-bordered eastern region that we now call China. Indeed, at that time China still took up only the easternmost part, much less than half, of the territory of today's China.

---

[104] And to that tradition of preservation we owe these fascinating insights into the Sumerian world of Noah, Sargon, Shulgi, etc., that would otherwise now be lost
[105] Wilkinson, p.671
[106] Carruthers, vol.2, p.415.

Fig.85: Ancient China C.500 BC within the borders of today's China[107].

The entire Western half of China had by that time been settled by what can only be called an entire subcontinent of European peoples, a population of extraordinary size, wealth and cultural diversity; a civilization arguably as large as that in South-Eastern Europe at that time. These were nations that have been virtually completely unknown and left out of mainstream history, whose story has been hidden, until now. This is their story, and it is an astonishing one.

---

[107] Image used courtesy of www.chinahighlights.com.

The European Civilization that lived in China

The European culture that dwelt in Western China for the first half of human post-flood history was based around the Tarim Basin. This was a region not easily accessible to the Chinese. Whilst the verdant eastern part of the country well supported a settled population, immediately to its west the land became rocky, arid and treacherous, with only one major desert pass leading westward, the 'Hexi Corridor', a dangerous and thankless journey, to the easternmost cities of the Tarim Basin civilization ('Tocharia'). The Tarim Basin itself would not become a part of China until the distant 8th Century AD. This map of the Silk Road illustrates the limited geographical reach of the early Chinese culture:

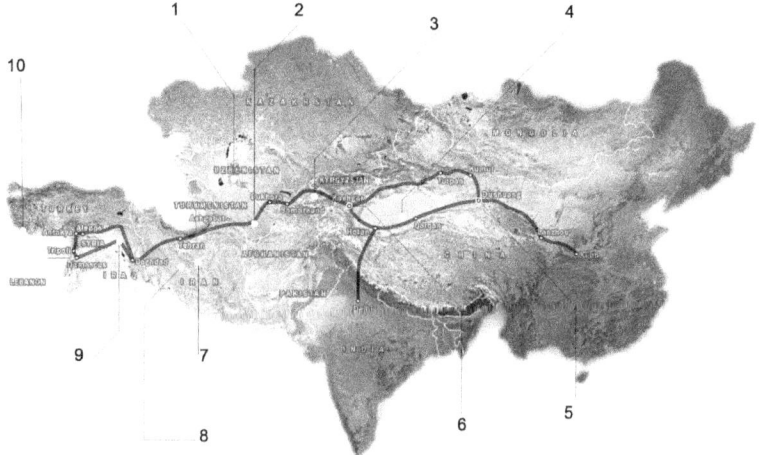

Fig.86: Map of the Silk Road, showing the fertile Chinese heartland around the Yellow and Yantze Rivers at the bottom right, with the road's eastern terminus at the ancient Chinese capital of Shang An. Note the commanding position of Tocharia right at the centre of the road [108].

The studious, urbanised and academic Han Chinese[109] were not highly motivated to broach this rough and dangerous terrain very far. Instead they sold their silk to middle men, for the prized

---
[108] Image © Asian Geographic Magazines Pte Ltd.
[109] The Han Chinese, who considered themselves distinctly descended from the Yellow Emperor, were a significant ethnic nation of China long before the dynasty of that name took control of the Qin's imperial apparatus in C.200 BC.

mineral *jade*; middle men until now virtually invisible to history, because of the giant mountain wall that also shielded them from western awareness. These were the proto-European nations of China. To give some idea of their diversity in the region, here is a list of the main nations of this civilization:

Yuezhi (around the Jade Gate and Qilian Mountains)[110]
Issedones (AKA 'Jushi', 'Wusun' and 'Kunmis/Kunmings') (generally in Turpan[111])
Kushans (from Kucha)
Kashgarians (from Kashgar AKA Shule)
Arsi/Agni (from Karashar, who may be the same as the Yuezhi)
Loulanians (from Loulan AKA Shanshan)
Khotanese (from Khotan AKA Yutian)
Suocheans (from Yarkand AKA Suoche)
Yuebanians (from Yueban)
Tashkurgians (from Tashkurgan)
Sutians (from Sute)
Sarikolans (from Sarikol)

The Chinese Book of Later Han states there were thirty-six Kingdoms in all in the 'western regions' (Tarim Basin)[112].

As well as these of course there were the Sogdians to the West[113], North of them the Saka (that we are positing were virtually identical with the Cimmerians). To the West of them were the Massagetae (also probably part of this same group). And to the East and North-East the Donghu (probably eastern-marauding

---

[110] Birrell translates 'Yuezhi' as 'Moonbranch' (Classic of Mountains and Seas, p.151, 240)
[111] 'Jushi' was possibly another name for the 'Wusun' (although it may simply be a variant of 'Yuezhi'). Wusun and Jushi are called distinct nations (for example in the Book of Later Han (C.440 AD, section 27), but it is in practice difficult to differentiate the two, who were certainly related and overlapping cultures, that were also related to the Yuezhi. In general 'Wusun' meant settlements further north and west and 'Jushi' meant settlements further south, around Karashar and Turfan.
[112] Ibid, section 1
[113] Sogdiana was known to the Chinese after around 100 BC as the Kingdom of 'Kangju'

Scythians). All these were distinct nations who had probably dwelt in this area since the super-ancient era before 1750 BC, and certainly since 1000 BC. Indeed, 'Tukriš' (Tocharia) was well-known even to Akkad/Babylonia in extreme antiquity[114], and 'Turrukkeans' are mentioned in connection with the reign of first Assyrian Emperor Shamshi-Adad C.1800 BC[115].

The sheer volume of the heretofore unknown history of European peoples in this area defies belief.

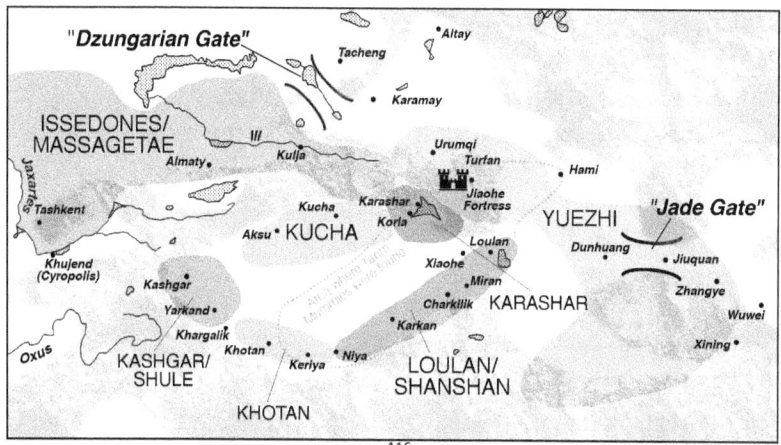

Fig.87: Tocharia's main oasis kingdoms[116]

---

[114] Steinkeller, 1982, p.248. It was listed in the Sumerian myth of Enki and Ninhursanga, as the furthest distant land to Sumer named.

[115] Potts, 2016, p.156-157. Potts calls them 'a Zagros people', a guess with very little apparent justification. Just as with the baffling failure of Steinkeller to perceive that 'Marhaši' clearly refers to Margiana (at least in the limited understanding of the Mesopotamians), although he has all the extensive evidence assembled (Steinkeller 1982; 2006, p.1-2), that seems to be part of a general academic myopia. Essentially it stems from an intertial unwillingness to comprehend that significant heretofore unidentified but extensive and powerful civilizations existed in the north of the habitable world from far-ancient times. Perhaps a feature of academic (and Greco-Roman) pride, in that they have been missed for so long. The discoveries of BMAC however are beginning to see the light dawn in some conventional academics' minds that this was indeed the case.

[116] These are approximations, of the centres of the regions of these nations. It is likely for example that the Yuezhi controlled or extended to a larger region than this, but we cannot be sure in what direction. 'Mountain Stone Rock' by the3rdSequence (https://www.the3rdsequence.com/texturedb/) is licenced under CC BY 4.0 (http://creativecommons.org/licenses/by/4.0)

309

La Couperie states:

"In the western part of the Tarym valley, cities still mentioned during the First Han dynasty [200-0 BC], in the eastern vicinity of the present Khotan, Yarkand, and Kashgar, were gradually sand buried in the following centuries. It is there that Bactro-Chinese coins older than the Christrian era, also manuscripts of the fifth century, and other antiquities have been dug out in recent years. The Annals of the pre-cited dynasty recorded that in Yen-Ki (Karashar) and the various kingdoms of these western regions, the land was covered with cities, villages, cultivated fields, and domestic animals.[117] ... The foregoing notes make it therefore certain that the Eastern Turkestan was different in antiquity of what it is at present, and that numerous states have arisen and disappeared there in the course of ages."[118]

Tocharia was a 'Jade Civilization' or at least a Jade economy, because it appears to have grown rich substantially as a consequence of early China's insatiable appetite for Jade. As La Couperie explains:

"Jade so-called, i.e., nephrite, which was not found by the Chinese in China, notwithstanding some unfounded statements to the contrary, was in all times known and highly prized by the Chinese, who looked upon it as symbolizing power and authority[119].

With the exception of unimportant beds, in the Caucasus, and in the rivers of the Yablono and Saiansk mountains, East and S. W. of Lake Baikal, which were not known in olden times, the true jade or nephrite exists only in what is known as Chinese Turkestan [Tocharia]. Mount Mirdjai reputed to be a mass of jade, and famous in the geographical romances of ancient China, mount

---

[117] La Couperie, p.309
[118] Ibid, p.310
[119] See for example Book of Documents, p.39-40. La Couperie argues the primaeval (Yellowite) Chinese even prized and traded in Jade when they lived in Elam/Susiana, and that that may have been a factor in their choosing to emigrate to China (p.32, 309)

Sertash, both at 74 miles from Yarkand, and the rivers Ulgunkash and Karakash near Ilchi, were the principal if not the sole source from where nephite jade was exported in the west and in the east.[120] This jade traffic was, according to all probabilities, of a second and third-hand kind, which could not provide a regular channel for the introduction of S.W. Asiatic civilisation into the East... [i.e. the middle men controlled both communication and trade into and out of China].

Once in China, the Chinese...received nephrite-jade from their rear. The legendary accounts on the subject are not all inventions, and there is doubtless some truth underlying the magnified and fabled reports. In the ninth year of Shun, Si Wang Mu [Chinese culture's mythical Queen who lived in a luxurious paradise in the western mountains – Ed] sent envoys with presents consisting of white jade rings, or archers' thimbles in jade, a tube of white jade, and topographical maps. Si-Wang-Mu, whatever unknown personage the name may have described originally, became the impersonation of the queen rulers, whose princedoms lay on the North of Tibet along Kuenlun, and who have had occasionally some intercourse direct and indirect with the Chinese states. A Si-Wang-Mu was reported to have presented Huang-ti [Yellow Emperor] with topographical maps.

...A Si-Wang-Mu appears again in connection with a journey which King Muh, fifth ruler of the Chou dynasty [C.950 BC], made in the West of China, along the Kuenlun range, where he was presented by her with some jade objects and some skilful workmen and where he examined their calendar and books. This journey which I am inclined to look upon as more important than is commonly believed, has been made the theme of all sorts of fables, extravaganzas and marvels, among which the historical truth and its particulars are probably lost irretrievably to history[121].

---

[120] See also Hill's comments in his preface to Fan Ye's 'Book of Later Han'
[121] Si Wang Mu was undoubtedly a Queen of one of the nations of the Tocharian Civilization, whose legend largely appears to stem from the aforementioned 950 BC westward trip of King Muh, who encountered her there then, and probably has been immortalised into other versions of her based on that. It is interesting to note

...there are some other proofs of jade traffic from Turkestan. Some of them are found in the Tu Rung or Tribute of Yu [part of the Book of Documents], a work of the Shang dynasty, where it is recorded that the western provinces of Yungtchou and Tsiang-tchou, corresponding to Shensi and Kansuh [Gansu Province] and to north Szetchuen respectively, produced to the Chinese court, jade stones of several forms. This jade, since it is not found in China proper, could only reach these provinces through the trade from Turkestan.

Chou Sin, the last ruler of the Shang Dynasty (circa 1120 BC) received as present from the Tan-tchi country, probably through the Chou people who made him some presents from the West in several instances, a pillow in Jade shaped like a tiger. This was undoubtedly procured by the same traffic.

Kuan-tze, an important writer of the seventh century B.C., states that Jade comes to China from the Yu-she mountains, in the far West, where the sun sets.

All the information we possess here on the Jade traffic shows it to be a second-hand one [i.e. through middle-men]; and however ancient it may have been, the amount of knowledge which has reached the Chinese through this channel cannot have been of importance, and must have consisted only of partial, incomplete notions, sometimes transmogrified on the way."[122]

Jade from Tocharia was traded the other way, too:

"The precious nephrite worked in the forms wrongly known as celts: neatly polished, with edges sharp and intact, is found along the route from Khotan in Turkestan, its starting point, to the Jaxartes, to the Oxus, then south of the Caspian sea, in Babylonia

---

the 'Queen' connections between Si Wang Mu and Cyrus's nemesis Massagetian Queen 'Tomyris'. Whether the Tocharians were already established when the Yellow Emperor passed through the region is a moot point.

[122] La Couperie, p.31-33. His interest was primarily in the ancient transmission route of Mesopotamian culture into China.

and Assyria, along the Northern Asia Minor shores, bordering upon ancient Troy, then passes to the Peloponnesus, where it directs its course to Crete, and, not touching Egypt, passes from Greece to Italy, whence it is distributed among the Helvetian lakes, the Megalithic monuments of Armorica &c., &c."[123]

The Tocharian region was well-known to the Han Chinese as the source of their precious jade, separated from them by the 'flowing sands' – i.e. the Gobi Desert flowing into the Tarim Basin. There are several mentions of this region in the 'Classic of Mountains and Seas', most featuring jade, such as:

"Going west, the River Peach runs on for 400 leagues to a place called Flowing Sands, and after 200 leagues it reaches Mount Hornetmother... On the summit of Mount Hornetmother are quantities of jade, and on its lower slopes are numerous green semi-precious stones, but there is no water...Three hundred and fifty leagues further west is a mountain called Mount Jade. This is where Queen Mother of the West lives.[124]...Within the West Sea region, in the middle of the Flowing Sands, there is a country named Chasmmarket."[125] (probably Kashgar) The Jade Civilization was all the while protected on all sides by the very mountains that the jade was dug out from. The mountain wall had essentially two passes westward: either directly through the Tarim Basin, along a mountainous road that led eventually to the Ferghana Valley or Bactria on the other side of the mountains (the furthest reach of Alexander the Great and the Greek imperialists) or north of the formidable Tian Shan Mountain range through the six mile wide 'Dzungarian Gate' pass through the Alatau mountain range, leading to the Eurasian steppe[126].

---

[123] La Couperie, p.33
[124] i.e. 'Si Wang Mu'. Classic of Mountains and Seas, p.24
[125] Classic of Mountains and Seas, p.191
[126] [from C.2000 B.C to C.800 B.C.] "there was *no other channel* than that of the eastern traffic of nephrite-jade originally from the Khotan region [between China and Bactria]." After this from C.800 BC there were sporadic but ineffective attempts to reach Patna in India from Szetchuen in China, then from C.300 BC increasing routes from Szetchuan and Yunnan in China through the mountains to

313

Whoever controlled this access between two worlds would be fabulously wealthy.

And it appears they were, because this trade route was bossed by the mysterious 'Great Yuezhi', (the 'Great Asia') a hugely powerful and populous nation based near Dunhuang around the Jade Gate[127], so as to control all traffic through it. They were the dominant military and political culture of the region, under whose oversight and protection the other oasis kingdoms thrived. Like the other nations of Tocharia, they spoke an Indo-European language.

Who were they? For millennia the Yuezhi operated unmolested in their far-eastern HQ, hidden from the eyes of the outside world by its mountain wall defences, who knew of them only through faint rumour and legend. Indeed their very existence was doubted in the Western world until the discovery of the Tarim Mummies in the 20th Century, and their fundamental ethnic and cultural identity has always remained a mystery.

Until now. We can exclusively reveal that the Yuezhi were none other than the direct forbears of the modern Swedes, Danes and Norwegians. Known sporadically in the West as the Seres, Hyperboreans, Asii and Aorsi, the term they used for themselves was 'Æsir' - Asians, from which many of the others derive.

Some may scoff at this identification, but there is absolutely no doubt, the evidence is conclusive.

The Icelandic history of Snorri Sturluson maintains with sober constancy that the Scandinavian people originally dwelt in the east

---

India became tentatively usable (La Couperie, p.63, 73.) Nb. La Couperie does not mention the northern 'Dzungarian Gate' Silk Road route. Throughout antiquity there were 'guerilla' attempts to find a southern back route through India, but this was not established until C.0 BC (see also Ptolemy, p.37-38). The discovery of the possibility of such a route - that could circumvent the Tocharian Silk Road - was a major achievement of the famous Chinese explorer and ambassador Zhang Qian who was sent westward in 138 BC, of whom more later.

[127] i.e. in the Qilian Mountains of Gansu Province (Shiji, 3, p.234)

on the other side of 'Swithiod the Great'[128] (Russia):

"The country east of the Tanaquisl [Tanais or Don River at the north-east corner of the Black Sea] in Asia was called Asaland, or Asaheim, and the chief city in that land was called Asgaard."[129] Commentators have also located the 'Hyperboreans' (the Greeks' name for Scandinavians) near the Dzungarian Gate[130]. Herodotus describes the journey of Aristeas, an explorer of the 7th Century BC:

"This Aristeas, possessed by Phoibos, visited the Issedones; beyond these live the one-eyed Arimaspoi[131], beyond whom are the [Griffins] that guard gold, and beyond these again the Hyperboreoi, whose territory reaches to the sea. Except for the Hyperboreoi, all these nations are always at war with their neighbors."[132]

The 'Boreas' to the Greeks was the 'North Wind' that blew out of a distant northern mountain cave, beyond where the Hyperboreans lived. Dzungaria (i.e. the area of the Dzungarian Gate, in many ways the 'door' to the world inside the mountain wall) is characterised by its constant, fierce winds (as well as gold

---

[128] Cognate with 'Scythia'
[129] Heimskringla, vol.1, p.270
[130] Ruck (p.227), Bolton, and Lehtinen (p.180) have made this identification.
[131] The 'Arimaspoi' who 'pushed the Issedones from their lands' (Herodotus, p.250), thereby triggering the 8th Century BC Massagetae>Scythian>Cimmerian movements, are thought possibly to refer to 'Ariama-Aspa' meaning 'horse-lovers' (i.e. possibly the huns) rather than 'Arima-Spou', 'one-eyed' but that this got lost in translation. Another connection to Herodotus' Arimaspoi is suggested by Strabo's discussion of the 'Arimi' (vol.2, p.304, 336, 403-5), a people who are associated with the resting place of 'Typhon', a Greek version of Thor (who slew Dionysious/Magog), and fittingly also with Anatolia around Mysia, but whose exact location is mysterious. Aristeas' 'Arimaspoi' meanwhile are located in Tocharia near the city of Turfan, where the Yuezhi/Æsir, the self-identifying offspring of Thor, were headquartered. Bolton notes that in other accounts 'Hyperboreans and Arimaspi are closely conjoined', and in fact the Arimaspi, elsewhere described as 'fair-haired', are called a 'Hyperborean tribe' (Bolton, p.23).
[132] Herodotus, p.250. As we have previously seen, Herodotus also identifies the Saka/Massagetae as the Issedones here, that may mean that both Hyperboreans and 'Arimaspi' refer to the Yuezhi, or the terms were confused (see Bolton, p.23)

deposits). Beyond the Dzungarian Gate, lived the Æsir.

The gold mentioned in these accounts is also discussed in the Chinese 'Classic of Mountains and Seas':

"West of the Flowing Sands [probably the Gobi Desert[133]] is Mount Bird. Three rivers rise on it. Here there is yellow gold, and fine jade, jasper, cinnabar goods, silver, and iron, which are all in the river currents of Mount Bird."[134]...

"On the summit of Mount Carobriver [later identified as being north of the Tarim Basin] are quantities of green male-yellow, precious pearl-like gems, and yellow gold and jade. Granular cinnabar is abundant on its south face and there are quantities of speckled yellow gold and silver on its north face."[135] This gold-mining region was known to Mesopotamian sources as 'Harali', the 'gold-bearing mountain' of 'Tukriš'[136]. The name 'Tukriš', otherwise Tocharia or Tocharistan, has the same linguistic origin as 'Turk'. 'Turk' was later co-opted as an ethnonym by other nations who succeeded to the area, but it was originally a term for the ancient Scandinavians, i.e. those who lived in Tocharia, the name being derived from that of their ancient ancestor Thor (pronounced in English 'Tour')[137].

---

[133] But could also refer to the Tarim Basin
[134] Classic of Mountains and Seas, p.191
[135] Ibid, p.22
[136] Steinkeller, 1982, p.248
[137] The derivation of the word 'Turk' appears to be as follows: the original of 'Turk' was 'Toxri', and it was the Old Turkish (i.e. before they were known as 'Turks') name for the Tocharians, i.e. the exonym given to the Tarim Basin/Gansu dwellers by others, while 'Æsir' AKA 'Ārśi' (or in some constructions 'Agni') was the name they used for themselves (Mallory & Mair, p.281-2). The Turks, being later mistaken for this people, co-opted the ethnonym for themselves (see e.g. Yarshater, p.576)

Further confirmation of this Tocharian 'Gold Mountain' comes from the Bible. It relates that the Israelite King Solomon (C.950 BC), when building his Temple for God, ordered gold to be brought specifically from 'Ophir'[138]. The location of Ophir has often been thought mysterious, however we know from Josephus that a son of Joktan, whom Thackeray identified as Ophir[139], went to the far east, specifically to 'Serica', the land of the Seres[140], i.e. Tocharia. These were the famous 'King Solomon's Mines'. Solomon had the gold, as well as precious jewels, from Ophir brought to Israel by ship, suggesting that it was transported through the Tirassian maritime trade routes via the Aral, Caspian and Black Seas[141]. The fame and excellence of Tocharian minerals appears to have been unmatched in the ancient world. Tocharian jade has also been found in the oldest layers of the City of Troy, witnessing that Scandinavians were transiting between the two centres as early as 1700 BC[142]. Along with their domination of the silk trade westwards, the Yuezhi's Tocharian operation had a good claim to being the world's pre-eminent logistics and supply hub.

---

[138] Tanakh, p.235-6; 288; 294

[139] Josephus book, vol.4, p.72. Ophir is listed as a son of Joktan in the Tanakh, p.6

[140] In fact the 'land of silk' or 'where the silk comes from'. But the 'Seres' of 'Serica' known to the Greeks were not the Chinese, as is clear from both Pliny, who describes them as 'above the ordinary height with flaxen hair and blue eyes' (Pliny, vol.2, p.54-55) and Ptolemy who lists 'Sinae' (Chinese) and 'Seres' as two separate peoples, and lists 'Serica' as in 'the northernmost parts of Greater Asia' along with Sarmatia and Scythia (p.159) and in his list of towns of 'Serica' (different from and hard to cross-identify with the Chinese list above) he names both 'Issedon Serica' (i.e. the Issedone or Massagetian city in Tocharia (so far unidentified) and 'Sera metropolis', the Greek understanding of the capital city of Serica, together (p.146). Therefore the Mediterranean conception of 'Serica' certainly included the Scandinavian Tocharia, and may have been identical with it. It is possible that 'Sera metropolis' did intend to mean Shang'An (from Ptolemy's distance estimates, p.33), but 'Seres' still referred to Tocharians, being their only contact with it. This understanding goes to show how completely the Tocharians controlled the trade in silk westwards - that they were known as 'the silk people' in the west, rather than its manufacturers, the Chinese. For further discussion of the term 'Seres' see La Couperie, p.226-7

[141] A trade route like this is mentioned by Strabo, vol.1, p.113

[142] "Thus the material of the implements discovered affords us interesting hints of a trade route leading to Central Asia existing as early as the oldest period of the city." [i.e. Troy], Schuchhardt, p.38

The Chinese were very aware of this power base to their north-west, even from furthest antiquity. The two oldest sources that mention the 'Western Regions', both probably from around 500-100 BC or earlier, are cryptic but colourful. These are the geographical work 'Classic of Mountains and Seas' and the 'Narrative of the Son of Heaven Called Muh', an apparently contemporary account of the aforementioned trip to the west undertaken by King Muh, the fourth King of the Chou dynasty, in C.950 BC. The flamboyant and poetic Classic and the pedestrian and functional Narrative have very different styles, but they corroborate one another in describing the same distinctive geographical features, as well as referring to powerful and mysterious rulers in the area.

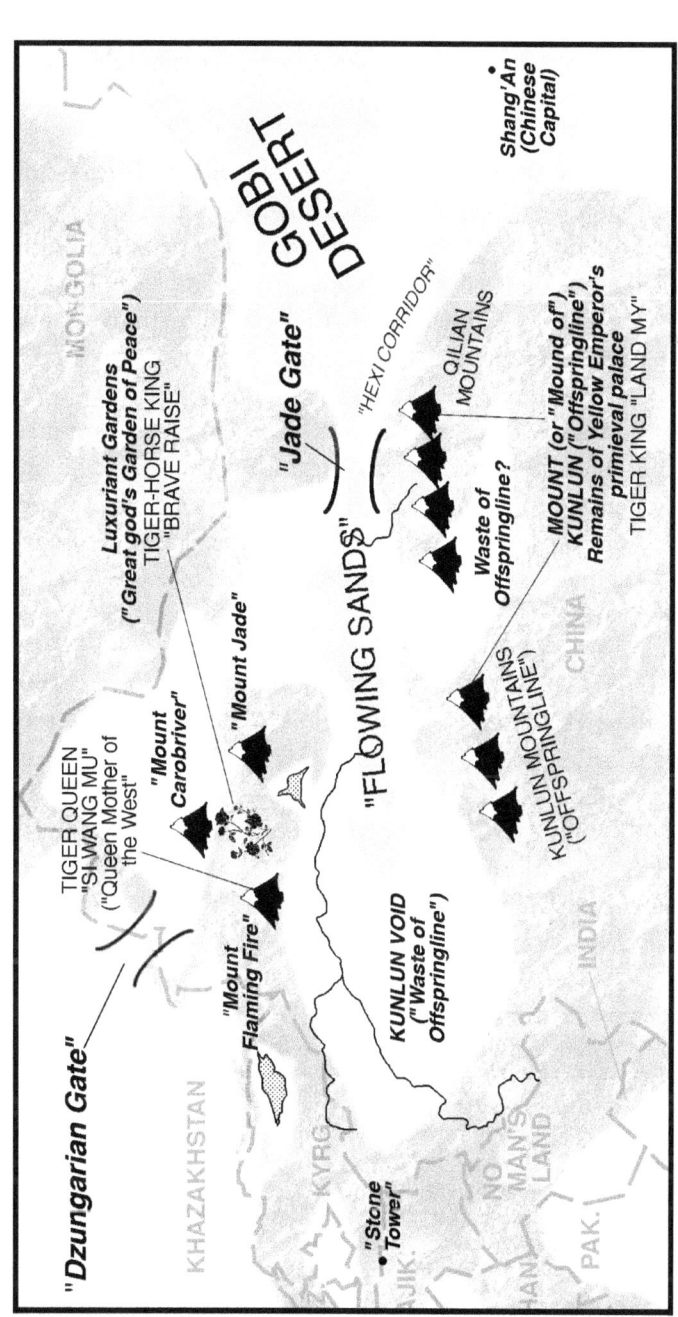

Fig.88: Some of the local landmarks of Tocharia known to the ancient Chinese (with the exception of 'Stone Tower', that was known to the Greeks). Some of these locations such as the Mound and Waste of Offspringline and Stone Tower are educated guesses, others like Mount Jade and the Luxuriant Gardens are known with some certainty. Incuded are the approximate locations of the Black (left) and Sarlet (right) rivers. (For Copyright info see footnote on following page)

The Chinese seem to have perceived the Scandinavian Kings as 'Tiger'-themed, as they are all described with this characteristic in the 'Classic'. The most ferocious-sounding is the ruler of the Kunlun Mount or Mound:

"...on the margins of the Flowing Sands, beyond the River Scarlet and before the River Black there is a huge mountain. Its name is the Mound of Offspringline. Here there is a god-human with a human face and a tiger's body which is striped and has a long tail, and it is flecked with white all over. This god-human lives on the mountain of the Mound of Offspringline"[143]

"...Four hundred leagues southwest[144] is called the Mound of Offspringline. This is in truth the Great God's City Here Below. The deity Land My presides over it. In appearance, he has a tiger's body and nine tails, a human head, and tiger claws. This deity presides over the Nine Parts of the Sky and the Great God's Park for the Seasons."[145]

When the Yuezhi are first mentioned in later, more prosaic Chinese histories, they are headquartered in the Qilian Mountains at the very north-eastern corner of the Himalayan Plateau, ideally situated to police the Silk Road from Shang'An to the Tarim[146]. This fits well with the Classic of Mountain and Seas' descriptions of the 'Tiger King' presiding over that area in antiquity. While the Qilian are generally understood to be further east than the Kunlun

---

'Mountain Stone Rock' by the3rdSequence (https://www.the3rdsequence.com/texturedb/) is licenced under CC BY 4.0 (http://creativecommons.org/licenses/by/4.0)

[143] Classic of Mountains and Seas, p.176. This location is also described as 'South of the West Sea' This sea may be Lop Nur, at the eastern end of the Tarim Basin. All but dried up today, it was a huge saltwater late in antiquity.

[144] Of Mount Carobriver, that does make this identification of Mount Kunlun questionable. However, the description goes on to describe 'Flowing Sands' and 'Mound Whitejade' as hundreds of miles further west.

[145] Classic of Mountains and Seas, p.23

[146] Shiji, 3, p.234

range, it is not clear if ancient writers made this distinction[147]. Certainly the 'Mound of Offspringline' was on the south side of the Tarim Basin, like the Qilian mountains, and it appears to have been the military strongpoint for the Great Yuezhi.

When King Muh passed through this region, it was near there that he undertook his famous visit to the remains of the Yellow Emperor's palace (that by then would have been perhaps a thousand years old). The location is described as "at the outlying hills of Kwan-lun in front of the river [Red]. Here there is the mountain of Yin-nao".[148]

It is unlikely that the Yuezhi would have selected the exact same place for their base as the Yellow Emperor had, and indeed they weren't at the palace when Muh visited. The narrative only recorded that the area was inhabited by the 'Chu-tsih' people and their King 'Wu', who lived on the 'heights of Kwan-lun'.

On the north side of the Tarim Basin is the highly identifiable 'Mount Jade', a hard-to-miss natural formation of gemstones that most visitors comment on. While the Classic of Mountains and Seas mentions jade on virtually every page, and refers to Tocharia in general as the 'Land of Mount Whitejade'[149], it only calls one mountain 'Mount Jade', and this is in the area of the well-known jade formation[150].

---

[147] Although if 'West Sea' is Lop Nur, this would tend to locate the 'Mound of Offspringline to the westward of the two options.
[148] Narrative of the Son of Heaven called Muh, p.229-230. A 'Mount Chung' also seems to have been in this area, about which the record states: 'Mount Chung is (one of) the highest mountains in the world.'
[149] Classic of Mountains and Seas, p.151. 'Mount Whitejade' may be one and the same as 'Mount Jade', although the characteristic white (and black) jade that Tocharia was famous for is more associated with mines on the south side of the Tarim Basin, around Khotan and Yarkand in the west, and 'Golmund' (near the Qilian Mountains) in the east, whereas 'Mount Jade' is on the north side.
[150] Ibid, p.24

The Narrative of Muh describes his progress from the Hwang Ti's palace. First he goes westward, then north, then east, crossing the River Black:

"He then followed the course of the river Hoh (Black). On Kwei-tsz (257th day), he reached the mountain of K'iun-yuh (lit. plenty of gems) which was guarded by the (chief of the) Yung...(shing) tribe...(On this mountain is a place) which the ancient Kings called their record-office. There are but few plants and trees there and more-over there are neither birds nor wild animals. Here there is, however, a tree...which the people of the Western Desert call[151]...In this place the Son of Heaven, by setting people to work the gem stone (mines), obtained three car-loads of gem-slabs, also gem utensils and dresss ornaments, gems being piled up to the number of ten thousand pieces."[152]

Marching westward from here he encounters the 'I-lu' tribe, then the Yin-han tribe, then "On Kwei-ch'eu (276th day), the Son of Heaven forthwith marched westwards. Ping-shan (279th day), he reached K'u-shan (Mount Brinjal), which the people of the Western Desert call Meu-yuen (Luxuriant Garden). The Son of Heaven here rested and hunted. Here it was that he tasted brinjal."[153]

Returning to the Classic of Mountains and Seas, this appears to be the same area where it says there lived another King:

"Three hundred and twenty leagues further west is a mountain called Mount Carobriver...On the summit of Mount Carobriver are quantities of green male-yellow, precious pearl-like gems, and yellow gold and jade. Granular cinnabar is abundant on its south face and there are quantities of speckled yellow gold and silver on

---

[151] This is thought to have been a special tree involved somehow in the spiritual life of the Jushi, perhaps similar to the later Saxon 'Irminsul', and perhaps even related in conception to the Norse 'world-tree', the ash 'Yggdrasil' (Poetic Edda, p.9)
[152] Narrative of the Son of Heaven called Muh, p.232. La Couperie also discusses this mountain, p.269
[153] Ibid, p.233. 'Brinjal' is related to the area's unique herbs, see later

its north face. In truth, this is the Great God's Garden of Peace. The deity Brave Raise presides over it. In appearance, this deity has a horse's body and a human face, with tiger markings and bird wings. He journeys around the four seas and his voice is like a booming crash. Mount Carobriver looks on Mount Offspringline to the south and the glare from it is dazzling, and its misty aura is haunting."[154]

This could well be referring to the Issedones, known in China as 'Wusun' or 'Jushi', as it mentions that, though he has 'tiger markings' he has a horse's body, similar to how many of the Issedones/Massagetae/Saka/Cimmerians had adopted the Scythian horse-warfare style. He also 'journeys around the four seas'. This could not be a more apt description of the Issedones/Saka's venturing far and wide westward, and how they got there: by sea. One can only speculate what 'four seas' might be referred to here, but the whole picture very much fits the Issedone's profile as 'outliers' and perhaps trade representatives of the Yuezhi, who were spread all over the place here and there as a consequence of seabourne enterprise, much like Anglo-Saxons are today.

However, the 'gardens' referred to, that can with some certainty be identified as today's Yulduz plateau south of Urumchi[155], possibly had a significance to all of the Scandinavian nations of Tocharia. 'Carobriver' or 'Brinjal' may have been to some extent a 'sacred mountain' to them[156], and the gardens certainly seem to play a central role in this area as their 'homeland'[157]. It may have been the

---

[154] Classic of Mountains and Seas, p.22-23
[155] La Couperie, p.273
[156] Ibid, p.269
[157] Notably this seems to have been the source of the Cinnabar or whatever was the key ingredient in the Yuezhi's 'elixir of life' or 'returning life spice'. About this La Couperie has this to say: "K'u shan, 8874-cl. 46 Bas., litt., Bitter's Mount, cannot be understood as Mount Brinjal as translated by Dr. Eitel (probably because of K'u-kwa, 8874, cl. 97 Bas. litt., bitter gourd, which was wrongly supposed to be the *solanum melangena* or brinjal. For instance in Doolittle's Vocab.) But Dr. Bretsehneider, Botan Sinic, ii., 387, tells us that the K'u kwa is the *momordica charantia*, which, the Pen tsao kang-muh of 1578 says, was introduced from the

'meeting point' or 'joining point' of the Yuezhi and Wusun nations[158].

After this stop King Muh goes to visit the 'Si Wang Mu', who certainly seems to be the head honcho in this area. Notably unlike all the other 'chiefs' he has met, Muh to some extent 'pays homage' to Si Wang Mu, as well as receiving homage from him:

"He then marched westwards. On Kwei-hai (286th day), he reached the people (called?) Si-wang-mu...(Having selected) as a lucky day, the Kiah-tsz (287th day), the Son of Heaven paid a visit to (the chief of) Si-wang-mu. Accordingly, holding the white rank-token and the round rank-token in his hands, he went to see (the chief of) Si-wang-mu, and (in token of his) friendly feelings he made an offering (to the chief) of 100 pieces of silk ribbons and 300 pieces of...ribbons. (The chief of) Si-wang-mu made repeated obeisances and accepted the presents"[159]

---

south, and therefore cannot be the intended plant, which I think was one of those producing *asafœtida*, for which the region north of Karashar has been renowned since antiquity. *Asafœtida*, from the Persian *aza*, mastic, which is largely used as a condiment by Asiatics, was with fir-bark and birds' fat the principal ingredients [sic] of the famous fir-balsam employed as a successful drug against consumption; it was therefore a life-prolonging medicine, and gave rise to the opinion amongst the Chinese of the contending states period, that Si Wang-mu...was in possession of the drug of immortality." (p.269-270)

[158] In general with the Yuezhi towards the south and east, and the Jushi/Wusun sprawling north and west, perhaps dominating the north side of the Tarim Basin. Notably 'Mount Jade' (the nearby landmark) in Chinese is 'Yushan', possibly being a source of 'Jushi' and 'Wusun'. The Book of Han (C.111 AD) states that a Jîh-ch'uh (Jushi) prince had a 'Slaves' Protector General' who ruled from Yanqi (Karashar) (Vol.10, p.21). Perhaps the division of labour was that the Yuezhi would guard the Jade Gate while the Issedones guarded the Dzungarian Gate, and this may have been the meaning of the Greek understanding of the 'Arimaspoi', the guardians of the gold. It is of no small significance that precisely in this area of the 'Luxuriant Gardens' were the easternmost headwaters of the Ili River system, from where a boat launched could travel downstream westward, perhaps communicating somehow with the headwaters of the Jaxartes River near the Issyk Kul lake, from where it was a straight journey downstream to the Aral Sea, that led to the Caspian and Black Seas. It is suggested that this was the route by which Jade and Gold from Tocharia reached Troy and Israel.

[159] Narrative of the Son of Heaven called Muh, p.233. A fascinating record of what must have been a fairly early transaction of the Silk Road.

This is followed by extremely tender and friendly exchanges, including mutual poetry composition, before King Muh takes his leave. Si-wang-mu perhaps later returned the honour by visiting King Muh's court at Shang'An.

The Chinese may have seen rulers (or, to them, 'deities') as having a continuity beyond individuals, so that these locations were known to be ruled by Kings with these characteristics, regardless of which particular ruler was reigning at the time. This for instance may explain the prodigious Chinese writings about the 'Queen Mother of the West' or 'Si Wang Mu', that seem all to have come from this initial report of King Muh's visit to the west, as well as a record in the Bamboo Annals that messengers from the 'Si Wang Mu' presented white jade rings and thimbles to the court of Shun, the fifth of the Five Emperors (C.1800 BC)[160]. Both of these descriptions of the western monarch are a lot less melodramatic than later, 'spiritualized' ones[161], and the translators are quick to point out that there is nothing in the text that describes a 'Queen' at all, only a ruler, and that the nation itself appears to have been known as 'Si Wang Mu'[162].

---

[160] Bamboo Annals, p.115
[161] For example in the Zhuangzi (C.330 BC), Si Wang Mu is listed along with other spiritual luminaries as one who had attained 'the way', the beginning of her long symbolic association with Taoism (Zhuangzi, p.56)
[162] Bamboo Annals, p.115, Legge states: 'the characters are merely the name of a state or kingdom in the distant west'. And in Narrative of the Son of Heaven book, p.233, Eitel states: 'These three characters probably are merely a transliteration of a name belonging to a polysyllabic non-Chinese language. The meaning of the individual characters chosen to represent that foreign name, ought not to prejudice the reader. There is nothing in this or any other *ancient* text to indicate that Si-wang-mu was a woman. Taking this name like other names in our text, it seems to me best to treat Si-wang-mu as the name of a tribe whose chief went by the same name.'

It is possible that when the Chinese first encountered the kingdom of Si-Wang-Mu (perhaps as early as the Yellow Emperor, or at least only some generations later, according to the Bamboo Annals) its ruler was a Queen. Or the feminisation (and 'deification') of 'Si Wang Mu' may have come later. The Oracle Bones (C.1500 BC) contain a reference to a 'western mother'[163] as the subject of 'offerings', but it is not clear if this is related. It has been suggested that the supernatural 'Queen Mother of the West' concept is a version of a Mesopotamian Moon goddess[164] (a variation of the pagan fertility goddess archetype), with whom the Tocharian kingdom was conflated because it was a major power in the west. Nevertheless, the Classic of Mountains and Seas has this to say about the fabled Queen:

"Three hundred and fifty leagues further west is a mountain called Mount Jade. This is where Queen Mother of the West lives. In appearance, Queen Mother of the West looks like a human, but she has a leopard's tail and the fangs of a tigress, and she is good at whistling. She wears a victory crown on her tangled hair. She presides over the Catastrophes from the Sky and the Five Destructive Forces."[165]

"...Queen Mother of the West leans against her raised seat. She wears a victory headdress and holds her staff. To her south there are the three green birds which gather food for Queen Mother of the West. The place where Queen Mother of the West resides lies north of the Waste of Offspringline."[166]

---

[163] in the context of making 'offerings to the eastern mother and the western mother'
[164] by Su Xuelin and Ling Chunsheng (Ye and Liu, p.595)
[165] Classic of Mountains and Seas, p.24. Nb. while Si-wang-mu is described here as living on Mount Jade, the later quote locates her at Mount Flamingfire.
[166] Ibid, p.145. Huainanzi also states 'The Queen Mother of the West dwells at the edge of the Flowing Sands.' (p.167)

"...Beyond it [a gulf that encircles the Mound of Offspringline], there is Mount Flamingfire. If you throw something at it, it immediately burns up. There is someone wearing a victory headdress. She has tiger fangs and a panther's tail. She lives in a cave. Her name is Queen Mother of the West. This mountain possesses all the myriad creatures that there are on earth."[167]

If at some point a Queen did rule the 'Si-wang-mu' with whom the Chinese had an encounter, she certainly made an impression![168]

Then we come to the mysterious and dramatic 'Waste of Offspringline". Perhaps the most spectacular yet obscure feature of Tocharia mentioned in the Classic of Mountains and Seas. It is tentatively identified here as the Tarim Basin itself, based on 1) the statement that the 'flowing sands' flow 'through' it[169]; 2) its definition as a 'void' or 'waste', suggestive of an emptiness within something[170], rather than a plateau; 3) the description of its size (see below) being approximately that of the Basin (remembering that the desert would have been smaller in the ancient past). However, it is also certainly possible that the 'waste' refers to the 'Taidam Basin' (labelled on the map above with a question mark) or even perhaps the Himalayan Plateau in toto, although this would seem to be too large.

"Offspringline Waste lies to its [Forkedtongue Country's] east. This mountainous Waste has four sides. One author says it lies to the east of Forkedtongue, and that the Waste is four-sided. Yi the Archer and Chisel Tooth fought in the Wilderness of Longlivedbloom. Yi shot him dead. The Wilderness lies to the east of Offspringline Waste."[171]

---

[167] Classic of Mountains and Seas, p.176
[168] The 'victory headdress' that is so insisted upon, does sound unlikely for a man, and is reminiscent of Queens' regalia such as that of Elizabeth I.
[169] Classic of Mountains and Seas, p.139
[170] The term might be translated as 'the void of inner Kunlun'
[171] Classic of Mountains and Seas, p.110

"Within the seas[172], the Waste of Offspringline lies to the northwest of Chiefbirdland. The mountainous Waste is the Great God's City on Earth Below. The Waste of Offspringline is 800 leagues square and 80,000 feet high[173]. On its summit there is the tree-barley which is forty feet high and five spans wide. There are nine wells on each face of the Waste of Offspringline, and their railings are made of jade. Each face of the mountainous Waste has nine gates, and at each of these gates there is an Openbright animal which guards the dwelling place of the hundred deities. The deities stay on the sheer cliffs of eight mountain nooks bordering on the River Scarlet. Apart from the humane god, Yi the Archer, no one else could climb up the sheer cliffs of these mountain ridges."[174]

The sumptuous descriptions of the wealth of Tocharia from the Israelite, Greek and Chinese conceptions are added to by Indian sources, that refer in particular to the city of Khotan, at the southwest of the Tarim Basin, a trade contact of theirs[175]. La Couperie describes: "Kuvera, the god of wealth of Brahmanic pantheon, corresponding to the Avestic Khshathra-Vairya...and also called a Vis Ravana or Vaisrava, moreover Ruler of the North, and described as a magnificent deity residing in the splendid city Alaka..., otherwise Khotan-Kustana. He was supposed to be a local deity of pre-Aryan[176] origin, and was worshipped by the first

---

[172] A bizarre description for such a landlocked region, this can perhaps only mean 'within' Lop Nur, that would make some kind of sense.
[173] A Chinese League ('Li') is now 500 metres, but in the past was around a third of a mile, putting the Kunlun Void at roughly 270 square miles, slightly smaller than the size of the Tarim Basin. Of course this cannot necessarily be taken at face value, especially considering the exaggerated height given (a Chinese foot = 9-9 ½ inches)
[174] Classic of Mountains and Seas, p.140
[175] From Khotan a 'southern route' of the Silk Road went south to India (see fig.86, above)
[176] Writing before the discovery of the Tarim Mummies and other evidence highlighted in this book, La Couperie was unaware of the Scandinavian civilization that lived around the Tarim Basin, i.e. the Tocharians. He calls them 'pre-Aryan' presumably because in later centuries, as part of Buddhist expansion into China, Indo-Aryans would make their way to or through the Tarim from India, with many of the extant remnants of the Tocharian language found there from the 5th-6th centuries AD being Buddhist texts. See also Mallory & Mair, p.116, 279

king spoken of, in the Legends, whose date, according to Buddhist sources, was 234 years after the Buddha's Nirvana, or about 238 B.C. The same sources either collected from Hiuen Tsang's report or from Tibetan documents, make this king contemporary and victorious of a son of Asoka [founder of a large North-Indian empire – Ed.] who had been sent there."[177]

The Yuezhi or 'Æsir' therefore controlled the economic and political activity of the extensive, globally-reaching and wealthy Tocharian civilization, a role in which they were apparently aided by their ubiquitous neighbours the 'Jushi', 'Wusun' or 'Issedones', and had apparently done so since before 1500 BC.

---

[177] La Couperie, p.74-75

As for the possible location of an historical 'Ásgard', the legendary home city of the Æsir[178], there are a few places of interest. Running from east to west the Yuezhi started off in the Qilian Mountains, that may have been the location of their original capital. There is also the spectacular fortress city of Jiaohe, near Turfan and 'Mount Jade', that may have been built by the Yuezhi to control the Silk Road:

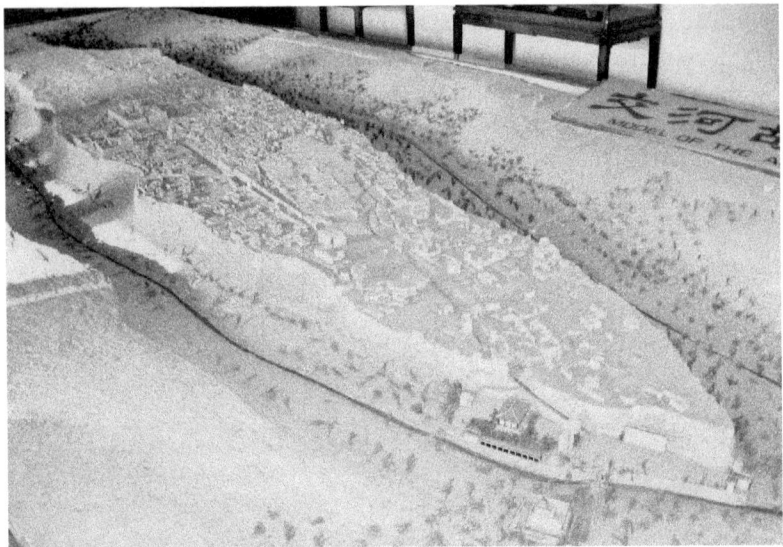

Fig.89: A model of the Jiaohe fortress city[179]

Another good idea would be to dredge the Issyk Kul lake[180], where in 2007 a Russian archaeological expedition discovered:

"sensational finds, including the discovery of major settlements, presently buried underwater.... formidable walls, some stretching for 500 meters-traces of a large city with an area of several square

---

[178] Like Troy before its discovery in the 19th Century or Leif Eriksson's colony in Newfoundland before its discovery, it would be foolish and to risk being found on the wrong side of history to presume that Ásgard was not a real place.
[179] Image by Colegota from Wikimedia Commons (https://en.wikipedia.org/wiki/File:Turpan-jiaohe-maqueta-d01.jpg) (desaturated, cropped), used under CC BY SA 2.5 ES (https://creativecommons.org/licenses/by-sa/2.5/es/deed.en)
[180] Visible on the above map (Fig.88) as the ellipse-shaped lake north-west of the Tarim Basin.

kilometres... Scythian burial mounds, eroded by waves over the centuries, and numerous well preserved artifacts-bronze battleaxes, arrowheads, self-sharpening daggers, objects discarded by smiths, casting molds, and a faceted gold bar, which was a monetary unit of the time."[181]

Somewhat more prosaicly, Heyerdahl & Lillieström note William B. Williams' research that the original name of Kiev was 'Azagarium'[182]. Kiev was certainly a vital node in the ancient Scandinavians' transit network, and may also have been the historical 'Ásgard'. Although if so the Russians seem to have forgotten it.[183]

There is no guarantee that any of these were 'Ásgard'[184] but it certainly would make a fascinating study.

The Yuezhi had built up their mountain-protected trading paradise really from the dawn of post-diluvian history, while orchestrating arguably the world's biggest mining and logistics operation. But since the fall of Troy and the increasing curtailment of Thraco-Cimmeria in the West by creeping imperial encroachment, with settlements there now more or less limited to the Crimean Peninsula and some other isolated trading centres around Sakasena and Azerbaijan, the Tocharian base of operations had taken on greater significance; it had become the world centre of the ancient Scandinavians, the global Scandinavian HQ.

This was not particularly a bad thing. Living around what some have called 'the celebrated garden of central Asia'[185], the Yuezhi enjoyed unparalleled levels of wealth and success. However, this prosperous and time immemorial set-up for the proto-Scandinavians and their Tarim Basin neighbours was not to last for much longer.

---

[181] Lukashov
[182] p.112, as per Ptolemy, p.80
[183] Russian Primary Chronicle, p.54-55
[184] Prose Edda (p.21), perhaps over-simplifying, asserts that Ásgard was Troy
[185] La Couperie, p.276

The Xiong Nu

Towards the end of the 3rd Century BC changes were afoot in the Chinese world. During the early history of China there was one gap in their mountain wall of protection and that was directly north of their settlement, through the 'Ordos Plateau'. This area had been the roaming ground for the horse-riding 'Donghu', very likely the furthest east-roaming Scythians or Saka from the steppe.

Fig.90: Bronze 'Donghu' figure from the 1st Century BC 'Ordos Loop' area directly north of Shang'An[186].

These nomads would occasionally make raids into Chinese territory. But by the middle of the 1st Millennium BC they were gradually being driven out by a home-grown Chinese version, who

---

[186] Wikimedia image by PHGCOM (https://commons.wikimedia.org/wiki/File: BronzeManOrdos3-1stCenturyBCE.JPG) (desaturated), used under CC BY SA 3.0 Unported (https://creativecommons.org/licenses/by-sa/3.0/deed.en)

may have taken their lead from the Scythian tactics, the 'Xiong Nu'. At that time they were still vassals of the Yuezhi, but this loose amalgam of raiders would continue to grow in size and aggression and would eventually come to be known by their westernised name: 'the Huns'.

The origins of the Xiong Nu are extremely obscure, and there are four basic possibilites:

1) They were an offshoot from Chinese culture, that had adopted Scythian horse archery tactics and to some extent intermarried with the Donghu[187]
2) They were essentially Indo-European, 'Scythian' (Donghu) who over the centuries had become increasingly sinicised and intermarried with the Han Chinese
3) Their defining characteristic was as a mixed-race 'outcast' group who were welcomed in neither culture and therefore had become hard-bitten outlaws. This is supported by the steady growth of their numbers and their 'confederate' organisation as a military group that did not require a high level of ethnic homogeneity within their number but rather only adherence to the rapacious 'Hun' mentality.
4) The Xiong Nu were of entirely separate descent and constituted a separate nation whose homeland was north of China.

Interestingly genetic studies of the paternal Y-DNA haplogroups of samples thought to represent the remains of various Eurasian Steppe nomads found that while the Huns' successors the Turks and Mongols shared virtually identical haplogroups (mainly C-M217, N-M231 and O-M175), the Huns were mainly Q1a and Q1b-M378. (With the Han Chinese as O2-M122). While pointing out the unreliability of DNA samples taken from the deceased, Professor Nathanael Jeanson identifies Q1 (Xiong Nu),

---

[187] Sima Qian in his 'Records of the Grand Historian' supported this view, believing the Xiong Nu to be descended from 'Chunwai', a descendant of Yu the Great and the 'Xia' dynasty (Shiji, 3, p.129). While this doesn't tell us much (because Yu is Noah), it suggests a descent from Shennong/Jie.

O2 (Han) and R1 (Tocharians including Afanasievo) as coming from three different branches of the descendants of the Shemite Joktan (most likely through his son Ophir who is recorded as emigrating to this area[188]). If this is so, then much of the area's populations were probably descended from an original Joktanian colony, possibly to be associated with Afanasievo and/or the Yellow Emperor, some of whom (Tocharians) settled in the Tarim, some of whom went east to join the Shennong Chinese colony (Han and Koreans) and some went North-East into Mongolia (Xiong Nu). C and D haplogroups (characterising Tibetan and Japanese populations) according to this research were descended from Ham. This all suggests that both options 1) and 3) above are somewhat accurate.

Either way, this outlaw confederacy burgeoned during the 'Warring States' period of civil war in Chinese history between 475 and 221 BC. When that period ended with the Qin dynasty establishing a tyrannical dominance as the first Chinese 'Empire', the Xiong Nu didn't go away. In fact the Qin government exacerbated the problem by preventing the Xiong Nu, living in the Ordos region, from trading with Chinese peasants. They raided South into China instead. But, free from the distraction of civil war, the newly centralized government could now take concerted steps against the growing Xiong Nu menace. What it did was to join the disparate sections of the northern border walls into one long wall: the Great Wall of China.

---

[188] Josephus book, vol.4, p.72

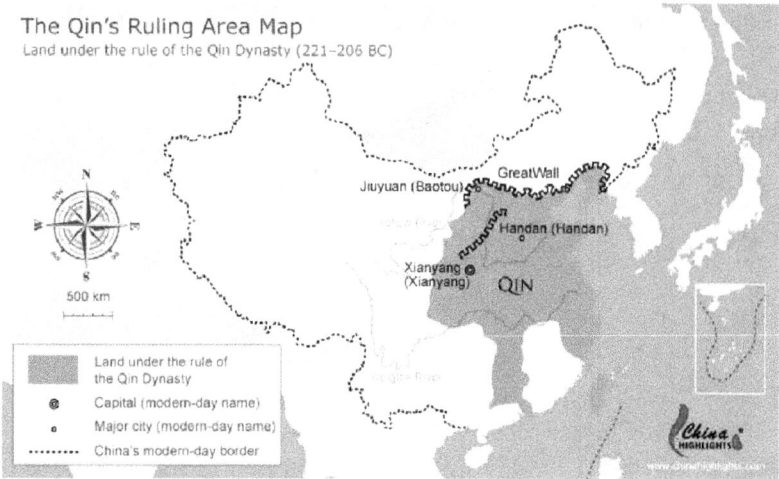

Fig.91: the Qin Empire C.200 BC and the Great Wall[189]

In 215 BC Emperor Qin ordered his general Meng Tian to expel the Xiong Nu from the Ordos Loop. This was done and the Xiong Nu were forced into Mongolia[190]. As a result of this, the defeated Xiong Nu leader's son Modu[191], when he took over as leader, reorganised the Xiong Nu for the first time into a powerful confederate state.

Modu launched an all-out war on both the Chinese and the Yuezhi, who were first attacked by his father Touman in 209 BC, with the Xiong Nu defeated and Touman possibly dying in the war or possibly being killed by Modu.

The authoritarian Qin Chinese dynasty didn't last long and fell in 207 BC leading to a short period of conflict. During this in 203 BC Modu attacked the Yuezhi again, this time taking territory from them and probably pushing them out of the Hexi Corridor.

---

[189] Image used courtesy of www.chinahighlights.com
[190] Shiji, 3, p.133-134
[191] AKA 'Maodun'

The more moderate Han dynasty took the hegemony of China in 202 BC, and was immediately attacked by a massive 320,000 strong Xiong Nu army. The new Emperor Gaozu came close to being toppled completely, instead agreeing to all Modu's terms including paying taxes to the Xiong Nu.

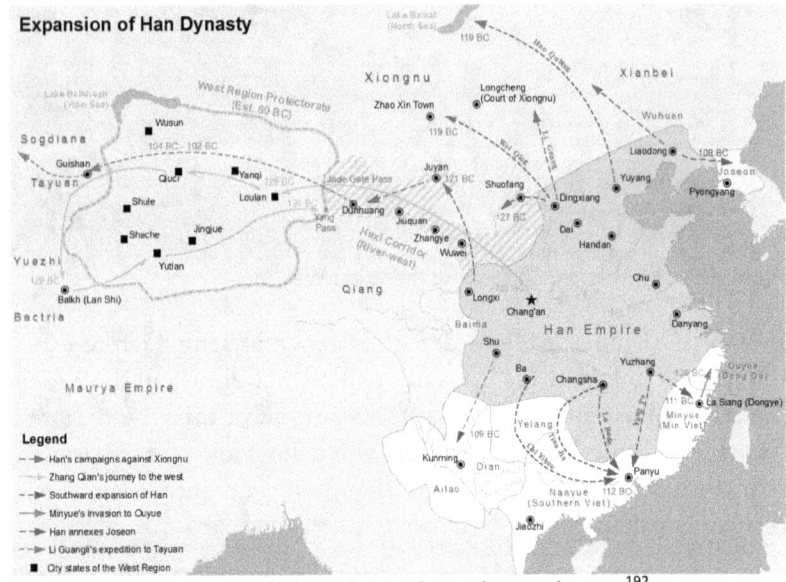

Fig.92: the chaotic state of China during the early Han dynasty[192]

In 176 BC the now considerably strengthened Xiong Nu under Modu attacked the Yuezhi for a third time, and finally overcame them, in what was a catastrophic defeat for the Yuezhi[193]. Their reign as Lords of Tocharia was over. Modu died in 174 BC, being replaced by his son Laoshang Chanyu. Laoshang allegedly then killed the King of the Yuezhi and made a drinking cup out of his skull[194].

---

[192] Wikimedia image by SY (https://commons.wikimedia.org/wiki/File:Han_Expansion.png) (desaturated), used under CC BY SA 4.0 International (https://creativecommons.org/licenses/by-sa/4.0/deed.en)

[193] Shiji, 3, p.140. Later Xiong Nu records make reference to various victories over the 'Az people', a group referred to as the 'far-away Az', who at one time appear to have been closer, on the borders of the Xiong Nu (Orkhon Inscriptions, p.866, 869, 873). These are probably references to the Yuezhi.

[194] Shiji, 3, p.231, 234

In 173 BC the Yuezhi attacked and displaced the Wusun – perhaps perceived as having taken part in their earlier defeat. Then in 165 BC began a vast migration westward – the exodus of a huge nation. First they settled in the Ili Valley north of the Tian Shan, displacing the Wusun/Saka there, but it was to be only a temporary stop

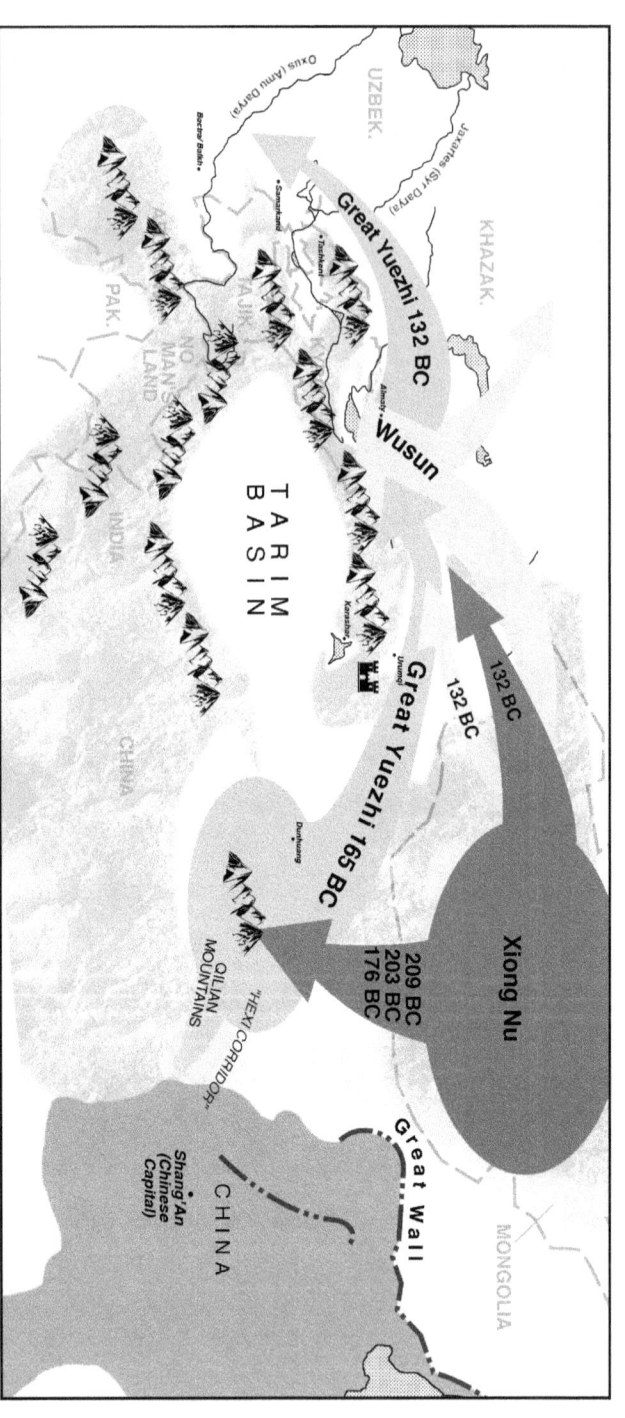

Fig.93: The momentous people movements in Western China during the 2nd Century BC that resulted from the building of the Great Wall of China and the growth of the 'Xiong Nu'. (See footnote on following page for copyright information)

The Great Yuezhi move house

In 132 BC the Wusun, now in full alliance with the Xiong Nu, invaded the Ili River Valley, forcing the Yuezhi to move once again, a bigger move this time. They would emerge west of the Tian Shan mountains for the first time, thus appearing on the radar of the western civilizations. Westward from the Ili Valley they rounded the Tian Shan and crossed the Jaxartes River where they faced: guess who? You've guessed it, the Iranians. Yes the Yuezhi are the Turans of Iranian legend.

When the massive and powerful nation of the Yuezhi rolled into Transoxiana, it was not a welcome event for the Parthians[195]. And so the first half of the Kayanian dynasty story from the Shahnameh, now correctly placed in its historical context of the Parthian dynasty's struggles with their northern neighbour across the Oxus River, the Thor-descended Æsir, can be told. The Æsir in turn were also not in a particularly good mood, having recently suffered epochal, catastrophic, civilization-destroying national defeat. It wasn't the recipe for a good relationship.

'Mountain Stone Rock' by the3rdSequence (https://www.the3rdsequence.com /texturedb/) is licenced under CC BY 4.0 (http://creativecommons.org /licenses /by/4.0)

[195] To give some idea of the size of this population movement, the Book of Han (Vol.10, p.40)) numbers the Yuezhi in this area after the move as 400,000 people, with 100,000 men under arms. A huge number, much larger than that of any of the Tocharian city-state nations listed. Particularly as the nearby neighbouring co-refugee nations, spread along the path of migration, the Jushi (numbering 30,000 people (Book of Later Han, Sections 23-27)), Wusun (630,000 people, originally 'Sacae' (Book of Han, Vol.11, p. 83-84)) the Kangju (an offshoot of the Yuezhi, 600,000 people, resident after the migration in the location of Sogdiana, north of the Yuezhi (Ibid, p.42)) and the Yancai (Alans, a 'dependency' of Kangju, to its north-west (Book of Later Han, Section 19) were probably related and to some extent subordinate to the Yuezhi. A remnant 'lesser' Yuezhi (cf. this 'Great' Yuezhi) stayed at or south of the Qilian Mountains (Shiji, 3, p.234)

In 127 BC an embassy from China visited the Yuezhi court in Transoxiana offering an alliance against the Xiong Nu, but the son[196] of the slain King refused it. By then the King, it seems, had other plans.

The Ambassador was the famous traveller Zhang Qian, whose long trip, including two periods of captivity and imprisonment by the Xiong Nu, changed the face of China by opening it up to the outside world. He went west to seek out an alliance with the Yuezhi, to re-open the Silk Road trade, that had been closed off by the Xiong Nu's possession of the Hexi Corridor. His description of his findings in Bactria (called by the Chinese 'Daxia') are recorded in the 'Shiji':

"Daxia is situated over 2,000 *li* (roughly 700 miles) south-west of 'Da Yuan' [Ferghana, probably meaning 'Great Javan/Ion', i.e. the closest area touching the Greek Empire or Greek culture, that had influenced Ferghana for 200 years by that point[197]], south of the Gui [Oxus] river. Its people cultivate the land, and have cities and houses. Their customs are like those of Dayuan. It has no great ruler but only a number of petty chiefs ruling the various cities. The people are poor in the use of arms and afraid of battle, but they are clever at commerce. After the Great Yuezhi moved west and attacked and conquered Daxia, the entire country came under their sway. The population of the country is large, numbering some 1,000,000 or more persons."[198]

That the 'Turans' of the Shahnameh are the 'Yuezhi' of Chinese records is backed up by copious references in the Shahnameh, such as for example that the initial Turan invasion came from 'Turan and China', and that the Turan King's chief advisor Piran hailed from Khotan.

---

[196] Or possibly Grandson
[197] La Couperie, p.221
[198] Shiji, 3, p.235. Note that Bactria, that had previously been under the control of the Greco-Bactrian Kingdom, though reduced to an Iranian vassal state by this time, was distinct from Iran proper, whose defence against the Yuezhi was more robust than this.

Finding Odin

We noted earlier that Thor Heyerdahl in his book 'Jakten På Odin' (the Hunt for Odin) travelled to Azerbaijan and Asov, identifying these as centres of 'Æsir' proto-Norse culture[199]. Indeed they were. But at this point in history, with the Troad and Thrace having been comprehensively overrun by Greeks and foreigners, the Crimea was possibly the last major bastion in the West of the maritime culture of the Tirassians. But it was not the dwelling place of the figure who would become something akin to the 'Scandinavian Moses' for them, who would lead his people out of wretched homelessness and peril in Asia to a new homeland in the far north of Europe. As we shall see, he was indeed a real person, but grew up much further east.

We note from the Shahnameh that the Iranian word for everything bad in the world was 'Azzhi' – surely not a coincidence that this was the self-identification of the Yuezhi/Æsir. Similarly the most despised characteristics within Norse cosmology were summed up by the word 'Sid' meaning cowardly deviousness, connivingness or witchcraft including sexual perversion, qualities they associated very directly with their southern neighbours the 'Vanir' (from which we get our word 'vain'). And this would arguably have been to the Yuezhi typical qualities of the 'magic'-studying Iranians, especially with a now 'orientalized' or homosexual, effete urban influence from the Greeks, not to mention the allegations of incest in the Shahnameh[200].

But do the 2nd Century BC events that would transpire between the Yuezhi and the Indo-Iranians across the Oxus River match the story of the Iranian war against the Turans? And can the Kings of the Indo-Iranian Parthian Empire really be the characters

---

[199] Heyerdahl & Lillieström, p.131, 156, 147

[200] p.440-441. 'Vanir' may also come from the culture memory of the Cimmerians' dust-up with Urartu AKA the 'Kingdom of Van' in the 8th Century BC (as proposed by Heyerdahl and Lillieström, p.131-133). Although we can now positively identify Snorri's 'Æsir' with the Yuezhi, in many ways their war with the Iranians was a continuation of the earlier one further west, and they may have associated the Urartian 'Vanir' with their later, related opponents in Iran.

described in the Shahnameh as the early Kayanian Kings, simply listed way out of sequence in the historical narrative? Let us take a look at some descriptions of the resulting war, that began immediately in 132 BC as soon as the Yuezhi/Æsir arrived in Transoxiana as an inherent part of their migration, from two parallel sources that this author contends represent the recorded histories of the two opposing sides in the war. Firstly the Iranian history in the Shahnameh of Ferdowsi, then the Heimskringla written by the primary source for ancient Scandinavian history, the 12th Century Icelandic skald Snorri Sturluson:

From the Shahnameh:

"But the tidings spread, even into Turan, that Minuchihr the just [the last successful Iranian King before the Kayanians – Ed.] was departed, and that the hand of Nauder was heavy upon the land. And Poshang, who was of the race of Tur, heard the news thereof with gladness, for he deemed that the time was ripe to remember the vengeance that was due unto the blood of his sire. Therefore he called about him his warriors, and bade them go forth to war against Iran, saying the time was come to avenge his father and draw unto himself the heritage[201]. And while his son Afrasiyab made ready the host to fulfil the desire of his father, there spread the news that Sam the Pehliva had been gathered unto the dust, and that Zal tarried in his house to build him a tomb. And the news gave courage unto Afrasiyab and his men, and they made haste to gain the frontier.

But the grandson of Feridoun had learned of their coming, and he prepared him to meet the foes of his land. Then he sent forth an army that overshadowed the earth in its progress. But the army of Afrasiyab was great also, and it covered the ground like unto ants and locusts. And both hosts pitched their tents in the plains of Dehstan and made them ready for the fight. And the horses neighed loud, and the pawing of their hoofs shook the deep places of the earth, and the dust of their trampling uprose even unto

---

[201] Pushang's father is named as 'Zadsham', but this may be a reference to Tur.

heaven. Then when they had put their men into array, they fell upon each other, and for two days did they rage in fierce combat, neither did the victory lean to either side. And the clamour and confusion were mighty, and earth and sky seemed blended into one. And the carnage was great, and blood flowed like water, and heads fell from their trunks like unto autumn leaves that are withered. But on the third day it came about that the upper hand was given unto the men of Turan, and Nauder the King, and the flower of his army with him, fell into the hands of the foe.

Then Afrasiyab cut off the head of Nauder the Shah, and sat himself down upon the throne of light. And he proclaimed himself lord of Iran, and required of all men that they should do him homage, and pour gifts before his face." [202]

An important thing to note from this Iranian version is that the Iranian land it names as captured by the Turans is 'Dahestan'. This was the region of the 'Dahae' or what the Greeks called 'Hyrcania', the ancestral base of the Parthian Kings[203].

The conflict seems to have begun with an initial huge battle, won by the Yuezhi, but followed after a few years by increasingly attritious victories and losses on both sides. The Shahnameh continues:

"Zal [Iranian champion[204]] heard about what had happened to Aghriras [Afrasiab's brother] and said, "His good fortune grows dim, and his throne desolate." He had the brazen trumpets blown,

---

[202] Shahnameh, p.112-125. The version quoted here is abridged by Helen Zimmern of Sattor.com (p.36-7) from the somewhat long-winded original
[203] Today's south-west Turkmenistan, on the corner of the Caspian Sea
[204] In fact Zal is the King of 'Sistan', i.e. Afghanistan. There is evidence he came from the Wusun (as Chinese histories record a similar 'bird-raised' origin story for a famous Wusun chief, 'Kunmo' (Shiji 3, p.237-8, cf. Shahnameh, p.63-64), i.e. he was Saka. Many of the Jushi/Wusun had been pushed southwards by the Yuezhi incursion into their Ili River territory C.165 BC, moving to and settling in Afghanistan, where they became an important aid to the Iranians when dealing with their new enemy to the north, the Yuezhi, with whom the Jushi/Wusun had much more experience. Thus 'Sakastana' became 'Sistan' (Bosworth, p.247)

and drums strapped onto his war elephants, and he drew up his army that glittered as splendidly as a rooster's eye. He led his men toward Pars, seething with anger as he marched. From sea to sea the plains were filled with men, and the faces of the sun and moon were obscured by dust. When Afrasyab learned that Zal had mobilized his forces, he prepared for the defense of Rey. The advance troops of the two armies fought day and night, and many warriors and chieftains were killed on both sides."[205]

Fig.94: A supposedly 'Scythian' copper helmet from Samarkand, 6th to 1st Century BC. In fact the Scythians were not known for wearing helmets, and this almost certainly belonged to the invading Yuezhi[206]

Now from the Scandinavian side:

"[The Æsir King] went out with a great army against the Vanaland people; but they were well prepared, and defended their land; so that victory was changeable, and they ravaged the lands of each other, and did great damage. They tired of this at last, and on both sides appointed a meeting for establishing peace."[207]

And the description of the peace in the Shahnameh (as spoken by Kay Kawad):

---

[205] Shahnameh, p.127-128
[206] Wikimedia image by ALFGRN (https://en.wikipedia.org/wiki/File: Scythian_helmet,_copper_alloy,_Samarkand,_6th-1st_century_BCE.jpg) (desaturated), used under CC BY SA 2.0 (https://creativecommons.org/licenses/by-sa/2.0/deed.en)
[207] Heimskringla, vol.1, p.272

"Verily not my people sought out this war but Afrasiyab, who deemed that he could wrest unto himself the crown of Iran, and could subdue the masterless land unto his will. And he hath but followed in the footsteps of Tur his father, for even as he robbed the throne of Irij, so did Afrasiyab take from it Nauder the Shah. And I say to you that I need not make peace with you because of any fear, but I will do it because war is not pleasing unto me. I will give unto you, therefore, the farther side of the river, and it shall be a boundary between us, and I pray that Afrasiyab may find rest within his borders."[208]

Now let us compare the descriptions from the two sides of the highly specific characteristics of the aggressive young invading King of the Turans/Æsir, who does not seem to have been a particularly pleasant human being:

From the Encyclopaedia Iranica:

"According to *Dēnkard* III.110 (tr. J. de Menasce, Paris, 1973, p. 113), Afrāsīāb was a demon (*dēv*) incapable of changing his nature and therefore unable to reach salvation...

"In the *Šāh-nāma*, Afrāsīāb is portrayed as a tenacious, shrewd, and resourceful king of great valor who commands the loyalty of his warriors and presents the Iranians with a redoubtable and worthy enemy. The title that *Mojmal* (p. 417) mentions for him in the list of kings' titles, *jahāngīr-e vadkerd*, "wicked world-conqueror," succinctly sums up his portrayal. The author of *Mojmal* adds (p. 44) that Afrāsīāb had fought more than one thousand and one hundred battles, in all of which he was victorious. Although depicted essentially as a villain, he is not without saving graces. He can be wise, as when he urges his father to sue for peace, or kind, as when he receives Sīāvoš; but he is also impetuous, suspicious, and cruel. The contrast between him and Kay Kosrow lies mainly in the latter's piety, justice, and humanity (see e.g. V, pp. 317ff., 376ff.)

---

[208] Shahnameh, p.139, again from the Zimmern version, p.42

...In the Iranian tradition Afrāsīāb's mythical aspects are eliminated or reduced, but Pahlavi books, and occasionally also Perso-Arab sources, retain scattered references to his demonic and magical powers. Theodor Bar Kōnay refers to Afrāsīāb's having turned into a dove, an ant, and an old dog (Benveniste, "Le témoignage," p. 192)"[209]

And a description in the Shahnameh by Iranian champion Qaren of his failure to get to grips with Afrasiab in the fateful battle where the Turans conquered the Iranians:

"today when battle overtook Pashang's son [Afrasiab], and part of his army was destroyed, he chose fresh troops, then saw me with my ox-headed mace and came after me eager to fight. I came so close to him that we looked one another in the eye, but then he wove a magical spell, and both light and color disappeared before my sight. Night fell and the world turned dark, and my arm was unable to strike. It seemed that time itself was ending, and that the sky had retreated beneath the earth, and we had to draw back from the battle in the dust and darkness."[210]

---

[209] Yarshater, p.571; 574
[210] Shahnameh, p.164

Now from the 'Heimskringla' of Snorri Sturluson:

"When sitting among his friends his countenance was so beautiful and dignified, that the spirits of all were exhilarated by it, but when he was in war he appeared dreadful to his foes. This arose from his being able to change his skin and form in any way he liked. Another cause was, that he conversed so cleverly and smoothly, that all who heard believed him. He spoke everything in rhyme, such as now composed, which we call scald-craft. He and his temple priests were called song-smiths, for from them came that art of song into the northern countries. Odin could make his enemies in battle blind, or deaf, or terror-struck, and their weapons so blunt that they could no more but than a willow wand; on the other hand, his men rushed forwards without armour, were as mad as dogs or wolves, bit their shields, and were strong as bears or wild bulls, and killed people at a blow, but neither fire nor iron told upon themselves. These were called Berserker.

...Odin could transform his shape: his body would lie as if dead, or asleep; but then he would be in shape of a fish, or worm, or bird, or beast, and be off in a twinkling to distant lands upon his own or other people's business. With words alone he could quench fire, still the ocean in tempest, and turn the wind to any quarter he pleased."[211]

Any reasonable observer must admit that there is a remarkable similarity between Afrasiab, the wicked Turan King, and 'Odin of Asaland', the ancient hero of the Scandinavian people[212].

---

[211] Heimskringla, vol.1, p.276-277
[212] This is not to comment on the historicity or otherwise of the strange phenomena witnessed, but rather to note that the descriptions, being conceptually identical, are a perfect match. It is likely that his capital was in the region of the city of Samarkand, as it is the location of an ancient ruined, pre-Mongol city bearing the name, 'Afrasiab'. See also Book of Han, vol.10, p.41

But this alone is not enough to make a positive identification, as many ancient heroes (and so-called 'gods') are credited with all kinds of supernatural powers by later chroniclers, notwithstanding that those described here are particularly specific and matching.

To remove all doubt however, let us compare more of the parallel passages that describe the conflict both from the Iranian side and from the Scandinavian Heimskringla, really to put this argument to bed:

From the Encyclopaedia Iranica:

"The first attack of Afrāsīāb against Iran takes place under Manōčehr's son and successor Nōḏar, who proves an inept and wayward king. When Pašang, the Turanian monarch, senses the weakness in Iran, he appoints his ambitious and vengeful son, Afrāsīāb, to head a mighty army, which invades Iran at Dahestān and Āmol (*Šāh-nāma* II², pp. 5ff.). Nōḏar is defeated, seized, and finally put to death, and 1,200 Iranian veterans are made captive; they are saved from execution only by the ardent intercession of Afrāsīāb's goodhearted and righteous brother Aḡrēraṯ, who pleads for them to be imprisoned in a cave under his custody (II², p. 29). Afrāsīāb assumes the kingship of Iran and rules over it for twelve years...

However, according to the more genuine Iranian tradition preserved in Pahlavi books and Islamic histories (e.g., *Bundahišn* 33.5-6; *Šahrastānīhā ī Ērān*, par. 35; *Zand ī Vahman Yašt* 5.7; *Mēnōg ī xrad* 27.44; Ṭabarī, I, pp. 434-36; Bīrūnī, *Āṯār*, p. 220; Taʿālebī, *Ġorar*, p. 107; Ebn Meskawayh, *Tajāreb*, facsimile ed., I, Leiden and London, 1909, pp. 18, 19)Afrāsīāb's attacks took place towards the end of Manōčehr's reign; Manōčehr was besieged and detained in the Padašxwār mountains in Ṭabarestān and, according to the *Bundahišn*, ibid., his two sons, Fryā and Nōḏar, were killed[213]. The genuineness of this tradition is shown not only by its prevalence in the sources, but also by the fact that Nōḏar's name does not appear among the kings in the Pahlavi books, nor do his sons Tūs and Gostahm attain kingship. The tradition followed by Ferdowsī and also by Ṭaʿālebī (who is aware of the variance between the two accounts, *Ġorar*, p. 107) has obviously been fashioned and recorded in the sources to remove the odium of defeat from the otherwise illustrious Manōčehr."[214]

And now from the Heimskringla (emphases added):

"both sides appointed a meeting for establishing peace, made a truce, and exchanged hostages. The Vanaland people sent their best men, Njord the Rich, and his son Frey...

Odin placed Njord and Frey as priests of the sacrifices, and they became Diar [Judges] of the Asaland people. Njord's daughter Freya was priestess of the sacrifices, and first taught the Asaland people the magic art, as it was in use and fashion among the Vanaland people. While Njord was with the Vanaland people *he had taken his own sister in marriage, for that was allowed by their law*; and their children were Frey and Freya. But among the Asaland people it was forbidden to intermarry with such near relations."[215]

---

[213] Bundahishn, p.172, 186
[214] Yarshater, p.572
[215] Heimskringla, vol.1, p.272-3. A perfect match with Iranian royal incest habits (Shahnameh, p.440-441); of which Frey and Freyja are also accused in the Poetic Edda (p.162)

Nōḍar and Fryā
Njord and Frey

These two virtually identical names, together with the same extensive surrounding circumstances are, this author proposes, irrefutable evidence that this is the same sequence of events seen from two opposing perspectives, and that the 'Afrasiab' of Iranian history is one and the same with the Odin of Scandinavian mythology[216]. One can see how the great bitterness caused by the recent traumatic national calamity at the hands of the Xiong Nu shaped the changeable character of this unusual leader of dubious morality, who would stop at nothing to win in battle and avoid further disaster to his people.

The Historical Kayanians

Clearly though, there is a tremendous amount of historical rumour, misattribution and translational detritus to be cleared away before we can see the events clearly. Not least in the fact that the renderings of the Iranian Pahlavi script's place and people names into English are enormously varied, so that they often appear differently even in different translations. In addition to which the understanding of the Parthian Arsacid dynasty that comes down to us in the western tradition is essentially the 'GRHF', Hellenized view of them that is substantially inadequate in understanding an entirely foreign, culturally distinct history that has as much in common with Chinese or Indian culture as it has with the Greek.

---

[216] There is one potential reference to Afrasiab in the ancient 'Yasna' (p.246): "the fell Turanian Frangrasyan (the murderous robber)". Either this is a different Turanian king, or an archetype of the Turanian aggressor, whom Afrasiab came to embody more than anyone since Tur himself. Or, perhaps more likely, this is evidence that elements were inserted into the Yasna at a later date, probably during the tremendously chaotic attempt to reconstruct the Iranian canon after the Greek book-burnings (roughly 100 BC-700 AD). Indeed, it is proposed here that the above proofs mean that this reference cannot have been written until after this time (i.e. C.120 BC). Similarly with mentions of 'Frangrasyan' in the much later (C.0-500 AD) Yashts (e.g. p.301).

To save time in unpacking this vast mulch of complex historical information, we will give a brief summary of who was who:

Manuchehr, the King of Persia in the Shahnameh, was Mithridates I (reigned 165-132 BC), the great scion of the Arsacids who restored lustre to the Iranian civilization after its 200 year-long depredations at the hands of the Greeks, including a significant restoration of Iranian culture that understood itself as being a continuation from the Persian Empire. As we can see, the dates involved fit like a glove. 132 BC was exactly the year that the Yuezhi rounded the Tian Shan and descended on Transoxiana and Parthia. The Shahnameh and other texts' mention of Dahestan as an Iranian centre confirms this, and its location near the South-East corner of the Caspian Sea, captured by Afrasiab/Odin who ruled there for perhaps 12 years[217], confirms the incredible military victory won by the Yuezhi and how far they got[218].

This defeat was a huge national disaster for the Iranians, a catastrophe not much better than the Yuezhi had just suffered at the hands of the Xiong Nu. This national shame accounts for the great pains Ferdowsi took to inflict a literary reposte to Afrasiab by having him coming back into the story again and again facing succeeding Iranian Kings until he is finally fully defeated by Kay Khosrow[219]. As we shall see, the Shahnameh's version of events is highly historically flawed, and Kay Khosrow in particular is probably a largely poetic 'wishful thinking' idealised amalgam of

---

[217] Although his headquarters is generally understood to have been at Samarkand, AKA 'Kangdiz' (see later)
[218] Strabo (vol.2, p.245) describes the participants in this conflict from the Greek perspective: "The best known tribes [of Nomads] are those who deprived the Greeks of Bactriana [in fact the Parthians had already liberated Bactria from the Greeks by this time, but Strabo is in denial about this, as Greek culture often was regarding Greek reverses], the Asii, Pasiani, (Asianī?) Tochari, and Sacarauli, who came from the country on the other side of the Iaxartes, opposite the Sacae and Sogdiani, and which country was also occupied by the Sacæ; some tribes of the Dahæ [i.e. Parthians] are surnamed Aparni, some Xanthii, others Pissuri" [i.e. the three tribes united by Arsaces].
[219] Although this is probably based on references in the Yashts that may be as old as 550 AD (e.g. p.304, 307)

characters that did not actually exist as a single historical figure[220]. Essentially he is a Cyrus the Great character with elements of Mithridates II, thrust out of time into the narrative in order to restore the honour of victory for the Iranians over the Turans who had shockingly humbled them so badly. This casts extreme doubt over whether 'Afrasiab' was ever actually killed by the Iranians, though it is possible.

As the Encyclopaedia Iranica article states, the military defeat was of Manuchehr/Mithridates himself, killing or capturing him and ending his reign. This is rather hushed up because of the shame of the massive Mesopotamian Empire at a point of greatness being immediately humbled by totally unknown, upstart 'barbarian' new arrivals from beyond the known world, hence the Turans regularly being referred to in Hellenic sources as 'Scythians', 'northern raiders' or 'nomads'. They just didn't know who they were.

The comprehensive victory for the Yuezhi included the capture of their territory (including Bactria, ending the already ailing 'Greco-Bactrian Kingdom'), their throne and two royal heirs. As in the Encyclopaedia article, Nodar/Njord may never have ruled. Or he may be Artavan 1 (AKA the Greek 'Artabanus') who ruled Parthia 127-124 BC, who was then killed by the Yuezhi. The genealogy of the Arsacid Parthian Kings is a nightmarish quagmire (on top of the fact that according to the Greeks they spent half their time murdering their relatives to obtain the throne, although this is possibly an ethnocentric slander), but what we know is that Artavan was Mithridates' brother. The 'two sons' of Manuchehr (Fry and Nodar) recorded in the Bundahisn and the 'father and son' recorded in the Heimskringla then could either be an error in that Nodar was in fact Fry's Uncle, or in that Nodar was a brother of Fry and a separate person from Artavan. Nodar/Njord either:

---

[220] A poetic 'blending' of historical characters across time is a feature of Iranian history. For example the archer who let fly the arrow establishing the border with the Turans at the Oxus River is often poetically associated with 'Arash', an idealised version of Arsaces, the founder of the Parthian Empire.

a) was killed immediately in or soon after the battle of 132 BC
b) lived on to fight against the Yuezhi occupation until 124 BC, or
c) (as in the Icelandic sources) was captured by the Yuezhi and lived on with them in captivity, being granted a position of dignity.

Frya/Frey was 'Phraates II' (this is the Hellenized rendering) who ruled Parthia 132-127 BC. Although according to both Iranian and Scandinavian sources this reign was very much as some kind of vassal under, or rebel towards, the new Yuezhi rulers of Iran.

Fig.95: Phraates II, the historical 'Inge Frey'[221]

What is incredible is that this figure, existing for millennia unknown as a minor King of a forgotten Asian fiefdom, came to extreme prominence and importance in the Scandinavian world. Whereas Njord's post-war existence is uncertain, there is no doubt that Frey lived on amongst the Yuezhi for many years, despite Greek history recording that he died in the war. 'Inge Frey' is one of the chief figures of Scandinavian history. He was taken to Scandinavia and became the Patriarch of the ancient Swedish

---

[221] Image used by kind permission of Classical Numismatic Group, LLC (https://cngcoins.com). Among his achievements, in 129 BC Freyr, probably aided by Afrasiab, was able decisively to defeat and destroy the Seleucid Empire at the Battle of Ecbatana, finally vanquishing the Greeks from Iran.

Royal house that later became the Royal house of Norway through Harald Hårfagri: the 'Ynglings' (another example of Magogians becoming leadership groups of other nations[222]). He was also very significant in Norse mythology, like Odin coming to be worshipped as a god (ancestor worship was a peculiar weakness of the Indo-Europeans), and our English day 'Friday' is named after him[223].

As per the Heimskringla, the character is usually divided into two in Scandinavian tradition, the male 'Frey' and female 'Frejya', who became the Norse 'goddess' of fertility. (Notably Freyja is not mentioned by the Iranians[224]). Whether Freyja's 'sexually perverse' reputation in Norse culture (typical of its view of the Vanir in general) came from the siblings being the product of Njord's incest with his own sister[225], or because of their own possibly imagined incest[226], 'Freyja"s sexual behaviour was seen as in some way relevant to the witchcraft that she is recorded as first bringing into Scandinavian culture[227].

---

[222] This is possibly an explanation for the term 'Gog and Magog' in Biblical prophecy

[223] "Yngvefrey, whom the Swedes, long after his time, worshipped and sacrificed to, and from whom the race or family of the Ynglings take their name." (Heimskringla, vol.1, p.263). 'Friday' is also sometimes said to be named after his proposed sister, Frejya.

[224] It could be that Freyja is a later poetic invention, similar to Horsa and Remus. Or that somehow they are the same person, with Freyja as a 'femalisation' of Frey, related to the strange, feminine qualities the Æsir associated with the Vanir.

[225] Heimskringla, vol.1, p.273. As discussed, a memory of Iranian incestuous royal history that echoes that of the Emperor Darius (Shahnameh, p.440-1)

[226] Poetic Edda, p.162

[227] Heimskringla, p.273

Extraordinarily, that was not the end of Frey, as it is highly likely that he returned to Iran late in life to take the throne again as King Sinatruces in 75 BC (Shahnameh's 'Zav'), ruling for 5 years as a wise King who brokered peace with the Turans[228]. Again, the dating is virtually exact as Sinatruces was famously 80 when he took the throne[229] (having spent most of his life living with the 'Saka'), that would give him a birth year of 155 BC, making him 23 at the time of the Yuezhi invasion.

Following the rule by the Yuezhi, according to the Greek history, came Parthian King Mithridates II, ruling from 124-91 BC. As previously, the Greek reluctance to understand that a nation from outside their awareness could actually have been ruling all of Parthia during this time makes them assign Parthian Kings to cover this period, when in reality they were under occupation. If the Iranian twelve years tradition is to be believed, Mithridates II won Iran back to the Parthian dynasty in 120 BC. Mithridates II then is the 'Kay Kawad' ('Qabod') of the Shahnameh, the restorer of Iranian fortunes, re-establisher of their nation and first Shah of the 'Kayanian' Kings[230].

---

[228] Indeed with Afrasiab himself (Shahnameh, p.128-9), entirely in keeping with Frey having been adopted by Odin and taken to Sweden to rule there during the intervening time.

[229] Ibid: "Zav ascended the throne on an auspicious day...An old man in his eightieth year, Zav reigned for only five years. In that time he made the world young again with his justice and goodness; he stopped the army from committing crimes and prevented them from arbitrarily arresting people and killing them, and he communicated in his heart with God."

[230] His name however seems to be entirely borrowed from the later Sasanian monarch 'Kavad I' (488-531 AD, whose reign does not resemble 'Kay Kawad''s). This is the beginning of Ferdowsi's morphing of the Kayanian narrative forward in time. Soon after 'Kay Kawad' he leaps 600 years ahead to join this 'Turan war'-era history seamlessly onto that of the Sasanian Kings from Kavad I onwards. Boyce believed the borrowing was in the other direction, i.e. the Sasanians were named after the legendary Kayanians. However it is by no means clear that the Kayanians were yet known so specifically in the 5th Century AD, if at all. Certainly the versions in the Denkard, Bundahisn and Shahnameh (C.1000 AD) must be based on the later Sasanian Kings because of a) their interractions with the Chionites (a nation not known before around the time of Christ (e.g. Bundahisn, p.173)) and b) Khosrow's Zoroastrianism (Denkard, p.5-7). Mithridates II may also be a model for 'Kay Khosrow', in that he was a successful Iranian King who lived after the

After his rule a period of less stable government followed, with the Greeks assigning it to Kings Gotarzes (reigning 90-80) and his son Orodes (reigning 80-75 BC), almost certainly the figures listed as great warriors rather than Kings in the Shahnameh and other Iranian sources: Godarz/Gudarz and Geew/Giv. According to the Shahnameh the actual King during this time was the hapless 'Kay Kavus', whose ill-advised adventuring all but lost the empire. Perhaps the most likely historical personage of this era resembling him is Mithridates III (C.90-80 BC)[231].

Fig.96: Sinatruces, the aged 'Inge Frey'[232]

Yuezhi invasion and at the time of 'Afrasiab'. Whereas the more obvious Sasanian inspirations for 'Khosrow' (see later) could only poetically be linked to these events.

[231] Sellwood famously termed the period from 88-57 BC the 'Parthian Dark Age' because of our lack of information about it (p.2, 9). This is probably because the Yuezhi were really ruling the region at the time, with various token puppets and nominal Kings filling the Parthian throne as it suited their interests, and this fact has been obscured by later historians to save face. The career of Ferdowsi's 'Kay Kavus' is also largely based on that of the later Sasanian monarch Kavad I (488-531 AD), in particular his losing the throne, being imprisoned, then being freed and regaining it.

[232] Image used by kind permission of Classical Numismatic Group, LLC (https://cngcoins.com).

Following the return of Frey (the reign of Sinatruces 75-69 BC[233]), there were a succession of unsuccessful monarchs in Iran, including Phraates III, 69-57 BC (Frey's son) and Orodes II, 57-37 BC, none of whom particularly match the imposing character of 'Kay Khosrow', the central or at least climactic figure of the Shahnameh, although an argument could be made. Rather these rather wretched dynasts variously presided over a period of slow national decline and ignominy only really halted by the incoming Sasanian dynasty in 224 AD, by which time Afrasiab would have been long gone (although Iranian sources attribute to him a lifespan of four hundred years[234]).

Orodes II married an 'Indo-Scythian princess' who gave birth to his heir Phraates IV (reigning 37-2 BC) that could conceivably be an origin of Kay Khosrow's birth story (although also lifted from that of Cyrus the Great and Sargon the Great), but this Phraates' reign was nothing to write home about either. Therefore the only historical figure who can really have been the model for the Shahnameh's Kay Khosrow is the much later Sasanian King Khosrow I (reigned 531-579 AD), who is after all the most famous 'Khosrow' in Iranian history and much like the 'Kayanian' Khosrow was a successful and long-reigning monarch and famous champion of Zoroastrianism[235].

---

[233] Further evidence that Sinatruces was the aged Phraates II AKA Frey is given by Sellwood (p.8) who notes evidence that Sinatruces was a son of Mithridates I.
[234] Yarshater, p.571
[235] While in the 6th Century AD Sasanian history, Khosrow is simply the son and heir of Kavad, in the Bundahisn (p.172-3) and Shahnameh, another king is inserted between them: Kay Kavus, who seems to have been used to portray the Sasanian King Kavad I. The historical Kavad turned on his general and friend 'Siyavash', allowing him to be executed, and married a Hephthalite King's daughter. Meanwhile in the Shahnameh, Kavus has a son called Siyavash (whom he also betrays), who marries Afrasiab's daughter. Afrasiab then kills Siyavash but Siyavash's son and Afrasiab's grandson becomes Kay Khosrow, who kills Afrasiab. All of this seems to be a transparent fictionalization of the Sasanian history, with Afrasiab inserted as the convenient, colourful and perennial villain. However there may be details from the story that preserve some aspects of genuine Afrasiab history, learned by Kavad during his stay as a refugee among the Hephthalites, who by then had occupied the old Yuezhi fortresses. Ferdowsi's version embellishes the Bundahisn's, that must be based on the Yashts (p.304, 307) where we first hear of Siyavash being Khosrow's father and Khosrow at least capturing Afrasiab. While

However it is also highly likely that the composite 'Kay Khosrow', based on Khosrow I, Cyrus, Mithridates II and others, was also intended to flatter his other namesake Khosrow II (reigned 590-628 AD), who according to Theodor Nöldeke was the patron of the now lost work of Iranian history 'Khwaday Namag' that formed the basis of Ferdowsi's 'Shahnameh'. The initial conception of the work then may have been as a glorious history of the Iranian Kings, with the inconveniently 'ruffian' Arsacids transformed into the 'Kayanians' (to avoid them getting too much credit[236]), but with Khosrow I as their crowning peak, who, to some extent resembling his grandson Khosrow II, would also please that incumbent sovereign[237]. Khosrow II's mother was of Arsacid stock, so a project that drew so heavily on the Arsacids (albeit in disguised form), or at least much of the arc of their story, may have been acceptable to him for this reason also, as well as simply the motivation of sponsoring a great work of Iranian history.

Khosrow II's Iran was facing overthrow by Muslim Arabs from the west, so he would also have seen the utility in producing a grand Iranian history, even one that focused on a previous dynasty, before the 'lights went out' in Iran, hence the 'Khwaday Namag', and from there the 'Shahnameh'[238].

---

this may be seen as evidence of a more ancient 'Kayanian' tradition, and the divergence with known Sasanian history is notable, in reality the mention of Khosrow, and in particular Siyavash, two similarly linked Sasanian historical figures from the 6th Century, is too much of a coincidence, and must mean that this section of the text was written after the 6th Century AD.

[236] The Sasanians, surprisingly, are one of the main causes of the 'Dark Age' lack of information regarding the Arsacid era. They 'denigrated Parthian achievements while expunging as many traces of them as came to hand' (Sellwood, p.2)

[237] Although it could be that Khwaday Namag had a more faithful and accurate version of Iranian history, and the historical editorializing originated after the Muslim conquest, during which much of the original source material was destroyed.

[238] In the 9th Century Zoroastrian work of history the 'Denkard', an extensive description of Khosrow's aggressive advancement of Zoroastrianism (that makes it impossible for his reign to have preceded that of Kay Lohrasp/Vishtaspa, the original sponsor of the religion) in a list of other monarchs, is placed in the sequence as follows: Vishtasp, Darai, (Alexander's vandalism), Ardashir (founder of the Sasanian dynasty), Shahpuhr, Shahpuhr II, Khosraw ('son of Kobad') (Denkard, p.5-7). While the list does not state that it is chronological, nevertheless the order

Basically Ferdowsi has fashioned a 'perfect Iranian dynasty' (the Kayanians) using materials from all three of the major Iranian dynasties (Achaemenid, Arsacid & Sasanian), not being too fussy about whether the position they occupy in his narrative is the same as the position they occupied in history. And he has taken this dynasty and transported it back in time to the mythological era before the recorded history of Iran, presumably to give his semi-fictional Kayanians the lustre of being even more ancient than Cyrus[239]. This is some time between the barely remembered first founders of the nation and the beginnings of national historical memory with the Achaemenids. Fascinatingly, he then closes the work with a more humdrum, prosaic version of the actual history as he knew it, of Cyrus, Darius, Artaxerxes, the 'Ashkanians' (Parthians), then Ardeshir the Sasanian, etc, despite the fact that he has already indiscriminately pilfered the best bits of their stories for the prior mythologisation section. He has therefore included both a romanticised ideal version and the more factual version of Iran's history into one narrative. No wonder this has confused Iranologists for millennia[240].

---

is highly significant, and it is suggested that this is the true sequence, i.e. that 'Kay Khosrow' is primarily the Sasanian Zoroastrian champions Khosrow I (531-579) and Khosrow II (590-628 AD)

[239] This is in accordance with the 'Newton Principle' that historians tend to elongate the antiquity of their nations' histories to add grandeur (Newton)

[240] The Shahnameh is not the earliest source to have this chronology, it can clearly be seen as deriving from (or being coterminous with) the Bundahishn (also compiled in the 9th Century AD at the same time as the Shahnameh, but probably from older sources). Bundahishn Chapter 33 (p.172-176) is a grand sweep of Iranian history describing roughly the whole timeline of the Shahnameh, and it also has Kay Khosrow's reign being succeeded by Vishtaspa's. Therefore this error/choice of placing the Kayanians much earlier in history was commonplace during the Viking Age Samanid and Ghaznavid dynasties' efforts at reconstructing Iranian history, influenced by foggy but powerful culture-memories of the recent antagonisms with the Turans, that had also been inserted into the Avesta during the centuries following them (i.e. 100 BC-600 AD; see for example Yasna, p.246; Yashts, p.304, 307). Like the Denkard, the Bundahishn goes on (glossing over the Arsacids/Parthians) to describe the encroachments of the Arabs and the reigns of the Shahpurs and Perez (4th-5th Centuries AD), then it describes the coming of 'Khosraw son of Kavat' again, who again does great deeds (p.174). This double-mention is a tacit admission of the confusion as to the historical record among Iranian historians of the time. The argument that these are two separate Khosrows, an ancient and a latter, is forestalled by the presence of Siyavash in the 'early'

The placement of essentially two Cyrus the Great figures (Khosrow and Bahman) after the events of the Turan war (Manuchehr/Nodar, etc) must have been to present the glory of their rules as a latter-day resurgence in fortunes to the ancient Iranian story, basically to give it a happy ending rather than the catalogue of degeneration from the heights of the Persian Empire under successive foreign invaders that was the somewhat depressing reality. The true Iranian history, not helped by the confusions added to it by some of its own chroniclers, is still even now only in the process of being unearthed from the heavy-handed treatment it received from those foreign invaders. In this undertaking the superb work done by Ehsan Yarshater's Encyclopædia Iranica project at Columbia University deserves special mention.

Before leaving this story we should remember the Chinese Embassy to the Yuezhi court in 128 BC, by the famous Chinese explorer and emissary Zhang Qian. The King visited by them appears to have been the 'Pushang' of the Shahnameh, Afrasiab's father (with Afrasiab being the grandson of the Yuezhi King killed by Modu in China). Whilst the Chinese witness that he was not interested in joining the Chinese for revenge against the Xiong Nu is at odds with the Shahnameh's version of Pashang as a vengeful and war-mongering King who continually pushed his son into military conflict with the Iranians, the timing is highly relevant. In 128 BC the Yuezhi would have been flush with the spoils of their

---

account (as above). The Bundahishn narrative, that focuses on the contributions of monarchs towards Mazdaism/Zoroastrianism, arguably provides the reason why the historical Arsacids are so glossed over (and placed as primaeval kings instead): they were not Zoroastrians, but Mithraists, hence the names of their most famous Kings: 'Mithridates'. This fact was probably an embarrassment to the writers of the Bundahisn. By contrast, as discussed, the legendary 'Kay Khosrow' (based in part on Mithridates II) was a hero of Zoroastrianism (Denkard, p.5-7); one of many anachronisms that expose the chronological misplacement (he supposedly lived before the religion was promulgated by his successor Vishtaspa (Bundahisn, p.173)). Others include Khosrow's predecessors' interactions with the Chionite Huns (C.50 BC-400 AD), and the aforementioned presence of Siyavash (who lived in the 5th century AD) as Khosrow's father. For a fuller discussion of the confused Iranian timeline as it relates to the dating of Zoroaster, see Appendix 6: Zoroaster Revisited.

overwhelming victory over the extensive, ancient and established Indo-Iranians and sitting in occupation over them.

Such a titanic upturn in fortunes must have made a return to the struggles of China seem an unattractive proposition. Zhang Qian, the Chinese envoy, reported that Bactria (Chinese 'Daxia') was entirely in the possession of the Yuezhi[241]. This area would henceforth become known as Tocharistan or Tochestan: the 'Turkestan' of the Iranian chronicles, that would be co-opted subsequently as the self-identifcation of the 'Turks' and is also related to today's place-name 'Tajikistan'. Meanwhile seemingly other Tocharians had moved into what had been the Kingdom of Sogdia, now termed by the Chinese visitor 'Kangju'[242] (centred around today's city of Tashkent) and described by him as the second state of Transoxiana after the Yuezhi. The Saka (probably AKA the Massagetae), migrating ahead of the Yuezhi (and now apparently increasingly acting in concert with them) had moved Southward to occupy the area that became known as 'Sakestan' or 'Sistan' AKA today's 'Afghanistan'[243]. The Yuezhi conquest of Parthia therefore was the foundation for what would become the Kushan Empire, that would be led by the previous inhabitants of the Tarim Basin's Kingdom of Kucha.

---

[241] Shiji, 3, p.235
[242] Ibid, p.234
[243] Bosworth, p.247; Book of Han, vol.10, p.69, vol.11, p.84

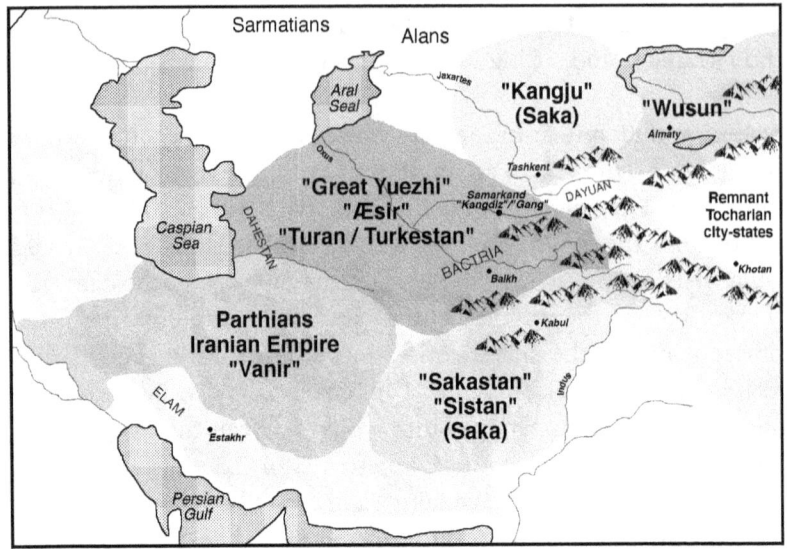

Fig.97: The geopolitical situation in the Transoxiana area following the Yuezhi invasion. Although Parthian Emperor Mithridates II was able nominally to push the Yuezhi back to the Oxus River C.120 BC, after his reign ended C.90 BC the state of affairs reverted back to that pictured here again until the year 57 BC. Afrasiab or his successors held the reigns of power in the region during this whole period, a situation about which GRHF historians were largely in denial[244].

Zhang Qian's trip west to visit the Yuezhi was actually a highly significant event in Chinese history, marking the first time their cultural awareness went beyond the borders of the mountain wall. It formed a major basis for the geographical information included in the 'Shiji' and laid the foundation, until then entirely remote, for the eventual Chinese expansion into the Tarim region. Soon after this, around 50 BC, the Han Chinese administration began co-opting the Silk Road trade route as a direct operation of its government. One other reason for Pushang[245] declining the Chinese offer of an alliance with them against the Xiong Nu was quite probably that by 128 BC he was already involved with, if not the initiator of, ambitous plans that were now underway for a wholesale northern migration of the Yuezhi.

---

[244] 'Mountain Stone Rock' by the3rdSequence (https://www.the3rdsequence.com/texturedb/) licensed by CC BY 4.0 (http://creativecommons.org/licenses/by/4.0)
[245] Or possibly it may have been Afrasiab himself

The Canter of the Sarmatians

The Asians were now caught in a vast pincer movement between the Roman Empire to their West and the Chinese Han dynasty, driving its anti-social Hun horse confederacies ahead of it, to their East. It was clear to many that this situation was not going to get any better for them as long as they remained in Asia.

Indeed, the westward migrations detonated by the Xiong Nu expansion into Tocharia had already in part begun and were in motion many hundreds of years earlier, as the Massagetae>Scythian>Cimmerian push of the 8th Century BC had already shown.

This people movement, that for a thousand years seems continually to have pushed nomadic nations westward from the Altai Mountain region, would, beginning symbolically when the Sarmatians crossed the Don River around 200 BC, massively pick up speed until the entire Eurasian landmass was engulfed in the swirling maelstrom of population movements that would become known as the Age of Migrations or Dark Ages.

The westward movement, that would turn into a gigantic, thousand year-long exodus of Indo-European peoples into Europe, was begun in earnest in the 3rd Century BC by a group of people who like so many have obscure origins but whose influence would be enormous on western culture. Amongst other things the Sarmatians would bring with them into Europe the military concept of the 'knight' (i.e. heavily-armoured, mounted lancers in orderly charges to break the enemy line – the Sarmation 'Cataphract') that would come to define the later Medieval or Middle Ages period of European history from 1066 to 1485 AD. When in the 3rd Century BC they saddled their horses and started cantering westward, the whole world took notice.

Because of the vastness of the Eurasian steppe, and the fact that from this point onwards many large nations were in motion upon it, mixing and admixing, this region of history, typified by the vague and amorphous 'Sarmatian' designation, becomes *extremely* complicated.

Who were the Sarmatians? Well their origins are reasonably simple: they were the offspring of the Scythians and Amazons mentioned earlier, whom Herodotus called 'Sauromatae'.

Herodotus's origin story for how the Amazons came to be in 'Scythia' is worth revisiting. He relates that at some point a group of Amazons having been captured at Thermodon by Greeks, overcame the Greek sailors of the ships they were being transported back to Greece on, turned the ships around and having no navigation skills ended up on the north shore of the Black Sea, where they encountered 'Scythians':

"The Scyths could not tell what to make of the attack upon them – the dress, the language, the nation itself, were alike unknown – whence the enemy had come even, was a marvel. Imagining, however, that they were all men of about the same age, they went out against them, and fought a battle. Some of the bodies of the slain fell into their hands, whereby they discovered the truth. Hereupon they deliberated, and made a resolve to kill no more of them, but to send against them a detachment of their youngest men, as near as they could guess equal to the women in number, with orders to encamp in their neighbourhood, and do as they saw them do – when the Amazons advanced against them, they were to retire, and avoid a fight – when they halted, the young men were to approach and pitch their camp near the camp of the enemy. All this they did on account of their strong desire to obtain children from so notable a race."[246]

---

[246] Herodotus, p.285. Quote taken from the 1862 John Murray Edition

Eventually the Scythians gained the trust of the Amazons: "The two camps were then joined in one, the Scythians living with the Amazons as their wives; and the men were unable to learn the tongue of the women, but the women soon caught up the tongue of the men."

But the Amazons were not willing to become simply Scythian wives nor return with their husbands to the traditional Scythian lands. Instead they persuaded the Scythians to bring their inheritances from home to live separately with the Amazons.

However, when the Scythians returned with their inheritances, the Amazons had changed their minds and reneged on the arrangement, preferring to return to a women-led society. After explaining this to their hapless Scythian suitors, who let them go, they journeyed north-eastwards from the Maeotian Lake to re-start Amazon society, carrying with them the offspring of their union with the Scythians, who would become the Sauromatae nation:

"Crossing the Tanais [Don River] they journeyed eastward a distance of three days' march from that stream, and again northward a distance of three days' march from the [Maeotian Lake]. Here they came to the country where they now live, and took up their abode in it. The women of the Sauromatae have continued from that day to the present to observe their ancient customs, frequently hunting on horseback with their husbands, sometimes even unaccompanied; in war taking the field; and wearing the very same dress as the men." [247]

Remarkably, it is in this exact location at Voronezh in Russia that extraordinary archaeological finds of female warriors have been found[248] with artifacts such as the head-dress in the image below, a testament to the last known centre of the Amazons' female warrior society.

---

[247] Herodotus, p.286. Quote taken from the 1862 John Murray Edition
[248] Volodin & Okorokov

Fig.98: Reconstruction of the golden headdress of the 'Amazon Queen' found in Kharkov near the Don River and dated to the 4th Century BC [249]

These events likely took place early, perhaps the 7th or 8th Century BC or even before. That would explain why both the Goths (Jordanes) and the Scythians (Herodotus) were claimed to be the 'husbands' of the Amazons (in 'Scythia' at least, as opposed to in their earlier, southern habitations of Anatolia and the Caucasus Mountains), in that the Amazons in fact met a Magogite group that were progenitors both of the later Scythians and of the Goths. i.e. some time before 600 BC at least, when the Scythians proper took possession of the Pontic Steppe.

---

[249] Image by Babenko, p.62. Used with permission

While there is a persistent effort to differentiate the later-appearing 'Sarmatians' from the 'Sauromatae' of Herodotus's tale (Hippolytus of Rome stated that they were descended from Ashkenaz, for example), the fact that they sprang from precisely the same location a few hundred years later and have virtually exactly the same name, that also means 'ruled by women' in Greek[250], makes such a position fairly untenable. Perhaps this reluctance to recognise the Amazon parentage of the Sarmatians is motivated by the customary academic unwillingness to find genuine historical origins for people groups and therefore to keep them 'mysteriously appearing' on the scene of history.

However, it appears that the Sarmatians' famous migration, that would sweep with it so many other nations, was motivated by a variety of factors, among them an influx into the Sarmatian lands of new groups from the north and east, who were then more or less assimilated into the Sarmatian horde and contributed to the big move west. It is suggested that these admixtures of different populations changed considerably the nature of the Sarmatians, and at least got them moving.

---

[250] "Sarmatai Gynaikokratoumenoi", Gluhak, p.132

Fig.99: Image of a Sarmatian from a 1st Century AD or later drinking horn in Kuban[251]

---

[251] Hermitage, St. Petersburg, after Rostovtseff.

So who were the newly arriving nations, and where had they come from? Well this is where it gets complicated. They are generally listed as:

Alans
Roxalani
Aorsi
Iazyges
Asoi/Asii
Sirakoi[252]

The problem is that according to Chinese and other sources, the Alans, Roxalani ("Rukh-As" Alani, i.e. fair-haired Az Alans, possibly the origin of the term 'Rus' and therefore 'Russia')[253], Aorsi and Asoi/Asii were all the same people. Strabo said that the 'upper Aorsi' 'ruled over most of the Caspian Coast'[254]. The Chinese almost certainly knew the Aorsi as 'Yen-ts'ai' or 'An-ts'ai' and reported them as living about 700 miles North-West of Sogdiana (known as 'K'ang-chu' to the Chinese. i.e. northern Transoxiana)[255]. Meanwhile the Alans are stated to be 'related' to the Asioi who invaded Bactria in the 2nd Century BC and were pushed west by the Kanchu people as they expanded from Ferghana to the Aral Sea[256]. The Alans are also said to have been the result of the merger of an unknown group with the

---

[252] Ptolemy, p.144-5; Strabo, vol.1, p.451, 172; vol.2, p.219, 239, 245
[253] MacKenzie, p.16; Heyerdahl & Lilleström, p.248. Ammianus (4th Century AD) confirms the Alans had blond hair (vol.3, p.393).
[254] To be contrasted with the 'lower Aorsi', a less powerful group, whom he said lived close to the Black Sea; this could well be a reference to the western and eastern wings of the Tirassian populations i.e. Cimmerians and Yuezhi, or at least the later migrating Iazyges/Aorsi and the Yuezhi. This is highly likely, as he adds the detail that the upper Aorsi controlled the northern route of the Silk Road, importing Indian and Babylonian merchandise by camel through Armenia and Media and so becoming very wealthy. He claimed King Spadines of the Don River Aorsi could muster 200,000 mounted warriors, while the upper Aorsi had even more (Strabo, vol.2, p.239).
[255] Book of Han, vol.10, p.44; Book of Later Han, Section 19
[256] Melyukova, p.97-117; Olbrycht, p.105–107.

Massagetae[257]. Ptolemy and Chinese sources state the Aorsi to have essentially merged with, assimilated with or changed their name to, the Alans ('Alanorsi': Ptolemy, 'Alan-Liao': Chinese) by about 100 AD. So basically we are dealing with our old friends the Saka. Or at least Scandinavian outliers of the main Yuezhi juggernaut, 'who moved ahead of it as it took over Bactria in the mid-2nd Century BC. But also who had already variously spread over the region for many centuries past, from the Saka's control of the eastern seaboard of the Caspian Sea (also presumably guarding the Uzboy River[258] that was probably a major southern shipping route east to the Tian Shan), to the Massagetae's ancient residence north of the Jaxartes.

The relationship between the Saka and the Yuezhi is complex. To some extent Saka/Massagetae appear to have associated themselves with the Yuezhi and been a peripheral part of their civilization (as against for example the Xiong Nu), but they also fought against them as they pushed westwards displacing the Saka first in the Ili River Valley then in Bactria (as above, as the Yuezhi pushed westwards to the Aral Sea, this reference appears to make Yuezhi cognate with the Chinese 'Kangchu', or at least that the Kangchu were a part of the Yuezhi). The Shahnameh is very notable for its depiction of the Kings of 'Sistan' (Afghanistan) who arguably were first wave Saka initially displaced from the Ili River Valley, aiding the Iranians against the Yuezhi, although this may be an anachronism more suited to the situation a thousand years later when the poem was composed.

These 'Sarmatian' elements of the Yuezhi periphery however seem to be even more closely associated with the Yuezhi than the traditional 'Saka'; a 'horse-Yuezhi'. The Yuezhi's name for themselves, the 'Æsir' must surely be the original not only of the

---

[257] Olbrycht, p.105–107; or simply 'they are Massagetae' (Cassius Dio, v.8, p.451; Ammianus, vol.3. p.387)

[258] The Uzboy River, like most of the Aral Sea, has now dried up, but in ancient times it connected the Aral to the Caspian Sea, possibly at some times even bypassing it to connect directly with the Oxus River (Polybius, vol.4, p.221). As such it would have been a major trade artery for the Yuezhi/Saka maritime network.

Chinese term 'Yuezhi' but also of the correlate terms 'Aorsi', 'Asioi/Asii' and 'Iazyges', suggesting these groups were the very same people, or at least a component of them[259].

From the Xiong Nu's earliest assaults on the ancient Yuezhi heartlands around 210 BC, it appears that many contingents of 'Yuezhi' (whether they be identical with the Saka/Cimmerians/Massagetae or not) rode out westwards, scouting and seeking possibilities for new lands. This would make perfect sense. If they were unable to resist the Xiong Nu, where were the Yuezhi going to go? Perhaps this had always been the role of the Saka. It is entirely possible that the Saka/Cimmerians' primary distinction from the Yuezhi was simply that they were land-based whereas the Yuezhi were water-based. Perhaps they were used as auxiliaries protecting the southern maritime trade routes through the Jaxartes, Aral, Uzboy, Caspian, Volga, Don and Black Sea. This would certainly explain all of the disparate locations where they pop up (Crimea, Sea of Asov, Azerbaijan, Gobustan peninsula, Caspian Sea coast, Ili River) that without the maritime network seem hard to explain.

This really leaves only the Sirakoi, who were perhaps a more Indo-Iranian group to be identified with the Apasiacae of pre-Yuezhi Sogdiana, but more likely just another variant of 'Yuezhi' with a name closer to 'Seres' from 'Serica'.

The movement west from Transoxiana and the Aral Sea region of the Saka/Alans/Aorsi, carrying with it once it reached the north

---

[259] See for example Heyerdahl & Lillieström, p.124, 161, 244-250. While the name 'Alan' appears to be an Iranian exonym used by non-Alans meaning 'warrior' (Ibid, p.162), otherwise it seems the Alans were simply land-based 'Æsir'/'Aorsi' (i.e. 'Alanorsi'), living in wagons, having been pushed westward by the Huns. Ammianus' colourful description of them (vol.3, p.389-395) is of an entirely Scandinavian nation, with details such as that their 'populous and extensive nations...stretch all the way to the river Ganges'; they 'do not know the meaning of slavery'; and, reminiscent of the macho values of the later Vikings, 'the man is judged happy who has sacrificed his life in battle, while those who grow old and depart from the world by a natural death they assail with bitter reproaches, as degenerate and cowardly'.

of the Caucasus the large Scytho-Amazon Sauromatae population, would continue unabated (with various of its sub-groups taking precedence at different times) all the way to Europe; the 'Iazyges', the first batch of overland 'Asian' migrants, reaching it in the mid 1st Century BC, and attacking the Roman Empire at the River Danube. It is possible that the sales pitch of the Iazyges to the Sauromatae was something along the lines of: 'the Xiong Nu are coming, you have to move!' Although it is unclear to what extent the Sauromatae were simply pushed out of the Southern Ural-Volga River region by the migrating Iazyges, Aorsi, Alans, etc, leaving them with no choice[260].

What is clear is that after crossing the Don River westward in 200 BC, the Sarmatians rolled into the northern Caucasus/ north of the Black Sea region that had been dominated by the Scythians for 400 years. The Scythians had been having troubles of late and their power had dwindled. By this time certainly the Irish 'Nelite' faction had left. They had suffered defeats at the hands of the creeping GRHF encroachment up the west coast of the Black Sea by Philip of Macedon in 339 BC and again by Lysimachus in 313 BC. They also lost out during the Bosporan Civil War of 309 BC. All this meant that the Sarmatian migration into the area in the 2nd Century BC was relatively unopposed and the Scythians were more or less assimilated into Sarmatian rule. Indeed it appears as though the Sarmatians (substantially composed of their ancient paternal kindred after all) taking over the area may have been something of a relief for the beleaguered Scythians. It certainly provided a huge boost, at least temporarily, for the free northern peoples' strength in the area. No longer were they under pressure from the Romans, rather the Romans were now themselves under

---

[260] This probably explains the distinction between 'Sauromatae' and 'Sarmatian': the former being the original Scythian-Amazons, and the latter being the much larger, mixed influx of horsemen westward across the steppe, of whom the 'Sauromate' were now merely only one component, whose leadership had now been co-opted by Scandinavians, of whom the latest-arriving and ultimately most powerful group were the incoming 'Alans'. Whereas outsiders, being perhaps not able or interested enough to perceive this change in leadership, continued calling dwellers in that region a version of the old 'Sauromatae', that became 'Sarmatian'.

pressure from the Sarmatians. The Iazyges' movements into Europe in particular would be one of the earliest signs of the defeat of the Roman Empire and the beginning of the 'Dark Ages'[261]. Greek cities on the northern Black Sea coast were forced to pay heavy taxation to their new Sarmatian overlords, and the Sarmatian influx also took possession of the northern Caucasus, a region previously dominated by the Kaskians and Togarmanians.

Over subsequent centuries, the Aorsi and later the Alans would create a vast commercial network across the steppe from Europe to the Urals and across to Transoxiana, an update of the existing Yuezhi maritime route but now with control of the land as well as the rivers. That is, until the Huns arrived, when this plan of consolidating in the Sea of Grass would turn out to be a pretty bad one.

Roman Encroachment

By the late 2nd Century BC the situation for the Asians living in the area of the Greco-Roman client state the Bosporan Kingdom, the Cimmerians or Crimeans, was not looking good. Sandwitched into the Crimean Peninsula they had been able to maintain enough of a tentative foothold to avoid the GRHF imperial creep. But it was getting closer. The old trade connection with Athens and its allies that had propped up the tyrannical Bosporan Kingdom slave state regime located in hostile Scythian terrain was faltering under the growth of the empire of the Roman Republic. That meant the Kingdom, and the region surrounding it, was close to falling to Roman rule. Meanwhile the Pontic Kingdom on the other (South) side of the Black Sea whose Greco-Iranian Pontid tyrants had fought off the Roman menace successfully for centuries was finally approaching capitulation as well[262].

---

[261] Especially their surprise defeat of a Roman Army under Marcus Fronto, the Roman Governor of Lower Moesia, in 169 AD, after which point the Roman Empire was largely on the defensive against invading Gothic, Sarmatian, Scandinavian and to some extent Celtic armies.

[262] These were the 'Mithridatic Wars' fought by King of Pontus Mithridates Eupator between 120 BC and 63 BC. If Mithridates was defeated, the whole Black Sea region would fall to the Romans.

Similar problems were facing their sister colony of Saka/Cimmerians in Azerbaijan[263], sandwiched as it was between the Parthian Empire to its east and the Armenian Kingdom to its west, that had previously acted as a buffer against the Roman tyranny, but this also was now under threat if the Pontic Kingdom fell to the Romans.

All of this was symptomatic of a domino, knock-on effect that was slowly creeping towards the Cimmerians' ancient homes in the Crimea and Azerbaijan. It was time to get out. But where to? Someone they knew of in the wider 'Asian' world had a plan. It was crazy and daring and sounded far-fetched, but at this point, what did the Cimmerians have to lose? This was the life's work of a bold eastern Yuezhi leader who was planning a vast national exodus of the Æsir out of Asia altogether, to a far, far off land beyond the reach and even awareness of Mediterranean and Mesopotamian nations, indeed beyond the scope of most global knowledge altogether. And if they wanted in, they could be part of it.

At some point Odin must have come west to lay out his plans. And possibly to garner support for a first phase of the exodus[264]. Azerbaijan and the Crimea areas would be staging posts for the escape, as supplies and people were probably needed from these regions, and the Crimean rivers, the Dnieper and Don may have formed part of the evacuation route. On today's maps, the Volga River appears to be the best of the Tirassians' 'superhighway' options for transversing Russia northward. If this was the main way taken, the Azerbaijani populations from the Caspian Sea and the Crimean settlements from the Don River would have been

---

[263] The descendants of the settlement at 'Gamir'
[264] Heyerdahl and Lillieström found copious evidence of his presence in this area (p.137), including remnant Asian populations in Azerbaijan such as the Christian 'Udin' people (p.140), for whom he was a national hero (p.147). They even speculated (p.285-287) that he may have been "Oltak/Olcaba", a powerful visiting noble and patron of the Mithridates regime, who is accused by both Plutarch (vol.2, p.214) and Appian (vol.2, p.389-90) of an abortive assassination attempt on the Roman General Lucullus, C.72 BC

'feeder' influxes added to the leading force arriving into the Caspian from the east via the Uzboy River.

Indeed it seems as though the grand vision was more attractive to the Black and Caspian Sea-dwelling Asians than their eastern cousins, the main bulk of the 'Great Yuezhi'. The idea was apparently a harder sell to the vast population out east, still very dominant and established in Bactria and for whom the peril of their hazardous temporary position caught between advancing empires would have been seemed more remote and less clear-cut.

Therefore the first phase of this people movement would have to be undertaken by the Cimmerians alone, to provide proof of concept for the sceptical main body of Yuezhi in Transoxiana. If the unbelievable plan actually worked and the Cimmerians came back alive, then they would consider it. With the Romans on their doorstep, the Cimmerians were ready to take the risk.

Northward to Liberty

Odin must already have made trips to Scandinavia. As the testimonies of him report, he was a far traveller. He also was possibly aware of the legacy, given down the ages, of Noah, who decreed that his sons would divide the Earth into three territories, and that the inheritance of Japheth would be in Europe, defined as being west of the Don River.

Having grown up directly in the fallout from the catastrophic Yuezhi defeat by the Xiong Nu and subsequent vast people movement from his nation's ancient homeland in China, this teaching may have come to mind when considering where, possibly, the Yuezhi people could go to be safe. Whilst the very many optimistic and enterprising planners of the Yuezhi civilization would have got to work building a new centre in their new home of Transoxiana, that indeed appeared to have great prospects for wealth and stability, providing a new base from which the ancient trading nation could maintain its monopoly on the Silk Road trade in the beautiful surrounds of ancient Bactria, and with every possibility of increased expansion south into India and the boundless untold potential of that continent, it would seem that Odin was not convinced.

Thinking long term and pragmatically, the Chinese Empire were already on the cusp of taking on the Silk Road trade for themselves, having recently made contact with the Iranians during the westward expedition of Zhang Qian in 128 BC, the same trip where they offered an alliance agreement to (probably) Odin's father, Pushang/Friallaf. The trade would not last for long. In addition, the Yuezhi economic dominance had also relied on their simultaneous control, or at least free commercial transit, of maritime trade into the Black Sea. But with the Roman Legions on the doorstep of the Cimmerian Bosporus, this was no longer a realistic expectation for the future.

Finally and most pressingly, Odin had encountered the Xiong Nu. This ferocious and insatiable outlaw band of robbers, having hit upon a winning formula with which to devastate their previous economic superiors, would not long be satisfied with the ill-gotten gains they had already aquired. Even if the Chinese could control them, the Xiong Nu would be hot on the heels of the Yuezhi before too long, and they would be required to move again. Even if this took hundreds of years, it meant the Yuezhi as a nation would be doomed.

History has well borne out this analysis. The Chinese eventually defeated the Xiong Nu by 50 BC, making their first military forays into the Tarim Basin into what is now the Xinjiang Province of China in the process - based on the information brought back by Zhang Qian - and expelling the Xiong Nu from the interior of the mountain wall. From this defeat however, they regrouped and began the inevitable expansion westward.

The optimists among the Yuezhi who had gone west across the Steppe, primarily the 'Aorsi' groups and the Alans, had established a huge dominion for themselves by 375 AD, and indeed had enjoyed it for a couple of centuries. But it was all for nothing when at that time the Hun hordes had appeared on the horizon, massacred the Alans east of the Don and enslaved or subjugated the rest, in preparation for the continued westward invasion that would get all the way to France before being decisively defeated by Gothic-led forces at the Battle of the Catalaunian Plains in 451 AD. But that victory would be small comfort to the previous, Indo-European occupants of the Eurasian Steppe, whose ancient cities and populations, devastated by the pestilential torrent of horse banditry, still lay under their tyrannical power and more or less would for the next few hundred years.

The idea of a wholesale northern exodus of the Yuezhi people to a land apparently all but totally unknown to most civilizations on earth – owing no doubt to its having been substantially covered by the Scandinavian ice cap until around 1000 BC at least, and even at this time it was virtually a frozen wasteland[265], was a gigantic risk, to say the least. But apparently the harsh lessons learnt by the Yuezhi heir (we do not know when or if he inherited the throne of 'Asaland') had led him to rationalize that anything was worth not having his nation suffer such devastation again. A home in the frozen tundra was at least a home!

---

[265] Note Herodotus' account of Scythian descriptions of the land to their north being impassable on account of the 'feathers' that fell from the sky with such thickness that one could not even see through them (p.258)

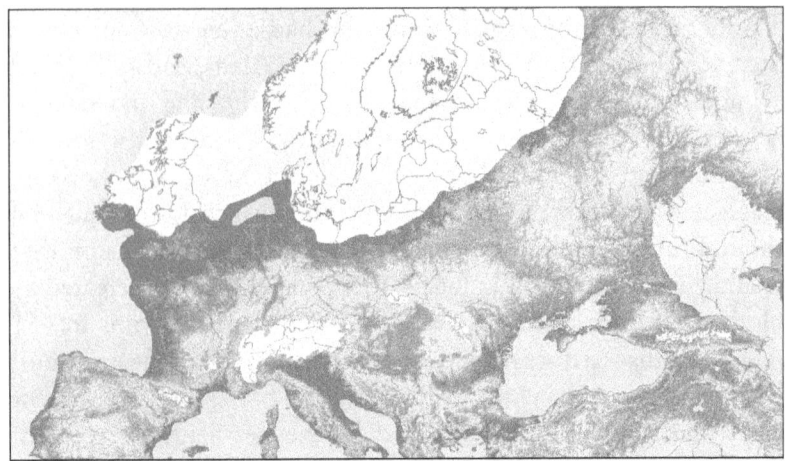

Fig.100: showing the 'Scandinavian Ice Cap' C.2300 BC. Increased waterways would have been available to cross Russia from south-east to north-west even 2200 years after this at the time of the Scandinavian exodus[266]

Snorri Sturluson takes up the story:

"There goes a great mountain barrier from north-east to south-west, which divides the Greater Swithiod [today's Russia – Ed.] from other kingdoms. South of this mountain ridge it is not far to Turkland, where Odin had great possessions. In those times the Roman chiefs went wide around in the world, subduing to themselves all people; and on this account many chiefs fled from their domains. But Odin having foreknowledge, and magic-sight, knew that his posterity would come to settle and dwell in the northern half of the world. He therefore set his brothers Ve and Vilje over Ásgard; and he himself, with all the gods and a great many other people, wandered out, first westward to Gardarike [North-Western Russia around Novgorod – Ed.], and then south to Saxland. He had many sons; and after having subdued an extensive kingdom in Saxland, he set his sons to rule the country."[267]

---

[266] Image by San Jose/Ulamm from Wikimedia Commons (https://en.wikipedia.org/wiki/File:Weichsel-Würm-Glaciation.png) (desaturated), used under CC BY SA 3.0 Unported (https://creativecommons.org/licenses/by-sa/3.0/deed.en)
[267] Heimskringla, vol.1, p.273-274

"Odin had second sight, and his wife also; and from their foreknowledge he found that his name should be exalted in the northern part of the world and glorified above the fame of all other kings. Therefore, he made ready to journey out of Turkland, and was accompanied by a great multitude of people, young folk and old, men and women; and they had with them much goods of great price. And wherever they went over the lands of the earth, many glorious things were spoken of them, so that they were held more like gods than men. They made no end to their journeying till they were come north into the land that is now called Saxland; there Odin tarried for a long space, and took the land into his own hand, far and wide."[268]

Note the 'great mountain barrier' mentioned that must surely be the mountain wall of the Pamirs and Tian Shan, suggesting that there was still substantial holdings 'south' of it (i.e. in today's China).

---

[268] Prose Edda, p.7

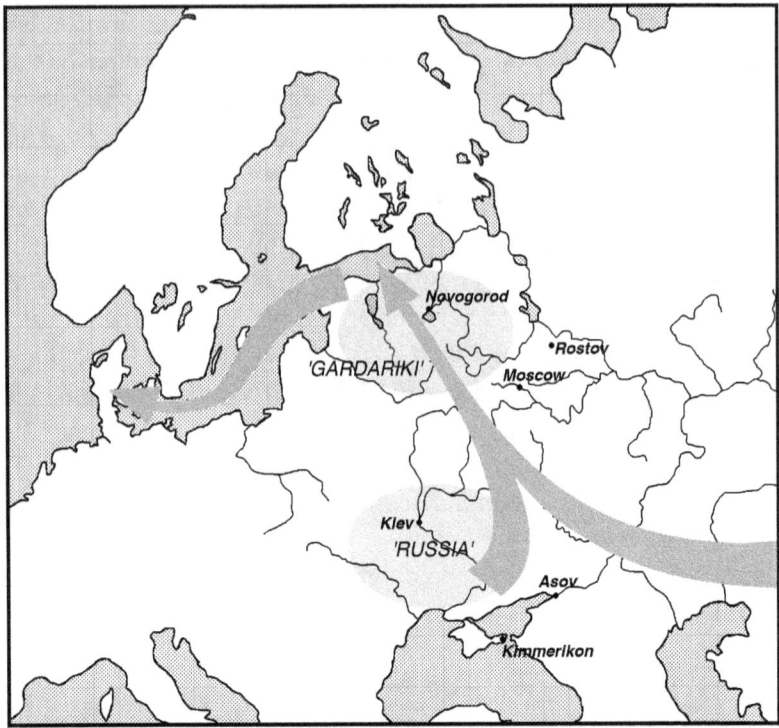

Fig.101: estimated route of the first northern migration of the Scandinavians using the river 'highways' of Russia

The route north for this first expedition, that would have taken place some time around 120-115 BC, was probably the Volga River, via Lakes Ilmen and Lagoda, into the Baltic Sea. This is suggested by the mention of 'Gardarike' ('fortress kingdom'), the Scandinavian settlement south of the Gulf of Finland that had been centred around 'Hólmgarðr' (Novgorod) for at least a thousand years preceding the time Snorri was writing.

But it could just as easily have been the Don, Dniepr, Dvina or Vistula rivers. The overwhelming number of waterways transversing 'the Great Swithiod' (the 'Great Scythia', AKA Russia) make it impossible to know which of the hundreds of potential routes was the one taken by Odin to reach Jutland with the first contingent of Scandinavian settlers for Western Europe[269]

Novgorod in the north and Kiev in the south were the first major city-states of the river-based Scandinavian nation of 'Russia'[270]. When they were first settled by Æsir is not known[271], but their populations and significance would certainly have been greatly enhanced by their utility in this migration effort, in which both must surely have been involved. The mention of going 'first westward to Gardarike' suggests a route directly from Transoxiana, but perhaps not without stopping at the Black Sea or at least the closest intersection of the Volga with the Don, to pick up the Cimmerians.

For it is all but an historical certainty that they constituted the greater part of this first migratory trip. Their presence was immediately missed in the Bosporan Kingdom, where the Scythians overthrew the city there and killed the King in 108 BC[272], and immediately witnessed in Europe, as we shall see. This

---

[269] Heyerdahl and Lillieström favour the Dniepr or Don (p.36-7, 216). They also point out the fact that the route north of the Scandinavian Peninsula entirely, via the White Sea east of Finland, was open as early as the early centuries AD, as proven by the voyages of first 'Njord', then Tore Hund and Ottar (p.86-96; 212-13). However it was probably still ice-locked at the time of Odin.

[270] Note however that 'Rus' was probably an exonym; used by non-Scandinavians to describe them (although cf. 'Rostock', 'Roskilde'). The city of Moscow (and the nation of 'Muscovy') was at that time a largely unrelated settlement of descendants of Meschech (though they were likely aware of the migration and perhaps aided it). The Huns all but destroyed Kiev during the Dark Ages, but it was re-established from Scandinavia afterwards, to become the medieval state of 'Kievan Rus'. After Scandinavian Russia was once again all but destroyed by the Mongols in the 13th Century AD, Muscovy under Ivan the Terrible in the 16th Century AD took the leadership of the region, including of the disparate, remnant states of 'Russia'.

[271] Syrian historians C.555 AD already name the populations south of Kiev (possibly the ancient 'Ásgard') as 'Hros'/'Rus' (Heyerdahl & Lillieström, p.112)

[272] Perhaps as little as 10 years after the escape of the Cimmerians and Azerbaijani Saka-Sunni northwards, the thread of the existing status quo in the Black Sea region

author proposes that the terms 'Cimmerians', 'Crimea' and 'Cimbri' are too similar for it reasonably to be disputed that they are all references to the same historico-geographical group.[273] As well as the overwhelming supporting evidence that the European 'Cimbri' of Roman and other records are the very same 'Cimmerians' of the Cimmerian Bosporus[274]. Frankly, to continue to attempt to resist this clear witness of history at this stage begins to look like unscientific, ideological dogma.

The description of Odin leaving his possessions in the care of his brothers gives some impression of the hazardousness of the undertaking. There would have been many who would have thought him a fool, or insane. The account's mention of leaving 'Ásgard' itself, ancient city of the Æsir, may be an historical flourish, in that the Yuezhi had had to abandon their ancestral lands. Or it could mean that at this time they still had access to their ancient capital, possibly in the Tian Shan. Or that new settlements in Transoxiana had taken on the meaning of 'Ásgard'

---

snapped. Exactly how much of this was caused by their departure from the scene is hard to know. However Kimmerikon on the southern shore of the Kerch peninsula had been an important stronghold defending the Bosporan Kingdom from the Scythians. Without the Cimmerians' presence the Greeks apparently were not able to hold them off. In 108 BC the Bosporan Kingdom's ailing Spartocid dynasty was overthrown by the Scythians and its last dynast Pairisades V was killed by the Scythian leader Saumacus. But before succumbing he bequeathed the Bosporan throne to the Greco-Iranian tyrant of the Pontic Kingdom on the other (south) side of the Black Sea, Mithridates, who sent his son to rule the Bosporus. However only a couple of decades later in 89 BC Roman legions arrived in Anatolia and engaged Pontus in the Mithridatic Wars, that led to the decisive defeat of Pontus and its allies (including the conquest of Athens) by the Roman Republic. In 66 BC Mithridates of Pontus himself fled to the Bosporan Kingdom, bringing the full weight of the Roman legions down on the Crimean region. By the mid-1st Century BC the Crimea was directly under the jackboot of imperial Rome.

[273] As also testified to by Poseidōnios of Apameia (Greek Historical Fragments, vol.1, p.245), and agreed with by Strabo (vol.1, p.450), who also indicates that the Cimmerians/Tauri had departed from the Crimean peninsula by the time of his writing (C.7 BC), and indeed arguably only such a circumstance could account for the detailed information on it that he possesses (vol.1, p.476, 478)

[274] See for example Heyerdahl & Lillieström, p.198-199, 237-243. At some point 'Azer' people from Azerbaijan also joined the migration, as it is remembered there to this day, even enshrined in a local aphorism: "those who go north, don't come back" (Ibid, p.147-8)

as the nation's capital.

Thor Heyerdahl, whose last energies were expended in the efforts to locate the jumping off point for the migration of the historical Odin, failed to find it in either Azerbaijan or Asov, but nevertheless identified them as key nodes in the Tirassian maritime trade network that would have played important roles in this huge people-moving endeavour, that must have been years in the planning[275].

Heyerdahl was of the opinion that it would have utilized the infamous 'collapsible ship' described by Snorri:

"Odin had a ship which was called Skidbladnir, in which he sailed over wide seas, and which he could roll up like a cloth."[276]

Or crafts like it. Whether it did or not, the description is highly consistent with a route through Russia to the Baltic, then 'south', probably to the south-east corner of Jutland, where, disembarking, they would find themselves the founding members of the culture that would become known as the Saxons, AKA the 'Sakaceni', one of several ancient names for the Cimmerians.

---

[275] Heyerdahl found overwhelming evidence of a Scandinavian presence in the city of Asov (south of the Don River) around the time of the migration, coming to the conclusion that Odin had probably lived and reigned there (p.122, 131, 147, 156, 270-271), but he was unable precisely to pin down the enigmatic patriarch. This is because, as we have seen, Odin almost certainly grew up in the Issyk Kul region, and reigned primarily at Samarkand, much further east.
[276] Heimskringla, vol.1, p.277-8; Heyerdahl & Lillieström, p.50, 187

The Cimmerians announce their arrival in Europe

The Cimmerians, once established in Jutland, did what they were used to doing in Asia: they raided southwards. The invasions of the 'Cimbri' south from Jutland into 'Germania' and then into Roman Gaul starting in 113 BC caused a major upset in Roman politics. This hitherto unknown nation from north of Roman awareness cut through the existing Roman defences like a hot knife through butter, and were an entirely different consideration from the populations they had already encountered in the region.

Facing the Cimbrians to their south were two classes of European 'Gomerans'. On the west were the Gauls, on the east the 'Germani', as the Romans called them: unconquered Celts and Scythians. The Germani included the Belgians, who had already crossed the Rhine to the west, near the Gauls, 'long ago'. Caesar noted that while the Gauls failed to withstand the Scandinavian assault, the 'German' Belgians did, resisting it and maintaining defences against it[277]. The Germani were most probably Tungrians of today's east Belgium (Tongeran) and Cologne, along with Ashkenazian and Riphathian Scythians who had migrated all the way from the steppe, pushed by the Sarmatians, and proto-Franks from Pannonia. The distinction of their martial abilities likely stems from their identity as free peoples rather than from any major ethnic difference with the Gauls.[278]

The Cimbri approached the Roman frontier at Noricum and attacked a Roman subject tribe the Taurisci. A Roman force reinforced them and requested them to leave. This they did, until betrayed by the Romans and attacked anyway, at which point the Cimbrians prompty defeated the Romans.[279]

---

[277] p.93-95. This distinction is a good example of the difference between the original meaning of 'German' as 'Gomeran' and the later conflation of it with the Scandinavian descendants of the Jutland landing, who, often coming from the direction of 'Germany', were frequently misidentified as 'Germans' by the Romans. See also Appendix 7: Who was who in Dark Ages Europe?

[278] Their fundamentally Celtic identity is noted by Strabo (vol.1, p.443)

[279] Beck, p.368.

The Cimbri then went west into Gaul, fighting and defeating numerous Roman armies (in 109 and 107 BC). At Arausio in 105 BC the Romans lost as many as 80,000 men in a devastating rout[280].

Rome was in a panic expecting imminent conquest, but the Cimbri instead headed to Spain for further looting. However, they were unable to overcome the Celtiberians (descendants of Ashkenaz and presumably Tubal).

This had given the panicked Romans time to prepare a defense. The Cimbrians crucially divided their forces, with one army being defeated at Aquae Sextiae (today's Aix–en-Provence) in 102 BC when the Romans took as prisoner the leader of the Cimbrians' partners the 'Teutones' (possibly the 'Tauri') recorded as 'Teutobod' by the Romans, and the other army, after penetrating the Alps, being defeated at the Battle of Vercellae in 101 BC. The Cimbrian leaders named by the Romans as 'Boiorix' and 'Lugius' were killed on the battlefield.

However Justin still reports the Cimbri as plundering Italy during the 'Social War' (90-88 BC)[281]. In short the Cimbri seem to have taken to Roman-occupied Europe like children in a candy store, apparently feeling loosened from the constraints that had been upon them in the more hostile Asia.[282]

After this, Jutland became known as the 'Cimbrian Peninsula'[283] The Cimbri were (of course) still there around the beginning of the next millennium, as described by Augustus, and Ptolemy's map duly places them at the north of the peninsula in today's 'Himmerland', that was named after them.

---

[280] Livy, vol.14, p.79
[281] Justin, p.378
[282] Nb. There is still a 'Cimbrian language'-speaking population in Italy today. It would be interesting to compare it with the languages of Tocharia.
[283] Ptolemy, p.81; Strabo, vol.1, p.449-50

This then was the first Scandinavian settlement in Europe (not counting ancient Thrace), from whom the nations of the Saxons, the Jutes, the Angles, the Dutch (in particular the Frisians), the Lombards (probably AKA Widsith's Heathobards), the Westphalians and the Old Prussians derive.

The Icelandic sources go on to describe the settlement of this area:

"He had many sons; and after having subdued an extensive kingdom in Saxland, he set his sons to rule the country. He himself went northwards to the sea"[284]

"In that land Odin set up three of his sons for land-wardens. One was named Vegdeg: he was a mighty king and ruled over East Saxland; his son was Vitgils; his sons were Vitta, Heingistr's father, and Sigarr, father of Svebdeg, whom we call Svipdagr. The second son of Odin was Beldeg, whom we call Baldr[285]: he had the land which is now called Westphalia. His son was Brandr, his son Frjódigar, (whom we call Fródi), his son Freóvin, his son Uvigg, his son Gevis (whom we call Gave)[286]. Odin's third son is named Sigi, his son Rerir. These the forefathers ruled over what is now called Frankland; and thence is descended the house known as Völsungs. From all these are sprung many and great houses.

Then Odin began his way northward, and came into the land which they called Reidgothland; and in that land he took possession of all that pleased him. He set up over the land that son of his called Skjöldr, whose son was Fridleifr;--and thence descends the house of the Skjöldungs: these are the kings of the Danes. And what was then called Reidgothland is now called Jutland."[287]

---

[284] Heimskringla, vol.1, p.274
[285] AKA 'Barðr'
[286] This genealogy from 'Bældæg' is confirmed in the Anglo-Saxon Chronicle (p.2)
[287] Prose Edda, p.8. There is evidence that the Jutes and Angols (descendants of Vegdeg and Baldr) were the original occupiers of Jutland, with the Skjöldungs rather establishing the Danish royal house at Leidre on the island of Sealand; and that Dan

The names of the 'land-wardens' set up as local rulers of the conquered territory match exactly English records of the ancient patriarchs of the various nations of Jutland who eventually, under the leadership of Offa of Angol in the 4th Century AD, would coalesce into the mutual defense and liberty alliance to be known as 'Angol-land' – the Jutes at the north of the peninsula, the Angols in the centre and the Saxons to the South. This coalition of nations, probably pressured by the expanding empire of Denmark-based tyrant Dan Mikillati ('the magnificent') would later follow its leaders the Jutes Hnaef and then Hengest who had established a daring foothold initially as a mercenary in the neighbouring island of Britain, to migrate there wholesale from 449 AD[288], conquering and changing the name of the main trunk of the island to be the new 'Angol-land' ('England').[289]

Odin's son 'Baldr''s stated inheritance in Westphalia is significant in that Bardowick and the Bardengau are probably named after him[290] (the sources also mention a residence of his at Breidablik in Sweden). Baldr was a significant figure in Norse mythology, coming to symbolise in the nascent pre-Christian era of Scandinavian history, but nevertheless when Christianity was known, a type of Christ – an innocent beloved son who was struck down in his youth. It is not impossible that Baldr is one and the same with Boiorix, the fallen Cimbrian general[291].

Mikillati's (4th Century AD) expansion pushed the Jutes out and added Jutland to the Danish possessions.

[288] In fact this traditional date (from Bede (p.49-51)) is now understood to be somewhat late. The emigration probably began as early as 400 AD.

[289] When the English were defeated and enslaved by the Normans in 1066 AD, a sizeable contingent of refugee English nobles, probably led by one Sigurd Earl of Gloucester, emigrated by ship to the Crimea, apparently in the belief that they had their origins there (Shepard, Saint Edward's Saga).

[290] Though it is also claimed that these toponyms are derived from the Langobards and/or Heathobards ('long-beards'/'war-beards'), later Cimbrian-derived nations descended from Baldr mentioned by Widsith (C.600 AD, p.195) among others

[291] This is consistent with Livy's description of Boiorix as 'a savage youth' (vol.14, p.79). Boiorix is likely a Celticisation of another word, possibly bestowed on him by the Celtic populations of the surrounding region or by the Romans whose understanding of the distinctions between the nations they encountered in Europe was limited.

To what extent Odin took part in the Cimbrian invasion of Gaul is at present obscure, but it is almost certain that he led the initial migration, as described in Snorri's Heimskringla. He may then have left the campaign in the charge of his sons and continued north house-hunting a more suitable location for the main party of the Yuezhi. Heyerdahl and Lillieström note that the Cimbrian onslaught took place at a critical moment during Mithridates Eupator's confrontation with Rome, and may have been planned to coincide with it, as suggested by Justin.[292]

---

[292] Justin, p.368

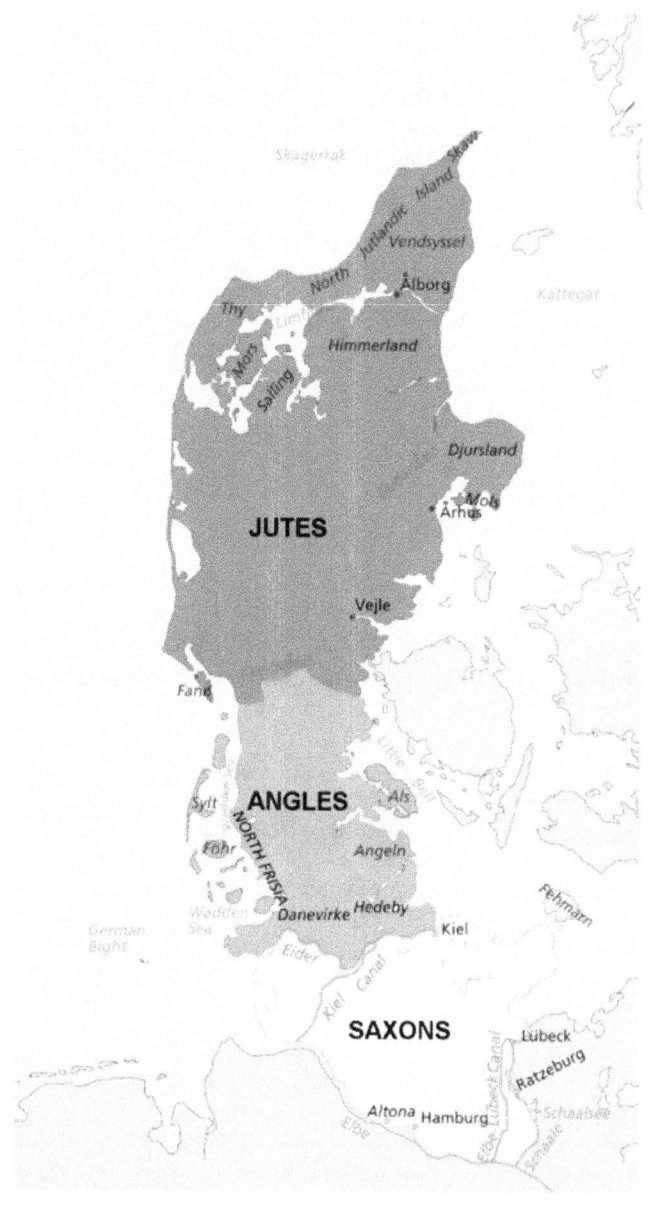

Fig.102: the Cimmerian/Cimbrian colonies of Jutland, whose populations would become 'England'[293].

---

[293] Wikimedia image by TharkunColl (https://commons.wikimedia.org/wiki/File:Angles_saxons_jutes.png) (desaturated), used under CC BY SA 3.0 Unported (https://commons.wikimedia.org/wiki/File:Angles_saxons_jutes.png)

The Founding of Sweden

The story continues with Odin, having delegated Saxland to others, travelling 'northward, where the land is called Sweden'. Here he meets a King Gylve. This could potentially be a King of the Goths, if indeed they were already there (although the earlier description of Reidgothland suggests their presence there as well). Odin negotiates with Gylve for his people to move there. Gylve, seeing he has no real choice, agrees. This then was likely the preparations for the larger exodus of the main body of the Æsir. Odin selects for himself Sigtuna, five miles from today's Stockholm, to be his capital.

While the text does not mention another trip by Odin back to Asia to bring out the great body of the people, it is most likely that this occurred as there appears to be a gap in time between the initial settlement in Saxony and Jutland and the settlement of Old Sigtuna in Sweden, with the Jutland/Saxony arrival of the Cimbri in roughly 115 BC and the founding of Sweden possibly as late as 60 BC[294].

---

[294] A picture emerges of Odin taking an initial, largely military 'task force' over the Baltic (the Jutland trip), to scout the best location and make arrangements there subsequently to bring out the main Yuezhi population, including women and children. The location he chose, today's Stockholm, is precisely the nearest point on the Scandinavian peninsula (and straight due west) from their probable embarkation point in the Gulf of Finland. This first 'scouting and preparation' trip could explain Odin's 'long absence' from Asaland: "Often he went away so long that he passed many seasons on his journeys...It happened once when Odin had gone to a great distance, and had been so long away that the Asas doubted if he would ever return home, that his two brothers took it upon themselves to divide his estate; but both of them took his wife Frigg to themselves. Odin soon after returned home, and took his wife back." (Heimskringla, p.271-20). This absence may have stretched to decades. Frey, who accompanied Odin on the first expedition, returned to Iran to assume the throne there in 75 BC, 40 years later. Soon after this, there is the potential 'sighting' of Odin in Pontus C.72 BC, at Mithridates' court (as per Plutarch (vol.2, p.214) and Appian (vol.2, p.389-90)). Both of these events might have taken place during the interval between the primary (scouting) and secondary (main) Scandinavian migrations. And, though it may be a poetic addition, the Shahnameh clearly states that Frey's negotiations establishing peace between the Iranians and Æsir in Transoxiana, after he regained the Iranian throne in 75 BC, were with Afrasiab personally (p.128-9), presenting prima facie evidence that Odin was present in Samarkand as late as the 70s BC.

Either way the text continues:

"Odin had with him one of his sons called Yngvi, who was king in Sweden after him; and those houses come from him that are named Ynglings. The Æsir took wives of the land for themselves, and some also for their sons; and these kindreds became many in number, so that throughout Saxland, and thence all over the region of the north, they spread out until their tongue, even the speech of the men of Asia, was the native tongue over all these lands. Therefore men think that they can perceive, from their forefathers' names which are written down, that those names belonged to this tongue, and that the Æsir brought the tongue hither into the northern region, into Norway and into Sweden, into Denmark and into Saxland. But in England there are ancient lists of land-names and place-names which may show that these names came from another tongue than this."[295]

Yngvi then is the captured Parthian prince Phraates II or 'Frey'[296]. The Heimskringla states that he lived in 'Upsal' in Sweden and also ascribes a Swedish residence to 'Njord' (though it seems to include an exhaustive list of the medieval Scandinavian pagan pantheon including Thor himself). The text is adamant that the Æsir language, the 'speech of the men of Asia' was spread out over the region. This certainly matches the spread of the Scandinavian base-language from this area. And it is correct that in Britain, ancient pre-English Byrthonic place names were well in evidence. Was the Scandinavian language itself the language of the Yuezhi in Asia? That is harder to say, although the field of linguistics does provide spectacular evidence of the Æsir migration from the far east, as Tocharian, a 'centum' language, has (otherwise unaccountably) more in common with the Indo-European languages of *Western Europe* than with any languages in between[297].

---

[295] Prose Edda, p.9
[296] This suggests that other of Odin's 'sons' to whom he gave thrones in Europe may also have been lieutenants rather than actual blood relatives.
[297] Mallory & Mair, p.121-2: "somehow people speaking a 'European' language had managed to trek their way from Europe to the Tarim Basin." Actually it was the

The Scandinavian sources go on to state that Odin proceeded to establish 'the same law in his land that had been in force in Asaland' (Heimskringla) or indeed Troy (Prose Edda), with twelve 'doomsmen', 'Diar', 'Drottnir' or judges of the land as there had been there.

Of the end of Odin the Heimskringla records that he 'went northwards to the sea, and took up his abode in an island which is called Odin's in Fyen'. This is the Danish island of Odense, a sometime home of the King. But it is not impossible that he returned to Asia after establishing the Swedish colony and may even have met his end as recorded in the Shahnameh, but this is more likely wishful thinking on the part of the Iranians. Rather the Heimskringla reports that 'Odin died in his bed in Sweden...and said he was going to Godheim.' It continues: 'Then began the belief in Odin, and the calling upon him.'[298]

This account relates that he was succeeded as King of Sweden by none other than Njord, the Shahnameh's 'Nodar', emphatically stated there to have been killed during the Turan war. Nevertheless Heimskringla adds the detail that after a good rule as King he died of sickness. Then Frey took over as King (or rather 'Drot') and was a particularly wise ruler:

---

other way around. Mallory & Mair's chart on p.288 clearly shows a closer relationship between Tocharian and the Scandinavian languages (here erroneously labelled 'Germanic') than with any other language group. There are also copious evidences of the Xiong Nu writing in 'Rune'-style script in that area (Tonyukuk and Orkhon inscriptions, C. 8th Century AD). The oldest Scandinavian runes proper have been dated to C.150 AD and were found on the island of Odense, Denmark, Odin's retirement home (Heyerdahl & Lillieström, p.222), suggesting he may have been the originator of the cypher/ script himself. The lack of earlier remnants of runes may also be because they were recorded on perishable material (Ibid).

[298] Heimskringla, vol.1, p.281. 'Godheim' is defined as the 'Great Swithiod' i.e. Russia, and "the Swedes believed that he was gone to the ancient Ásgard, and would live there eternally."

"Frey built a great temple at Upsal, made it his chief seat, and gave it all his taxes, his land, and goods. Then began the Upsal domains, which have remained ever since. Then began in his days the Frode-peace; and then there were good seasons, in all the land, which the Swedes ascribed to Frey, so that he was more worshipped than the other gods, as the people became much richer in his days by reason of the peace and good seasons".[299]

This again is an exact match for the qualities of peace-making and wise, prosperous rulership ascribed to Sinatruces' rule in Iran. An interesting description follows of the events surrounding his death:

"Frey fell into a sickness; and as his illness took the upper hand, his men took the plan of letting few approach him. In the meantime they raised a great mound, in which they placed a door with three holes in it. Now when Frey died they bore him secretly into the mound, but told the Swedes he was alive; and they kept watch over him for three years. They brought all the taxes into the mound, and through the one hole they put in the gold, through the other the silver, and through the third the copper money that was paid. Peace and good seasons continued."[300]

These unusual details could very possibly be a memory of a cunning contrivance whereby Frey was whisked out of the country to return to his native land, so that the Swedes would not panic about losing the 'peace and good seasons' that had accompanied his tenure.

---

[299] Heimskringla, vol.1, p.282
[300] Ibid, p.283

It would make perfect sense for Frey, upon hearing of the sad state of affairs in Iran, where they lacked a solid leader, to want to return there, make peace between the two sides – between whom he was now the perfect mediator – and restore good rule to Iran. It is entirely possible that Odin accompanied this trip back to 'Swithiod'[301].

The journey back, though a long one, was clearly an open route for some time, as Heimskringla records that Frey's grandson Swegde returned there on a five-year trip 'where he found many of his connections' and brought back a wife from Vanheim.

Frey was succeeded by his son Fjolne, while the Danish domain was held by the descendants of Skjöld[302], ruled from Leidre in Sjælland where Skjöld's grandson Fredfrode had a large hall. This became the capital of Denmark, and Skjöld's descendant Hrothgar was still King there 600 years later as witnessed in the Anglo-Saxon epic poem 'Beowulf'[303]. These then became the bases of the subsequent Scandinavian nations, the centres in Sigtuna (traditionally ruled by the Ynglings), Leidre (the Skjöldings), Himmerland (the Vitgilsings) and Bardenwick (Baldrings). From here spread out the Svear, Danes, Angles, Saxons, Jutes, Frisians, Lombards and Wulflings that would develop into the later Scandinavian nations of the Swedes, Danes, Norwegians, English, Dutch and Icelanders[304].

---

[301] As discussed there is some evidence of Odin being active up to and beyond the time of Frey's 'death' in Sweden and subsequent return to Iran.
[302] Prose Edda states that Fredfrode, reigning after his father Friedlief, Skjöldr's son, "succeeded to the kingdom after his father, in the time when Augustus Caesar imposed peace on all the world; at that time Christ was born." (p.161)
[303] Heimskringla, vol.1, p.274; Beowulf, p.1-3
[304] Further evidence in support of the Scandinavian exodus comes in the form of archaeo-genetics. We previously discussed how the original settlements of Thor in Thrace correlate with the 'Cucuteni-Trypillia' archaeological horizon, associated archaeo-genetically with Y-DNA haplogroup I, found most strongly in the Scandinavian countries. Outside Scandinavia, the British Isles, Iceland and Europe, it is only found in numbers in two other places in the world: a small amount in the far north-east in Siberia, and a larger amount in Sogdiana/Bactria around Samarkand: the precise final Asian jumping-off point for the Æsir before their migration (Jeanson, plates 225 and 106). Heyerdahl and Lilliestrőm also found grave

For the achievement of the 'Scandinavian Exodus' in preserving his people and for being a teacher and patriarch, Odin was celebrated in no small measure (and in true Indo-European default fashion eventually worshipped as a pagan idol before their conversion to Christianity[305]), by the future descendants of the populations he had settled in Scandinavia. The English day 'Wednesday' is named after him.

---

evidence in Sweden that supports a Swedish arrival at this time (p.42-44, 23)

[305] The above accounts of the Swedes' reactions to the passing of both Odin and Frey perfectly describe how this process occurred throughout human history.

The End of Thrace and Dacia

The huge Sarmatian wave of immigration from the Steppe impacted Europe at exactly the same place previous waves had: Dacia or the region around the Danube River, roughly today's Romania, that would become route one for western-migrating Dark Age invasive nations for the next 600 years. The Dacians, probably descendants of the Goths[306], already squeezed into this area by GRHF creep to their south (in the form of the weak Greek client state the Odrysian Kingdom), expanding Celts to their west and the Scythians to their North, were put under severe pressure by this massive new influx.

The Iazyges had sought territory inland, transiting straight through Dacia around the south of the Carpathian Mountains and settling on the plains there south of the Tiszra river. Subsequent waves of Sarmatians, Aorsi and Alans would continue to challenge Dacia's ability to maintain itself as a distinct and contiguous polity. This swirling Sarmatian/Dacian movement would develop into the complex 'Chernyakhov' archaeological culture, and would ultimately be the ethnogenesis of the Lithuanian and Slavic peoples.

---

[306] Although many would find a distinction between the origins of the two

From the mid 2nd Century BC Dacian fortunes improved somewhat, as a couple of Dacian leaders arose who were able to fight back against this uncomfortably 'hemmed in' predicament. First 'Rubobostes' asserted the independence of the Dacians, particularly against western Celtic belligerence and influence. This was followed up by Dacia's greatest leader 'Burebista' from around 70 BC. Burebista expelled the Celts, reformed the Dacians' morality and built a network of mountain fortresses in the Orastie Mountains to provide some protection and stability for Dacia against foreign incursions. His capital was possibly in today's Popesti. Burebista led highly successful military expeditions westward into inland Europe, in particular defeating the Celtic Boii (in 50-40 BC) and Bastarnae. He then conquered virtually all of the western Black Sea Greek port colonies, assigning to himself the title 'King of Kings'.

Fig.103: Left: the 'Dacian Draco' totem used in battle to frighten the enemy[307]. Such 'battlefield theatre' would be employed for millennia by the Goths, as for example in the dress of the 17th Century 'Winged Hussar' at right[308]

---

[307] After Rostovtseff
[308] Detail from Kaczor Batowksi's 'Atak Husarii' (1917). Public Domain image from Wikimedia Commons (https://en.wikipedia.org/wiki/File:Atak_husarii.jpg)

However, this Dacian expansion would not halt the tide of invasion for long. This era was arguably the high-point of Roman power. The Romans had conquered Thrace in 70 BC, taking the boundary of empire right up to Dacia's southern border. While Burebista made a deal with one of the three 'Triumvirs' (dictators) of post-Republican Rome, Pompey, the fragile Roman Triumvirate (a consequence of Roman general Julius Caesar's 'breaking' of the old Roman Republic in 50 BC) soon degenerated into infighting and a massive civil war from 49-45 BC. Especially after one Triumvir, Crassus, was unexpectedly killed fighting the Parthian Empire, leaving just two Triumvirs left. Burebista was on the wrong side of these events as Caesar got the better of Pompey, although arguably the contest was closer to a draw resulting in a split into two spheres of influence: the western or European Roman Empire led by Caesar and the Eastern or Anatolian Roman Empire led by Pompey, that was in reality a continuation of the Greek Empire and came to be known as the Byzantine Empire.

Either way Dacia was in Caesar's domain. Aware of the significant power of the Dacian ruler, Caesar planned a massive invasion of Dacia. Fortunately for the Dacians, he was assassinated in 44 BC. But then so was Burebista, so it was a stalemate. However the Dacians had secured something approximating independence for the next 150 years, a highly complex period in western history.

At the end of that 150 years however, the imperial creep caught up with Dacia. In 101-106 AD Roman Emperor Trajan led a huge army and conquered the Dacians, turning much of their territory into a Roman Province, with the rest of it following soon after. Dacia was no more.

More About the Goths

It is time for another word about those foils of clear, linear history, the Goths. One of the main reasons for the difficulties historians have in understanding their trajectory through history is that there really is only one source: Jordanes' 'Getica', written approximately 551 AD. Jordanes, a Goth himself of some sort, gives a comprehensive and colourful description of the ancient history of the Gothic nation up to his day. But much like that other Magogian tome, the 'Lebor Gabála Érenn' of Irish history, the chronology of events within the 'Getica' is far from clear, with geographical settlements mentioned multiple times from different eras of human history without a straightforward explanation of what happened between them or how they got from one to the other.

Jordanes' history is reasonably clear as to Geography. He mentions three locations where the Goths dwelt:

a) 'Scandza' AKA Southern Sweden (Scandia, the origin of 'Scandinavia')[309]
b) The Maeotian Lake (the Sea of Azov at the north-east corner of the Black Sea)[310]
c) Moesia (a region of South-Eastern Europe near Thrace)[311]

These are easy to identify. The problem is the chronology of when the Goths were situated at these three places. Jordanes says that the ancient home of the Goths was 'Scandza'[312]. From here they emigrated to Poland at the Vistula River, and from there to the Maeotian Lake. Here they were sometime husbands to the Amazons[313]. After this they went to Moesia. It is not clear whether these were separate forays from Sweden but the context suggests they were consecutive places of occupation and they moved from

---

[309] Jordanes, p.55
[310] Ibid, p.59
[311] Ibid, p.61
[312] Ibid, p.53
[313] Ibid, p.62

one to the other, with one final move back to the northern shore of the Black Sea, the 'Pontic coast' 'in Scythia'.

There's just one problem with this. Sweden was covered by a giant ice cap and therefore uninhabitable until probably 1000 BC. Meanwhile the Amazons' main activity is generally associated with the period 1500 BC to 500 BC. After this there is not much record of them; as discussed they were very likely existing largely as the founders of the 'Sauromatae' culture of the South Urals, with possibly some remnant left in the Caucasus Mountains. So the chronological crossover potential between these cultures is slim. If the Amazons emigrated to Scythia perhaps 1000 AD at the latest, when exactly were the Goths in 'Scandza'? Realistically, it cannot have been before 500 BC. And by this point the Amazons were no longer a separate polity in Scythia but rather part of the Sauromatians. Moreover, there is no trace in history known to this writer of the Goths still being in 'Scythia' by 500 BC. Not north of the Black Sea and not in Caucasia (where they might conceivably have still had contact with Mountain-dwelling Amazons).[314]

---

[314] At one point it was thought that Alans and Roxalani were Goths, part of the Dark Age Gothic migrations. The Alans had a state north of the Caucasus Mountains called 'Alania', a precursor to the modern state of Ossetia. However the Alans were not Goths but rather a people from the far east, as previously discussed. And regardless of this, 'Alania' was not formed until the time of the Hunnic invasion of the 'Pontic Steppe' (Scytho-Sarmatia) during the 4th Century AD when the Alans fled there from the Huns – much too late to be part of Jordanes' 'ancient' Maeotian Gothic homeland.

It is proposed then that the 'Scandza' dwelling was a later phase of Gothic movement. And that the Maeotian Lake phase was the earlier one. This indeed fits perfectly with other history:

- The Goths primaevally migrating north through the Caucasus (possibly as part of the 'Yamnaya horizon' of Japhetic peoples) and then staying in the area of the Maeotian Lake close to the nexus of this initial spread
- The coincidence with the Amazons fits perfectly with Greek and other witnesses of their activities during very ancient antiquity. Indeed, it is quite possible that the Amazon prisoner escape and adventure in 'Scythia' was earlier rather than later and therefore it interacted not so much with the later 'Scythians' but rather with a pre-Scythian, Magogian culture living around the Maeotian Lake sometime before 800 BC. This would happily explain why both Goths and Scythians were claimed as being the husbands of these escaped women: the men involved may have been ancestors of both.
- Neither the Tirassian expansion from Thrace and the Tyras River in the west, nor the later Scythian expansion from the Volga River in the east, had yet come to dominate the Maeotian Lake region. A Gothic residence there during very ancient antiquity is therefore eminently plausible.

And this proposition also fits perfectly with what we know of the people movements when the Scythian 'Empire' did sweep westward around 600 BC; it carried before it the Tirassians but also the 'Getae', who would largely form the Kingdom of Dacia.

This would perfectly explain Jordanes' description of the Goths moving to 'Moesia', that is in the region of Dacia. Conventional historians vehemently deny that the Dacians were Goths or could be made up of Goths, but it is increasingly hard to support that insistence. While 'Dacians' proper could refer to other ethnic components of the emerging Kingdom, clearly the term 'Getae' is very close to 'Goths' or 'Geats' as they were variously known, and they were living in the same area of south-east Europe that Jordanes says the Goths moved to after Lake Maeotis, which is also highly likely to have been the location that the 'Getae' were pushed to by the Scythian expansion. So realistically, it is the same group of people or a very closely associated group.

Most conventional history tentatively accepts Jordanes' 'Scandza' origin for the Goths, and with it implicitly his confusing though more or less apparent assertion that this is the very beginning of their history[315]. But such a tepid, uncritical, non-committal and vague semi-consensus is highly inadequate as it leaves a jarring gap in the explanation of Gothic origins. Because how did they get there? Unless it is asserted that they 'evolved' separately in frozen Sweden, then they must have come from somewhere. It is proposed here that they were hiding in plain sight largely in Dacia, and to some extent to its north.

Probably the most confusing aspect of the Goths' story that has confounded commentators for centuries, is that there was a second, later and much more famous, residence at the Maeotian Lake.

Around 100 AD the celebrated Goths of the Dark Ages made their first appearance on the stage of history, establishing a colony/invasion bridgehead at the mouth of the Vistula River in Poland, apparently from 'Scandza'. Jordanes calls this area 'Gothiscandza' and states that the leader that achieved the emigration was one Berig[316]. From here they migrated south to the Maeotian Lake[317], defeating and displacing the Sarmatians and dwelling there in supremacy until 376 AD when the Hunnic hordes finally appeared on the horizon from the east, having overrun the Alans on the other side of the Don River. The Huns captured half of the Goths (the 'Ostrogoths') and pushed the other half (the 'Visigoths') down to (you guessed it) Dacia, again, where they crossed the Danube

---

[315] Jordanes, p.53, 57
[316] Ibid, p.57, 78
[317] Ibid, p.58

into Roman territory and began wreaking havoc on it, decisively defeating the Roman legions at the Battle of Adrianople in 378 AD, an event that militarily marked the beginning of the end of the Roman Empire. Other nations that developed out of the Vistula beachhead who were either fully Gothic as well or had been partners with the Visigoths and Ostrogoths in some sort of alliance with them[318] were the Gepids, Vandals and probably the Burgundians, who all also dispersed among the disintegrating Roman Empire and became involved in large-scale migrations and political regime change.

One can see why with this well-established trajectory of Gothic movement from the Maeotian Lake westwards into Dacia it is a bit hard to believe that it all happened in almost exactly the same way a thousand years before! But indeed it seems that it was so. Twice the poor Goths were expelled from their beloved Maeotian homeland[319].

---

[318] In particular during the 'Marcommanic Wars' of 166-180 AD
[319] Indeed Jordanes tacitly acknowledges this. In a second statement that appears to contradict his earlier one that the Goths originated in 'Scandza', he says (not mentioning Scandza) that their 'first abode' was near Lake Maeotis, their second in Moesia, Thrace and Dacia, and their third again in Scythia (p.60)

So the Jordanes chronology is exactly right, except for the timing of the residence in Sweden. This didn't happen first, but later. One question remains then: when did the Goths settle 'Scandza', AKA the region of Götaland and the island of Gotland? There are really four possibilities:

1) They were there from very ancient times, before 1000 BC
2) They moved there sometime following the Getic retreat to Dacia/Moesia caused by the Scythian expansion C.600 BC
3) They caught wind of the Scandinavian exodus plans and joined them, migrating to Sweden around 120 BC
4) They were never there. The Gothic settlement of Scandza began later, during the Dark Ages, and the Vistula colony was established directly from Dacia up the 'Gothic corridor', perhaps a slower migration from the 5th Century BC onwards, that also produced a settlement at the same time in Scandza.

1 can be dispensed with as it is all but impossible considering the climate of the time. 3 is an intriguing possibility. In support of it is the close relationship between the Goths and the Scandinavians/Thracians. They had been their neighbours since time immemorial and there was considerable cultural cross-pollination between the Thracians and Dacians/Getae. For example Dacia or the Getae were frequently referred to in ancient sources as being 'part of' Thrace[320], the Dacians' state being located in the ancient Thracian homelands south of the 'Tyras' River; some type of hybrid group known as the 'Tyragetae' dwelling along that river; and most dramatically of all, the Gothic language (that almost certainly started with 'Gutnish') being a Scandinavian language (not an Indo-Iranian, Magogian one). And of course there is the fact of their later peaceful dwelling in Sweden with their northern Æsir neigbours, such was the close relationship between the Thracians/Scandinavians and the Getae/Goths. When the Dacian territory was most under threat around 120 BC from surrounding Romans, Celts, Scythians and Sarmatians, the

---

[320] For example by Herodotus (p.279): "the Getae... are the noblest as well as the most just of all the Thracian tribes"

Dacians may well have been attracted to the idea of joining the northern escape plan then being formulated by their neighbours the Thraco-Cimmerians of the Black Sea.

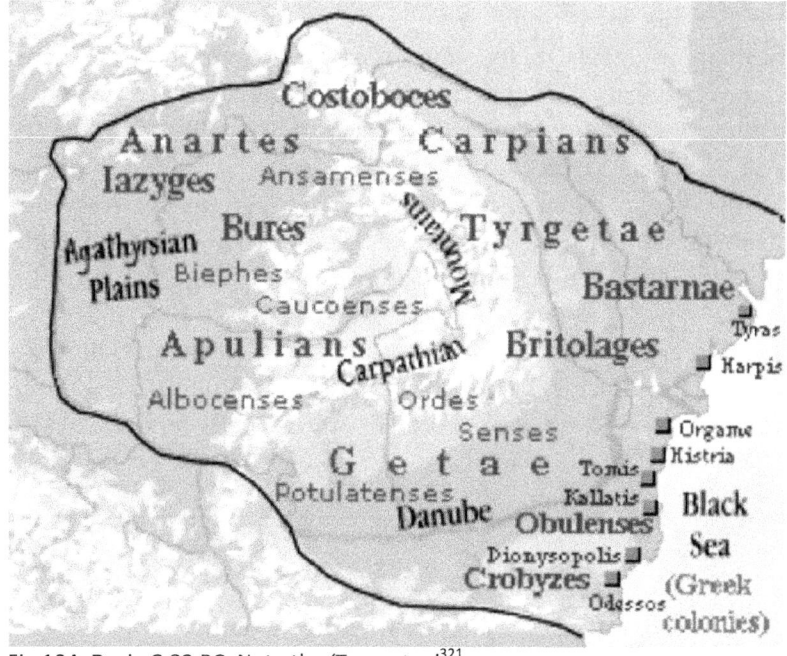

Fig.104: Dacia C.82 BC. Note the 'Tyragetae'[321]

However, against this argument is the witness of the Scandinavian sources that there was already a Gothic King (Gylve) present in Sweden when Odin first travelled there looking for land for his people, with whom he came to terms[322]. This of course may be

---

[321] Wikimedia image by Bogdangiusca (https://commons.wikimedia.org/wiki/File:Dacia_82_BC.png) (desaturated), used under CC BY SA 3.0 Unported (https://creative commons.org/licenses/by-sa/3.0/deed.en)

[322] Prose Edda also states that "One of Odin's sons, named Skjöldr,--from whom the Skjöldungs are come,--had his abode and ruled in the realm which now is called Denmark, but then was known as Gotland." (p.161). This suggests that the Goths had settled not only Scania but also the Danish Islands – possibly this is connected with 'Scandza' in some ancient sources being described as an island. It goes on to say "for Gautland or Gotland was named after Odin's name, and Sweden from the name of Svidurr, which is also a title of Odin's. At that time all the mainland which he possessed was called Reid-Gotaland, and all the islands, Ey-Gotaland: that is now called the Realm of Danes or of Swedes." (p.234). This suggests an

incorrect, or the King could be from an entirely separate nation. The account though is consistent with a pre-existing Gothic settlement in south-east Sweden[323]. The language similarity could also be explained by the influx of Æsir into Sweden. By all accounts the Scandinavian exodus was a large group, that dominated the Scanian peninsula and became the senior partner in Sweden's future national character. It would make perfect sense that their southern neighbours gradually learnt and used their language for ease of commerce etc. in the region. This can be tested by looking at the language of the Getae/Dacians. Assumedly it is not Scandinavian. If not, then the question can be asked: how long would it take the Goths to transition to a new language?

2 and 4 are similar. They posit a northward movement, hitherto hidden from history, of Goths from Dacia through the 'Gothic corridor' to the Baltic, some time between 500 BC and 100 AD.

---

understanding that 'Ey-Gotaland' was the Danish islands with possibly the 'Gotland' of the Edda referring to the Danish island of Odense, as opposed to today's island of 'Gotland' to the east of Sweden.

[323] The Edda also states that "The Goths are named after that king who was called Goti, from whom Gotland is named: he was so called after Odin's name, derived from the name *Gautr*". This remarkable claim is that the name of the 'Goths' was one bestowed on them by Odin himself. However this does not seem compatible with earlier descriptions of populations living in Moesia as 'Getae' much earlier (by for example Herodotus). Certainly it is highly likely that a King Goti, if he existed, lived earlier than the Scandinavian exodus and was a different person from the distinctly named 'Gylve'. Otherwise it is very hard to explain both the pre-existence of the obviously related Getae and also the clear ethnic distinction between the 'Svear', i.e. 'Scandinavian' Swedes (named after 'Svidurr', it says), and their Gothic neighbours in Gotland. Snorri's testimony that the 'Got' name derived from Odin certainly seems questionable and is perhaps an ethnocentric boast, considering the Goths' extremely distinct culture from the Scandinavians.

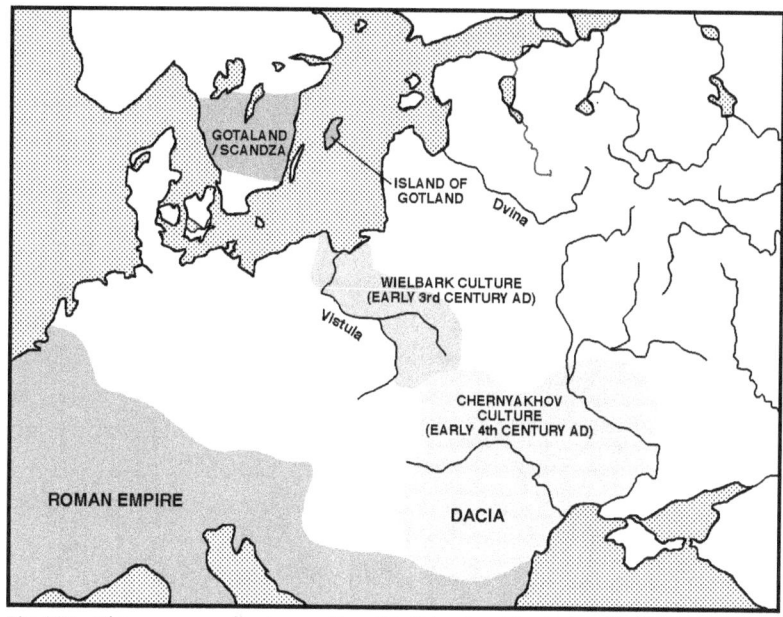

Fig.105: This map well shows the 'Gothic Corridor' that links Dacia with 'Scandza' (Götaland) in Southern Sweden, via the Dniester and Vistula Rivers[324]

This slow migration north independently from the Æsir is very likely the truth. Although it is highly complex to pin down exactly when or how this happened. The migration north and 're-migration' south from the Vistula may have been gradual and overlapping processes. With the partially intermixing influx of Sarmatians to the area this whole region would develop into the Chernyakhov culture of the 4th Century AD that would become the medieval Polish-Lithuanian Commonwealth. Goths essentially make up the main national character of today's Poland.

This 'soft' or slow migration north theory has multiple factors in its favour. For instance the general Chernyakhov cultural region that grew out of it, and the appearance, though rare, of Goths in the area of Poland before 100 AD[325]. In particular Strabo mentions 'Gutones' (usually recognised as Goths) alongside 'Lugii' (that

---

[324] Adapted from a Wikimedia map by Wiglaf/Dbachmann, used under CC BY SA 3.0 Unported (https://creativecommons.org/licenses/by-sa/3.0/deed.en)
[325] Heather, p. xiv, 2, 21, 30.

some equate with Vandals) as part of a military faction under the control of the 'Marcomanni' around 15 AD[326]. It seems possible that Greco-Roman sources were simply not aware of how far back from the coast 'Dacia' extended. It may have extended, one way or another, all the way to the Baltic coast and the mouth of the Vistula.

So was there ever an early settlement in 'Scandza', or did the Vistula Goths migrate there directly from Dacia? Because of the Heimskringla witness regarding King 'Gylve' and the pre-existence of a Gothic settlement at the time of the Æsir arrival, Jordanes' testimony about Berig's embarkation point being 'Scandza' and the fact of the Scandinavian 'Gothic' language (now largely extinct) – i.e. they must have dwelled next to the Æsir at some point to pick up their language (as testified to by Sturluson), it is conjectured that the Goths did indeed settle 'Scandza' before the arrival of the Æsir, so some time prior to 120 BC.

This explanation for the origins and movements of the Goths ties in well with their later activities. Why for example, on establishing the beach-head at the Vistula, did they head to the Maeotian Lake? Well, because it was their ancient homeland, famous in Gothic self-identity, even down to the time of Jordanes. Also, its current occupants the Sarmatians/Scythians had been largely responsible for pushing them out of it before, in the 7th-6th Centuries BC, as well as adding insult to injury by then invading their Dacian territory in the 2nd Century BC as well. Finally as to the timing of the Vistula Gothic outbreak, it coincides almost exactly with the Roman conquest and occupation of Dacia around 100 AD. Whether Berig's invasion of the mainland was in response to this, in an attempt to establish an alternate continental presence or base, or merely as a shift of focus once the Dacian territory had been overrun, is yet to be revealed.

---

[326] Strabo, vol.1, p.444-5, writing C.7 BC. Pliny (vol.1, p.345-6) around 100 AD, backs up this assertion with a similar grouping of nations identified in the same area: Gutones and Burgundiones both belonging to the Vandili. So it would seem that the Vandals were a Gothic leadership group of some sort at this time.

The Yuezhi part ways

Sweden, Russia or India? These were more or less the options facing the main Yuezhi population in 1st Century BC Tocharistan. Or, they could stay put, in the comfortable environs of Bactria. Except, that is, for the tidal wave of Huns heading in their direction, that would be arriving sooner or later.

The argument for a need for a wholesale northern migration out of Asia altogether was weakened by the fact that from the Yuezhi's holdings north of the Oxus River at the west but also in the east spreading down to the Saka state of 'Sakastan'/'Sistan' (today's Afghanistan) was emerging a highly prosperous trade state. This was an expansion out of and evolution from the previous Tocharian role as the trade middle-men of the Silk Road. With the Tarim Basin Silk Road bottleneck having been taken over by the Xiong Nu and soon after sporadically by the Han Chinese empire, the mercantile city-state cultures that had previously been based there resolved to adapt their business model and instead become middle-men between India and China instead, their territory now wrapped around the western side of the Himalayan Plateau. This undertaking, that became a huge empire, was led by the merchants of the largest of the Tarim Basin city-states, Kucha[327], and it would become known as the Kushan Empire.

---

[327] According to the Book of Later Han (Section 1), there were "Thirty-six Kingdoms of the Western Regions". Of those that were based in the Tarim Basin, the Book of Han (completed 111 AD) states that Kucha was the largest, with a population of 81,317, including 21,076 persons able to bear arms (vol.11, p.94). And this of course probably only refers to the city of Kucha itself, whereas much of their holdings and presumably personnel would have moved west with the Yuezhi.

The Kushan Empire

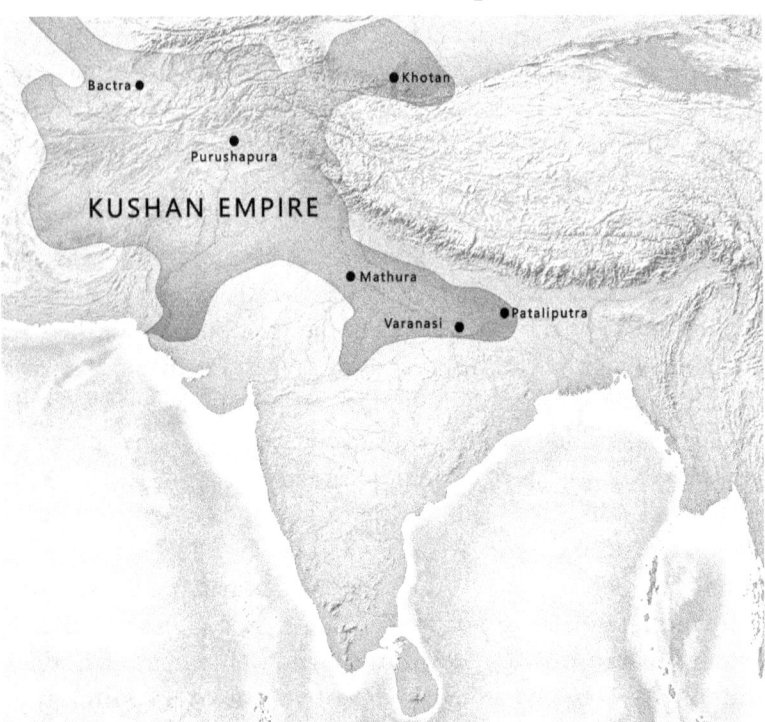

Fig.106: The Kushan Empire C.50 BC-200 AD[328]

The Kushan Empire was a 'tail' or 'Indian Summer' to the ancient Tarim Basin trading prosperity of the Tocharians, now forestalled, and represented the second of three major Indo-European incursions into the vast and fertile subcontinent of India that would have a huge influence on its culture and political history (the other two being the Vedic Aryans and the British Empire). From India the Kushans would transport goods up through the region of Yuezhi control and into the Tarim (apparently often by the mountainous, southern Gandhara route directly from India into today's China) where the ancient cities, though now under increasing foreign pressure from Chinese expansion and Xiong Nu raids, were still able to operate to some extent as independent

---

[328] Wikimedia image by Koba-chan (https://en.wikipedia.org/wiki/File:Map_of_the_Kushan_Empire.png) (desaturated), used under CC BY SA 3.0 Unported (https://creativecommons.org/licenses/by-sa/3.0/deed.en)

trading states right up to their absorption into the Chinese Empire in the 8th Century AD[329]. They would also bring cultural ideas as well - the Kushans were the main transporters of the growing Indian spiritual philosophy of Buddhism through their Empire into China.

By their conquest of Bactria and Sogdiana, the Tocharians succeeded for a few centuries in simply moving their 'middle-man' role westward, thereby continuing to be the main or even only trading agents between China in the east and the growing Roman Empire in the west, in addition to their trade with their immediate western neighbours the Iranians (the 'Vanir') whose Parthian Empire was superceded by the Sasanian Empire in the 3rd Century AD.

The foundation of the Kushan Empire is clouded in the mists of the climactic events of the 2nd and 1st Centuries BC, that followed the Yuezhi conquest of Iran. In Chinese history the five main nations that made up the Yuezhi were Xiūmì (休密), Guìshuāng (貴霜), Shuāngmǐ (雙靡), Xìdùn (肸頓), and Dūmì (都密)[330]. Of these 'Guishang' was the Kushans. The beginning of the supremacy of the Kushans coincides apparently exactly with the departure of the Æsir, the northern exodus migration group. This suggests that the Kushan contingent, faction or leaders were previously under the authority of Odin's father (named 'Pushang' in the Shahnameh, very close to 'Guishang' perhaps indicating some connection) and that once his heir left they assumed control of the future direction of the remaining Yuezhi nation that stayed behind. It may be that the Kushan Empire was an outgrowth of the rule of the 'Ve and Vilje' named in the Heimskringla as Odin's brothers whom he left in charge of 'Asaland' when leaving for the north.

---

[329] Kujula Kadphises sent armed forces to defend Kucha from Chinese imperial attack in the 1st Century AD, but failed to prevent its capture. Chinese control in the Tarim however was only sporadic and the city-states soon had their independence back.
[330] Book of Later Han, Section 13

The Chinese source (basically the Book of Later Han, from 440 AD) describes the figure that first rose to prominence as the founder of the Kushan Empire, one 'Kujula Kadphises':

"More than a hundred years later [than the Yuezhi conquest of Bactria], the *xihou* ('Allied Prince') of Guishuang [AKA Kucha]..., named Qiujiu Que [the Kujula Kadphises of coins]..., attacked and exterminated the four other *xihou* ('Allied Princes'). He set himself up as king of a kingdom called Guishuang [Kushan][331]...He invaded Anxi (Parthia) and took the Gaofu (Kabul) region. He also defeated the whole of the kingdoms of Puta (Parthuaia[332]), and Jibin (Kapisha-Peshawar). Qiujiu Que (Kujula Kadphises) was more than eighty years old when he died." [333]

In other words Kujula Kadphises "founded by means of the submission of the other Yueh-chih clans the Kushan Empire"[334]

It seems likely that the Kushan primacy amongst the remaining Yuezhi groups (that had not left for Scandinavia) may have been more or less immediate[335], (notwithstanding the reigns of Ve and Vilje, that are nowhere mentioned by outside sources), but that Kujula's conquering of the wider territory to become known as the 'Empire' of the Kushans was not until the latter half of the 1st Century BC or the 1st Century AD.

---

[331] Hill claims this was in Badakhshan (north-eastern Afghanistan)
[332] Hill gives a date of 55 AD for this
[333] Book of Later Han, Section 13
[334] Grousset, p.32
[335] As they were arguably the next most powerful 'Yuezhi' group after the Pushang/Odin-led 'Æsir', who do not appear to correspond particularly with any of the other five 'Allied Princes' of Yuezhi-controlled Bactria. The Iranian sources suggest rather that the 'Æsir' were a supervening group in overall military command of the Yuezhi as a whole, as indeed they had been in Tocharia. As we shall see, it is possible that the Kushans, subordinate to the Yuezhi, are not rightly called 'Yuezhi' at all, but rather were one amongst a group of Tocharian nations who had migrated west with the Yuezhi, under their protection.

Kujula may be one and the same as the 'Heraios' who appears on coins and reigned 1-30 AD, or his son. This is hard to say as the Greek nomenclature of the Kushan coinage is quite different from that of the Chinese sources. They go on:

"His son, Yan Gaozhen (Vima Taktu), became king in his place. He returned and defeated Tianzhu (Northwestern India) and installed a General to supervise and lead it. The Yuezhi then became extremely rich. All the kingdoms call [their king] the Guishuang (Kushan) king, but the Han call them by their original name, Da Yuezhi"[336]

This trade Empire would reach its largest territorial extent under the reign of 'Kanishka the Great' ruling from roughly 127-150 AD. By the 2nd Century AD the Kushan Empire stretched from eastern India to the Aral Sea where they would have traded with their Yuezhi-related cousins the Alans.

The Kushans' culture was characterised by an undiscriminating, cleptomaniacal use of many aspects of the cultures around them that would eventually result in their slow dilution and dispersion into those cultures as they dived fully into the coin-minting, self-aggrandising, Greco-Iranian, Babylonian pursuit of empire-building. While their main identity was distinctly Tocharian, nevertheless they minted coins in the Greek style using the Greek alphabet and adopted Bactrian as their administrative trade language (though Kanishka also added Kushan language inscriptions to his coins). Spiritually they would come to be associated variously with Shaivism, Iranian Zoroastrianism and Indian Buddhism, amongst other beliefs. Their capitals were at Bagram in today's Afghanistan and Charsadda in today's Pakistan.

---

[336] Book of Later Han, Section 13. As discussed, this may be a mistake on the part of the Chinese, as the real 'Yuezhi' may all have departed for Scandinavia by this time, leaving the Kushans, a different but previously subordinate group, in the driving seat in Transoxiana.

Fig.107: Gold coin from the reign of Kushan Emperor Kanishka the Great, 127-150 AD.[337]

Eventually, the 'Vanir' got the better of the Kushans, with the new Iranian Sasanian Empire invading and defeating the Kushan Empire around 230 AD and pushing them out of Bactria and Pakistan, meanwhile from the other side the Gupta empire pushed them out of eastern India.

Soon after this (350-375), the northern part of the previous territory of the Kushan Empire was indeed comprehensively overrun by the expected 'great invasion', a massive wave of huns from the north-east (in this case the 'Xionites'/'Kidarites'). Kushan rulers continued on in the Punjab of India based at Taxila until completely conquered by the Kidarites by 410 AD. The area roughly congruent with the Kushans' whole empire was soon after taken over by the Hephthalite empire. The Hephthalites (aka 'white huns'[338]) were probably led by descendants of the Israelite

---

[337] Image used by kind permission of Classical Numismatic Group, LLC (https://cngcoins.com).

[338] Nb. this designation does not refer to skin colour but rather to a cardinal point on maps, where 'Black Huns' were the northern branch, 'Blue Huns' the eastern, 'Red Huns' the southern (probably the Kidarites/ Alchon/ Chyon) and 'White Huns' the western. However Procopious wrote that they were white-skinned and were not nomads. Also "they are ruled by one king, and since they possess a lawful constitution, they observe right and justice in their dealings both with one another and with their neighbours" (Procopius, Vol.1, p.15)

tribe of Naphtali, who had previously settled in the region, particularly in the ancient Bactrian capital of Bukhara, as traders[339]. Their rule displaced the Iranians and other huns from 'Tokharistan' (roughly the territory of the previous 'Turans' between the Oxus and Jaxartes Rivers, particularly Bactria, Sogdiana and Ferghana) and ruled the region with a cultural and ethnic fusion of Shemite/Israelite, Bactrian/Iranian, Yuezhi and Hunnic traditions. They carried on wars with the Iranians (now under the Sasanian dynasty) much like the Turans had before them.

The Hephthalites were in turn displaced in Bactria/Sogdiana and the Tarim by an essentially Mongol invasion from the north from the mid 6th Century AD[340]. This Hunnic/Mongol residency in 'Tokharistan' was the origin of the name 'Turk' and 'Turkish', as the invading Mongols took on aspects of the culture of the previous inhabitants whose ancient borders they now occupied, especially the original and now semi-legendary 'Turans' or 'original Turks/Tocharians' of Tokharistan. Particularly after the latters' exploits were immortalised in Persian epic histories such as the 'Khwaday Namag' and 'Shahnameh', the Mongols were happy to be identified and even confused with the 'Turks' by outside populations, calling themselves by that name from then on.

---

[339] They may be related to the Silk Road traders living in Bactria who were referred to as 'skilled in commerce' in Shang Qian's report of 120 BC (Shiji, 3. p.235). Their presence in this area fits the general Semitic presence and heritage in Bukhara including Bactria's probable original founding by the Shemite 'Gather', as well as the Apocrypha's (p.65) and Josephus' (Vol.6, p.147) descriptions of the 'lost tribes' as dwelling in 'Arzareth', beyond the Euphrates, 'a year and a half's journey'. With 'Eretz' meaning in Hebrew 'the land of', Bactria had been indeed by that time the 'land of' the 'Arz' AKA 'Æsir'.
[340] This would become known as the 'Western Turkic Khaganate'.

The total destruction of the Kushan state by 400 AD and its subsequent comprehensive fall first to the Huns, then to the Mongols/Turks and then to the Arabs strongly vindicates the 'exodus party' in foreseeing the region's fundamental indefensibility and the wisdom of a wholesale migration to Europe. The society and culture of those who stayed behind was destroyed so thoroughly that for millennia, indeed even until today, it was barely remembered that they were ever there.

Scandinavian Family Portrait

As mentioned above, identifying and dating the early Kushans is extremely difficult, that is all the more frustrating as these individuals may have the most direct and significant bearing on Scandinavian history. In particular, the question arises of whether the personages portrayed on Yuezhi/Kushan coins, statues and tapestries lived before or after the Scandinavian exodus to Northern Europe. In one sense it does not make much of a difference in that either way as Tocharians they were to some extent 'proto-Scandinavians', but it bears on the question of whether or not they were the direct ancestors of today's Scandinavians.

Fig.108: Kushan King 'Heraios', possibly 'Kujula Kadphises', on a coin from some time between 100 BC and 150 AD[341]. Note the 'diadem' tied around the head, a symbol of rank or perhaps even royalty

An amazing feast of visual insights into the world of the Yuezhi, in the form of a stash of carpets and wall hangings portraying Yuezhi kings and warriors, was discovered in the 1920s in Xiong Nu burial mounds at Noin-Ula in Outer Mongolia, apparently

---

[341] Image used by kind permission of Classical Numismatic Group, LLC (https://cngcoins.com).

taken there as spoils of war from Samarkand, the Yuezhi capital, by its later occupiers the Huns.

Fig.109: Image of a Yuezhi/Kushan King from a carpet found in Noin-Ula in Mongolia, probably looted from Samarkand[342]

Note how both of the above pictures, from the coin and the carpet, feature apparently the same perennially moustachioed individual. Was this Kajula Kadphises, 'Heraios', or both? Or, did all Yuezhi/Kushan nobles look exactly alike?

---

[342] From a carpet found at the Xiong Nu centre at Noin Ula in Mongolia. Public Domain image from Wikimedia (https://en.wikipedia.org/wiki/File:Noin-Ula_nobleman_and_priest_over_fire_altar.jpg)

Fig.110: a horse warrior from the same Noin-Ula carpet. Remarkably he is wearing the characteristic 'Cataphract' full-body armour later made famous by the Alans/Sarmatians[343]

---

[343] Public domain image from Wikimedia (https://en.wikipedia.org/wiki/File:Noin -Ula_horseman.jpg)

Fig.111: Detail from another Noin-Ula carpet: a highly lifelike warrior sporting the regulation Yuezhi moustache[344]

These carpets, apparently prized by the Xiong Nu, provide a unique window into the world of the Yuezhi, and establish beyond any doubt that modern 'Westerners' lived and thrived in the far east in remote antiquity in great numbers, in civilizations all but lost to history until these remains were unearthed (and even today

---

[344] Erdene–Ochir, p.254-55 & Yatsenko, p.45

they are glossed over, perhaps out of academic embarrassment), and in fact, it was their ancient homeland, whence they first arrived in 'the west', only around two thousand years ago.

A still more extraordinary discovery came to light between 1959 and 1963, when Russian archaeologist Galina Pugachenkova excavated what had been a Yuezhi country Palace or Hall at Khalchayan near the town of Denov, around 130 miles south-east of Samarkand.

The Palace had contained 3-dimensional friezes along 3 of its 4 interior walls, with the fourth painted. The paint had largely worn away, but the remains of the statue-friezes could be reconstructed into what had been a unique group family or court portrait.

It has been argued that these figures must be derived stylistically from the previous Greco-Bactrian occupants of Bactria, but in fact both in construction and in style they owe as much or more to Chinese sculpture, like the Qin Emperor's 'terracotta army'[345].

Fig.112: Reconstruction of the Khalchayan frieze[346]

---

[345] Qingbo, p.27-28
[346] Pugachenkova, p.137. © Pugachenkova Estate

421

While noting, with some surprise, that the subjects belong to the 'Caucasian' ethnic group, Pugachenkova pays tribute to the 'lost' or 'forgotten' nature of this culture:

"But to the vast artistic heritage of ancient art, we do not find exact correspondences to all these persons; they are far from the ideals of Greco-Roman sculpture and from the magnificent beauty of Indian statues...Khalchayan sculpture introduces new material into the history of Central Asian ancient culture"[347]

Fig.113: The cast of 1st Century BC Samarkand. But who were they?[348]

---

[347] Pugachenkova, p.31
[348] As reconstructed from the ruins by Pugachenkova, Ibid, p.51, 61, 71

The famous statue reliefs and wall paintings found at Denov in Uzbekistan at the 'Khalchayan' site provide mind-blowing evidence of the ancient proto-Scandinavians. The reception hall there was apparently decorated to commemorate and celebrate the initial Yuezhi conquest of Tocharistan (Transoxiana), in particular over the Saka who had preceded them there[349]. Therefore it is almost certainly a glimpse into the culture of the Æsir and the ancient Swedes.

Further light may be brought to bear on the the identity of the portraitees by a passage of Ferdowsi's Shahnameh concerning the character of 'Siyavash'. One of the epic poem's main characters, Siyavash is an ill-fated hero who is persecuted for his integrity in his homeland of Iran and so flees to the court of Afrasiab in Turan, where he marries Afrasiab's daughter. Initially he is given territory in 'the land that stretches toward China' and told to build himself a dwelling there. But this site is seen as inauspicious, and soon Afrasiab, who has developed a fondness for Siyavash, recalls him: "Since you left I am never happy. I have identified a place here in Turan where you could live". Ferdowsi continues:

"He came to the chosen place, named Khorram-e Bahar (The Joy of Spring), and there constructed a city of palaces, porticoes, public squares, orchards and gardens; the place was like a paradise, and in the desert wastes he made roses, hyacinths, and tulips grow. On his palace walls he had frescoes painted showing royal battles and banquets. One was of King Kavus with his crown, torque, and royal mace; Rostam stood next to his throne, and with him were Zal, Gudarz, and the rest of Kavus's entourage. On the opposite wall Afrasyab was painted, together with his warriors and the chieftains Piran and Garsivaz. At each corner of the city was a dome that reached to the clouds; and there, their heads among the stars, musicians would sit and sing. The city was called Seyavashgerd, and the world rejoiced in its existence."[350]

---

[349] This at least is the theory of Abdullaev (Abdullaev)
[350] Shahnameh, p.256-7. Note the Scandinavian language name of the settlement, 'Seyavashgerd": the 'guarded area' or 'garden' of Seyavash. Unexplainable in an Iranian poem, unless the language of the characters described was Scandinavian.

Is this then a contemporary depiction of Odin on his throne? Well, although that is not entirely impossible, probably not. Yet there are some remarkable parallels between the Shahnameh text and the Khalchayan remains:

- Khalchayan is 'in the land of Turan', very close to 'Kangdiz', the capital of the Yuezhi, that was probably at Samarkand, but has also been theorised to have been at Dalmerzin Tepe, only a few miles from Denov and Khalchayan[351]. And the settlement of Khalchayan is in every other way an exact fit for Seyavashgerd; in particular both featured orchards[352].
- Like the description of the Parthian/Iranian/Vanir King Kavus in the Shahnameh, the King on the Khalchayan frieze has royal headgear (a 'crown' of sorts) and a mace.
- Were we instead to associate the King with Odin, this would fit with Pugachenkova's identification of the woman next to the seated Queen as the royal daughter, and the young man to her left as her husband, the son-in-law of the King (i.e. in the story, Siyavash)

---

[351] By Pugachenkova - at least as the capital of the later Kushans. The question of the location of the main citadel or stronghold of Afrasiab, known as 'Kang' or 'Kangdiz' (Shahnameh, p.247) is not entirey settled. It was almost certainly the northern and most ancient part of the modern city of Samarkand (originally the capital of the Sogdians), a section even today called 'Afrasiab', where stands the 'Castle of Afrasiab', an impressive hill fortress with high walls. Yet there are other testimonies that somewhat contradict this. For example the Chinese 'Shiji' states that the newly arrived Yuezhi 'set up the court of their King on the northern bank of the [Oxus] river' (3, p.234), i.e. considerably further South than Samarkand, suggesting today's city of Termiz, directly south of Denov/Dalmerzin, but possibly this was only the initial settlement. The Shahnameh also describes an occasion when Afrasiab "evacuated Bokhara, Soghd, Samarkand, Chaj, and Sepanjab, moving toward Gang" (p.237), indicating that 'Gang' ('Kangdiz') was north of Samarkand. However these aside the identification of the 'Castle of Afrasiab' as Odin's 'Kangdiz' is fairly solid.

[352] Pugachenkova writes: "The salient features of Khalchayan's layout are as follows: a citadel encompassed by strong walls and a moat; regularly planned town blocks; large architectural ensembles in combination with estates surrounded by orchards and fields, stretching along a network of *aryks* (irrigation canals). The close links between towns and farmlands, demonstrated by the organic inclusion of farming estates into town limits, is in general a characteristic of town planning in Central Asia in antiquity." (p.127)

Unfortunately, the preponderance of evidence does not necessarily support the theory that one of the main characters in the Khalchayan frieze is the legendary Odin.

Firstly, 'Siyavash' was a real person, but, bizarrely, one who lived 500 years later, in the 5th-6th Centuries AD. The inclusion of him in the Shahnameh as part of 1st Century BC history is a later fictionalisation by the 6th Century author of the 'Khwaday Namag' (on which the Shahnameh is based), intended to tie the reign of the 'victorious' 'Kay Khosrow' (mainly Khosrow I, the author's patron, who reigned 531-579 AD), to that of the Iranians' legendary nemesis 'Afrasiab', thus symbolically gaining final victory over him, despite having to vault over five centuries of history to do it. (This motivation apparently explains much of the Bundahisn and Shahnameh's convoluted historical contortions)[353]

Nevertheless, the access that the 6th Century AD authors of the 'legendary' version had to otherwise lost information regarding Yuezhi-era art provides the tantalising possibility that some accurate memetic material was transmitted by them.

---

[353] In the 'historical' version, Sasanian King Kavad I (probably a leading inspiration for the Shahnameh's hapless 'Kay Kavus') was overthrown and imprisoned by the nobility in 496 AD. Aided by his general Siyavash, he escaped to the Hephthalites (the successors of the Yuezhi in the Transoxiana area north of the Oxus river), where he married the 'barbarian' King's daughter, much like Siyavash in the Shahnameh. Kavad was then able to regain his throne in Iran (498 AD). Twenty years later in 520 AD, in connection with the negotiations concerning Kavad's son, Khosrow (who would become Khosrow I), Siyavash was unfairly accused of acting in bad faith and executed. Unlike the romanticized 'Kay Khosrow', Khosrow I's mother was not in fact the daughter of this 'barbarian' King, but of an Iranian noblewoman. Also in contrast with the Sasanian history the author of the Khwaday Namag and/or Ferdowsi, makes Siyavash, not Kawad, the father of 'Kay Khosrow', perhaps in recognition that Siyavash, not Kavad, was the more noble in their dealings with one another, and therefore more worthy to be the father of Kay Khosrow, the main triumphant Iranian champion of the Shahnameh. Interestingly, the historical Sasanians whose experiences informed the writing of the Shahnameh, in particular Kavad and probably Siyavash, had the opportunity of seeing the Hephthalite Kingdom up close during Kavad's exile, and may well have been shown the Khalchayan frieze remains, and informed who it portrayed. Pugachenkova states that over the centuries the role of the palace changed from being that of a reception hall to being a more sacred museum or 'house of deified ancestors' (p.102)

Secondly, both Pugachenkova (1971) and Abdullaez (2007), in attempting the difficult task of interpreting the Khalchayan friezes' sporadic, incomplete and complex internal textual evidence, concluded that the court scene was probably a work of the very early Kushan ascendancy (that would be perhaps 20-50 years after the departure of the Æsir for Sweden).

Largely these interpretations rest on the categorisation of ethno-cultural distinctions between the figures portrayed. Pugachenkova found three different ethnic types, while Abdullaez proposed four, with distinctions based more often than not on different styles of facial hair!

Firstly, there are the Kushans. These are typified by the 'classic' appearance, familiar from coins struck by (probably) their later descendants Heraios and Kajula Kadphises: moustache, no beard, diadem tied around the head, 'pyjama'-style Kaftan clothing and evidence of skull deformation indicating contact or cultural cross-pollination with the huns.

Secondly, there is one figure, standing at the right hand of the King, who can almost certainly be identified (from extant coins) as a monarch of the subjugated Iranians, owing to his long, wavy hair, wider diadem, and beard.

Thirdly, there are other subjugated people, without skull deformation, and with shorter hair and beards, whom Pugachenkova identifies as the local Bactrians, but who may be the Massagetae/Saka. They are represented by the noble couple at the far left of the court frieze, who are also on thrones, but are less prominent than the main King and Queen.

Finally, Abdullaev proposes that a fourth type, the 'enemies' of the Kushans, are depicted with faces grotesquely contorted in semi-caricature, and distinguished by their having side whiskers and wearing cataphract armour. These, he argues, are the Massagetae/Saka, and this is in concert with a theory that the 'horse' frieze was originally a battle scene between two different nations, the Kushans (in the PJs) and the Massagetae/Saka (in the cataphract armour), representing the Yuezhi's initial displacement of the Saka from the Oxus region, pushing them southward into Afghanistan ('Sakastan'/'Sistan').

The obvious great depth of unknown meaning in the curious and extensive details of the artwork make this theory something of a stretch, that the extant evidence cannot fully support[354]. In truth we can only make two very clear identifications:

---

[354] It appears to be contradicted by, for example, a) figures of the 'Kushan' type being depicted wearing cataphract armour on the Noin-Ula carpets, who are themselves in combat with side-whisker-sporting warriors (who are usually identified as Sogdians or Scythians); b) the 'King' in the Khalchayan frieze quite possibly having side whiskers himself; c) the standing cataphracted warrior from Khalchayan being of the third, not the fourth, type.

1) Arguably the most notable figure of the piece, the 'young Kushan prince' (standing at the right hand of the seated figure on the second panel above), is quite possibly Heraios/ Kujula Kadphises himself, the ubiquitously moustachioed and ever-present founder and image of the Kushan empire; or another scion of the early Kushans from this same line. (Pugachankova makes the genealogy Heraios->Kadphises I->Kadphises II[355], but this period of history is very obscure). His strong resemblance to a Buddhist 'Boddhisatva' statue found in Gandhara, India, the region that Heraios/Kujula conquered, makes this identification even stronger. If the Khalchayan frieze celebrates a Kushan victory over an enemy, it is perhaps more likely this one, Kujula's later victory over the other four 'Yuezhi' 'allied princes', rather than the earlier one of the Yuezhi over either the Iranians, Bactrians or Saka[356].

---

[355] Pugachenkova, p.46

[356] i.e. as previously quoted: "more than a hundred years later, the *xihou* ('Allied Prince') of Guishuang...attacked and exterminated the four other *xihou* ('Allied Princes'). He set himself up as king of a kingdom called Guishuang" (Book of Later Han, Section 13). If 'Saka' are portrayed they may however have been one of the five previously allied 'Yuezhi' nations; certainly they held Afghanistan before the Kushans.

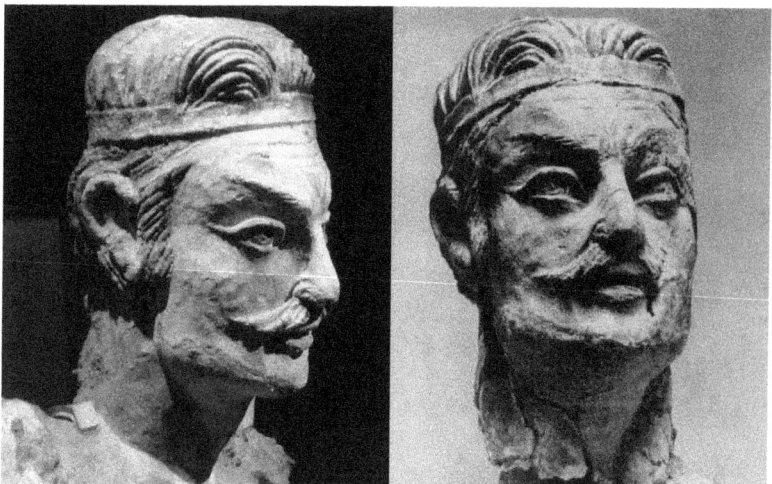

Fig 114: the 'young prince' from Khalchayan. It is proposed that this is Heraios AKA Kujula Kadphises, the brutal conqueror of the other four Allied Tocharian powers after the departure of the Æsir, and founder of the Kushan Empire[357]

Fig 115: the resemblance between the Khalchayan prince and the 'Gandhara Boddhisatva' in India is remarkable. However it could be that many Kushan princes looked alike.[358]

---

[357] Figs 114 & 115 at left: Wikimedia images by ALFGRN, used under CC BY SA 2.0 (https:// creativecommons.org/licenses/by-sa/2.0/deed.en). Fig 114 at right, Pugachenkova, plate 64. © Pugachenkova Estate

[358] Fig 115, right: Wikimedia image by Sailko, used under CC BY SA 3.0 Unported (https://creativecommons.org/licenses/by-sa/3.0/deed.en)

Fig 116 (above). The head shows evidence of infant skull deformation, a Hunnic affectation, indicating the great effect the culture of the surrounding Huns had on the Yuezhi/Kushans.

Fig 117 (right): The prince holds a suit of cataphract armour at his feet. This is claimed by Abdullaev to be a sign of his conquest over the cataphract-wearing Saka. However the cataphract armour seems to have been in more common use than by this one group only. Artwork shows that it was also used by Yuezhi and/or Kushans, and by the Alans, who migrated west around this time, possibly influenced by this Kushan victory.

(Pugachenkova, plates 63 and 61. © Pugachenkova Estate)

Fig 118: The Iranian King standing at the right hand of the enthroned King. The dependant state of this figure (and his rather pained expression) confirm that the 'Vanir' were still very much under the thumb of the Æsir's Kushan co-Tocharians, even after the Æsir had left the region[359].

Fig 119: Because 1st Century BC Iranian Kings seem to have been all but indistinguishable in appearance, it is hard to identify exactly who this monarch was. Pugachenkova favoured Phraates IV, but it could just as easily be a likeness of any of the Kings that followed the reign of Sinatruces (i.e. Frey). Sinatruces' son, Phraates III (reigning 69-57 BC), is pictured at left. After him came Mithridates IV, Orodes II, then Phraates IV (38-2 BC), pictured at right[360].

---

[359] Pugachenkova, plate 59. © Pugachenkova Estate
[360] Images used by kind permission of Classical Numismatic Group, LLC (https://cngcoins.com)

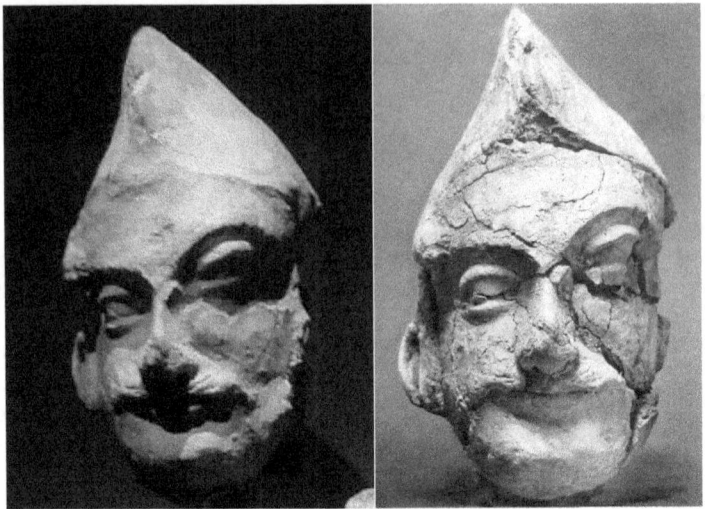

Fig. 120: The enthroned King. Who was he?[361]

The figure of the enthroned King at the centre of the frieze is somewhat mysterious. It is almost impossible that he is is an Iranian King, as suggested by the Shahnameh's account of King 'Kavus' being represented like this with 'crown' and mace, because of his entirely 'aniranian' appearance. The pointed cap suggests a possibly Scandinavian origin, while the side whiskers also seem somewhat to differentiate him from the surrounding Kushans. Is this Odin? The context of the rest of the Khalchayn frieze however points to the work of the Kushans, in which case this King may be either an older version of the 'Heraios'/'Kajula Kadphises' figure, to whom he bears some resemblance, or perhaps his predecessor.

This predecessor could conceivably be one of the Kushans' previous Æsir overlords, i.e. Afrasiab or one of his brothers Ve or Vilje. But if this is a celebration of Kushan victory, would the Kushans really be honouring a different nation's leaders? Whose recent absence alone has enabled the Kushans to take over in Transoxiana, possibly by overthrowing the heirs of Ve and Vilje? Remembering that in Tocharia, as in Transoxiana, while the Kushans were under the protection of the Yuezhi and dependent on them, the 'Ārśi' and 'Kuśiññe' were not only separate nations, they had entirely separate

---

[361] Left: Wikimedia image by ALFGRN used under CC BY SA 2.0 Generic (https://creativecommons.org/licenses/by-sa/2.0/deed.en). Right: Pugachenkova, plate 55. © Pugachenkova Estate

languages, that may not even have been mutually comprehensible³⁶². Judging from the distinctly 'Kushan' characteristics of for example the 'Kushan prince' figure, it may be that the Chinese were wrong to continue calling the Kushans 'Yuezhi', even after the Æsir had left for Sweden. In other words, they may have been substantially different nations.³⁶³

Abdullaez's theory³⁶⁴ is that the Kushans were celebrating a victory over the Saka. Maybe, but if so why is the apparently Kushan King wearing a pointed hat, the traditional headgear of the Scandinavian Saka? The Khalchayan frieze poses more questions than answers, and we may be certain that we do not have the full story yet.

Fig.121: Another intriguing image from Noin-Ula, usually interpreted as Yuezhis (left) in combat with bearded Sogdians (i.e. Scottish Scythians, right). But the blonde, cataphracted Yuezhi (left), being attacked by the ginger-haired Sogdian, is different from the dark-haired, moustachioed Kushan (right), shown as more victorious³⁶⁵

---

³⁶² Mallory & Mair, p.275
³⁶³ As per Mallory & Mair, Tocharian A, 'Ārśi' or 'Agnean', was the older language, from the eastern Tarim, centred at Karashar but with roots even further east in Gansu, the primaeval homeland of the Yuezhi, whereas 'Kuśiññe', a later, more western variant, was centred at 'Kucha', home of the Kushans - an ethnonym Henning believed may have derived from *'Guti'* (Ibid, p.276-284); i.e. the Kushans may be descended from the Gutians, arriving from the west later than the Æsir.
³⁶⁴ Abdullaev, p.94
³⁶⁵ Public domain image from Wikimedia Commons

Figs. 122 and 123: A decidedly English-looking Saka, in full cataphract armour, from the more damaged southern wall of the Palace. Pugachenkova expresses some surprise at the high-tech, fully-formed and sophisticated military technology on display, that owes more to ancient Chinese traditions of warfare than anything from the west[366].

Pugachenkova states: "the statues obviously depict some kind of local, unaffected by influence, purely Bactrian armored weapons, maybe existing precisely in the northern Bactrian regions. The type of armored weapons depicted in the sculpture of Khalchayan would remain in the Central Asian environment throughout the era of the Great Kushan...which, judging by the Khalchayan sculpture, had a fully developed character in the 1st century BC, and probably formed much earlier. The sculpture of Khalchayan reveals an almost unknown page in the history of Bactrian-Yuezhi military affairs."[366]

---

[366] Left: Public Domain image from Wikimedia Commons, used under CC0 1.0. Right: Pugachenkova, p.73. © Pugachenkova Estate. Text: Pugachenkova, p.72

It is suggested that the 'sudden' appearance of this martial gear demonstrates that it was not 'Bactrian', but rather had recently arrived fully-formed with the Yuezhi from beyond the mountain wall, battle-tested for centuries against the Xiong Nu and Chinese, and contributing significantly to the shock defeat of the Parthian Empire at the hands of the newcomers.

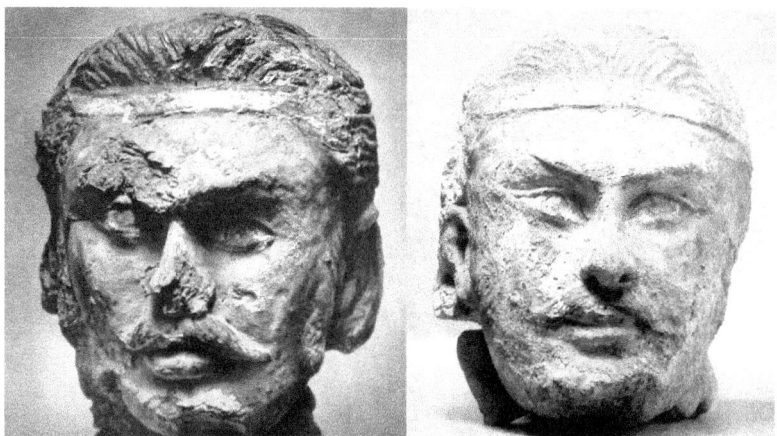

Fig 124: Two more heads, of the horse-riders from the third panel at Khalchayan[367]. Which figures they belonged to is not exactly certain (an earthquake destroyed the complex in the 3rd Century AD). Abdullaev's theory posits that the left-hand, 'ugly', 'grotesque' and side-whiskered head was the central cataphracted rider, and therefore a Saka and an enemy, while the focused visage of the right-hand head was that of a victorious Kushan. Yet they look remarkably similar. And why would Kushan artists place their enemy's soldier at the front and centre of the frieze?

If, as Abdullaev theorises[368], the 'horse panel' depicts the initial battle wherein the arriving Yuezhi displaced the Saka (C.132 BC), rather than the later Kushan rise to ascendancy perhaps 100 years later (C.50-20 BC), then these could yet be depictions of Æsir, i.e. non-Kushan 'Yuezhi', before their emigration.

---

[367] Pugachenkova, plates 78 and 79, © Pugachenkova Estate
[368] Abdullaev, p.89, 91

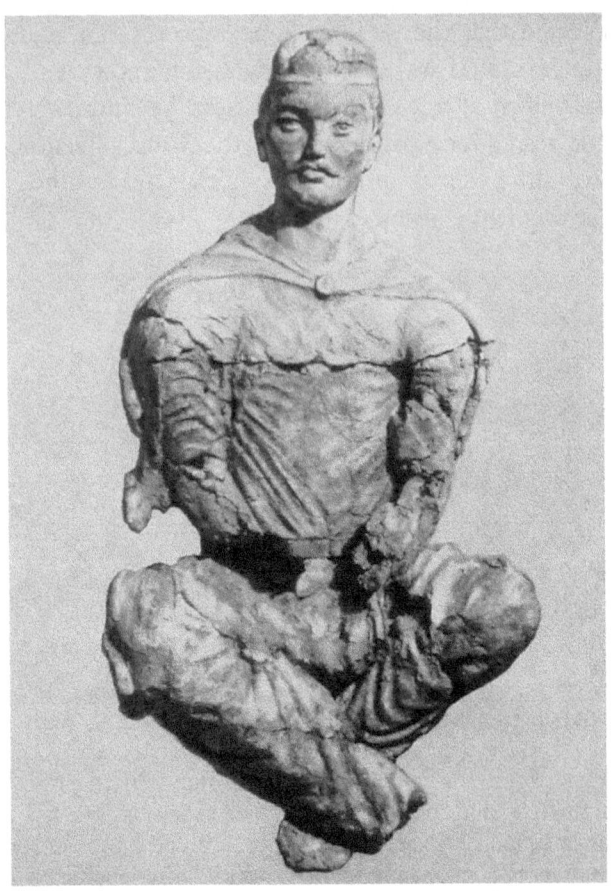

Fig 125: One of the more mysterious figures from the Khalchayan frieze, the seated noble from the second panel. A glum 'Siyavash', perhaps?[369]

By any measure the Khalchayan find is a remarkable discovery that sheds invaluable light on the Yuezhi/Kushan world. At furthest distance, it is no more than fifty years from the date when Odin left this very throne in the hands of those depicted; at closest he himself is portrayed, as one of the frieze's central figures.

---

[369] Pugachenkova, plate 68. © Pugachenkova Estate. It is tempting to see in the Khalchayan 'Court' panel the Parthian 'Kavus' and his court, and in the second panel Afrasiab with his 'warriors', as this seems to fit quite well. However, the 'King' does not look very Iranian at all, while this seated figure in the second panel is but a young man, this could surely not be Odin. If the 'Kushan Prince' was Odin, why is he not seated in the position of authority? Also, unlike in the Shahnameh, the panels do not face each other, and are statues rather than paintings.

So it seems like so many of his pursuers we may have just missed out on getting a look at the historical Odin. But let us summarise some of the information we have about this globally significant historical figure, now that he has conclusively been identified as Iranian history's 'Afrasiab'.

Snorri Sturluson makes Odin, whose real name he says was 'Voden'[370], an 18th generation descendent of Thor[371], who he says was a grandson of 'Menon' of the Trojan War era who was born in Troy. As discussed earlier, this is an unlikely scenario as it would seem to require Thor having been born in a city named after himself[372]. Meanwhile in the Bundahisn, Afrasiab is only a 6th generation descendant of Tur[373].

The names mentioned in the two genealogies do not match, with Odin's father called 'Friallaf' (or 'Frithowulf') by Snorri and 'Pushang' in the Iranian version. Neither do the names of Odin's sons, although some of his later offspring bear some resemblance in the two accounts, such as the Prose Edda's 'Svebdeg' and 'Freóvin' and the Bundahisn's 'Šēdag' and 'Frašāward'. There is

---

[370] Prose Edda, p.7. It has been suggested by Heyerdahl and others that 'Odin' may have been a title rather than a name (it could be interpreted as meaning 'Oathen', i.e. 'Oath'd' or 'sworn'), that Heyerdahl believed he found in Herodotus' 'Budini' and Alexander's 'Odena' peoples (p.147). Meanwhile the Iranian 'Afrasiab' has been proposed to mean 'beyond the black water' (Yarshater, p.576), that could also be a title, possibly related to the river flowing to the north of Samarkand (or even the 'Black River' that flows west to east through the Tarim Basin).
[371] The genealogy is given as Thor-Loridi-Einridi-Vingethor-Vingener-Moda-Magi-Seskef-Bedvig-Athra-Itermann-Heremod-Skjaldun-Bjaf-Jat-Gudolfr-Finn-Friallef-Odin. (Prose Edda, p.7). Somewhat more poetically, in the 'Gylfaginning', Odin is said to be a three-generation (Búri-Borr-Odin) son of the same 'primordial cow' that nurtured Ymir (Noah), shortly after the ice age (Ibid, p.18-19)
[372] Prose Edda, p.6. 'Teucer 2' in our earlier discussion of Thor. As previously argued, and backed up by the Iranian evidence, it is much more likely that the 'original' Thor (there were and still are many later figures named after him) was a more ancient figure: the 'Tiras' of the Tanakh, 'Tur' of the Bundahisn (brother of Magog), 'Teucer 1', 'Thrax', 'Ares', 'Typhon' of the Greeks, the original of 'Tukriš' known to the Sumerians, etc., after whom Thrace and Troy were originally named.
[373] The genealogy is given as Tur-Durosasp-Spenasp-Turag-Zadshun-Pushang-Afrasiab (Bundahisn, p.186). Nb. 'Tur' in the Shahnameh is 'Tuz' in the Bundahisn, the Shahnameh versions are used here for consistency.

however corroboration that Odin had two brothers, 'Ve' and 'Vilje/Vili' in the Scandinavian accounts[374], and 'Aghiras' and 'Garsewaz' in the Iranian[375]. The Bundahisn also tells us that Pushang had a brother, Wesag, whose son Piran was the Khotan-dwelling main advisor to Afrasiab in the Shahnameh.

It is certain that Odin was a major player in the Yuezhi invasion of Bactria in 132 BC, but whether he was yet 'King' of the Yuezhi[376] at that time, is still in doubt. This is because of the Shahnameh, in which 'Pushang', Afrasiab's father, plays a large role as King of the Turans during the initial invasion of Transoxiana, with Afrasiab as military general and prince only[377]. Meanwhile the Chinese 'Shiji' makes it very clear that the Yuezhi King whose Bactrian court Zhang Qian arrived at in 128 BC was the son of the Yuezhi King whom the Xiong Nu 'Chanyu' (warlord) had previously killed. If we could presume that this happened during the Xiong Nu attack on the Yuezhi in the Ili River valley, that occurred immediately prior to the Yuezhi's migration to Transoxiana, we could speculate that Odin, not his father, was King of the Yuezhi already by 132 BC. However, the Shiji only says the previous Yuezhi King was killed 'some time after' 174 BC[378]. This is a span of 42 years, so it is perhaps more

---

[374] Heimskringla, vol.1, p.271-2. As per Laing and Anderson, these names mean 'Sancity' and 'Will' (Ibid); Prose Edda, p.19

[375] Bundahisn, p.186; Shahnameh, p.113; 232. The Shahnameh relates that Afrasiab killed Aghiras for some infraction during the Iranian war (Ibid, p.127)

[376] A note about the word 'King'. It seems to have been transferred to Europe from the far east exclusively by the Æsir, being entirely different from Celtic (variously) 'Ri,', Flath', Matern' and 'Errega', Roman 'Rex', Frankish 'Dux' (Duke), Iranian 'Shah', Sanskrit 'Raja' and Slavic 'Kral'. It apparently meant 'warlord' or 'holder of militiary supremacy' and was a common term among the nations of western China, including the Scandinavians (proto-'King': 'Kong', 'Konung', etc), the Huns ('Chanyu' that became 'Khan'), the Wusun (Kun-mo/Kwan-mo (Book of Han, vol.10, p.68)) and (claims La Couperie, p.278) the Chinese ('Kam-mu', that became 'Kwam-mu' then 'Wang-Mu' and finally 'Wang' (cf. the Hamitic Hittites' 'Wanaka')) and also stood somewhat for the ethnic designation of Yuezhi/Wusun in general, in particular the later 'lesser' Yuezhi who continued on in south-west China, the 'Kunmings' (La Couperie, p.250, Book of Han, vol.10, p.68).

[377] Shahnameh, p.113

[378] Shiji, 3, p.231, 234. After Modu first defeated the Yuezhi (176 BC), and after Modu had been succeeded by his son (174 BC).

likely that 'Pushang'/'Friallef' had taken over as King earlier than 132 BC, and that therefore the Chinese envoy had spoken with Pushang, not Odin, in 128 BC, and that consequently Odin was the grandson, not the son, of the slain King[379]. This would make more sense considering Odin's potentially very long subsequent career.

The question of exactly how long is a difficult one. Although the Heimskringla records him passing away peacefully in Sweden, ceding the Swedish throne to Njord[380] (that would perhaps have been around 100-90 BC), circumstantial evidence suggests this is somewhat early, as there are lingering hints of his influence continuing well into the 1st Century BC.

These include the possibility of a second trip back to 'Asaland' to bring out the main body of the Æsir people, after the land arrangement with Gylfe had been negotiated[381]; the aiding of his protégé Frey's restoration to the throne of Iran in 75 BC (no small task, requiring as it did a permanent altering of the Iranian royal line of succession); the subsequent settling of the peace treaty with the now-installed Frey in Transoxiana (that the Shahnameh says was made with Afrasiab personally[382]); possible continued post-Mithridates II (the Shahnameh's 'Kay Kabod', who reigned 124-

---

[379] This agrees with hints in the Shahnameh that Pushang is angry about his father, 'Zadsham', alluding to an association of him with military defeat: "When the Turkish commander Pashang heard of this, he decided to invade Iran. He talked constantly of his father, Zadsham, and sighed bitterly over what had happened to Tur, remembering all that Manuchehr and his army had done." Afrasiyab also mentions Zadsham: "If Zadsham had but drawn his warlike sword, the world would not be ruled by Persia's lord: If he'd been eager for a warrior's fame, Turan would not be overwhelmed with shame" (p.112-3). Perhaps the fate of 'Zadsham' at the hands of the Huns explains Pushang's war-lust in the Shahnameh, that says his "heart was filled with hatred and his head with thoughts of war" (p.129)
[380] Heimskringla, vol.1, p.281.
[381] The name 'Sweden' comes from the national/ethnic designation 'Svear', that Snorri claims came from another name of Odin's: 'Svidurr' (Prose Edda, p.234), but it may also have come from the Norse 'Svær' meaning 'massive' or 'main', as in the main contingent of the Æsir emigrants.
[382] Shahnameh, p.128-9

87 BC) harassment of the Iranians[383]; the proposed 'sighting' of Odin as 'Olcaba' in Caucasia in 71 BC[384]; and the late Kushan takeover of Transoxiana, that, were the Æsir gone by 100 BC, could be expected to have occurred earlier[385].

---

[383] Described in the Shahnameh, p.179, 190. The Bundahisn, however, though oblique, suggests there was no further war with Afrasiab after the reign of Mithridates II: "When Manuščihr [Mithridates I] was killed [132 BC], Frāsyāb came again and terribly destroyed and desolated Iran. He held back the rain from Iran until Uzaw, son of Tahmāsp, came. He drove out Frāsyāb and caused the rain that they call "new rain." After Uzaw, Frāsyāb again caused grave evil to Iran until Kawād took the throne." (p.172). The Bundahisn's cryptic brevity makes it hard to interpret, but if Kawad is Mithridates II, then (dispensing with later 'appearances' of Afrasiab in the narrative, that seem to relate to 6th Century AD events), his 'vanquishing' of Afrasiab (traditionally 120 BC) may have been the catalyst for Afrasiab to make the move to Scandinavia. But who is 'Uzaw'? Bundahisn (p.192) states that Uzaw ruled for five years. This then is surely Sinatruces (Frey's second reign), AKA the Shahnameh's 'Zav', ruling 75-69 BC. In this case, Afrasiab 'again caused grave evil to Iran' *after* this time. But it names the next Iranian monarch as 'Kawād' (i.e. Mithridates II), who should already have reigned before Zav/Uzaw. Perhaps then, 'Uzaw's reign could be the *first* reign of Frey (132-127 BC, also 5 years, although in what sense did he 'drive out' the Turanians? The only alternative (i.e. it being the second reign) would be that Bundahisn's 'Kawād' refers to an AD, Sasanian figure, again making Afrasiab's involvement in the later 'grave evil', largely fictional). In which case Kawād is still Mithridates II, and there was also no post-Sinatruces (i.e. 69 BC) interventions of Afrasiab in Iranian history.
[384] Heyerdahl and Lilliestrőm, (p.285-287). This raises the subject of the war between Mithridates VI Eupater of Pontus (reigned 120-63 BC) and the Romans. The Prose Edda makes it abundantly clear that one of the main motivations for the Scandinavian exodus was the encroachment of Roman tyranny, and this was an issue sensitively dependent on the evolving situation of Mithridates' campaigns. Indeed, the Roman menace was held at bay by Mithridates' forces for fifty years until his defeat in 66 BC. This makes the sometime presence of Odin at Mithridates' court entirely plausible, and adds believability to the identification of him as Olcaba. If it was him, he would indeed have been antagonistic to the Roman General Lucullus, whom he is accused of attempting to assassinate. One could even theorise that the return of Frey to the throne of Iran was a major play in this power politics chess game, as Frey's son Phraates III immediately entered the conflict on the side of Mithridates, intriguing against the pro-Roman Tigranes the Elder of Armenia. Also Mithridates was only defeated in 66 BC, an event that might be seen as a major motivation for the migration to Scandinavia (i.e. the second, main trip, to Sweden).
[385] Much like the Scythian conquest of the Crimea immediately after it had been vacated by the Cimmerians, the Kushan takeover in Bactria can reasonably be assumed to have followed fairly closely on the heels of the Æsir leaving. If so, the Æsir did not complete their exodus until much later than 115 BC.

It might well be argued that Odin cannot still have been active so far into the 1st Century BC, as he would have been approaching a hundred years old by that time. On that subject, Chinese history records that in 87 BC the King of the Yuezhi at Bactria sent four ounces of a spice called 'King-tsing' to China, an unidentified delicacy whose name translates as 'returning life spice' or 'rejecting death spice'[386].

What happened to the Scythians?

So the Scandinavians had made their escape from Asia. But what happened to the vast hordes of Iranian-Scottish bow and arrow-wielding horsemen who once abounded on the Sea of Grass and had been synonymous with it? Well, their fate was various.

Firstly of course they found a home in Scotland. Whilst the Indo-Iranian 'Milesians' who arrived in Ireland C.600-300 BC often preferred to remain on that island, the Scottish contingent, descended from Riphath, tended to be more likely to make their way across the Irish Sea to make a home with their nearer relatives the red-headed 'Cruithne' or 'Picts' who had anciently settled the highlands of Scotland and were descended from Riphath's elder brother Ashkenaz. This migration was highly accelerated by the spread to the Scottish islands and south-west of Scotland of the Irish-Scottish-Shemite 'Dalriada' Empire beginning in the 5th Century AD under Fergus Mor, until it was destroyed by Norwegian colonists C.839 AD.

---

[386] La Couperie, p.229-231. This may well have a connection to Tocharian herbs previously associated with the 'elixir of life' such as cinnabar, 'jade grease', 'brinjal' and Asafœtida. The idea of long life resulting from imbibing certain nutrients is very ancient, and reflected in the Epic of Gilgamesh, where the titular adventurer, living around 2100 BC, seeks out his reportedly still living ancestor Noah (Utnapashti). When Gilgamesh finds him, Noah and his wife feed him and give him new clothes. Noah also shares with him some of the precious herb that will preserve his life. Unfortunately Gilgamesh, being proud and bombastic, promptly neglects it and it is stolen by a snake (Epic of Gilgamesh, p.691-723). Iranian history also records that Noah used a life-preserving foodstuff, known to them as 'Haoma' (Yasna, p.231-239)

Many Scythians over the centuries went south from the Sea of Grass, becoming involved in mainstream Indo-Iranian politics where they provided a constant admonition to the effete Persians to 'keep it real' as nomadic horse archers on Persia's northern border. In particular the Parthian Arsacid dynasty is thought to have been part of a group that had recently migrated southward from the regions around Sogdiana, the ancient crucible of the Scythians, when it took possession of Parthia in 238 BC.

Other Scythians would migrate west into Europe during 200 BC-200 AD, firstly following the Sarmatians into areas like today's Bulgaria and the Balkans, and also quite probably making their way northwards to form a large part of the population of Austria and Southern Germany. This may be the derivation of the term 'Ripuarian Franks' (i.e. descended from Riphath) that the Romans used for certain populations east of the Rhine River, that would match the Scythians' original 'Riphean Mountains' (i.e. Ural Mountains) homeland.

The Scythians who stayed on the Steppe were not so fortunate. After diminishing their power resisting constant Greco-Roman encroachments they were absorbed by the westward-migrating Sarmatians in the 2nd Century BC. This arrangement north of the Black Sea continued for a few centuries of relative prosperity until it was comprehensively obliterated by invasion during the dark ages. First by the southward-migrating Goths C.200 AD, then finally and catastrophically by the Huns around 375 AD, when much of the existing Indo-European culture of the area was wiped out or essentially enslaved by a vast tidal wave of Turkic horse confederacies. Any surviving Scythian populations, most of whom fled Northwards into the great plains of Russia, would have to wait until the 9th Century AD when returning Scandinavians from northern Europe would re-establish the first Indo-European state in the area following the Hunnic Khaganates, the 'Kievan Rus', based in the Dnieper river city of Kiev, that would develop into the modern state of Russia.

The Japhetic Spread

It is time for a final look at the macro movements of the Indo-Europeans - the descendants of Japheth - in prehistoric Asia. This is informed by our earlier discussion of the super-ancient 'Gutians' who overran the evil empire of Nimrod C.2000 BC. It seems clear now that the Gutians, after being themselves finally turfed out of Babylonia, went north through the Caucasus Mountains and became the Goths. This means that their empire-busting credentials are impeccable and unparalleled, as they destroyed both the Akkadian and Roman empires.[387] It also has a significant effect on our understanding of early post-flood Japhetic people movements.

In particular it means that the 'Yamnaya' horizon – the original spread of Indo-Europeans north from the Caucasus after the flood, probably did *not* include the proto-Goths/Gutians[388]. Because at the time when the Yamnayans were first exploring Eurasia, the Gutians were still heavily involved in Mesopotamian politics, and therefore were still south of the Caucasus.

This means that the leaders of the Yamnaya horizon were almost certainly the descendants of Gomer. This fits perfectly with Scythian memories of a progenitor who had three sons[389]. While Togarmah remained largely in the Caucasus region, the other two brothers, Ashkenaz and Riphath, pushed northwards to become the Celts and Scythians respectively, with Ashkenaz migrating west into central Europe, and Riphath migrating east onto the Eurasian Steppelands, the 'Sea of Grass'.

---

[387] And, arguably, through Polish 'Perestroika', the USSR in the 20th Century AD
[388] This is also suggested by our understanding that the Goths were descended from Dionysius/Magog, during his cross-continental tour to India and back, and therefore would have both originated and remained south of the Caucasus for some time after the flood, much later than the Yamnaya horizon.
[389] i.e. 'Targitaus' (Gomer), son of Papaios (Japheth), whose sons were Leipoxais, Arpoxais and Colaxais, that are very likely the same as Agathyrsus, Gelonus and Scythes (though Herodotus gives these alternate names as sons of Heracles), AKA Ashkenaz, Togarmah and Riphath (Herodotus, p.247-9)

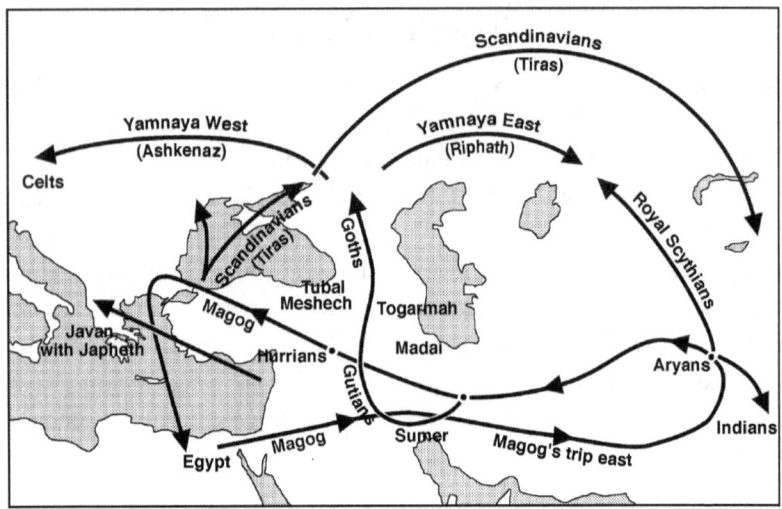

Fig.126: Early spread of the Indo-Europeans from the Ark/Babel, with particular regard to Caucasia

This understanding of the trajectory of Gomer is instructive, as we now know that Galatia in western Anatolia was probably not an early Gomeran settlement (but rather a result of 3rd Century BC Gaulic migration), whereas we might expect to find remnants of his descendants in eastern Anatolia, near the Caucasus, from where many of them went north through the mountains to Europe and Asia. And indeed, this is the location of 'Gamir', at the foot of the mountains, as discussed earlier, a place name almost certainly derived from 'Gomer'. Appropriately, descendants of Togarmah, Gomer's son, dominate the region, with both Armenians and Georgians descended from him. Albanians also, to the east of Armenia, are thought to have descended from Gomer, and this may be a connection with the ancient name of Scotland, 'Alban', whose 'Cruithne', early Celtic settlers were Gomerans.

Many have argued that this Gomeran origin of 'Gamir' means that the Cimmerians must also be Gomerans, and that this must be the origin of the name 'Cimmerian'[390]. However, it should be noted that the Cimmerians, in contrast to the nations recently mentioned, were not 'from' Gamir, but were new arrivals in this region, who had been pushed south by the Scythians from their home in Thraco-Cimmeria[391]. It could be argued that they were merely retracing their Gomeran ancestors' route of migration, however this does not explain their strong associations with Scandinavian maritime culture, nor their antagonism with the Riphathian Scythians, who were descended from those very Gomeran ancestors.

Moreover, Dark Age sources provide further evidence that the Crimea/Asov Cimmerian settlement was a colony founded from the Black Sea, much earlier than the Cimmerians' association with 'Gamir'. Indeed, they relate the founding of this original Cimmerian colony, presumably the one referred to by Homer, directly to the fall of Troy.

---

[390] The Behistun inscription of Persian Emperor Darius the Great's reference to them as 'Gimera' seems to support this (p.161-2).
[391] And the mention of them in Homer's 'Odyssey', C.750 BC (p.250), as 'Cimmerians', who dwelt at the northern edge of the world, leaves precious little time, if any, for them to have taken on that name based on their new, temporary, base in Gamir, where they arrived only around C.722 BC.

The 'Liber Historiae Francorum', a history of the Franks from the 8th Century AD, states that after the Trojan defeat, one party left westward, while a second party went north:

"Priam and Antenor, two of the other Trojan princes, embarked on ships with twelve thousand of the men remaining from the Trojan army. They departed and came to the banks of the Tanais [Don] river. They sailed into the Maeotian swamps [of the Sea of Azov], penetrated the frontiers of the Pannonias which were near the Maeotian swamps and began to build a city as their memorial. They called it Sicambria and lived there many years growing into a great people."[392]

This surely is the origin of 'Cimmeria', a term that seems to be related to 'Trojan'. This can be seen from the fact that the Britons, named after their King Bryt, also refugees from Troy, also called themselves by a variation of this same word; in the Welsh language even today, the self-identifying name of the Welsh or British people is 'Cymru'[393].

---

[392] Liber Historiae Francorum, p.23. Interestingly, on an 1154 AD map by Al-Idrisi, a settlement on the Don river is labelled 'Troy' (Heyerdahl and Lillieström, p.81)

[393] If 'Cimbrian' came from 'Gomer', it is hard to explain why the Dardanian and/or Tirassian Trojan royal family would have so named their nation.

The Telescoping of Generations and the 'gods' of Ancient Pantheons

After the flood, a curious phenomenon occurred that explains much about human beings' later view of super-ancient history and their ancestors, whom they often worshipped as gods. At some point in the 300 years or so after this cataclysmic event, human lifespans grew shorter. In the Bible's account, it states that "the Lord said, My spirit shall not always strive with man, for that he also is flesh; yet his days shall be an hundred and twenty years."[394] This statement is recorded as taking place before the flood. However it is not clear when this lifespan change among human beings would occur.

Noah is listed as living for nine hundred and fifty years[395], his son Shem for 600 years, his great great great grandson Peleg for 239 years[396], and his great great great great great great great great great grandson Abraham for 175 years[397] with Noah passing away around the time that Abraham was born, roughly 2050 BC. People born after about 2000 BC then, seem to have begun living to around the prescribed 120 years. But people born before then were living longer[398]. People born earlier were living longer and people born later were living shorter lifetimes. So for 5-600 years after the flood (the period of 'super-ancient' history) there exists a situation where there are a lot of people all living together at the same time, from very many generations. Perhaps ten generations of the same family being alive at the same time. Moreover, there is a point in history (let's say 1900 BC to 1750 BC) when later-born generations are dying before the most ancient generations (such as the grandsons and granddaughters of Noah): a telescoping generational overlap.

---

[394] Tanakh, p.4
[395] Ibid, p.6
[396] Ibid, p.7
[397] Ibid, p.16
[398] Most sources agree that this change occurred during the lifetime of Joktan, being the explanation of his name, that refers to diminishment. Pseudo-Philo (p.90-91) and Jerahmeel (Yosippon book, p.61) confirm that Joktan was contemporaneous with the tower of Babel incident.

Leaving a 'gap' during which (perhaps at 1750 BC) let's say Japheth, Gomer, Togarmah, Kartli and Mts'xet'os (all born before 2000 BC) are still alive, but Mts'xet'os's son (born let's say in 2000 BC), his grandson (1950 BC) and his great grandson (1900 BC) have died, leaving only his great great grandson (born 1850 BC), his great great great grandson (1800 BC) and his great great great grandson (1750 BC) to interact with the most ancient generations on earth, still alive 600 years after the flood[399].

During this era then was seeded the memetic germination of the 'gods' of ancient pantheons such as Zeus, Thor, Shennong, Dionysius, Poseidon and the Titans/Frost Giants.

Imagine the intimidation factor of meeting your great great great, great, great, great, great grandfather (when you never met your great grandfather, your great great grandfather or your great great great grandfather because they lived too long ago), who has been alive for hundreds of years. His wisdom and knowledge, as well as his physical size (with height following virtually the same trajectory of degeneration as age) would have seemed divine and certainly as though from a 'different realm'.

The slow morphing of these people, the memories of whose acts reverberated down the ages, into otherworldly 'gods' in their descendants' perceptions, who were truly 'larger than life' to later eras, is attributable substantially to this period of human memory, and many of the stories of the 'gods' come from that time. Especially when the true explanation of these stories was closed off from acceptable discussion, after the promoters of the 'enlightenment' during the early 19th Century got their grips on the means to censor intelligent, critical enquiry, with the fanatical dogma of secular modernism. That effort has increasingly been to attempt to 'mythologise' all of history out of existence, so that

---

[399] If the Septuagint turns out to be the accurate chronology, the 'telescoping' effect would be lessened, but still a major factor. As discussed, this effect is documented in, for example, the Epic of Gilgamesh, in which Gilgamesh seeks out his ancestor Noah, who is many hundreds of years older than he is (p.691-723)

more and more of it can be dismissed as purely imaginary and conceptual; so that, with their heritage thus lost to them, human beings can more easily be enslaved. Because for a people to be enslaved, they first have to be separated from their history and heritage.

Conclusion

Empires come and go, and for what? God's eternal plan doesn't change. All we need to know about our fate here in this world can be learned from the humble altar of Noah in the mountains of Ararat.[400]

---

[400] N 39.63414 E 43.98658

APPENDIX 1: Plato on the 'gods' of Super-Ancient History

Plato, while a bit of a space cadet, was also very talented at prose and communication. Here he describes the situation of the super-ancient world:

"In the days of old the gods had the whole earth distributed among them by allotment[1]. There was no quarrelling; for you cannot rightly suppose that the gods did not know what was proper for each of them to have, or, knowing this, that they would seek to procure for themselves by contention that which more properly belonged to others. They all of them by just apportionment obtained what they wanted, and peopled their own districts; and when they had peopled them they tended us, their nurselings and possessions, as shepherds tend their flocks, excepting only that they did not use blows or bodily force, as shepherds do, but governed us like pilots from the stern of the vessel, which is an easy way of guiding animals, holding our souls by the rudder of persuasion according to their own pleasure;-thus did they guide all mortal creatures. Now different gods had their allotments in different places which they set in order...

[They] put into their [childrens'] minds the order of government; their names are preserved, but their actions have disappeared by reason of the destruction of those who received the tradition, and the lapse of ages. For when there were any survivors, as I have already said, they were men who dwelt in the mountains; and they were ignorant of the art of writing, and had heard only the names of the chiefs of the land, but very little about their actions. The names they were willing enough to give to their children; but the virtues and the laws of their predecessors, they knew only by obscure traditions; and as they themselves and their children lacked for many generations the necessaries of life, they directed their attention to the supply of their wants, and of them they

---

[1] This agrees with the division of the earth by lot to the sons of Noah, and by them to their sons.

conversed, to the neglect of events that had happened in times long past; for mythology and the enquiry into antiquity are first introduced into cities when they begin to have leisure, and when they see that the necessaries of life have already been provided, but not before. And this is reason why the names of the ancients have been preserved to us and not their actions." [2]...

"For many generations, as long as the divine nature lasted in them, they were obedient to the laws, and well-affectioned towards the god, whose seed they were; for they possessed true and in every way great spirits, uniting gentleness with wisdom in the various chances of life, and in their intercourse with one another. They despised everything but virtue, caring little for their present state of life, and thinking lightly of the possession of gold and other property, which seemed only a burden to them; neither were they intoxicated by luxury; nor did wealth deprive them of their self-control; but they were sober, and saw clearly that all these goods are increased by virtue and friendship with one another, whereas by too great regard and respect for them, they are lost and friendship with them. By such reflections and by the continuance in them of a divine nature, the qualities which we have described grew and increased among them; but when the divine portion began to fade away, and became diluted too often and too much with the mortal admixture, and the human nature got the upper hand, they then, being unable to bear their fortune, behaved unseemly, and to him who had an eye to see grew visibly debased, for they were losing the fairest of their precious gifts; but to those who had no eye to see the true happiness, they appeared glorious and blessed at the very time when they were full of avarice and unrighteous power."[3]

---

[2] Plato, vol.3, p.530
[3] Plato, vol.3, p.542-543. Note the parallel description of the exact same process of history in the Huainanzi (C.150 BC), p.98-100 and p.297. Compare also Huainanzi p.224 with Tanakh, p.4

Note some points about which Plato is particularly candid:

1) The 'gods' (in this case Poseidon and Atlas, i.e. Ham and one of his sons[4]) existed from the *beginning* of the time period remembered[5]. The account is one of constructing a Kingdom from scratch, with (to the writer) admirable values that only *later* fell away, by *degeneration*, over time.

2) The 'gods' lived a long time, and the people surrounding them, the subjects of their Kingdom, were their *descendants*; their *children* ('seed').

3) As Plato relates, the 'gods' eventually were no longer there anymore. We know, because their values, influence and presence went away, hence the lament at the end of the account. Where had they gone? There is only one answer: they died, because they were human beings. Thereafter, Plato describes how through *degeneration*[6] and loss of memory of them and their teachings and values, the righteousness of behaviour of their *descendants* 'began to fade away.' There really is no other interpretation of these passages.

---

[4] Possibly Put or Canaan
[5] Though his children Hephaestus and Athene are also called 'gods'
[6] Of course Plato with his famous idealism believed that the 'gods' were fundamentally different from their offspring, 'fully divine' in the Greek conception. But nothing else in the testimony about them, neither in Plato nor elsewhere, supports this. Other than being relatively more prodigious than their offspring, they were exactly the same. If they had been divine, they would not have died.

APPENDIX 2: The Trojan War Through the Eyes of the Hittites

There are essentially three sets of evidences of the Trojan War. We have the Epic Cycle, that is Homer's Iliad and Odyssey and the six other major epic poems (many of them lost or only partially surviving) that made up the cultural foundation of the ancient Greek Civilization. We have the archaeological evidence of the many layers of the remains of the ancient city of Troy at Hissarlik in today's western Turkey. And we have the real-time record of imperial interactions with the various entities to its west of the Hittite Empire based in Hattusa in today's central Turkey.

Of these, the most reliable in terms of providing definite anchor points in time are the Hittite records, because:

a) They are primary sources written in situ, whereas the Iliad, the earliest written poem of the Epic Cycle, was only put to paper in the 8th Century BC, some 350-400 years after the events it described[1].
b) While the Epic Cycle is a highly dramatized and subjective poetic narrative, the Hittite documents are real-world communications between parties to the events.
c) The Hittite records form part of a large and internally consistent corpus of administrative documentation that exists within a systematic structure continuing over many hundreds of years, making them highly cross-referenceable by a dedicated army of Hittitologists. This allows for the construction of a prosaic, linear timeframe (by the succession dates of the Hittite Emperors mentioned if nothing else). This cannot provide dates in absolute terms but can at least claim a reasonable level of dating accuracy relative to other major events of the period that involved the Hittite Empire.

---

[1] Not taking into account the possible 'New Chronology' of David Rohl

For these reasons our best timeline structure for analysing forensically the political interactions of Western Anatolia during the period 1350-1200 BC comes from the drier Hittite records (while the other sources often add colour and meaning.)

There are 6 primary Hittite source documents (cuneiform clay tablets) for this study:

1. The *'Indictment of Madduwata'* (CTH147). of C.1390 BC
   - A long compendium of the sins of a hapless sub-King of South-Western Anatolia, written by the Hittite Emperor Arnuwanda I to the subject Madduwata
2. The *'Ten Year Annals'* and *'Extensive Annals'* of Mursili II', Years 3-4 (CTH61) of C.1310 BC
   - A self-aggrandising list of his own achievements by Hittite Emperor Mursili II
3. The *'Manapa-Tarhunta Letter'* (CTH191) of C.1295 BC.
   - A letter from Manapa-Tarhunta, sub-King of the 'Seha River Land' that lay between Mira in the South and Troy in the North, to the Hittite Emperor (probably Mursili II)
4. The *'Alaksandu Treaty'* of C.1280 BC
   - A treaty written by the Hittite Emperor Muwatalli II between himself and Alaksandu, the King of Troy
5. The *'Tawagalawa Letter'* (CTH181) of C.1250 BC
   - A letter from the Hittite Emperor (probably Hattusili III) to the (unnamed) King of Achaea (Mycenaean Greece)
6. The *'Milawata Letter'* (CTH182) of C.1230 BC
   A letter from the Hittite Emperor (probably Tudhaliya IV) to a sub-King of Western Anatolia, probably Kupanta Kurunta of Mira

These communications contain snapshots (though scant and haphazard) of the complex political maneuverings in the region during this period. They concern the political interplay between the Hittite Empire, the Kingdom of Troy, the Achaeans, the ancient Minoan colony of Miletus, the island of Cyprus and the Arzawan capital of Ephesus, as well as the various loyalties of many local sub-Kings.

There follows a very brief digest of the 'news' to be gleaned from the respective documents that is relevant to the Trojan War issue:

Indictment of Madduwata
C.1400 BC: Attarsiya/Atreus, a 'man of Achaea' with 100 chariots has captured Miletus and put the Hittite vassals in the region to flight. He has also been raiding Alashiya (Cyprus) that the Hittite Emperor considers Hittite subject territory[2].

Annals of Mursili II
C.1322 BC: The King of Arzawa (a vassal state created by the Hittite Empire in the wake of its conquest of Troy-based predecessor the Assuwa alliance), Uhha-Ziti, has defied the Hittite Emperor Mursili II (calling him a 'child') and gone over to the Achaean side, leading a widespread uprising against Hittite power in the area.

Hittite Emperor Mursili, marching to reconquer the area, has witnessed a 'lightning bolt' (probably the meteorite) strike Ephesus, the capital of Arzawa, injuring Uhha-Ziti. Uhha-Ziti's sons Piyama-Kurunta and Tapalazunauli battle Mursili but lose. Uhha-Ziti and his sons flee to the Achaean-controlled islands offshore. Uhha-Ziti dies soon afterwards.[3]

Manapa-Tarhunta Letter
C.1295 BC: There has been an attack on Troy and it appears to have been conquered by enemies of the Hittite Empire.

---

[2] Hittite Correspondence, p.69
[3] Ibid, p.10

Meanwhile Piyama-Radu, a warlord in the area, has conquered the Seha River area, placing its Hittite vassal King under the authority of Atpa, King of Miletus, before attacking the island of Lesbos. There is a strong suggestion that Troy was conquered by Piyama-Radu, in league with the Achaeans.[4]

Alaksandu Treaty
C.1280 BC: King Alaksandu is in power in Troy, and has been since the reign of the new Hittite Emperor's father Mursili II (whose reign ended C.1295 BC). The new Emperor wishes to continue this treaty agreement with Alaksandu. He reassures Alaksandu that dynastic succession is not that big a deal. The Emperor recalls that (a previous King of Troy) Kukkuni and his grandfather, Hittite Emperor Suppiluliuma I, were friends[5].

Tawagalawa Letter
C.1250 BC: Piyama-Radu has continued to raid against Hittite power in the region. Now he has fled to Miletus, whose King Atpa seems to be sympathetic to Piyama-Radu. Piyama-Radu was in a bad mood with the Hittite Emperor in that the Emperor sent the Crown Prince to talk to Piyama-Radu and bring him to the Emperor (the Emperor asserts at Piyama-Radu's request), but Piyama-Radu rebuffed the Crown Prince, with the words "Bestow kingship on me here on the spot! if not, I will not come."[6]

The Emperor himself then went to Miletus, but before he got there, Piyama-Radu had fled by boat to Achaea. So the Emperor could only make his feelings known to King Atpa and (apparently his brother) Awayana who were still present. He accuses them in the letter of 'covering up the matter – because [Piyama-Radu] is their father-in-law'.[7]

---

[4] Hittite Correspondence, p.140
[5] Hittite Treaties, p.87
[6] Hittite Correspondence, p.103
[7] Ibid. p.105

The Emperor puts extreme pressure on the recipient of the letter – the King of Achaea – to deal with the Piyama-Radu situation. He accuses the King of Achaea of providing support to Piyama-Radu:

"While he leaves behind his wife, children, and household in my brother's land, will your land support him? This person keeps attacking my territory. But if I... it to him, he returns to your land. Do you approve, my brother? Did you now [...] this?"[8]

He urges the King of Achaea to say to Piyama-Radu:

"The King of hatti has persuaded me about the matter of the land of [Troy] concerning which he and I were hostile to one another, and we have made peace. Now(?) hostility is not appropriate between us."[9]

This language would appear to suggest that the Hittites are asking the Achaean King to turn Piyama-Radu over to Hittite control as the Hittite Emperor's condition for making peace with Achaea.

The letter ends with what looks like a threat towards the Achaean colony of Miletus ('or else!')

---

[8] Hittite Correspondence, p.115
[9] Ibid

Milawata Letter

C.1230 BC: The Hittites have attacked and overthrown Miletus. They also seem now to be back in control of Troy.

"I, My Majesty, thereby established] once more the sea [as my frontier...]"[10]

Whatever happened to Alaksandu, the Hittite Emperor is now planning to reinstall on the throne of Troy a previously deposed vassal King of Troy, Walmu.

"[he shall] now be king of the land of [Troy], as he was formerly. he shall now be our military vassal, as he [was] formerly."[11]

---

[10] Hittite Correspondence. p.125
[11] Ibid. p.130

Interpretation

It is proposed that the relations between Piyama-Radu, Alaksandu, Atreus, Troy and the Hittites gleaned from these documents is such that it is close to impossible not to see in Piyama-Radu the Homeric Priam of Troy.

And that the events of the 13th Century BC represented the final attempts by the indigenous Trojans to maintain/assert their independence after the disastrous defeat of the Assuwan League in the 1400s.

Sandwiched between the Hittites' aggression and the growing Greek influence in the region, the Trojan royal family had probably been attempting, ever since the defeat of Assuwa (that represented their last 'true' independence) and commencing in earnest with Uhhi-Ziti in 1322 BC, to elicit support from their kinsmen Japhethite (and Javanite) Greeks for their reconquest of/reinstatement in Troy.

This may have succeeded with the capture of Troy by Piyama-Radu/Priam in C.1295 BC, with his successor the Greek-named Alaksandu installed as King, whom the Hittites were forced (temporarily) to accept.

Weight is added to all this by the remarkable scholarly acceptance of the identification of Alaksandu as Homer's 'Alexandros of Ilios' AKA Paris of Troy[12]. If Priam did conquer Troy at this time, it makes perfect sense for him to put in his son as King.

---

[12] Hittite Correspondence book, p.2

That would make Kukkunni either:

a) the last non-Hittite puppet King of Troy (perhaps King at the time of the Assuwan League), and possibly Priam's father or Grandfather, or
b) a Hittite puppet King, perhaps Walmu's father or antecedent. This is the more likely as it is suggested by the letter that the Hittite Emperor wishes to continue cordial diplomatic relations with the Trojan throne *despite* that Alaksandu is *not* a descendant of the Hittites' previous preferred ruler.

However, many commentators take the Alaksandu Treaty as being that of a puppet ruler, with Alaksandu/Paris then having been installed by the Hittites after they reconquered Troy or otherwise sorted out whatever happened in 1295 BC. But this does somewhat call into question the status of Walmu. When for example with this interpretation could he previously have been the Hittite's puppet or vassal King of Troy?

A couple of other notes:
- Dodan, son of Javan, settled the Troad when welcomed there by Teucer/Thor in far ancient antiquity, according to Greek history. So the Trojans being pre-war allies of the Greeks against the Hittite Empire does make sense: there was an ethnic tie of Javanite ancestry in the Troad.
- There is the appearance of a stretching of time between 1300BC and 1250BC that suggests that some dating in the Hittite chronology may be off. For example Piyama-Radu himself, after conquering (Troy) in 1295 BC is still active and warring in 1250 BC. Likewise Atpa the King of Miletus doesn't seem to have aged much during this time either. Walmu also, if we are to read him as being the same puppet King of Troy that was deposed in 1295BC (though many commentators see there being two overthrows of the Hittite-backed Trojan regime during this time, not one) is still available to go back to his old job some 65 years later.

So where does all this leave the Iliad narrative?

Well, cloudy. The information is still extremely incomplete. We just don't really know exactly how it all fits together. From the evidence above, it would appear that Priam himself could have conducted the Iliad's famous 'Greek' invasion and conquest of Troy, in 1295 BC, aided by the Achaeans.

Yet there is certainly scope to construct the traditional narrative out of these elements, even if it is fairly tenuous. The details in the last two letters are particularly unusual and hint at intrigues so far hidden from us behind the scenes.

In essence it seems that some major changes happened between these two letters, dated 1250 BC and 1230 BC (or possibly between the 1280 BC treaty and the 1250 BC letter). Either way, by the time of the Milawata letter in C.1230 BC:

i) the Greeks are now allies of the Hittites
ii) the 'previous disagreement' between the Hittites and the Greeks over Troy is now settled
iii) Alaksandu is gone from the Kingship of Troy
iv) Piyama-Radu is also completely gone from the scene, not so much as mentioned.
v) A new and seemingly more aggressive Hittite Emperor (Tudhaliya IV) is in power (interestingly the penultimate generation of Emperors before the destruction of Hattusa by the Sea Peoples - his two sons would be the last two Hittite Emperors)

In short, could the Achaeans have taken the Queen's shilling and betrayed the Trojans by attacking them for the Hittites? Hatusili III's letter to the Achaean King (the Tawagalawa letter) seems to be a subtly calculated threat. He offers peace with the Hittite Empire more or less if the Achaeans hand over Piyama-Radu, possibly also threatening the Achaean colony of Miletus if rebuffed. By the next letter, the threat has been carried out, Miletus has been conquered by the Hittites.

In the intervening years, could the Achaeans have grown weary of their beleaguered, always in trouble, eastern cousins? An increasing liability to Greek Anatolian ambitions and with an old-fashioned attachment to the past that was out of step with Greek realpolitik? Especially after what appears to have been a particularly ham-fisted diplomatic face-plant by Priam. Namely insulting the Hittite Crown Prince then running straight to the Achaean court, thus dropping the Achaeans right in it with the Hittites. Who are consequently about to invade the Achaeans' Miletus territory in retaliation, whose Kings indeed have been harbouring the Trojan partisans as accused.

It looks as though it might have been wiser of Priam to accept the Crown Prince deal. Having rejected it, perhaps he had no bargaining chips left. It is fascinating to see how Piyama-Radu and his party were at this point being hosted by the Achaeans, precisely primed for the events that cause the war in the Iliad. If Paris then eloped with an Achaean princess and absconded back to Troy with Priam following, that could certainly have been the straw that broke the camel's back for the previously close allies. Especially if the Hittites had started demolishing Miletus. Could Agamemnon[13] have invaded and conquered Troy during 1250 BC to 1230 BC and handed it over to the Hittites in order to placate them and in the hopes of getting Miletus back?[14] Did Hattusili and Agamemnon essentially carve up Troy between them? It would certainly explain the wrath of the Sea Peoples towards these two empires in particular.[15]

---

[13] An 'Agapurusiya' features in the Milawata letter. But his role is obscured by missing text.

[14] Such a dating interestingly would fit exactly with Strabo's estimate of sixty years between the Trojan War and the 'Return of the Heracleidae', i.e. the destruction of Mycenae, C.1180 BC (though Thucydides has eighty years) (Strabo, vol.2, p.339-340)

[15] While the conquest of Miletus by the Hittites doesn't seem to fit with this theory, another Hittite letter, Aht27B, from the Hittite Emperor to King Ammurapi, the last King of Ugarit, requests war provisions (copper) from Ugarit for Achaeans who were then in Lukka (Hittite Correspondence, p.257). This suggests that the Hittites were still at this late stage in league with Achaeans of some description who were then in South-West Anatolia, and also in league with Ugarit. In other words that the 'anti-Sea Peoples' league consisted of Hatti, Achaea and Ugarit.

And how does this fit with the archaeological remains? Again, extremely hard to say. Troy VIh was destroyed (including by earthquake damage) around 1300-1250 BC. Troy VIIa was destroyed C.1190 BC. Of course these dates are still highly approximate. The first destruction could have been Priam's invasion of 1295BC. The second could have been a projected Greek naval assault that overthrew the re-established Trojan royal house.

Some argue that archaeology reveals Troy VII to have continued after the destruction of Mycenae (the Greek capital). This would arguably mean the Troy VIh destruction was the 'Trojan War' and possibly Troy VIIa was destroyed by the Sea Peoples themselves. Or indeed both could have been the result of 'friendly fire' if the 1295 BC attack was indeed by Piyama-Radu and there was no later Greek attack. Or, was the Greek conquest of Troy C.1240 BC by deceit as described in the Epic Cycle and therefore left no major destruction of the city (although most accounts of the war do include such a destruction). This would make the 1295 BC event Priam's 'reconquest' of Troy and the 1190 BC event the Sea Peoples' revenge on the now Hittite and Greek-held city.

The fact is we cannot accurately lay down the true sequence of events with the information currently available. Nevertheless there is compelling evidence to support the theory that the above reviewed period of instability during the 13th Century BC in Western Anatolia constitutes, one way or another, the factual basis for the Epic Cycle's retrospective narrative.

And that as more evidence is discovered, the missing details will be filled in and judging by the emphatic historical consensus will likely support the fundamental narrative of the Iliad: a fratricidal conquest of Troy by her erstwhile allies and supporters the Achaeans.

APPENDIX 3: Logic Chain on the Cause of the Bronze Age Collapse

It has been established beyond reasonable doubt that:

i) the Sea Peoples were primarily Trojans (or 'wider Trojans' i.e. 'Asians').

ii) the 'Bronze Age Collapse' was caused by the invasions of the Sea Peoples.

Therefore the Bronze Age Collapse was caused by whatever it was that angered or motivated the Trojans in their attack. What could that be, but some offence to the entity that united and defined them: the city of Troy.

Therefore the Bronze Age Collapse was caused by something that happened to the city of Troy.

There is some basis to theorise that this was a conquest of Troy by the Hittites, (C.1240 BC).

However,

a) Troy had already, previously been conquered or at least 'annexed' by the Hittites (who put in place the vassal Walmu), assumedly after the defeat of the Assuwan League (C.1400 BC) *without* eliciting such a response from the Sea Peoples, nor anything like it.

Also, remarkably few Hittite artefacts have ever been found at the archaeological site of Troy. In other words the previous 'annexation' consisted of 'paper control', a remote relationship of vassalage and service, not conquest.

Notably the big 'sea change' in the nature of artefact findings at the Hissarlik site of Troy came after the Troy VIIa destruction event of C.1190 BC. After this the record shows an influx of new kinds of cosmopolitan ware at Troy from foreign cultures that previously were not present. However, these are not from the Hittite Empire (that of course no longer existed at this point in time) but rather from the Aegean and Mediterranean World.

(It is plausible that the Troy VIIa destruction event of C.1190 BC was caused by the Sea Peoples, for example by the Phrygian invasion of Asia, in some kind of 'friendly fire' event. But this does not alter the discussion of what was the initial *causal* event of these subsequent invasions.)

b) Secondly, a primarily Hittite proposed conquest of Troy substantially places Troy in an alliance with the Greeks. This alliance is admittedly present in the Hittite records, albeit under extreme pressure arguably to breaking point by 1250 BC. But this Greek-Trojan alliance is fundamentally incompatible with the absolute destruction of both the Hittite Empire *and* Mycenaean Greece by the Sea Peoples. By contrast a purely Hittite conquest of Troy would have seen a Greek-Trojan 'Sea Peoples' invasion and destruction of Hatti only, in response. But that is not what we see in the evidence. What we see is a (primarily) non-Greek destruction of *both* Hatti *and* Mycenaean Greece by Trojans. Indeed, what appears to be a destruction of Hatti *and its allies*.

So whatever happened C.1240 BC was something of a different character to previous Hittite claims on Troy.

The only realistic explanation for all this evidence is that the causal event of the Bronze Age Collapse was:

- upon Troy, and
- by a combination of Greeks and Hittites

That fits with the Homeric, classical Greek memory of an Achaean conquest of Troy, in an epochal event momentous enough to echo down the centuries.

APPENDIX 4: Investigation into the Trojan Roman origin story

The famous story of Rome being founded by descendants of Aeneas and/or other Trojan veterans of the Trojan war cannot be supported historically. This is fundamentally because the most ancient witnesses do not agree with it but rather attest to facts incompatible with it. What is more, the further back in time one goes, the more the story diverges and indeed outright contradicts and renders impossible the later imperial-era Trojan Roman origin story.

The following points are relevant to this discussion:

1. The earliest witnesses have Aeneas remaining in the Troad area:

   Homer[1] (C.750 BC), as per Strabo[2] and Banier[3]
   Acusilaus[4] (C.525 BC)
   Hegesippus of Mecyberna (C.300 BC): Aeneas went to Thrace only[5]
   Agathocles (C.300 BC): one of the first to mention Italy, but also an authority for the fact that Aeneas is buried in Berecynthia, near Troy[6]
   Antigonus (C.210 BC[7]): Rome founded by 'Romus', son of Jupiter (no mention of Aeneas or the Trojans)[8]
   Demetrius of Scepsis[9] (C.175 BC) Aeneas dwelt in Scepsis, in the Troad[10]

---

[1] Iliad: p.513
[2] Strabo, vol.1, p.377-378
[3] Banier, vol.4, p.314-317
[4] Greek Historical Fragments, vol.1, p.103, Fr.26
[5] Dionysius, vol.1, p.157
[6] Greek Historical Fragments, vol.4, p.290, Fr.8. Mount Berecynthus was in Phrygia, across the Hellespont
[7] Cornewall-Lewis, vol.1, p.94-95
[8] Greek Historical Fragments, vol.4, p.305, Fr.1
[9] Strabo, vol. 2, p.376-377
[10] Strabo adds that the family of Ascanius (son of Aeneas) 'reigned, it is said, a long time at Scepsis'

See also Hellanicus' (C. 450 BC) detailed (and apparently complete) story of Aeneas' migration to Thrace only[11]

2. The above-mentioned trajectory of historical witness testimonies, to the effect that the older the witness, the less it attests to the Trojan Roman origin story:

Homer (750 BC): Aeneas staying in the Troad area after the war[12]
Thucydides (450 BC): Trojan veterans settling in Sicily[13]
Aristotle (350 BC): Greeks holding Trojan women captive run aground in Italy (no mention of Rome)[14]
Callias (300 BC): Trojan woman 'Rome' marries the Latin King Latinus (no mention of Aeneas)[15]
Agathocles (C.300 BC): Aeneas buried in Phrygia but a mention of Italy[16]

Then only after 300 BC, after:
a) the destruction of Roman historical records by the Celts in 390 BC
b) the possible erection in Rome of the Romulus and Remus wolf statue in 294 BC[17]
c) the beginnings of Roman entry into the Hellenic world following the invasion of Italy by Pyrrhus in 281 BC, for the acceptance of which they needed a plausible heroic origin story connecting them to the Greek world,

do we find the fully-fledged story being told by Romans (only) of the Trojan origins of Rome:

---

[11] Dionysius, vol.1, p.145-155
[12] Iliad, p.513
[13] Thucydides, vol.2, p.179
[14] Dionysius, vol.1, p.237-239
[15] Ibid, p.239; Greek Historical Fragments, vol.2, p.383
[16] Greek Historical Fragments, vol.4, p.290, Fr.8. It is worth noting that the most ancient versions of the Aeneas story involve Aeneas as a traitor to the Trojans and to Priam, indeed as the one who procured the defeat of Troy for the Greeks (Iliad, p.513; Menecrates of Xanthus (Dionysius, vol.1, p.157))
[17] Cornewall-Lewis, vol.1, p.108

Fabius Pictor (C.210 BC)
Nævius in a dramatic play (C. 210 BC)[18]
Cincius (C.200 BC)
Cato the Elder (C.180 BC)
Piso (C.140 BC)

Indeed from the available sources it is quite possible that Fabius Pictor was the very first to come up with the idea, around 210 BC: at least six hundred years after the events he was supposedly recording.

Finally come the Augustinian-era flatteries of the Julio-Claudian dynasty as being Trojan descendants, that sought fully to embed the story into the Roman mind as historical:

Dionysius (C.20 BC)
Virgil (C.20 BC)
Livy (C.10 BC)[19]

It should be noted that these works came after more significant losses of Roman civic records, with the Ærarium/Tabularium burnt in 83 BC during the civil war of Sulla and the Capitol burnt in 69 BC by the Vitellians[20]. The highly volatile civil war era (49-31 BC) that followed also included much destruction, and the subsequent reign of Augustus was no stranger to book-burning[21]. The sources for the Annales Maximi of the Pontifex Maximus[22] are also largely a product of the Augustinian era[23]. Such limitations on recorded history arguably served the purposes of the Julio-Claudians in casting themselves in the most prominent, ancient and distinguished light

---

[18] Cornewall-Lewis, vol.1, p.56
[19] The 'Tabula Iliaca' discovered at Bovillae is also a product of this same period
[20] Cornewall-Lewis, vol.1, p.149
[21] Such as the burning of the history of Labienus (Ibid, p. 52)
[22] the Roman pagan high priest
[23] Frier, p.iv-vii. And again, no earlier than Pictor

possible, by removing evidence that may have exposed the Aeneas story as a nationally convenient fabrication no older than perhaps 350 BC at the earliest (see the quote from Plutarch below).

Nb. Dionysius has an incongruous statement that he claims to be from Hellanicus and/or Damastes (i.e. C.450 BC), about which Cornewall-Lewis writes this:

"An isolated legend which connects Æneas with the Molossians, is cited by Dionysius from the author of the work on the Priestesses of Argos; that is, apparently, the ancient historian Hellanicus. According to this story, Æneas went from the Molossian country to Italy with Ulysses in order to found Rome, which he named after a Trojan woman. Whatever may be the origin of this account, it is not credible that the genuine Hellanicus should have recorded the foundation of Rome."[24]

This refers to the fact that until the 4th Century BC and as late as the invasion of Italy by Pyrrhus in 281 BC the Greeks had barely heard of Rome nor the Romans[25].

3. An alternate founding narrative that is likely as old as the Aeneas one, that has Rome founded by sons of Ulysses, for example in Xenagoras[26] (C.150 BC) and mentioned by Plutarch[27].

4. Trojan culture was highly distinct from, indeed quite opposite to, Roman (AKA Latin) culture; The evidence of the main ethnic descent of the Latins/Romans is that they

---

[24] Cornewall-Lewis, Vol.1, p.314
[25] Ibid, p.58-67
[26] Dionysius and Greek Historical Fragments vol. 4, p.527, Fr. 6
[27] Plutarch, vol. 1, p.28. Another founding narrative related by Strabo, citing Coelius (C.50 BC)) states that Rome was a Greek colony planted by Evander during Heracles' visit to Italy driving the cattle of Geryon C.1350-1300 BC (Strabo, vol.1, p.343).

were descended from Kitt, son of Javan[28]. As such they were closely related culturally to their cousin nation the Greeks, who were mainly descended culturally and ethnically from Elisha (probably Hellen and Aeolus), son of Javan[29]. While a component of the Trojans was descended from Javan's son Dodan, the Trojans' defining identity was as the cultural and ethnic heirs of Thor (Teucer, Thrax, Ares). Hence arguably their animosity with the Greeks. This is demonstrated by the Latins having battled with their neighbours the Etruscans, who are much better attested as having descended from the Trojans. A Trojan origin of the Latins/Romans does not therefore make sense in the context of:

a) their hostility to the Etruscans
b) their close association with the Greeks

Further, there is a lack of any significant linguistic or ethno-cultural evidence of a change in the distinctly Kittian culture of the Latins by some outside, Trojan settlement. The Latins spoke the Latin language seemingly throughout their history, not any version of ancient Anatolian. Indeed there is apparently complete continuity of Latin, Kittian culture from its arrival in Italy[30] down to classical times, including its use of Rome's peculiar deities Saturn and Janus, neither of which are associated with the Troad. Claims of relics for example of altars to Aeneas in Latium are highly subjective and find their equivalents in a multitude of sites around the Mediterranean that purport to relate to visits by (usually) Ulysses or Aeneas, owing to the extraordinary popularity of Homer and the Epic Cycle in the region during antiquity, the poems' position as the foundation of classical

---

[28] As for example in the Dead Sea Scrolls and Yosippon
[29] E.g. Josephus, vol.4, p.62-63
[30] As argued in the main text, likely memorialised in the 'rape of the Sabine women' story.

culture, and therefore the many civic claims of association with it. Rome, being militarily the strongest city during this period, was able to promote its claims the most effectively.

Quotes:

Strabo[31]- Homer redacted:

"Sophocles, in his play, The Capture of Troy, says, that a panther's skin was placed before Antenor's door as a signal that his house should be spared from plunder. Antenor and his four sons, together with the surviving Heneti, are said to have escaped into Thrace, and thence in to Henetica on the Adriatic; but Æneas, with his father Anchises and his son Ascanius, are said to have collected a large body of people, and to have set sail. Some writers say that he settled about the Macedonian Olympus; according to others he founded Capuæ, near Mantineia in Arcadia, and that he took the name of the city from Capys. There is another account, that he disembarked at Ægesta in Sicily, with Elymus, a Trojan, and took possession of Eryx and Lilybæus, and called the rivers about Ægesta Scamander and Simois; that from Sicily he went to Latium, and settled there in obedience to an oracle enjoining him to remain wherever he should eat his table. This happened in Latium, near Lavinium, when a large cake of bread which was set down instead of, and for want of, a table, was eaten together with the meat that was laid upon it.

Homer does not agree either with these writers or with what is said respecting the founders of Scepsis. For he represents Æneas as remaining at Troy, succeeding to the kingdom, and delivering the succession to his children's children after the extinction of the race of Priam:

---

[31] vol.2, p.377-378

"the son of Saturn hated the family of Priam: henceforward Æneas shall reign over the Trojans, and his children's children to late generations."

In this manner not even the succession of Scamandrius could be maintained. He disagrees still more with those writers who speak of his wanderings as far as Italy, and make him end his days in that country."

Plutarch[32] records an incidental admission:

"But a writer named Clodius, in a work on chronology asserts that the ancient registers disappeared in the destruction of the city by the Gauls, and that those now extant have been falsified, for the purpose of honouring particular persons, by placing them in the first and most distinguished families."

Cornewall-Lewis[33] aptly sums up the situation:

"But when the memory of the event was extinct, and no written record of the fact had been preserved, the imagination of mythologists and antiquarians was actively employed in supplying the void, and manufacturing an article to satisfy the public demand."

Dionysius[34] doth protest too much:

"The arrival of Aeneas and the Trojans in Italy is attested by all the Romans and evidences of it are to be seen in the ceremonies observed by them both in their sacrifices and festivals, as well as the Sibyl's utterances, in the Pythian oracles, and in many other things, which none ought to disdain as invented for the sake of embellishment."

---

[32] vol. 1, p.91
[33] vol.1, p.404
[34] vol.1, p.159-161

APPENDIX 5: Historical Correction in Classical Chinese Chronology

Here we must take a quick detour regarding the figure of Yu the Great. The 'traditional' Chinese chronology, that was highly settled and authenticated at a state-wide level during the Han dynasty (C.200 BC-200 AD)[1], runs thus:

Ruler	Date
Fuxi	2952 BC[2]
Nuwa	(no traditional date)
Shennong	(no traditional date)
Yellow Emperor	2697 BC[3]
Yao	2357 BC[4]
Shun	2255 BC[5]
Yu the Great/ Xia dynasty	2205[6]/2070 BC[7]
Shang dynasty	1766[8]/1600 BC
Chou dynasty	1122[9]/1046 BC

[1] i.e. the *order* was codified (in the Book of Han (111 AD) (Wilkinson, p.672)). The actual dates listed here as 'traditional', still tacitly acknowledged and used as a rule of thumb in all discussions of Chinese history (although the last three were 'revised down' by the recent Xia–Shang–Zhou Chronology Project (1996-2020)), only began to be used much later. The actual origin of these specific, 'traditional' dates is wrapped in Olympic levels of petty obfuscation, but Mungello (p.124) traces the earliest two dates back to the Jesuit Martino Martini in a 1658 AD work, the later dates in the chronology appearing earlier. Although increasingly cringed at in its most ancient section, the chronology nevertheless continues to be the basis of conventional Chinese history. For example the XSZ Project, while fiddling with some dates (in particular acknowledging Pankenier's brilliant archaeo-astronomical proof for the accession of the Zhou at 1046 BC), substantially retains and restates the traditional chronology unchanged.

[2] Mungello, p.124
[3] Wilkinson, p.671; Mungello, p.124; La Couperie, p.6
[4] Date first arrived at by physician Huangfu Mi (C.250 AD)(Wilkinson, p.671)
[5] Date was probably established by the medieval era (Ibid, p.671 & 673)
[6] Date was probably established by the medieval era (Ibid, p.671 & 673)
[7] These last three dates were revised down by approximately 200 years each by the XSZ Chronology Project (1996-2000) (Lee, p.18)
[8] Listed in the 1938 'Cihai' dictionary (Mungello, p.132)
[9] This date appears to derive from the data of astronomer Li Xin (C.50 AD), that was incorporated into the Book of Han (Wilkinson, p.673)

And this is where it all gets difficult. Because this neatly delineated Han history, epitomised and directed by the 1st Century BC 'Shiji', that is ubiquitous in all discussions of ancient Chinese history, now commonly called the 'classical' chronology, codified after the reprehensible 'destruction of the books' wherein all ancient classics were burnt by the first Chinese imperial tyranny the 'Qin', C.213 BC[10], has Yu as a relatively recent 'historical' figure, called in as a lay or non-royal specialist to help with a flood, perhaps a thousand years after the primaeval narratives of Fuxi, Nuwa and Shennong occurred. Narratives that Sima Zhen in his 7th Century AD Introductory Chapter to the Shiji appended to the beginning of the story, before the Shiji proper starts with the characters of Shennong and the Yellow Emperor. But the (allegedly) older, pre-Qin 'Classic of Mountains and Seas' does not mention Fuxi, Nuwa or Shennong at all[11]. Neither does the Book of Documents, that also apparently preceded the Qin book destruction. In the Classic of Mountains and Seas, the figure of Yu is given absolute primacy in all issues relating to the flood.

In other words, perhaps owing to the tyrannical destruction of the books of classics by the Qin Emperor in 213 BC[12], we may be staring down the barrel of a major error in historical chronology that requires serious correction. One all the more startling because of the highly polished and settled nature of 'classical' Chinese history, taught to legions of Mandarins for millennia. But perhaps not such a drastic one, as the 'classic' dates for Yu (C. 2205/2070 BC) are still fairly accurate[13], with the true dating probably being slightly older.

---

[10] Allen, p.8
[11] Except for a single, offhand mention of a very differentiated version of Nuwa as 'Nu Kua'.
[12] A measure of the wickedness of this loathesomely ignorant historical vandalism (recommended to the Qin emperor by his minister Li Sze) is that the I Ching was one of the only classics preserved precisely *because* it was a book of witchcraft (i.e. divination), rather than a treatment of more wholesome subjects such as music, poetry or history, as were the others (I Ching book, p.2; Wilkinson, p.372).
[13] The classical Chinese chronology is in remarkable agreement for example with the traditional Jewish chronology (settled upon by Medieval scholars R. Abraham bar Hiyya and Maimonides (Guggenheimer, p.269), that places Adam (Fuxi) at 3760

The classical Han narrative as above described relates the reign of the Yellow Emperor, then after a number of centuries Yu (named in the Shiji as Yellow's great, great grandson[14]) is called upon to help with flood earthworks. Yu then founds the Xia (AKA 'Hsia' - meaning 'Summer') dynasty, that lasts for 471 years, ending with his descendant 'Bold'. Bold's reign gives way to the Shang (beginning C.1600 BC) and Chou (beginning C.1000 BC) dynasties, of which there is copious historical evidence. But this is not the case for the preceding Xia dynasty. Anne Birrell describes the problem (emphases added):

"Traditionally, this mythical dynasty (Hsia) lasted for 471 years, with seventeen kings. It formed the first part of the Golden Age of Antiquity, together with the historical eras of the Shang (Highest) and Chou (Round) dynasties. Primitive cultures once erroneously designated as 'Hsia' are now known by the name of their archaeological site, such as the Erh-li-t'ou culture. *No evidence exists, either archaeological or a written historical record, for the verification of the Hsia.*"[15]

So this famous dynasty, founded by one of the most important characters in Chinese history (Yu the Great), has absolutely no historical evidence supporting it, despite the fact that in the classical schema it immediately precedes well known and well-evidenced historical states.

It does not seem too impertinent to ask, therefore, whether the only reason flood-battler Yu was apportioned his position in the classical chronology (i.e. after Shun and immediately before historical records began in earnest with the Shang), might have been because the role of mythical flood progenitor, i.e. Noah, was perceived to have already been taken by Fuxi and Nuwa, figures

---

BC (p.281) and the flood at 2104 BC (p.3) respectively. However, if the Chinese dates derive from the Jesuits, the significance of this is lessened considerably.
[14] Shiji, 1, p.21. Although see footnote 56, below
[15] Classic of Mountains and Seas book, p.262. See also Wilkinson, p.678

from the I Ching[16], who were assumed to have lived earlier than the Yu narratives.[17]

Perhaps the key piece of evidence suggesting an alternative placement of Yu's story in the chronology is the name of his dynasty, 'Xia' (meaning 'Summer'). This name is also the name of 'Greater Summer' ('Ta Xia'[18]), an area of the world well known to the ancient Chinese and described by Anne Birrell thus:

"The name of a western region in Central Asia, identified as Bactria, modern Afghanistan's northern region; also part of the Roman Orient. The name derives from a mythical dynasty, Hsia (Summer). Kuo notes that the capital city of Greater Summer was two to three hundred leagues (li) across, and that the state was divided into numerous kingdoms. He also notes that its temperate climate is suitable for grain crops."[19]

Basically, this sounds a whole lot like Sumer, the original, one-language, post-flood civilization located in Mesopotamia between the Tigris and Euphrates rivers, indeed founded and nurtured by Noah himself[20].

It seems that the reason for the missing 'Xia' dynasty in the second millennium BC can only be that Yu did not live at the time of the

---

[16] I Ching, p.382-383, part of the supposedly Confucius-written portion, therefore deriving from C.450 BC or earlier. Note Nuwa does not appear here, but he is 'part of' the Fuxi story, as elaborated by the Huainanzi (C.150 BC) and Sima Zhen in his 7th Century AD introduction to the Shiji.
[17] In other words, not being able to leave the I Ching's Shennong out (seen as the founder of the nation), the I Ching's Fuxi/Shennong narrative was given primacy.
[18] Classic of Mountains and Seas, p.151
[19] Classic of Mountains and Seas book, p.227
[20] Nb. the coincidence of the names 'Sumer' and 'Summer' is irrelevant to this identification of Yu/the Chinese conception of central Asia with Noah/ post-flood Mesopotamia. Kramer (p.298) argued that the name 'Sumer' derives from 'Shem'.

semi-historical Yao and Shun Emperors at all, nor after the famous Yellow Emperor, nor after his predecessor the Yan (Flame) Emperor, nor even after Shennong himself. Because Yu was actually Noah, and preceded everybody in the post-diluvian world.

And the descriptions of his efforts with earthworks to drain flooded areas and so prepare them for grain cultivation can only refer to Noah's own industry in husbanding not China, but Mesopotamia, the very centre of the world, in super-ancient antiquity, before the Tower of Babel incident had even separated the nations into their seventy different languages, as the careful Father of the entire world community, now known to us as 'Sumer'[21]. 'Xia': 'Summer', was Noah's own dynasty, and 417 years would be about right to fit with other testimonies of the time

---

[21] Aside from the overwhelming descriptions of Yu as the one who dealt with the Great Flood, Chinese history also includes many other details about Yu/Noah that corroborate the identification, such as a) the memory of his issues with wine: "Yu had a penchant for licentiousness and inebriation" (Lüshi Chuqiu, p.251; Wu, p.111; Tanakh, p.6); b) Yu is given instruction in the 'five elements' (Book of Documents, p.139-143) while Nuwa 'smelted together five-coloured stones' in order to fix the world after the flood (Huainanzi, p.224); c) anachronisms such as: the name of 'Xie'/'Hsia', a contemporary of Shun's yet apparently named after Yu's dynasty, that was not yet founded if Yu was after Shun (see later); the association of the term 'the Four Mountains' or 'Four Peaks' with Yu (for example Zuo book, p.196) yet in the classical chronology, in use before Yu's reign (Documents, p.34-35); in the Shiji, chapter 2: "Yu is stated to be the grandson of Chuan-hsu, yet Shun, whom he succeeded on the throne, is, as we saw in the last chapter, seven generations from Chuan-hsu" (Allen, p.59); in the Huainanzi, an apparent quote lists Yu as before Shennong (p.55); Huangfu Mi states that Shennong "rules Xia, so he is called Yan Emperor" (section 1) when according to conventional chronology, Xia was not established by Yu until after Shennong; the Bamboo Annals describe a pre-flood Yu interacting with 'a tall man, with a white face and a fish's body' (p.117), clearly one of the same beings discussed by Berossus, only present in the antediluvian era (p.13-14). Another interesting detail is Yu's height, given in the Bamboo Annals (p.117) as approximately 16 ft (9 cubits 6 inches) (although it should be noted that Yao, stated erroneously as having been earlier than Yu, is stated to have been taller: 17 ft (p.112), while Shun, stated as having succeeded Yao and preceded Yu, is ascribed a height of 10½ ft (p.114). The preoccupation of Yu with drainage, irrigation and land cultivation fits perfectly the evidence of the earliest period of Sumerian settlement, when the as yet undeciphered pre-Babel mono-language was spoken, that provided the names of most of the first settlements and rivers of Sumer (Kramer, p.40-41; Rohl, 1999, p.132)

between the flood and the Tower of Babel, the troubles resulting from that debacle often witnessed as following soon after Noah's passing, some 350 years after the flood[22].

In other words the reason there is no evidence of the Xia dynasty in China is because *it was not in China*, but rather in Mesopotamia[23]. So where does this leave the story of Fuxi, Nuwa and Kun Kung? Well, it would appear that it is a parallel retelling, with much less detail, of the same story, so that both Nuwa and Yu represent the historical Noah; the two alternative versions apparently deriving from the varying accounts in the I Ching on the one hand[24] and the Book of Documents and Classic of Mountains and Seas on the other.

This means that the early years of China's formation are truncated and simplified, the era of the Yellow Emperor and the rest of the Five Emperors now appearing as more formative on it than previously thought, with the descent from his rule to the Shang and the classical Han now unencumbered by misplaced flood story impositions that belong earlier, but also now somewhat floating and without a distinct position in the chronology, having been detached from their erstwhile rank in the traditional lineage (i.e. before Yu).

---

[22] For example Pseudo-Philo, p.89. Alternatively, the 417 years also fits the time between the establishment of Nimrod's empire (C.2000 BC – still based in 'Ta Xia' i.e. Mesopotamia, and so associated by the Chinese with the Government established by Noah) and the Chinese break with it under Tang of Shang.

[23] The great 'capital cities' of Xia from the Mountains and Seas account, therefore, would be referring to the likes of Sumerian urban centres Ur, Uruk and Eridu. And we ought not to look for correlations between Xia rulers and Bronze Age leaders, so much as for correlations between Xia rulers and the Sumerian King List. In fact an extensive and detailed interpretation of just such an identification has already been put forth by French scholar La Couperie (and previously alluded to by James Legge, amongst others (Bamboo Annals book, p.189)), who went so far as to identify both the Yellow Emperor and Shennong as Mesopotamian figures, the Elamite chief 'Hu Nak Kunte' and Sargon the Great respectively (La Couperie, p.319-322). These identifications are arguable (see main text), however his proofs that Chinese culture derives directly from the Mesopotamian are beyond dispute (p.9-25, 277, 291-302).

[24] Followed (in its 'Fuxi-(Nuwa)-Shennong-Yellow Emperor' narrative) by the Huainanzi (C.150 BC) and Sima Zhen (C.700 AD)

With the 'Xia' identified as the historical Sumer, we can project that it would have ended with the Tower of Babel and the subsequent tyranny of Nimrod. Not surprisingly, we also find this event reflected in the Chinese 'Yu' narrative, in the story of how the Shang dynasty won its independence from the Xia. The Shiji describes how the Xia dynasty eventually became tyrannical, so that one 'Tang' takes up the leadership of the Chinese and defeats the final Xia dynast 'Jie' at the battle of Mingtao (traditionally dated to 1675 BC), establishing the Shang dynasty[25]. Tang is a (thirteen generation) descendant of one 'Xie'[26], who was 'awarded' the territory of the Shang for helping Yu (Noah) with flood recovery services[27]. We can with some confidence equate (the Shiji's) 'Xie' with (the I Ching's) Shennong[28].

Jie of Xia bears all the hallmarks of being a version of the tyrannical Nimrod[29], or at least a closely-related Babylonian tyrant, whether Bel, Ninus, etc. of the house of Nimrod, similarly engaged in attempting to hold together a 'world empire' by force, after the nations had split up according to language[30]. He is recorded as having alienated the common people by using their labour to undertake a huge and unpopular building project, the 'Tilt Palace', that is possibly a memory of the Tower of Babel at Eridu[31].

---

[25] Shiji, 1, vol.1, p.38
[26] Whose name associates him with the Xia dynasty, but according to the 'Documents' and Shiji, he preceded it (Shiji, 1, vol.1, p.14). He is also named as Yao's brother (Shiji, 1, p.41)
[27] Shiji, 1, vol.1, p.41-42
[28] Shennong (Xie) would therefore have rendered this assistance to his own great Grandfather, Noah (Yu). The 13 generations between Xie and Tang fit perfectly with the dates for Noah we have from other histories. With Noah passing away C.2050 BC, 13 generations of 30 years each would take the date of Tang down to 1660 BC, very close to the classical dates for the Battle of Mingtao (1766/1600 BC). This would seem a very late date for Nimrod, but entirely within the scope of late Babelite tyrants, the tyrannical legacy of Nimrod's regime continuing to be based in Babylonia until the rise of the Assyrian Empire C.1500 BC.
[29] For example in the description of him in the Huainanzi, p.209
[30] Or at least a memory of the excesses of the Babylonian imperial system, of which Xia was known to be a continuity
[31] "In his 3rd year, he built the K'ing palace, and pulled down the Yung tower", Bamboo Annals, p.125.

The Battle of Mingtao then, represents the Shennongite (and Yellowite) Chinese winning their independence from the now tyrannical ex-Babel empire of Nimrod (or one of his descendants), AKA Jie of Xia, under the leaderhip of Tang[32].

The reason why Yellow Emperor and the rest of the Five Emperors are not particularly mentioned in this story (aside from their being 'I Ching characters' rather than 'Documents characters'), and for their 'floating' detachment from it, is that they were in China, part of the fledgling Yellow River Civilization, while the story of the Xia dynasty (founded previously by Yu) started in Mesopotamia. That is why though overlapping in time, the two stories rarely interact. Both Xie (Shennong) and the Yellow Emperor lived during the Sumerian/Akkadian/Babylonian era, prior to the Battle of Mingtao and the establishment of China as an independent state[33], but were later than Yu. Tang, a descendant of Shennong, later fought off the late Babelite depredations (or at least the remnants of the 'Xia-authorised' (i.e. by Noah through Shennong) original settlement/imperial outpost in China) and established the Shang dynasty, the first actual Chinese state proper, following on from the (Noahide) community traditionally founded by Shennong and later taken over by Yellow in primaeval antiquity.[34]

---

[32] Tang is also credited by some with having written the I Ching, or some part of it. This would make sense as the Shang dynasty are associated with pagan witchcraft, the famous 'Oracle bones' representing the earliest Chinese written records, another method of 'divination', having been found at the last of the Shang 'five cities' sites, Yin. Being pagans, the Shang practised human sacrifice and possibly cannibalism (Chong, p.47). But the compilation of the I Ching's main section is usually attributed to King Wen of Zhou, father of the founder of the Chou dynasty (King Wu), and his son the Duke of Chou, C.1000 BC.

[33] With Shennong probably living before the separation of the nations at Babel (C.2050), or if not, soon after it. His direct connection to Yu (Noah) suggests his wish to continue Yu's legacy (i.e. the 'Xia'), and the Chinese wish to continue his legacy, hence the copious Yu literature transmitted through Chinese history, in particular the 'clean-up' operation after the flood, that Shennong (Xie) may have been an eye-witness to (See Shiji, 1, vol.1, p.41-42)

[34] But in fact probably founded by Yellow, long after Shennong's lifetime, as per La Couperie.

This fits perfectly with the archaeological evidence, which knows of no definite Xia remains within China at all[35], but can trace with some precision the emergence of the Shang state from the very earliest, most primitive sites in China, all found around the 'S' bend of the Yellow River (AKA the 'Ordos Loop' or 'Ordos Plateau'), just upstream from the original Chinese settlement[36]. These archaeological sites correspond roughly to the 'five cities' of Shang, with Longshan to Erlitou probably the remains of the Yellow Emperor and Five Emperor-era settlements, that were then followed by the 'five cities':

1) 'Bo'[37] = Erligang culture of the Yanshi/ Shang City sites
2) 'Ao' = Xiaoshuangqiao site
3) 'Yan' = Near modern Qufu
4) 'Xiang' = Huanbei on the Huan river
5) 'Yin' = Yinxu, the final and greatest incarnation of Shang (the move here took place C.1300 BC)[38], and where the Oracle bones (containing the earliest Chinese script) were found. (Although also the one that became corrupt and lost the empire, as it was overthrown by Wu of Zhou C.1046 BC.)

This correction, exposing a significant error in the 'Shiji''s timeline, arguably calls into question the entire traditional Chinese historical chronology of events in the very ancient past before the Shang, and perhaps even before the Han, as was strongly argued by Herbert Allen, the first translator of the early chapters of the

---

[35] Haw, p.17. While the Erlitou site is tentatively accepted as being Xia, it only testifies to a small, local centre interacting with a diverse, multicultural local population (basically it's a palace), not at all the grand, sprawling remains of a long and powerful imperial state (like those of Shang, see for example Wilkinson, p.678-9). However, it is exactly consistent with being the local outpost of a *foreign* great empire. Lee (p.23-25) illustrates the current confusion around the substantially missing Xia in Chinese archaeology.

[36] Near the later Chou imperial centre, named (it is proposed) after Shennong: 'Shang'An', and traditionally believed to have been founded by him.

[37] Shiji, 1, vol.1, p.43 onwards

[38] Under 19th Shang King Pan Gen. This date is agreed with by the XSZ Chronology Project (Lee, p.28)

Shiji into English, who believed all Chinese Classics 'reappearing' after 213 BC were forged.[39]

It seems that the newly aggressive and centralised imperialism of the classical era was tremendously culturally destructive not only in the West but also in the East as well.[40]

However, Allen's extreme view is perhaps throwing the baby out with the bathwater. What Birrell describes is a Han-derived 'Confucian mythological system' that bears only partial relation to the prior, organic, ancient and true history of China, and that it was this 'Confucian construct' that ascribed Yu his new, later position in the 'historicized' chronology[41]. The Han dynasty, lasting roughly from 200 BC to 200 AD, consolidated, centralised and organised Chinese society as far as they were able to into one uniform whole, and, while eschewing the naked, beastial empire-building of the Qin tyranny, also suppressed much of Chinese idiosyncrasy, individualism and variety in favour of the proposed benefits of a Confucian conception of temperate, balanced, ordered, bureaucratic, administrative and centralized Government. This resulted in the established, 'traditional' Chinese chronology, that stems from this Han period.

Or does it? It is easy to attribute the erroneous 'Yellow-Yao-Shun-Yu' sequence to the Han period because of the burning of the books that preceded it, that certainly caused much historical information to be lost and would explain the historical error, as it calls into question the veracity of all post-Han 'rediscovered' classics (as per Allen). However this assumption is premature, as

---

[39] Allen (p.9-12) cited Sima Qian and Kung Ankuo (a claimed descendant of Confucius and 'finder'/recoverer of about a third of the chapters of the Book of Documents during the Han era), as the chief suspects. Allen cast aspersions on the accepted story that after the overthrow of the Qin, the Book of Documents and some other ancient classics were discovered hidden in a compartment behind a wall and brought out to much acclaim.
[40] La Couperie suggests many of the tyrannical, 'imperialistic' ideas (such as book burning) were received into China by the Qin via a fledgling coastal interaction with sailors from the Mediterranean, influenced by Alexander (p.36, 203-6)
[41] Classic of Mountains and Seas book, p.272

there are strong proofs that the sequence was already an established part of Chinese traditional chronology by the beginning of the Han dynasty (C.200 BC) and long before the 'Shiji' (91 BC). From whom and how far back then did this error originate? To investigate this we must take a deep dive into the swamp that is Chinese historiography.

Unfortunately, as a result of endless 'rewrites', 'rediscoveries', 're-edits', etc. down the ages, Chinese historiography is a ridiculous quagmire, archetypical of the infamous Chinese 'inscrutability'. In service to clarity of argument, a general list is presented here (in an attempted chronological order) of some of the main ancient Chinese historical written sources (as such a list seems painfully absent from the vast, voluminous ocean of Chinese historical commentary, despite its immense and unwieldy size!):

Historical Work	Author/Editor	Date
Classic of Mountains and Seas	Unknown	> 1000 BC
I Ching	Wu and Wen of Chou	C.1000 BC
Book of Documents	Confucius	C.500 BC
Analects	Confucius	C.500 BC
Commentary on the Spring and Autumn Annals	Zuo Qiuming	C.450 BC
Mencius	Mencius	C.325 BC
Bamboo Annals	Unknown	C.299 BC
Lüshi Chunqiu	Lü Buwei	C.239 BC
Huainanzi	Liu An	C.150 BC
Shiji	Sima Qian	C.91 BC

It should be noted with regard to this list:

a) Virtually all works come complete with subsequent layers of later built-in commentary of varying age and authority, but the rough dates listed are intended to reflect the main 'trunk' of the work, that constitutes the bulk of its original information of historical interest.

b) The provenance of the Bamboo Annals has for at least two hundred years been the subject of a debate arguably as interminable and entangled as any in world intellectual pursuit. But most commentators tacitly accept that the original autographs of the annals (unearthed in 280 AD), whatever they were (nobody knows) were probably authentic records written around 299 BC, when the annals stop.

c) Such a list is of necessity incomplete, as there are numerous smaller pieces of evidence, such as the oracle bones, that while being earlier, are usually petty records of pagan rites, divinations, or court and administrative proceedings, that (in the awareness of this writer) do not impact on the primary issues of ancient history under review.

d) The Book of Documents is given this late date based on its opening section, that is most relevant here. Later sections of the work such as the 'Tribute of Yu' and the 'Great Plan' probably originated in a much earlier epoch.

So, working from the oldest, which of these ancient classics[42] that pertain to history are found actually to be in error in this issue of the dating of Yu the Great? The Mountains and Seas plainly describes Yu as Noah, taking on all the flood works, exactly as would have been observed and recorded by his close descendants[43].

---

[42] Nb. this list is irrespective of the famous 'Five Classics' list. Only three of the 'Five Classics' appear on this list of specifically *historical* sources: the I Ching, the Book of Documents and the Commentary on the Spring and Autumn Annals. Confusingly the 'Classic of Mountains and Seas', customarily so-called, is not one of the 'Five Classics'.

[43] The credentials of Yu as Noah are even more extensive in the 'Mountains and Seas' than in the 'Documents'. He is described as having variously 'blocked', 'dammed' or 'stemmed' the floodwaters (p.186,196) and afterwards been the first to 'fix the contours of the Nine Provinces into equal divisions.' (p.195)

The I Ching tells us about Fuxi and Shennong being succeeded by Yellow Emperor, Yao and Shun without mentioning Yu[44]. When it comes to the Book of Documents however (that Sima Qian seems to have relied on most for his chronology in the Shiji), questions might be asked about the pre-Yu deliberations of the figures of Emperors Yao and Shun, such as:

"The Ti (Yao) said, 'Ho! (President of) the Four Mountains, destructive in their overflow are the waters of the inundation. In their vast extent they embrace the hills and overtop the great heights, threatening the heavens with their floods, so that the lower people groan and murmur! Is there a capable man to whom I can assign the correction (of this calamity)?' [45]

This seems a rather understated response to the imminent global catastrophe. In answer to this, 'Khan'[46] is appointed, who labours for nine years apparently against the flood, but with no success. Yu then takes over, and the matter has been dealt with without being mentioned much thereafter. Yao is then succeeded as 'Ti' by Shun. Later:

"Shun said, 'Ho (President of) the Four Mountains, is there any one who can with vigorous service attend to all the affairs of the Ti, whom I may appoint to be General Regulator, to assist me in (all) affairs, managing each department according to its nature?' All (in the court) replied, 'There is Po-Yu, the Minister of Works.' The Ti said, 'Yes. Ho! Yu, you have regulated the water and the land. In this (new office) exert yourself.' Yu did obeisance with his head to the ground, and wished to decline in favour of the Minister

---

[44] I Ching, p. 382-3. Indeed, the I Ching does not mention the flood at all, skirting over it while moving seamlessly from Fuxi to Shennong
[45] Book of Documents, p.34-35
[46] Yu's father (Book of Documents book, p.35)

of Agriculture, or Hsieh[47], or Kao-yao. The Ti said, 'Yes, but do you go (and undertake the duties).'"[48]

Again, a relaxed, office-casual approach to what would appear to have been a rather tumultuous moment. One is left to wonder precisely who this Yao and Shun were who are pictured 'appointing' Noah to these roles, if indeed, as described, they in fact preceded Noah's rule. Shun for example is present both for the original 'inundation' and subsequent 'hiring' of Yu, as well as for the assumedly post-flood 're-hiring' of him as an agricultural planner (assumedly a memory of his work in Sumer.) Allen believed that Sima Qian's quoting of this text and many others from the 'Documents', virtually verbatim and without credit, is evidence that the passages were written in their current form by Sima Qian.[49]

Certainly the somewhat comically administrative nature of this account, with Yu presented as a 'Minister of Works' is highly characteristic of the bureaucratic fastidiousness associated with the culture of the Han, and with Chinese imperial culture from the Han onwards, but not really before. This is circumstantial evidence that Allen may be correct, but arguably these are cosmetic issues. Granting that this might be a textbook case of 'Chinese Whispers', the 'Documents', regardless of its transmission, begins with the flood, as it might be expected to. Even if the 'dialogue' was fleshed out by later chroniclers, that seems insufficient grounds to impugn the fundamental integrity of the work as preceding both the Qin and Han upheavals. However, the placement of Yao and Shun before Yu may create problems for the veracity of the Book of Documents' early section.

---

[47] The aforementioned 'Xie'. As his name suggests, part of the Xia dynasty era, thought by the Shang to be their ancestor (Book of Documents book, p.42-3 and La Couperie, p.5). An anachronism as he appears in the 'Documents' and 'Shiji' as a contemporary of Shun and Yu (founder of the Xia dynasty).
[48] Book of Documents, p.42
[49] Allen, p.12

As discussed, if Yu is Noah, who are Yao and Shun? Moreover, we already know from the much older I Ching that Yao and Shun succeeded the reign of the Yellow Emperor[50]. Therefore to place them before Yu is to repeat, or invent, the error of misplacing Yu in the narrative.

But any idea that this error first occurred during the Han era and/or by Sima Qian in his writing of the Shiji, is refuted by the presence of the same error in the 'Analects'[51], the 'Spring and Autumn Commentary'[52], the Mencius[53], the 'Bamboo Annals'[54] and the 'Lüshi Chunqiu'[55], five other ancient sources on the list that precede the Han by hundreds of years. While the credibility of the Analects and Spring and Autumn Commentary may be impugned by the 'burning of the books' and subsequent 'rediscovery' controversy (as per Allen), and that of the Bamboo Annals by their 'unearthing' and subsequent version confusion, no such controversy attends the Lüshi Chunqiu, as this was the work of the Qin Emperor's own kingmaker, and therefore didn't get burnt by the Qin necessitating a possibly dubious rediscovery. The error then did not originate post book-burning, and so there is no remaining reason to continue to think it was added to the Book of Documents after that work's main compilation.

All the evidence suggests then that the mistaken historical chronology that places Yu after the Five Emperors first appears no later than the writings of Confucius.

---

[50] I Ching, p.383
[51] p.140
[52] p.453, in this single instance
[53] p.250
[54] p.117
[55] p.74, 293

It is, therefore, at the door of the 'Great Sage' of Chinese philosophy himself, masterful and monumental though his achievements were, that the chief blame must currently be laid for the error of interposing the Yu flood story and attendant Xia dynasty into Chinese history immediately prior to the Shang dynasty and crucially *after* Shennong and the Yellow Emperor, who must in fact have been Yu's descendants[56].

The issue seems to have been that, as discussed, 'Yu' and 'Nuwa' were different labels for the same person – Noah. Drawn from 'Tribute of Yu' and the Classic of Mountains and Seas tradition[57], and the I Ching tradition (followed by the Huainanzi) respectively. That is why the Mountains and Seas does not mention Fuxi or Nuwa[58], and the I Ching does not mention Yu.

But Confucius (or someone[59], let's call them the 'editor') has mistakenly combined the two accounts, leaving Yu and Nuwa as two separate characters, not realising they are one and the same, and so ending up with two Noahs[60].

---

[56] For example, as Allen points out, in Chapter 2 "Yu is stated to be the grandson of Chuan-hsu, yet Shun, whom he succeeded on the throne, is, as we saw in the last chapter, seven generations from Chuan-hsu" (Allen, p.59)

[57] Indeed the 'Mountains and Seas' is claimed (by Han era editor Liu Hsin (C.0 BC)) to have been substantially written by Yu (Noah) himself. (Classic of Mountains and Seas book, p.xxxviii-xxxix)

[58] Or at least barely, there is a single, brief mention of the femalised version of Nuwa (Nu Kua), as part of a local tradition, in the 'Mountians and Seas' (p.173), relating the idea that ten 'gods' came from her 'guts'. Birrell quotes the commentator Kuo that 'In one day she made seventy metamorphoses, and her belly was transformed into these gods' (Ibid, p.223). This seems to be a memory of the seventy nations that came from Noah. This albeit scant 'double appearance' of Noah in the Mountains and Seas material may nevertheless have influenced the editor of the 'Documents'.

[59] i.e. a prior chronicler whom he followed.

[60] At least after the error was compounded by Sima Zhen's addition of Fuxi and Nuwa to the beginning of the Shiji, based on Confucius' work (Sima Zhen, p.269)

Apparently basing their synthesis fundamentally on the Yu 'stream'[61], perhaps because of the source text of the 'Tribute of Yu'[62] (that, it is proposed, describes Noah clearing up after the flood), that was placed as one of the early sections of the 'Book of Documents', and also because of the source text of the 'Great Plan' section[63] (words of wisdom from Noah supposedly received from God), this editor wisely excludes (I Ching characters) Fuxi and Shennong from his narrative, being unsure of their place in it[64]. (Assumedly 'Nuwa' already existed in some tradition at that time, but not in the I Ching, adding to the confusion[65]). While the

---

[61] Although the 'Mountains and Seas' was not collated into one volume until 0 BC by Liu Hsin the Han librarian, the material is a lot older and may have influenced the editor of the 'Documents'; clearly the story of Yu was already long venerated, such as in the 'Tribute of Yu' and the 'Great Plan', that were constituent parts of the 'Documents'.

[62] Book of Documents, p.64-75

[63] Ibid, p.139-149. Also considered to be of great antiquity.

[64] because, it is proposed, the two cycles occurred in different parts of the world and so did not directly interrelate – Shennong to the Yellow Emperor, Yao and Shun were largely in China, while Yu's story took place earlier in Mesopotamia, notwithstanding La Couperie's claims that Shennong and Yellow both lived in Mesopotamia, with Yellow migrating to China. Even if this were the case, Yu's Mesopotamian narrative is still somewhat split geographically from the Chinese narrative beginning with the Yellow Emperor, Yao and Shun. The migration and its timing was a great source of confusion for Chinese scholars in the past, and even today.

[65] i.e. if Nuwa was in the I Ching, it would have been easier to identify him as the same person as Yu. Further complexity is added by the fact that it was Confucius who supposedly also edited the 'I Ching'. However, if this were so, it was clearly not in the same interventionist capacity as with the editing of the 'Book of Documents', because the I Ching's chronology does not fit the chronology of that work. The erroneous presence of Yao and Shun in the wrong place in the 'Documents' testifies both to the hand of 'the editor' in that work and to the veracity of the I Ching's historical portion, that doesn't contain it. In other words, if 'the editor' of the 'Documents' had also altered the I Ching, he would have made the two fit better together. The extra presence of the Fuxi/Shennong story in the I Ching, in fact a parallel account of the Yu story in the Documents, is the very text that exposes the editor's own error in misplacing the Yu cycle when writing the chronology of the 'Documents' (and of which he must therefore have been ignorant). So either the two texts were 'edited' by different people, or by the same person, but whereas the 'I Ching' was largely a collation of existing stories, the 'Documents' introductory section was a substantial reconstruction. Or, the 'reconstruction' was undertaken by an earlier hand than that of Confucius, and he merely 'curated' both sets of documents.

collections of Yu stories - the 'Tribute', 'the Great Plan' and also probably the traditions that would later form the 'Classic of Mountains and Seas' - were chaotic and haphazard, essentially a random collection of mythological stories and documents, the I Ching by contrast has a straight, linear timeline from Fuxi to Shun. In constructing his timeline from the Yu side however, this editor, wishing to impose (arguably a very Confucian) order on the chaotic Yu information, has erroneously added the characters of Yao and Shun (who appear in *both* traditions[66]) at the *beginning* of the Yu narrative, thus introducing the linear I Ching timeline (and therefore its logical consequences) into the Yu narrative *in the wrong place* (i.e. before Yu/Noah).

In making this 'join', it appears the editor has also artificially manufactured the (previously quoted) 'connecting scene' (complete with dialogue) that presents Yao and Shun's rule transitioning seamlessly into the Yu flood cycle, (now by necessity curtailed into a local and Chinese event), that became the first section, or 'introduction'[67] to the Book of Documents.

Over the millennia, this mistake has had the logical consequence of creating the aforementioned 'double narrative' of Yu/Nuwa, because later chroniclers followed the Book of Documents' lead. Sima Qian in the Shiji added the Yellow Emperor and the next two Emperors on to the beginning of this already artificially elongated timeline, understandably extrapolating back from Yao[68]. Then, Sima Zhen's introductory chapter to the Shiji, written

---

[66] The 'Mountains and Seas' source material would have featured Yellow, Yao, Shun and Yu as great primaeval Patriarchs, but because of its disjointed nature, it would have been difficult to draw from it exactly who preceded who. Significantly, Yao and Shun do *not* appear in the 'Tribute of Yu' (Book of Documents, p.64-75), nor in the 'Great Plan' (Ibid, p.137-149) at all, which are thought to be the oldest documents in the Book of Documents.

[67] i.e. parts I and II of the Book of Documents/ Shu-Ching (p.31-63) Notably this section of the Book of Documents bears a certain resemblance to the same events summarised in Confucius' 'Analects' (p.140)

[68] Based on an apparently already existing 'Five Emperors' chronology, partly probably from the I Ching and possibly also from the Bamboo Annals (p.108-114) or their source text.

C.700 AD, added yet further material (of Fuxi and Nuwa) to the beginning of this same narrative, compounding the problem.[69]

Of course this synthesis may already have existed, but the circumstantial documentary evidence (Confucius being the avowed editor of the 'Book of Documents'), combined with the weight of Confucius' authoritative and decisive editorial impact on the Chinese written canon at precisely this point in time, make him the chief suspect.

It is extremely significant that neither the I Ching, the Classic of Mountains and Seas, the Tribute of Yu nor the Great Plan are tainted by the erroneous Confucian chronology[70], and they arguably contain the most ancient material of Chinese history. The character of Yu as a lowly administrative official and later entrant in the saga is nowhere to be found in them.

Sima Qian expresses some hesitancy in following the chronology of the Book of Documents in his explanatory coda at the end of chapter 1 of the Shiji (emphases added):

"Students generally observe that the five gods[71] are the most ancient. Now the 'Book of History' [i.e. Book of Documents] only speaks of Yao and those subsequent to him. Again the writings of the various schools referring to Yellow Emperor *are not canonical teaching*[72]; and the literary gentlemen are reluctant to speak of

---

[69] Sima Zhen, p.269-274
[70] Nor were the 'Mountains and Seas' or I Ching destroyed in the Qin bookburning; the Mountains and Seas because it had not yet been compiled into book form by Liu Hsin (C. 0 BC) from 'archaic graphs' in the Han court library, and the I Ching because it was a book of witchcraft divination and so exempt.
[71] i.e. the Five Emperors: 1) Yellow (Yu-Hsiung ('Having Bears')), 2) (his Grandson) Chuan-hsu ('High Male'), 3) (his Great Grandson) K'u (High H), 4) (K'u's son) Yao (Tao-Tang), 5) (a Commoner) Shun (Yu-Yu ('Possessor of Forresters')). As listed in the Shiji (Allen, p.38; Shiji, 1, vol.1, p.17, Sima Zhen book, p.294) and Bamboo Annals (p.108-114)
[72] A curious turn of phrase, as the Yellow Emperor is placed right at the beginning of the Shiji as its first and most prominent character. Perhaps this is evidence of Sima Qian's reluctantance to include this 'folk' figure, but he may have felt forced to because of Yellow's popularity and indelible association with Chinese nationality,

him...The notables and elders whom I have addressed have one and all frequently talked of the places where Yellow Emperor, Yao, and Shun dwelt; their traditions and teachings were certainly diverse, but in a general way those who do not vary from the ancient texts are right...

The 'Book of History' [i.e. 'Documents'] is defective, and there are lacunæ, but what has been omitted may occasionally be found in other accounts. I have collected the several doctrines, and, after arranging and selecting the statements which are the most correct, I have in this way compiled the original records, which stand at the beginning of my book."[73]

Sima Qian's displeasure about the authority of the 'Five Emperors' tradition is notable[74], perhaps because they *do not include Yu* (i.e. Noah) (see footnote on previous page for a list of the five Emperors), who would be the sixth. If Yu was such a great Emperor and succeeded Shun, why on earth would he not be included in this distinguished grouping? The reason is because he *didn't*. Sima Qian perhaps reluctantly lists a sixth great Emperor in his chronology[75], but the tradition is unmistakable that there were only five.

But what does Sima Qian mean by 'canonical teaching' and 'literary gentlemen'? Well these can only refer to the teachings and

---

which possibly left him uncomfortable with the final result, sensing that Yellow's inclusion was half-baked and not historical. And so it turned out to be, but only because it was added in the wrong place.

[73] Shiji, 1, vol.1, p.17. The translation quoted is Allen's revised one, from Allen, p.38-39

[74] He twice mentions two works of history that feature them about which he is ambivalent, the 'Virtues of the Five Emperors' and the 'Genealogies and names of the Emperors', expressing his opinion that while 'not all without basis' they are dubious, despite possibly being 'handed down' by Confucius. (Allen, p.38-39)

[75] Shiji, 1, vol.1, p.17. Nb some translations do not translate 'Ti' as 'Emperor' in the case of the (first-named) Yellow Emperor, so that only five 'emperors' appear in the list, perhaps reflecting something in Sima Qian's text that wishes to minimise the obvious mathematical problem of having one too many Emperors. However 'Ti' surely means 'Emperor' in 'Huangti' as much as it does in the names of the other Emperors, as indeed it is translated by Allen (p.38).

person of Confucius himself, for the Chinese the ultimate 'literary gentleman', upon whom increasingly the suspicion of originating this error falls. Sima Qian is clearly deferring here to the authority of his illustrious predecessor, arguably the founder of the whole Han mindset upon which much of imperial Chinese thinking has been based ever since.

It seems probable that the 'Book of Documents' was not so much counterfeited or ghost-written by Sima Qian and its 'discoverer' Kung Ankuo after the book-burning, as Allen proposed, as first suffered this error in chronology while being edited by Confucius.

La Couperie states:

"There is no doubt that we are indebted to him [Confucius] for a mangled preservation of the Shu King [Book of Documents] which has come down to us still more dilapidated, but which otherwise might have been entirely lost, between his time and the Fire of Literature in 213 B.C. Nothing has been found which throws any suspicion on the statement made on the matter by his kinsman and descendant Kung Ngan Kwoh [Kung Ankuo], who re-edited the classics, circa 150 b.c.[76] "He (Kung-tze [i.e. Confucius]) examined and arranged the grand monuments and records, deciding to commence with Yao and Shun, and to come down to the times of Tchou. When there was perplexity and confusion, he *mowed* them. Expressions frothy and unallowable *he cut away*. What embraced great principles he retained and *developed*. What were more minute and yet of importance he carefully selected. Of those deserving to be handed down to after ages, and to supply permanent lessons, he made in all one hundred books, consisting of Canons, Counsels, Instructions, Announcements, Speeches and Charges."

---

[76] An intriguing statement that suggests the 'Documents' could have been edited at this point, as part of the process of its 'discovery'. However, as we have seen, the erroneous chronology preceded this as it was already present in the Lüshi Chunqiu of 239 BC (p.74, 293).

One third of these documents have been lost since Confucius' time, but they have never been intended to form a continuous Record. It was not a history of China which he compiled, but a collection of texts countenancing his views." Any how besides later suppressions he has deliberately left aside and ignored any thing from old traditions, such as those which were preserved in the San fen or 'Three eminences' concerning Fuh-hi, Shen-nung and Hwang- ti, and in the Wu Tien or 'Five causes', any thing concerning Shao Hao, Tchwen Hiuh and Kao-sin, keeping only extracts from those of Yao and Shun." This method has deprived us of many a valuable tradition which in their capacity of state documents and mementos would have permitted [us] to check the exuberancy or supply the insufficiency of the accounts which have been transmitted to posterity from irregular sources.

Besides the mowing, cutting away, and developing processes of editorship, the pruning pencil of the sage had recourse to another means to instil his views; this consisted in changing a word for another, or in the alteration of an ideogram by the addition or change of one of its component parts, a process impossible except with an ideographic writing like that of the Chinese.

With reference to the Western foreigners, founders of the Chinese civilization[77], let us understand the position assumed by Confucius. His almost complete silence towards them can be explained as the natural feeling of a Chinese among the Chinese, such as he was, and thus would confirm our discoveries about their foreign origin....

---

[77] This is a reference to La Couperie's theory that the Han Chinese, in the person or community of the Yellow Emperor (Huangti), were 'Baks' who emigrated from Elam in (or near) Mesopotamia in far-ancient antiquity.

Hwang-ti and his son Shao-Hao were foreigners, born outside of China; their immediate successors Tchuen-hiuh, Kao-yang and Ti Kao-Sin were yet too much of strangers; Yao was more of a Chinese, but he was still too closely connected with his foreign forefathers. Such was not the case with Shun, who was a descendant of native princes, and his association in the government by Yao has placed the latter on a different footing than his predecessor in the eyes of the patriotic Chinese. Hence it has happened that Yao and Shun have almost always been spoken of together. And it is a fact that the really Chinese history can hardly be said to begin before them. As to the myths and legends which Huang-ti and his Bak families had brought from the West, they were no part of the Chinese heirlooms, concerning as they did foreign folklore and traditions, or the past history of the Baks themselves. The consideration of these facts ought to justify the silence of the great philosopher of Lu [Confucius], towards the myths, legends, and traditions anterior to the age of Yao and Shun, which were found in the ancient literature.

The objections of Confucius to all that was unclear to his mind, or unsatisfactory to the sternness of his doctrines, and to all recits tinged with fables and wonderism, has thrown uselessly a discredit on ancient fragments of early ages. These early documents, which as natural in the case, could be but mixed up with stories of extraordinary feats and events, have not received the care and attention which would have secured for several centuries, at least to some extent, their safety and transmission to after ages."[78]

And from the Shiji (emphases added):

"During the time of Confucius the House of Chou had declined, the ancient rites and music were forgotten, and many of the songs and records were missing. He verified the rites of the Three Dynasties and compiled the Book of Documents, *arranging the records chronologically from the time of Yao and Shun* to that of Duke Mu of Chin, *marshalling the facts in good order*. He said, "I can

---

[78] La Couperie, p.139-142.

speak about the rites of Hsia, but the records of Chi are too scanty to verify. I can speak about the rites of Yin, but the records of Sung are too scanty to verify. Had they been complete, I should have been able to check them"...Thus both the Book of Documents and the Book of Rites were compiled by Confucius."[79]

Unfortunately the Shiji's very authority, resting upon Confucius, has led to this flaw going unquestioned for thousands of years. Chinese culture's idolatry of parentage and ancestors[80] (as we have seen ancestor-worship is common in all human cultures as the main default character of the descent into paganism, but idolatry of parents is particularly pronounced in the Sinite world), may also be partly to blame. This tendency has led to an uncritical, overly docile and submissive approach that, because of its unwillingness to criticise established authority (indeed its elevation of it into a cult) has rarely questioned the veracity of historical information, rather contenting itself simply to prune, collate and prettify it, as attractively and with as much grandeur as possible.

Confucius was not an historian, but a philosopher. His interest was in establishing a reliable aesthetic and cultural basis for compliance and conformity. Drawing from Taoism[81], he was perhaps more concerned with form and seemliness, than with Truth.

Nevertheless, it is proposed, the issue was not so much one of 'forging' as Allen believed, but rather of 'inaccurate compiling and consolidation of sources', notwithstanding the immense influence this small mistake may have had in the history of China.

---

[79] Shiji, 2, p.21-22
[80] Codified as the doctrine of 'Filial Piety'.
[81] That, argues La Couperie, was introduced into China from India (p.120-122)

APPENDIX 6: Zoroaster Revisited

Having established that the Kayanians are in fact a memory largely of the Arsacid and Sasanian dynasties of 200 BC-600 AD, and the Shahnameh's narrative (based on the Bundahisn's prior erroneous information) contains a massive chronological jump backwards in time five hundred years right in the middle of it[1], where does that leave our provisional dating of the life of Zoroaster, the founder of Zoroastrianism, to around 650 BC, based on his contemporary relationship to Vistaspa, who in turn was dated by the Shahnameh's King list to around 100 years before Cyrus? Well, basically, in tatters!

---

[1] And indeed the entire 'Pahlavi', 'AD' corpus of Zoroastrian writings and codifications that all essentially stemmed from the Sasanian 'reboot' of Zoroastrianism C.100-600 AD (more specifically probably 270-400 AD (Darmesteter in Gathas book, p.xxxvii-xxxviii)). Judging by the spectacular irregularity in the historical timeline of Iranian history now discovered, that reboot may have constituted a wholesale reconstruction of the Zoroastrian narrative (particularly the historical narrative) from highly piecemeal and incomplete fragments salvaged from the destruction of Alexander and later invaders. This 'new orthodoxy' of Zoroastrianism and Zoroastrian history was then codified and consolidated into later Zoroastrian lore mainly through the Bundahisn and 'Denkard' religious texts and the Shahnameh epic historical poem.

Further evidence that the events of the 'earlier' Kayanian narrative in the Shahnameh actually occurred *later* (132 BC-600 AD), and the 'later' Achaemenid narrative actually occurred *earlier* (550-350 BC), comes in the form of the many 'Kayanian anachronisms' in the Shahnameh text. Such as, for example:
- The use of a 'Rumi' (Roman) helmet during the Kayanian era (p.191, 182), whereas Darab (Darius), supposedly later, battles with Greece (p.448)
- The Alans being named 'lords of the Steppe' (p.374), that did not occur until around 200 BC at the earliest
- The mother of Esfandiyar (supposedly Bahram AKA Cyrus the Great's predecessor on the Iranian throne, in reality the last king of the 'new narrative' before it jumps back to Cyrus) is called 'the daughter of Caesar' (p.391)
- That same Esfandiyar and his predecessor Vishtaspa fight against 'Arjasp', who now rules in Turan (p.373). The Yashts (p.117) identify Arjasp as a leader of the Huns: "That I may put to flight the (H)yaona murderer, Areaspa...". These Chionite (Red) Huns featured in Transoxianan history only around C.50 BC-400 AD. So this interaction is totally impossible for a pre-Cyrus date Vishtaspa and Esfandiyar, but entirely in keeping with the Kayanians as the Arsacids, with a dating at the end of the Arsacid era (C.0 BC). Arjasp's appearance with that of the Huns in the Yashts also clearly shows that some parts of the Yashts were added no earlier than 50 BC (as also in the case of their mentions of Afrasiab)

503

It should be stated up front that the dating of Zoroaster is one of the knottiest problems in world history and is unlikely to be resolved in this discussion. Nevertheless, it is a discussion worth having, because the new information about the identity of the Kayanians throws significant light on the Zoroaster dating controversy. The battle lines of this debate were drawn during the 20th Century, with two main schools of thought:

<u>1) Zoroaster lived and taught approximately 650 BC</u>
This is the conventional, argued to be the 'sensible', dating, the provisional dating we ascribed earlier, for the conventional reasons. Some of its proponents were:

Henning (1951)[2]
Gershevitch (1995)[3]

<u>2) Zoroaster lived and taught significantly earlier than this, earlier than 1000 BC</u>
This is a view increasingly put forward by academics looking at other, disparate disciplines and sources that call into question whether the 'awareness' of Zoroaster testified to by them could have been so late. Some of its proponents were:

Boyce (1955)[4], Henning's student
Nyberg (1937)[5]

---

[2] Henning
[3] Gershetitch
[4] Boyce, 1955 and 1984
[5] Nyberg

The Vistaspa Question

The question becomes, *at what exact point*, in the Shahnameh's narrative (see p.227) does it jump backwards in time? Is it:

a) Before Kay Lohrasp, therefore the reigns of Lohrasp, Vistaspa (Gostasp) and Esfandiyar are 'attached' to the *beginning* of the (later in the narrative but earlier in history) Achaemenid portion of the Bundahisn/Shahnameh's narrative ('the narrative'). Or

b) After Esfandiyar and before Kay Bahman, therefore the above Kings are 'attached' to the *end* of the (earlier in the narrative but later in history) Kayanian (Arsacid/Sasanian) portion of the narrative?

Aside from this having some effect on the identity of Cyrus the Great in the narrative (if (a), Cyrus is probably Vistaspa, if (b), Cyrus is probably Kay Bahman), this has great significance for the discussion of the dating of Zoroaster.

This is because of the contemporary relationship between Vistaspa and Zoroaster[6].

To wit: if a) is true, there is still a possibility that Vistaspa and therefore Zoroaster lived around 650 BC. But if b) is true, that is extremely unlikely if not impossible.

This is because if the dynastic, 'King' Vistaspa of the Shahnameh was part of the 'late' history, he would have lived around the time of Christ, and this is much too late for this Vistaspa to have been a contemporary of Zoroaster, because the figure of Zoroaster appears in historical records as early as 400 BC[7]

---

[6] Vishtaspa is known from the Gathas and subsequent Avesta as the original patron or supporter of Zoroaster and his teachings (Gathas, p.22, 142, 185)

[7] For example in Plato and Xanthus (both writing C. 400 BC). Plato in Alcibiades 1 calls Zoroaster 'the son of Oromasus' (Plato, vol.2, p.488). For the Xanthus quote, see below. Countering this is the notable fact that Herodotus, writing a generation earlier, who discusses the Medo-Persian Empire extensively, makes not one mention of Zoroaster nor Zoroastrianism. He only states that "The customs

That date might seem to indicate that the conventional dating is accurate. But we must remember that our main reason for arriving at that date is because of Vistaspa. If this Vistaspa, the dynastic, political Vistaspa of the Shahnameh, lived hundreds of years later, that reason falls away, and the question of Zoroaster's antiquity is once again 'open'. And there are many other evidences that come into play that suggest a more ancient dating, as we shall see.

Arguing against the 'dropping' of the 7th-6th Century BC dating of Vistaspa are the somewhat anomalous statements of Herodotus regarding one 'Hystaspes', whom he (generally) states was the father of Darius[8]. This would seem to relate quite well to the Shahnameh's 'Vistaspa' being an Iranian ruler closely preceding Darius. Oddly he also later states that in Darius' army: "The Bactrians and the Sacae had for leader Hystaspes, the son of Darius and of Atossa, the daughter of Cyrus."[9] This confusion (i.e. Hystaspes now as the son of Darius not his father) may be merely a typo or a symptom of the ambiguity resulting from the obfuscation of the ugly truth about Darius's incestuous dynastic parentage (for example if Atossa is Humay). But the reference to Hystaspes being 'leader' of the Bactrians and Sacae certainly places Hystaspes – possibly Vistaspa – in a role of local leadership in Bactria, around this time. Perhaps as some kind of 'under-King',

---

which I know the Persians to observe are the following: they have no images of the gods, no temples nor altars, and consider the use of them a sign of folly. This comes, I think, from their not believing the gods to have the same nature with men, as the Greeks imagine. Their wont, however, is to ascend the summits of the loftiest mountains, and there to offer sacrifice to Jupiter, which is the name they give to the whole circuit of the firmament. They likewise offer to the sun and moon, to the earth, to fire, to water, and to the winds. These are the only gods whose worship has come down to them from ancient times. At a later period they began the worship of Urania, which they borrowed from the Arabians and Assyrians. Mylitta is the name by which the Assyrians know this goddess, whom the Arabians call Alitta, and the Persians Mitra." (Herodotus, p.61)

However this can perhaps be attributed to Greek lack of awareness of monotheism. For example, Darius is discussed at length by Herodotus, and we know from Darius's monumental inscriptions that he did indeed know of and worship Ahura Mazda.

[8] Herodotus, p.81,92-93, 208, 216, 219
[9] Herodotus, p.455

renowned in 'Iran' (and therefore featuring in the Shahnameh) but not so much in the Empire as a whole.

Herodotus' contribution muddies the idea that Vistaspa/Hystaspes was part of the later grouping (and also the attribution of this Hystaspes as a very ancient figure as other Greek sources might suggest, see later) that might otherwise be very persuasive.

The reason being that there are also good reasons to think that 'this' (i.e. kingly) Vistaspa was part of the later grouping. In particular the well-attested role of Vistaspa in fighting against the 'Hyaona', who have been well identified as the Chionite Huns, and their leader 'Arjasp'. This is attested both in the Shahnameh[10] and in no less distinguished an authority than the Yashts[11] and is integral to and inseparable from the 'story' of Vistaspa in the Shahnameh. The Chionites took over the territory of 'Turan' and invaded Bactria around 50 BC[12]. This part of the narrative then would make perfect sense as following on from the Kayanian/Arsacid cycle that covered the period 200-0 BC.

Is this enough to 'sever' Vistaspa from the earlier pre-Achaemenid section of the Shahnameh? And if so are we then free to consider 'this' Vistaspa (he of the Shahnameh, often known as 'Gostasp') as a *wholly different person* from the Vistaspa featured in the Gathas themselves, the foundation texts of Zoroastrianism, as one of its first friends and supporters? It is notable that the Gathas' Vistaspa does not appear to be such a political leader, rather simply a disciple or convert of Zoroaster's, even a holy man, but by the time of the writing of the Yashts, as part of the 'renewal' of Zoroastrianism from around the time of Christ, Vistaspa has been converted into a military Prince, as he would appear in the Bundahisn and Shahnameh, fighting against the enemies of Iran

---

[10] Shahnameh book, p.369-70; 754
[11] Yashts, p.117
[12] The Chionites, attacking with their 'Chinese cavalry' (Shahnameh, p.373) appear to have co-ruled Transoxiana with the Kushans from around 50 BC-0 BC, with the Hunnic push from the north a motivating factor in the Kushans' expansion into India. One tradition has Arjasp as Afrasiab's grandson (Tafażżoli)

contemporary with that very period of revival, the Chionites, suggesting that this later, warrior Vistaspa, was *also* a 'champion', this time a military one, of Zoroastrianism, one indeed connected with that very revival. This could certainly account for some of the confusion. But what of Herodotus' statements? Could there be *three* Vistaspas? A Gathic one, an Achaemenid one and a Hun-fighting one?

This confusion, in particular the firm identification of at least one Vistaspa as contemporary with the Chionite invasion of Bactria C.50 BC, entitles us to look at the significant evidence for the presence of Zoroaster in history *before* 650 BC, and arguably even before 1000 BC.

Evidence for a pre-1000 BC Zoroaster

1) The 'fire temple' at Gonur.

Viktor Sarianidi's discovery of 'BMAC' sites in the Turkmenistan desert include sites that have been well dated to around 2000 BC. These include a 'fire temple' at the main 'Gonur Depe' site[13]. This is evidence that some kind of Zoroastrian-style fire fixation was present in Iran in super-antiquity.

However, this does not necessarily mean that Zoroaster himself was involved. Certainly worship of 'Ahura Mazda' (often under the single name 'Ahura' or 'Asura', by whom the Iranians more or less meant 'God') existed from this time. Whether or not this means Zoroaster's religious reforms and codification had occurred yet is unclear[14]. Similarly, it is possible that fire had some spiritual significance to the Indo-Iranians and/or BMAC residents prior to Zoroaster. Nevertheless, it is circumstantial evidence.

---

[13] Sarianidi, 2008, p.60-61

[14] Forms of Ahura Mazda are attested in records of the Assyrian Emperor Ashurbanipal (C.630 BC) and possibly as early as 1760 BC in Babylonian documents relating to the conquering Kassites (Boyce, 1975, vol.1, p.14)

2) The mentions of one 'Hystaspes' in Greek sources

Lactantius (C.250 AD) refers to and explicitly cites Hystaspes, a very ancient king of Media, as the author of an apocalyptic dream which foretold the ultimate extinction of sinners and the end of the world[15]. Note: 'very ancient'

Ammianus Marcellinus[16] tells us that "To this science, derived from the sacred lore of the Chaldaeans, in ages long past the Bactrian Zoroaster made many contributions, and after him the wise king Hystaspes". While Ammianus calls Vistaspa/Hystaspes a 'King', he also adds the details:
   a) in ages long past
   b) Zoroaster was a Bactrian

3) The associations with Shem.

As has frequently been mentioned, Josephus tells us that Bactria was founded by Shem's son Gether/Gather[17]. This is intriguing information, because Bactria is famously one of the 16 perfect lands of the Avesta, the homelands of the (Japhetic) Aryans. How then is this Shemite involved? Very early in time, perhaps 2000 BC or even earlier, a BMAC city 'Dashly' was established on the Oxus, near the site of what would later become the Bactrian capital city of Balkh (AKA Bactra).

Meanwhile, the hard drinking, hard fighting Aryans of the Bactrian region were at some point converted to a legalistic, monotheistic and self-reflective religious order, Zoroastrianism, of a character that is extremely Semitic in substance and practice. Its affect on the Aryans can perhaps be gauged somewhat by the comparison between the Zoroastrian convert BMAC Aryans and the non-Zoroastrian SIIVA Aryans of India (who either fell away from Zoroastrianism or Asura-worship or its spread did not reach

---

[15] Lactantius, vol.1, p.465, 469; vol.2, p.162
[16] Ammianus Marcellinus, vol.2, p.367
[17] Josephus, vol.4, p.71

them). In other words, Aryans without Zoroastrianism fell towards idolatry, tribalism and superstition. Whereas those with it, in the north around BMAC and what would become Iran, retained some notion of 'God' and with it justice, law and humility.

The point being that quite possibly or even probably, the Zoroastrian influence was a 'foreign' one, one quite possibly brought in by a non-Aryan outsider, and very possibly a Shemite one at that, because of the decidedly Shemite preoccupations of much of Zoroastrian teaching, particularly in its early, 'Gathic' form. Possibly this was from the West, after the founding of Arya by Dionysius.

The (medieval) 'Book of Zoroaster' tells us that Zoroaster was not from Bactria, but arrived there from somewhere else and made it his home[18]. It describes Zoroaster arriving at Balkh and meeting and befriending Vistaspa (here now endowed with his possibly later-added royal status as no less than 'King of Earth').

All of this raises the possibility that Zoroaster was a Shemite, and possibly of the lineage described by Josephus as descending from Shem through his son Gather. The 'Vistaspa' of the Gathas, then, was potentially the first Iranian (or Indo-European) who received the Shemite teaching of Zoroaster.

But there's more to this Shemite connection:

Moses of Khorene expands somewhat on Josephus, telling us[19] that one of Shem's youngest sons, 'Tarban' "dwelt for a few days on the confines of Bactria, and one of his sons remained there...and the district is called Zaruand up to now."[20]

---

[18] Book of Zoroaster, p.490, 498-499
[19] From "a book about Xisut'ra [Noah] and his sons that now can nowhere be found, in which, they say, is the following account..." Moses of Khorene, p.79
[20] Although it is possible that this reference is confusing an area of Armenia with Bactria

Moses also tells us that Shem was known in the 'eastern regions' as 'Zrvan'[21]. Zurvanism is a form of Zoroastrianism, dealing with the fundamental *source* of both Ahura Mazda (i.e. the 'God' of Zoroastrianism) and Ahriman (the 'devil' of Zoroastrianism), with that source being a prior, pre-existing 'Father' of both: 'Time' (Zurvan); a name quite possibly alluding to Shem's great antiquity as a Patriarch, i.e. 'Oldest One'. (Cf. Greek 'Cronus' (Noah), also meaning 'Time'.)

Moses, quoting Berossus, also tells us[22] that "when they [Shem, Ham and Japheth] had divided the whole whole world under their dominion...Zrvan prevailed and ruled over the other two." Then Moses continues (without Berossus): "Zradasht, the magus and king of the Bactrians, who are the Medes [Nb. this throwaway statement is in contrast to the general impression that Bactria was founded by Shemites, but see later], said that he [Zrvan/Shem] was the origin and father of the gods."

Another Shemite influence has been pointed out by La Couperie, who notes that Shemite Elam/Susiana (to the South-West of Iran, where 'Persia' would eventually be) was the homeland of the 'Bak' peoples:

"It is in this region that the ethnic *Bak*, name of the tribes which went to N. W. China, was in existence and was best preserved, e.g. Bakhdi (Bactra), Bakhtan, Bakthyari, Bagdad, Bagistan (Bag or Bak+stan,) i.e., land of Bak, Bak mes nagi, i.e., country of the Baks."[23]

La Couperie believed these Baks were the founders of China, who apparently founded Bactria on the way.

All of this strongly associates Bactria, at a very early date, with a Shemite influence, possibly of Zoroaster, or one of his kinsmen.

---

[21] Moses of Khorene, p.80
[22] Ibid, p.78
[23] La Couperie, p.26

As per the various sources, a Shemite settled in Bactria, founded Bactria and Zoroaster is described as 'king of the Bactrians'. The point being that for Bactria, that we know was a very early part of BMAC, to have had much of an existence *prior* to this Shemite influence, would make these strong statements about Bactria's founding highly nonsensical. Therefore, it would seem that this Shemite influence was very early. Of course, it is possible that Gether, Tarban or some other Shemite helped found Bactria in far ancient antiquity, and that his distant descendant Zoroaster grew up there and became a religious holy man. However, this does not fit with the descriptions of Zoroaster *himself* arriving at Balkh/Bactria as a stranger[24]. All of this connotes that it is hard not to see Zoroaster as being involved somehow in this very early formation of Bactria, perhaps being identical with 'Gather', or a close descendant, and therefore having lived as long ago as perhaps 2000 BC. This would be an extreme construction, but the various Shemite references do make later dates problematic.

Indeed, they continue:

The Book of Jubilees clearly states that when the world was apportioned by Noah, Shem's portion was Asia[25]. In the Bundahisn, however, we read "Zoroaster is the master of the continent of Xwanirah [Asia] and also of all righteous people in the material world. All mastery comes from Zoroaster; that is, all received the *dēn* [i.e. Law or Godly teaching[26]] from him."[27]

This is highly reminiscent of Moses of Khorene's statement above that Shem was "the origin and father of the gods." Such statements begin to suggest that Zoroaster was himself Shem! While not entirely impossible this does seem unlikely, but they certainly perpetuate the idea of a very early post-Shem dating for Zoroaster,

---

[24] For instance in the Book of Zoroaster, p.490
[25] Jubilees, p.68-73. See also Moses of Khorene p.79
[26] Or possibly Spirit or Soul righteousness
[27] Bundahisn, p.155

whose teachings and remit are so closely associated with his illustrious possible ancestor.

However these super-ancient Shemite associations contradict more conventional understandings of Zoroaster's origins. The question of his ethnic and geographical background is a complex one that also involves two other debates: the 'Ragha' issue and the 'Median Magi' issue.

The second tier of the Avesta, the Yasna, states that Zoroaster's 'domain' within the Aryan community was at 'Ragha':

"(Question.) How are the chiefs (constituted)? (Answer.) They are the house-chief, the village-chief and the tribe-chief, the chief of the province, and the Zarathustra as the fifth. That is, so far as those provinces are concerned which are different from, and outside of the Zarathustrian regency, or domain. [Ragha which has four chiefs (only) is the Zarathustrian (district)]. (Question.) How are the chiefs of this one constituted? (Answer.) They (are) the house-chief, the village-chief, the tribe-chief, and the Zarathustra as the fourth."[28]

Note however that this calls Ragha the 'district' of Zoroaster, without precisely naming it as where he came *from*. Nevertheless Ragha is one of the '16 perfect lands' of the Iranians named in the Vendidad[29]. Therefore in terms of the geographical origins of Zoroaster, one might think that this would put an end to the debate. But not so, as the controversy extends to where exactly 'Ragha' was. And there have been two, widely divergent views:

a) (Arguably the 'traditional' view[30]) Ragha is 'Rey', far to the West of Arya, near Mount Damavand, south of the Caspian Sea.

---

[28] Yasna, p.265
[29] Vendidad, p.4-10
[30] Possibly a product of early interpreters of Iranian history failing to appreciate that the Iranians had moved west over time (for example to Persia), and that many of the most ancient Iranian 'lands' mentioned were further east, around Bactria and Tajikistan.

This western (and 'foreign') origin would fit with the above 'Shemite' hypothesis, but it is also supported by the 'Median Magi' theory. Basically the 'priest' class of Zoroastrian society, the 'Magi', were ethnically distinct – they were Medians[31]. So the argument goes that this hereditary priesthood, being the repositories of Zoroaster's teachings down the ages, must themselves have been descended from Zoroaster, and therefore Zoroaster was of the Magi – a Mede (and therefore neither a Shemite nor a Dionysian Aryan).

This is in perfect accord with Moses of Khorene's earlier statement, that "Zradasht, the magus and king of the Bactrians, *who are the Medes*, said that he [Zrvan/Shem] was the origin and father of the gods."[32] This seems to lean towards an understanding that 'Magi' from Media, led by Zoroaster, moved east and settled in Bactria, indeed becoming 'the Bactrians', along with their religion, Zoroastrianism.

Based on statements about the Median Magi in particular by Ammianus[33], James Darmesteter (translater of much of the Avesta) states categorically that Zoroaster was a Median, from and based in either 'Shiz' in Media Atropane or in Rey[34]. However, as previously quoted, Ammianus himself states that Zoroaster was a Bactrian, but this is explained if the 'Bactrians' were simply displaced Medes.

Foltz also suggests a Western origin for 'Mazdaism', albeit at a later date:

"Beginning in the Achaemenid period (C.550-350 BCE), evidence of Mazda-worship is strongest in the western parts of

---

[31] The Magi are named by Herodotus as being one of the original six Median tribes conquered by Deioces (p.47)
[32] Moses of Khorene, p.78
[33] Ammianus Marcellinus, vol.2, p.367-369
[34] Vendidad book, p.xlvi-li

Iran; further east, Mithra appears to have been the more prominent god."³⁵

b) The 'newer' or 'eastern' view³⁶ is that 'Ragha', being one of the '16 perfect lands' of the Aryans, must have been near the other lands, that over time have increasingly been identified with localities around Bactria, Margiana, Afghanistan and Tajikistan, the centres of 'BMAC'³⁷.

In particular, this view is drawn from plain statements in the Bundahisn, that Zoroaster was born in Arya:

"The Dārāja River is in Ērānwēz [Iran/Arya], and the house of Pōrušāsp, the father of Zoroaster, was built on its banks"³⁸ and "The bank of the Dārāja River is the master of river banks, for the house of Zoroaster's father was on that bank, and *Zoroaster was born there.*"³⁹

On this basis others have understandably argued that Zoroaster was born in Arya, at the heart of the earliest Indo-Iranian culture, and therefore presumably was himself much more likely to have been an Aryan descendant of Dionysius⁴⁰. So interpreted, the 'Daraja' River is said to be none other than the Oxus (Iranian 'Amu Darya')⁴¹

Mitigating against this, however, are the inaccuracies in the Bundahisn historical record previously discovered. They call into question the reliability of the Bundahisn's historical information, in particular its genealogical lists. For example, its named father of

---

³⁵ Foltz, p.20
³⁶ Held by among others Darmesteter's colleague H.L. Mills, writing only a decade later (1887) (Gathas book, p.xxxviii, xxxiii)
³⁷ See its placement here on the map on page 208
³⁸ Bundahisn, p.65
³⁹ Ibid, p.93
⁴⁰ One might argue that the name 'Gathas' suggests an association with the ancient 'Gutians' or Goths, descendants of Dionysius.
⁴¹ Darmesteter's view was that this was 'the Darah river, which falls from the Sebîlân mount into the Aras', near the Caspian Sea (Vendidad book, p.xlix)

Zoroaster 'Pōrušāsp' is later identified as being a twelfth-generation descendant of Manuchir[42], who we now know is based on the historical Mithridates I (165-132 BC)

It is certainly consistent with the overall 'romantic Iranian mythic history' theme and intention of the whole Pahlavi, post-Sasanian 'reboot' of Iranian culture and Zoroastrianism (roughly the Zoroastrian corpus written from 0-1100 AD), entirely understandable after the wanton destruction of their heritage by the Greeks and Arabs, to have wished to locate Zoroaster himself slap-bang at the heart of the birthplace of Iranian culture.

4) The Ninus/Semiramis connection

Eusebius's Chronicle Canons[43] (C.300 AD) date Zoroaster (also described here as 'King of the Bactrians') as being contemporary with 'Ninus'. It states: "The magus Zoroaster, king of the Bactrians, is considered important, against whom Ninus fought".

The salient information here is that Ninus 'fought' against Zoroaster. This statement potentially provides another super-ancient reference for Zoroaster. While the antiquity of Ninus is also highly controversial (see the footnotes on pages 9-10), with two schools of thought: one that Ninus was Nimrod or within a few generations of him, so lived C.2000 BC, the other that Ninus was associated with the founding (or 're-founding') of the City of Babylon C.850 BC[44]. But Eusebius also states that exactly contemporary with the Zoroaster entry: "Abraham, a Chaldaean by birth, wears away his youth among the Chaldaeans". This throws the cat among the pigeons because Abraham cannot have been as late as 850 BC, nor even really 1500 BC. Eusebius, then, for whatever reason, clearly believes Zoroaster to have lived close to 2000 BC.

---

[42] Bundahisn, p.188. i.e. in accordance with the erroneous 'reboot' chronology
[43] Eusebius, Chronicle Part 2, p.16/17
[44] This second option is called into question by the statement by Ctesias that his 'Ninus' (probably the blueprint for the use of this name) built the city of Nineveh (p.115), a feat ascribed in the Bible only to Nimrod (Tanakh, p.6).

Eusebius's companion Chronicle Part 1 adds more information:

"After that he [Cephalion, C.0 BC] also gave an account of the family of Samiram [i.e. Semiramis]; and of Zaravyšt the Magus and his war against the Bactrian King and defeat by Samiram..."[45]

This suggests that Zoroaster defeated (and therefore possibly displaced) the 'Bactrian King', but then was himself in turn defeated by Semiramis. However, this narrative, probably deriving from Hellanicus (C.450 BC) and Ctesias (C.350 BC), is further fleshed out by Ctesias, who explains that it was during Ninus's war to conquer Bactria that he met Semiramis (who was then married to one of Ninus's underlings), as it was she who came up with the stratagem to defeat the Bactrians (in particular the city of Bactra), who were otherwise impregnable in their fortress.

Although Zoroaster is not mentioned in the account of this war, it seems likely to have been the 'war against the Bactrian King' and the 'defeat by Semiramis' referred to. This then casts Zoroaster, if he was thus defeated by Semiramis, as a native Bactrian, if not its 'King' during this contest. Ctesias gives the King of Bactra's name as 'Exaortes'[46], but this may have been the king of the city only, not of the whole of Bactria, that might have been Zoroaster. Or, having lived previously, he could have been perceived as its king, as the society was still based on his 'righteous' teachings, in contrast to the besieging hordes of satanic Babylon.

This narrative, featuring Ninus as a super-ancient Nimrod with his wife Semiramis, is a staple that appears in many other texts, Zoroaster also popping up sometimes in association with it. For example in this confused fragment from Ioannis Antiocheni, writing around 600 AD:

"But Zeus, having first given Assyria to his brother Ninus, was carried away to his father Cronus, and he remained there, having

---

[45] Ctesias, p.113 & Eusebius, Chonicle Part 1, p.17
[46] Ctesias, p.118

forgiven him by his father, and disappeared. But Ninos became 'Pean (sic) [and] Semiramis, the mother of the house: whence the law of Persians marries mothers. Then Zoroaster the astronomer also appeared, who was dying in the fire of heaven, saying that the Assyrians should keep his own ashes, for in this way their kingdom would not be extinguished."[47]

Note the reference to Zoroaster being a source for the origin of the fire cult.

5) Eudoxus', Hermippus', Xanthus' and Hermodorus' statements about Persian history

Pliny (writing around 100 AD) states:

"Eudoxus...informs us that this Zoroaster existed six thousand years before the death of Plato, an assertion in which he is supported by Aristotle. Hermippus, again, an author who has written with the greatest exactness on all particulars connected with this art [magic – Ed.], and has commented upon the two millions of verses left by Zoroaster, besides completing indexes to his several works, has left a statement, that Agonaces was the name of the master from whom Zoroaster derived his doctrines, and that he lived five thousand years before the time of the Trojan War."[48]

While Diogenes Laertius (writing around 250 AD) reports quite assertively right at the start of his book 'Lives of Eminent Philosophers':

"The date of the Magians, beginning with Zoroaster the Persian, was 5000 years before the fall of Troy, as given by Hermodorus the Platonist in his work on mathematics; but Xanthus the Lydian reckons 6000 years from Zoroaster to the expedition of Xerxes, and after that event he places a long line of Magians in succession, bearing the names of Ostanas, Astrampsychos, Gobryas, and

---

[47] Greek Historical Fragments, vol.4, fragments 3 & 4, p.541
[48] Pliny, vol.5, p.422

Pazatas, down to the conquest of Persia by Alexander."⁴⁹

These are some startling statistics! Many commentators believe that the translations should read '500' and '600' rather than '5000' and '6000'. But regardless of this, the statements stand that:

a) Zoroaster lived before the fall of Troy (C.1200 BC); even a considerable age before it, and
b) There was a considerable amount of time between both Zoroaster and Plato, and Zoroaster and Xerxes. As Plato lived C.400 BC, and Xerxes reigned approximately 500 BC, the conventional dating of Zoroaster would be only perhaps 100-200 years before this. That is a long way off 6000 years, or even 600.

6) The linguistic and content relationship of the Gathas to the Rigveda

Linguistically, the Gathas (supposedly written by Zoroaster) and the Rigveda are very similar, and present two closely related cultures, fairly recently separated. The question then becomes, which is older? Linguistically, they would seem to be fairly evenly matched. This itself is evidence that the Gathas are very ancient, as the Rigveda has been dated variously to between 2000 and 1000 BC.

Mills, the translator of the Gathas, has this to say about the comparative linguistics of the two texts (emphases added):

"the oldest *Riks* [i.e. of the Rigveda – Ed.] have now an established antiquity of about 4000; were the hymns sung on the other side of the mountains [i.e. the Hindu Cush] as old? *The metres of these latter are as old as those of the Rig-veda, if not older, and their grammatical forms and word structure are often positively nearer the original Aryan from which both proceeded.*"⁵⁰

---

⁴⁹ Diogenes Laertius, vol.1, p.5
⁵⁰ Gathas book, p.xxxvi

In other words, in terms of linguistics, the Gathas are older. However, most modernist scholars, Mills included, believed the *Rigveda* to be older. This was apparently for one basic reason: their content. Mills states:

"I would not call [Zoroaster] a reformer; he does not repudiate his predecessors. The old Aryan Gods retire before the spiritual Ahura; but I do not think he especially intended to discredit them."[51]

In other words, as Mills acknowledges, Zoroaster [i.e. the author of the Gathas] *does not mention the 'old Aryan gods' at all*. How, then, are we to understand that they were the 'old Aryan gods'? It would seem that this belief, that the pagan 'gods' (of, for example, the Rigveda), are 'old' in relation to the Gathas, that in turn, being monotheistic, must therefore be newer, or more recent than the Rigveda, is circular reasoning.

Mills, again in his introduction to the Gathas, continues (emphases added):

"If it were not for two circumstances, we should be forced to ask very seriously which were the older, and to abandon altogether our mention of later dates. Those circumstances are *the absence of the Aryan gods from the Gâthas*; and, secondly, their abstract conceptions. These latter are so little offset with *expected puerilities* that it is often hard to believe that the Gâthas are old at all."[52]

---

[51] Gathas book, p.xxiv
[52] Ibid, p.xxxvi

So, it is only Mills' 'expectation' that super-ancient peoples would *not* have the sophistication of his own revered generation, that they should be 'puerile' and pagan simply because they were older – the modernist 'myth of progress'– that causes him to abandon the philological evidence of his own eyes.

This same circular reasoning is also present in his colleague James Darmesteter's introduction to his translation of the Vendidad. Even while acknowledging that the Avesta does not derive from the Vedas and that monotheism came down from the original proto-Indo-Iranian religion[53], and that 'the change took place, not in Iran, but in India'[54], Darmesteter continues to refer to the 'older religion of the Vedas' and to decide that the Vedic understanding of words (for example 'dev'/'deva': 'demon' in the Avesta but a 'god' in the Vedas) was the 'primitive meaning' from which the other degenerated (in the case of 'dev' largely it seems by his assumption that a meaning 'to shine' was incompatible with 'demon'[55]).

If there are any linguistic reasons for placing the Rigveda earlier than the Gathas, they remain startlingly absent from these comments by Mills and Darmesteter. Despite their clear statements of evidence to the contrary, their understanding of the spiritual development of the writers of the Gathas and Rigveda remains: polytheism->dualism->monotheism.

The assumption that this must be so comes apparently only from the ideology of their era (the 1880s), a modernist teleology of human progress (co-terminous with the then-fashionable Darwinian racism) that assumes a trajectory from pagan polytheism towards monotheism. However this seems to rest upon nothing but supposition and Victorian evolutionist ideological preference, as remarkably no explanation for it is ever offered by these writers, and the very content of the Avesta plainly testifies that the true trajectory is in precisely the opposite direction.

---

[53] Vendidad book, p.lviii-lix
[54] Ibid, p.lxxx
[55] Ibid, p. lxxix-lxxxxi

The Gathas, the oldest part of the Avesta, contain the *least* pagan idolatry, (i.e. worship of entities other than God, or at least 'Ahura Mazda'), while the latest-written parts of the Avesta contain the *most* other entities worshipped. This also helps us relate the (very pagan) Rigveda chronologically to the Gathas.

While the Gathas only worship Ahura Mazda, the later-introduced portions of the 'Yasna' ritual, the second tier of the Avesta added after the Gathas, repeatedly and explicitly address the following objects of worship as well:

Mithra (traditionally the sun, that would suggest Nimrod as a commonly-understood human 'embodiment')[56]
Haoma (the ritual elixir drug drink AKA the Rigveda's 'Soma')
Fire
The 'Immortals' (apparently the righteous dead who have obtained eternal life)
'Obedience' personified ('Sraosha')
Rashnu (the 'most just')
The *'Fravashis'* of the Saints
Frushaostra (Frashostar), a disciple of Zoroaster

And many others besides[57]

---

[56] The precise relationship between the worship of Mithra (AKA Mitra or Mithras) and Zoroastrianism is another controversial topic. Many such as Foltz (e.g. p.19-21) would argue that Mithra-worship preceded Mazdaism, citing early witnesses such as its appearance on the Mitanni Treaty of 1350 BC (p.20). However relative to the potential antiquity of the Gathas, 1350 BC is in fact a fairly late date. Herodotus states that the 'Persians' only began to worship Mitra 'at a later date', having 'borrowed' the practice from the Arabians and Assyrians (p.61, see footnote 7, above, for full quote). (This would explain a proposed connection to Nimrodian sun-worship – Mithra being a sun deity (note the Mithraic solar disk on Cyrus's tomb entrance, e.g. Foltz, p.21-23), whose festival at the time of the Winter Solstice between 21-25 December is the basis for the modern festival of Christmas), although confusingly Herodotus refers to Mithra as a 'goddess'. Foltz himself however, while convincingly demonstrating that Mithraism was very present during the Achaemenid era (p.21-22), also admits that Mithraism grew in stature under the later Arsacids and only displaced Mazda as the primary deity of the Parthians and Sogdians with the teachings of Mani (founder of Manicheanism) during the 3rd century AD (p.23). Mithraism is associated with contractual binding and with soldiers, and was very popular in the Roman Army during this time.
[57] e.g. Yasna, p.219; 258-259

This huge change in spiritual perspective and priority argues strongly for a period of at least 200 years between the writing of the Gathas and the writing of the newer portions of the 'Yasna'. This trend is dismissed by the aforementioned translators as being the 'old gods' somehow 'coming back' (at which they express some mystified head-scratching[58]), but there is no rational reason to think so. Rather, it is rational to conclude that they have 'crept in' *later*, where they *weren't* present (being not mentioned) before.

When we turn to the Rigveda, we have a text that takes the second tier of the Avesta's numerically increasing idolatry yet further. Most of the Yasna's idols are also worshipped in the Rigveda, with great numbers of others besides. (In particular, as previously discussed, Iranian ancestors of every stripe.)

In other words a trajectory or trend can clearly be seen that starts with the 'one God' concept, and over time degenerates into a 'multi-god' or 'multiple object of worship' understanding and practice.

This means that the likely relative chronology of the texts is that the Gathas came first, then possibly roughly contemporaneously (noting their shared worship of the likes of Mithra and Haoma/Soma), the rest of the 'Yasna' and the Rigveda.

Many commentators have expressed certainty that the Rigveda must have come first because of the lack of Zoroastrian content in it, the rationale being that the 'split' between the Iranians and Indians must therefore have occurred prior to Zoroastrianism's introduction. However, this does not necessarily follow. It is quite possible that either:

a) there was a considerable amount of time after the split before the Rigveda was written, or

---

[58] e.g. Gathas book, p.231

b) the Gathas found their acceptance in only a section of the Indo-Aryan community, and the Indian contingent were not part of that section and so only peripherally connected to it[59].

As discussed, considering the startling similarities between the subject matter of the *second* tier of the Avesta (the Yasna) and the Rigveda, it seems most likely that of the three sets of text, these two (the Yasna and Rigveda) are the most closely contemporary with one another, and that therefore the Gathas must pre-date the Rigveda, so that one of the above two possibilities must have occurred.

It is notable for example that whereas neither Mithra nor Haoma appear in the Gathas at all[60], 'Asura' or 'Surya' does appear in the Rigveda[61], but rarely, either as just another among a number of 'gods', or in woebegone asides, as though it were a forgotten, prior belief. For example:

"Wise Asura, thou King of wide dominion, loosen the bonds of sins by us committed."[62]

and

"Asura, the gentle leader. Where now is Surya, where is one to tell us to what celestial sphere his ray hath wandered?"[63]

---

[59] As discussed, Zoroaster's geographical base and so presumably also his influence was arguably towards the West side of 'Bactria'. It is possible that Zoroastrianism never significantly penetrated the Indian Dionysian colonies. But this is no reason to suppose that the Rigveda preceded it. As we saw, Magog/Dionysius founded both India and Iran on the same trip, neither colony necessarily migrating to the other (see the map on page 221). Zoroastrianism may have been established in Bactria after this colonisation, slowly degenerated there, then still later the Indo-Aryans wrote their Rigveda, following their later incursions further into India.

[60] Though some have attempted to construct a mention of Haoma in Yasna 32.14

[61] As does another cognate of 'God': 'Varuna', usually as a representative of 'law' and often hyphenated/mitigated with one of the pagan idols, i.e. 'Mitra-Varuna' or 'Indra-Varuna'.

[62] Rigveda, vol.1, p.42

[63] Ibid, p.65

Or even used in comparison to assert that the 'newer' 'gods' are now superior to 'Asura'[64], or are themselves 'Asuras'.[65]

In other words, there is in reality no barrier purely from the relative 'theological' content of the writings, to ascribing to the Gathas a greater antiquity than the Rigveda. If anything, rather the reverse.

7) The Apocalyptic internal textual evidence.

Renowned Zoroastrian scholar Mary Boyce believed that the internal evidence, particularly from the eschatological elements of the Avesta and Zand, pointed to a dating for Zoroaster of around 1400 BC, (considerably earlier than most commentators[66]), believing that the tumultuous nature of Zoroaster's 'apocalyptic vision' could only have been birthed during the 'revolutionary' era of the coming of the Bronze Age.[67]

Conclusion
The way seems clear, then, to ascribe a much older date to the lifetime and ministry of Zoroaster than has generally been accepted before.

---

[64] Rigveda, vol.1, p.235
[65] Rigveda, vol.3, p.51-53
[66] Although as discussed, Mills also, when shorn of his Victorian modernist and evolutionary prejudices, dated the Gathas philologically to between 2000 and 1200 BC. (Gathas book, p.xxxvi-xxxvii)
[67] Boyce, 1984, p.75

APPENDIX 7: Who was who in Dark Ages Europe?

During the Dark Ages, an era defined at a wide extent as lasting from 200 BC to 793 AD, a huge number of nations entered continental Europe from the East. Refugees from their previous home as the main occupants of the vast Eurasian landmass, they were fleeing the oncoming Westward invasion of the 'Xiong Nu' – the Hamitic and Shemitic peoples excluded from the Han Chinese Shang-An Empire to their South and South-East by the newly-built Great Wall of China, and known to us as the Huns, Turks and Mongols. The refugees fleeing from these Xiong Nu were almost exclusively Japhetic, and this era, rightly termed the 'Age of Migrations' represents a period in time when the large majority of the Japhetic world arrived, seeking pasture grounds and new homelands, into a Europe already long-occupied by their minority Japhetic cousins Ashkenaz (Germany, France and central Europe), Tubal (Spain and Italy), Tarsus (Spain), Javan (Greece and Macedonia) and Tiras (Thrace and Dacia).

This vast jumble of incoming nations has led to significant confusion about their origins and ethnic descent, with many cultures leaving us only their names and some information about their geographical location and movements. Overwhelmingly they did not write much down and what we know of them is basically from foreign observers. Huge swathes of their prior Asian history has been lost in the great turmoil of the era. Conventional history has also tended to conflate and guess at their origins, further exacerbating the confusion. So let's sort it out. It should be noted that we can with some confidence look to ethnic descent as the main component of national identity among these nations at the time, as this history occurred prior to their significant involvement in any institutional programmes of multi-national political unionism such as Romanism, Republicanism or Communism (*Nb. this probably does not in fact apply to the Franks, who seem indeed to have been a product of this kind of system, nor to the Steppe horse groups, who were multi-national confederacies, though not unionised). Obviously, this is an estimation and a generalisation!

	Existing European Nation			
Biblical Nation/ Patriarch	Ashkenaz (Hallstatt and LaTene cultures)	Elisha	Dodan	Kitt
Nation	Celts/ Basques/ Aquitanians/ Picts	Mainline Greeks	British (could originally be Thracian, but very hard to say)	Romans/ Italians
	Celts/ Gauls: Rheginians, Boii, Helvetii, Gotini, Taurisci, Divico, Tougeni, Osi, Arveni	Possibly Macedonians	Possibly proto-Franks: Salians, Dardanoi, Sicambri	Possibly Proto-Franks
	Celts/ Belgians: Bellovaci, Suessiones, Nervii, Atrebates, Ambiani, Morini, Menapii, Caleti, Velocasses, and Veromandui			
	Celts/ Belgians/ Germans:			

	Tungri: Condrusi, Eburones, Caeroesi, Paemani, Segni, Usipetes; Bructeri, Bastarnae; Elements of Chatti/ Suevi/ Semnones, Quadi, Marcomanni, Alamanni			
	Possibly proto-Franks: Salians, Germans (as above)			

Biblical Nation/ Patriarch	Existing European Nation			
	Tubal	Tiras	Riphath	Magog
Nation	Spanish/ Iberians	Thracians	Scots	('Milesian') Irish
	Possibly Romans/ Italians	Etruscans	Possibly Proto-Franks: Ripuarians	Dacians/ Getae
				Possibly Macedonians
				Possibly Danaan Greeks

Biblical Nation/ Patriarch	Dark Age invasive nation			
	Riphath	Magog	Tiras	Shennong, Heth or Joktan
Nation	Scythians	Goths/ Geats Getae: Visigoths, Ostrogoths	Cimbri	Huns/ Xiong Nu
	Ripuarian Franks	Vandals	Teutones	Bulgars
	Ampsivarii	Gepids	Chauci	Turks
	Ubii	Royal Scythians	Cherusci	Tartars
	Chattuari	'Sauromatae' Sarmatians	Atuatuca	Magyars
	Hermanduri	Burgundians	Frisians	Pechenegs
		Heruli	Angles	Khazars
		Possibly Avars	Saxons	Pannonian Avars
			Jutes	
			Lombards	
			Heatho-bards	
			Old Prussians	
			Avars	
			Sarmatian: Alans/ Roxalani, Iazyges, Aorsi, Massa-getae	
			Svear/ Swedes	
			Danes	

1) Scythians

This label represents arguably the largest grouping that entered Europe during this time. However, their exact make-up has proven to be one of the knottiest issues in ancient history. The upshot of the various arguments seems to be that Scythians was a catch-all term for Japhetic horse nations of the Sea of Grass (Scythian meaning essentially 'rider-shooter'), made up overwhelmingly of descendants of Riphath and Magog, who confederated culturally and often geographically and militarily, but retained distinct ethnic and national identities. The Scythians began entering Europe around 200BC with the Sarmatians, and devastated the existing nations of Thrace and Dacia, (although these nations survived in some form until the Magyar invasion around 800AD). They then largely skirted to the North of the Balkans and went on to contribute to the modern nations of Austria and Germany, and pushing further West probably made up a significant component of the 'Ripuarian' (eastern) Franks, whose name suggests a derivation from Riphath.

It is likely that all the Riphathian nations listed above, as well as the Avars, Alans and Sarmatians, would have been recognizably thought of as 'Scythians' at the time. Once they had established themselves in Europe and began pushing Westward and Southward from around 100 AD onwards so as to interact with the Roman Empire, they were known less as Scythians as they had in the main to change from their previous 'rider-shooter' ways to suit the more urban and mountainous environment. The Riphathian Scythian language is likely to have been similar to modern Scots Gaelic. The Magogian Scythians may also have spoken a version of Uralic or Iranian. These Magogian Scythians seem to have been the group from whom the 'Royal Scythians' came, a faction recorded as having led the Scythians in some form during their time in the Sea of Grass. As time went on, 'Scythian' seems to have also been used for increasingly Hamitic/Joktanite 'rider-shooters' as well, as more of these nations passed through the Sea of Grass, although only when the prevailing culture was still Japhetic. From the time when the main invasion of Huns took control of the territory (around 376 AD), changing it fundamentally to a Shennong or Joktan-led culture, the groups in control are usually referred to as 'Khaganates' rather than being elements of 'Scythia'.

Another interesting study is the place of the 'Slavs' among the Scyths. This group, the ancestors of today's Russians and Eastern Europeans, first crops up in the Russian Primary Chronicle as the 'Sclaveni', a Northern Steppe nation pushed Southward into the Sea of Grass by the invasion of the Goths from Scandinavia in the 1st Century AD. They may well have made up a significant portion of the Scythians from this point until the invasion of the Huns in the 4th Century AD. It is entirely possible, even likely, that the Slavs themselves were mixed-race Japhethites and Hamites or, at a pinch, Uralics. So the make-up of the Scythians through time from perhaps 1500 BC to 400 AD (the 'end' of the Scythians as their former territory was now overrun by Hunnic Shennongites and Joktanites) can roughly be projected as: Scots (Gomer>Riphath) – Iranians (Magog) – Slavs (?) – Huns (Shennong and Joktan). It is also notable that in Russian history 'Scythia' is essentially understood as meaning the area of 'Russia', with the 'Scythians' in many respects seen as being the precursors of today's Russians (therefore associating them yet more with 'Slavs'). In Roman geography of the time such as that of Pomponius Mela (writing in 37 AD), this is also the understanding conveyed, with 'Scythia' extending to the top of what we would call 'Russia' reaching his version of the Arctic Sea, that he calls the 'Scythian Ocean'[1]. However it should be said that this only conveyed the limited understanding of the Romans; as in many other parts of his geography the labels only go so far as the Roman awareness of the world

---

[1] Pomponius Mela, p.37

extended. So for example Mela thought the Caspian Sea extended as far as the Arctic Ocean, calling it the 'Caspian Gulf', therefore it could be said that the 'Northern-most' border of his understanding was somewhere in mid-Asia.

2) Goths

The Goths are an interesting study in that they are Magogites that are less usually associated with the Scythians in that they were not a 'horse-nation' (Jordanes emphatically denies that they were Scythians[2]). They appear to have previously culturally assimilated themselves closely with the Tirassians, with whom they had long been neighbours in Asia in Pontus and in Thrace/Dacia (e.g. 'Tyragetae'). Jordanes claimed that they had dwelt in Scandinavia for millennia (Southern Sweden – Gothland) and migrated Southward to Pontus and Thrace from there. However it is also possible that Jordanes is mistaken in this and that the reverse is true, with them arriving in Sweden with the Tirassians in the 2nd Century BC or not long before, from Asia and/or Dacia (and this is supported by Russian history that has them invading inwards from the Baltic coast at the Vistula no earlier than around 100 AD). Either way Gothic, a well-attested but now extinct language, was a Scandinavian language adopted from their neighbours rather than a Magogian one. This language formed one of the bases of the modern German language. The Goths celebrated an ancient ancestor 'Telefus'[3], and were 'of the Arian Faith'.

---

[2] Jordanes, p.58
[3] Who is claimed to have taken part in the Trojan War on the side of the Trojans (Jordanes, p.66-67)

3) <u>Avars</u>

The Avars have traditionally been grouped with the Hamite/Joktanite invaders, however this is in flat contradiction to the still existing nation of Avars in Caucasia and Dagestan, who are a Japhetic nation (possibly descended from the Goths or perhaps from the Alans/Alanorsi who migrated there ahead of the Huns in the 4th Century AD). It seems highly unlikely that two nations with the same name could both be so similarly geographically and culturally situated. Particularly as Jordanes states that in antiquity (from prior to 1000BC) the nation of the Amazons lived in this area of Caucasia, who were married to the Goths at this point in history. This ethnic/cultural connection between Magogite nations would make sense. It should also be noted however that that Caucasian region is also the traditional homeland of Togarmah nations like Armenia and Georgia, so that both Avars and Amazons may have been descended from Togarmah as much as from Magog. Nevertheless on balance it is probably most likely that they were Magogians.

Note the distinction between 'Avars' and 'Pannonian Avars'. The Pannonian Avars are in fact recognized as being a different group, the aforementioned Hamite or Joktanite invaders from the traditional North-East Asian homelands East of the Altai Mountains in the Amur River basin. As with so often in relation to steppe-dwelling peoples, an earlier Japhetic group characterizes the lifestyle so much that later, ethnically very different nations are often called by the same name as the earlier groups. So it is the Japhetic Avars we are concerned with here, who are very likely Magogian or Tirassian and probably like the other Goths settled somewhere between Sogdiana and the Maeotic Lake, migrating Southward into North Caucasia by the middle ages to escape the Huns.

4) Franks

The Franks are mysterious in that they are unlikely to have been Tirassians because of their horse-cultural identity, their close relationship with the Roman Empire and their differing cultural heritage (they primarily celebrated an ancient ancestor 'Mannus', a son of 'Tuisco' - some argue these could be Odin and Thor, although see later). However their identification as Riphathian Scythians is also not entirely satisfactory. The Scythians constitute a large component of modern Austria and Germany (who populated it in the centuries before Christ, joining its original Celtic settlers, who are the other main component) and the Franks are also involved with the establishment of those nations, but it looks as though the Franks (or rather 'Frankishness') later conquered the Scythian peoples of Germany and Austria for Rome (turning them into 'Ripuarian Franks'), rather than being 'part' of the Scythian influx. The Franks also seem to be less Celtic (Gomerian) than their co-invaders such as the Alamanni. Michael the Syrian in his enormous compendium of history, the 'Chronicle', states plainly that the Franks were Edomites, descended from Esau![4]

In fact, further investigation reveals evidence that 'Franks' was more of a cultural than an ethnic concept: Procopius describes it as simply the new name for Germans[5], with 'Germans' (see below) meaning to the Romans primarily 'Rhineland Celts or Scythians' rather than 'Scandinavians'. 'Franks' therefore would seem to have meant something like 'Romanised Germans', that ethnically would similarly have been a mix between Celts, Scythians and Italians/Romans, from many centuries of intermarrying and hostages being brought up within the Empire, indeed remarkably similar ethnically to today's French. They seem to have 'originated' or rather are first described as living in what is now Belgium and to have

---

[4] Chronicle of Michael the Syrian (C.1150 AD), p.16
[5] Procopius (C.552 AD), vol.2, p.23

emerged from within the Empire as it withdrew, rather than having entered from without (Gregory of Tours states that they 'came from Pannonia'[6]), so that they were not a 'nation' so to speak, but rather a semi-ethnic but mostly geographic element of ex-Roman subsidiaries, clients and foederati, an emphatically Rome-oriented, mostly political construct. In other words a faction of the Empire.

Their appearance as 'defenders of the Rhine' unsuccessfully attempting to stop the famous crossing of the river by Vandals, Alans and others in 405/6 backs this up, and also arguably precludes their membership in this Rhine-crossing 'Suevi' faction – see below. Also many of the earliest attested Franks are in fact Roman Generals like Richimer and Aegidius. Therefore it looks like the Franks did not in fact exist as a non-Roman entity, they were merely a regional successor state to the Romans. Hence the lack of a distinct 'national' history pre-dating their appearance around 388 AD (when they invaded the Roman Province of Germany under Genobaud, Marcomer and Sunni[7]). The attempt to make them one of the Dark Age invading nations (rather than the name for the left behind, culturally Roman and semi-Roman peoples of Northern Gaul) appears in this light to be almost deliberately misleading, as they share almost no national distinctives, other than that their Kings had long hair[8]. In the light of this evidence it is probable that they

---

[6] Gregory of Tours, p.80. This is today's western Hungary, eastern Austria and east of northern Italy, on the west bank of the Danube. Notable in that it means the 'Franks' started off on the Roman side of 'Germania', invading into it, not the other way around. Pannonia was 'Romanised' in the 2nd Century BC.

[7] Gregory of Tours, p.120

[8] The sole source for a national origin story for the Franks is the 'Liber Historiae Francorum', that has them as refugee Trojans who became mercenaries for Valentinian (C.364-375 AD, who it says named them 'Franks') before turning against him and moving to Belgium. However there are a number of holes in this story, such as its confusion between Pannonia (in today's western Hungary) and the Maeotian Swamp (Sea of Azov), and the total lack of any history between the Trojan era and the Dark Ages, that suggests a later Roman invention of this story

were not a product of recent Eastern immigration at all, but rather only of cultural mixing between Italy/ the Roman Empire and the previous inhabitants of Gaul, the Gauls. Their Celtic element, often downplayed, is highlighted by their first appearance during the campaign of the Roman Imperial pretender Maximus (388 AD), a decidedly Celtic figure[9], although in fact they seem to have sided against him.

So, the Frankish 'nation' was largely a non-ethnic construct manufactured by the Romans, from ex-Roman foederati and dependents, as the Roman Empire collapsed in Europe, as a successor state, made up mainly of mixed Javanic/Gomeran Celtic peoples[10] In light of this, the transmission of the information relating to the Trojan colony of 'Sicambria' via the Franks (in the Liber Historiae Francorum[11]) is unusual. The Frank's fundamentally Roman cultural leaning can be seen from the repetition of Rome's own 'Aeneas' story in the same narrative. But clearly there was a tradition preserved by someone either of the Scandinavian experience after the Trojan War, or of another group that came west from Cimmeria, presumably at or after the time of the Scythian invasions in the 8th Century BC, into Europe around the Danube and Pannonia (today's western Hungary), blending with the Romanised Celts there in the melting pot that would become the proto-Franks, while retaining this memory[12]. And indeed, one of these proto-Frank groups that settled in Belgium along with other 'Germans' (as the Romans called them[13]) such as the Tuncteri, Tungrians and Salians, was known as the 'Sicambri'.

---

to give some national substance to this key Foederati group that were supporting Roman interests.

[9] Gregory of Tours, p.120

[10] Often synonymous with both Pannonian 'Isataevones' and the original 'Germans', see below

[11] p.23

[12] As discussed the Liber Historiae Francorum text provides virtually no information connecting the founding of 'Sicambria' with the later Franks

[13] See 'Germans' below.

It is suggested that this Trojan tradition may have come through the Pannonian 'Dardanoi', who may be supposed to have been related to Dodan, who according to the Greek and British histories, was the patriarch of the Trojan royal family, and therefore they were aware of the Trojan history. Or, it may simply have been politically expedient for the Romans to try to define the 'Franks' as being a nation, and one that had a Scandinavian ancestry, in order to try to persuade Scandinavians to submit to the empire.

Further understanding of the origin of the Franks as elements of the Roman Empire comes via the title 'Dux' ('Duke'; Latin 'leader'). The earliest Frankish leaders were unquestionably and particularly known as 'Dukes' rather than Kings or Princes, and this became the traditional name for all Frankish leaders that lasted for many centuries. The title first began to be used as part of the administrative reforms of the Roman Emperor Diocletian (reigned 284-305 AD). With the fast-collapsing Empire, Diocletian separated the civil and military rule, naming the solely military rulers of a province 'Dux'. It is proposed that this was the origin of the Franks, as 'Duxes' of the Roman Empire. The timing would fit perfectly as within that same century the first Frankish 'Dukes' would come to prominence during the campaign of Maximus (388 AD).

5) <u>Bulgars</u>
Almost always claimed as Hamites, speaking as they probably did a version of the Oghuric branch of Turkish, it is nevertheless quite possible that, like the Avars, their original ethnicity was Japhetic but they were previously enslaved by Turks and had adopted cultural elements from the Turks so were perceived as being part of them by outsiders. There seems to be a distinct effort in conventional history to identify South-East Europe-invading nations as Turkic if at all possible, when closer inspection reveals the definite possibility that they were originally Magog or Togarmah nations, who had not moved fast enough to stay ahead of the Huns and/or

Turks. If this historical revision is appropriate, it would also apply to the Avars, Khazars and possibly the Tartars. The meaning of 'Bulgar' in the Turkic language is 'mixed', so the compromise is probably that these Steppe unions were all to some extent mixed ethnicity.

6) Vandals

The vandals are included here under the Magogites after Procopius, "History of the Wars Book III" wherein he identifies them as being the same basic nation as the Goths and Gepids[14]. He also adds that they dwelt for a while "about the Maeotic Lake" but because of hunger moved "to the country of the Germans, who are now called Franks, and the river Rhine, associating with themselves the Alani, a Gothic people."[15] This is an interesting connection as it supports Jordanes' strong assertions about the Goths living at the Maeotic Lake, and adds to that area's amazing centrality and significance to the ancient world (it looms huge in early maps!) however it does not help with the difficult question of when exactly they were there – was it only in ancient antiquity and then they moved to Scandinavia then beachheaded the Vistula River with the Goths? (Russian Primary Chronicle says so) Or had they moved from an ancient homeland in Scandinavia to Maeotis, and from there to Western Europe? It is also interesting in that the Alans are called by Mackenzie a faction of the Sarmatians[16], who also dwelt at the Maeotic Lake, leaving it around 250 BC. Pomponius Mela states that at the time of his writing (37 AD), the Sauromatae lived there (and also around the mouth of the Vistula)[17]. These are also called Goths by some sources, who nevertheless insist they are distinct from the Sarmatians. It does appear that Goths of all kinds had a substantial history at the lake, particularly on its Eastern side

---

[14] Procopius, vol.2, p.10-11
[15] Ibid, p.23.
[16] Mackenzie, p.16
[17] p.66

stretching down into Caucasia to the Caspian Gate, home of the Amazons; one that appears likely to have been before any emigration to Scandinavia.

7) Turks

A considerable amount has been written in support of the theory that the Turks were originally Japhetic in origin, specifically being descended from Togarmah. While there is no doubt that the earliest 'Turk/Hun/Mongol' horse-riding confederation that we know of, the Xiong Nu of C.200 BC, spoke a Turkic (not Indo-European) language, it is not possible to rule out some sort of early connection with Togarmah. Although the Togarmah homelands were in Caucasia and today's Eastern Turkey not Mongolia making such a connection seem unlikely, the Xiong Nu were probably even at that time an ethnically mixed grouping of Hamite, Semitic and Japhetic origin. If this is true then Togarmah may have been a prominent Japhetic component of this mix, defining them as different from the neighbouring Han Empire, and therefore being a source of pride remembered among Turks to this day. It seems unlikely, for example, that their Japhetic component could have come from the Yuezhi, considering their hostile relationship with them. As previously discussed, the ethnonym 'Turk' (that may have suggested 'Togarmah' to some) in fact comes from the Xiong Nu's partial adoption in Transoxiana of the reputation of its previous occupants, the 'Tocharians', i.e. the proto-Scandinavians

8) Germans

A note about the term 'Germany'/'Germanic'. This is one of the most misguiding labels in this whole area of study.

a) It is a Roman designation for the land beyond the Danube and Rhine (and to some extent an area on the West of the Rhine), but a designation made largely before the Dark Age invasive migrations.

b) Consequently the term almost certainly referred to the nations of Gomer ('Gomeran-ia'), i.e. Celtic nations, not Dark Age newcomers. This is attested in both Tacitus and Caesar, who write that 'Germans' was a Gaulic name for

541

the 'Tungri', a label for the Celtic, Belgic nations in the Northern Rhine area whom Caesar first encountered there, such as the Eburones whom he fought around 57 BC. Tacitus and Caesar both state that this probably non-Gallic but still Celtic and Celtic-speaking group was the origin of the term 'Germany', and that the 'Germani' were well established there and not recent arrivals[18].

Caesar clearly distinguishes between the Germani and the incoming Cimbri and Teutones invading from the North, including the Cimbrian 'Aduatuci', and notes that the Belgian Germani had had to defend themselves against the Cimbri invasion (and had done so successfully unlike the Gauls). It is also notable that the Germani are stated to have originally arrived from the East (not the North). This is suggestive of a Scythian (Riphathian or Ashkenaz) origin, and sometime before 115 BC. In short, the 'Germans' were Celts, or at least Gomerans[19].

c) Further, many of the Dark Age newcomers now commonly called 'Germanic' with the intention of conveying the mistaken post-Victorian idea that 'Germanic' = 'Scandinavian', were not in fact of Scandinavian descent either, but (generally) rather Scythian or at least Magogite (such as the Goths and Vandals) or even products of the Empire itself (such as the Franks), and that this was the understanding of the Romans themselves when labeling a group 'Germanic', rather than 'Scandinavian'. For example the Roman court historian Velleius Paterculus, who accompanied a Roman expedition as prefect of the cavalry between AD 9 and 16, says that under Tiberius the "power of the Langobardi was

---

[18] Caesar, p.93-95; Tacitus, p.265, 267. Tacitus states that the Germans were the original inhabitants of the country

[19] Cassius Dio also repeatedly refers to many 'German' tribes as 'Celts'. He also states: "The Rhine issues from the Celtic Alps, a little outside of Rhaetia, and proceeding westward, bounds Gaul and its inhabitants on the left, and the Germans on the right, and finally empties into the ocean. This river has always down to the present time been considered the boundary, ever since these tribes gained their different names; for very anciently both peoples dwelling on either side of the river were called Celts." (vol.3, p.269, 381, 383)

broken, a race surpassing even the Germans in savagery"[20]. The Langobards almost certainly *were* Scandinavians, so this statement reveals the Roman understanding at the time, but now little understood, that Germans and Scandinavians were entirely different.

The original 'Germans' were in fact centred on today's Liege/Tongeran (named after the Tungri) and stretched to Cologne, in other words essentially the area we know today as East Belgium. They included the Tuncteri, Tungri, Salians and Ripuarians (before they became 'Franks'), Bructeri, possibly the Bastarnae. 'Chatti'/'Suevi' was a related, catch-all term for the polyethnic group of central Europe.

d) The situation is further confused by the fact that the Romans, having named the area beyond their Rhineland border with the Belgians and Scythians 'Germania', soon afterwards as the Dark Ages began, through to the 3rd and 4th Centuries AD, faced new nations emerging from beyond that border. The Romans (and even more so later writers) understandably called these attackers 'Germans' and 'Germanic' nations as well, not realising that they were not really 'Germans' at all, but rather groups invading *through* 'Germania', from the other side of it, from lands and nations that the Romans did not know about. This Roman lack of understanding, their failure to perceive that these new nations rather than being 'Germans', were new arrivals from the other side of 'Germania' who were themselves as new to 'Germania' as they were to the Romans[21] and about whom in fact the Romans knew nothing, contributed significantly to the Romans' disastrous losses against them. They found to their cost

---

[20] p.271

[21] Tacitus hints at this, explaining that the original term 'German' was applied to the Tungri, then other tribes arrived whom the Gauls also called 'German' out of fear of the Tungrians; then the new tribes, having learned that the term inspired fear, began to call themselves 'German' also. He then lists some other nations, including the (Gothic) Vandals and the Suebi, and states that for them, the name 'German' was 'new and a recent addition' (p.267). Thus the confusion began.

that everything they knew about 'Germania' did not in fact apply to these new nations at all, because they were not 'Germans', and that unlike the recently defeated Gauls and (true) Germans (Tungrian/Belgian Celts), who were indigenous and had had settled structures and an ordered, established society, these new nations emerging from 'Germania' had shifting populations, often didn't know or have relations with one another at all, and were constantly on the move. This later confusion is exhibited by Tacitus, who calls Celtic Tencteri, Goths, Uralic Finns, Scandinavian Cimbri (who it seems from his commentary he hasn't actually seen close up) and many others such as the Suevi, all 'Germans' or at least inhabitants of 'Germania'[22], which, practically, is what was often meant by the term. While noting the sometimes gaping cultural differences between them, he nevertheless is incapable of distinguishing them as being fundamentally different nations with totally separate origins.[23]

Strabo, writing less than 50 years after Caesar, is a case in point. He refers to the Cimbrians as 'Germans'[24] (assumedly because they often came from beyond the Romans' 'German' border, basically the Rhine). But this is only as accurate as his statement that the Tauri were 'Scythians'[25]. In fact the Tauri (Cimmerians) and Scythians were antagonistic nations with very different origins, but 'Scythians' had become an imprecise catch-all term used by GRHF historians who were ignorant of the distinction. 'German' took on a similarly lazy (and related) meaning in Europe[26]. Despite this usage, Strabo goes on

---

[22] p.309, 317, .267, 315, 331. The Tencteri may be similar to or identical with the Tungri, also with the Chatti/Suevi, with whom they were neighbours.
[23] Where he discusses an homogenous 'German' culture, it involves the worship of 'Mannus', the same deity worshipped by the Franks, rather than the Scandinavian deities that would at have included Odin.
[24] Strabo, vol.1, p.445
[25] Ibid, p.478
[26] The distinction between the two, Tacitus admits, deriving purely from the fact that the Scythians/Sarmatians lived on horseback, whereas the groups he was categorising as 'Germans' went on foot. (p.331) This seems to be and was a fairly

to note that the Germans are fundamentally Celtic in character, differentiated only from the occupied Gauls on the west of the Rhine by their being more fierce, larger and 'more ruddy in countenance'[27], that is usually understood to mean red-haired and pale-skinned, characteristics usually associated with the Celts, i.e. populations descended from Gomer, in particular through Ashkenaz. Tacitus is also very clear that the Germans, near universally, had red hair[28].

At the very least, the catch-all Roman concept of 'Germans', that included Celts, Goths and Finns as well as Scandinavians, does not leave 'German' as a national designation at all. Rather, much like the Frankish state, 'Germany' was a Roman creation, in fact nothing more than an administrative subdivision of the Roman Empire. This can be seen from the medieval name of Germany, the multi-ethnic legal construct known as 'the Holy Roman Empire', as well as the title of early German rulers: 'Herzog', a version of the Roman 'Dux' or 'Duke'. During the 19th Century, for various 'Kulturkampf' reasons, an attempt was made to draw a national personality for this Roman province from Scandinavian history, despite most of its population, especially in the south, not being Scandinavian at all. This ill-fitting cultural appropriation led to huge confusion, and not a little self-conscious aggrandising on the part of the consequently insecure German state leadership, with disastrous results.

---

arbitrary distinction, that could quite easily have changed in the course of a few generations, as the Scythians and Sarmatians arrived in Europe. Indeed, Strabo describes Germans as wandering with cattle in a way that is hard to distinguish from Scythians/Sauromatae (vol.1, p.445)

[27] Strabo, vol.1, p.443. He also opines that the term 'Germani' comes from a Latin construction meaning 'genuine'. If this is so, it nevertheless applied to populations in Europe prior to the arrival of the Scandinavians in Jutland. It would also mean that 'German' and 'Frank' were virtual synonyms, raising the definite possibility that this was the same label in two different languages (witness their shared worship of 'Mannus')

[28] p.269. Indeed his description of them is hard to distinguish from Livy's description of the Gauls who invaded Anatolia in 278 BC (vol.11, p.55-57)

'Germany', therefore, is an entirely Roman idea. It is fundamentally an arbitrary imperial construct, a 'slave compound' in fact, that exists only for the purposes of its Roman masters, notwithstanding the many and continued, virulent attempts to promote it into being a real nation. That is why its name is drawn from a Roman exonym, and one originally intended to convey the meaning of a Celtic people at that, as opposed to the character that subsequent observers, motivated by political considerations, have attempted artificially to paint onto it. Those populations that the Romans originally wished to enslave in their compound 'Germania', the 'Franco-Germans', worshipped 'Mannus' and 'Tuisco' but had no knowledge of Odin, confirming that they were not Odinite Scandinavians (i.e. nations deriving from the Danish and Swedish colonies). They were mainly Celts, with some overland migrants, an admixture of Roman, Celtic, Pannonian and Scythian peoples.

It is tempting to see in the Roman invention of 'Germany', (particularly during its 19th Century phase), a campaign perhaps specifically positioned and marketed so as to ensnare and thereby enslave Scandinavians into Greco-Roman Homosexual Fascism. (See also below, 'Ingaevones, Herminones & Istaevones')

9) Lombards

The Lombards are one of the few nations of the Dark Ages commonly painted with the catch-all term 'Germanic' for whom a credible Scandinavian (that is usually wrongly intended by the term) history is present. A great number of these 'Germanic' nations on closer inspection are more likely to have been Scythian or Belgian Celtic. The Lombards however have a few things in their favour pointing to a more authentic descent from Tiras rather than Riphath or Ashkenaz: i) their name is Scandinavian: "Long-beard", at least that is the meaning usual given, ii) they are known to have celebrated Norse ancestors, rather than the curious, apparently Frankish, ancestor "Mannus", iii) while the Lombards are regularly stated as having come from Sweden relatively recently but yet contradictorily are evidenced as dwelling on the banks of the Elbe near Saxony as early as the 1st Century AD, Paul the Deacon in his history actually calls this place where they lived "Scandinavia". The lesser-known fact that Saxony (and the Bardengau, where they were probably based) was at that time part of Scandinavia, not 'Germany' (arguably until it was conquered by the Franks in the 8th Century AD), unintentionally corroborates the Lombard origins as Saxony, probably descended from Baldr or Vegdeg. iv) the flag of Lombardy/ Northern Italy is identical to that of the English St. George cross. v) The 'Heathobards', that could arguably refer to the Langobards, are included in Widsith's comprehensive list of Scandinavian nations as dwelling in a similar area[29].

Having said this, there is of course a caveat. Lebor Gabála Érenn describes the proto-Scots battling with Langobards in Northern Spain around 350 BC. While that work is riddled with inconsistencies and contradictions, it also contains much valuable information and this witness cannot be completely discounted.

10) Marcomanni

The Marcomanni are one of four groups (along with the following two plus the Suevi) who seemed to constitute a mixed-race general 'trunk' of central European nations who are hard to identify as belonging to any specific ethnic group, and were probably political groupings brought together for actions against the Romans across the Rhine and Danube frontier. The name Marcomanni has been claimed to be a Scandinavian word ('Mark-man', i.e. 'Border-man' or 'Border-men'). According to Tacitus and Strabo they were Suebian, a similarly ambiguous group (see below).

---

[29] Widsith, p.195

11) Quadi
    Also part of the 'Suevi'/'Marcomanni' group (Strabo[30] and Tacitus)
12) Alemanni
    Similar to the 'Marcomanni', the name may be derived from 'All Men', indicating that possibly this was another 'catch-all' term for a mixed population. This group came to make up a basis of today's Switzerland and Alsace. They also, according to Walafrid Strabo[31], were 'Suebi'/'Suevi' (see below). Although this identification is not so certain. It is not impossible that they were part of the Thuringian and therefore Saxon/Danish group. The reason for this is the somewhat elastic meaning of 'Suebian'. The original (Caesar's) 'Suebi' were Celts. Later the term was expanded to a 'larger' 'Suebia' that took up most of central Europe during much of the Dark Ages (see below). After much population movement, the label was later retained for a more specific area, the area of the Alemanni in today's Switzerland and Alsace (later called the Duchy of Swabia). These Alemannian 'Suebians' were more likely to have derived from the Scandinavian/Jutland colony because a) they were further west and b) this is the area where the 'Pforzen Buckle' (Est. late 500s AD) was found, containing an inscription in the 'Elder Futhark' Runic alphabet, that is generally associated with Scandinavian culture, although this of course is many hundreds of years after the Scandinavians had arrived in Europe, and by that time they had raided all over the continent.
13) Sarmatians and Alans
    One of the very hardest groups of all to identify, the Sarmatians entered Scythia from the East and essentially took it over around 250 BC.

    Hippolytus of Rome stated that they were descended from Ashkenaz. Mackenzie in his history of the Soviet Union has them categorically as of Iranian (Magogian)

---

[30] vol.1, p.444
[31] Greenwood, p.498

origin[32]. This is somewhat more convincing as they came from the East, 'Central Asia'. However it is still not quite satisfactory in explaining the mixed testimony we have of them. He adds more detail: "The Sarmatians were nomadic cattle-breeders who lived in felt huts mounted on wheels to facilitate easy and rapid movement as they followed their wandering herds of cattle and horses"[33]. Tacitus also says they "pass their time in wagons and on horseback"[34]. Now this sounds a lot more like Scottish culture (Gomer>Riphath) than Iranian. However this is really not enough information to make a definitive statement of any kind about their origins, other than that they were apparently distinct from Goths, Germans/ Celts and Thracians.

Mackenzie also says that the Alans were a faction of the Sarmatians, one of the last of them to enter the Eurasian plain, and one of the tribes of the Alans was the 'Rukhs-As', that may be the origin of the term 'Rus', and so 'Russia', though he says this theory is now discredited. Finally he mentions another tribe of Sarmatians called Roxolani. These can now be understood as the above-mentioned break-off of the Alans, i.e. 'Rox-Alani'. The Messagetae became part of the Alan group. There are multiple intriguing possibilities here, mostly connected with the question 'where exactly did the Sarmatians emerge from?':

a) they were Iranians and came from the culture of Khorasan, Margiana and Bactria, possibly Sogdiana, a group of people fairly similar then to the Parthians, who may have been the 'Royal Scythians' discussed earlier. This is supported by the fact that when they entered Europe around 50 BC they were known for their Cavalry. Indeed arguably they brought the military concept of the 'knight' (i.e. heavily-armoured,

---

[32] Mackenzie, p.15
[33] Ibid, p.15
[34] Tacitus, p.33

mounted lancers in orderly charges to break the enemy line) into Europe (it possibly having originated further East with the Parthians or Sogdanians), although the first record of them having developed this is in 35 AD as mercenaries for an Iberian King by Tacitus.

b) they were Ashkenazi or Riphathian, a group of 'original' ('Scottish') Scythians who had kept their powder dry somewhere East of the Caspian, again probably Sogdiana (that has been called the homeland of the Scythians before), and were now migrating West ahead of the Huns (but this is quite early for that movement)

c) They could even be elements of the 'Great Yuezhi', although again, the Yuezhi did not start losing wars to the Huns/Xiong Nu until around 175 BC, so it is hard to understand why they would be migrating West so early. Support for this connection is the name of a group of the Sarmatians who settled near Dacia in the Tisza River valley in 44 BC. They were called the 'Iazyges'. Still another, even closer name is given to a larger, more powerful, further Eastern group: the 'Aorsi', that the Chinese may have known as 'Yen-ts'ai' or 'An-ts'ai' and reported as living about 700 miles North-West of Sogdiana (known as 'K'ang-chu' to the Chinese. i.e. Transoxiana)[35], around the turn of the millennium. Strabo is a source for this that the 'lower Aorsi' lived close to the Black Sea and the more powerful group, the 'upper Aorsi' lived further East and ruled over most of the Caspian Coast[36]. This name evidence is close to overwhelming that they must have had some connection to the Yuezhi. Essentially, whatever their ethnicity, this element at least of the Sarmatians was almost certainly part of the Yuezhi network, and their location, dominating the trade from Black to Caspian Seas (virtually indistinguishable

---

[35] Book of Han, vol.10, p.44; Book of Later Han, Section 19
[36] Strabo, vol.2, p.239

from that of the Alans, and indeed, arguably also the earlier Massagetae) confirms this. Perhaps one faction of the Yuezhi left early or immediately upon the defeat to the Xiong Nu and went West overland, indeed they must have left earlier that that. This then would be a third, 'early leaving' faction of Yuezhi, neither i) staying East til 115 BC, nor ii) migrating South to create the Kushan Empire, but iii) going West around 300 BC either from Yuezhi territory or from an already-established base North-East of the Caspian Sea. If so this Western or early-leaving, or non-migrating, more horse-based faction of the Yuezhi fell on hard times. By the time of their leader in Dacia "Banadaspus" the Iazyges were impoverished and at the mercy of the Romans, Banadaspus having lost a war with them (the 'Marcomannic War' in 169-175 AD) after they fought alongside the Romans in the Dacian wars (around 100 AD). Roman protection saw them soon destroyed as a nation by the Goths and then the Huns – although they ended up in the region of today's Czech Republic so perhaps survived in some form.

It is hard to reconcile them as Yuezhi because of their early appearance. However, sources have them as dwelling near the Sea of Azov (Maeotian Lake) around 300 BC. If so they could easily have been a remnant of Tirassians having been connected to the Cimmerians and part of the same network around the Crimea/Asov, who may have left there for Scythia prematurely, a couple of centuries before the main Cimmerian exodus[37]. Although if this was true one would expect them to have a greater commonality with

---

[37] However Strabo (vol.1, p.471) reports that the Roxolani fought against the armies of Mithridates Eupator under a leader 'Tasius', alongside the Scythian leader Palacus. This would apparently have put them on the opposite side of the conflict from the Cimmerians (who seem to have supported Mithridates during the Mithridatic wars against Rome), although this may have been earlier in Mithridates' reign, before 100 BC, so predating the Mithridatic Wars.

the Thracians, whom they lived close to after entering Europe. The Yuezhi connection is more convincing. The Aorsi also did not survive as a distinct group. They are reported by Ptolemy and Chinese sources to have essentially merged with, assimilated with or changed their name to, the Alans ('Alanorsi': Ptolemy, 'Alan-Liao': Chinese) by about 100 AD.

The Sarmatians probably also roamed further north than this, that perhaps takes the discussion into the territory of the early 'Slavs' (AKA 'Sclaveni', 'Veneti' and later 'Wends'). The early 'Sclaveni' were witnessed as occupying the 'Venedic Bay' (Gdansk) area east of the Vistula river (Pliny, Tacitus & Ptolemy), where they may have fed into later nations such as Lithuania and Belarus.

d) They were Gothic, and (more or less) identical with the Sauromatae, a Gothic people that sources do state emphatically were different to the Sarmatians, but it is not easy to see how. Pomponius Mela, writing around 37 AD, states that the Sauromatae dwelt 'beside the Tanais', near the Maeotic Lake. The Alans are attested as being a Gothic people by Procopius[38]) so this does fit. However it doesn't explain their curiously Scottish 'cowboy' lifestyle and distinct, non-assimilatory culture in South-East Europe, an area full of Goths with whom one would have expected them to make common cause (although those were 'migratory' Goths). All of this really suggests a 'horse-Yuezhi' origin, those that had drifted West overland, but having absorbed very many traits of the Scythian lifestyle, such as a focus on horsemanship. This would make the Yuezhi the migrators (to Scandinavia), and Aorsi/Alans the overland, early-leaving group, choosing to take their chances staying in Eurasia, that turned out to be a bad move. The Alans are described

---

[38] Procopius, Vol.2, p.23

by the Roman Ammianus as having 'yellow hair'[39]. While more 'Scythian' or 'Hunnic' cultural elements like long hair and even skull deformation are reported among the Sarmatians, the essential picture (especially Iazyges, Aorsi and Alans) is of bearded, trouser and skin-wearing Northerners.

e) All of this ambiguity about these strangely 'Western' frontier-dwellers appearing out of nowhere adds to the 'Lost Tribes of Israel' speculation, that 'Sarmatians' is 'Samaritans'. Frustratingly, like the Scythians and Cimmerians, they do appear on the scene at exactly the right time for this origin, in the late 8th Century BC.

Much of this confusion is clarified by the Amazon origin story of the Sauromatae: the 'Sauromatae' (probably meaning 'ruled by women') were initially Magogian in paternity, but were later taken over by the vast Westward migration of the 'horse Yuezhi', including Iazyges, Aorsi and Alans, into whose ranks they were subsumed and became merely a component part. This larger grouping nevertheless retained, possibly as an exonym used primarily by outside observers, a version of the same name, that at this point became 'Sarmatians' rather than 'Sauromatae'.

In conclusion then, the 'Sarmatians', understood as being the group typified by the Alans and their various subgroups (as opposed to the earlier 'Sauromatae') can be satisfactorily identified (despite Procopius) as being largely 'Alanorsi' i.e. Aorsi (Yuezhi) who had taken to the Steppe (apparently directly from Tocharia) and to some extent adopted the horse culture of the Scythians.

14) <u>Burgundians</u>

The Burgundians are another group that are very hard to pin down. Their later, better attested, trajectory would appear to make them Franks; appearing at the Rhine in the late 3rd Century and later being relocated to an area within the Empire and operating as Foederati (Roman

---

[39] Ammianus Marcellinus, vol.3, p.393

Hirelings). Later still they established Burgundy, that is still a region of France.

However there are other evidences that seem to suggest that their earlier history was similar to that of the migratory Goths:

a) the best evidence is the name of the island of Bornholm, East of Sweden, in Old Norse: "Borgundarholmar". This island seems to have been vacated by around 200 BC.

b) They are frequently found in the company of other Magogians like the Vandals and Gepids (albeit they seem to be much more Rome-friendly than these other groups – notwithstanding that apparently some Burgundians fought with Attila)

c) It appears that they could have settled in the Vistula basin (from Bornholm) and migrated Southward during the 2nd Century AD with many other (Gothic) nations, through 'Germany' and towards the Roman border.

d) They are featured in Volsungasaga, in the story of the destruction of the Burgundian King Gunnar (who, with the Alan King Goar had set up a Roman puppet Emperor Jovinus) and his wife Gunnhild and their Kingdom based at Worms, by the Huns around 437 AD. The fact that this Kingdom is recognised in Scandinavian Saga history and features Scandinavian names (though they could be anthropomorphized) is further evidence that the Burgundians came from Bornholm and were known to the Scandinavians.

However when this destruction happened, the majority of the Burgundian nation was destroyed. It could be that at this time 'Burgundians' became more a term sought out by those seeking to establish a successor state drawing on the prestige of the previous one, who may themselves have been more Frankish in origin. This would explain the more Frankish behaviour of becoming Foederati and getting involved in Roman politics⁴⁰. In other words the Burgundians, unlike other Northern invaders, dove in to central European politics and intrigue so thoroughly that their distinctives were soon destroyed and they became just another faction of Roman/Frankish politics⁴¹. This is well summarised by Susan Reynolds (speaking about Ian Wood and Walter Goffart):

"Wood suggests that those who were called Burgundians in their early sixth-century laws were not a single ethnic group, but covered any non-Roman follower of Gundobad and Sigismund. Some of the leaders of Goths and Burgundians may have descended from long-distant ancestors somewhere round the Baltic. Maybe, but everyone has a lot of ancestors, and some of theirs may well have come from elsewhere. There is, as Walter Goffart has repeatedly argued, little reason to believe that sixth-century or later references to what look like names for Scandinavia, or for places in it, mean that traditions from those particular ancestors had been handed through thick and thin."⁴²

If the origins of the Burgundians (at least before their destruction by Attila) were Bornholm, it is likely that they were Getic rather than Scandinavian because of their Arian Faith, usually a mark of having been a part of the Getic 'Vistula' settlement around 100 AD.

15) Heruli

Not an easy group to identify, as the information on them is scant. Mainly known from Jordanes' description of them as being the tallest of the residents of Sweden. They were probably Goths, although Jordanes does not explicitly claim them as such (whereas he claims just about everyone else), but their height seems comparable to his description

---

⁴⁰ Although as discussed, quite possibly this behaviour itself made one a 'Frank'.
⁴¹ See also Pliny book, vol.1, p.346
⁴² Reynolds, p.35

of the eight foot tall Goth 'Maximin', who became Roman Emperor in 235 AD[43].

16) Pechenegs

The Pechenegs are one of the later of the many post-Hunnic, Hamitic or semi-Hamitic 'Khaganates' that in turn dominated the area between the former 'Scythia' (roughly today's Ukraine), and the former 'Thrace', (roughly today's Bulgaria), along the North and West coasts of the Black Sea. They followed the Huns, the Bulgars and the Avars, and preceded the Slavs, the Khazars and the Mongols.

17) Khazars

An amazingly central and influential group, as discussed the Khazars are a favourite of anti-Semitic propaganda as they converted to the religion of Judaism around 900 AD, apparently in a commercial and strategic move to allow them to remain a neutral trading party between the 'Christian' Byzantine Empire to their South and West and the Seljuk Sultanate and other Muslim entities to their East. As with so many of the Eurasian Steppe federations their ethnicity is debated and was probably mixed, with Japhetic elements from perhaps Togarmah (a descent from his son Caucus is suggested by their name, though unlikely if early on they warred with the Caucasians and other Togarmanians and conquered them) and Eastern, Hamitic and Shemitic elements from the Huns and Turks, with whom they shared substantial cultural similarities.

18) Tartars, Uyghurs

Another name for the Turks, closely associated with the earlier Xiong Nu AKA Huns and later Mongols, from Mongolia, and to some extent synonymous with them. 'Tartar' or 'Tatar' was generally a later name in this continuum, mainly used to mean Mongols of the medieval era of Ghengis Khan and the 'Golden Horde'. 'Uyghur' is a modern, 20th Century, western/Russian (often linguistic) 'rebranding' of the Turks, specifically those who had

---

[43] Jordanes, p.74-76

settled in the Tarim Basin, based on the name of the (744-840 AD) Mongolian 'Uyghur Khaganate' (empire). The earliest of these groups are usually known as Xiong Nu or Huns. As discussed, they are strongly associated with mixed-race, 'bandit' horse confederacies located in Mongolia, but they also had an ethnic homogenaeity that probably originated with descendants of Ham or Joktan.

19) Istaevones, Herminones & Ingaevones

These are the three labels for the three[44] main macro groups put together by Pliny[45] and Tacitus[46] under the Romans' somewhat catch-all term 'Germanic', as the races facing them in Europe appeared to them to be. As we have seen, 'German', though originally used to refer to European Celtic populations, ultimately came to signify nothing more than captives of the Roman Province of 'Germania', rather than any homogenous ethnicity.

Pliny admits that the Romans were in near perfect confusion as to the identities of and connections between the groups that were or had been beyond the Rhine, and that they therefore termed them 'Germans'[47], after the Celts that they had originally called 'Germans'. Through many mistakes, however, it is possible to interpret their three main categories thus:

Istaevones = Franco-Germans (i.e. the Rhineland Celts and Pannonians who were the original 'Germans' - possibly named after the Roman term for the Danube, the 'Ister').

Herminones = Goths

Ingaevones = Scandinavians (i.e. of the Odinite Danish and Swedish colonies – named after Inge Frey)

The Istaevones are somewhat mysterious as they were very early on a categorisation of Romanised central Europeans rather than independent, external nations.

---

[44] Though sometimes expanded to five - Pliny adds two more categories: the 'Vandili' (Vandals) and 'Peucini' (Bastarnae)
[45] vol.1, p.345-348
[46] p.267
[47] vol.1, p.345

Nevertheless they appear to have had some indigenous existence beforehand. Firstly it should be noted that the Germans and Franks were almost certainly the same people[48], who lived on or just over the Rhine and Danube, from the south-east of Europe up to Tongeran in Belgium, interacting fairly closely with the Romans. Secondly that 'Franks' at least was predominantly a term for culturally Romanised people, of almost any derivation, but primarily from this southern region of Celts, where 'German' was likely to be used for less Romanised members of this group (though it subsequently became a term for all inhabitants of the conquered Roman catchment area of 'Germania'). Thirdly that the worshipped ancestor-'god' Mannus is another factor that joins both 'Franks' and 'Germans', showing them to be fundamentally the same people.

Tacitus lists these three groups (Istaevones, Herminones and Ingaevones) as the progeny of three sons of an ancestor 'Mannus', however:

a) his casual mention that there may have been many other 'sons' corresponding to other 'German' groups, naming Marsi, Gambrivii, Suebi and Vandilii as other 'race names'[49], exposes his ignorance about whether these are really 'sons' of a common ancestor or merely random separate groups of unknown origin.

b) only the 'Istaevones' actually appear to have worshipped Mannus. That the Romans believed this to be a universal, 'German' (in their conception) ancestor shows both the origins of their confusion in calling all these nations 'Germans' and also their general lack of understanding of the world to their north, only the 'Istaevones' of the border having apparently been available to them for close study. This explains a lot about Tacitus' descriptions of the 'Germans', that in fact are mainly probably descriptions of the Istaevones, not the Scandinavians or Goths, whose habits indeed were markedly different. (And as we know

---

[48] Procopius, vol.2, p.23
[49] Tacitus, p.267

were paternally descended from entirely different patriarchs: Tiras and Magog, suggesting the Istaevones were from another sibling, possibly Gomer).

Who was 'Mannus' then? This is a huge question. The proposition that this was Odin fails because of the fact that he was not worshipped by the Odinites. If 'Mannus' was indeed a common ancestor of the three groups (though not worshipped as 'Mannus' by the other two), he could only be Japheth. And this conclusion is backed up by the comparisons that have been drawn between Mannus' father, 'Tuisco' (in Franco-German mythology) and the Norse version of Noah, 'Ymir'[50]. This then would make the forefather of the 'Istaevones' likely Gomer (or Ashkenaz or Riphath specifically)[51], indicating indigenous 'Celtic' settlers from long ago, or more recently arriving 'Scythians' who had moved into Austria and southern Germany pushed by the Sarmatians; but still much earlier than the other two groups, the 'Herminones' (i.e. those descended from Magog) and 'Ingaevones' (Tiras) who would have been largely unknown in western Europe before C.150 BC. These 'Istaevones' were as discussed the first 'Germans' encountered by the Romans, who defined the term based on them, and even those who derived from the Scythians (joining their Ashkenazite cousins), would have been in place along the border by 100 BC.

The later Roman three-way distinction for 'Germans' was further fleshed out (probably by another Roman writer, in Italy or Byzantium) in the 'Frankish Table of Nations' C.500 AD[52], that confirms that two out of the Romans' three 'German' nationalities were certainly not Scandinavian, contrary to the banal Victorian error of equating 'Germanic' with 'Scandinavian'. It calls the three brothers 'Erminus', 'Inguo' and 'Istio'. This suggests that

---

[50] North, p.269
[51] Or possibly, as discussed, Javan, after the early (2nd Century BC) Pannonian group the 'Dardanoi', that could have been connected to Dardan, son of Javan
[52] Müllenhoff, p.163-164, also transmitted with some variations in Nennius (C.600 AD, p.11) and the Lebor Gabála Érenn (vol.1, p.23,157,161)

'Istio' is not Gomer but perhaps Javan, as it lists the nations deriving from him as Romans, Britons, Franks and Alemanni[53]. However, it should be remembered that this entire schema was a Roman one, externally attempting to construct the backgrounds of foreign nations about whom they were substantially ignorant.

20) <u>Semnones and Suevi/Suebi</u>

The Suevi, though ubiquitous in Roman accounts of groups they encountered during the (especially early) Dark Ages, are another nation that are hard to pin down.

They are known in two versions, Caesar's Suevi (writing C.50 BC), a more specific, more Celtic group (the 'Chatti'), and the later use of the term as a catch-all, general designation, that incorporated sometime separate groups the Marcomanni, Quadi, Hermunduri, Semnones, Alamanni, Bavarians and Naristi, with the Juthungi being a constituent group of the Semnones. Later still, the term became all but ubiquitous for Franco-Germanic groups in the south and east near the source of the Danube, and gave its name to the Duchy of Swabia in this area.

This influential group were possibly Riphathian Scythians who settled in what is now Germany in the centuries before Christ. They may have been part of the 'Magogian' beachhead settlements from Sweden at the Vistula river mouth along with the Goths, Gepids, Vandals and Burgundians. Tacitus in his book 'Germania' does label this 'early', 'central' group as 'Irminones' or 'Herminones', suggesting a descent from Magog, but also includes that they worshipped their ancestor 'Mannus'; the same figure worshipped by the Franks, but unknown to the Goths and Scandinavians. In general it seems they were present in Central Europe earlier than the Magogites and are more often associated with the first contingent of

---

[53] Nb. the Frankish Table of Nations is frequently mistakenly added into attempted genealogies much later by subsequent chroniclers, unaware that it probably represents the sons of Japheth. For example in Nennius the 'Mannus' equivalent 'Alanus' comes as a 17th generation descendant of Javan (p.11), and in the LGE 'Elinus' is a great grandson of Riphath (p.23)

'Germania'-dwelling nations to interface with the Romans along their Rhine/Danube border like the Marcomanni and Quadi (who are variously described as being constituent parts of the Suevi), suggesting a Celtic, Pannonian or Scythian origin, before the Vistula Magogians really got moving. Tacitus also points out that the Semnones considered themselves to be "the most ancient and noble of the Suevi" and that in their evil pagan rites they asserted "that it was here where the race arose" [54]. This is suggestive of a longer residency in the area than the hundred or so years at most that they would have been there had they recently arrived from Scandinavia or the far east, and could indicate a connection with the similarly-named 'Senones' Celts who conquered Rome in 390 BC under 'Bren', that would also explain their national pride.

It is notable also in discussing this early, central group, that Tacitus' description of much of their behaviour sounds distinctly Celtic in character, such as the entertainment of young men dancing naked around drawn swords and spears, reminiscent of Scottish highland dancing, and the ubiquitous sport of horsemanship.

Another possibility is that they were Scandinavian and came from Sweden. In this case the name 'Suevi' could be related to the 'Svear', one of the founding nations of Sweden, after whom it is named, possibly connected to or descended from 'Svidurr', the figure (another name of Odin') described in the Prose Edda as being the eponym of the country. However, this can really be discounted, as Tacitus makes it fairly clear that the 'Suiones' (Swedes) who live 'in the ocean' are a different group[55].

They could be Sarmatians, however a Sarmatian origin would not be easy to reconcile with the early date that the 'Suevi' appear. Caesar C.50 BC wrote about them as the main and substantial body of the 'Germans' he

---

[54] Tacitus, p.319
[55] Tacitus, p.327. Here he describes a longship

faced[56], at a time when arguably the first Iazyges were only entering Europe at its very south-east. Although there was certainly contact between the two, with Tacitus reporting that nations living near the Quadi (as the easternmost of the Suevi) paid tribute to the Sarmatians to their east[57]. He also makes this comment about the differences between the pedestrian 'Germans' (of whom the Suevi were a major contingent) and the Sarmatians:

"And yet these peoples are preferably entered as Germans, since they have fixed abodes, and carry shields, and delight to use their feet and to run fast: all of which traits are opposite to those of the Sarmatians, who live in wagons and on horseback."[58]

On the whole, most of the ambiguity surrounding the Suevi can be explained by the use of the 'Suevi' name as a generic term that included many different groups of differing and mixed ethnicity, hence the strangely 'Celto-Scythian' personality of the Suevi.

They dwelt in a region that was semi-Celtic, essentially the melting pot of the early dark ages between the Danube and today's Czech Republic, where Celtic Helvetii and Boii (and Tectosages - Caesar) had recently vacated, but where other Celts still lived. Cassius Dio refers to them straightforwardly as Celts[59]. This is consistent with them (in their other name possibly as 'Chatti[60]') having previously been neighbours with the Tuncteri and Usipi[61] further north-west (where Caesar encountered them), on the Rhine banks. The Tuncteri and Usipi, along with the Tungri, Batavians and Salians, were

---

[56] Caesar, p.85
[57] Tacitus, p.323
[58] Ibid, p.331
[59] vol.3, p.269, 381, 383
[60] Tacitus book, p.306-7
[61] Tacitus, p.309

probably the original Celtic 'Germans' (AKA 'Istaevones') whom the Romans met.

As with those groups, the Suevi were also intimately involved with the emergence of the Franks, a further identification of them with the 'Istaevones'. The notion of 'Franks' seems to have been as a franchise outgrowth of the Roman Empire, in some way connected to the Celt Magnus Maximus's campaign to become Emperor in 388 AD. Two of the first well-known Franks who came to prominence during this incident, Marcomer and Richimer, both had Suevian connections. Caesar's Suevi (i.e. the more specific version) have been identified as the 'Chatti' (later called a constituent group of the Suevi). Marcomer, the father of Pharamond, the first 'long-haired' King of the Franks, living in the 4th Century AD, was a leader of the Amsivarii and Chatti. Meanwhile Richimer, the Suebian general who was de facto ruler of the ailing Roman Empire during the mid-5th Century AD, shares his name with Ricimer (or Ricomer, apparently an early form of the later Norman 'Richard'), who lived during the late 4th Century AD, and whose son was Theodomer, King of the Franks. This underlines the nature of the concept of Franks as fundamentally Roman vassals or retainers, the term likely being synonymous with that function.

There is an argument for a Scandinavian connection to the Suevi, based on an area in Saxony called the 'Schwabengau'. However the presence of Suevians this far north does not fit with its distance from their general area around the Duchy of Swabia, and can in fact be explained by later colonisation of the area by Suevi after its conquest by the Frankish Empire C.532 AD. This makes perfect sense in that the Franks essentially were Suevians to a significant extent, and the Empire was amongst other things a pushback against the Scandinavian settlers by the

---

[62] Tacitus book, p.306-7
[63] Gregory of Tours, p.122

now Romanised Celts (or at least 'Istaevones': Tungri, Salians, Batavians, etc) who occupied the region of Belgium.

This is why the Suevi are never included among the 'Ingaevones' and are described by Tacitus as having Celtic red hair and by Caesar as being 'Germans' like those (Tungri) who first fought the Scandinavians (i.e. the Cimbri) when they first arrived in Europe. Strangely the Lombards, who were 'Ingaevones' are often included in lists of Suevi. However the Lombards seem to have been the furthest south and east-wandering of the Scandinavian colony, and this only demonstrates the generic, mixed-ethnicity nature of the central-European 'Suevian' tag.

There are also many sources who simply identify the Suevi as 'Herminones'; i.e. Goths, and this is the group (of the three Roman categories) that the Suevi are given as belonging to by Pliny. However, an identification of the Suevi as Goths is extremely unlikely, owing to Tacitus' clear delineation between the ending of the Suevian territory and the beginning of that of the 'Gotones' to its north[65]. But this adds further to the understanding of the Suevi in the final analysis as a melting pot, a catch-all term for groups occupying this central area of Europe, as Tacitus acknowledges[66].

All in all, the story of the Suevi is a textbook example of how many previously free peoples of central Europe were corrupted and increasingly enslaved by the Roman Empire. Firstly by accepting their enemies' name for them: 'Germans'. Thereafter having slowly become self-identiying 'Germans', they then became 'Franks', and finally 'Romans'.

---

[64] But like the Vandals are one of the nations that are swapped between groups depending on the version of the 'Frankish Table of Nations' one reads. LGE for example has the Lombards as Herminones (sons of 'Airmen'), vol.1, p.161.
[65] Pliny, p.317-5
[66] Tacitus, p.317

21) Cimbri

The Cimbri are relatively easy to identify: all evidence points to them having migrated from the Crimea ('Cimmeria') around 115 BC to Jutland, immediately launching an invasion Southward into Gaul and the Mediterranean Roman Empire. It also seems highly likely that the Chauci and Cherusci also came from this group, looking at their geographical spread Southward from Jutland. Their movements before then, however, are somewhat more difficult to establish.

Essentially the Cimbri, or a group associated with them, ruled and dominated the Black Sea Coast from the Maeotian Lake (Sea of Asov) Westward to the mouth of the Danube, i.e. Thrace, including Dacia in between. This has given rise to the term 'Thraco-Cimmerian'. It seems accurate, the only issue being where the Cimmerians ended and the Thracians began. Some would see the Cimmerians as the direct successors to the Thracians, and this is probably broadly correct. Although conventional history would contrast Thrace as a fairly ancient state, probably a direct outgrowth of the Troas, but one under increasing pressure from Greece, Macedon and Rome, and having already been substantially Hellenised in the centuries before Christ, whereas Crimea is seen more as a colony of the Cimmerians, who arrived there from Phrygia in the 7th Century BC, having come Southward through the Caucasus Mountains invading Urartu, then Assyria, then Phrygia, so essentially less Hellenised/Romanised (although the Pontid Greeks under Mithridates II moved in soon after the Cimbri had vacated the Crimea in 108 BC).

However this is largely a wish to see the Thracians as having petered out in situ, and a reluctance to follow the clear thread of evidence leading to where the Scandinavian nation spread out to from Thrace: the Crimea, right next door. The Iliad's mention of this colony at the edge of the world previously alerted us to the fact that the Cimmerians were *already there, before* their southern adventure. It may be that 'Thraco-Cimmeria' was only separated into two groups by the Scythian invasion from the east in the 8th Century BC, that pushed the 'Getae' south-westwards towards Thrace, and restricted the Cimmerians to their Crimean peninsula, so that henceforth communication between them and their Thracian cousins was usually across the sea. The Thracians and Cimmerians were perhaps slightly different groups, but there was obviously a cultural similarity and mutual support with a substantial shared history between them, even after this. For example the Thracian King Sparatocos became the King of Cimmerian Bosporus in 438 BC (although this was by then a Greek colony in the Crimean area), establishing a long dynasty.

As we have seen, the term 'Cimbri' almost certainly relates to *Troy*, as 'Sicambria' is attested as being the name of the Don river settlement founded by Trojan refugees after the Trojan War,[67] and it was also remembered by the Trojan Welsh (the Britons were pushed into Wales by the Scandinavian English in the 5th-7th Centuries AD) as their national name: 'Cymru'. Ironically it was also 'Cimbri', (but from the aforementioned Scandinavian Asov/Crimean colony, rather than from the captured Trojan royal family via Greece), who pushed the Welsh out of England and into Wales! This Cimbrian connection may have played a part in the initial agreement between Vortigern (the British King) and Hengest (the Jutish Sea-King) for the English to migrate to the island of Britain C.400 AD[68].

---

[67] Liber Historiae Francorum, p.23
[68] Vortigern, beleaguered by attacks from Picts and Scots, agreed to let Hengist and his flotilla have the Isle of Thanet in Kent (Nennius, p.17, Bede, p.51). Symbolically, over hundreds of years, silt built up and eventually joined the Isle of Thanet to the mainland, and likewise Hengist got the whole island. See also Gildas, p.19-22, Anglo-Saxon Chronicle, p.13

Aside from the fascinating testimony of the English nobililty returning to exactly this location after being defeated and overrun by the Normans in 1066 AD[69], it is interesting to note that the very first book printed in the English language was William Caxton's 1474 'Recall of the Histories of Troy'.

---

[69] Shepard; Saint Edward's Saga

Bibliography

This Bibliography lists the ancient sources referred to in the text in the order of the estimated date they were written down, from oldest to newest. They are named primarily for the original author, as far as can be ascertained. Secondly the specific published volume where the ancient text has been accessed from is listed. Non-ancient sources are then listed alphabetically.

Sumerian King List (Weld-Blundell Prism), written C.1900 BC
Langdon, S (Ed). *Oxford Editions of Cuneiform Texts, Volume II, The Weld-Blundell Collection.* Oxford University Press, London (1923)

Epic of Gilgamesh, written C.1800 BC
George, A.R. *The Babylonian Gilgamesh Epic.* Oxford University Press, New York (2003)

Weidner Chronicle, written C.1800 BC
Hallo, W.W. (Ed). *The Context of Scripture, Vol.1.* Brill, Leiden (2003)

Sumerian Documents, written C.2100 BC-1700 BC
Black, J.A., et al. *Electronic Text Corpus of Sumerian Literature.* Online Edition (https://etcsl.orinst.ox.ac.uk/datclist.htm). Oxford (1998)

Hittite Myths, written C.1700-1200 BC
Hoffner, H.A. *Hittite Myths, 2nd Edition.* Society of Biblical Literature, Atlanta (1998)

Gathas, written C.1500 BC
Mills, L.H. *Sacred Books of the East Vol.31: The Zend-Avesta, Part III.* Clarendon, Oxford (1887)

Hittite Correspondence, written C.1390-1230 BC
Beckman, G.M. et al. *The Ahhiyawa Texts.* Society of Biblical Literature, Atlanta (2011)

Hittite Treaties, written C.1390-1230 BC
Beckman, G.M. *Hittite Diplomatic Texts, 2nd Edition.* Scholars, Atlanta (1999)

Egyptian Correspondance, written C.1350 BC
Moran, W.L. *The Amarna Letters.* Johns Hopkins University Press, Baltimore (1992)

Egyptian Inscriptions, written C.1300-1000 BC
Breasted, J. H. *Ancient Records of Egypt.* University of Chicago Press, Chicago (1906)

Classic of Mountains and Seas, written C.1900-0 BC
Birrell, A. Penguin, London (1999)

Yasna, written C.1300 BC
Mills, L.H. *Sacred Books of the East Vol.31: The Zend-Avesta, Part III.* Clarendon, Oxford (1887)

Rigveda, written C.1300 BC
Griffith, R.T.H. *Hymns of the Rigveda.* E.J. Lazarus & Co, Benares (1889)

Egyptian Wall Reliefs, written C.1200 BC
Nelson, H.H., et al. (The Epigraphic Survey). *Medinet Habu-Volume I: Earlier Historical Records of Ramses III.* University of Chicago Press, Chicago (1930)

Tanakh (Old Testament), written C.1600-400 BC
Young, R. *Young's Literal Translation of the Holy Bible, 3rd Edition.* Baker Book House, Grand Rapids (1989)

Book of Jubilees, written C.1500-100 BC
Charles, R.H. Adam and Charles Black, London (1902)

I Ching (Book of Changes), written C.1000-350 BC
Legge, J. *Sacred Books of the East, Vol.16: The texts of Confucianism, Part II.* Clarendon, Oxford (1882)

Narrative of the Son of Heaven Called Muh, written C.900 BC
Eitel, E.J. China Review, Vol. 17, p.223-240, 247-258. China Mail, Hong Kong (1888)

Black Obelisk of Shalmaneser, written C.825 BC
Luckenbill, D.D. *Ancient Records of Assyria and Babylonia, Vol.1.* University of Chicago Press, Chicago (1926)

Karatepe Inscription, written C.800 BC
Hallo, W.W. (Ed). *The Context of Scripture, Vol.2.* Brill, Leiden (2003)

Homer, 'Iliad', written C.750 BC
Fagles, R. Penguin, New York (1990)

Homer, 'Odyssey', written C.725 BC
Fagles, R. Penguin, New York (1997)

Hesiod, 'Theogony', written C.700 BC
Most, G. W. Harvard University Press, Cambridge, Mass. (2006)

Assyrian Correspondence, written C.700 BC
Parpola, S. *State Archives of Assyria, Vol. 1: The Correspondence of Sargon II, Part I: Letters from Assyria and the West.* Helsinki University Press, Helsinki (1987)

Assyrian Divination Records, written C.675 BC
Starr, I. *State Archives of Assyria, Vol. 4: Queries to the Sungod: Divination and Politics in Sargonid Assyria.* Helsinki University Press, Helsinki (1990)

Birth Legend of Sargon, written C.600 BC
Pritchard, J.B. (Ed.) *Ancient Near Eastern Texts, 3rd Edition.* Princeton University Press, Princeton (1969)

Aethiopis, written C.600 BC
West, M.L. *Greek Epic Fragments.* Harvard University Press, Cambridge, Mass. (2003)

Bacchylides, written C.550 BC
Poste, E. Macmillan, London (1898)

Behistun Inscription, written C.500 BC
King, L.W. & Thompson, R.C. *The Sculptures and Inscription of Behistun.* Harrison & sons, London (1907)

Book of Documents/ Shu-Ching, written C.2100-100 BC
Legge, J. *Sacred Books of the East, Volume 3: Sacred Books of China, Part I.* Clarendon, Oxford (1879)

Confucius, 'Analects', written C.475 BC
Watson, B. Columbia University Press, New York (2007)

Herodotus, 'Histories', written C.430 BC
Rawlinson, G. Roman Roads Media, Moscow, Idaho (2013)

Thucydides, 'History of the Peloponnesian War', written C.400 BC
Jowett, B. Clarendon, Oxford (1900)

Plato, 'Dialogues', written C.400 BC
Jowett, B. *The Dialogues of Plato, 3rd Edition.* Oxford University Press, London (1892)

Zuo, 'Commentary on the Spring and Autumn Annals', written C.390 BC
Durrant, S., et al. *Zuo Tradition: Zuozhuan.* University of Washington Press, Seattle (2016)

Ctesias, 'Persica', written C.400-358 BC
Llewelyn-Jones, L. & Robson, J. *Ctesias' History of Persia: Tales of the Orient.* Routledge, London (2010)

Xenophon, *'Anabasis'*, written C.370 BC
Brownson, C.L. G.P. Putnam's Sons, New York (1921)

Greek Historical Fragments, written C.600-100 BC
Muller, C. Firmin Didot, Paris (1841)

Apocrypha, written C.500 BC-125 BC
Komroff, M. Barnes & Noble, New York (1992)

Zhuangzi, *'Zhuangzi'*, written C.330 BC
Mair, V.H. *Wandering On The Way*. Bantam, New York (1994)

Mencius, *'Mencius'*, written C.325 BC
Legge, J. *The Chinese Classics, Vol.II*. Hong Kong University Press, Hong Kong (1960)

Bamboo Annals, written C.299 BC
Legge, J. *The Chinese Classics, Vol.III, Part I*. London Missionary Society, Hong Kong (1865)

Berossus, *'Babylonaica'*, written C.290-275 BC
Burstein, S.M. *The Babylonaica of Berossus*. Undena, Malibu (1978)

Manetho, *'Aegyptiaca'*, written C.275 BC
Waddell, W.G. *Manetho*. Harvard University Press, Cambridge, Mass. (1964)

Lü Buwei, *'Lüshi Chunqiu'*, written C.239 BC
Knoblock, J. & Riegel, J. *The Annals of Lü Buwei*. Stanford University Press, Palo Alto (2000)

Apollonius Rhodius, *'Argonautica'*, written C.200 BC
Coleridge, E.P. George Bell and sons, London (1889)

Polybius, *'Histories'*, written C.150 BC
Paton, W.R. William Heinemann, London (1922)

Liu An, *'Huainanzi'*, written C.139 BC
Major, J.S., et al. Columbia University Press, New York (2010)

Sima Qian, *'Shiji'/ 'Records of the Grand Historian'*, written C.91 BC
1: Nienhauser, W.H., et al. *The Grand Scribe's Records*. Indiana University Press, Bloomington (1994-2019)
2: Yang, H. & Yang, G. *Records of the Historian*. Commercial, Hong Kong (1974)
3. Watson, B. *Records of the Grand Historian: Han Dynasty II, 2nd Edition*. Columbia University Press, Hong Kong (1993)

Diodorus Siculus, *'Historical Library'*, written C. 50 BC
Booth, G. *The Historical Library of Diodorus the Sicilian*. W. McDowall, London (1814)

Caesar, G.I., *'Gallic Wars'*, written C.50 BC
Edwards, H.J. William Heinemann, London (1919)

Dionysius of Halicarnassus, *'Roman Antiquities'*, written C.20 BC
Cary, E and Spelman, E. Harvard University Press, Cambridge, Mass. (1960)

Livy, *'From the Founding of the City'*, written C.10 BC
Foster, B.O. 8th *Edition*. Harvard University Press, Cambridge, Mass. (1976)

Strabo, *'Geography'*, written C.7 BC
Hamilton, H.C. & Falconer, W. Henry G. Bohn, London (1854)

Dead Sea Scrolls, written C.2500 BC - C.30 AD
Vermes, G. *The Complete Dead Sea Scrolls in English*, 5th *Edition*. Penguin, New York (1998)

Velleius Paterculus, *'Compendium of Roman History'*, written C.30 AD
Shipley, F.W. William Heinemann, London (1924)

Pomponius Mela, *'Chronography'*, written C.50 AD
Romer, F.E. *Pomponius Mela's Description of the World*. University of Michigan Press, Ann Arbor (1998)

Josephus, *'Antiquities of the Jews'*, written C.94 AD
Thackeray, H.ST.J. & Marcus, R. *Josephus*. William Heinemann, London (1930)

Brit Chadashah (New Testament), written C.30-100 AD
Young, R. *Young's Literal Translation of the Holy Bible, 3rd Edition*, p.589. Baker Book House, Grand Rapids (1989)

Vendidad, written C.1000 BC-500 AD
Darmesteter, J. *Sacred Books of the East Vol.4: The Zend-Avesta, Part I: The Vendidad*. Clarendon, Oxford (1880)

Tacitus, P.C., *'Germania'*, written C.98 AD
Hutton, M. William Heinemann, London (1914)

Apollodorus, *'Library'*, written C.100 AD
Frazer, J.G. William Heinemann, London (1921)

Plutarch, *'Parallel Lives'*, written C.100 AD
Dryden, J; Clough, A.H. J.M. Dent & Sons, London (1910)

Pliny, *'History of Nature'*, written C.100 AD
Bostock, J. & Riley, H.T. *The Natural History of Pliny.* Henry G. Bohn, London (1855)

Ban Gu & Zao, *'Book of Han' ('Hanshu')*, written C.111 AD
Wylie, A. Journal of the Anthropological Institute of Great Britain and Ireland, Vols. 3, 5, 10, 11. Trübner & Co., London (1874-1882)

Pseudo-Philo, *'Biblical Antiquities'*, written C.50 -150 AD
James, M.R. *The Biblical Antiquities of Philo.* SPCK, London (1917)

Ptolemy, *'Geography'*, written C.150 AD
Stevenson, E.L. Dover, New York (1991)

Peshitta, written C.150 AD
Bauscher, G.D. *The Aramaic-English Interlinear Peshitta Old Testament.* Lulu, Morrisville, N.C. (2017)

Arrian, *'Anabasis of Alexander'*, written C.150 AD
Robson, E.I. *Arrian.* Harvard University Press, Cambridge, Mass. (1966)

Justin, written C.150 AD
Codrington, R. *The History of Justin.* W.W., London (1672)

Appian, *'Roman History'*, written C.150 AD
White, H. William Heinemann, London (1912)

Yashts, written C.0-500 AD
Darmesteter, J. *Sacred Books of the East Vol.23: The Zend-Avesta, Part II* Clarendon, Oxford (1883)

Wen-tzu, written C.200 AD
Cleary, T. *Wen-tzu: Understanding the Mysteries.* Shambhala, Boston (1992)

Cassius Dio, *'Roman History'*, written C.200 AD
Cary, E. *Dio's Roman History.* William Heinemann, London (1914)

Diogenes Laertius, *'Lives and Opinions of Eminent Philosophers'*, written C.250 AD
Hicks, R.D. William Heinemann, London (1925)

Huangfu Mi, *'Diwang Shiji/Imperial Century'*, written C.250 AD
Xu, Z. *Diwang shiji jicun.* Zhonghua, Beijing (1964)

Liezi, written C.300 AD
Graham, A.C. *The Book of Lieh-tzu.* John Murray, London (1960)

Lactantius, written C. 300 AD
Fletcher, W. *The Works of Lactantius.* T & T Clark, Edinburgh (1871)

Eusebius, *'Chronicle, Part I'*, written C.311 AD
Bedrosian, R. *Eusebius' Chronicle.* Online edition (https://archive.org/details/EusebiusChroniclechronicon/mode/2up). Long Branch, New Jers. (2008)

Eusebius, *'Chronicle, Part II'*, written C.311 AD
Pearse, R. *The Chronicle of St. Jerome.* Online edition (https://www.tertullian.org/ fathers/jerome_chronicle_00_eintro.htm). Ipswich, Suffolk (2005)

Eusebius, *'Preparation for the Gospel'*, written C.325 AD
Gifford, E.H. Oxford University Press, Oxford (1903)

Ammianus Marcellinus, *'Achievements'*, written C.375 AD
Rolfe, J.C. William Heinemann, London (1935)

Augustine of Hippo, *'City of God'*, written C.426 AD
Dods, M. T & T Clark, Edinburgh (1871)

Fan Ye, *'Book of Later Han' ('Hou Hanshu')*, written C.440 AD
Hill, J.E. *The Western Regions according to the Hou Hanshu.* Online edition (https://depts.washington.edu/silkroad/texts/hhshu/hou_han_shu.html). Cooktown, Qld. (2003)

Moses of Khorene, *'History of the Armenians'*, written C.490 AD
Thompson, R. W. Harvard University Press, Cambridge, Mass. (1978)

Gildas, written C.500 AD
Giles, J.A. *The Works of Gildas and Nennius.* James Bohn, London (1841)

Jordanes, *'Getica' (*or *'Origins and Deeds of the Goths')*, written C.550 AD
Mierow, C.C. *The Gothic History of Jordanes.* Princeton University Press, Princeton (1915)

Procopius, *'History of the Wars'*, written C.552 AD
Dewing, H.B. William Heinemann, London (1914)

Widsith, written C.600 AD
Gummere, F.B. *The Oldest English Epic.* Macmillan, New York (1922)

Gregory of Tours, *'History of the Franks'*, written C.600 AD
Thorpe, L. Penguin, London (1974)

Beowulf, written C.700 AD
Thorpe, B. Barron's, Great Neck, N.Y. (1962)

Sima Zhen, *'Introductory Chapter to the 'Shiji''*, written C.720 AD
Allen, H.J. *Ssŭma Ch'ien's Historical Records. Introductory Chapter, Part I.* Journal of the Royal Asiatic Society, Vol. 1894, p.269-295. Royal Asiatic Society, London (1894)

Tonyukuk Inscription, written C.720 AD
Ross, E.D. Bulletin of the School of Oriental and African Studies, University of London, Vol. 6 (1), p.37-43. Cambridge University Press, Cambridge (1930)

Liber Historiae Francorum, written C.727 AD
Bachrach, B.S. Coronado, Lawrence, Kan. (1973)

Bede, *'Ecclesiastical History of the English People'*, written C.731 AD
Colgrave, B. & Mynors, R.A.B. Clarendon, Oxford (1969)

Orkhon Inscriptions, written C.735 AD
Ross, E.D. Bulletin of the School of Oriental and African Studies, University of London, Vol. 5 (4), p.861-876. Cambridge University Press, Cambridge (1930)

Bundahishn, written C.750-850 AD
Agostini, D. & Thrope, S. Oxford University Press, New York (2020)

Anglo-Saxon Chronicle, written C.891-1070 AD
Swanton, M. Phoenix Press, London (2000)

Denkard, written C.1000 AD
Sanjana, P.B. (Tr.) & Petersen, J.H. (Ed.) *Denkard, Book 4*. Online Edition (http://www.avesta.org/denkard/dk4.pdf). Boston (1998)

Ferdowsi, *'Shahnameh'*, written C.1000 AD
Davis, D. Penguin USA, New York (2006)

Welsh Chronicle, written C.50-1100 AD (at the latest)
Cooper, W.R. *The Chronicle of the Early Britons*. Online edition (https://archive.org/ details/chronicle_of_the_early_britons 2002). Ashford, Surrey (2002)

Life of Kartli, written C.800-1400 AD
Bedrosian, R. *Juansher's Concise History of the Georgians*. Online edition (http://www.attalus.org/armenian/gc1.htm). New York (1991)

Nennius, *'History of the Britons'*, written C.900 AD
Giles, J.A. *The Works of Gildas and Nennius*. James Bohn, London (1841)

Pictish Chronicle, written C.1000 AD
Skene, W.F. *Chronicles of the Picts, Chronicles of the Scots*. T. Constable, Edinburgh (1867)

Lebor Gabála Érenn, written C.1050 AD
Macalister, R.A.S. Dublin University Press, Dublin (1938)

Russian Primary Chronicle (or 'Tale of Bygone Years'), written C.1115 AD
Cross, S.H. & Sherbowitz-Wetzor, O.P. Mediaeval Society of America, Cambridge, Mass. (1953)

Chronicle of Michael the Syrian, written C.1150 AD
Bedrosian, R. *The Chronicle of Michael the Great, Patriarch of the Syrians.* Online edition (https://archive.org/details/ChronicleOfMichaelTheGreat PatriarchOfTheSyrians). Long Branch, N. J. (2013)

Poetic Edda, written C.1175 AD (at the latest)
Bellows, H.A. Oxford University Press, New York (1923)

Yosippon, written C.1200 AD
Gaster, M. *Chronicles of Jerahmeel.* Royal Asiatic Society, London (1899)

Sturluson, S., *'Prose Edda',* written C.1230 AD
Brodeur, A.G. Oxford University Press, New York (1916)

Sturluson, S., *'Heimskringla',* written C.1230 AD
Laing, S. & Anderson, R.B. (2nd Edition) John C. Nimmo, London (1889)

Book of Zoroaster, written C.1275 AD
Wilson, J; Eastwick E.B. (Tr.) *The Parsi Religion.* American Mission Press, Bombay (1843)

Saint Edward's Saga, written C.1300 AD
Dasent, G.W. *Icelandic Sagas, Vol. III.* Eyre & Spottiswoode, London (1894)

Book of the Bee, written C.1400 AD
Budge, E.A. (Ed). *Texts, Documents and Extracts, Semitic Series, Vol I, Pt. II.* Clarendon, Oxford (1886)

Abdullaev, K. *Nomad Migration in Central Asia.* Proceedings of the British Academy, 133: 91. Oxford University Press, London (2007)

Allen, H.J. *Early Chinese History: Are the Chinese Classics Forged?* SPCK, London (1906)

Allentoft, M.E, et al. *Population genomics of Bronze Age Eurasia.* Nature 522 (7555) p.167–172. Nature Research, London (2015)

Archibald, Z. H. *The Odrysian Kingdom of Thrace: Orpheus Unmasked.* Clarendon, Oxford (1998)

Asimov, I. *Asimov's Chronology of the World.* HarperCollins, New York (1991)

Babenko, L.I. *Womans' Headdress of the 4th Century B.C. from burial mound No.8 near Pesochin Village in Kharkov.* Archaeology 4, p.59-69. National Academy of Sciences of Ukraine, Kiev (2002)

Banier, A. *The Mythology and Fables of the Ancients Explain'd from History.* A. Millar, London (1739)

Beckwith, C. I. *Empires of the Silk Road: A History of Central Asia from the Bronze Age to the Present.* Princeton University Press, Princeton (2009)

Bloch, E. *Sex between Men and Boys in Classical Greece: Was It Education for Citizenship or Child Abuse?* Journal of Men's Studies, Vol. 9 Issue 2, p.183-204. Sage, Thousand Oaks, Calif. (2001)

Beck, F.G.M. *Cimbri.* In Chisholm, H (Ed.) *Encyclopædia Britannica. Vol. 6 (11th ed.).* Cambridge University Press, Cambridge (1911)

Bodde, D. *Myths of Ancient China* in Kramer, S.N. (Ed.) *Mythologies of the Ancient World.* Doubleday Anchor, New York (1961)

Bolton, J.D.P. *Aristeas of Proconnesus.* Clarendon, Oxford (1962)

Bosworth, C.E. *Arachosia.* In Yarshater, E (Ed.) *Encyclopædia Iranica, Vol.2.* Routledge & Kegan Paul, London (1987)

Boyce, M. *Zariadres and Zarēr.* Bulletin of the School of Oriental and African Studies, University of London, Vol. 17, p.463-77. Cambridge University Press, Cambridge (1955)

Boyce, M. *A History of Zoroastrianism.* Brill, Leiden (1975)

Boyce, M. *Textual Sources for the Study of Zoroastrianism.* Manchester University Press, Manchester (1984)

Boyce, M. *On the Antiquity of Zoroastrian Apocalyptic*. Bulletin of the School of Oriental and African Studies, University of London, Vol. 47, p.57-75. Cambridge University Press, Cambridge (1984)

Brzezinski, R., Mielczarek, M. & Embleton, G. *The Sarmatians*. Osprey, Oxford (2002)

Carruthers, D. *Unknown Mongolia: A Record of Travel and Exploration in North-West Mongolia and Dzungaria, 2nd Edition*. Hutchinson & Co, London (1914)

Champollion, J-F. *Monuments of Egypt*. Firmin Didot, Paris (1844)

Chong, K.R. *Cannibalism in China*. Longwood Academic, Wakefield, N.H. (1990)

Cline, E.H. *1177 BC: The Year Civilization Collapsed*. Princeton University Press, Princeton (2014)

Cornewall-Lewis, G. *An Inquiry into the Credibility of the Early Roman History*. John W. Parker and Son, London (1855)

Cram, G.F. *Cram's Atlas of the World*. G.F. Cram, New York (1901)

Dickinson, O. *The Aegean Bronze age*. Cambridge University Press, Cambridge (1994)

Domeier, N. & Schneider, D.L. (Tr.) *The Eulenburg Affair*. Camden House, Rochester, N.Y. (2015)

Erdene–Ochir, N-O. *Felt rugs, silks and embroideries of the Xiongnu*. In Eregzen, G (Ed.) *Treasures of the Xiongnu. Culture of Xiongnu, the first Nomadic Empire in Mongolia*. Institute of Archaeology, Mongolian Academy of Sciences, Ulanbaatar (2011)

Feldman, M, et al. *Ancient DNA sheds light on the genetic origins of early Iron Age Philistines*. Science Advances 5 (7). AAAS, Washington D.C. (2019)

Foltz, R. *Religions of Iran*. Oneworld, London (2013)

Frier, B.W. *Libri Annales Pontificum Maximorum: The Origins of the Annalistic Tradition*. University of Michigan Press, Ann Arbor (1999)

Gallego Romero, I, et al. *Herders of Indian and European Cattle Share their Predominant Allele for Lactase Persistence*. Molecular Biology and Evolution, 29 (1), p.249–260. Oxford University Press, Oxford (2011)

Ganor, N.R. *Who Were the Phoenicians?* Kotarim, Glil Yam (2009)

Gangal, K., Sarson, G.R. & Shukurov, A. *The Near-Eastern Roots of the Neolithic in South Asia*. PLOS ONE, 9 (5). PLOS, San Francisco (2014)

Gelabert, P. *Genomes from Verteba cave suggest diversity within the Trypillians in Ukraine.* Scientific Reports 12 (1): 7242. Nature Research, London (2022)

Gershevitch, I. *Approaches to Zoroaster's Gathas.* Iran, Vol. 33, p.1-29. Taylor & Francis, London (1995)

Gibbon, E. *The History of the Decline and Fall of the Roman Empire.* Strahan & Cadell, London (1776-1788)

Gill, J. *Exposition of the Old Testament.* Gill, London (1764)

Girardot, N.J. *The Victorian Translation of China.* University of California Press, Berkeley (2002)

Glassner, J. *Mesopotamian Chronicles.* Society of Biblical Lit., Atlanta (2004)

Gluhak, A. *The origin of the ethnonym Croat.* Jezik, 37 (5), p.129–138. Croatian Philological Society, Zagreb (1989)

Greenwood, T. *The First Book of the History of the Germans: Barbaric Period.* Longman, Rees, Orme and Co., London (1836)

Grosswald, M. *New approach to the Ice Age paleohydrology of northern Eurasia.* In Benito, G., Baker, V. R. & Gregory, K. J. (Eds.) *Paleohydrology and Environmental Change,* p. 199–214. John Wiley & Sons, Chichester (1998)

Grousset, R. & Walford, N. (Tr.) *The Empire of the Steppes: A History of Central Asia.* Rutgers University Press, New Brunswick, N.J. (1970)

Guggenheimer, H.W. *Seder Olam: The Rabbinic View of Biblical Chronology.* Rowman & Littlefield, Lanham, Md. (2005)

Hallo, W. W. *The Ancient Near East: A History.* Harcourt Brace Jovanovich, New York (1971)

Hallo, W.W. (Ed). *The Context of Scripture.* Brill, Leiden (2003)

Harden, M. *Praeludium.* The Future, Vol. 57, p.251. Zukunft, Berlin (1906)

Haw, S.G. *Beijing: A Concise History.* Routledge, London (2007)

Heather, P. *The Goths.* Blackwell, Oxford (1996)

Henning, W.B. *Zoroaster: Politician or Witch-Doctor?* Oxford University Press, London (1951)

Hewsen, R. H. *Armenians on the Black Sea: The Province of Trebizond,* in Hovannisian, R.G. (Ed.) *Armenian Pontus: The Trebizond-Black Sea Communities,* p.39. Mazda Pub., Costa Mesa, Calif. (2009)

Heyerdahl, T. & Lillieström, P. *The Hunt for Odin*. Dejavu, Stockholm (2001)

Holden, A. *The Abduction of the Sabine Women in Context*. American Journal of Archaeology, Vol. 112, p. 121-142. AIA, Washington D.C. (2008)

Huggett, R.J. *Fundamentals of Geomorphology*. Routledge, London (2003)

Igra, S. *Germany's National Vice: Homosexuality in Nazi Germany*. Quality, London (1945)

Ivantchik, A. *The Cimmerians in the Near East*. Fribourg University Editions, Fribourg (1993)

Ivantchik, A. & Licheli, V. *Achaemenid Culture and Local traditions in Anatolia, Southern Caucasus and Iran: New Discoveries*. Brill, Leiden (2007)

Jacobovici, S. & Halpern, E. (Producers). *Quest for the Lost Tribes*. Alliance Atlantis; A+E; CBC, Ottawa (1998)

Jacobsen, T. *The Reign of Ibbi-Suen*. Journal of Cuneiform Studies, Vol. 7:2, p.36-47. American Schools of Oriental Research, Chicago (1953)

Jeanson, N.T. *Traced: Human DNA's Big Surprise*. Master Books, Green Forest, Ark. (2022)

Kajuri, M. (Tr.) *Shahnameh*. Razi, Tehran (1850)

Keating, G. & Comyn, D (Tr.) *The History of Ireland*. Irish Texts Society, London (1902)

Kitchen, K. *Pharaoh Triumphant: The Life and Times of Ramesses II, King of Egypt*. Aris & Phillips, London (1982)

Khaleghi-Motlagh, D. *Bahman*, in Yarshater, E (Ed.) *Encyclopædia Iranica, Vol. 3*. Routledge & Kegan Paul, New York (1989)

Kramer, S.N. *The Sumerians: Their History, Culture and Character*. University of Chicago Press, Chicago (1963)

Kroonen, G., et al. *Indo-European cereal terminology suggests a Northwest Pontic homeland for the core Indo-European languages*. PLOS ONE 17(10). PLOS, San Francisco (2022)

La Couperie, T. *Western Origin of the Early Chinese Civilization*. Asher & Co., London (1894)

Laufer, B. *Jade: A Study in Chinese Archaeology and Religion*. Field Museum of Natural History, Chicago (1912)

Lee, Y.K. *Building the Chronology of Early Chinese History*. Asian Perspectives, 1:41, p.15-42. University of Hawai'i Press, Honolulu (2002)

Lehtinen, I. *Traces of the Central Asian culture in the North: Finnish-Soviet Joint Scientific Symposium held in Hanasaari, Espoo.* p.14–21. Finno-Ugrian Society, Helsinki (1986)

Leibold, J. *Narratives of Racial Unity in Republican China: From the Yellow Emperor to Peking Man.* Modern China, Vol. 32, No. 2, p.181-220. Sage, Thousand Oaks, Calif. (2006)

Li, C, et al. *Evidence that a West-East admixed population lived in the Tarim Basin as early as the early Bronze Age.* BMC Biology 8 (15), p.15. Biomed Central, London (2010)

Li, C, et al. *Analysis of ancient human mitochondrial DNA from the Xiaohe cemetery: Insights into prehistoric population movements in the Tarim Basin, China.* BMC Genetics 16, p.78. Biomed Central, London (2015)

Lively, S. & Abrams, K.E. *The Pink Swastika, 4th Edition.* Veritas Aeterna, Sacramento (2002)

Lukashov, N. *Remains of ancient civilization discovered on the bottom of a lake.* 27th Dec, RIA Novosti, Moscow (2007)

MacKenzie, D. & Curran, M. W. *A History of Russia, the Soviet Union, and Beyond, 4th Edition.* Wadsworth, Belmont, Calif. (1993)

Madella, M. & Fuller, D.Q. *Palaeoecology and the Harappan Civilisation of South Asia: a reconsideration.* Quaternary Science Reviews 25, 1283–1301. Elsevier, Amsterdam (2006)

Mair, V. H. *Mummies of the Tarim Basin.* Archaeology 48 (2), p.28–35. AIA, Washington D.C. (1995)

Mallory, J.P. & Mair, V.H. *The Tarim Mummies.* Thames & Hudson, London (2000)

Maspero, G., McClure, M.L. (Tr.) & Sayce, A.H. (Ed.) *Ancient History of the Peoples of the Classical Orient*: Vol 1: *The Dawn of Civilization.* D. Appleton & Company, New York (1894); Vol 2: *The Struggle of the Nations.* SPCK, London (1896); Vol 3: *The Passing of the Empires.* SPCK, London (1900)

Mathieson, I. *The Genomic History of Southeastern Europe.* Nature 555 (7695), p.197–203. Nature Research, London (2018)

Mathisen, R. W. *Ancient Roman Civilization.* Oxford University Press, New York (2019)

Melyukova, A. I., Sinor, D. (Ed.) & Crookenden, J. (Tr.) *The Cambridge History of Early Inner Asia. Vol. 1.* Cambridge University Press, Cambridge (1990)

Mitchum, R. *Lactose Tolerance in the Indian Dairyland.* Science Life, University of Chicago Medicine, Chicago (2011)

Müllenhoff, K. *Germania Antiqua.* Weidmann, Berlin (1873)

Mungello, D.E. *Curious Land: Jesuit Accommodation and the Origins of Sinology.* University of Hawaii Press, Honolulu (1989)

Newton, I. *The Chronology of Ancient Kingdoms.* Tonson, Osborne, Longman, London (1728)

North, R. *Heathen Gods in Old English Literature.* Cambridge University Press, Cambridge (1997)

Nyberg, H. *Ancient Religions of Iran.* Church of Sweden Board of Deacons, Stockholm (1937)

Oettinger, N. *Before Noah: Possible Relics of the Flood myth in Proto-Indo-Iranian and Earlier* in Jamison, S.W., Melchert, H.C. & Vine, B. (Eds.) *Proceedings of the 24th Annual UCLA Indo-European Conference.* Hempen, Bremen (2013)

Olbrycht, M. *Notes on the presence of Iranian peoples in Europe and their Asiatic relations.* In Pstrusinska, J. & Fear, A. (Eds.) *Krakov Celto-Asiatic Collection.* Księgarnia Akademicka, Krakov (2000)

Pellechia, T. *Wine: The 8,000-Year-Old Story of the Wine Trade.* Running Press, London (2006)

Petrie, W.M.F. *Neglected British History.* Oxford University Press, London (1917)

Peyrot, M. *The deviant typological profile of the Tocharian branch of Indo-European may be due to Uralic substrate influence.* Indo-European Linguistics 7 (1), p.72–121. Brill, Leiden (2019)

Pollini, J. *The Warren Cup: Homoerotic Love and Symposial Rhetoric in Silver.* Art Bulletin 81.1, p.21–52. CAA, New York (1999)

Potts, D.T. *Puzur-Inšušinak and the Oxus civilization (BMAC): Reflections on the geo-political landscape of Iran and Central Asia in the Ur III period.* Journal of Assyriology and Near Eastern Studies 98, p.165–94. De Gruyter, Berlin (2008)

Potts, D.T. *The Archaeology of Elam: Formation and Transformation of an Ancient Iranian State, 2nd Edition*. Cambridge University Press, New York (2016)

Pritchard, J.B. (Ed). *Ancient Near Eastern Texts, 3rd Edition*. Princeton University Press, Princeton (1969)

Pugachenkova, G.A. *The Sculpture of Khalchaian*. Iskusstvo, Moscow (1971)

Qingbo, D. *Sino-Western Cultural Exchange as Seen through the Archaeology of the First Emperor's Necropolis*. Journal of Chinese History 7, p.21–72. Cambridge University Press, Cambridge (2022)

Raghavan, M., et al. *Upper Palaeolithic Siberian genome reveals dual ancestry of Native Americans*. Nature 505 (7481), p.87–91. Nature Research, London (2014)

Rainey, A. F. *Unruly Elements in Late Bronze Canaanite Society* in Wright, D. P., Freedman, D. N. & Hurvitz, A. (Eds.) *Pomegranates and Golden Bells*, p.481-496. Eisenbrauns, Winona Lake, Ind. (1995)

Reynolds, S. *Our Forefathers? Tribes, Peoples and Nations in the Historiography of the Age of Migrations*. In Murray, A.C. (Ed.) *After Rome's Fall: Narrators and Sources of Early Medieval History*. University of Toronto Press, Toronto (1998)

Rohl, D.M. *A Test of Time*. Century, London (1995)

Rohl, D.M. *Legend: The Genesis of Civilization, 2nd Edition*. Century, London (1999)

Rohl, D.M. *The Lords of Avaris*. Century, London (2007)

Ruck, C.A.P. *Poets, Philosophers, Priests*. In Wasson, R.G., et al. *Persephone's Quest: Entheogens and the origins of Religion*, p.227–230. Yale University Press, New Haven, Conn. (1986)

Sandars, N.K. *The Sea Peoples, 2nd Edition*. Thames and Hudson, London (1985)

Sarianidi, V. *Margiana and Soma-Haoma*. Electronic Journal of Vedic Studies, Vol. 9, Issue 1, p.53-73. HASP, Heidelberg (2003)

Sarianidi, V. & Hramov, V.H. (Ed.) *Margush: Mystery and Truth of the Great Culture*. TDH, Asgabat (2008)

Scanlon, T.F. *The Dispersion of Pederasty and the Athletic Revolution in Sixth-Century BC Greece*. In Verstraete, B.C. and Provencal, V. (Eds.) *Same-Sex Desire and Love in Greco-Roman Antiquity and in the Classical Tradition of the West*. Haworth Press, New York (2005)

Schlegel, G. *China or Elam*. T'oung Pao, Vol.II, p.244. Brill, Leiden (1891)

Schuchhardt, C. *Schliemann's Excavations*. Macmillan & Co., London (1891)

Sellwood, D. *The Drachms of the Parthian "Dark Age"*. Journal of the Royal Asiatic Society of Great Britain and Ireland, 1, p.2-25. Cambridge University Press, Cambridge (1976)

Shepard, J. *Another New England? – Anglo-Saxon Settlement on the Black Sea*. Byzantine Studies, Vol.1(1), p.18-39. University of Pennsylvania Press, Philadelphia (1974)

Sigrist, M. *Isin Year Names*. Andrews University Press, Berrien Springs, Mich. (1988)

Steinkeller, P. *The Question of Marhaši: A contribution to the historical geography of Iran in the third millennium BC*. Journal of Assyriology and Near Eastern Studies 72, p.237-64. De Gruyter, Berlin (1982)

Steinkeller, P. *New light on Marhaši and its contacts with Makkan and Babylonia*. Journal of Magan Studies 1, p.1-17. CDLI, Oxford (2006)

Steinkeller, P. *New light on Šimaški and its rulers*. Journal of Assyriology and Near Eastern Studies 97, p.215-32. De Gruyter, Berlin (2007)

Steinkeller, P. *The Divine Rulers of Akkade and Ur: Toward a Definition of the Deification of Kings*. In Steinkeller, P. *History, Texts and Art in Early Babylonia: Three Essays*. De Gruyter, Boston (2017)

Steinkeller, P. *The Birth of Elam in History*. In Álvarez-Mon, J (Ed.) *The Elamite World*, p.177-203. Routledge, London (2018)

Strasser, O. *The Gangsters Around Hitler*. W.H. Allen, London (1942)

Sulimirski, T. & Taylor, T. F. *The Scythians*. In Boardman, J., Edwards, I.E.S., Hammond, N.G.L., Sollberger, E. & Walker, C.B.F. (Eds.) *The Cambridge Ancient History, Vol. 3*. Cambridge University Press, Cambridge (1991)

Szemerényi, O. *Four old Iranian ethnic names: Scythian – Skudra – Sogdian – Saka*. Austrian Academy of Sciences, Vienna (1980).

Tafażżolī, A. *Arjāsp*. In Yarshater, E. (Ed.) *Encyclopædia Iranica, Vol.2*. Routledge & Kegan Paul, London (1987)

Van Dijk, J. *Išbi'erra, Kindattu, the Man of Elam and the Fall of the City of Ur*. Journal of Cuneiform Studies, Vol.30, 4, p.189-208. American Schools of Oriental Research, Chicago (1978)

Volodin, S.A. & Okorokov, K.S. *Reconstruction of a Scythian period calathus from the burial ground Devitsa V in the Middle Don area.* In Kashuba, M.T. et al. (Ed.) *Antiquities of the Northern Black Sea Region, the Caucasus and Central Asia.* Institute of the History of Material Culture, Russian Academy of Sciences, St. Petersburg (2024)

Wachsmann, S. *The ships of the Sea Peoples (IJNA, 10.3: 187-220): additional notes.* International Journal of Nautical Archaeology and Underwater Exploration, 11.4, p.291-304. Taylor & Francis, London (1982)

Wilkinson, E. *Chinese History: A New Manual.* Harvard University Press, Cambridge, Mass. (2013)

Wilson, C. *Ancient DNA reveals that Jews' biblical rivals were from Greece.* New Scientist, No.3237. New Scientist, London (2019)

Wood, M. *In Search of the Trojan War.* University of California Press, Berkeley (1998)

Woolley, C.L. *The Sumerians.* W.W. Norton & Co., New York (1965)

Woudhuizen, F.C. *The Ethnicity of the Sea Peoples.* Erasmus University, Rotterdam (2006)

Wreszinski, W. *Atlas of Ancient Egyptian Culture.* J. C. Hinrichs, Leipzig (1935)

Wu, K.C. *The Chinese Heritage.* Crown, New York (1982)

Yarshater, E. *Afrasiab.* In Yarshater, E. (Ed.) *Encyclopædia Iranica, Vol.1.* Routledge & Kegan Paul, London (1985)

Yatsenko, S.A. *Yuezhi on Bactrian embroidery from textiles found at Noyon Uul, Mongolia.* Russian State University for the Humanities, Moscow (2012)

Ye, S. & Liu, W. *Classic of Mountains and Seas and the Origin of White Jade Worship.* Journal of Literature and Art Studies, Vol.6, 6, p.579-596. David, Wilmington, Del. (2016)

www.ingramcontent.com/pod-product-compliance
Lightning Source LLC
Chambersburg PA
CBHW072334300426
44109CB00042B/1299